THE COLLECTED WORKS OF

F. A. Hayek

VOLUME XVII

THE CONSTITUTION OF
LIBERTY

The Definitive Edition

PLAN OF THE COLLECTED WORKS
Edited by Bruce Caldwell

The plan is provisional. Minor alterations may occur in titles of individual books, and several additional volumes may be added.

THE COLLECTED WORKS OF

F. A. Hayek

VOLUME XVII

THE CONSTITUTION OF
LIBERTY

The Definitive Edition

EDITED BY

RONALD HAMOWY

The University of Chicago Press

RONALD HAMOWY is professor of history emeritus at the University of Alberta and affiliate professor of economics at George Mason University. He is a fellow in social thought at the Cato Institute and has written numerous articles and books on social theory, including *The Scottish Enlightenment and Spontaneous Order* and *The Political Sociology of Freedom: Adam Ferguson and F. A. Hayek*. He is the editor of the Liberty Press edition of *Cato's Letters*.

The University of Chicago Press, Chicago 60637
The University of Chicago Press, Ltd., London
© 1960, 2011 by the University of Chicago
All rights reserved. Published 2011
Printed in the United States of America

20 19 18 17 16 15 14 13 12 11   1 2 3 4 5

ISBN-13: 978-0-226-31537-9 (cloth)
ISBN-13: 978-0-226-31539-3 (paper)
ISBN-10: 0-226-31537-1 (cloth)
ISBN-10: 0-226-31539-8 (paper)

Library of Congress Cataloging-in-Publication Data

Hayek, Friedrich A. von (Friedrich August), 1899–1992.
  The constitution of liberty : the definitive edition / edited by Ronald Hamowy.
    p. cm. — (The collected works of F. A. Hayek ; v. 17)
  ISBN-13: 978-0-226-31537-9 (cloth : alk. paper)
  ISBN-10: 0-226-31537-1 (cloth : alk. paper)
  ISBN-13: 978-0-226-31539-3 (pbk. : alk. paper)
  ISBN-10: 0-226-31539-8 (pbk. : alk. paper) 1. Liberty. 2. Rule of law.
3. Social policy. I. Hamowy, Ronald, 1937– II. Title. III. Series: Hayek,
Friedrich A. von (Friedrich August), 1899–1992. Works. 1989 ; v. 17.
  HB171 .H426 1989 vol. 17
  [JC585.H29]
  320.01'1—dc22

2010020835

♾ The paper used in this publication meets the minimum requirements of the American National Standard for Information Sciences— Permanence of Paper for Printed Library Materials, ANSI Z39.48-1992.

THE COLLECTED WORKS OF F. A. HAYEK

Founding Editor: W. W. Bartley III
General Editor: Bruce Caldwell

Published with the support of

The Hoover Institution on War, Revolution, and Peace
Stanford University

The Cato Institute

The Earhart Foundation

The Pierre F. and Enid Goodrich Foundation

The Heritage Foundation

The Morris Foundation, Little Rock

CONTENTS

PART II.   *Freedom and the Law*

PART III.   *Freedom in the Welfare State*

POSTCRIPT

EDITORIAL FOREWORD

Many scholars view *The Constitution of Liberty* to be F. A. Hayek's greatest work. It is a great pleasure to present here, as volume 17 in the series, *The Collected Works* version of the book.

I was delighted when Ronald Hamowy agreed to serve as the editor of the volume. Hamowy did his Ph.D. under Hayek at the Committee on Social Thought at the University of Chicago and was on the scene in 1960 when *The Constitution of Liberty* was published. Indeed, he wrote one of the first critical reviews of the book, one that so impressed Hayek that he penned a reply.[1] Because of his intimate knowledge of the material, Hamowy is in many respects the ideal choice as editor.

Those familiar with the original 1960 version of *The Constitution of Liberty* will notice some differences between it and *The Collected Works* edition. The most prominent of these is that the endnotes of the 1960 volume have been transformed into footnotes in the present one. The decision to make such a dramatic change was not made lightly. The endnotes ran to over one hundred pages, and there was some fear that when set as footnotes they might overwhelm the text. As I read through the manuscript that Hamowy had prepared, though, it quickly became apparent how useful it was to have the notes immediately available. Hayek's text typically does not provide any clues as to what one is going to find in the endnotes. One would never try to check every one, and because of that, much is missed. The problem was remedied by turning them into footnotes. I have read *The Constitution of Liberty* a number of times. In looking over Hamowy's manuscript, I learned a number of things I never knew before, simply because I had Hayek's notes right there before me. It greatly enhanced my reading experience and my engagement with Hayek's ideas.

As he indicates in his "A Note on the Notes," editor Hamowy checked Hayek's notes for accuracy, making additions when Hayek omitted material and silently correcting any bibliographical errors that Hayek may have made.

---

[1] See Ronald Hamowy, "Hayek's Concept of Freedom: A Critique," *New Individualist Review*, 1 (April 1961): 28–31; F. A. Hayek, "Freedom and Coercion: Some Comments and Mr. Hamowy's Criticism," *New Individualist Review*, 1 (Summer 1961): 28–30, reprinted in *Studies in Philosophy, Politics, and Economics* (Chicago: University of Chicago Press, 1967), pp. 348–50.

But Hamowy did much more than this—translating passages, adding more than two hundred citations from the 1971 German edition of the book, and providing explanatory information when appropriate.

In his notes, Hayek quoted from sources in many different languages, including German, French, Italian, Spanish, Russian, Greek, and Latin. A number of scholars contributed at the copyediting stage, and at very short notice, to ensure that any typos or other errors that crept into the manuscript were corrected. I am indebted to Professors Marina Bianchi, Linda Danford, Hansjoerg Klausinger, Susan Shelmerdine, and Pedro Schwartz for their invaluable and timely assistance.

There are a number of others who contributed. Kevin Welding and Nicolas Venditti prepared an initial version of the master text, and Chandran Kukathas did some early work on the volume prior to passing on the job of editor to Ronald Hamowy. David Pervin of the University of Chicago Press oversees the whole *Collected Works* series and has been a frequent source of assistance and sound advice. His counterpart at Routledge, Thomas Sutton, has managed the distribution of the volume outside of North America. Perhaps my greatest debt, however, is to the meticulous and unflappable Rhonda Smith, who brilliantly coordinated and executed the immensely complicated task of copyediting the manuscript.

Given the new placement of the notes, and the immense amount of work that so many people have put into this volume, we have decided to label *The Collected Works* version of Hayek's great book *The Definitive Edition*.

Bruce Caldwell
Greensboro, North Carolina

INTRODUCTORY ESSAY

In September 1989 the Solidarity party, an arm of the Polish anticommunist labor movement, took control of the government in Poland after the party had earlier won all parliamentary seats. In the same month, Hungary opened its borders with Austria, thus permitting huge numbers of refugees to flee Eastern Europe and particularly East Germany. Two months later the Berlin Wall was opened and the East German government collapsed. Also, in the same month that Solidarity achieved a massive election victory in Poland, Alexander Dubček, who had been taken into custody by occupying Soviet forces in Czechoslovakia in 1968, addressed a rally of 300,000 in Prague. Mounting protests against the communist regime throughout Czechoslovakia finally led to the resignation of its Communist government in late December. These events throughout Eastern Europe soon spread to the Soviet Union where pressures for reform had been building. Finally, in December 1991, the Soviet Union was officially abolished and Russia, the Ukraine, and Byelorussia created the Commonwealth of Independent States, thus bringing to an end seventy-four years of Communist control. Despite the appearance of impregnability, the swiftness with which these governments collapsed is testimony to how corrupt and diseased their internal structures were.

Few Western social theorists foresaw just how feeble the economic framework of communist nations in fact was. It had been assumed by millions that planned economies could somehow put an end to the depredations associated with capitalism and could open the way to a more just and fair distribution of wealth and, while it might require temporary sacrifice and hardship, would in the end result in a better world. Nor was this view limited to those living in Eastern Europe. Most Western intellectuals were equally convinced that socialism offered a realistic, and in many way superior, alternative to the free market.

While most intellectuals were prepared to accept the fact that there was nothing inherent in socialist economies that prevented this outcome, F. A. Hayek, in a series of penetrating analyses, had demonstrated that such planning was impossible in the absence of a price system such as only free markets could provide. In the absence of prices that accurately reflect people's preferences for various goods and services, government direction of the economy can only lead to increasing malinvestment and disorder. This constituted a crucial failing that made the ultimate disintegration of communist societies inevitable. Hayek had been preceded in his analysis by his mentor at the University of Vienna, Ludwig von Mises, whose seminal work on socialism was first published in the early 1920s. To those persuaded by the arguments put forward by Mises and Hayek, the collapse of the Communist governments of Eastern Europe came as less of a surprise than to many others. Indeed, the great contribution of these two thinkers is that they demonstrated that government attempts to plan the economy were inevitably doomed to fail.

Mises had argued in a seminal article published in 1920[1] that productive efficiency was contingent on knowing the real prices of the factors of production, since without such prices it would be impossible to know how to rationally allocate resources. With all productive resources owned by a central authority and in the absence of market-generated prices, the calculation of real costs would be impossible and thus render production essentially random. To these conclusions Hayek added the notion that the market was itself essentially a discovery process providing information that would otherwise not exist on the relative value of goods. This information, he contended, could only be supplied by free markets since it was impermanent and widely dispersed among a host of individuals, many of whom were not even aware that they possessed any relevant knowledge, knowledge that emerged only as a product of the market process itself. As one economist has written of Hayek's conclusions: "Persons embedded in a competitive process can, by virtue of their very rivalry with one another, impart information to the system of relative prices that in the absence of competition they would have no way of obtaining."[2] Without a price system socialist economies lacked the ability to coordinate the actions of consumers and producers and were thus doomed to substantial misallocations of resources. These insights, together with Hayek's conclusions regarding the business cycle, were on the verge of dominating academic economics when, in the early 1930s, the world found itself in the midst of the

[1] "Die Wirtschaftsrechnung im sozialistischen Gemeinwesen," *Archiv für Sozialwissenschaft und Sozialpolitik*, 47 (1920): 86–121. The article was translated into English in 1935 and published under the title "Economic Calculation in the Socialist Commonwealth," published in *Collectivist Economic Planning: Critical Studies of the Possibilities of Socialism*, F. A. Hayek, ed. (London: Routledge and Kegan Paul), pp. 87–130. Mises's conclusions were expanded two years later in *Die Gemeinwirtschaft: Untersuchungen über den Sozialismus* (Jena: Gustav Fischer, 1922), translated into English by Jacques Kahane in 1936 as *Socialism: An Economic and Sociological Analysis* (London: Jonathan Cape).

[2] Don C. Lavoie, "Economic Calculation and Monetary Stability," *Cato Journal*, 3, no. 1 (Spring 1983): 164. Hayek first discusses the question of economic calculation in "The Nature and History of the Problem," pp. 1–40, and "The Present State of the Debate," pp. 201–43, in *Collectivist Economic Planning*, F. A. Hayek, ed.

Great Depression. In 1936 John Maynard Keynes published his *General Theory of Employment, Interest, and Money*. Released at the Depression's height, the academic world found in Keynes's recommendations regarding deficit spending and vigorous government activity a formula that had far more appeal than did Hayek's analysis of the causes of the business cycle and the need to allow the market to correct itself without more monetary intervention. The result was that Keynes's theory of underinvestment and underconsumption during periods of slow or negative economic growth came to dominate economic theory for several decades.[3]

Hayek's analysis of the role of the price system and its effect on the operation of socialist societies, however, was not limited to economic issues. Alarmed by the spectacular growth of government involvement in the economy in Great Britain and the United States, in part as a reaction to the Great Depression and the Second World War, Hayek published *The Road to Serfdom* in 1944, his first work aimed at an audience broader than academic economists. The prevailing orthodoxy during the period held that National Socialism was, in every crucial respect, the antithesis of welfare socialism. Welfare statism had captured the imagination of most intellectuals during the Depression and remained popular during the struggle against Nazi Germany. This view was exacerbated by the barrage of propaganda issued by the allied governments during the war, when it was felt necessary to paint England, the United States, and Stalinist Russia as similar in their approach to economic and social problems, in contrast to Nazi Germany and Fascist Italy. It was generally thought that only through vigorous government intervention was it possible to forestall the more destructive aspects of unbridled capitalism, which, if left unchecked, would bring privation and misery to the great mass of people. Equally important, only government direction could galvanize and coordinate the productive facilities of a nation so as to minimize waste and maximize wealth creation.

Reaction to the essay was, with few exceptions, both hostile and swift, both in Britain and in the United States.[4] Most of the book's readers were appalled

---

[3] The claim that Hayek's writings in political and social theory reflected a rigidity that fatally compromised his conclusions is without merit. Nor were his arguments in the field of economics "muddled." To contend, as does Robert Skidelsky ("Hayek versus Keynes: The Road to Reconciliation," in *The Cambridge Companion to Hayek*, Edward Feser, ed. [Cambridge: Cambridge University Press, 2006], pp. 82–110), that these failings are what account for the success of Keynesianism while Austrianism was relegated to the margins of the discipline is to misconstrue the political history of the 1930s, when massive government intervention in all aspects of social and economic life became fashionable, and the attractions of Keynesianism to professional economists who saw in Keynes's conclusions an opportunity to henceforth play prominent roles in shaping fiscal policy.

[4] Indeed, a new low in academic discourse was probably set by Herman Finer, university professor of political science at the University of Chicago, whose venomous book, *The Road to Reac-*

that Hayek could suggest that any approach to social problems as benign as welfare socialism was similar to a movement as pernicious as was National Socialism. Hayek had contended that distrust of the market and the disdain that was felt for individual decision making were common to both fascism and welfare-statism, which destroyed the spontaneous order inherent in free and undirected markets and led to a wide array of unforeseen and undesired consequences. These, in turn, led to more controls on people's actions and increasingly greater limits on freedom. Public response to *The Road to Serfdom* doubtless contributed to Hayek's decision to devote more of his time and energies to discussing why socialist societies, by their nature, rested on coercion and to lay bare the principles of a free and open society. The upshot of this decision was *The Constitution of Liberty*, which was published in 1960, wherein he sought more fully to examine the demarcation between the amount and area of government intervention that he regarded as consistent with a free society and governmental actions that illegitimately encroached on personal liberty.

Bruce Caldwell, in his excellent study of Hayek's social and economic thought,[5] has suggested that *The Constitution of Liberty* most likely constituted a part of Hayek's broader project to respond to the increasingly fashionable view that the application of the methodology of the natural sciences to social phenomena, in the form of social planning by a team of experts, could in theory solve all problems of human organization. This conclusion was predicated on the assumption that the laws of human interaction were analogous to the laws of physics, which, once uncovered, would permit the engineering

---

tion (Boston: Little, Brown and Co., 1945), was written as a response to Hayek's book. The following quotation from chapter 2, entitled "The Reactionary Manifesto," will give some idea of how scurrilous Finer's essay is. He writes: "Here is a joy for all conservatives. In spite of the world's desperate travail to overthrow Hitler and Mussolini and what they stood for, many conservatives need the new joy because secretly they have just lost the old one.

"We now live in a world without Hitler. His removal has swept away the inhibition against open avowal of his doctrines of contempt for the majority and equality and popular sovereignty. There will be a babel of antidemocratic statements within a few months; murmurings can already be heard. For a time the bitterness of the reactionaries has been merely bridled, out of expediency, while the power and repute of the majority have been magnified, because it is the majority that fights world wars" (pp. 15–16). There follow another 212 pages containing a seemingly endless series of ad hominem assaults on Hayek's scholarship and motives in writing *The Road to Serfdom*. Despite the unscholarly nature of Finer's attack, his colleague at Chicago, Charles E. Merriam, in his review of Finer's essay, referred to it as "highly skilled" and to Hayek's book as "an over-rated work of little permanent value." (Review of Barbara Wootton, *Freedom Under Planning*, and Herman Finer, *The Road to Reaction*, in *American Political Science Review*, 60 [1946]: 133, 135.) It is interesting that almost three-quarters of a century after Finer's diatribe first saw print, this mediocre academic is remembered solely because of the malevolence of his condemnation of Hayek's essay.

[5] *Hayek's Challenge: An Intellectual Biography of F. A. Hayek* (Chicago: University of Chicago Press, 2004), pp. 288–89.

of social relationships with the same predictability of outcome as obtained with respect to the physical world. To this view Hayek gave the name scientism.[6] In addition to being subject to the classic arguments against reductionism, Hayek contended that scientism disregards the fundamental fact that coherent patterns in human affairs are often the result of the interaction of numerous individuals, none of whom sought to achieve the resulting overall end. Or, as Adam Ferguson noted two hundred years earlier, complex social arrangements, while indeed the product of the action of human beings, are not the result of any conscious plan.[7]

This insight into the nature of social organization, that the level of complexity of institutions put them beyond the ability of any one mind or group of minds to comprehend and design, pervades all of Hayek's social theory and plays a crucial role in shaping the political conclusions he draws in *The Constitution of Liberty*. What he attempts in this work is nothing less than laying bare the political machinery necessary for a free society, treated in both its historical and philosophical dimensions. This is a monumentally ambitious project and if, in the end, Hayek occasionally falters and slips, as he indeed does, these failures are more reflections of the complexity of his enterprise than of weaknesses in his reasoning.

At no point in his autobiographical writings does Hayek indicate when he originally conceived of writing *The Constitution of Liberty*. Caldwell suggests the possibility that Hayek intended it to serve as a response to a challenge laid down by the socialist economist H. D. Dickinson in 1940 that those who opposed a collectivist economic system and embraced free markets were incapable of offering a positive program that would "guarantee the ordinary man a reasonable security of livelihood and prevent the accumulation of wealth (and, what is still more important, the concentration of power over wealth) in the hands of a minority of the community."[8] The central problem faced

---

[6] F. A. Hayek, "Scientism and the Study of Society," *Economica*, n.s., 9 (1942): 267–91; n.s., 10 (1943): 34–63; n.s., 11 (1944): 27–39; reprinted in *The Counter-Revolution of Science: Studies on the Abuse of Reason* (2nd ed.; Indianapolis, IN: Liberty Fund, 1979), pp. 19–363, and *Studies on the Abuse and Decline of Reason, Collected Works* edition, pp. 75–166.

[7] As Ferguson put it in 1767: "The establishments of men, like those of every animal, are suggested by nature. . . . [They] arose from successive improvements that were made, without any sense of their general effect; and they bring human affairs to a state of complication, which the greatest reach of capacity with which human nature was ever adorned, could not have projected." *Essay on the History of Civil Society*, Fania Oz-Salzberger, ed. (new ed.; Cambridge: Cambridge University Press, 1996), p. 174.

[8] H. D. Dickinson, "Book Review: *Freedom and the Economic System*," *Economica*, n.s., 7 (November 1940): 437. In the year prior to writing this review of Hayek's essay, Dickinson had published *The Economics of Socialism* (Oxford: Oxford University Press, 1939), in which he argued that socialist economies were quite capable of replicating the economic calculations that are required to establish a price system.

by proponents of an economic system based on private property wherein the "ballot of the market" prevails, Dickinson maintains, "involves not only outrageous plural voting, but also the wholesale intimidation of the smaller voters by a few great pluralists."[9] It is a tribute to Dickinson's obtuseness, and to those who shared his sympathies, that they appeared oblivious to how these problems would be avoided in an economy where all decisions concerning the production and distribution of wealth would be centralized in the hands of a few bureaucrats acting under the direction of a central committee. In addition, as Hayek was keenly aware, there is something distastefully naïve in the view that political power is invariably more benign than is economic power.

Despite the problems implied by Dickinson's collectivist alternative, Hayek was determined to reply to the critics who claimed that a free market economy would, if left unchecked, turn the great majority of the population into helots, forced to act at the mercy of a few plutocrats. Caldwell notes that Hayek's interests in political and social theory were part of a broader concern with a larger enterprise that Hayek came to refer to as the Abuse of Reason project. While never completed, the project served to direct him into investigating new areas of thought.[10]

R. M. Hartwell, a close friend of Hayek's and one of Great Britain's leading economic historians, records, in his history of the Mont Pèlerin Society, that by the time the Society was founded in 1947, Hayek had already "moved towards the writing of *The Constitution of Liberty*."[11] And in his autobiographical notes Hayek recounts that the structure of the work occurred to him during a car trip through southern Europe that he and his wife made in 1954–55. During that fall and winter, the Hayeks had the opportunity to motor through France, Italy, and Greece following the route taken by John Stuart Mill one hundred years earlier.[12] The book had its genesis, according to Hayek's biographer, in early 1953; in November of that year Hayek wrote to the economist Fritz Machlup that he was "beginning to have definite plans for that positive complement to *The Road to Serfdom* which people have so long [been] asking me to do."[13] While touring southern Europe, he had taken this occasion to make a side trip to Cairo to deliver the Commemoration Lectures at the Na-

[9] Dickinson, "Book Review," p. 436.

[10] Caldwell, *Hayek's Challenge*, p. 181.

[11] R. M. Hartwell, *The History of the Mont Pèlerin Society* (Indianapolis, IN: Liberty Fund, 1995): p. 16.

[12] F. A. Hayek, *Hayek on Hayek: An Autobiographical Dialogue*, Stephen Kresge and Leif Wenar, eds. (Chicago: University of Chicago Press, 1994), pp. 129–30.

[13] Quoted in Ebenstein, *Hayek's Journey: The Mind of Friedrich Hayek* (New York: Palgrave Macmillan, 2003), pp. 141–42. "The work that eventually would become *The Constitution of Liberty* would be titled, Hayek wrote in the 1953 letter to Machlup, 'Greater than Man: The Creative Powers of a Free Civilization.' It would be composed of parts titled 'The Role of Reason,' 'The Role of Morals,' 'The Role of Force,' and 'The Role of Material Resources.'"

tional Bank of Egypt, and these lectures later formed a segment of *The Constitution of Liberty*. The book's detailed organization, however, took shape during 1954–55.

In the preface to the Cairo lectures, Hayek notes that he was invited to deliver them some time earlier and his comments "were the tentative results of a study on which I have been engaged for some time but which is not yet concluded. I have availed myself of the opportunity to give an outline of conclusions at which I have arrived though they may still require modification in some respect."[14] The National Bank of Egypt lectures were to serve as Hayek's treatment of the nature and history of the rule of law. Indeed, Hayek himself noted in his application to the Guggenheim Foundation, to whom he had applied for funding for the 1954–55 trip, that one of its purposes was to investigate how spontaneously generated rules and customs developed in more traditional societies, which, he added, was a crucial element of a more extensive study he had been engaged in for years.

The Cairo lectures, four in number, served as earlier drafts of chapters 11, 12, 13, 14, and 16 of *The Constitution of Liberty* and are, in most respects, quite close to, albeit truncated versions of, what was finally published in 1960. In fact, the published version of these lectures even contained a good number of footnotes. Lecture one concerns itself with a historical survey of the rule of law and its relation to a free society in both Great Britain and America, topics that received far fuller discussion in chapters 11 and 12. One of the lectures' earliest paragraphs harks back to Hayek's concerns when writing *The Road to Serfdom*. He notes in the lecture that:

> The main reason why I have decided to approach my subject historically is to make you aware how greatly the whole framework of governmental power already has changed, how little the legal position even in the freest countries still corresponds to the ideals and concepts to which we still pay lip-service. I want to draw your attention to a silent revolution, which during the past two or three generations, has proceeded in the sanctuaries of the law largely unobserved by the general public. This revolution has gradually whittled away most of the guarantees of individual liberty for which at one time those people had been willing to fight. It is a peculiar kind of revolution in which what is often regarded as the most conservative of professions, in working out the implications of the popular will, have more completely changed the legal framework of governmental power than either the sovereign people or its representatives ever comprehended. The crucial steps were changes in the juridical attitude on issues which to the laymen must

---

[14] F. A. Hayek, *The Political Ideal of the Rule of Law*, (Cairo: National Bank of Egypt, Fiftieth Anniversary Commemorative Lectures, February 1955), preface.

have appeared nice legal points which only the lawyer could understand or care for, but on which in fact the foundations of their liberty depended.[15]

Hayek then discusses the classical notion of isonomy. He there argues that the claim that individual liberty, as it is understood in the modern world, was unknown to ancient Greece has no merit, certainly not when one looks at Athens during the period of its greatness. This Greek conception was particularly significant in shaping seventeenth-century English political thought, by which it entered Locke's treatises on government and ultimately eighteenth-century British and American theories of liberty.

Lecture two is devoted to an analysis of the English tradition of law, which spawned personal freedom, as it was transmitted to readers on the Continent, especially through the works of Montesquieu and Kant. While the German liberal tradition, Hayek noted, crystallized in the notion of the *Rechtsstaat*, French liberalism was crucially shaped by the events of the French Revolution, which appears to have concluded that "since at least the control of all power had been placed in the hands of the people, all safeguards against any abuse of that power had become unnecessary."[16] With certain exceptions, most notably Alexis de Tocqueville and Benjamin Constant, French liberal thinkers abandoned the British notion that social and political institutions should be grounded in those traditional arrangements that were compatible with individual autonomy. In its place it substituted the idea that a free society could, and should, be constructed *de novo*, without reference to existing social formations. This distinction, which reflects the primary concern of Hayek's *The Counter-Revolution of Science*,[17] plays a critical role in Hayek's understanding of the nature of freedom.

In lecture three, Hayek considers the attributes of a legal system consistent with a society operating under the rule of law. "The end," he noted, "is to limit coercion by the power of the state to instances where it is explicitly required by general abstract rules which have been announced beforehand and which applied [*sic*] equally to all people, and refer to circumstances known to them."[18] These criteria, Hayek claims, generality, equal applicability, and certainty, constitute the underlying structure of any free society and occupy a crucial role in Hayek's discussion of freedom in *The Constitution of Liberty*. In the same lecture, Hayek introduced the notion of spontaneously generated orders, arguing that not every social arrangement, despite the consistency of its elements, requires that it be the product of a designing intelligence. Indeed,

---

[15] Ibid., p. 3.
[16] Ibid., p. 17.
[17] F. A. Hayek, *Studies on the Abuse of and Decline of Reason, Collected Works* edition, pp. 75–166.
[18] *The Political Ideal of the Rule of Law*, p. 34.

the knowledge necessary to produce such arrangements "can exist only dispersed among all the different members of society and can never be concentrated in a single head, or be deliberately manipulated by any man or group of men."[19] Law particularly is an institution of such complexity that in a free society its particulars can take their form only through an evolutionary process, the result of which is a consistent set of rules that is the product of each of us pursuing our individual ends. Both these themes, the formal nature of the rule of law and the claim that law in a free society results from a spontaneously generated order, were central to Hayek's discussion of the constitution of liberty.

After laying bare the elements of a society in which people can be said to be free, Hayek turns to a discussion of the arguments put forward by the opponents of the rule of law in lecture four. Socialists, he notes, have always objected to the principle of equality of legal treatment inasmuch as treating people, who are inherently unequal, equally will invariably result in inequality. What socialists have sought ever since the French Revolution is not equality before the law but rather equality of outcome. Their contempt, he argues, is succinctly encapsulated in Anatole France's reference to "the majestic equality of law, which prohibits both rich and poor from sleeping under bridges, begging in the streets, and stealing bread."[20] This attitude pervades modern social and political theory and is a logical extension of the view that sufficient proof of the unfairness of any society is that the outcomes that befall the individuals that comprise it are unequal.

In addition, particularly in Great Britain and the United States, the transformation of governmental edicts from general rules enacted by the legislature to the *ad hoc* directives of regulatory agencies, whose decisions in any particular instance are unpredictable, enlarges and intensifies the arbitrary nature of our interactions with the state. In particular, large areas of the economy are increasingly shaped by the decisions of these tribunals, whose outcomes cannot be foreseen. The result is not only the deterioration of the rule of law but also the erosion of the spontaneous order of the market that makes rational investment possible.

The arguments that Hayek put forward in the Cairo lectures in 1955 served as a *précis* of the theoretical portions of *The Constitution of Liberty*, which he completed four years later. The purpose of both works is, as Hayek himself maintains, "to assist the formation of a spontaneous order and to restrict the use of coercion as much as possible" and thus "to adjust our rules so as to make the spontaneous forces of society work as beneficially as possible."[21] In

---

[19] Ibid., p. 31.

[20] "La majestueuse égalité des lois, qui interdit aux riches comme aux pauvres de coucher sous les ponts, de mendier dans les rues et de voler du pain." *Le Lys Rouge* (Paris: Calmann-Lévy, 1894), pp. 117–18; quoted in *Political Ideal of the Rule of Law*, p. 50.

[21] *Political Ideal of the Rule of Law*, p. 58.

the period between 1955 and 1959, Hayek applied himself to expanding the Cairo lectures into a systematic presentation of the nature of free societies, taken in both their historical and theoretical dimensions. During that period he published a number of articles in both English and German that were to serve, in expanded and somewhat revised form, as chapters in *The Constitution of Liberty*. In 1956 Hayek's comments on progressive taxation, sections of which were reprinted as chapter 20, appeared in a collection of essays issued in honor of Ludwig von Mises[22] and in the following year a slightly longer version of chapter 3, on "the common sense of progress," was published in the German journal *Ordo*.[23] In 1958 three more chapters were released, the first a version of chapter 4, on "freedom, reason, and tradition," in *Ethics*; the second, incorporated into chapter 6, on "equality, value, and merit," which was published in *Ordo*; and the third, which was to serve as a draft of chapter 2, on "the creative powers of a free civilization," as part of an anthology edited by the noted journalist Felix Morley.[24] Finally, in 1959, the year in which Hayek completed the manuscript of *The Constitution of Liberty*, two further sections, chapter 5 on "responsibility and freedom" and chapter 8 on "employment and independence," were published, the first in an anthology and the second in the periodical *Schweizer Monatshefte*.[25] These essays, together with the material that earlier appeared in *The Political Ideal of the Rule of Law*, constitute approximately one half of the larger work. Finally, on May 8, 1959, his sixtieth birthday, Hayek completed the preface to what was to prove his most important work in social theory and submitted the manuscript of *The Constitution of Liberty* to the University of Chicago Press.

Hayek divides his monograph into three parts. The first is devoted to a discussion of the value of freedom, the second to the connection between freedom and law, and the third to personal liberty and its relation to the welfare

[22] "Progressive Taxation Reconsidered," in *On Freedom and Free Enterprise: Essays in Honor of Ludwig von Mises*, Mary Sennolz, ed. (Princeton, NJ: D. Van Nostrand Company, 1956), pp. 265–84.

[23] "Grundtatsachen des Fortschritts" [The Fundamental Facts of Progress], *Ordo: Jahrbuch für die Ordnung von Wirtschaft und Gesellschaft*, 9 (1957): 19–42. *Ordo*, in which Hayek frequently published, was founded in 1948 by Walter Eucken and Franz Böhm, both of the University of Freiburg, and was Germany's leading neoliberal journal, a consistent opponent of central planning and defender of unhindered markets. See Henry R. Oliver, Jr., "German Neoliberalism," *Quarterly Journal of Economics*, 74 (1960): 117–49.

[24] "Freedom, Reason, and Tradition," *Ethics*, 68 (1958): 229–45; "Gleichheit, Wert und Verdienst" [Equality, Value, and Merit], *Ordo: Jahrbuch für die Ordnung von Wirtschaft und Gesellschaft*, 10 (1958): 5–29; and "The Creative Powers of a Free Civilization," in *Essays on Individuality*, Felix Morley, ed. (Philadelphia: University of Pennsylvania Press, 1958), pp. 183–204 [Liberty Fund edition, pp. 261–89].

[25] "Verantwortlichkeit und Freiheit" [Responsibility and Freedom], in *Erziehung zur Freiheit*, Albert Hunold, ed. (Erlenbach-Zürich: Eugen Rentsch, 1959), pp.147–90, and "Freiheit und Unabhängigkeit" [Freedom and Independence], *Schweizer Monatshefte*, 39 (May 1959): 89–103.

state. Sections one and two are primarily philosophical and, to a lesser degree, historical, while the arguments put forward in section three are, in the main, economic. To this discussion Hayek appends a massive scholarly apparatus, comprising no less than 1,900 citations in eight languages, the results of a lifetime of scholarship.

Hayek begins his analysis of the nature of a free society by attempting to define personal freedom. One is free, he maintains, when one is not coerced. And coercion, he continues, "occurs when one man's actions are made to serve another man's will, not for his own but for the other's purpose,"[26] but only when the possibility of alternative action is open and only when that alternative action serves the other person's desires. As Hayek puts it, coercion implies "that I still choose but that my mind is made someone else's tool, because the alternatives before me have been so manipulated that the conduct that the coercer wants me to choose becomes for me the least painful one."[27] It is clear that what Hayek wishes to do is to construct a definition of freedom that precludes only those actions that aim at placing others in positions where they feel forced to act in a specific way and where there exists no effective alternative to their so acting. While there are theoretical problems with this formulation if interpreted in its strictest sense,[28] it can at the least suffice as a rough guide to determining whether people are for the most part free.

This definition of coercion serves as the basis of Hayek's extensive discussion of the rule of law. As he previously argued in *The Political Ideal of the Rule of Law*, the legal rules of any society said to be operating under the rule of law must meet three criteria, that they be general, equally applicable, and certain. "Law in its ideal form," Hayek writes, "might be described as a 'once-and-for-all' command that is directed to unknown people and that is abstracted from all particular circumstances of time and place and refers only to such conditions as may occur anywhere and at any time."[29] In a free society, government edicts must take the form of general rules that prohibit specific action, rather than *ad hoc* commands, and once having been formulated in this way they largely deprive such rules of their coercive nature. "Insofar as the rules providing for coercion are not aimed at me personally but are so framed as to apply equally to all people in similar circumstances," he maintains, "they are no different from any of the natural obstacles that affect my plans."[30]

---

[26] This volume, p. 199.

[27] Ibid.

[28] See my "Freedom and the Rule of Law in F. A. Hayek," *Il Politico*, 36 (1971): 349–76, in which I argue that Hayek's claim that the rule of law is a sufficient condition for a free society is untenable inasmuch as the criteria he posits for the rule of law are, if analyzed, consistent with a regime that even Hayek would regard as clearly unfree.

[29] This volume, p. 218.

[30] This volume, p. 210.

Much has been written regarding Hayek's description of the rule of law and of its intimate connection with a free society, most taking issue with his conclusion that general rules are, at least in their effect, noncoercive.[31] The logic of Hayek's argument is such that freedom is a consequence of a certain set of formal restrictions on legislative activity. He writes: "The conception of freedom under the law . . . rests on the contention that when we obey laws, in the sense of general abstract rules laid down irrespective of their application to us, we are not subject to another man's will and are therefore free."[32] This clearly freights the rule of law with far too extended a function. For example, it is not too difficult to imagine the rule of law, as Hayek understands it, as perfectly consistent with a regime operating under, say, Islamic religious law, a society which in almost every respect is coercive and lacking in all spontaneity. Indeed, this is the gravamen of most of the reviews of *The Constitution of Liberty*, which point out that Hayek makes too much of the rule of law as a guardian of personal freedom.

Why Hayek chose to define freedom under law so broadly is something of a mystery. He had been more guarded in the Cairo lectures where he noted that it was still possible that the rule of law, no matter how carefully one crafts its provisions, was still compatible with "a great deal of silly and harmful legislation."[33] And at another point he conceded that it alone is hardly a sufficient condition for a free society. "The Rule of Law," he asserts, "gives us only a necessary and not a sufficient condition of individual freedom: within the scope that it leaves for legislation and administration these might still become very irksome and harmful. But it still seems to me not only an essential minimum condition of freedom but in practice also to secure what is most important."[34] However, he removed these qualifications four years later by logically linking personal liberty with the rule of law.[35]

[31] See especially Professor Bruno Leoni's penetrating study *Freedom and the Law* (Princeton, NJ: D. Van Nostrand Company, 1961). At one point Leoni writes: "We cannot help admitting that general rules, precisely worded (as they can be when written laws are adopted), are an improvement over the sudden orders and unpredictable decrees of tyrants. But, unfortunately, all this is no assurance that we shall be actually 'free' from interference by the authorities" (p. 75).

[32] This volume, p. 221.

[33] *Political Ideal of the Rule of Law*, p. 47.

[34] Ibid., p. 46.

[35] J. W. N. Watkins has suggested one reason why Hayek made such far-reaching claims for the rule of law. He writes: "Hayek has been over-impressed by the following logical consideration: a prohibition leaves an agent free to act in any of the indefinitely large number of ways compatible with not acting in the prohibited way, whereas a positive command leaves him unfree to act in any of the indefinitely large number of ways incompatible with acting in the commanded way. This seems to suggest that a prohibition is infinitely less coercive than a command. But we must not be dazzled by the largeness of the number of alternative courses left open by a prohibition. After all, the agent can select only one of them. To measure the degree of penalisation which a prohibition involves, what we have to weigh against the prohibited alternative is

In the year following publication of *The Constitution of Liberty*, Hayek had the occasion to clarify these rather far-reaching claims in response to one of the earliest critiques of his definition of coercion and its logical relation to a society operating under the rule of law. Writing in the *New Individualist Review*, a publication founded by several of his graduate students at the University of Chicago, Hayek maintained:

> It was not the main thesis of my book that "freedom may be defined as the absence of coercion." Rather, as the first sentence of the first chapter explains, its primary concern is "the condition of men in which coercion of some by others is reduced as much as is possible in society." I believe I am etymologically correct in describing such a state as one of liberty or freedom. But this is a secondary issue. The reduction of coercion appears to me an objective of the first importance in its own right and it is to this task that the book addresses itself.
>
> I sympathize with those who are disappointed with my admission that I know of no way of preventing coercion altogether and that all we can hope to achieve is to minimize it or rather its harmful effects. The sad fact is that nobody has yet found a way in which the former can be achieved by deliberate action. Such a happy state of perfect freedom (as I should call it) might conceivably be attained in a society whose members strictly observed a moral code prohibiting all coercion. Until we know how we can produce such a state all we can hope for is to create conditions in which people are prevented from coercing each other. But to prevent people from coercing each other is to coerce them. This means that coercion can only be reduced or made less harmful but not entirely eliminated.[36]

Hayek's concept of the rule of law is predicated on his belief that rights are neither abstract nor do they exist prior to the establishment of government. Rights, at least as they are understood in the Anglo-Saxon world, are essentially procedural and, as Burke earlier maintained, the product of the evolution of political institutions whose current constitution reflects the growth and arrangement most consistent with our understanding of the nature of a free society. A central aspect of Hayek's conception of rights is that their most crucial element is the manner by which government chooses to inter-

---

not the whole class of unprohibited alternatives but just the unprohibited alternative which he dislikes least." "Philosophy," in *Agenda for a Free Society: Essays on Hayek's "The Constitution of Liberty,"* Arthur Seldon, ed. (London: Published for the Institute of Economic Affairs by Hutchinson, 1961), p. 39.

[36] "Freedom and Coercion: Some Comments on a Critique by Mr. Ronald Hamowy," in *New Individualist Review*, 1 (1961): 28; reprinted in *Studies in Philosophy, Politics, and Economics* (Chicago: University of Chicago Press, 1967), pp. 348–49.

vene in our lives, which, Hayek suggests, is more significant than the extent of its intervention.

A central premise of *The Constitution of Liberty* is the distinction Hayek draws between, on the one hand, Anglo-American notions of a liberal society and, on the other, what he describes as the French conception of a free society. The first has as its models the political insights of, among others, Adam Smith, Adam Ferguson, David Hume, and Edmund Burke, while the second is indebted to the French Enlightenment thinkers, particularly Rousseau and the physiocrats. As he had earlier discussed in his 1945 lecture, "Individualism: True and False,"[37] and which he touches on in his *Political Ideal of the Rule of Law*,[38] we are heir to two distinct theories of liberty, one of which traces its roots to an empirical, evolutionary approach to politics, the other to a rationalist conception of social life. Hayek offers a succinct analysis of the distinction between these two notions of individualism:

> It is the contention [of the true individualist tradition] that, by tracing the combined effects of individual actions, we discover that many of the institutions on which human achievements rest have arisen and are functioning without a designing and directing mind; that, as Adam Ferguson expressed it, "nations stumble upon establishments, which are indeed the result of human action but not the result of human design"; and that the spontaneous collaboration of free men often creates things which are greater than their individual minds can ever fully comprehend. This is the great theme of Josiah Tucker and Adam Smith, of Adam Ferguson and Edmund Burke, the great discovery of classical political economy which has become the basis of our understanding not only of economic life but of most truly social phenomena.
>
> The difference between this view, which accounts for most of the order which we find in human affairs as the unforeseen result of individual actions, and the view which traces all discoverable order to deliberate design is the first great contrast between the true individualism of the British thinkers of the eighteenth century and the so-called "individualism" of the Cartesian school.[39]

This emphasis on the historical development of procedural rules is in some ways an extension of Hayek's broader insights into the issue of the disper-

---

[37] "Individualism: True and False," in *Individualism and Economic Order* (London: University of Chicago Press, 1948), pp. 1–32. The essay, originally delivered as the twelfth Finlay Lecture at University College, Dublin, on December 17, 1945, and published by Hodges, Figgis, and Company, Dublin, was later reprinted as the prelude to *Studies on the Abuse and Decline of Reason*, pp. 46–74.

[38] *Political Ideal of the Rule of Law*, pp. 11–18.

[39] "Individualism: True and False," in *Individualism and Economic Order*, pp. 6–8, and *Studies on the Abuse and Decline of Reason*, pp. 52–54.

sal of knowledge within society. The function of social, and particularly of political, rules is to create the conditions within which the discrete knowledge we each possess regarding how a free society consistent with social order can best flourish. In this project abstract notions of freedom serve no purpose. Hayek is particularly disturbed by the conception of "social justice," the notion that a just society obtains only when society's advantages and assets are evenly distributed among all its members. Most advocates of social justice regard this condition, in which each of us is possessed of our "fair share" of the wealth of the community, as the only one consistent with a truly just social order. Thus, the benefits to which we are entitled are as much a function of our existence within a community as of our own efforts. Conversely, the theory embraces the view that should a member of the group be handicapped in some manner or another, efforts should be made to socialize this disadvantage so that all share its burden equally. This view is currently embraced by most social theorists who see in it the overarching standard by which political action should be guided. As Hayek was later to point out in his extensive treatment of the subject, "it is perhaps not surprising that men should have applied to the joint effects of the actions of many people, even where these were never foreseen or intended, the conception of justice which they developed with respect to the conduct of individuals towards each other."[40]

Social justice implies nothing less than that the government be given plenary powers to control the distribution of all wealth, of all that is good in society. Rather than providing the same circumstances for all, the state "should aim at controlling all conditions relevant to a particular individual's prospects and so adjust them to his capacities as to assure him of the same prospects as everybody else."[41] Previously it had been a central element of our understanding of justice that only those responsible for a particular outcome should be held to account. "Social justice," on the other hand, holds that the whole group of which the victim is a member should be recompensed, while the group to which the perpetrator belongs should all be equally penalized. This is a particularly pernicious aspect of current views of justice, that it can as easily be accomplished should rewards and punishments be visited on collectivities as on individuals. This constitutes a reversion to the most primitive aspects of the Old Testament, prior to the introduction of the idea of personal responsibility, in which the sins of certain individuals issued in punishment of the whole community. It is the antithesis of the idea of justice based on a theory of individual rights that holds that only those responsible for a wrong should be held to account. Doubtless that is why the idea of punishing

---

[40] *Law, Legislation, and Liberty.* Vol. 2, *The Mirage of Social Justice* (Chicago: University of Chicago Press, 1976), p. 62.
[41] This volume, p. 155.

hostages is so abhorrent to our sense of fairness and equity and why we have traditionally regarded personal innocence as an absolute bar to punishment.

Hayek undertakes his examination of social and political arrangements, including legal rules, by investigating their origins and evolutionary development and their interactions such that when taken together allow a community to adhere. Despite the complexity of these institutions and rules, which become increasingly elaborate as societies evolve, they are both internally consistent and to great extent compatible one with the other. Were they not, societies would prove inherently unstable and would soon disintegrate. These consistencies and compatibilities intuitively suggest that these social arrangements must have been the product of a designing intelligence. However, Hayek argues, it is exactly their complexity that points to the fact that they did not come about through conscious deliberation inasmuch as their level of intricacy is such that they are beyond the capacity of any mind or group of minds to design. Rather, complex social structures originate as a result of numerous discrete individual actions, none of which aims at the formation of coherent social arrangements. Their shape and function, which in the aggregate form ordered arrangements, are the end result of countless individual actions each of which seeks ends distinct from the social patterns that emerge. This is the evolutionary dynamic that makes for viable social and political institutions and creates the conditions for a society governed by the rule of law and not the commands of men.

The third section of *The Constitution of Liberty* is devoted to the implications Hayek's theoretical analysis has for issues of public policy, all of especially significant contemporaneous importance. More specifically, Hayek's discussion centers on the rise of the welfare state, labor unions and employment, social security, taxation and redistribution, the monetary framework, housing and town planning, agriculture and natural resources, and education and research. In each of these chapters he examines the effects of existing governmental interventions both in terms of its effects on the principles of the rule of law enunciated in his earlier chapters and its general economic effects. In each instance Hayek evaluates the impact of each of the many incursions into free markets and the effects of their replacement by private arrangements. When Hayek originally wrote these sections in 1959, it was thought unimaginable by many that, for example, rent controls could be dismantled without serious negative effects on the supply of housing for the less affluent, nor was it thought that progressive taxation could have a profound effect on incentives and on the total production of wealth in society. We, reading these chapters fifty years later, are the beneficiaries of several of Hayek's insights into the dangers that follow the erosion of market forces, including the baleful effects in cost and efficiency of agricultural subsidies, the dire consequences that follow from the exceptional immunities accorded labor unions and the long-term dangers of a system of unfunded entitlements.

Hayek concludes *The Constitution of Liberty* with a postscript entitled "Why I Am Not a Conservative," in which he explicates the distinction between the political position he embraces and modern conservatism, with which it might easily be confused. Until the early twentieth century and especially during the nineteenth century, when it most fully flourished as a doctrine governing political life in Europe, the views that coincided with those put forward by Hayek were called "liberal." Liberalism had little in common with contemporaneous conservatism, which was marked by opposition to rapid changes in political and social life, by a propensity to support traditional institutions, and by a distrust of any spontaneously generated arrangements as opposed to those directed by a supervising authority. Most importantly, conservatism as a political philosophy lacks any principles to guide its adherents regarding in which direction society should move. In sum, conservatism tends to favor authority over liberty and over the free interaction of individuals. In the first decades of the twentieth century, as Hayek points out, radicals and socialists in the United States usurped the name "liberal" from those who supported free markets and minimal government and by doing so left true liberals without a recognizable designation. The effect has been to mistakenly attach the label "conservative" to those who are in fact precursors to nineteenth century liberalism, namely "Old Whigs," which is how Hayek regarded himself.

Upon completion of the printing of *The Constitution of Liberty* in December 1959, Hayek directed that the University of Chicago Press send out advance copies of the book to some fifty-five fellow academics, journalists, and heads of foundations. In addition, he personally presented copies to another two dozen colleagues at the University of Chicago and to close personal friends. Its official publication date was February 9, 1960. Despite efforts by both Hayek and the Press, the book was reviewed in only a dozen or so journals and periodicals, a shockingly small number given the reception accorded by the public to Hayek's earlier essay, *The Road to Serfdom*. Intellectuals in both Europe and the United States appear to have remained wedded to the view that an extensive welfare state was necessary to insure economic stability and the public's social welfare and that any defense of free markets bordered on the crackpot, unworthy of comment. In the spring of 1960 Hayek wrote a friend that "so far the response has not been encouraging. If it were not for a few friends like Henry Hazlitt [columnist for *Newsweek* magazine] and John Davenport [the assistant managing editor of *Fortune*], the book would not yet have had a decent review and I shall have to get help of all interested in the principles I have been trying to expound if it is to become widely known."[42]

---

[42] Hayek to William H. Brady, Jr., Chicago, March 22, 1960. Three weeks earlier Hayek had written to John Davenport: "What had made me despondent was particularly that the *Wall Street Journal*, on which I had placed much hope, has so far taken no notice. Is there a chance that *Time* or perhaps even *Life* may do something? . . . Apart from the discussions [by my friends at *Newsweek* and the *Journal of the American Medical Association*] and a few flattering notices by

Among the reviews that Hayek mentions in his correspondence is that by Sidney Hook, at one time a prominent Marxist and later a staunch defender of the Cold War. For some reason, the editor of the *New York Times Book Review* selected Hook, a firm supporter of "intelligent social control," to review Hayek's monograph, despite Hook's vigorous bias. The review, as predictable, was quite negative and, given that it appeared so soon after the publication of the book and in such an influential publication, doubtless played a role in the poor reception *The Constitution of Liberty* originally received. For these reasons it is worth quoting sections of it:

> It is demonstrable that Hayek suffers from the defects of the very rationalism he condemns. His antitheses between tradition and reason, experience and experiment, are analytically untenable and historically unjustifiable. Intelligent social control always learns from experience and history. It no more need take the form of a Utopian blueprint than concern for history need make a fetish of the past. . . .
>
> The conception of "self-regulating forces" in history and society is largely mythical. We would still be living in a state of slavery had we relied on them. . . .
>
> As a cautionary voice Mr. Hayek is always worth listening to. He is an intellectual tonic. But in our present time of troubles, his economic philosophy points the road to disaster.[43]

Hayek was particularly upset because Hook's review was in such sharp contrast to several of the letters he received from academics with whose work Hayek was familiar but whom he had not personally met. For example, the eminent mathematician H. B. Phillips, at one time chairman of the mathematics department at the Massachusetts Institute of Technology, whose interests extended to political theory, wrote Hayek a glowing letter, maintaining that "without doubt this is the greatest book ever written on liberty and liberal views in politics, and its value is greatly increased by the objective form of presentation, entirely free from the emotionalism which usually spoils discussions of this kind."[44] In mid-March the University of Chicago arranged that *All Things Considered*, which was broadcast on WTTW, the PBS television sta-

---

local dailies there has so far been only Sidney Hook in the *New York Times*." Chicago, March 4, 1960. Friedrich von Hayek Collection. Hoover Institution Archives, box 62, folder 7. Some two weeks following the date of this letter, on March 16 and 17, the *Wall Street Journal* reprinted two excerpts from Hayek's book.

[43] "Of Tradition and Change: *The Constitution of Liberty* by F. A. Hayek," *New York Times Book Review*, February 21, 1960, p. 6.

[44] H. B. Phillips to F. A. Hayek, South Lincoln, MA, March 30, 1960. Friedrich von Hayek Collection. Hoover Institution Archives, box 62, folder 7.

tion in Chicago, would devote its program to a discussion of *The Constitution of Liberty*. Among the discussants was Warner Wick, professor of philosophy at the University and an authority on metaphysics and logic, who wrote Hayek: "I offer this [note] in thanks and appreciation for your book and the occasion which led to my being pushed into reading it. In my humble judgment, it deserves to become a classic statement of a position that few people now think of as even relevant to our times. I hope it shakes many from their dogmatic slumbers."[45]

Hayek's essay received only a handful of reviews in the more scholarly journals, but these were mixed. Jacob Viner, possibly the most distinguished historian of economic thought in the United States, wrote in the *Southern Economic Journal* that *The Constitution of Liberty* had shown the author to be in principle capable of a major contribution to social theory "by virtue of his learning, his analytical skills, and his dialectical virtuosity."[46] However, while Hayek's arguments in favor of limited government are impressive, he is far too doctrinaire in his conclusions. "He writes," Viner maintains,

> with every appearance that in reaching his conclusions he has taken adequately into consideration all the values that are relevant, and all the conjectures that are actually or potentially important except major emergency situations such as war or danger of war. He manages also to reach his conclusions without giving evidence that to do so he had found it necessary to labor with the weighing of competing values. Great as are the merits of his case, they are not overwhelming enough, I think, to explain how Hayek succeeded in reaching substantially unconditional conclusions and in avoiding what is, in social thought, the generally unavoidable and troublesome necessity of coping with major conflicts between values.[47]

Reviewers generally could not help having been impressed by Hayek's erudition and cogency but had serious reservations about his conclusions and largely because of this found them unconvincing.[48] Several were essentially negative[49] while others—whose comments reduced to ad hominem attacks—

[45] Warner Wick to F. A. Hayek, Chicago, March 16, 1960. Friedrich von Hayek Collection. Hoover Institution Archives, box 62, folder 7.

[46] "Hayek on Freedom and Coercion," *Southern Economic Journal*, 27 (1961): 236.

[47] Ibid., p. 230.

[48] See, e.g., Pierre Bauchet, *"The Constitution of Liberty,"* *Revue économique*, 13 (1962): 143–44; Charles S. Hyneman, *"The Constitution of Liberty,"* *Midwest Journal of Political Science*, 5 (1961): 86–87; H. B. Mayo, *"The Constitution of Liberty,"* *Canadian Journal of Economics and Political Science*, 27 (1961):115–16; and Edmund L. Pincoffs, *"The Constitution of Liberty,"* *Philosophical Review*, 70 (1961): 433–34.

[49] Sidney C. Sufrin, "Some Reflections on Hayek's *The Constitution of Liberty*," *Ethics*, 71 (1961): 201–4.

were clearly motivated by the worst kind of ideological bias. Thus, Leslie Lipson, professor of political science at the University of California at Berkeley, ostensibly an authority on the history of political theory, wrote of Hayek: "His basic principles are a strange medley. They are a blend of the utopian, the nostalgic, and the inhumane—all of which is oddly described as liberalism. . . . There is a strange unrealism in this book. Its author clings to a never-never-world of illusion and doctrine, which not only cannot be created now, but in fact never did exist. He argues for a dream and is a slave to fantasy." Lipson concludes that "it is sad to discover that *The Constitution of Liberty*, as one man sees it, becomes the institution of private selfishness."[50]

British academics were more favorably disposed towards Hayek's book than were those in America. In February 1961, Lord Robbins offered an on the whole quite positive review of *The Constitution of Liberty* in one of the leading British economics journals. He wrote in part:

> This is a book which certainly rises to the high plane of the matters with which it elects to deal and which, by reason both of the depth of its analysis and the width of its learning, must surely take an honourable place among the standard works on the subject. Nor is the tone less impressive than the content. . . .
>
> [*The Constitution of Liberty*] is a work which surely no one with even a bare minimum of magnanimity and sense of what is fine can read without gratitude and admiration—gratitude for a splendid contribution to the great debate, admiration for the moral ardour and intellectual power which inspired it and made it possible.[51]

This more positive public reception of *The Constitution of Liberty*, especially in Great Britain, was encouraged by the appearance, in the early summer of 1961, of a collection of essays centering on Hayek's book. The work was published by the Institute of Economic Affairs in London[52] and comprised ten essays edited by Arthur Seldon, whose aim was to make Hayek's monograph more easily accessible to a larger audience. Each essay is devoted to a particular aspect of *The Constitution of Liberty*, explicating and expanding on Hayek's discussion: the individual in society, philosophy, law, objectives, the monetary framework, taxation, social welfare, the legal status of trade unions, human rights in industry, and agriculture. While the authors, scholars of some standing, were, for the most part, sympathetic to Hayek's conclusions, they were not uncritical where they regarded Hayek's arguments as flawed

---

[50] Leslie Lipson, "*The Constitution of Liberty*," *American Political Science Review*, 54 (1960): 1008.

[51] Lord Robbins [Lionel Robbins], "Hayek on Liberty," *Economica*, n.s., 28 (1961): 66, 81.

[52] Arthur Seldon, ed., *Agenda for a Free Society: Essays on Hayek's "The Constitution of Liberty."*

or as warranting greater precision. Possibly the book's most interesting essay is that on Hayek's political philosophy, written by J. W. N. Watkins, reader in the history of philosophy at the University of London. In a tightly argued article Watkins points out the theoretical problems with Hayek's notion of coercion and with the relationship between freedom and the rule of law. But despite these telling criticisms, Watkins was enthusiastic about Hayek's monograph. He writes: "In any circumstances *The Constitution of Liberty* would have been an important book. Given the condition of political philosophy in the English-speaking world today, it is outstandingly important."[53]

While the initial reception accorded *The Constitution of Liberty*, with a few notable exceptions, was somewhat tepid, its reputation as a major treatise on law and politics grew in the years following its publication, in part because of the recognition accorded Hayek's other writings and in part because of the ingenuity of Hayek's arguments. Over the course of the next fifteen years Hayek's views were often cited in discussions in books and articles in economics, political theory, and law. The originality and insights that he brought to bear on crucial questions in these fields were increasingly appreciated as his analysis took on an authority with which serious scholars were expected to contend. Between 1960 and 1974, several hundred articles were published that referred to Hayek's published work. In addition, several books centering on Hayek's thought appeared during that period, among them *Agenda for a Free Society*, a critical evaluation of the arguments put forward in *The Constitution of Liberty*, surely a signal honor accorded a recently published book. As the *Times Literary Supplement* pointed out: "Few writers earn the distinction of having one of their books singled out as the subject of a compilation of laudatory criticisms within a year of its publication."[54] All this, together with the growing respectability of Hayek's economic and political conclusions eventuated in his being awarded the Nobel Prize in 1974 for his "penetrating analysis of the interdependence of economic, social, and institutional phenomena."

Hayek's reputation continued to grow between 1974 and his death in 1992, accelerated both by the international recognition accorded him and by the events in eastern Europe that offered startling proof of Hayek's claims regarding the impossibility of rational calculation in socialist economies. Within a few years of his being awarded the Nobel Prize, a number of books were published that offered an overview of Hayek's work, the best of which are those by Norman Barry, released in 1979, and by John Gray, which appeared in 1984,

---

[53] "Philosophy," *Agenda for a Free Society*, 31. Watkins was not alone in praising Hayek. Writing in the same anthology, Arthur Shenfield, the economic director of the Federation of British Industries, maintained that "*The Constitution of Liberty* is one of the great books of our time, profound in analysis, ample in scholarship, noble in spirit" ("Law," *Agenda for a Free Society*, 51).

[54] "The Rule of Law," *Times Literary Supplement*, October 20, 1961.

both academics sympathetic to Hayek's conclusions.[55] Since he received the Nobel Prize, Hayek's international reputation has reached a level unmatched by all but a few scholars. Over the course of the next two decades *The Constitution of Liberty* has been translated into all the major European languages in addition to Chinese and Japanese.[56] At present there are no less than 250 books and separately bound shorter monographs in twelve languages devoted to Hayek's work.

When, in the spring of 1959 Hayek completed the manuscript of the *Constitution of Liberty*, he must have realized that it was and would continue to be his most ambitious and important work, in which he set out to sketch the structural outlines of a free society that would provide for the greatest amount of individual liberty consistent with the complexities of modern life. He would have been the first to concede that there were flaws in his analysis, some of them perhaps grave. However, inasmuch as the history of the first half of the century had offered every indication that the nations of the world had settled on a path that would eventuate in the victory of the total state, the need to offer some alternative to this alarming course appeared especially acute. At this point, fifty years later, there seems little doubt that this book, if it did not reverse that process, at least slowed it considerably. We are, all of us who value freedom and an open society and who believe in the primacy of the individual over the state, greatly indebted to Professor Hayek for *The Constitution of Liberty*, thus bringing to bear his tremendous erudition in the cause of liberty.

Ronald Hamowy
Rockville, Maryland

---

[55] Norman P. Barry, *Hayek's Social and Economic Philosophy* (London: Macmillan, 1979), and John Gray, *Hayek on Liberty* (Oxford: Basil Blackwell, 1984). See also Gray's extended essay "F. A. Hayek and the Rebirth of Classical Liberalism," *Literature of Liberty*, 5 (1982): 19–101. Alas, since writing his essay on Hayek, Gray appears to have abandoned his earlier libertarian leanings and has embraced a somewhat dim-witted mix of fashionable and often contradictory views on the need for brotherhood directed by an authoritarian state. His attacks on what he calls the "Enlightenment Project" are, in the end, simply recapitulations of the old arguments that individuals cannot be trusted to make their own decisions and that a kind and beneficent government, directed by right-thinking bureaucrats, is far more likely to establish a livable and sustainable society than are individuals left to their own devices.

[56] See *The Constitution of Liberty* Editions and Translations section of this volume.

THE CONSTITUTION OF LIBERTY: EDITIONS AND TRANSLATIONS

English

The Constitution of Liberty. Chicago: University of Chicago Press, 1960. x + 568 pages.

The Constitution of Liberty. Phoenix edition, paperback. Chicago: University of Chicago Press, paperback, 1978. x + 568 pages.

The Constitution of Liberty. Gateway edition, paperback. Chicago: Regnery, 1972. x + 568 pages.

The Constitution of Liberty. Legal Classics Library, leather-bound edition for sale by subscription. New York: Gryphon Editions, 1999. x + 568 pages.

The Constitution of Liberty. London: Routledge and Kegan Paul, 1960. x +568 pages.

The Constitution of Liberty. London: Routledge and Kegan Paul, 1963. x + 568 pages.

The Constitution of Liberty. London: Routledge and Kegan Paul, 1976. x + 568 pages.

The Constitution of Liberty. Paperback. London: Routledge, 1990. x + 568 pages.

The Constitution of Liberty. New edition, Routledge Classics. London: Routledge, 2006. xiii + 498 pages.

The Constitution of Liberty. Beijing: Zhongguo she hui ke xue chu ban she, 1999. viii + 567 pages.

Why I Am Not a Conservative. CIS Occasional Papers, No. 41 (from the postscript to *The Constitution of Liberty*). St. Leonards, N.S.W.: Center for Independent Studies, 1992. 18 pages.

Responsibility and Freedom. President's Essay series (Chapter 5 of *The Constitution of Liberty*). Washington, DC: Heritage Foundation, 1993. 33 pages.

Freedom: A Philosophical Anthology. Ian Carter, Matthew H. Kramer, and Hillel Steiner eds. Contains a selection from Chapter 9: "Coercion and the State," pp. 104–9. Oxford: Blackwell Publishers, 2007. 6 pages.

Chinese

Zi you de xian zhang. Translated by Dewei Zhou. Taipei: Taiwan yin hang jing ji yan jiu shi, 1973. xxii + 618 pages.

Zi you zhi xu yuan li. Translated by Zhenglai Deng. 2 volumes. Beijing: Sheng huo, du shu, xin zhi san lian shu dian, 1997.

Zi you xian zhang. Beijing: Zhongguo she hui ke xue chu ban she, 1998. xxiii + 597 pages.

French

La Constitution de la liberté. Translated by Raoul Audouin and Jacques Garello with the collaboration of Guy Millière. Paris: Litec, 1993. xxvii + 530 pages.

German

Der Verfassung der Freiheit. 1st edition. Tübingen: J. C. B. Mohr and P. Siebeck, 1971. xvi + 530 pages.

Der Verfassung der Freiheit. 2nd edition. Tübingen: J. C. B. Mohr and P. Siebeck, 1983. xvi + 530 pages.

Der Verfassung der Freiheit. 3rd edition. Tübingen: J. C. B. Mohr and P. Siebeck, 1991. xvi + 530 pages.

Der Verfassung der Freiheit. 4th edition, volume 3 of the Gesammelte Schriften in deutscher Sprache. Translated by Alfred Bosch. Tübingen: J. C. B. Mohr and P. Siebeck, 2005. xx + 575 pages.

Italian

La società libera. Translated by Marcella Bianchi and Lavagna Malagodi. Firenze: Vallechi, 1969. 603 pages.

La società libera. Translated by Marcella Bianchi and Lavagna Malagodi. Formello: SEAM, 1998. 647 pages.

Perché non sono un conservatore. [Postscript: "Why I Am Not a Conservative."] Rome: Ideazione, 1971. 85 pages.

Japanese

Jiyu no kachi. [Of Part 1: The Value of Freedom]. Translated by Kenzo Kiga and Katsujiro Koga. Tokyo: Shunjusha, 1986. 241 pages.

Jiyu no kachi. [Of Part 1: The Value of Freedom]. Translated by Kenzo Kiga and Katsujiro Koga. Tokyo: Shunjusha, 1997. 241 pages.

Jiyu no kachi. [Of Part 1: The Value of Freedom]. Translated by Kenzo Kiga and Katsujiro Koga. Tokyo: Shunjusha, 2007. 250 pages.

Jiyu to ho. [Of Part 2: Freedom and Law.] Translated by Kenzo Kiga and Katsujiro Koga. Tokyo: Shunjusha, 1987. 254 pages.

Jiyu to ho. [Of Part 2: Freedom and Law.] Translated by Kenzo Kiga and Katsujiro Koga. Tokyo: Shunjusha, 1997. 254 pages.

Jiyu to ho. [Of Part 2: Freedom and Law.] Translated by Kenzo Kiga and Katsujiro Koga. Tokyo: Shunjusha, 2007. 273 pages.

Fukushi kokka ni okeru jiyu. [Of Part 3: Freedom in the Welfare State.] Translated by Kenzo Kiga and Katsujiro Koga. Tokyo: Shunjusha, 1987. xxxvi + 266 pages.

Fukushi kokka ni okeru jiyu. [Of Part 3: Freedom in the Welfare State.] Translated by Kenzo Kiga and Katsujiro Koga. Tokyo: Shunjusha, 1997. xxxvi + 266 pages.

Fukushi kokka ni okeru jiyu. [Of Part 3: Freedom in the Welfare State.] Translated by Kenzo Kiga and Katsujiro Koga. Tokyo: Shunjusha, 2007. xxxvi + 277 pages.

Polish

Konstytucja wolności. Translated by H. Lapszyc. Warsaw, Wroclaw: Wers, 1987. 337 pages.

Konstytucja wolności. Translated by Janusz Stawiński. Warsaw: Wydawnnictwo Naukowe PWN, 2006. 526 pages.

Spanish

Los fundamentos de la libertad. Translated by José Vicente Torrente. 2 volumes. Valencia: Fomento de Cultura Ediciones, 1961.

Los fundamentos de la libertad. 2nd edition. Translated by José Vicente Torrente. Madrid: Unión Editorial, 1975. 510 pages.

Los fundamentos de la libertad. 3rd edition. Translated by José Vicente Torrente. Madrid: Unión Editorial, 1978. 548 pages.

Los fundamentos de la libertad. 4th edition. Translated by José Vicente Torrente. Madrid: Unión Editorial, 1982. 548 pages.

Los fundamentos de la libertad. 5th edition, volume 18 of the Obras completas. Translated by José Vicente Torrente. Madrid: Unión Editorial, 1991. 510 pages.

Los fundamentos de la libertad. 5th edition, 2 volumes. Translated by José Vicente Torrente. Barcelona: Folio, 1997. 510 pages.

Los fundamentos de la libertad. 6th edition. Translated by José Vicente Torrente. Madrid: Unión Editorial, 1998. 541 pages.

Los fundamentos de la libertad. 7th edition, 2 volumes. Translated by José Vicente Torrente. Madrid: Unión Editorial, 2006. 541 pages.

Swedish

Frihetens grundvalar. Translated by Barbro Ahlstrom and Carl Johan Ljungberg. Stockholm: Ratio, 1983. 521 pages.

Frihetens grundvalar. Translated by Barbro Ahlstrom and Carl Johan Ljungberg. Stockholm: Timbro, 1999. 611 pages.

A NOTE ON THE NOTES

Hayek's *Constitution of Liberty* is unquestionably his most important work in social philosophy, the one for which he is most likely to be remembered. I have therefore made every attempt to ensure the accuracy of his citations and quotations and to include crucial bibliographical material missing from the 1960 edition. In addition to the footnotes that appear in this edition, Hayek added approximately 200 citations to the first German edition of *The Constitution of Liberty*, published in 1971. I have included these here.

In the German edition, Hayek duplicated the footnote numbering found in the 1960 English edition, adding new material either to existing footnotes or interpolating new notes by situating them between existing notes and affixing a letter after the number of the previous note. Thus, if a note were added between footnotes 12 and 13, it would be indicated as footnote 12a. I have renumbered these new notes so all notes are now numbered consecutively. Thus, the footnote numbering in this edition will not necessarily correspond to that in the 1960 edition. All material Hayek added to the German edition is shown here in **sans serif font**.

The footnoting style to which Hayek adhered is that which predominates in Britain, where surnames are prefixed solely by initials and where no publisher or subtitles are given. I have always found the use of initials infuriating since, *inter alia*, it makes it extremely tedious to uncover other publications by the same author (consider, for example, an author cited solely as "D. Brown"). As a consequence, I have added first and middle names where these were available, even in those instances where they are rarely if ever used, as in "Wystan Hugh Auden" or "Herbert Lionel Adolphus Hart." In addition, the titles of the monographs Hayek cites have been given in full, including subtitles. I realize that in a number of cases this might well present the reader with superfluous knowledge, but I thought it best for consistency's sake to provide this information, especially in light of its utility in consulting online library catalogs. Finally, publishers' names have been added to all books, as have the page numbers on which articles in journals and anthologies fall. Unfortunately, Hayek's notes contain a large number of bibliographical errors—page and volume numbers of his quotations, titles, and even, in some instances, the names of journals. All 1,900 citations have been checked for accuracy and all errors and omissions have been silently corrected. Hayek was in the habit, here and elsewhere in his writings, of employing the abbreviation "cf." as a synonym for "see" in instances where the citation or quotation supports the contention made in the text. This has been left unaltered.

Where Hayek quotes in a foreign language, I have added a translation of the quotation. In instances where he has quoted from a source other than in English but has himself translated the material, I have included the quotation in the original language. Hayek occasionally quotes from a work that itself contains a quotation; I have tried to check the original quotation for accuracy and indicate its source. Lastly, in those instances where Hayek cites an author whose work is currently available in an edition published by the Liberty Fund of Indianapolis (e.g., Lord Acton, Adam Smith, Edmund Burke), I have keyed Hayek's references to these readily available, inexpensive editions.

Ronald Hamowy
Professor Emeritus of History, University of Alberta
Affiliate Professor of Economics, George Mason University

EDITOR'S ACKNOWLEDGMENTS

The editing of Hayek's *Constitution of Liberty* has proved a major undertaking, involving, as it has, checking each of Hayek's 1,900 citations in eight languages, the accumulated research of many decades of reading in a wide variety of fields, among them economics, history, political theory, theoretical psychology, sociology, and law. I would not have been able to accomplish this task without the help of a number of people—librarians, scholars, and students—and would be remiss if I failed to acknowledge their assistance. I wish to thank Ms. Silvia Brandolin, of the Banca Nazionale del Lavoro; Ms. Hannah Chandler, Ms. Christine Mason, and Mr. Andrew Milner, of the Bodleian Library, Oxford; Mr. Michael Chambers and Ms. Lalitha Fernando, of the British Library; Ms. Naomi Woodburn and Mr. Colin T. Clarkson, of the Cambridge University Library; Ms. Ingemar Schmart, of the Deutsche Zentralbibliothek für Wirtschaftswissenschaften; Ms. Carol Leadenham, of the Hoover Institution Library and Archives; Ms. Emily Howie, of the Library of Congress; Ms. Anna Plattner, of the Österreichische Nationalbibliothek; Mr. Robert Nef, of the *Schweizer Monatshefte;* Ms. Sabine Tolksdorf, of the Abteilung Historische Drucke, Staatsbibliothek zu Berlin; the staff of the *Times Literary Supplement;* Ms. Emma Taylor, of the University of Glasgow Library; Ms. Amy Tomaszewski, of the College of Law, and Ms. Julia Dolinnaya, of the Slavic Research Service, both of the University of Illinois Library; Ms. Kate Wilcox-Jay, of the Institute for Historical Research, University of London; the staff of the University of Michigan Library; and Mr. Geoffrey P. Williams, of the State University of New York at Albany Library.

Additionally, I am indebted to Professor William Bartley and Mr. Joel Fonstad, of the Department of English, University of Saskatchewan; Mr. Alex Biscaro, of the Swiss Embassy, Washington, DC; Professor Gerhard Ens, of the Department of History, University of Alberta; Professor Ralph Lerner, of the Committee on Social Thought, University of Chicago; Professor Roderick Long, of the Department of Philosophy, Auburn University; Professor Sam Peltzman, of the Business School, University of Chicago; Professor Donald Rutherford, of the Department of Economics, Edinburgh University; Professor Stephen Stigler, of the Department of Statistics, University of Chicago;

Professor Viktor J. Vanberg of the Institut für Allgemeine Wirtschaftsfor-schung, University of Freiburg; and Professor Gerald Stourzh, of the Depart-ment of History, University of Vienna, for their generous help.

My debt is greatest to Professors Doris Bergen, of the History Department, University of Toronto, and Daniel Gargola, of the History Department, University of Kentucky, who were unstinting in their assistance in uncover-ing and translating many of Hayek's German and classical citations. In addi-tion, I must express my special thanks to the staff of the American University Library in Washington, DC, and particularly to its interlibrary loan depart-ment, for their patience and unfailing help in providing me the bibliograph-ical assistance needed to complete an examination of Hayek's innumerable citations. I am deeply grateful to the Cato Institute, and especially to Joey Coon, Ryan Hagemann, Susanna Morrison, Daniel Robinson, David Rob-inson, Charlotte Rommerskirchen, Marian Wirth, and Jessica Wright, for supplying much-needed editorial assistance. I should also like to thank the Department of Economics at George Mason University and particularly its chairman, Professor Donald J. Boudreaux, for granting me affiliation with the department, thus permitting me the use of the university's facilities. Above all, I am indebted to the Earhart Foundation, for its generosity in underwriting the costs of this project, thus making it possible for me to devote my full time to its completion.

Finally, this task would have been impossible without the constant support, encouragement, and patience of my dear friend and companion, Mr. Clem-ent Ho.

LIBERTY FUND EDITIONS CITED

Where the books Hayek cited have been issued in editions published by the Liberty Fund, I have added that information in the notes. What follows is a listing of Liberty Fund editions referred to.

Lord Acton
> *Lectures on the French Revolution*. Foreword by Stephen J. Tonsor. Indianapolis, IN: Liberty Fund, 2000.
>> Chapter 24, n. 14
>
> *Selected Writings of Lord Acton*. Edited by J. Rufus Fears. 3 volumes. Indianapolis, IN: Liberty Classics, 1985.
>> Vol. 1. *Essays in the History of Liberty*.
>>> Chapter 4, n. 21
>>> Chapter 9, n. 9
>>> Chapter 11, n. 4
>>> Chapter 11, n. 18
>>> Chapter 11, n. 90
>>> Chapter 12, epigraph n.
>>> Chapter 12, n. 5
>>> Chapter 12, n. 7
>>> Chapter 12, n. 8
>>> Chapter 12, n. 36
>>> Chapter 16, epigraph n.
>>> Postscript, epigraph n.
>>> Postscript, n. 17
>>
>> Vol. 2. *Essays in the Study and Writing of History*.
>>> Chapter 1, n. 25
>>> Chapter 9, n. 4

Jacob Burckhardt
> *Reflections on History*. Introduction by Gottfried Dietze. Indianapolis, IN: Liberty Classics, 1979. (This edition is similar to the edition published in 1943 by Pantheon Books under the title *Force and Freedom: Reflections on History*.)

Chapter 9, n. 4

Chapter 9, n. 20

Edmund Burke

The Selected Works of Edmund Burke. Foreword and notes by Frances Canavan. 3 volumes. Indianapolis, IN: Liberty Fund, 1960.

Vol. 1. *Thoughts on the Cause of the Present Discontents and The Two Speeches on America*

Chapter 12, n. 2

Vol. 2. *Reflections on the Revolution in France*

Introduction, n. 7

Chapter 4, n. 20

Vol. 3. *Letters on a Regicide Peace*

Chapter 19, n. 37

Chapter 23, epigraph n.

A Vindication of Natural Society. Edited by Frank N. Pagano. Indianapolis, IN: Liberty Fund, 1982.

Chapter 4, n. 42

Chapter 9, n. 4

Miscellaneous Writings. Foreword and notes by Frances Canavan. Indianapolis, IN: Liberty Fund, 1999.

Chapter 4, n. 29

Further Reflections on the Revolution in France. Edited by Daniel E. Ritchie. Indianapolis, IN: Liberty Fund, 1992.

Chapter 4, n. 36

Chapter 12, n. 4

Sir Edward Coke

Selected Writings of Sir Edward Coke. Edited by Steve Sheppard. 3 volumes. Indianapolis, IN: Liberty Fund, 2005.

Vol. 1.

Chapter 4, n. 20

Chapter 11, n. 37

Chapter 11, n. 43

Chapter 11, n. 45

Chapter 11, n. 46

Edward S. Corwin

The "Higher Law" Background of American Constitutional Law. Amagi series. Indianapolis, IN: Liberty Fund, 2008.

Chapter 11, n. 6

Chapter 11, n. 35

Chapter 12, n. 11
Chapter 12, n. 42

Albert Venn Dicey
  Introduction to the Study of the Law of the Constitution. Introduction and appendix by
  A. V. Dicey; foreword by Roger E. Michener. Indianapolis, IN: Liberty Fund,
  1982.
  Chapter 11, n. 7
  Chapter 13, n. 4
  Chapter 14, n. 4
  Chapter 14, n. 8
  Chapter 16, n. 36
  *Lecturers on the Relation between Law and Public Opinion in England during the Nineteenth
  Century.* Edited by Richard VandeWeting. Indianapolis, IN: Liberty Fund, 2008
  Chapter 3, epigraph n.
  Chapter 4, n. 47
  Chapter 7, n. 13
  Chapter 7, n. 15
  Chapter 18, n. 3

Alexander Hamilton, John Jay, James Madison
  The Federalist, or the New Constitution. Gideon Edition. Edited by George W. Carey
  and James McClellan. Indianapolis, IN: Liberty Fund, 2001
  Chapter 12, n. 10
  Chapter 12, n. 32
  Chapter 15, epigraph n.

Wilhelm von Humboldt
  The Limits of State Action. Edited by John Wyon Burrow. Indianapolis, IN: Liberty
  Fund, 1993. (Originally published in English translation as *The Sphere and Duties
  of Government.*)
  Chapter 13, n. 21
  Chapter 24, n. 3

David Hume
  Essays. Edited by Eugene Miller. Indianapolis, IN: Liberty Fund, 1987. (Unlike
  the 2-volume Green-Grose edition used by Hayek, the Liberty Fund edition
  does not include either Hume's *Enquiry Concerning Human Understanding* or his
  Enquiry Concerning the Principles of Morals.)
  Introduction, n. 9
  Chapter 3, epigraph n.
  Chapter 3, n. 10

Chapter 3, epigraph n.
Chapter 4, n. 26
Chapter 4, n. 30
Chapter 7, epigraph n.
Chapter 11, n. 34
Chapter 11, n. 81
Chapter 11, n. 81
Chapter 12, n. 30
History of England from the Invasion of Julius Caesar to the Revolution of 1688. Foreword
by William B. Todd. 6 volumes. Indianapolis, IN: Liberty Fund, 1983.
Chapter 11, n. 83
Chapter 12, n. 10

Bertrand de Jouvenel
The Ethics of Redistribution. Introduction by John Gray. Indianapolis, IN: Liberty
Fund, 1990.
Chapter 8, n. 13
On Power: The Natural History of Its Growth. Foreword by D. W. Brogan. Indianapolis,
IN: Liberty Fund, 1993.
Chapter 6, n. 13
Chapter 9, n. 3
Sovereignty: An Inquiry into the Political Good. Translated by J. F. Huntington. India-
napolis, IN: Liberty Fund, 1997.
Chapter 1, n. 14

William Edward Hartpole Lecky
Democracy and Liberty. Introduction by William Murchison. 2 volumes. Indianapolis,
IN: Liberty Classics, 1981.
Chapter 20, n. 17

Jean Louis de Lolme
The Constitution of England. Edited and with an introduction by David Lieberman.
Indianapolis, IN: Liberty Fund, 2007.
Chapter 1, n. 11

Frederic William Maitland
A Historical Sketch of Liberty and Equality. Indianapolis, IN: Liberty Fund, 2000.
Chapter 2, n. 10
Chapter 9, epigraph n.

Charles Howard McIlwain
Constitutionalism: Ancient and Modern. Indianapolis, IN: Liberty Fund, 2007.

Chapter 10, n. 21
Chapter 11, n. 75
Chapter 12, n. 11

John Stuart Mill
  The Collected Works of John Stuart Mill. 8 volumes. Indianapolis, IN: Liberty Fund.
    Vols. 2 and 3. *Principles of Political Economy, with Some of Their Application to Social Philosophy.* Edited by V. W. Bladen and J. M. Robson, 1965.
      Chapter 3, n. 9
      Chapter 7. n. 7
      Chapter 15, n. 3
      Chapter 15, n. 4
      Chapter 20, n. 6
    Vol. 4. *Essays on Economics and Society.* Edited by J. M. Robson, 1965.
      Chapter 4, n. 31
    Vol. 10: *Ethics, Religion, and Society.* Edited by J. M. Robson, 1965.
      Chapter 7, n. 14

John Milton
  Areopagitica and Other Political Writings of John Milton. Foreword by John Alvis. Indianapolis, IN: Liberty Fund, 1999.
    Chapter 5, n.10
    Chapter 9, n. 4

Ludwig von Mises
  Anti-capitalistic Mentality. Edited by Bettina Bien Greaves. Indianapolis, IN: Liberty Fund, 2006.
    Chapter 8, n. 10
  Human Action: A Treatise on Economics. Edited by Bettina Bien Greaves. 4 volumes. Indianapolis, IN: Liberty Fund, 2007.
    Vol. 1.
      Chapter 7, n. 9
    Vol. 2.
      Chapter 8, n. 5
      Chapter 19, n. 10
      Chapter 21, n. 1
    Vol. 3.
      Chapter 20, n. 28
    Vol. 4.
      Chapter 17, n. 21
  Nation, State, and Economy: Contributions to the Politics and History of Our Time. Translated by Leland B. Yeager. Indianapolis, IN: Liberty Fund, 2006.
    Chapter 24, n. 4

Planning for Freedom: Let the Market System Work. Edited by Bettina Bien Greaves.
Indianapolis, IN: Liberty Fund, 2008.
Chapter 20, n. 4

Socialism: An Economic and Sociological Analysis. Translated by Jacques Kahane; fore-
word by F. A. Hayek. New edition. Indianapolis, IN: Liberty Fund, 1960.
Chapter 1, n. 6
Chapter 4, n. 15
Chapter 9, n. 14
Chapter 10, n. 21
Chapter 18, n. 6 (German edition)
Chapter 19, n. 28
Chapter 23, n. 11

Felix Morley

Essays on Individuality. Edited by Felix Morley. Indianapolis, IN: Liberty Fund,
1977.
Chapter 2, epigraph n.
Chapter 8, n. 10

Michael Polanyi

The Logic of Liberty: Reflections and Rejoinders. Foreword by Stuart D. Warner. India-
napolis, IN: Liberty Fund, 1998.
Chapter 2, n. 2
Chapter 3, n. 8
Chapter 9, epigraph n.
Chapter 10, n. 25
Chapter 24, n. 14

David Ricardo

The Works and Correspondence of David Ricardo. Edited by Piero Sraffa with the collab-
oration of M. H. Dobb. 11 volumes. Indianapolis, IN: Liberty Fund, 2004.
Vol. 9. *Letters 1821–1823*
Chapter 21, n. 16

Algernon Sidney

Discourses Concerning Government. Edited by Thomas G. West. Indianapolis, IN: Lib-
erty Fund, 1996.
Title page, epigraph n.
Chapter 11, n. 59

Adam Smith

The Glasgow Edition of the Works and Correspondence of Adam Smith. 7 volumes. Indianapolis, IN: Liberty Fund.

Vol. 1. *The Theory of Moral Sentiments*. Edited by David Daitches Raphael and
Alec Lawrence Macfie, 1977.
Chapter 6, n. 11

Vols. 2a and 2b. *An Inquiry into the Nature and Causes of the Wealth of Nations*. Edited
by R. H. Campbell and A. S. Skinner, 1982.
Chapter 3, n. 9
Chapter 4, n. 26
Chapter 10, n. 15
Chapter 11, n. 84
Chapter 15, n. 5
Chapter 24, n. 13

Vol. 5. *Lectures on Jurisprudence*. Edited by Ronald Lindley Meek, David Daitches
Raphael, and Peter Gonville Stein, 1982
Chapter 22, n. 2

Herbert Spencer
The Principles of Ethics. Introduction by Tibor R. Machan. 2 volumes. Indianapolis, IN: Liberty Classics, 1978. (The section on justice appears in vol. 2,
pp. 19–279.)
Chapter 15, n. 11

James Fitzjames Stephen
Liberty, Equality, Fraternity. Edited by Stuart D. Warner. Indianapolis, IN: Liberty
Fund, 1993.
Chapter 7, n. 9

Emer de Vattel
*The Law of Nations, Or, Principles of the Laws of Nature, Applied to the Conduct and Affairs
of Nations and Sovereigns*. Edited and with an introduction by Béla Kapossy and
Richard Whatmore. Indianapolis, IN: Liberty Fund, 2008.
Chapter 12, n. 9

Friedrich A. Hayek

THE CONSTITUTION OF LIBERTY

Our inquiry is not after that which is perfect, well knowing that no such thing is found among men; but we seek that human Constitution which is attended with the least, or the most pardonable inconveniences. —Algernon Sidney

This quotation is taken from Algernon Sidney, *Discourses Concerning Government* (London. Printed and are to be sold by booksellers of London and Westminster, 1698), chap. 3, sec. 18, p. 142 [*The Works of Algernon Sidney*, Thomas Hollis, ed. (London. Printed for W. Strahan Iun., 1772), p. 151 (Liberty Fund edition, p. 180).]

To the unknown civilization that is growing in America.

PREFACE

The aim of this book is explained in the Introduction, and my chief obligations are acknowledged in the few paragraphs that follow this preface. All that remains for me to do here is to issue a warning and to present an apology.

This book is not concerned mainly with what science teaches us. Though I could not have written it if I had not devoted the greater part of my life to the study of economics and had not more recently endeavored to acquaint myself with the conclusions of several other social sciences, I am not concerned here exclusively with facts, nor do I confine myself to statements of cause and effect. My aim is to picture an ideal, to show how it can be achieved, and to explain what its realization would mean in practice. For this, scientific discussion is a means, not an end. I believe I have made honest use of what I know about the world in which we live. The reader will have to decide whether he wants to accept the values in the service of which I have used that knowledge.

The apology concerns the particular state at which I have decided to submit the results of my efforts to the reader. It is perhaps inevitable that the more ambitious the task, the more inadequate will be the performance. On a subject as comprehensive as that of this book, the task of making it as good as one is capable of is never completed while one's faculties last. No doubt I shall soon find that I ought to have said this or that better and that I have committed errors which I could myself have corrected if I had persisted longer in my efforts. Respect for the reader certainly demands that one present a tolerably finished product. But I doubt whether this means that one ought to wait until one cannot hope to improve it further. At least where the problems are of the kind on which many others are actively working, it would even appear to be an overestimate of one's own importance if one delayed publication until one was certain that one could not improve anything. If a man has, as I hope I have, pushed analysis a step forward, further efforts by him are likely to be subject to rapidly decreasing returns. Others will probably be better qualified to lay the next row of bricks of the edifice to which I am trying to contribute. I will merely claim that I have worked on the book until I did not know how I could adequately present the chief argument in briefer form.

Perhaps the reader should also know that, though I am writing in the United

States and have been a resident of this country for nearly ten years, I cannot claim to write as an American. My mind has been shaped by a youth spent in my native Austria and by two decades of middle life in Great Britain, of which country I have become and remain a citizen. To know this fact about myself may be of some help to the reader, for the book is to a great extent the product of this background.

F. A. Hayek
Chicago
May 8, 1959

ACKNOWLEDGMENTS

So much of what I have been trying to say in this book has been said before in a manner on which I cannot improve, but in places widely dispersed or in works with which the modern reader is not likely to be familiar, that it seemed desirable to expand the notes beyond mere references into what is in part almost an anthology of individualist liberal thought. These quotations are meant to show that what today may often seem strange and unfamiliar ideas were once the common heritage of our civilization, but also that, while we are building on this tradition, the task of uniting them into a coherent body of thought directly applicable to our day is one which still needed to be undertaken. It is in order to present the building stones from which I have tried to fashion a new edifice that I have allowed these notes to run to this length. They nevertheless do not provide a complete bibliography of the subject. A helpful list of relevant works can be found in Henry Hazlitt, *The Free Man's Library: A Descriptive and Critical Bibliography* (Princeton, NJ: Van Nostrand, 1956).

These notes are also far from being an adequate acknowledgment of my indebtedness. The process in which I formed the ideas expressed in this book necessarily preceded the plan of stating them in this form. After I decided on this exposition I read little of the work of authors with whom I expected to agree, usually because I had learned so much from them in the past. In my reading I rather aimed at discovering the objections I had to meet, the arguments I had to counter, and at finding the forms in which these ideas have been expressed in the past. In consequence, the names of those who have contributed most to shaping my ideas, whether as my teachers or as fellow strugglers, appear rarely in these pages. If I had regarded it as my task to acknowledge all indebtedness and to notice all agreement, these notes would have been studded with references to the work of Ludwig von Mises, Frank H. Knight, and Edwin Cannan; of Walter Eucken and Henry C. Simons; of Wilhelm Röpke and Lionel Robbins; of Karl R. Popper, Michael Polanyi, and Bertrand de Jouvenel. Indeed, if I had decided to express not my aim but my indebtedness in the dedication of this book, it would have been most appropriate to dedicate it to the members of the Mont Pèlerin Society and in particular to their two intellectual leaders, Ludwig von Mises and Frank H. Knight.

There are, however, more specific obligations which I wish to acknowledge here. Edward C. Banfield, Chester I. Barnard, W. H. Book, John Davenport, Pierre F. Goodrich, Walter Fröhlich, David Grene, Floyd A. Harper, David G. Hutton, Arthur Kemp, Frank H. Knight, William L. and Shirley Letwin, Fritz Machlup, Laurence W. Martin, Ludwig von Mises, Alexander Morin, Felix Morley, Sylvester Petro, J. H. Reiss, Gerald Stourzh, Ralph Turvey, C. Y. Wang, and Richard Ware have read various parts of an earlier draft of this book and assisted me with their comments. Many of them and Aaron Director, Victor Ehrenberg, Duncan Forbes, Milton Friedman, Morris Ginsberg, Claude W. Guillebaud, Bruno Leoni, John U. Nef, Margaret G. Reid, Max Rheinstein, Hans Rothfels, Helmut Schoeck, Irene Shils, T. F. T. Plucknett, and Jacob Viner have supplied me with important references or facts, though I hesitate to mention their names since I am almost bound to forget some of the many who have helped me in this way.

In the final stages of the preparation of the book I have had the invaluable benefit of the assistance of Mr. Edwin McClellan. It is mainly due to his and (I understand) Mrs. McClellan's sympathetic efforts to straighten out my involved sentences if the book is more readable than I could ever have made it. It has received further polish from the hands of my friend Henry Hazlitt, who was good enough to read and comment upon part of the final typescript. I am also indebted to Mrs. Lois Fern for checking all the quotations in the notes and to Miss Vernelia Crawford for preparing the Subject Index.

Though the book is not the product of the now common kind of collective effort—I have never learned even to avail myself of the aid of a research assistant—it has in other ways greatly benefited from opportunities and facilities which various foundations and institutions have provided. To the Volker, Guggenheim, Earhart, and Relm foundations I owe in this connection a great debt. Lectures given at Cairo, Zurich, Mexico City, Buenos Aires, and Rio de Janeiro and at various American universities and colleges have provided an opportunity not only to try out on audiences some of the ideas expounded in the book, but also to gain experiences that were important in writing it. Places of publication of earlier drafts of some of the chapters are mentioned in the notes, and I am grateful to the various editors and publishers for permission to reprint them. I also wish to acknowledge the help of the University of Chicago Library, on which I have relied almost exclusively in the work on this book, and whose Inter-Library Loan Service has invariably procured whatever I needed; and to the Social Science Research Committee and the typing staff of the Social Science Division of the University of Chicago who have provided the funds and the labor for typing successive drafts of this book.

My greatest debt, however, is to the Committee on Social Thought of the University of Chicago and to its chairman, Professor John Ulrich Nef, who made it possible for me for some years to regard as my main task the completion of this book, which was facilitated rather than hindered by my other duties on the Committee.

BIBLIOGRAPHICAL ABBREVIATIONS

Acton, *Historical Essays*
  John Emerich Edward Dalberg Acton, Baron Acton. *Historical Essays and Studies.* Edited by John Neville Figgis and Reginald Vere Laurence. London: Macmillan and Co., 1907.

Acton, *History of Freedom*
  John Emerich Edward Dalberg Acton, Baron Acton. *The History of Freedom and Other Essays.* Edited by J. N. Figgis and R. V. Laurence. London: Macmillan and Co., 1907.

  The Liberty Fund has published a three-volume collection of Acton's essays under the general title *Selected Writings of Lord Acton,* J. Rufus Fears, ed. (Indianapolis, IN: Liberty Classics, 1985). The individual volumes are titled: Vol. 1: *Essays in the History of Liberty;* Vol. 2: *Essays in the Study and Writing of History;* and Vol. 3: *Essays in Religion, Politics, and Morality*

Bagehot, *Works*
  Walter Bagehot. *The Works and Life of Walter Bagehot.* Edited by [Mrs.] Russell Barrington. 10 vols. London: Longman, Green, and Co., 1910.

Burke, *Works*
  Edmund Burke. *The Works of the Right Honourable Edmund Burke.* New edition. 16 vols. London: Rivington, 1815–27.

  The Liberty Fund has published a number of essays by Burke in several volumes. They are, in three volumes, *The Selected Works of Edmund Burke,* foreword and notes by Frances Canavan (Indianapolis, IN: Liberty Fund, 1960); another volume containing *A Vindication of Natural Society,* Frank N. Pagano, ed. (1982); yet another volume entitled *Miscellaneous Writings,* foreword and notes by Frances Canavan (1999); and, finally, a volume titled *Further Reflections on the Revolution in France,* Daniel E. Ritchie, ed. (1992).

Dicey, *Law of the Constitution*
  Albert Venn Dicey. *Introduction to the Study of the Law of the Constitution,* 9th ed. Introduction and appendix by E. C. S. Wade. London: Macmillan and Co., 1939.

The ninth edition, published in 1939, some 25 years after the eighth edition had appeared, was edited by Emlyn Capel Stewart Wade and contains a new introduction and appendix that replaced those written by Dicey and that appeared in earlier editions. The Liberty Fund has issued a reprint of the eighth edition containing Dicey's original material (Indianapolis, IN: Liberty Fund, 1982) with a foreword by Roger E. Michener.

Dicey, *Law and Public Opinion*

Albert Venn Dicey. *Lectures on the Relation between Law and Public Opinion in England during the Nineteenth Century*, 2nd ed. London: Macmillan and Co., 1914.

The Liberty Fund republished the 1917 edition, with a new introduction by Richard VandeWeting, in 2008.

Encyclopedia of the Social Sciences

Edwin R. A. Seligman and Alvin Johnson, eds. *Encyclopedia of the Social Sciences*. 15 vols. New York: Macmillan Company, 1930–35.

The *Encyclopedia* was reissued in 1937 and reprinted in 1951.

Hume, *Essays*

David Hume. *Essays: Moral, Political, and Literary*. Edited by Thomas Hill Green and Thomas Hodge Grose. 2 vols. London: Longmans, Green, and Co., 1875. Vol. 2 contains *inter alia* the *Enquiry Concerning Human Understanding* and the *Enquiry Concerning the Principles of Morals*.

Essays (not including either the *Enquiry* or the *Principles*) was republished by the Liberty Fund in a new edition by Eugene Miller in 1987.

Hume, *Treatise of Human Nature*

David Hume. *A Treatise of Human Nature*. Edited by Thomas Hill Green and Thomas Hill Grose. 2 vols. London: Longmans, Green, and Co., 1890.

Locke, *Second Treatise*

John Locke. *The Second Treatise of Civil Government* and *A Letter Concerning Toleration*, 3rd ed. Edited by John Wiedhofft Gough. Oxford: Basil Blackwell, 1946.

Menger, *Untersuchungen*

Carl Menger. *Untersuchungen über die Methode der Socialwissenschaften, und der Politischen Oekonomie insbesondere*. Leipzig: Duncker und Humblot, 1883.

This work has been translated into English by Francis J. Nock and published under the title of *Problems of Economics and Sociology*. Edited by Louis Schneider. Urbana: University of Illinois Press, 1963.

Mill, *Principles*

John Stuart Mill. *Principles of Political Economy, with Some of Their Applications to Social Philosophy*. Edited by Sir William James Ashley. London: Longmans, Green, and Co., 1909.

A new edition of Mill's *Principles* constitutes volumes 2 and 3 of the *Collected Works of John Stuart Mill*, Vincent Wheeler Bladen and John Mercel Robson, eds., published by the University of Toronto Press in 1965 and reprinted by the Liberty Fund in 2006.

Montesquieu, *Spirit of the Laws*
Charles de Secondat, Baron de Montesquieu. *The Spirit of the Laws*. Translated by Thomas Nugent. 2 vols. in one. Hafner Library of Classics. New York: Hafner Publishing Co., 1949.
The French edition used is that contained in volume 2 of the Pléiade complete works: "De l'Esprit des Lois," in *Œuvres Complètes*, Roger Caillois, ed. Bibliothèque de la Pléiade. 2 vols. Paris: Éditions Gallimard, 1951.

Smith, *Wealth of Nations*
Adam Smith. *An Inquiry into the Nature and Causes of the Wealth of Nations*. Edited by Edwin Cannan. 2 vols. London: Methuen and Co., 1904.
The Liberty Fund republished the Glasgow edition of the works and correspondence of Adam Smith in paperback in 1960. *The Wealth of Nations*, edited by R. H. Campbell and A. S. Skinner, constitutes volumes 1 and 2.

Tocqueville, *Democracy in America*
Alexis de Tocqueville. *Democracy in America*. Translated by Henry Reeve. Edited by Phillips Bradley. 2 vols. New York: Alfred A. Knopf, 1945.
The French edition used is that contained in volume 2 of the Pléiade complete works: "De la démocratie en Amérique," in *Œuvres*, André Jardin, ed. Bibliothèque de la Pléiade. 2 vols. Paris: Éditions Gallimard, 1992.

[vol.] *U.S.* [pp.]
United States Reports: Cases Adjudged in the Supreme Court. Washington: Government Printing Office. (According to American standard legal practice, references to this and such earlier reports of federal cases as "Dallas," "Cranch," "Wheaton," and "Wallace," and to reports of cases in state courts, are *preceded* by the number of the volume and followed by the number of the page on which the report of the case begins and, where necessary, the page to which reference is made.)

INTRODUCTION

What was the road by which we reached our position, what the form of government under which our greatness grew, what the national habits out of which it sprang? . . . If we look to the laws, they afford equal justice to all in their private differences. . . . The freedom which we enjoy in our government extends also to our ordinary life. . . . But all this ease in our private relations does not make us lawless as citizens. Against this fear is our chief safeguard, teaching us to obey the magistrates and the laws, particularly such as regard the protection of the injured, whether they are actually on the statute book, or belong to that code which, although unwritten, yet cannot be broken without acknowledged disgrace. —Pericles

If old truths are to retain their hold on men's minds, they must be restated in the language and concepts of successive generations. What at one time are their most effective expressions gradually become so worn with use that they cease to carry a definite meaning. The underlying ideas may be as valid as ever, but the words, even when they refer to problems that are still with us, no longer convey the same conviction; the arguments do not move in a context familiar to us; and they rarely give us direct answers to the questions we are asking.[1] This may be inevitable because no statement of an ideal that is likely to sway men's minds can be complete: it must be adapted to a given climate of opinion, presuppose much that is accepted by all men of the time, and illustrate general principles in terms of issues with which they are concerned.

The quotation at the head of this section is taken from Pericles' Funeral Oration as reported by Thucydides ii.36.4 to ii.37.3, Richard Crawley, trans., *The Complete Writings: The Peloponnesian War* (New York: Modern Library, 1951), pp. 103–4.

[1] There are sayings which gain currency because they express what at one time seemed an important truth, continue to be used when this truth has become known to everybody, and are still used when, through frequent and mechanical use, they have ceased to carry a distinct meaning. They are finally dropped because they no longer provoke any thought. They are rediscovered only after they have been dormant for a generation and then can be used with new force to convey something like their original meaning—only to go through the same cycle once more if they are successful.

It has been a long time since that ideal of freedom which inspired modern Western civilization and whose partial realization made possible the achievements of that civilization was effectively restated.[2] In fact, for almost a century the basic principles on which this civilization was built have been falling into increasing disregard and oblivion. Men have sought for alternative social orders more often than they have tried to improve their understanding or use of the underlying principles of our civilization.[3] It is only since we were confronted with an altogether different system that we have discovered that we have lost any clear conception of our aims and possess no firm principles which we can hold up against the dogmatic ideology of our antagonists.

In the struggle for the moral support of the people of the world, the lack of firm beliefs puts the West at a great disadvantage. The mood of its intellectual leaders has long been characterized by disillusionment with its principles, disparagement of its achievements, and exclusive concern with the creation of "better worlds." This is not a mood in which we can hope to gain followers. If we are to succeed in the great struggle of ideas that is under way, we must first of all know what we believe. We must also become clear in our own minds as to what it is that we want to preserve if we are to prevent ourselves from drifting. No less is an explicit statement of our ideals necessary in our relations with other peoples. Foreign policy today is largely a question of which political philosophy is to triumph over another; and our very survival may depend on our ability to rally a sufficiently strong part of the world behind a common ideal.

This we shall have to do under very unfavorable conditions. A large part of the people of the world borrowed from Western civilization and adopted Western ideals at a time when the West had become unsure of itself and had largely lost faith in the traditions that have made it what it is. This was a time when the intellectuals of the West had to a great extent abandoned the very belief in freedom which, by enabling the West to make full use of those forces that are responsible for the growth of all civilization, had made its unprecedented quick growth possible. In consequence, those men from the less advanced nations who became purveyors of ideas to their own people

---

[2] The last comprehensive attempt to restate the principles of a free society, already much qualified and in the restrained form expected of an academic textbook, is Henry Sidgwick, *The Elements of Politics* (London: Macmillan, 1891). Though in many respects an admirable work, it scarcely represents what must be regarded as the British liberal tradition and is strongly tainted with that rationalist utilitarianism which led to socialism.

[3] In England, where the tradition of liberty lasted longer than in other European countries, as early as 1885 a writer whose work was then widely read among liberals could say of these liberals that "the reconstruction of society, not the liberation of individuals, is now their most pressing task" (Francis Charles Montague, *The Limits of Individual Liberty* [London: Rivingtons, 1885], p. 16. [Montague (1858–1935) was regarded as one of the leading liberals of his period.—Ed.]

learned, during their Western training, not how the West had built up its civilization, but mostly those dreams of alternatives which its very success had engendered.

This development is especially tragic because, though the beliefs on which these disciples of the West are acting may enable their countries to copy more quickly a few of the achievements of the West, they will also prevent them from making their own distinct contribution. Not all that is the result of the historical development of the West can or should be transplanted to other cultural foundations; and whatever kind of civilization will in the end emerge in those parts under Western influence may sooner take appropriate forms if allowed to grow rather than if it is imposed from above. If it is true, as is sometimes objected, that the necessary condition for a free evolution—the spirit of individual initiative—is lacking, then surely without that spirit no viable civilization can grow anywhere. So far as it is really lacking, the first task must be to waken it; and this a regime of freedom will do, but a system of regimentation will not.

So far as the West is concerned, we must hope that here there still exists wide consent on certain fundamental values. But this agreement is no longer explicit; and if these values are to regain power, a comprehensive restatement and revindication are urgently needed. There seems to exist no work that gives a full account of the whole philosophy on which a consistent liberal view can rest—no work to which a person wishing to comprehend its ideals may turn. We have a number of admirable historical accounts of how "The Political Traditions of the West" grew. But though they may tell us that "the object of most Western thinkers has been to establish a society in which every individual, with a minimum of dependence on the discretionary authority of his rulers, would enjoy the privileges and responsibility of determining his own conduct within a previously defined framework of legal rights and duties,"[4] I know of none that explains what this means when applied to the concrete problems of our time, or whereupon the ultimate justification of this idea rests.

In recent years valiant efforts have also been made to clear away the confusions which have long prevailed regarding the principles of the economic policy of a free society. I do not wish to underrate the clarification that has been achieved. Yet, though I still regard myself as mainly an economist, I have come to feel more and more that the answers to many of the pressing social questions of our time are to be found ultimately in the recognition of principles that lie outside the scope of technical economics or of any other single discipline. Though it was from an original concern with problems of

[4] Frederick Mundell Watkins, *The Political Tradition of the West: A Study in the Development of Modern Liberalism* (Cambridge, MA: Harvard University Press, 1948), p. x.

economic policy that I started, I have been slowly led to the ambitious and perhaps presumptuous task of approaching them through a comprehensive restatement of the basic principles of a philosophy of freedom.

But I tender no apologies for thus venturing far beyond the range where I can claim to have mastered all the technical detail. If we are to regain a coherent conception of our aims, similar attempts should probably be made more often. One thing, in fact, which the work on this book has taught me is that our freedom is threatened in many fields because of the fact that we are much too ready to leave the decision to the expert or to accept too uncritically his opinion about a problem of which he knows intimately only one little aspect. But, since the matter of the ever recurring conflict between the economist and the other specialists will repeatedly come up in this book, I want to make it quite clear here that the economist can not claim special knowledge which qualifies him to co-ordinate the efforts of all the other specialists.[5] What he may claim is that his professional occupation with the prevailing conflicts of aims has made him more aware than others of the fact that no human mind can comprehend all the knowledge which guides the actions of society and of the consequent need for an impersonal mechanism, not dependent on individual human judgments, which will co-ordinate the individual efforts. It is his concern with the impersonal processes of society in which more knowledge is utilized than any one individual or organized group of human beings can possess that puts the economists in constant opposition to the ambitions of other specialists who demand powers of control because they feel that their particular knowledge is not given sufficient consideration.

In one respect this book is, at the same time, more and less ambitious than the reader will expect. It is not chiefly concerned with the problems of any particular country or of a particular moment of time but, at least in its earlier parts, with principles which claim universal validity. The book owes its conception and plan to the recognition that the same intellectual trends, under different names or disguises, have undermined the belief in liberty throughout the world. If we want to counter these trends effectively, we must understand the common elements underlying all their manifestations. We must also remember that the tradition of liberty is not the exclusive creation of any single country and that no nation has sole possession of the secret even today. My main concern is not with the particular institutions or policies of the United States or of Great Britain but with the principles that these countries have developed on foundations provided by the ancient Greeks, the Italians of the early Renaissance, and the Dutch, and to which the French and

---

[5] On the problem of "expertocracy" see Manfred Kuhn, *Herrschaft der Experten? An den Grenzen der Demokratie* [Beiträge zur politischen Bildung No. 4] (Würzburg: Werkbund-Verlag, 1961), and Kuhn's earlier writings mentioned there.

the Germans have made important contributions. Also, my aim will not be to provide a detailed program of policy but rather to state the criteria by which particular measures must be judged if they are to fit into a regime of freedom. It would be contrary to the whole spirit of this book if I were to consider myself competent to design a comprehensive program of policy. Such a program, after all, must grow out of the application of a common philosophy to the problems of the day.

While it is not possible to describe an ideal adequately without constantly contrasting it with others, my aim is not mainly critical.[6] My intention is to open doors for future development rather than to bar others, or, I should perhaps say, to prevent any such doors being barred, as invariably happens when the state takes sole control of certain developments. My emphasis is on the positive task of improving our institutions; and if I can do no more than indicate desirable directions of development, I have at any rate tried to be less concerned with the brushwood to be cleared away than with the roads which should be opened.

As a statement of general principles, the book must deal mainly with basic issues of political philosophy, but it approaches more tangible problems as it proceeds. Of its three parts, the first endeavors to show why we want liberty and what it does. This involves some examination of the factors which determine the growth of all civilizations. The discussion in this part must be mainly theoretical and philosophical—if the latter is the right word to describe the field where political theory, ethics, and anthropology meet. It is followed by an examination of the institutions that Western man has developed to secure individual liberty. We enter here the field of jurisprudence and shall approach its problems historically. Yet it is neither from the point of view of the lawyer nor from that of the historian that we shall chiefly regard that evolution. Our concern will be with the growth of an ideal, only dimly seen and imperfectly realized at most times, which still needs further clarification if it is to serve as a guide for the solution of the problems of our times.

In the third part of the book those principles will be tested by the application of them to some of today's critical economic and social issues. The topics I have selected are in those areas where a false choice among the possibilities

---

[6] I also hope that I shall not lay myself open to the reminder addressed to Edmund Burke by Samuel Taylor Coleridge, particularly important in our time, that "it is bad policy to represent a political system as having no charm but for robbers and assassins, and no natural origin but in the brains of fools or madmen, when experience has proved that the great danger of the system consists in the peculiar fascination it is calculated to exert on noble and imaginative spirits; on all those who, in the amiable intoxication of youthful benevolence, are apt to mistake their own best virtues and choicest powers for the average qualities and attributes of the human character." (*The Political Thought of Samuel Taylor Coleridge*, Reginald James White, ed. [London: Jonathan Cape, 1938], pp. 235–36.)

before us is most likely to endanger freedom. Their discussion is meant to illustrate how often the pursuit of the same goals by different methods may either enhance or destroy liberty. They are mostly the kind of topics on which technical economics alone does not provide us with sufficient guidance to formulate a policy and which can be adequately treated only within a wider framework. But the complex issues which each of them raises can, of course, not be treated exhaustively in this volume. Their discussion serves mainly as an illustration of what is the chief aim of this book, namely, the interweaving of the philosophy, jurisprudence, and economics of freedom which is still needed.

This book is meant to help understanding, not to fire enthusiasm. Though in writing about liberty the temptation to appeal to emotion is often irresistible, I have endeavored to conduct the discussion in as sober a spirit as possible. Though the sentiments which are expressed in such terms as the "dignity of man" and the "beauty of liberty" are noble and praiseworthy, they can have no place in an attempt at rational persuasion. I am aware of the danger of such a cold-blooded and purely intellectual approach to an ideal which has been a sacred emotion to many and which has been stoutly defended by many more to whom it never constituted an intellectual problem. I do not think the cause of liberty will prevail unless our emotions are aroused. But, though the strong instincts on which the struggle for liberty has always nourished itself are an indispensable support, they are neither a safe guide nor a certain protection against error. The same noble sentiments have been mobilized in the service of greatly perverted aims. Still more important, the arguments that have undermined liberty belong mainly to the intellectual sphere, and we must therefore counter them here.

Some readers will perhaps be disturbed by the impression that I do not take the value of individual liberty as an indisputable ethical presupposition and that, in trying to demonstrate its value, I am possibly making the argument in its support a matter of expediency. This would be a misunderstanding. But it is true that if we want to convince those who do not already share our moral suppositions, we must not simply take them for granted. We must show that liberty is not merely one particular value but that it is the source and condition of most moral values.[7] What a free society offers to the individual is much

---

[7] Cf. Wystan Hugh Auden in his "Introduction," to Henry James, *The American Scene: Together with Three Essays from "Portraits of Places"* (New York: Charles Scribner's Sons, 1946), p. xviii; and see also Christian Bay, *The Structure of Freedom* (Stanford, CA.: Stanford University Press, 1958), p. 19: "Freedom is the soil required for the full growth of other values." (This latter work became available too late to admit of more than occasional references in the notes.) See also Edmund Burke, *Reflections on the Revolution in France* in *Selected Works*, Edward John Payne, ed. (3 vols.; Oxford: Clarendon Press, 1874), vol. 2, p. 122 [Liberty Fund edition, vol. 2, p. 201]: "The world on the whole will gain by liberty without which virtue cannot exist."

more than what he would be able to do if only he were free. We can therefore not fully appreciate the value of freedom until we know how a society of free men as a whole differs from one in which unfreedom prevails.

I must also warn the reader not to expect the discussion to remain always on the plane of high ideals or spiritual values. Liberty in practice depends on very prosaic matters, and those anxious to preserve it must prove their devotion by their attention to the mundane concerns of public life and by the efforts they are prepared to give to the understanding of issues that the idealist is often inclined to treat as common, if not sordid. The intellectual leaders in the movement for liberty have all too often confined their attention to those uses of liberty closest to their hearts, and have made little effort to comprehend the significance of those restrictions of liberty which did not directly affect them.[8]

If the main body of the discussion is to be as matter of fact and unemotional as possible throughout, its starting point will of necessity have to be even more pedestrian. The meaning of some of the indispensable words has become so vague that it is essential that we should at the outset agree on the sense in which we shall use them. The words "freedom" and "liberty" have been the worst sufferers. They have been abused and their meaning distorted until it could be said that "the word liberty means nothing until it is given specific content, and with a little massage it will take any content you like."[9] We shall therefore have to begin by explaining what this liberty is that we are concerned with. The definition will not be precise until we have also examined such other almost equally vague terms as "coercion," "arbitrariness," and "law" which are indispensable in a discussion of liberty. The analysis of these concepts has, however, been postponed to the beginning of Part II, so that the arid effort at clarification of words should not present too great an obstacle before we reach the more substantial issues.

For this attempt at restating a philosophy of men's living together which has slowly developed through more than two thousand years, I have drawn

[8] Cf. Alfred North Whitehead, *Adventure of Ideas* (Mentor Books; New York: New American Library, 1955), p. 73. "Unfortunately the notion of freedom has been eviscerated by the literary treatment devoted to it. . . . The concept of freedom has been narrowed to the picture of contemplative people shocking their generation. When we think of freedom, we are apt to confine ourselves to freedom of thought, freedom of the press, freedom of religious opinions. . . . This is a thorough mistake. . . . The literary exposition of freedom deals mainly with [the] frills. . . . In fact, freedom of action is a primary human need." [Hayek's footnote is to the first paperback edition of Whitehead's essay published by the New American Library in 1955 and now long out of print and extremely difficult of access. The original hardbound edition was published in New York by Macmillan in 1933. The quotation can be found on pp. 83–84 of the 1933 edition.—Ed.]

[9] Carl Lotus Becker, *New Liberties for Old* (New Haven: Yale University Press, 1941), p. 4.

encouragement from the fact that it has often emerged from adversity with renewed strength. During the last few generations it has gone through one of its periods of decline. If to some, especially those in Europe, this book should appear to be a kind of inquest into the rationale of a system that no longer exists, the answer is that if our civilization is not to decline that system must be revived. Its underlying philosophy became stationary when it was most influential, as it had often progressed when on the defensive. It has certainly made little progress during the last hundred years and is now on the defensive. Yet the very attacks on it have shown us where it is vulnerable in its traditional form. One need not be wiser than the great thinkers of the past to be in a better position to comprehend the essential conditions of individual liberty. The experience of the last hundred years has taught us much that a Madison or a Mill, a Tocqueville or a Humboldt, could not perceive.

Whether the moment has arrived when this tradition can be revived will depend not only on our success in improving it but also on the temper of our generation. It was rejected at a time when men would recognize no limits to their ambition, because it is a modest and even humble creed, based on a low opinion of men's wisdom and capacities and aware that within the range for which we can plan, even the best society will not satisfy all our desires. It is as remote from perfectionism as it is from the hurry and impatience of the passionate reformer, whose indignation about particular evils so often blinds him to the harm and injustice that the realization of his plans is likely to produce. Ambition, impatience, and hurry are often admirable in individuals; but they are pernicious if they guide the power of coercion and if improvement depends on those who, when authority is conferred on them, assume that in their authority lies superior wisdom and thus the right to impose their beliefs on others. I hope our generation may have learned that it has been perfectionism of one kind or another that has often destroyed whatever degree of decency societies have achieved.[10] With more limited objectives, more patience, and more humility, we may in fact advance further and faster than we have done while under the guidance of "a proud and most presumptuous confidence in the transcendent wisdom of this age, and its discernment."[11]

[10] David Hume, who will be our constant companion and sage guide throughout the following pages, could speak as early as 1742 (*Essays*, "Of Moral Prejudices," [Essay 2], vol. 2, pp. 371 and 373 [Liberty Fund edition, pp. 539 and 542]) of "that grave philosophic Endeavour after Perfection, which, under Pretext of reforming Prejudices and Errors, strikes at all the most endearing Sentiments of the Heart, and all the most useful Byasses and Instincts, which can govern a human Creature."(vol. 2, p. 371) "not to depart too far from the receiv'd Maxims of Conduct and Behaviour, by a refin'd Search after Happiness or Perfection" (vol. 2, p. 373).

[11] William Wordsworth, *The Excursion: Being a Portion of The Recluse; A Poem* (London: Printed for Longman, Hurst, Rees, Orme, and Brown, 1814), pt. 2, p. 62.

PART I

THE VALUE OF FREEDOM

Throughout history orators and poets have extolled liberty, but no one has told us why liberty is so important. Our attitude towards such matters should depend on whether we consider civilization as fixed or as advancing. . . . In an advancing society, . . . any restriction on liberty reduces the number of things tried and so reduces the rate of progress. In such a society freedom of action is granted to the individual, not because it gives him greater satisfaction but because if allowed to go his own way he will on the average serve the rest of us better than under any orders we know how to give.

—H. B. Phillips

This quotation is taken from Henry Bayard Phillips, "On the Nature of Progress," *American Scientist* 33 (1945): p. 255.

ONE

LIBERTY AND LIBERTIES

The world has never had a good definition of the word liberty, and the American people, just now, are much in want of one. We all declare for liberty; but in using the same word, we do not mean the same thing. . . . Here are two, not only different, but incompatible things, called by the same name, liberty. —Abraham Lincoln

1. We are concerned in this book with that condition of men in which coercion of some by others is reduced as much as is possible in society. This state we shall describe throughout as a state of liberty or freedom.[1] These two words have been also used to describe many other good things of life. It would therefore not be very profitable to start by asking what they really mean.[2] It

---

The quotation at the head of the chapter is taken from Abraham Lincoln, *The Writings of Abraham Lincoln*, Arthur Brooks Lapsley, ed. (Federal ed.; 8 vols.; New York: G. P. Putnam's Sons, 1905), vol. 7, p. 121. Cf. the similar remark by Montesquieu, *Spirit of the Laws*, bk. 11, chap. 2, vol. 1, p. 149: "there is no word that admits of more various significations, and has made more varied impressions on the human mind, than that of *liberty*. Some have taken it as a means of deposing a person on whom they had conferred a tyrannical authority; others for the power of choosing a superior whom they are obliged to obey, others for the right of bearing arms, and of being thereby enabled to use violence; others, in fine, for the privilege of being governed by a native of their own country, or by their own laws." ["Il n'y a point de mot qui ait reçu plus de différentes significations, et qui ait frappé les esprits de tant de manières, que celui de *liberté*. Les uns l'ont pris pour la facilité de déposer celui à qui ils avoient donné un pouvoir tyrannique; les autres, pour la faculté d'élire celui à qui ils dévoient obéir; d'autres, pour le droit d'être armés, et de pouvoir exercer la violence; ceux-ci pour le privilège de n'être gouvernés que par un homme de leur nation, ou par leurs propres lois."(vol. 2, p. 394)—Ed.]

[1] There does not seem to exist any accepted distinction in meaning between the words "freedom" and "liberty," and we shall use them interchangeably. Though I have a personal preference for the former, it seems that "liberty" lends itself less to abuse. It could hardly have been used for that "noble pun" (Joan Robinson, *Private Enterprise or Public Control* [Handbook for Discussion Groups, No. 11; London: Association for Education in Citizenship, 1943], p. 13) of Franklin D. Roosevelt's when he included "freedom from want" in his conception of liberty.

[2] The limited value of even a very acute semantic analysis of the term "freedom" is well illustrated by Maurice William Cranston, *Freedom: A New Analysis* (New York: Longmans, Green, and Co., 1953), which will be found illuminating by readers who like to see how philosophers have tied themselves in knots by their curious definitions of the concept. For a more ambitious sur-

would seem better to state, first, the condition which we shall mean when we use them and then consider the other meanings of the words only in order to define more sharply that which we have adopted.

The state in which a man is not subject to coercion by the arbitrary will of another or others[3] is often also distinguished as "individual" or "personal" freedom, and whenever we want to remind the reader that it is in this sense that we are using the word "freedom," we shall employ that expression. Sometimes the term "civil liberty" is used in the same sense, but we shall avoid it because it is too liable to be confused with what is called "political liberty"— an inevitable confusion arising from the fact that "civil" and "political" derive, respectively, from Latin and Greek words with the same meaning.[4]

---

vey of the various meanings of the word see Mortimer Jerome Adler, *The Idea of Freedom: A Dialectical Examination of the Conceptions of Freedom* (Garden City, NY: Doubleday, 1958), which I have been privileged to see in draft, and an even more comprehensive work by Harald Ofstad, *An Inquiry into the Freedom of Decision* (Oslo: Norwegian University Press; Stockholm: Svenska bokförlaget, 1961).

[3] See Aristotle, *Metaphysics*, 1.2.8 [982b]: "As man is free we say he exists for his own sake and not for another's." Gottfried Wilhelm Leibniz, "Über die Freiheit," in *Philosophische Werke: Hauptschriften zur Grundlegung der Philosophie*, Artur Buchenau and Ernst Cassirer, eds. (Leipzig: Verlag der Dürr'schen Buchhandlung, 1906), vol. 2, p. 497: "Daher kam ich der Meinung derer nahe, es sei für die Freiheit genug, daß das Geschehen dem *Zwange* nicht unterworfen ist, wenngleich es der *Notwendigkeit* untersteht." ["Thus, I approached the opinion of those it would suffice for liberty that events are not subordinate to *coercion*, albeit, they are subject to *necessity*."—Ed.]; Cf. Jeremy Bentham, *The Limits of Jurisprudence Defined: Being Part Two of an Introduction to the Principles of Morals and Legislation*, Charles Warren Everett, ed. (New York: Columbia University Press, 1945), p. 59: "Liberty then is of two or even more sorts, according to the number of quarters from whence coercion, which it is the absence of, may come." See also Georg Jellinek, *System der subjektiven öffentlichen Rechte* (2nd ed.; Tübingen: Verlag von J. C. B. Mohr, 1905), chap. 8, pp. 94–114: "Der negative Status (status liberatatis)"; Moritz Schlick, *Fragen der Ethik* (Vienna: J. Springer, 1930), p. 110: "Freiheit bedeutet ja den Gegensatz zum Zwang, der Mensch ist frei, wenn er nicht gezwungen handelt" ["Freedom means the opposite of compulsion; a man is free if he does not act under compulsion." *Problems of Ethics*, David Rynin, trans. (New York: Prentice Hall, 1939), p. 150—Ed.]; Frank Hyneman Knight, "The Meaning of Freedom," in *The Philosophy of American Democracy*, Charner Marquis Perry, ed. (Chicago: University of Chicago Press, 1943), p. 75: "The primary meaning of freedom in society . . . is always a negative concept . . . and coercion is the term which must really be defined"; and the fuller discussion by the same author in his review article "The Meaning of Freedom," a review of *Freedom: Its Meaning*, Ruth Nanda Anshen, ed. *Ethics*, 52 (1941): 86–109, and "Conflict of Values: Freedom and Justice," in *Goals of Economic Life*, Alfred Dudley Ward, ed. (New York: Harper, 1953); also Franz Leopold Neumann, *The Democratic and the Authoritarian State: Essays in Political and Legal Theory* (Glencoe, IL: The Free Press, 1957), p. 202: "The formula, freedom equals absence of coercion, is still correct. . . . [F]rom this formula there follows fundamentally the whole rational legal system of the civilized world. . . . It is *the* element of the concept of freedom that we can never give up"; and Christian Bay, *The Structure of Freedom* (Stanford, CA: Stanford University Press, 1958), p. 94: "Among all the freedom goals, the goal of maximizing everyone's freedom from coercion should take first priority."

[4] Currently the expression "civil liberty" seems to be used chiefly with respect to those exercises of individual liberty which are particularly significant for the functioning of democracy,

Even our tentative indication of what we shall mean by "freedom" will have shown that it describes a state which man living among his fellows may hope to approach closely but can hardly expect to realize perfectly. The task of a policy of freedom must therefore be to minimize coercion or its harmful effects, even if it cannot eliminate it completely.

It so happens that the meaning of freedom that we have adopted seems to be the original meaning of the word.[5] Man, or at least European man, enters history divided into free and unfree; and this distinction had a very definite meaning.[6] The freedom of the free may have differed widely, but only in the degree of an independence which the slave did not possess at all. It meant always the possibility of a person's acting according to his own decisions and plans, in contrast to the position of one who was irrevocably subject to the will of another, who by arbitrary decision could coerce him to act or not to act in specific ways. The time-honored phrase by which this freedom has often been described is therefore "independence of the arbitrary will of another."

This oldest meaning of "freedom" has sometimes been described as its vulgar meaning; but when we consider all the confusion that philosophers have

---

such as freedom of speech, of assembly, and of the press—and in the United States particularly with reference to the opportunities guaranteed by the Bill of Rights. Even the term "political liberty" is occasionally used to describe, especially in contrast to "inner liberty," not the collective liberty for which we shall employ it, but personal liberty. But though this usage has the sanction of Montesquieu, it can today only cause confusion.

[5] Cf. Sir Ernest Barker, *Reflections on Government* (London: Oxford University Press, 1942), pp. 1–2: "Originally liberty signified the quality or status of the free man, or free producer, in contradistinction to the slave." It seems that, etymologically, the Teutonic root of "free" described the position of a protected member of the community (cf. Gustav Neckel, "Adel und Gefolgschaft: Ein beitrag zur germanischen altertumskunde," *Beiträge zur Geschichte der deutschen Sprache und Literatur* 41 [1916], esp. 403: "'Frei' hiess ursprünglich derjenige, der nicht schutz- und rechtlos war" ["Originally the term 'free' referred to those who had neither legal protection nor rights."—Ed.]. See also Otto Schrader, *Sprachvergleichung und Urgeschichte. Linguistisch-historische Beiträge zur Erforschung des indogermanischen Altertums*. Vol. 2, part 2: *Die Urzeit*. (3rd ed.; Jena: H. Costenoble, 1907), p. 294, and Adolf Waas, *Die alte deutsche Freiheit. Ihr wesen und ihre geschichte* (Munich and Berlin: R. Oldenburg, 1939), pp. 10–15. Similarly, Latin *liber* and Greek *eleutheros* seem to derive from words denoting membership in the tribe. The significance of this will appear later when we examine the relation between law and liberty. See also Ruth Fulton Benedict, "Primitive Freedom," *Atlantic Monthly*, 169 (1942): 760: "So too in primitive societies there are civil liberties, the crux of which is that they are guaranteed to all men without discrimination. Wherever these privileges and protections to which all members have an inalienable right are important privileges in the eyes of that tribe, people regard themselves, whatever their form of government, as free men enjoying the blessings of liberty."

[6] Max Pohlenz, *Griechische Freiheit: Wesen und Werden eines Lebensideals* (Heidelberg: Quelle und Meyer, 1955), p. 7: "Historisch ist die Begriffsentwicklung aber so verlaufen, daß erst das Vorhandensein von Unfreien, von Sklaven, bei den anderen das Gefühl der Freiheit weckte." ["Historically, it was the existence of the unfree, the slaves, that first gave the others the feeling that they themselves were free."—Ed.]

THE CONSTITUTION OF LIBERTY

caused by their attempts to refine or improve it, we may do well to accept this description. More important, however, than that it is the original meaning is that it is a distinct meaning and that it describes one thing and one thing only, a state which is desirable for reasons different from those which make us desire other things also called "freedom." We shall see that, strictly speaking, these various "freedoms" are not different species of the same genus but entirely different conditions, often in conflict with one another, which therefore should be kept clearly distinct. Though in some of the other senses it may be legitimate to speak of different kinds of freedom, "freedoms from" and "freedoms to," in our sense "freedom" is one, varying in degree but not in kind.

In this sense "freedom" refers solely to a relation of men to other men,[7] and the only infringement on it is coercion by men. This means, in particular, that the range of physical possibilities from which a person can choose at a given moment has no direct relevance to freedom. The rock climber on a difficult pitch who sees only one way out to save his life is unquestionably free, though we would hardly say he has any choice. Also, most people will still have enough feeling for the original meaning of the word "free" to see that if that same climber were to fall into a crevasse and were unable to get out of it, he could only figuratively be called "unfree," and that to speak of him as being "deprived of liberty" or of being "held captive" is to use these terms in a sense different from that in which they apply to social relations.[8]

The question of how many courses of action are open to a person is, of course, very important. But it is a different question from that of how far in acting he can follow his own plans and intentions, to what extent the pattern of his conduct is of his own design, directed toward ends for which he has been persistently striving rather than toward necessities created by others

[7] Cf. Thomas Hill Green, *Lectures on the Principles of Political Obligation* [1895] (new imprint; London: Longmans, Green, and Co., 1911), p. 3: "As to the sense given to 'freedom,' it must of course be admitted that every usage of the term to express anything but a social and political relation of one man to others involves a metaphor. Even in the original application its sense is by no means fixed. It always implies indeed some exemption from compulsion by others, but the extent and conditions of this exemption, as enjoyed by the 'freeman' in different states of society, are very various. As soon as the term 'freedom' comes to be applied to anything else than an established relation between a man and other men, its sense fluctuates much more." Also, Ludwig von Mises, *Socialism* (new ed.; New Haven: Yale University Press, 1951), p. 191: "Freedom is a sociological concept. It is meaningless to apply it to conditions outside society" [pt. 2, chap. 9, sec. 3]; and p. 194: "This, then, is freedom in the external life of man—that he is independent of the arbitrary power of his fellows" [pt. 2, chap. 9, sec. 3] [Liberty Fund edition, pp. 169 and 171].

[8] Cf. Knight, "Review: The Meaning of Freedom," p. 93: "If Crusoe fell into a pit or became entangled in jungle growth, it would certainly be correct usage to speak of his freeing himself or regaining his liberty—and this would apply to an animal as well." This may well be established usage by now, but it nevertheless refers to a conception of liberty other than that of absence of coercion which Professor Knight defends.

in order to make him do what they want. Whether he is free or not does not depend on the range of choice but on whether he can expect to shape his course of action in accordance with his present intentions, or whether somebody else has power so to manipulate the conditions as to make him act according to that person's will rather than his own. Freedom thus presupposes that the individual has some assured private sphere, that there is some set of circumstances in his environment with which others cannot interfere.

This conception of liberty can be made more precise only after we have examined the related concept of coercion. This we shall do systematically after we have considered why this liberty is so important. But even before we attempt this, we shall endeavor to delineate the character of our concept somewhat more precisely by contrasting it with the other meanings which the word liberty has acquired. They have the one thing in common with the original meaning in that they also describe states which most men regard as desirable; and there are some other connections between the different meanings which account for the same word being used for them.[9] Our immediate task, however, must be to bring out the differences as sharply as possible.

2. The first meaning of "freedom" with which we must contrast our own use of the term is one generally recognized as distinct.[10] It is what is commonly called "political freedom," the participation of men in the choice of their government, in the process of legislation, and in the control of administration. It derives from an application of our concept to groups of men as a whole which gives them a sort of collective liberty. But a free people in this sense is not necessarily a people of free men; nor need one share in this col-

---

[9] The linguistic cause of the transfer of "free" and of the corresponding nouns to various uses seems to have been the lack in English (and apparently in all Germanic and Romance languages) of an adjective which can be used generally to indicate that something is absent. "Devoid" or "lacking" are generally used only to express the absence of something desirable or normally present. There is no corresponding adjective (other than "free" of) to describe the absence of something undesirable or alien to an object. We will generally say that something is free of vermin, of impurities, or of vice, and thus freedom has come to mean the absence of anything undesirable. Similarly, whenever we want to say that something acts by itself, undetermined, or uninfluenced by external factors, we speak of its being free of influences not normally connected with it. In science we speak even of "degrees of freedom" when there are several possibilities unaffected by the known or assumed determinants (cf. Cranston, *Freedom: A New Analysis*, p. 5). And see also the excellent essays by Stanley Isaac Benn and Richard Stanley Peters, *Social Principles and the Democratic State* (London: Allen and Unwin, 1959), p. 212: "any condition can be described as the absence of its opposite. If health is 'freedom from disease,' education 'freedom from ignorance,' there is no conceivable object of social organization and action that cannot be called 'freedom.' But the price of making 'freedom' all-embracing as a social end is to drain it of all prescriptive meaning, and to leave only the prescriptive overtones, to make it synonymous with terms of approval like 'good' and 'desirable.'"

[10] This sharp differentiation between "freedom," in the sense of alternately ruling and obeying, and "liberty," in the sense that we may live as we choose, occurs as early as Aristotle, *Politics*, 6.3 [1317b]. ["One factor of liberty is to govern and be governed in turn."—Ed.]

61

lective freedom to be free as an individual. It can scarcely be contended that the inhabitants of the District of Columbia, or resident aliens in the United States, or persons too young to be entitled to vote do not enjoy full personal liberty because they do not share in political liberty.[11]

It would also be absurd to argue that young people who are just entering into active life are free because they have given their consent to the social order into which they were born: a social order to which they probably know no alternative and which even a whole generation who thought differently from their parents could alter only after they had reached mature age. But this does not, or need not, make them unfree. The connection which is often sought between such consent to the political order and individual liberty is one of the sources of the current confusion about its meaning. Anyone is, of course, entitled to "identify liberty . . . with the process of active participation in public power and public law making."[12] Only it should be made clear that, if he does so, he is talking about a state other than that with which we are here concerned, and that the common use of the same word to describe these different conditions does not mean that the one is in any sense an equivalent or substitute for the other.[13]

[11] All these would have to be described as unfree by Harold Joseph Laski, who contended (*Liberty in the Modern State* [new ed.; London: Allen and Unwin, 1948], p. 48.) that "the right . . . to the franchise is essential to liberty; and a citizen excluded from it is unfree." By similarly defining freedom, Hans Kelsen ("The Foundations of Democracy," *Ethics*, 66, no. 1, pt. 2, [1955]: 94) triumphantly reaches the conclusion that "the attempts at showing an essential connection between freedom and property . . . have failed, though all those who have asserted such a connection have been speaking of individual and not political freedom."

[12] Edwin Mims, Jr., *The Majority of the People* (New York: Modern Age Books, 1941), p. 170.

[13] Cf. Montesquieu, *Spirit of the Laws*, bk. ix., sec. 2 (vol. 1, p. 150) [French edition, vol. 2, p. 394]: "In fine, as in democracies the people seem to act almost as they please, this sort of government has been deemed the most free, and the power of the people has been confounded with their liberty." ["Enfin, comme dans les démocraties le peuple paroît à peu près faire ce qu'il veut, on a mis la liberté dans ces sortes de gouvernements; et on a confondu le pouvoir du peuple avec la liberté du peuple."—Ed.]

See also Jean Louis de Lolme, *The Constitution of England, or, An Account of the English Government: In Which It Is Compared Both with the Republican Form of Government, and the Other Monarchies in Europe* [1784] (new ed.; London, G. G. and J. Robinson, 1800), bk. 2, chap. 5, p. 240 [Liberty Fund edition, p. 170]: "To concur by one's suffrage in enacting laws, is to enjoy a share, whatever it may be, of power: to live in a state where the laws are equal for all, and sure to be executed . . . is to be free." ["Contribuer, par son suffrage, à la sanction des lois, c'est avoir une portion quelconque de puissance, mais donc l'exercice de laquelle, encore une fois, on est très éloigné de voir toujours sa volonté réussir. Vivre dans un état où les lois sont égales pour tous, et sûrement exécutées . . . c'est être libre." Jean Louis de Lolme, *Constitution de l'Angleterre, ou état du gouvernement anglois, comparé avec la forme républicaine & avec les autres monarchies de l'Europe* (2 vols.; London: G. Robinson, J. Murray, 1785), vol. 1, p. 218.—Ed.]

Cf. also the passages quoted in nn. 2 and 5 to chap. 7. [The two passages to which Hayek refers appear in two footnotes to chapter 7 of book 2 of de Lolme's work. The footnotes are

The danger of confusion here is that this use tends to obscure the fact that a person may vote or contract himself into slavery and thus consent to give up freedom in the original sense. It would be difficult to maintain that a man who voluntarily but irrevocably had sold his services for a long period of years to a military organization such as the Foreign Legion remained free thereafter in our sense; or that a Jesuit who lives up to the ideals of the founder of his order and regards himself "as a corpse which has neither intelligence nor will" could be so described.[14] Perhaps the fact that we have seen millions voting themselves into complete dependence on a tyrant has made our generation understand that to choose one's government is not necessarily to secure freedom. Moreover, it would seem that discussing the value of freedom would be pointless if any regime of which people approved was, by definition, a regime of freedom.

The application of the concept of freedom to a collective rather than to individuals is clear when we speak of a people's desire to be free from a foreign yoke and to determine its own fate. In this case we use "freedom" in the sense of absence of coercion of a people as a whole. The advocates of individual freedom have generally sympathized with such aspirations for national freedom, and this led to the constant but uneasy alliance between the liberal and the national movements during the nineteenth century.[15] But though the

---

not numbered but Hayek is apparently referring to the following two quotations. The first is from Valerius Maximus, *Memorable Doings and Sayings* (bk. 3, sec. 7) and reads: "Valerius Maximus relates that the tribunes of the people having offered to propose some regulations in regard to the price of corn, in a time of great scarcity, Scipio Nasica over-ruled the assembly merely by saying: 'Silence, Romans! I know better than you what is expedient for the republic'—which words were no sooner heard by the people, than they showed by a silence full of veneration, that they were more affected by his authority, than by the necessity of providing for their own subsistence." (de Lolme, vol. 1, p. 256; Liberty Fund edition, p. 179). The second, from Livy, (6.16.3–4), reads: "The tribunes of the people," says Livy, who as a great admirer of the aristocratical power, "and the people themselves, durst neither lift up their eyes, nor even mutter, in the presence of the dictator." (de Lolme, vol. 1, pp. 257–58; Liberty Fund edition, p. 180)—Ed.]

[14] The full description of the proper state of mind of a Jesuit, quoted by William James from one of the letters of Ignatius Loyola (*Varieties of Religious Experience: A Study in Human Nature* [New York: Longmans, Green, and Co., 1902], p. 314) runs as follows: "In the hands of my Superior, I must be a soft wax, a thing, from which he is to require whatever pleases him, be it to write or receive letters, to speak or not to speak to such a person, or the like; and I must put all my fervor in executing zealously and exactly what I am ordered. I must consider myself as a corpse which has neither intelligence nor will; be like a mass of matter which without resistance lets itself be placed wherever it may please anyone; like a stick in the hand of an old man, who uses it according to his needs and places it where it suits him. So must I be under the hands of the Order, to serve it in the way it judges most useful." [James gives the source of Loyola's letter as Danielo Baroli, *Histoire de Saint Ignace de Loyola et de la Compagnie de Jésus, d'après les documents originaux*, translated from the Italian by P. L. Michel (2 vols.; Paris: Vaton, 1844), vol. 2, p. 13.—Ed.]

[15] This is the view that prevailed in Germany at the beginning of the century, despite being historically incorrect. Consider the comments of Friedrich Naumann, *Das Ideal der Freiheit* (Berlin-Schöneberg: Hilfe,

---

concept of national freedom is analogous to that of individual freedom, it is not the same; and the striving for the first has not always enhanced the second. It has sometimes led people to prefer a despot of their own race to the liberal government of an alien majority; and it has often provided the pretext for ruthless restrictions of the individual liberty of the members of minorities. Even though the desire for liberty as an individual and the desire for liberty of the group to which the individual belongs may often rest on similar feelings and sentiments, it is still necessary to keep the two conceptions clearly apart.

3. Another different meaning of "freedom" is that of "inner" or "metaphysical" (sometimes also "subjective") freedom.[16] It is perhaps more closely related to individual freedom and therefore more easily confounded with it. It refers to the extent to which a person is guided in his actions by his own considered will, by his reason or lasting conviction, rather than by momentary impulse or circumstance. But the opposite of "inner freedom" is not coercion by others but the influence of temporary emotions, or moral or intellectual weakness. If a person does not succeed in doing what, after sober reflection, he decides to do, if his intentions or strength desert him at the decisive moment and he fails to do what he somehow still wishes to do, we may say that he is "unfree," the "slave of his passions." We occasionally also use these terms when we say that ignorance or superstition prevents people from doing what they would do if they were better informed, and we claim that "knowledge makes free."

Whether or not a person is able to choose intelligently between alternatives, or to adhere to a resolution he has made, is a problem distinct from whether or not other people will impose their will upon him. They are clearly not without some connection: the same conditions which to some constitute coercion will be to others merely ordinary difficulties which have to be overcome, depending on the strength of will of the people involved. To that

---

1908), p. 5. He writes: "Freiheit ist in erster Linie ein nationaler Begriff. Das soll heißen: Lange ehe man über die Freiheit des einzelnen Volksgenossen stritt und nachdachte, unterschied man freie und unfreie Völker und Stämme." ["Liberty is primarily a term associated with the nation. That is to say that long before it was conceived and discussed in terms of the individual liberty of one's countrymen, it was employed to distinguish free and unfree peoples and tribes."—Ed.] It is significant, however, that this entailed that "Die Geschichte lehrt, daß der Gesamtfortschritt der Kultur gar nicht anders möglich ist als durch Zerbrechung der nationalen Freiheit kleinerer Völker," ["History instructs us that cultural progress is possible solely by crushing the national liberty of lesser peoples."—Ed.] and "Es ist kein ewiges Recht der Menschen, von Stammesgenossen geleitet zu werden. Die Geschichte hat entschieden, daß es führende Nationen gibt und solche, die geführt werden, und es ist schwer, liberaler sein zu wollen, als die Geschichte selber ist" ["It is not an eternal human right to be led by fellow tribesmen. History has decided that there are leading nations as well as such that are led, and it is difficult to wish to be more liberal than history itself." p. 13.—Ed.]

[16] The difference between this concept of "inner liberty" and liberty in the sense of absence of coercion was clearly perceived by the medieval Scholastics, which distinguished between *libertas a necessitate* [liberty to choose] and *libertas a coactione* [liberty from external compulsion].

extent, "inner freedom" and "freedom" in the sense of absence of coercion will together determine how much use a person can make of his knowledge of opportunities. The reason why it is still very important to keep the two apart is the relation which the concept of "inner freedom" has to the philosophical confusion about what is called the "freedom of the will." Few beliefs have done more to discredit the ideal of freedom than the erroneous one that scientific determinism has destroyed the basis for individual responsibility. We shall later (in chap. 5) consider these issues further. Here we merely want to put the reader on guard against this particular confusion and against the related sophism that we are free only if we do what in some sense we ought to do.

4. Neither of these confusions of individual liberty with different concepts denoted by the same word is as dangerous as its confusion with a third use of the word to which we have already briefly referred: the use of "liberty" to describe the physical "ability to do what I want,"[17] the power to satisfy our wishes, or the extent of the choice of alternatives open to us. This kind of "freedom" appears in the dreams of many people in the form of the illusion that they can fly; that they are released from gravity and can move "free like a bird" to wherever they wish, or that they have the power to alter their environment to their liking.

This metaphorical use of the word has long been common, but until comparatively recent times few people seriously confused this "freedom from" obstacles, this freedom that means omnipotence, with the individual freedom that any kind of social order can secure. Only since this confusion was deliberately fostered as part of the socialist argument has it become dangerous. Once this identification of freedom with power is admitted, there is no limit to the sophisms by which the attractions of the word "liberty" can be used to support measures which destroy individual liberty,[18] no end to the tricks by which

[17] Barbara Wootton, *Freedom under Planning* (London: Allen and Unwin, 1945), p. 10. The earliest explicit use of freedom in the sense of power which is known to me occurs in Voltaire, *Le Philosophe ignorant*, quoted by Bertrand de Jouvenel, *De la souveraineté, à la recherche du bien politique* (Paris: M. T. Génin, 1955), p. 315: "Être véritablement libre, c'est pouvoir. Quand je peux faire ce que je veux, voilà ma liberté." ["To be really free, is (to possess) power. When I can do what I wish to do, therein my liberty lies." Voltaire's essay appears in *Mélanges*, J. van den Heuvel, ed. (Paris: Gallimard, 1961), p. 887. There is a Liberty Fund edition of Jouvenel's work: *Sovereignty: An Inquiry into the Political Good*, J. F. Huntington, trans. (Indianapolis, IN: Liberty Fund, 1997). The reference is on p. 248.—Ed.] It seems ever since to have remained closely associated with what we shall later (chap. 4) have to distinguish as the "rationalist," or French, tradition of liberty. [The 1971 German edition reads: "The term's meaning has since then been linked with the tradition which we shall later describe (chap. 4) as the French or the "rational" tradition. It seems, however, that the notion that freedom is power can be traced back, as can so many modern anti-liberal views, to Francis Bacon."—Ed.]

[18] Cf. Peter Ferdinand Drucker, *The End of Economic Man: A Study of the New Totalitarianism* (London: William Heinemann, 1939), pp. 74–75: "The less freedom there is, the more there is talk of the 'new freedom.' Yet this new freedom is a mere word which covers the exact contradiction of all that Europe ever understood by freedom. . . . The new freedom which is preached in Europe

people can be exhorted in the name of liberty to give up their liberty. It has been with the help of this equivocation that the notion of collective power over circumstances has been substituted for that of individual liberty and that in totalitarian states liberty has been suppressed in the name of liberty.

The transition from the concept of individual liberty to that of liberty as power has been facilitated by the philosophical tradition that uses the word "restraint" where we have used "coercion" in defining liberty. Perhaps "restraint" would in some respects be a more suitable word if it was always remembered that in its strict sense it presupposes the action of a restraining human agent.[19] In this sense, it usefully reminds us that the infringements on liberty consist largely in people's being prevented from doing things, while "coercion" emphasizes their being made to do particular things. Both aspects are equally important: to be precise, we should probably define liberty as the absence of restraint and constraint.[20] Unfortunately, both these words have come also to be used for influences on human action that do not come from other men; and it is only too easy to pass from defining liberty as the absence of restraint to defining it as the "absence of obstacles to the realization of [our] desires"[21] or even more generally as "the absence of external impediments."[22] This is equivalent to interpreting it as effective power to do whatever we want.

This reinterpretation of liberty is particularly ominous because it has penetrated deeply into the usage of some of the countries where, in fact, individ-

---

is, however, the right of the majority against the individual." That this "new freedom" has been preached equally in the United States is shown by Woodrow Wilson, *The New Freedom: A Call for the Emancipation of the Generous Energies of a People* (New York: Doubleday, Page, and Co., 1913), esp. p. 26. A more recent illustration of this is an article by Allen Garfield Gruchy, "The Economics of the Natural Resources Committee," *American Economic Review*, 29 (1939): 70, where the author observes approvingly that "for the economists of the National Resources Committee economic freedom is not a question of the absence of restraint upon individual activities, but instead it is a problem of collective restraint and direction imposed upon individuals and groups to the end that individual security may be achieved."

[19] A definition in terms of absence of restraint in which this meaning is stressed, such as that of Edward Samuel Corwin, *Liberty Against Government: The Rise, Flowering, and Decline of a Famous Juridical Concept* (Baton Rouge: Louisiana State University Press, 1948), p. 7: "Liberty signifies the absence of restraints imposed by other persons upon our own freedom of choice and action."

[20] *The Shorter Oxford English Dictionary on Historical Principles* (2 vols.; Oxford: Clarendon Press, 1933), s.v. "coerce," gives as the word's first definition: "To constrain, or restrain by force, or by authority resting on force." [This definition is essentially the same as the one published in the complete *Oxford English Dictionary* (2nd ed.; 20 vols.; Oxford: Oxford University Press, 1989). It reads: "To constrain or restrain (a voluntary or moral agent) by the application of superior force, or by authority resting on force."—Ed.]

[21] Bertrand Russell, "Freedom and Government," in *Freedom: Its Meaning*, Ruth Nanda Anshen, ed. (New York: Harcourt, Brace, 1940), p. 251.

[22] Thomas Hobbes, *Leviathan; or, The Matter, Forme, and Power of a Commonwealth, Ecclesiasticall and Civil*, Michael Joseph Oakeshott, ed. (Oxford: B. Blackwell, 1946), p. 84.

ual freedom is still largely preserved. In the United States it has come to be widely accepted as the foundation for the political philosophy dominant in "liberal" circles. Such recognized intellectual leaders of the "progressives" as J. R. Commons[23] and John Dewey have spread an ideology in which "liberty is power, effective power to do specific things" and the "demand for liberty is the demand for power,"[24] while the absence of coercion is merely "the negative side of freedom" and "is to be prized only as a means to a freedom which is power."[25]

5. This confusion of liberty as power with liberty in its original meaning inevitably leads to the identification of liberty with wealth;[26] and this makes it

[23] John Rogers Commons, *Legal Foundations of Capitalism* (New York: Macmillan, 1924), esp. chaps. 2–4 [chap. 2, "Property, Liberty, and Value," pp. 11–46; chap. 3, "Physical, Economic, and Moral Power," pp. 47–64; chap. 4, "Transactions," pp. 65–142].

[24] John Dewey, "Liberty and Social Control," *The Social Frontier*, 2 (November 1935): 41–42. [The full quotation reads: "Liberty is not just an idea, an abstract principle. It is power, effective power to do specific things. There is no such thing as liberty in general; liberty, so to speak, at large. If one wants to know what the condition of liberty is at a given time, one has to examine what persons *can* do and what they *cannot* do. The moment one examines the question from the standpoint of effective action, it becomes evident that the demand for liberty is a demand for power."—Ed.] Cf. also his article "Force and Coercion," *International Journal of Ethics*, 23 (1916): 359–67: "Whether the use of force is justified or not . . . is, in substance, a question of efficiency (including economy) of means in the accomplishing of ends" (p. 362). "The criterion of value lies in the relative efficiency and economy of the expenditure of force as a means to an end" (p. 364). Dewey's jugglery with the concept of liberty is indeed so appalling that the judgment of Dorothy Fosdick, *What Is Liberty? A Study in Political Theory* (New York: Harper and Brothers, 1939), p. 91, is hardly unjust: "The stage, however, is fully set for this [identification of liberty with some principle, such as equality] only when the definitions of liberty and of equality have been so juggled that both refer to approximately the same condition of activity. An extreme example of such sleight-of-hand is provided by John Dewey when he says 'If freedom is combined with a reasonable amount of equality and security is taken to mean cultural and moral security and also material safety, I do not think that security is compatible with anything but freedom.' After redefining two concepts so that they mean approximately the same condition of activity he assures us that the two are compatible. There is no end to such legerdemain."

[25] John Dewey, *Experience and Education* (New York: Macmillan, 1938), p. 74. [The full quotation reads: "There can be no greater mistake . . . than to treat such freedom as an end in itself. It then tends to be destructive of the shared cooperative activities which are the normal source of order. But, on the other hand, it turns freedom which should be positive into something negative. For freedom from restriction, the negative side, is to be prized only as a means to a freedom which is power: power to frame purposes, to judge wisely, to evaluate desires by the consequences which will result from acting upon them; power to select and order means to carry chosen ends into operation (pp. 73–74).—Ed.] Cf. also Werner Sombart, *Der moderne Kapitalismus* (2 vols.; Leipzig: Duncker und Humblot, 1902), vol. 2 *Die Theorie der kapitalistischen Entwicklung*, p. 43, where it is explained that "Technik" is "die Entwicklung zur Freiheit" [the development towards freedom]. This idea is developed at length in Eberhard Zschimmer, *Philosophie der Technik. Vom Sinn der Technik und Kritik des Unsinns über die Technik* (Jena: Eugen Diederichs, 1914), pp. 86–91.

[26] Cf. Ralph Barton Perry, "Liberty in a Democratic State," in *Freedom: Its Meaning*, Ruth Nanda Anshen, ed. (New York: Harcourt, Brace, 1940), p. 269: "The distinction between 'welfare' and

possible to exploit all the appeal which the word "liberty" carries in the support for a demand for the redistribution of wealth. Yet, though freedom and wealth are both good things which most of us desire and though we often need both to obtain what we wish, they still remain different. Whether or not I am my own master and can follow my own choice and whether the possibilities from which I must choose are many or few are two entirely different questions. The courtier living in the lap of luxury but at the beck and call of his prince may be much less free than a poor peasant or artisan, less able to live his own life and to choose his own opportunities for usefulness. Similarly, the general in charge of an army or the director of a large construction project may wield enormous powers which in some respects may be quite uncontrollable, and yet may well be less free, more liable to have to change all his intentions and plans at a word from a superior, less able to change his own life or to decide what to him is most important, than the poorest farmer or shepherd.

If there is to be any clarity in the discussion of liberty, its definition must not depend upon whether or not everybody regards this kind of liberty as a good thing. It is very probable that there are people who do not value the liberty with which we are concerned, who cannot see that they derive great benefits from it, and who will be ready to give it up to gain other advantages; it may even be true that the necessity to act according to one's own plans and decisions may be felt by them to be more of a burden than an advantage. But liberty may be desirable, even though not all persons may take advantage of it. We shall have to consider whether the benefit derived from liberty by the majority is dependent upon their using the opportunities it offers them and whether the case for liberty really rests on most people wanting it for themselves. It may well be that the benefits we receive from the liberty of all do not derive from what most people recognize as its effects; it may even be that liberty exercises its beneficial effects as much through the discipline it imposes on us as through the more visible opportunities it offers.

Above all, however, we must recognize that we may be free and yet miserable. Liberty does not mean all good things[27] or the absence of all evils. It is

---

liberty breaks down altogether, since a man's effective liberty is proportional to his resources." This has led others to the contention that "if more people are buying automobiles and taking vacations, there is more liberty" (for reference, see chap. 16, n. 72 [Dwight Waldo, *The Administrative State: A Study of the Political Theory of American Public Administration* (New York: Ronald Press Co., 1948), p. 73]); and Robert Lee Hale, *Freedom through Law: Public Control of Private Governing Power* (New York: Columbia University Press, 1952), p. 385: "Inequalities of fortune . . . are inequalities in individual liberty."

[27] An amusing illustration of this is provided by Denis Gabor and André Gabor, "An Essay on the Mathematical Theory of Freedom," *Journal of the Royal Statistical Society*, Series A (General), 117 (1954): 32. The authors begin by stating that freedom "means the absence of undesirable restraints, hence the concept is almost coextensive with everything which is desirable" and then, instead of discarding this evidently useless concept, not only adopt it but proceed to "measure" freedom in this sense.

true that to be free may mean freedom to starve, to make costly mistakes, or to run mortal risks. In the sense in which we use the term, the penniless vagabond who lives precariously by constant improvisation is indeed freer than the conscripted soldier with all his security and relative comfort. But if liberty may therefore not always seem preferable to other goods, it is a distinctive good that needs a distinctive name. And though "political liberty" and "inner liberty" are long-established alternative uses of the term which, with a little care, may be employed without causing confusion, it is questionable whether the use of the word "liberty" in the sense of "power" should be tolerated.

In any case, however, the suggestion must be avoided that, because we employ the same word, these "liberties" are different species of the same genus. This is the source of dangerous nonsense, a verbal trap that leads to the most absurd conclusions.[28] Liberty in the sense of power, political liberty, and inner liberty are not states of the same kind as individual liberty: we cannot, by sacrificing a little of the one in order to get more of the other, on balance gain some common element of freedom. We may well get one good thing in the place of another by such an exchange. But to suggest that there is a common element in them which allows us to speak of the effect that such an exchange has on liberty is sheer obscurantism, the crudest kind of philosophical realism, which assumes that, because we describe these conditions with the same word, there must also be a common element in them. But we want them largely for different reasons, and their presence or absence has different effects. If we have to choose between them, we cannot do so by asking whether liberty will be increased as a whole, but only by deciding which of these different states we value more highly.

6. It is often objected that our concept of liberty is merely negative.[29] This is

[28] Cf. Lord Acton, *Lectures on Modern History*, John Neville Figgis and Reginald Vere Laurence, eds. (London: Macmillan, 1906), p.10 [The essay is from Acton's inaugural lecture on the study of history, delivered at Cambridge in June 1895 (Liberty Fund edition, *Essays in the Study and Writing of History*, p. 516)—Ed.]: "There is no more proportion between liberty and power than between eternity and time." Also Bronislaw Malinowski, *Freedom and Civilization* (New York: Roy Publishers, 1944), p. 47: "If we were carelessly to identify freedom with power, we obviously would nurse tyranny, exactly as we land into anarchy when we equate liberty with lack of any restraint." See also Frank Hyneman Knight, "Freedom as Fact and Criterion," in *Freedom and Reform: Essays in Economics and Social Philosophy*, Frank Hyneman Knight, ed. (New York: Harper and Brothers, 1947), p. 4ff.; Joseph Cropsey, *Polity and Economy: An Interpretation of the Principles of Adam Smith* (The Hague: M. Nijhoff, 1957), p. xi; and Martin Bronfenbrenner, "Two Concepts of Economic Freedom," *Ethics*, 65 (1955): 157–70.

[29] The distinction between "positive" and "negative" liberty has been popularized by Thomas Hill Green, "Lecture on 'Liberal Legislation and Freedom of Contract,'" [1880] in *The Works of T. H. Green*, Richard Lewis Nettleship, ed. (3 vols.; London: Longmans, Green, and Co., 1888), vol. 3, *Miscellanies and Memoir*, pp. 365–86. The idea which is there connected mainly with "inner freedom" has since been put to many uses. Cf. Sir Isaiah Berlin, *Two Concepts of Liberty: An Inaugural Lecture Delivered Before the University of Oxford on 31 October 1958* (Oxford: Clarendon Press, 1958), and, for a characteristic taking-over of the socialist arguments by the conservatives, Clin-

true in the sense that peace is also a negative concept or that security or quiet or the absence of any particular impediment or evil is negative. It is to this class of concepts that liberty belongs: it describes the absence of a particular obstacle—coercion by other men. It becomes positive only through what we make of it. It does not assure us of any particular opportunities, but leaves it to us to decide what use we shall make of the circumstances in which we find ourselves.

But while the uses of liberty are many, liberty is one. Liberties appear only when liberty is lacking: they are the special privileges and exemptions that groups and individuals may acquire while the rest are more or less unfree. Historically, the path to liberty has led through the achievement of particular liberties. But that one should be allowed to do specific things is not liberty, though it may be called "a liberty"; and while liberty is compatible with not being allowed to do specific things, it does not exist if one needs permission for most of what one can do. The difference between liberty and liberties is that which exists between a condition in which all is permitted that is not pro-hibited by general rules and one in which all is prohibited that is not explic-itly permitted.

If we look once more at the elementary contrast between freedom and slav-ery, we see clearly that the negative character of freedom in no way dimin-ishes its value. We have already mentioned that the sense in which we use the word is its oldest meaning. It will help to fix this meaning if we glance at the actual difference that distinguished the position of a free man from that of a slave. We know much about this so far as the conditions in the oldest of free communities—the cities of ancient Greece—are concerned. The numerous decrees for the freeing of slaves that have been found give us a clear picture of the essentials. There were four rights which the attainment of freedom reg-ularly conferred. The manumission decrees normally gave the former slave, first, "legal status as a protected member of the community"; second, "immu-nity from arbitrary arrest"; third, the right to "work at whatever he desires to do"; and, fourth, the right to "movement according to his own choice."[30]

This list contains most of what in the eighteenth and nineteenth centu-ries were regarded as the essential conditions of freedom. It omits the right to own property only because even the slave could do so.[31] With the addition of

---

ton Rossiter, "Toward an American Conservatism," *Yale Review*, 44 (1955): 361, who argues that "the conservative should give us a definition of liberty that is positive and all-embracing. . . . In the new conservative dictionary, *liberty* will be defined with the help of words like *opportunity*, *crea-tivity*, *productivity*, and *security*."

[30] William Linn Westermann, "Between Slavery and Freedom," *American Historical Review*, 50 (1945): 216.

[31] This was at least the case in practice, if perhaps not in strict law (cf. John Walter Jones, *The Law and Legal Theory of the Greeks: An Introduction* [Oxford: Clarendon Press, 1956], p. 282).

this right, it contains all the elements required to protect an individual against coercion. But it says nothing about the other freedoms we have considered, not to speak of all the "new freedoms" that have lately been offered as substitutes for freedom. Clearly, a slave will not become free if he obtains merely the right to vote, nor will any degree of "inner freedom" make him anything but a slave—however much idealist philosophers have tried to convince us to the contrary. Nor will any degree of luxury or comfort or any power that he may wield over other men or the resources of nature alter his dependence upon the arbitrary will of his master. But if he is subject only to the same laws as all his fellow citizens, if he is immune from arbitrary confinement and free to choose his work, and if he is able to own and acquire property, no other men or group of men can coerce him to do their bidding.

7. Our definition of liberty depends upon the meaning of the concept of coercion, and it will not be precise until we have similarly defined that term. In fact, we shall also have to give a more exact meaning to certain closely related ideas, especially arbitrariness and general rules or laws. Logically, we should therefore now proceed to a similar analysis of these concepts. We cannot altogether avoid this. But before asking the reader to follow us further in what may appear to be the barren task of giving precise meaning to terms, we shall endeavor to explain why the liberty we have defined is so important. We shall therefore resume our effort at precise definition only at the beginning of the second part of this book, where we shall examine the legal aspects of a regime of freedom. At this point a few observations anticipating the results of the more systematic discussion of coercion should be sufficient. In this brief form they will necessarily seem somewhat dogmatic and will have to be justified later.

By "coercion" we mean such control of the environment or circumstances of a person by another that, in order to avoid greater evil, he is forced to act not according to a coherent plan of his own but to serve the ends of another. Except in the sense of choosing the lesser evil in a situation forced on him by another, he is unable either to use his own intelligence or knowledge or to follow his own aims and beliefs. Coercion is evil precisely because it thus eliminates an individual as a thinking and valuing person and makes him a bare tool in the achievement of the ends of another. Free action, in which a person pursues his own aims by the means indicated by his own knowledge, must be based on data which cannot be shaped at will by another. It presupposes the existence of a known sphere in which the circumstances cannot be so shaped by another person as to leave one only that choice prescribed by the other.

Coercion, however, cannot be altogether avoided because the only way to prevent it is by the threat of coercion.[32] Free society has met this problem by

<hr />

[32] Cf. Frank Hyneman Knight, *Freedom and Reform: Essays in Economics and Social Philosophy* (New York: Harper and Brothers, 1947), pp. 193–94: "The *primary* function of government is to *pre-*

conferring the monopoly of coercion on the state[33] and by attempting to limit this power of the state to instances where it is required to prevent coercion by private persons. This is possible only by the state's protecting known private spheres of the individuals against interference by others and delimiting these private spheres, not by specific assignation, but by creating conditions under which the individual can determine his own sphere by relying on rules which tell him what the government will do in different types of situations.

The coercion which a government must still use for this end is reduced to a minimum and made as innocuous as possible by restraining it through known general rules, so that in most instances the individual need never be coerced unless he has placed himself in a position where he knows he will be coerced. Even where coercion is not avoidable, it is deprived of its most harmful effects by being confined to limited and foreseeable duties, or at least made independent of the arbitrary will of another person. Being made impersonal and dependent upon general, abstract rules, whose effect on particular individuals cannot be foreseen at the time they are laid down, even the coercive acts of government become data on which the individual can base his own plans. Coercion according to known rules, which is generally the result of circumstances in which the person to be coerced has placed himself, then becomes an instrument assisting the individuals in the pursuit of their own ends and not a means to be used for the ends of others.

---

vent coercion and so guarantee to every man the right to live his own life on terms of *free* association with his fellows." See also his discussion of the topic in the article quoted in n. 3 above ["The Meaning of Freedom," a review of *Freedom: Its Meaning*, Ruth Nanda Anshen, ed., *Ethics*, 52 (1941): 86–109].

[33] Cf. Rudolph Von Ihering, *Law as a Means to an End*, Isaac Husik, trans. (Boston: Boston Book Co., 1913), pp. 241–42; Max Weber, *From Max Weber: Essays in Sociology*, C. Wright Mills, ed. and trans. (New York: Oxford University Press, 1946), p 78: "A State is a human community that (successfully) claims the *monopoly of the legitimate use of physical force*"; Bronislaw Malinowski, *Freedom and Civilization* (New York: Roy Publishers, 1944), p. 265: the state "is the only historic institution which has the monopoly of force"; also John Maurice Clark, *Social Control of Business* (2nd ed.; New York: Whittlesey House, McGraw-Hill, 1939), p. 115: "Forcible coercion is supposed to be the monopoly of the state"; and Edward Adamson Hoebel, *The Law of Primitive Man: A Study in Comparative Legal Dynamics* (Cambridge, MA: Harvard University Press, 1954), chap. 2 ["What Is Law?" (pp. 18–28)].

TWO

THE CREATIVE POWERS
OF A FREE CIVILIZATION

Civilization advances by extending the number of important operations which we can perform without thinking about them. Operations of thought are like cavalry charges in a battle—they are strictly limited in number, they require fresh horses, and must only be made at decisive moments.

—A. N. Whitehead

1. The Socratic maxim that the recognition of our ignorance is the beginning of wisdom has profound significance for our understanding of society. The first requisite for this is that we become aware of men's necessary ignorance of much that helps him to achieve his aims. Most of the advantages of social life, especially in its more advanced forms which we call "civilization," rest on the fact that the individual benefits from more knowledge than he is aware of. It might be said that civilization begins when the individual in the pursuit of his ends can make use of more knowledge than he has himself acquired and when he can transcend the boundaries of his ignorance by profiting from knowledge he does not himself possess.

This fundamental fact of man's unavoidable ignorance of much on which the working of civilization rests has received little attention. Philosophers and students of society have generally glossed it over and treated this ignorance as a minor imperfection which could be more or less disregarded. But, though discussions of moral or social problems based on the assumption of perfect knowledge may occasionally be useful as a preliminary exercise in logic, they are of little use in an attempt to explain the real world. Its problems are dominated by the "practical difficulty" that our knowledge is, in fact, very far from perfect. Perhaps it is only natural that the scientists tend to stress what we do know; but in the social field, where what we do not know is often so much more important, the effect of this tendency may be very misleading. Many

The quotation at the head of the chapter is taken from Alfred North Whitehead, *An Introduction to Mathematics* (London: Williams and Norgate, 1911), p. 61. An earlier version of this chapter appeared as "The Creative Powers of a Free Civilization," in *Essays on Individuality*, Felix Morley, ed. (Philadelphia: University of Pennsylvania Press, 1958), pp. 183–204 [Liberty Fund edition, pp. 261–89].

of the utopian constructions are worthless because they follow the lead of the theorists in assuming that we have perfect knowledge.

It must be admitted, however, that our ignorance is a peculiarly difficult subject to discuss. It might at first even seem impossible by definition to talk sense about it. We certainly cannot discuss intelligently something about which we know nothing. We must at least be able to state the questions even if we do not know the answers. This requires some genuine knowledge of the kind of world we are discussing. If we are to understand how society works, we must attempt to define the general nature and range of our ignorance concerning it. Though we cannot see in the dark, we must be able to trace the limits of the dark areas.

The misleading effect of the usual approach stands out clearly if we examine the significance of the assertion that man has created his civilization and that he therefore can also change its institutions as he pleases. This assertion would be justified only if man had deliberately created civilization in full understanding of what he was doing or if he at least clearly knew how it was being maintained. In a sense it is true, of course, that man has made his civilization. It is the product of his actions or, rather, of the action of a few hundred generations. This does not mean, however, that civilization is the product of human design, or even that man knows what its functioning or continued existence depends upon.[1]

The whole conception of man already endowed with a mind capable of conceiving civilization setting out to create it is fundamentally false. Man did not simply impose upon the world a pattern created by his mind. His mind is itself a system that constantly changes as a result of his endeavor to adapt himself to his surroundings. It would be an error to believe that, to achieve a higher civilization, we have merely to put into effect the ideas now guiding us. If we are to advance, we must leave room for a continuous revision of our present conceptions and ideals which will be necessitated by further experience. We are as little able to conceive what civilization will be, or can be, five hundred or even fifty years hence as our medieval forefathers or even our grandparents were able to foresee our manner of life today.[2]

---

[1] Cf. Adam Ferguson, *An Essay on the History of Civil Society* (Edinburgh: Printed for A. Millar and T. Caddel in the Strand, and A. Kincaid and J. Bell, Edinburgh, 1767), p. 279: "The artifices of the beaver, the ant, and the bee, are ascribed to the wisdom of nature. Those of polished nations are ascribed to themselves, and are supposed to indicate a capacity superior to that of rude minds. But the establishments of men, like those of every animal, are suggested by nature, and are the result of instinct, directed by the variety of situations in which mankind are placed. Those establishments arose from successive improvements that were made, without any sense of their general effect; and they bring human affairs to a state of complication, which the greatest reach of capacity with which human nature was ever adorned, could not have projected; nor even when the whole is carried into execution, can it be comprehended in its full extent."

[2] Cf. Michael Polanyi, *The Logic of Liberty: Reflections and Rejoinders* (London: Routledge and Kegan Paul, 1951), p. 199 [Liberty Fund edition, p. 245]: "The conceptions by the light of

The conception of man deliberately building his civilization stems from an erroneous intellectualism that regards human reason as something standing outside nature and possessed of knowledge and reasoning capacity independent of experience. But the growth of the human mind is part of the growth of civilization; it is the state of civilization at any given moment that determines the scope and the possibilities of human ends and values. The mind can never foresee its own advance. Though we must always strive for the achievement of our present aims, we must also leave room for new experiences and future events to decide which of these aims will be achieved.

It may be an exaggeration to assert, as a modern anthropologist has done, that "it is not man who controls culture but the other way around"; but it is useful to be reminded by him that "it is only our profound and comprehensive ignorance of the nature of culture that makes it possible for us to believe that we direct and control it."[3] He suggests at least an important corrective to the intellectualist conception. His reminder will help us to achieve a truer image of the incessant interaction between our conscious striving for what our intellect pictures as achievable and the operations of the institutions, traditions, and habits which jointly often produce something very different from what we have aimed at.

There are two important respects in which the conscious knowledge which guides the individual's actions constitutes only part of the conditions which enable him to achieve his ends. There is the fact that man's mind is itself a product of the civilization in which he has grown up and that it is unaware of much of the experience which has shaped it—experience that assists it by being embodied in the habits, conventions, language, and moral beliefs which are part of its makeup. Then there is the further consideration that the knowledge which any individual mind consciously manipulates is only a small part of the knowledge which at any one time contributes to the success of his action. When we reflect how much knowledge possessed by other people is an essential condition for the successful pursuit of our individual aims, the magnitude of our ignorance of the circumstances on which the results of our action depend appears simply staggering. Knowledge exists only as the knowledge of individuals. It is not much better than a metaphor to speak of the knowledge of society as a whole. The sum of the knowledge of all the individuals exists nowhere as an integrated whole. The great problem is how we can

---

which men will judge our own ideas in a thousand years—or perhaps even in fifty years—are beyond our guess. If a library of the year 3000 came into our hands to-day, we could not understand its contents. How should we consciously determine a future which is, by its very nature, beyond our comprehension? Such presumption reveals only the narrowness of an outlook uninformed by humility."

[3] Leslie Alvin White, "Man's Control over Civilization: An Anthropocentric Illusion," *Scientific Monthly*, 66 (1948): 238; also his *The Science of Culture: A Study of Man and Civilization* (New York: Farrar, Straus, and Co., 1949), pp. 337 and 342.

all profit from this knowledge, which exists only dispersed as the separate, partial, and sometimes conflicting beliefs of all men.

In other words, it is largely because civilization enables us constantly to profit from knowledge which we individually do not possess and because each individual's use of his particular knowledge may serve to assist others unknown to him in achieving their ends that men as members of civilized society can pursue their individual ends so much more successfully than they could alone. We know little of the particular facts to which the whole of social activity continuously adjusts itself in order to provide what we have learned to expect. We know even less of the forces which bring about this adjustment by appropriately co-ordinating individual activity. And our attitude, when we discover how little we know of what makes us co-operate, is, on the whole, one of resentment rather than of wonder or curiosity. Much of our occasional impetuous desire to smash the whole entangling machinery of civilization is due to this inability of man to understand what he is doing.

2. The identification of the growth of civilization with the growth of knowledge would be very misleading, however, if by "knowledge" we meant only the conscious, explicit knowledge of individuals, the knowledge which enables us to state that this or that is so-and-so.[4] Still less can this knowledge be confined to scientific knowledge. It is important for the understanding of our argument later to remember that, contrary to one fashionable view,[5] scientific knowledge does not exhaust even all the explicit and conscious knowledge of which society makes constant use. The scientific methods of the search for knowledge are not capable of satisfying all society's needs for explicit knowledge. Not all the knowledge of the ever changing particular facts that man continually uses lends itself to organization or systematic exposition; much of it exists only dispersed among countless individuals. The same applies to that important part of expert knowledge which is not substantive knowledge but merely knowledge of where and how to find the needed information.[6] For

---

[4] See Gilbert Ryle, "Knowing How and Knowing That," [The Presidential Address] *Proceedings of the Aristotelian Society*, n.s., 46 (1946): 1–16; and now compare also Michael Polanyi, *Personal Knowledge: Towards a Post-critical Philosophy* (Chicago: University of Chicago Press, 1958).

[5] Cf. the often quoted observation by Frank Plumpton Ramsey, *The Foundations of Mathematics and Other Logical Essays* (London: Routledge and Kegan Paul, 1931), p. 287: "There is nothing to know except science." [The statement does not appear in *The Foundations of Mathematics*, as Hayek indicates, but in the Epilogue to Ramsey's collected essays, of which *The Foundations* is the central article and which gives its name to the anthology.—Ed.]

[6] On these different kinds of knowledge see my article "Über den 'Sinn' sozialer Institutionen" [On the Meaning of Social Institutions], *Schweizer Monatshefte*, October 1956, pp. 512–24, and, on the application of the whole argument of this chapter to the more specifically economic problems, the two essays on "Economics and Knowledge" and "The Use of Knowledge in Society" reprinted in my *Individualism and Economic Order* (Chicago: University of Chicago Press, 1948), pp. 33–56 and 77–91. See also Samuel Johnson's remark: "Knowledge is of two kinds: we know

our present purpose, however, it is not this distinction between different kinds of rational knowledge that is most important, and when we speak of explicit knowledge, we shall group these different kinds together.

The growth of knowledge and the growth of civilization are the same only if we interpret knowledge to include all the human adaptations to environment in which past experience has been incorporated. Not all knowledge in this sense is part of our intellect, nor is our intellect the whole of our knowledge. Our habits and skills, our emotional attitudes, our tools, and our institutions—all are in this sense adaptations to past experience which have grown up by selective elimination of less suitable conduct. They are as much an indispensable foundation of successful action as is our conscious knowledge. Not all these non-rational factors underlying our action are always conducive to success. Some may be retained long after they have outlived their usefulness and even when they have become more an obstacle than a help. Nevertheless, we could not do without them: even the successful employment of our intellect itself rests on their constant use.

Man prides himself on the increase in his knowledge. But, as a result of what he himself has created, the limitations of his conscious knowledge and therefore the range of ignorance significant for his conscious action have constantly increased. Ever since the beginning of modern science, the best minds have recognized that "the range of acknowledged ignorance will grow with the advance of science."[7] Unfortunately, the popular effect of this scien-

---

a subject ourselves or we know where we can find information upon it." (James Boswell, *The Life of Samuel Johnson, LL.D.: Comprehending an Account of His Studies and Numerous Works* [3 vols.; 2nd ed., rev. and aug.; London: Printed by Henry Baldwin, 1793], vol. 2, pp. 237–38).

[7] Giorgio de Santillana, *The Crime of Galileo* (Chicago: University of Chicago Press, 1955), pp. 34–35. Herbert Spencer also remarks somewhere: "In science the more we know, the more extensive the contact with nescience." [The quotation, as Hayek has it, is somewhat different from that written by Spencer. The wording as quoted by Hayek, in fact comes from the article on Herbert Spencer in the eleventh edition of the *Encyclopedia Britannica* (New York: The Encyclopedia Britannica Co., 1911) s.v. "Spencer, Herbert" by Ferdinand Canning Scott Schiller. Spencer's actual wording reads: "Regarding Science as a gradually increasing sphere, we may say that every addition to its surface does but bring it into wider contact with surrounding nescience." (*First Principles* [London: Williams and Norgate, 1862], pp. 16–17.)—Ed.]. See also Sir Karl Raimund Popper, "On the Sources of Knowledge and Ignorance," *Proceedings of the British Academy*, 46 (1960): 69: "The more we learn about the world, and the deeper our learning, the more conscious, specific, and articulate will be our knowledge of what we do not know, our knowledge of our ignorance"; and Warren Weaver, "A Scientist Ponders Faith," *Saturday Review*, 3 (January 1959): 9: "[is] science really gaining in its assault on the totality of the unsolved? As science learns one answer, it is characteristically true that it also learns several new questions. It is as though science were working in a great forest of ignorance, making an ever larger circular clearing within which, not to insist on the pun, things are clear. . . . But as that circle becomes larger and larger, the circumference of contact with ignorance also gets longer and longer. Science learns more and more. But there is an ultimate sense in which it does not gain; for the volume of the appreciated but not understood keeps getting larger. We keep, in science, getting a more and more sophisticated view of our essential ignorance."

tific advance has been a belief, seemingly shared by many scientists, that the range of our ignorance is steadily diminishing and that we can therefore aim at more comprehensive and deliberate control of all human activities. It is for this reason that those intoxicated by the advance of knowledge so often become the enemies of freedom. While the growth of our knowledge of nature constantly discloses new realms of ignorance, the increasing complexity of the civilization which this knowledge enables us to build presents new obstacles to the intellectual comprehension of the world around us. The more men know, the smaller the share of all that knowledge becomes that any one mind can absorb. The more civilized we become, the more relatively ignorant must each individual be of the facts on which the working of his civilization depends. The very division of knowledge increases the necessary ignorance of the individual of most of this knowledge.

3. When we spoke of the transmission and communication of knowledge, we meant to refer to the two aspects of the process of civilization which we have already distinguished: the transmission in time of our accumulated stock of knowledge and the communication among contemporaries of information on which they base their action. They cannot be sharply separated because the tools of communication between contemporaries are part of the cultural heritage which man constantly uses in the pursuit of his ends.

We are most familiar with this process of accumulation and transmission of knowledge in the field of science—so far as it shows both the general laws of nature and the concrete features of the world in which we live. But, although this is the most conspicuous part of our inherited stock of knowledge and the chief part of what we necessarily know, in the ordinary sense of "knowing," it is still only a part; for, besides this, we command many tools—in the widest sense of that word—which the human race has evolved and which enable us to deal with our environment. These are the results of the experience of successive generations which are handed down. And, once a more efficient tool is available, it will be used without our knowing why it is better, or even what the alternatives are.

These "tools" which man has evolved and which constitute such an important part of his adaptation to his environment include much more than material implements. They consist in a large measure of forms of conduct which he habitually follows without knowing why; they consist of what we call "traditions" and "institutions," which he uses because they are available to him as a product of cumulative growth without ever having been designed by any one mind. Man is generally ignorant not only of why he uses implements of one shape rather than of another but also of how much is dependent on his actions taking one form rather than another. He does not usually know to what extent the success of his efforts is determined by his conforming to habits of which he is not even aware. This is probably as true of civilized man as of primitive man. Concurrent with the growth of conscious knowledge there always takes place an equally important accumulation of tools in this wider sense, of tested and generally adopted ways of doing things.

Our concern at the moment is not so much with the knowledge thus handed down to us or with the formation of new tools that will be used in the future as it is with the manner in which current experience is utilized in assisting those who do not directly gain it. So far as it is possible to do so, we shall leave the progress in time for the next chapter and concentrate here on the manner in which that dispersed knowledge and the different skills, the varied habits and opportunities of the individual members of society, contribute toward bringing about the adjustment of its activities to ever changing circumstances.

Every change in conditions will make necessary some change in the use of resources, in the direction and kind of human activities, in habits and practices. And each change in the actions of those affected in the first instance will require further adjustments that will gradually extend throughout the whole of society. Thus every change in a sense creates a "problem" for society, even though no single individual perceives it as such; and it is gradually "solved" by the establishment of a new over-all adjustment. Those who take part in the process have little idea why they are doing what they do, and we have no way of predicting who will at each step first make the appropriate move, or what particular combinations of knowledge and skill, personal attitudes and circumstances, will suggest to some man the suitable answer, or by what channels his example will be transmitted to others who will follow the lead. It is difficult to conceive all the combinations of knowledge and skills which thus come into action and from which arises the discovery of appropriate practices or devices that, once found, can be accepted generally. But from the countless number of humble steps taken by anonymous persons in the course of doing familiar things in changed circumstances spring the examples that prevail. They are as important as the major intellectual innovations which are explicitly recognized and communicated as such.

Who will prove to possess the right combination of aptitudes and opportunities to find the better way is just as little predictable as by what manner or process different kinds of knowledge and skill will combine to bring about a solution of the problem.[8] The successful combination of knowledge and aptitude is not selected by common deliberation, by people seeking a solution to

---

[8] Cf. Homer Garner Barnett, *Innovation: The Basis of Cultural Change* (New York: McGraw-Hill, 1953): "Every individual is an innovator many times over" (p. 19) and "There is a positive correlation between individualism and innovative potential. The greater the freedom of the individual to explore his world of experience and to organize its elements in accordance with his private interpretation of his sense impressions, the greater the likelihood of new ideas coming into being" (p. 65).

their problems through a joint effort;[9] it is the product of individuals imitating those who have been more successful and from their being guided by signs or symbols, such as prices offered for their products or expressions of moral or aesthetic esteem for their having observed standards of conduct—in short, of their using the results of the experiences of others.

What is essential to the functioning of the process is that each individual be able to act on his particular knowledge, always unique, at least so far as it refers to some particular circumstances, and that he be able to use his individual skills and opportunities within the limits known to him and for his own individual purpose.

4. We have now reached the point at which the main contention of this chapter will be readily intelligible. It is that the case for individual freedom rests chiefly on the recognition of the inevitable ignorance of all of us concerning a great many of the factors on which the achievement of our ends and welfare depends.[10]

[9] Cf. Sir William Arthur Lewis, *The Theory of Economic Growth* (London: Allen and Unwin, 1955), p. 148: "These innovators are always a minority. New ideas are first put into practice by one or two or very few persons, whether they be new ideas in technology, or new forms of organization, new commodities, or other novelties. These ideas may be accepted rapidly by the rest of the population. More probably they are received with scepticism and unbelief, and make their way only very slowly at first if at all. After a while the new ideas are seen to be successful, and are then accepted by increasing numbers. Thus it is often said that change is the work of an elite, or that the amount of change depends on the quality of leadership in a community. This is true enough if it implies no more than that the majority of people are not innovators, but merely imitate what others do. It is, however, somewhat misleading if it is taken to imply that some specific class or group of people get all the new ideas." Also p. 172: "Collective judgement of new ideas is so often wrong that it is arguable that progress depends on individuals being free to back their own judgement despite collective disapproval. . . . To give a monopoly of decision to a government committee would seem to have the disadvantage of both worlds."

[10] One of the few authors who have seen clearly at least part of this was Frederic William Maitland, who stresses (*The Collected Papers of Frederic William Maitland, Downing Professor of the Laws of England* [3 vols.; Cambridge: Cambridge University Press, 1911], vol. 1, p. 107) that "the most powerful argument is that based on the ignorance, the necessary ignorance, of our rulers." [Maitland's quotation appears in *A Historical Sketch of Liberty and Equality*, Liberty Fund edition, p. 133.—Ed.] See, however, Bennett E. Kline and Norman H. Martin, "Freedom, Authority, and Decentralization," *Harvard Business Review*, 36 (1958), esp. 70: "the chief characteristic of the command hierarchy, or any group in our society, is not knowledge but ignorance. Consider that any one person can know only a fraction of what is going on around him. Much of what that person knows or believes will be false rather than true. . . . At any given time, vastly more is not known than is known, either by one person in a command chain or by all the organization. It seems possible, then, that in organizing ourselves into a hierarchy of authority for the purpose of increasing efficiency, we may really be institutionalizing ignorance. While making better use of what the few know, we are making sure that the great majority are prevented from exploring the dark areas beyond our knowledge." See also William Graham Sumner, "Speculative Legislation," *The Challenge of Facts and Other Papers* (New Haven: Yale University Press, 1914), p. 215: "It is characteristic of speculative legislation that it very generally produces the exact opposite of the result it was hoped to get

If there were omniscient men, if we could know not only all that affects the attainment of our present wishes but also our future wants and desires, there would be little case for liberty. And, in turn, liberty of the individual would, of course, make complete foresight impossible. Liberty is essential in order to leave room for the unforeseeable and unpredictable; we want it because we have learned to expect from it the opportunity of realizing many of our aims. It is because every individual knows so little and, in particular, because we rarely know which of us knows best that we trust the independent and competitive efforts of many to induce the emergence of what we shall want when we see it.

Humiliating to human pride as it may be, we must recognize that the advance and even the preservation of civilization are dependent upon a maximum of opportunity for accidents to happen.[11] These accidents occur in the combination of knowledge and attitudes, skills and habits, acquired by individual men and also when qualified men are confronted with the particular circumstances which they are equipped to deal with. Our necessary ignorance of so much means that we have to deal largely with probabilities and chances.

Of course, it is true of social as of individual life that favorable accidents usually do not just happen. We must prepare for them.[12] But they still remain chances and do not become certainties. They involve risks deliberately taken, the possible misfortune of individuals and groups who are as meritorious as others who prosper, the possibility of serious failure or relapse even for the majority, and merely a high probability of a net gain on balance. All we can do is to increase the chance that some special constellation of individual endowment and circumstance will result in the shaping of some new tool or the improvement of an old one, and to improve the prospect that such

---

from it. The reason is that the elements of any social problem which we do not know so far exceed those which we do know, that our solutions have a greater chance to be wrong than right."

There is one important respect in which the term "ignorance" is somewhat too narrow for our purposes. There are occasions when it would probably be better to speak of "uncertainty" with reference to ignorance concerning what is right, since it is doubtful whether we can meaningfully speak about something being right if nobody knows what is right in the particular context. The fact in such instances may be that the existing morals provide no answer to a problem, though there might be some answer which, if it were known and widely accepted, would be very valuable. I am much indebted to Mr. Pierre F. Goodrich, whose comment during a discussion helped to clarify this important point for me, though I have not been persuaded to speak generally of "imperfection" where I stress ignorance.

[11] Cf. John Archibald Wheeler, "A Septet of Sibyls: Aids in the Search for Truth," *American Scientist*, 44 (1956): 360: "Our whole problem is to make the mistakes as fast as possible."

[12] Cf. the remark of Louis Pasteur: "In research, chance only helps those whose minds are well prepared for it," quoted by René Taton, *Reason and Chance in Scientific Discovery* (London: Hutchinson, 1957), p. 91. [Pasteur appears to have originally made the statement in a lecture at the University of Lille on December 7, 1854. The original reads: "Dans les champs de l'observation le hasard ne favorise que les esprits préparés."—Ed.]

innovations will become rapidly known to those who can take advantage of them.

All political theories assume, of course, that most individuals are very ignorant. Those who plead for liberty differ from the rest in that they include among the ignorant themselves as well as the wisest. Compared with the totality of knowledge which is continually utilized in the evolution of a dynamic civilization, the difference between the knowledge that the wisest and that which the most ignorant individual can deliberately employ is comparatively insignificant.

The classical argument for tolerance formulated by John Milton and John Locke and restated by John Stuart Mill and Walter Bagehot rests, of course, on the recognition of this ignorance of ours. It is a special application of general considerations to which a non-rationalist insight into the working of our mind opens the doors. We shall find throughout this book that, though we are usually not aware of it, all institutions of freedom are adaptations to this fundamental fact of ignorance, adapted to deal with chances and probabilities, not certainty. Certainty we cannot achieve in human affairs, and it is for this reason that, to make the best use of what knowledge we have, we must adhere to rules which experience has shown to serve best on the whole, though we do not know what will be the consequences of obeying them in the particular instance.[13]

5. Man learns by the disappointment of expectations. Needless to say, we ought not to increase the unpredictability of events by foolish human institutions. So far as possible, our aim should be to improve human institutions so as to increase the chances of correct foresight. Above all, however, we should provide the maximum of opportunity for unknown individuals to learn of facts that we ourselves are yet unaware of and to make use of this knowledge in their actions.

It is through the mutually adjusted efforts of many people that more knowledge is utilized than any one individual possesses or than it is possible to synthesize intellectually; and it is through such utilization of dispersed knowledge that achievements are made possible greater than any single mind can foresee. It is because freedom means the renunciation of direct control of individual efforts that a free society can make use of so much more knowledge than the mind of the wisest ruler could comprehend.

---

[13] Cf. Abba Ptachya Lerner, "The Backward-leaning Approach to Controls," *Journal of Political Economy*, 65 (1957): 441: "The free-trade doctrines are valid as *general rules* whose general use is generally beneficial. As with all general rules, there are particular cases where, if one knew all the attendant circumstances and the full effects in all their ramifications, it would be better for the rule not to be applied. But that does not make the rule a bad rule or give reason for not applying the rule where, as is normally the case, one does not know all the ramifications that would make the case a desirable exception."

From this foundation of the argument for liberty it follows that we shall not achieve its ends if we confine liberty to the particular instances where we know it will do good. Freedom granted only when it is known beforehand that its effects will be beneficial is not freedom. If we knew how freedom would be used, the case for it would largely disappear. We shall never get the benefits of freedom, never obtain those unforeseeable new developments for which it provides the opportunity, if it is not also granted where the uses made of it by some do not seem desirable. It is therefore no argument against individual freedom that it is frequently abused. Freedom necessarily means that many things will be done which we do not like. Our faith in freedom does not rest on the foreseeable results in particular circumstances but on the belief that it will, on balance, release more forces for the good than for the bad.

It also follows that the importance of our being free to do a particular thing has nothing to do with the question of whether we or the majority are ever likely to make use of that particular possibility. To grant no more freedom than all can exercise would be to misconceive its function completely. The freedom that will be used by only one man in a million may be more important to society and more beneficial to the majority than any freedom that we all use.[14]

It might even be said that the less likely the opportunity to make use of freedom to do a particular thing, the more precious it will be for society as a whole. The less likely the opportunity, the more serious will it be to miss it when it arises, for the experience that it offers will be nearly unique. It is also probably true that the majority are not directly interested in most of the important things that any one person should be free to do. It is because we do not know how individuals will use their freedom that it is so important. If it were otherwise, the results of freedom could also be achieved by the majority's deciding what should be done by the individuals. But majority action is, of necessity,

---

[14] Cf. Rev. Hastings Rashdall, "The Philosophical Theory of Property," in *Property; Its Duties and Rights: Historically, Philosophically, and Religiously Regarded,* Charles Gore and Leonard Trelawney Hobhouse, eds. (new ed.; New York: Macmillan, 1915), pp. 61–62: "The plea for liberty is not sufficiently met by insisting, as has been so eloquently and humorously done by Mr. Lowes Dickinson (*Justice and Liberty: A Political Dialogue,* e.g. pp. 129 and 131), upon the absurdity of supposing that the propertyless labourer under the ordinary capitalistic regime enjoys any liberty of which Socialism would deprive him. For it may be of extreme importance that *some* should enjoy liberty—that it should be possible for some few men to be able to dispose of their time in their own way—although such liberty may be neither possible nor desirable for the great majority. That culture requires a considerable differentiation in social conditions is also a principle of unquestionable importance." [The full citation of the book quoted by Rashdall is: Goldsworthy Lowes Dickinson, *Justice and Liberty: A Political Dialogue* (London: J. M. Dent, 1908).—Ed.] See also Bennett E. Kline and Norman H. Martin, "Freedom, Authority, and Decentralization," p. 69: "If there is to be freedom for the few who *will* take advantage of it, freedom must be offered to the many. If any lesson is clear from history, it is this."

confined to the already tried and ascertained, to issues on which agreement has already been reached in that process of discussion that must be preceded by different experiences and actions on the part of different individuals.

The benefits I derive from freedom are thus largely the result of the uses of freedom by others, and mostly of those uses of freedom that I could never avail myself of. It is therefore not necessarily freedom that I can exercise myself that is most important for me. It is certainly more important that anything can be tried by somebody than that all can do the same things. It is not because we like to be able to do particular things, not because we regard any particular freedom as essential to our happiness, that we have a claim to freedom. The instinct that makes us revolt against any physical restraint, though a helpful ally, is not always a safe guide for justifying or delimiting freedom. What is important is not what freedom I personally would like to exercise but what freedom some person may need in order to do things beneficial to society. This freedom we can assure to the unknown person only by giving it to all.

The benefits of freedom are therefore not confined to the free—or, at least, a man does not benefit mainly from those aspects of freedom which he himself takes advantage of. There can be no doubt that in history unfree majorities have benefited from the existence of free minorities and that today unfree societies benefit from what they obtain and learn from free societies. Of course the benefits we derive from the freedom of others become greater as the number of those who can exercise freedom increases. The argument for the freedom of some therefore applies to the freedom of all. But it is still better for all that some should be free than none and also that many enjoy full freedom than that all have a restricted freedom. The significant point is that the importance of freedom to do a particular thing has nothing to do with the number of people who want to do it: it might almost be in inverse proportion. One consequence of this is that a society may be hamstrung by controls, although the great majority may not be aware that their freedom has been significantly curtailed. If we proceeded on the assumption that only the exercises of freedom that the majority will practice are important, we would be certain to create a stagnant society with all the characteristics of unfreedom.

6. The undesigned novelties that constantly emerge in the process of adaptation will consist, first, of new arrangements or patterns in which the efforts of different individuals are co-ordinated and of new constellations in the use of resources, which will be in their nature as temporary as the particular conditions that have evoked them. There will be, second, modifications of tools and institutions adapted to the new circumstances. Some of these will also be merely temporary adaptations to the conditions of the moment, while others will be improvements that increase the versatility of the existing tools and usages and will therefore be retained. These latter will constitute

a better adaptation not merely to the particular circumstances of time and place but to some permanent feature of our environment. In such spontaneous "formations"[15] is embodied a perception of the general laws that govern nature. With this cumulative embodiment of experience in tools and forms of action will emerge a growth of explicit knowledge, of formulated generic rules that can be communicated by language from person to person.

This process by which the new emerges is best understood in the intellectual sphere when the results are new ideas. It is the field in which most of us are aware at least of some of the individual steps of the process, where we necessarily know what is happening and thus generally recognize the necessity of freedom. Most scientists realize that we cannot plan the advance of knowledge, that in the voyage into the unknown—which is what research is—we are in great measure dependent on the vagaries of individual genius and of circumstance, and that scientific advance, like a new idea that will spring up in a single mind, will be the result of a combination of conceptions, habits, and circumstances brought to one person by society, the result as much of lucky accidents as of systematic effort.

Because we are more aware that our advances in the intellectual sphere often spring from the unforeseen and undesigned, we tend to overstress the importance of freedom in this field and to ignore the importance of the freedom of *doing* things. But the freedom of research and belief and the freedom of speech and discussion, the importance of which is widely understood, are significant only in the last stage of the process in which new truths are discovered. To extol the value of intellectual liberty at the expense of the value of the liberty of doing things would be like treating the crowning part of an edifice as the whole. We have new ideas to discuss, different views to adjust, because those ideas and views arise from the efforts of individuals in ever new circumstances, who avail themselves in their concrete tasks of the new tools and forms of action they have learned.

The non-intellectual part of this process—the formation of the changed material environment in which the new emerges—requires for its understanding and appreciation a much greater effort of imagination than the fac-

---

[15] For the use of the term "formation," more appropriate in this connection than the usual "institution," see my study on *The Counter-Revolution of Science: Studies on the Abuse of Reason* (Glencoe, IL: Free Press, 1952), p. 83. [*Collected Works* edition, vol. 13, p. 145.] [Hayek there writes of human institutions: "Though in a sense man-made, i.e., entirely the result of human actions, they may yet not be designed, not be the intended product of these actions. The term 'institution' itself is rather misleading in this respect, as it suggests something deliberately instituted. It would probably be better if this term were confined to particular contrivances, like particular laws and organizations, which have been created for a specific purpose, and if a more neutral term like 'formations' (in a sense similar to that in which the geologists use it, and corresponding to the German *Gebilde*) could be used for those phenomena, which, like money or language, have not been so created."—Ed.]

tors stressed by the intellectualist view. While we are sometimes able to trace the intellectual processes that have led to a new idea, we can scarcely ever reconstruct the sequence and combination of those contributions that have not led to the acquisition of explicit knowledge; we can scarcely ever reconstruct the favorable habits and skills employed, the facilities and opportunities used, and the particular environment of the main actors that has favored the result. Our efforts toward understanding this part of the process can go little further than to show on simplified models the kind of forces at work and to point to the general principle rather than the specific character of the influences that operate.[16] Men are always concerned only with what they know. Therefore, those features which, while the process is under way, are not consciously known to anybody are commonly disregarded and can perhaps never be traced in detail.

In fact, these unconscious features not only are commonly disregarded but are often treated as if they were a hindrance rather than a help or an essential condition. Because they are not "rational" in the sense of explicitly entering into our reasoning, they are often treated as irrational in the sense of being contrary to intelligent action. Yet, though much of the non-rational that affects our action may be irrational in this sense, many of the "mere habits" and "meaningless institutions" that we use and presuppose in our actions are essential conditions for what we achieve; they are successful adaptations of society that are constantly improved and on which depends the range of what we can achieve. While it is important to discover their defects, we could not for a moment go on without constantly relying on them.

The manner in which we have learned to order our day, to dress, to eat, to arrange our houses, to speak and write, and to use the countless other tools and implements of civilization, no less than the "know-how" of production and trade, furnishes us constantly with the foundations on which our own contributions to the process of civilization must be based. And it is in the new use and improvement of whatever the facilities of civilization offer us that the new ideas arise that are ultimately handled in the intellectual sphere. Though the conscious manipulation of abstract thought, once it has been set in train, has in some measure a life of its own, it would not long continue and develop without the constant challenges that arise from the ability of people to act in a new manner, to try new ways of doing things, and to alter the whole structure of civilization in adaptation to change. The intellectual process is in effect

[16] Cf. my article "Degrees of Explanation," *British Journal for the Philosophy of Science*, 6 (1955): 209–25, reprinted in *Studies in Philosophy, Politics, and Economics* (Chicago: University of Chicago Press, 1967), pp. 3–21 [Also reprinted in *Studies in Philosophy, Politics, and Economics*, pp. 22–42.—Ed.], and my "The Theory of Complex Phenomena," in *The Critical Approach to Science and Philosophy: Essays in Honor of Karl R. Popper*, Mario Augusto Bunge, ed. (New York: Free Press of Glencoe, 1964), pp. 332–49.

only a process of elaboration, selection, and elimination of ideas already formed. And the flow of new ideas, to a great extent, springs from the sphere in which action, often non-rational action, and material events impinge upon each other. It would dry up if freedom were confined to the intellectual sphere.

The importance of freedom, therefore, does not depend on the elevated character of the activities it makes possible. Freedom of action, even in humble things, is as important as freedom of thought. It has become a common practice to disparage freedom of action by calling it "economic liberty."[17] But the concept of freedom of action is much wider than that of economic liberty, which it includes; and, what is more important, it is very questionable whether there are any actions which can be called merely "economic" and whether any restrictions on liberty can be confined to what are called merely "economic" aspects. Economic considerations are merely those by which we reconcile and adjust our different purposes, none of which, in the last resort, are economic (excepting those of the miser or the man for whom making money has become an end in itself).[18]

7. Most of what we have said so far applies not only to man's use of the means for the achievement of his ends but also to those ends themselves. It is one of the characteristics of a free society that men's goals are open,[19] that new ends of conscious effort can spring up, first with a few individuals, to become in time the ends of most. It is a fact which we must recognize that even what we regard as good or beautiful is changeable—if not in any recognizable manner that would entitle us to take a relativistic position, then in the sense that in many respects we do not know what will appear as good or beautiful to another generation. Nor do we know why we regard this or that as good or who is right when people differ as to whether something is good or not. It is not only in his knowledge, but also in his aims and values, that man is the creature of civilization; in the last resort, it is the relevance of these individual wishes to the perpetuation of the group or the species that will determine whether they will persist or change. It is, of course, a mistake to believe that we can draw conclusions about what our values ought to be simply because we realize that they are a product of evolution. But we cannot

[17] See Aaron Director, "The Parity of the Economic Market Place," in *Conference on Freedom and the Law, May 7, 1953: Fiftieth Anniversary Celebration*, Thuman Welsey Arnold, et al. (University of Chicago Law School Conference Series, no. 13, Chicago: University of Chicago Press, 1953), pp. 16–25.

[18] Cf. my book *The Road to Serfdom* (Chicago: University of Chicago Press, 1944), chap. 7, pp. 88–100; reprinted as vol. 2 of *The Collected Works of F. A. Hayek*, Bruce Caldwell, ed. (Chicago: University of Chicago Press, 2007), pp. 124–33.

[19] See Sir Karl Raimund Popper, *The Open Society and Its Enemies* (American ed.; Princeton: Princeton University Press, 1950), esp. p. 195: "If we wish to remain human, there is only one way, the way into the open society. We must go into the unknown, the uncertain and insecure, using what reason we may have to plan for both, security *and* freedom."

reasonably doubt that these values are created and altered by the same evolutionary forces that have produced our intelligence. All that we can know is that the ultimate decision about what is good or bad will be made not by individual human wisdom but by the decline of the groups that have adhered to the "wrong" beliefs.

It is in the pursuit of man's aims of the moment that all the devices of civilization have to prove themselves; the ineffective will be discarded and the effective retained. But there is more to it than the fact that new ends constantly arise with the satisfaction of old needs and with the appearance of new opportunities. Which individuals and which groups succeed and continue to exist depends as much on the goals that they pursue, the values that govern their action, as on the tools and capacities at their command. Whether a group will prosper or be extinguished depends as much on the ethical code it obeys, or the ideals of beauty or well-being that guide it, as on the degree to which it has learned or not learned to satisfy its material needs. Within any given society, particular groups may rise or decline according to the ends they pursue and the standards of conduct that they observe. And the ends of the successful group will tend to become the ends of all members of the society.

At most, we understand only partially why the values we hold or the ethical rules we observe are conducive to the continued existence of our society. Nor can we be sure that under constantly changing conditions all the rules that have proved to be conducive to the attainment of a certain end will remain so. Though there is a presumption that any established social standard contributes in some manner to the preservation of civilization, our only way of confirming this is to ascertain whether it continues to prove itself in competition with other standards observed by other individuals or groups.

8. The competition on which the process of selection rests must be understood in the widest sense. It involves competition between organized and unorganized groups no less than competition between individuals. To think of it in contrast to cooperation or organization would be to misconceive its nature. The endeavor to achieve certain results by co-operation and organization is as much a part of competition as individual efforts. Successful group relations also prove their effectiveness in competition among groups organized in different ways. The relevant distinction is not between individual and group action but between conditions, on the one hand, in which alternative ways based on different views or practices may be tried and conditions, on the other, in which one agency has the exclusive right and the power to prevent others from trying. It is only when such exclusive rights are conferred on the presumption of superior knowledge of particular individuals or groups that the process ceases to be experimental and beliefs that happen to be prevalent at a given time may become an obstacle to the advancement of knowledge.

The argument for liberty is not an argument against organization, which is

one of the most powerful means that human reason can employ, but an argument against all exclusive, privileged, monopolistic organization, against the
use of coercion to prevent others from trying to do better. Every organization
is based on given knowledge; organization means commitment to a particular
aim and to particular methods, but even organization designed to increase
knowledge will be effective only insofar as the knowledge and beliefs on which
its design rests are true. And if any facts contradict the beliefs on which the
structure of the organization is based, this will become evident only in its
failure and supersession by a different type of organization. Organization is
therefore likely to be beneficial and effective so long as it is voluntary and is im-
bedded in a free sphere and will either have to adjust itself to circumstances
not taken into account in its conception or fail. To turn the whole of society
into a single organization built and directed according to a single plan would
be to extinguish the very forces that shaped the individual human minds that
planned it.

It is worth our while to consider for a moment what would happen if only
what was agreed to be the best available knowledge were to be used in all
action. If all attempts that seemed wasteful in the light of generally accepted
knowledge were prohibited and only such questions asked, or such experiments tried, as seemed significant in the light of ruling opinion, mankind
might well reach a point where its knowledge enabled it to predict the consequences of all conventional actions and to avoid all disappointment or failure. Man would then seem to have subjected his surroundings to his reason,
for he would attempt only those things which were totally predictable in their
results. We might conceive of a civilization coming to a standstill, not because
the possibilities of further growth had been exhausted, but because man had
succeeded in so completely subjecting all his actions and his immediate surroundings to his existing state of knowledge that there would be no occasion
for new knowledge to appear.

9. The rationalist who desires to subject everything to human reason is thus
faced with a real dilemma. The use of reason aims at control and predictability. But the process of the advance of reason rests on freedom and the unpredictability of human action. Those who extol the powers of human reason
usually see only one side of that interaction of human thought and conduct
in which reason is at the same time used and shaped. They do not see that,
for advance to take place, the social process from which the growth of reason
emerges must remain free from its control.

There can be little doubt that man owes some of his greatest successes in
the past to the fact that he has *not* been able to control social life. His continued advance may well depend on his deliberately refraining from exercising
controls which are now in his power. In the past, the spontaneous forces of
growth, however much restricted, could usually still assert themselves against

the organized coercion of the state. With the technological means of control now at the disposal of government, it is not certain that such assertion is still possible; at any rate, it may soon become impossible. We are not far from the point where the deliberately organized forces of society may destroy those spontaneous forces which have made advance possible.

THREE

THE COMMON SENSE OF PROGRESS

Man never mounts higher than when he knows not where he is going.

—Oliver Cromwell

The quotation at the head of the chapter is taken from Jean François Paul de Gondi de Retz, *Mémoires du Cardinal de Retz, de Guy-Joli, et de la duchesse de Nemours, contenant ce qui s'est passé de remarquable en France pendant les premières années du règne de Louis XIV* (6 vols. in 8; Nouvelle édition; Paris: Chez Étienne Ledoux, 1820), vol. 2, p. 497, where President Bellièvre is recorded as having said that Cromwell once told him "on ne montait jamais si haut que quand on ne sait où l'on va." [Pomponne de Bellièvre (1606–57), grandson of two chancellors of France and the first president of the Parlement of Paris, at one point served as French ambassador to England.—Ed.] The phrase apparently made a deep impression on eighteenth century thinkers, and it is quoted by David Hume (*Essays*, vol. 1, p. 124) [The essay in which Hume's reference falls originally appeared under the title "Whether the British Government Inclines More to Absolute Monarchy, or to a Republic," (Essay 9) in *Essays, Moral and Political* (Edinburgh: Printed by R. Fleming and A. Alison for A. Kincaid, 1741), p. 98n. (Liberty Fund edition, p. 50). In a footnote quoting Cromwell's statement to Bellièvre he there notes that "a Man, possess'd of usurp'd Authority, can set no Bounds to his Pretensions." Hume's footnote appears in all editions of his *Essays* until that of 1774, at which point it was dropped.—Ed.], Adam Ferguson (*An Essay on the History of Civil Society* [Edinburgh: Printed for A. Millar and T. Caddel in the Strand, London, and A. Kincaid and J. Bell, Edinburgh, 1767], p. 187), and (according to Duncan Forbes, "Scientific Whiggism," *Cambridge Journal*, vol. 7 [1954]: 654) also by Anne Robert Jacques Turgot. [Turgot comes very close to the idea in his *Plan de Deux Discours sur l'Histoire Universelle*, where he writes of men that "leur passions, leurs fureurs même, les conduits sans qu'ils sussent où ils allaient." The essay appears in Turgot's *Œuvres de Turgot et Documents le Concernant*, Gustave Schelle, ed. (5 vols.; Paris: Librairie Félix Alcan, 1913–23), vol. 1, p. 283. Ronald Meek in his edition of Turgot's essays, *Turgot on Progress, Sociology, and Economics* (Cambridge: Cambridge University Press, 1973), p. 69, translates Turgot's words as "Their passions, even their fits of rage, have led them on their way without their being aware of where they were going."—Ed.] It appears once more, appropriately, in Albert Venn Dicey, *Law and Public Opinion*, p. 231 [Liberty Fund edition, p. 164]. A slightly modified version occurs in Johann Wolfgang von Goethe's posthumously published *Maximen, Reflexionen: Goethe's Aufsätze zur Kultur-, Theater- und Literatur-Geschichte*, Grossherzog Wilhelm Ernst Ausgabe (2 vols.; Leipzig: Inselverlag, 1913–14), vol. 2, p. 626: "Man geht nie weiter, als wenn man nicht mehr weiss, wohin man geht." ["One never goes so far as when one doesn't know where one is going."—Ed.] Cf. in this connection also Giambattista Vico, *Opere di Giambattista Vico, ordinate ed illustrate coll'analisi storica della mente di Vico in relazione alla scienza della civiltà*, Giuseppe Ferrari, ed. (6 vols.; Milan: Società Tipog. de' Classici Italiani, 1852–54), vol. 5, p. 183. "Homo non intelligendo fit omnia." [The Latin should read: "Homo non intelligendo facit omnia," which translates as "Man unknowingly makes all things."—Ed.] Since there will

1. Writers nowadays who value their reputation among the more sophisticated hardly dare to mention progress without including the word in quotation marks. The implicit confidence in the beneficence of progress that during the last two centuries marked the advanced thinker has come to be regarded as the sign of a shallow mind. Though the great mass of the people in most parts of the world still rest their hopes on continued progress, it is common among intellectuals to question whether there is such a thing, or at least whether progress is desirable.

Up to a point, this reaction against the exuberant and naïve belief in the inevitability of progress was necessary. So much of what has been written and talked about it has been indefensible that one may well think twice before using the word. There never was much justification for the assertion that "civilization has moved, is moving, and will move in a desirable direction,"[1] nor was there any ground for regarding all change as necessary, or progress as certain and always beneficial. Least of all was there warrant for speaking about recognizable "laws of progress" that enabled us to predict the conditions toward which we were necessarily moving, or for treating every foolish thing men have done as necessary and therefore right.

But if the fashionable disillusionment about progress is not difficult to explain, it is not without danger. In one sense, civilization is progress and progress is civilization.[2] The preservation of the kind of civilization that we know depends on the operation of forces which, under favorable conditions, produce progress. If it is true that evolution does not always lead to better things, it is also true that, without the forces which produce it, civilization and all we value—indeed, almost all that distinguishes man from beast—would neither exist nor could long be maintained.

The history of civilization is the account of a progress which, in the short space of less than eight thousand years, has created nearly all that we regard as characteristic of human life. After abandoning hunting life, most of our direct ancestors, at the beginning of neolithic culture, took to agriculture and soon to urban life perhaps less than three thousand years or one hundred gen-

---

be no other opportunity to refer to Vico, it should be mentioned here that he and his great disciple, Ferdinando Galiani, constitute the only important parallel on the Continent to the anti-rationalist British tradition, which we shall consider more fully in the next chapter.

A German translation of an earlier and somewhat longer version of the present chapter has been published as "Grundtatsachen des Fortschritts," [The Fundamental Facts of Progress] in *Ordo: Jahrbuch für die Ordnung von Wirtschaft und Gesellschaft*, 9 (1957): 19–42.

[1] John Bagnell Bury, *The Idea of Progress: An Inquiry into its Origin and Growth* (London: Macmillan and Co., 1920), p. 2.

[2] Cf. John Stuart Mill, "Representative Government," in *On Liberty and Considerations on Representative Government*, Ronald Buchanan McCallum, ed. (Oxford: B. Blackwell, 1946), p. 121.

erations ago. It is not surprising that in some respects man's biological equipment has not kept pace with that rapid change, that the adaptation of his non-rational part has lagged somewhat, and that many of his instincts and emotions are still more adapted to the life of a hunter than to life in civilization. If many features of our civilization seem to us unnatural, artificial, or unhealthy, this must have been man's experience ever since he first took to town life, which is virtually since civilization began. All the familiar complaints against industrialism, capitalism, or overrefinement are largely protests against a new way of life that man took up a short while ago after more than half a million years' existence as a wandering hunter, and that created problems still unsolved by him.[3]

2. When we speak of progress in connection with our individual endeav-

---

[3] Cf. Adam Ferguson, *History of Civil Society*, p. 12: "If the palace be unnatural the cottage is so no less: and the highest refinements of political and moral apprehension, are no more artificial in their kind, than the first operations of sentiment and reason." Wilhelm Roscher, *Ansichten der Volkswirthschaft aus dem geschichtlichen Standpunkte* (Leipzig and Heidelberg: C. F. Winter, 1861), pp. 408–9, gives, as illustrations of the "pernicious refinements" against which austere moralists have thundered at one time or another, forks, gloves, and glazed windows; Plato in his *Phaedo* makes one of the speakers fear that the invention of writing, by weakening memory, would lead to degeneration! [Hayek is here confusing the *Phaedo* with the *Phaedrus*. It is in the *Phaedrus* that Socrates recounts the following: "The story is that in the region of Naucratis in Egypt there dwelt one of the old gods of the country, the god to whom the bird called Ibis is scared, his own name being Theuth. He it was that invented number and calculation, geometry and astronomy, not to speak of draughts and dice, and above all writing. Now the king of the whole country at that time was Thamus, who dwelt in the great city of upper Egypt which the Greeks called Egyptian Thebes, while Thamus they called Ammon. To him came Theuth, and revealed his arts, saying that they ought to be passed on to the Egyptians in general. Thamus asked what was the use of them all, and when Theuth explained, he condemned what he thought the bad points and praised what he thought the good. On each art, we are told, Thamus had plenty of views both for and against; it would take too long to give them in detail. But when it came to writing Theuth said, 'Here, O king, is a branch of learning that will make the people of Egypt wiser and improve their memories; my discovery provides a recipe for memory and wisdom.' But the king answered and said, 'O man full of arts, to one it is given to create the things of art, and to another to judge what measure of harm and of profit they have for those that shall employ them. And so it is that you, by reason of your tender regard for the writing that is your offspring, have declared the very opposite of its true effect. If men learn this, it will implant forgetfulness in their souls; they will cease to exercise memory because they rely on that which is written, calling things to remembrance no longer from within themselves, but by means of external marks. What you have discovered is a recipe not for memory, but for reminder. And it is no true wisdom you offer your disciples, but only its semblance, for by telling them of many things without teaching them you will make them seem to know much, while for the most part they know nothing, and as men filled, not with wisdom, but with the conceit of wisdom, they will be a burden to their fellows." (Plato, *Phaedrus*, 274cde-275ab). The translation is that of Reginald Hackforth and appears in *The Collected Dialogues of Plato, Including the Letters*, Edith Hamilton and Huntington Cairns, eds. (Bollingen Series; New York: Pantheon Books, 1961), p. 520.—Ed.]

ors or any organized human effort, we mean an advance toward a known goal.[4] It is not in this sense that social evolution can be called progress, for it is not achieved by human reason striving by known means toward a fixed aim.[5] It would be more correct to think of progress as a process of formation and modification of the human intellect, a process of adaptation and learning in which not only the possibilities known to us but also our values and desires continually change. As progress consists in the discovery of the not yet known, its consequences must be unpredictable. It always leads into the unknown, and the most we can expect is to gain an understanding of the kind of forces that bring it about.[6] Yet, though such a general understanding of the character of this process of cumulative growth is indispensable if we are to try to create conditions favorable to it, it can never be knowledge which will enable us to make specific predictions.[7] The claim that we can derive from such insight necessary laws of evolution that we must follow is an absurdity. Human reason can neither predict nor deliberately shape its own future. Its advances consist in finding out where it has been wrong.

Even in the field where the search for new knowledge is most deliberate, i.e., in science, no man can predict what will be the consequences of his work.[8] In fact, there is increasing recognition that even the attempt to make science

[4] If it were still possible to change an established usage, it would be desirable to confine the word "progress" to such deliberate advance toward a chosen goal and to speak only of the "evolution of civilization."

[5] See Alfred Louis Kroeber, *Configurations of Cultural Growth* (Berkeley: University of California Press, 1944), p. 839: "Progress . . . is something that makes itself. We do not make it." [Hayek is in error in citing this work. The quotation in fact appears in Kroeber's *Anthropology* (New York: Harcourt, Brace and Company, 1923), p. 133.—Ed.]

[6] Cf. John Bagnell Bury, *The Idea of Progress*, pp. 236–37: "Theories of Progress are thus differentiating into two distinct types, corresponding to two radically opposed political theories and appealing to two antagonistic temperaments. The one type is that of constructive idealists and socialists, who can name all the streets and towers of 'the city of gold,' which they imagine as situated just round a promontory. The development of man is a closed system; its term is known and is within reach. The other type is that of those who, surveying the gradual ascent of man, believe that by the same interplay of forces which have conducted him so far and by a further development of the liberty which he has fought to win, he will move slowly towards conditions of increasing harmony and happiness. Here the development is indefinite: its term is unknown, and lies in the remote future. Individual liberty is the motive force, and the corresponding political theory is liberalism."

[7] See Sir Karl Raimund Popper, *The Poverty of Historicism* (London: Routledge and Kegan Paul, 1957), and my *The Counter-Revolution of Science: Studies in the Abuse of Reason* (Glencoe, IL: Free Press, 1952). [*Collected Works* edition, vol. 13.]

[8] It has been well put by Irving Langmuir, "Freedom, the Opportunity to Profit from the Unexpected," reprinted in the [General Electric] *Research Laboratory Bulletin*, (Fall 1956): 4. "In research work, you cannot plan to make discoveries but you can plan work which would probably lead to discoveries." [These comments were originally made at a commencement address delivered before the Pratt Institute on June 1, 1956.—Ed.]

deliberately aim at useful knowledge—that is, at knowledge whose future uses can be foreseen—is likely to impede progress.[9] Progress by its very nature cannot be planned. We may perhaps legitimately speak of planning progress in a particular field where we aim at the solution of a specific problem and are already on the track of the answer. But we should soon be at the end of our endeavors if we were to confine ourselves to striving for goals now visible and if new problems did not spring up all the time. It is knowing what we have not known before that makes us wiser men.

But often it also makes us sadder men. Though progress consists in part in achieving things we have been striving for, this does not mean that we shall like all its results or that all will be gainers. And since our wishes and aims are also subject to change in the course of the process, it is questionable whether the statement has a clear meaning that the new state of affairs that progress creates is a better one. Progress in the sense of the cumulative growth of knowledge and power over nature is a term that says little about whether the new state will give us more satisfaction than the old. The pleasure may be solely in achieving what we have been striving for, and the assured possession may give us little satisfaction. The question whether, if we had to stop at our present stage of development, we would in any significant sense be better off or happier than if we had stopped a hundred or a thousand years ago is probably unanswerable.

The answer, however, does not matter. What matters is the successful striving for what at each moment seems attainable. It is not the fruits of past success but the living in and for the future in which human intelligence proves itself. Progress is movement for movement's sake, for it is in the process of learning, and in the effects of having learned something new, that man enjoys the gift of his intelligence.

The enjoyment of personal success will be given to large numbers only in a society that, as a whole, progresses fairly rapidly. In a stationary society

[9] Cf. Michael Polanyi, *The Logic of Liberty: Reflections and Rejoinders* (London: Routledge and Kegan Paul, 1951), p. 76 [Liberty Fund edition, p. 93], and the remarkable early discussion of these issues in Samuel Bailey, *Essays on the Formation and Publication of Opinions, and on Other Subjects* (London: Printed for R. Hunter, 1821), especially the observation in the Preface (pp. iv–v): "It seems to be a necessary condition of human science, that we should learn many useless things, in order to become acquainted with those which are of service; and as it is impossible, antecedently to experience, to know the value of our acquisitions, the only way in which mankind can secure all the advantages of knowledge is to prosecute their inquiries in every possible direction. There can be no greater impediment to the progress of science than a perpetual and anxious reference at every step to palpable utility. Assured that the general result will be beneficial, it is not wise to be too solicitous as to the immediate value of every individual effort. Besides, there is a certain completeness to be attained in every science, for which we are obliged to acquire many particulars not otherwise of any worth. Nor is it to be forgotten, that trivial and apparently useless acquisitions are often the necessary preparatives to important discoveries."

there will be about as many who will be descending as there will be those rising. In order that the great majority should in their individual lives participate in the advance, it is necessary that it proceed at a considerable speed. There can therefore be little doubt that Adam Smith was right when he said: "It is in the progressive state, while the society is advancing to the further acquisition, rather than when it has acquired its full complement of riches, that the condition of the labouring poor, of the great body of people, seems to be happiest and the most comfortable. It is hard in the stationary, and miserable in the declining state. The progressive state is in reality the cheerful and hearty state to all the different orders of the society. The stationary is dull; the declining melancholy."[10]

It is one of the most characteristic facts of a progressive society that in it most things which individuals strive for can be obtained only through further progress. This follows from the necessary character of the process: new knowledge and its benefits can spread only gradually, and the ambitions of the many will always be determined by what is as yet accessible only to the few. It is misleading to think of those new possibilities as if they were, from the beginning, a common possession of society which its members could deliberately share; they become a common possession only through that slow process by which the achievements of the few are made available to the many. This is often obscured by the exaggerated attention usually given to a few conspicuous major steps in the development. But, more often than not, major discoveries merely open new vistas, and long further efforts are necessary before the new knowledge that has sprung up somewhere can be put to general use. It will have to pass through a long course of adaptation, selection, combination, and improvement before full use can be made of it. This means that there will always be people who already benefit from new achievements that have not yet reached others.

3. The rapid economic advance that we have come to expect seems in a large measure to be the result of this inequality and to be impossible without it. Progress at such a fast rate cannot proceed on a uniform front but must take place in echelon fashion, with some far ahead of the rest. The reason for this is concealed by our habit of regarding economic progress chiefly as an accumulation of ever greater quantities of goods and equipment. But the rise of our standard of life is due at least as much to an increase in knowledge which

---

[10] Adam Smith, *The Wealth of Nations*, vol. 1, p. 83 [Liberty Fund edition, vol. 1, p. 99]. See by way of contrast John Stuart Mill, who in 1848 (*Principles*, IV, vi, 2, p. 749; Liberty Fund edition, *Collected Works*, vol. 3, p. 755) seriously contended that "it is only in the backward countries of the world that increased production is still an important object: in those most advanced, what is economically needed is a better distribution." He appears to have been unaware that an attempt to cure even extreme poverty by redistribution would in his time have led to the destruction of all of what he regarded as cultured life, without achieving its object.

enables us not merely to consume more of the same things but to use different things, and often things we did not even know before. And though the growth of income depends in part on the accumulation of capital, more probably depends on our learning to use our resources more effectively and for new purposes.

The growth of knowledge is of such special importance because, while the material resources will always remain scarce and will have to be reserved for limited purposes, the uses of new knowledge (where we do not make them artificially scarce by patents of monopoly) are unrestricted. Knowledge, once achieved, becomes gratuitously available for the benefit of all. It is through this free gift of the knowledge acquired by the experiments of some members of society that general progress is made possible, that the achievements of those who have gone before facilitate the advance of those who follow.

At any stage of this process there will always be many things we already know how to produce but which are still too expensive to provide for more than a few. And at an early stage they can be made only through an out-lay of resources equal to many times the share of total income that, with an approximately equal distribution, would go to the few who could benefit from them. At first, a new good is commonly "the caprice of a chosen few before it becomes a public need and forms part of the necessities of life. For the luxuries of to-day are the necessities of tomorrow."[11] Furthermore, the new things will often become available to the greater part of the people only *because* for some time they have been the luxuries of the few.

If we, in the wealthier countries, today can provide facilities and conveniences for most which not long ago would have been physically impossible to produce in such quantities, this is in large measure the direct consequence of the fact that they were first made for a few. All the conveniences of a comfortable home, of our means of transportation and communication, of entertainment and enjoyment, we could produce at first only in limited quantities; but it was in doing this that we gradually learned to make them or similar things at a much smaller outlay of resources and thus became able to supply them to the great majority. A large part of the expenditure of the rich, though not intended for that end, thus serves to defray the cost of the experimentation with the new things that, as a result, can later be made available to the poor.

The important point is not merely that we gradually learn to make cheaply on a large scale what we already know how to make expensively in small quantities but that only from an advanced position does the next range of desires and possibilities become visible, so that the selection of new goals and the effort toward their achievement will begin long before the majority can

---

[11] Gabriele de Tarde, *Social Laws: An Outline of Sociology*, Howard Crosby Warren, trans. (New York: Macmillan, 1907), p. 194.

strive for them. If what they will want after their present goals are realized is soon to be made available, it is necessary that the developments that will bear fruit for the masses in twenty or fifty years' time should be guided by the views of people who are already in the position of enjoying them.

If today in the United States or western Europe the relatively poor can have a car or a refrigerator, an airplane trip or a radio, at the cost of a reasonable part of their income, this was made possible because in the past others with larger incomes were able to spend on what was then a luxury. The path of advance is greatly eased by the fact that it has been trodden before. It is because scouts have found the goal that the road can be built for the less lucky or less energetic. What today may seem extravagance or even waste, because it is enjoyed by the few and even undreamed of by the masses, is payment for the experimentation with a style of living that will eventually be available to many. The range of what will be tried and later developed, the fund of experience that will become available to all, is greatly extended by the unequal distribution of present benefits; and the rate of advance will be greatly increased if the first steps are taken long before the majority can profit from them. Many of the improvements would indeed never become a possibility for all if they had not long before been available to some. If all had to wait for better things until they could be provided for all, that day would in many instances never come. Even the poorest today owe their relative material well-being to the results of past inequality.

4. In a progressive society as we know it, the comparatively wealthy are thus merely somewhat ahead of the rest in the material advantages which they enjoy. They are already living in a phase of evolution that the others have not yet reached. Poverty has, in consequence, become a relative, rather than an absolute, concept. This does not make it less bitter. Although in an advanced society the unsatisfied wants are usually no longer physical needs but the results of civilization, it is still true that at each stage some of the things most people desire can be provided only for a few and can be made accessible to all only by further progress. Most of what we strive for are things we want because others already have them.[12] Yet a progressive society, while it relies on this process of learning and imitation, recognizes the desires it creates only as a spur to further effort. It does not guarantee the results to everyone. It disregards the pain of unfulfilled desire aroused by the example of others. It appears cruel because it increases the desire of all in proportion as it increases its gifts to some. Yet so long as it remains a progressive society, some must lead, and the rest must follow.

---

[12] Regarding the curious conclusion reached by John Kenneth Galbraith from the fact that most of our needs are culturally determined, see my "The Non Sequitur of the Dependence Effect," *The Southern Economic Journal*, 27 (April 1961): 346–48.

The contention that in any phase of progress the rich, by experimenting with new styles of living not yet accessible to the poor, perform a necessary service without which the advance of the poor would be very much slower will appear to some as a piece of far-fetched and cynical apologetics. Yet a little reflection will show that it is fully valid and that a socialist society would in this respect have to imitate a free society. It would be necessary in a planned economy (unless it could simply imitate the example of other more advanced societies) to designate individuals whose duty it would be to try out the latest advances long before they were made available to the rest. There is no way of making generally accessible new and still expensive ways of living except by their being initially practiced by some. It would not be enough if individuals were allowed to try out particular new things. These have their proper use and value only as an integral part of the general advance in which they are the next thing desired. In order to know which of the various new possibilities should be developed at each stage, how and when particular improvements ought to be fitted into the general advance, a planned society would have to provide for a whole class, or even a hierarchy of classes, which would always move some steps ahead of the rest. The situation would then differ from that in a free society merely in the fact that the inequalities would be the result of design and that the selection of particular individuals or groups would be done by authority rather than by the impersonal process of the market and the accidents of birth and opportunity. It should be added that only those kinds of better living approved by authority would be permissible and that they would be provided only for those specially designated. But, in order for a planned society to achieve the same rate of advance as a free society, the degree of inequality that would have to prevail would not be very different.

There is no practicable measure of the degree of inequality that is desirable here. We do not wish, of course, to see the position of individuals determined by arbitrary decision or a privilege conferred by human will on particular persons. It is difficult to see however, in what sense it could ever be legitimate to say that any one person is too far ahead of the rest or that it would be harmful to society if the progress of some greatly outstripped that of others. There might be justification for saying this if there appeared great gaps in the scale of advance; but, as long as the graduation is more or less continuous and all the steps in the income pyramid are reasonably occupied, it can scarcely be denied that those lower down profit materially from the fact that others are ahead.

The objections spring from the misconception that those in the lead claim the right to something that otherwise would be available to the rest. This would be true if we thought in terms of a single redistribution of the fruits of past progress and not in terms of that continuous advance which our unequal society fosters. In the long run, the existence of groups ahead of the rest is clearly an advantage to those who are behind, in the same way that, if we could suddenly draw on the more advanced knowledge which some other men on a previously unknown continent or on another planet had gained under more favorable conditions, we would all profit greatly.

5. The problems of equality are difficult to discuss dispassionately when members of our own community are affected. They stand out more clearly when we consider them in their wider aspect, namely, the relation between rich and poor countries. We are then less apt to be misled by the conception that each member of any community has some natural right to a definite share of the income of his group. Although today most of the people of the world benefit from one another's efforts, we certainly have no reason to consider the product of the world as the result of a unified effort of collective humanity.

Although the fact that the people of the West are today so far ahead of the others in wealth is in part the consequence of a greater accumulation of capital, it is mainly the result of their more effective utilization of knowledge. There can be little doubt that the prospect of the poorer, "undeveloped" countries reaching the present level of the West is very much better than it would have been, had the West not pulled so far ahead. Furthermore, it is better than it would have been, had some world authority, in the course of the rise of modern civilization, seen to it that no part pulled too far ahead of the rest and made sure at each step that the material benefits were distributed evenly throughout the world. If today some nations can in a few decades acquire a level of material comfort that took the West hundreds or thousands of years to achieve, is it not evident that their path has been made easier by the fact that the West was not forced to share its material achievements with the rest—that it was not held back but was able to move far in advance of the others?

Not only are the countries of the West richer because they have more advanced technological knowledge, but they have more advanced technological knowledge because they are richer. And the free gift of the knowledge that has cost those in the lead much to achieve enables those who follow to reach the same level at a much smaller cost.[13] Indeed, so long as some countries lead, all the others can follow, although the conditions for spontaneous progress may be absent in them. That even countries or groups which do not possess freedom can profit from many of its fruits is one of the reasons why the importance of freedom is not better understood. For many parts of the world the advance of civilization has long been a derived affair, and, with modern

---

[13] See David Hume, "The Rise and Progress of the Arts and Sciences," *Essays: Moral, Political, and Literary* [Essay 14], vol. 1, p. 184 [Liberty Fund edition, p. 124]: *"That though the only proper Nursery of these noble plants be a free state, yet may they be transplanted into any government."*

communications, such countries need not lag very far behind, though most of the innovations may originate elsewhere. How long has Soviet Russia or Japan been living on an attempt to imitate American technology! So long as somebody else provides most of the new knowledge and does most of the experimenting, it may even be possible to apply all this knowledge deliberately in such a manner as to benefit most of the members of a given group at about the same time and to the same degree. But, though an egalitarian society could advance in this sense, its progress would be essentially parasitical, borrowed from those who have paid the cost.

It is worth remembering in this connection that what enables a country to lead in this world-wide development are its economically most advanced classes and that a country that deliberately levels such differences also abdicates its leading position—as the example of Great Britain so tragically shows. All classes there had profited from the fact that a rich class with old traditions had demanded products of a quality and taste unsurpassed elsewhere and that Britain, in consequence, came to supply to the rest of the world. British leadership has gone with the disappearance of the class whose style of living the others imitated. It may not be long before the British workers will discover that they had profited by being members of a community containing many persons richer than they and that their lead over the workers in other countries was in part an effect of a similar lead of their own rich over the rich in other countries.

6. If on an international scale even major inequalities may be of great assistance to the progress of all, can there be much doubt that the same is also true of such inequalities within a nation? Here, too, the over-all speed of advance will be increased by those who move fastest. Even if many fall behind at first, the cumulative effect of the preparation of the path will, before long, sufficiently facilitate their advance that they will be able to keep their place in the march. Members of a community containing many who are rich enjoy, in fact, a great advantage not available to those who, because they live in a poor country, do not profit from the capital and experience supplied by the rich; it is difficult to see, therefore, why this situation should justify a claim to a larger share for the individual. It seems indeed generally to be the case that, after rapid progress has continued for some time, the cumulative advantage for those who follow is great enough to enable them to move faster than those who lead and that, in consequence, the long-drawn-out column of human progress tends to close up. The experience of the United States at least seems to indicate that, once the rise in the position of the lower classes gathers speed, catering to the rich ceases to be the main source of great gain and gives place to efforts directed toward the needs of the masses. Those forces which at first make inequality self-accentuating thus later tend to diminish it.

Therefore, there must be two different ways of looking at the possibility of reducing inequality and abolishing poverty by deliberate redistribution—that is, from a long-term or a short-term point of view. At any given moment we could improve the position of the poorest by giving them what we took from the wealthy. But, while such an equalizing of the positions in the column of progress would temporarily quicken the closing-up of the ranks, it would, before long, slow down the movement of the whole and in the long run hold back those in the rear. Recent European experience strongly confirms this. The rapidity with which rich societies here have become static, if not stagnant, societies through egalitarian policies, while impoverished but highly competitive countries have become very dynamic and progressive, has been one of the most conspicuous features of the postwar period. The contrast in this respect between the advanced welfare states of Great Britain and the Scandinavian countries, on the one hand, and countries like Western Germany, Belgium, or Italy, is beginning to be recognized even by the former.[14] If a demonstration had been needed that there is no more effective way of making a society stationary than by imposing upon all something like the same average standard, or no more effective way of slowing down progress than by allowing the most successful a standard only a little above the average, these experiments have provided it.

It is curious that, while in the case of a primitive country every detached observer would probably recognize that its position offered little hope so long as its whole population was on the same low dead level and that the first condition for advance was that some should pull ahead of the others, few people are willing to admit the same of more advanced countries.[15] Of course, a society in which only the politically privileged are allowed to rise, or where those who rise first gain political power and use it to keep the others down, would be no better than an egalitarian society. But all obstacles to the rise of some are, in the long run, obstacles to the rise of all; and they are no less harmful to the true interest of the multitude because they may gratify its momentary passions.[16]

[14] Cf. the two important articles in the *Times Literary Supplement*: February 24, 1956, pp. 109–11, "The Dynamic Society," and December 28, 1956, pp. 773–75, "The Secular Trinity." The articles have also been published in pamphlet form by the *Times Literary Supplement*.

[15] See Kenneth Ewart Boulding, *Principles of Economic Policy* (Englewood Cliffs, NJ: Prentice-Hall, 1958), p. 94: "Equality . . . is a luxury of rich societies. If a poor society is to achieve anything at all it must develop a high degree of inequality—the small economic surplus must be concentrated in a few hands if *any* high-level achievements are to be made."

[16] Cf. Henry Christopher Wallich, "Conservative Economic Policy," *Yale Review*, 46 (1956): 67: "From a dollars-and-cents point of view, it is quite obvious that over a period of years, even those who find themselves at the short end of inequality have more to gain from faster growth than from any conceivable income redistribution. A speedup in real output of only one extra per-cent per year will soon lift even the economically weakest into income brackets to which no amount of redistribution could promote them. . . . For the economist, economic inequality

7. With respect to the advanced countries of the West it is sometimes contended that progress is too fast or too exclusively material. These two aspects are probably closely connected. Times of very rapid material progress have rarely been periods of great efflorescence of the arts, and both the greatest appreciation and the finest products of artistic and intellectual endeavor have often appeared when material progress has slackened. Neither western Europe of the nineteenth century nor the United States of the twentieth is eminent for its artistic achievements. But the great outbursts in the creation of non-material values seem to presuppose a preceding improvement in economic condition. It is perhaps natural that generally after such periods of rapid growth of wealth there occurs a turning toward non-material things or that, when economic activity no longer offers the fascination of rapid progress, some of the most gifted men should turn to the pursuit of other values.

This is, of course, only one and perhaps not even the most important aspect of rapid material progress that makes many of those who are in its van skeptical of its value. We must also admit that it is not certain whether most people want all or even most of the results of progress. For most of them it is an involuntary affair which, while bringing them much they strive for, also forces on them many changes they do not want at all. The individual does not have it in his power to choose to take part in progress or not; and always it not only brings new opportunities but deprives many of much they want, much that is dear and important to them. To some it may be sheer tragedy, and to all those who would prefer to live on the fruits of past progress and not take part in its future course, it may seem a curse rather than a blessing.

There are, especially, in all countries and at all times groups that have reached a more or less stationary position, in which habits and ways of life have been settled for generations. These ways of life may suddenly be threatened by developments with which they have had nothing to do, and not only the members of such groups but often outsiders also will wish them to be preserved. Many of the peasants of Europe, particularly those in the remote mountain valleys, are an example. They cherish their way of life, though it has become a dead end, though it has become too dependent on urban civilization, which is continually changing, to preserve itself. Yet the conservative peasant, as much as anybody else, owes his way of life to a different type of person, to men who were innovators in their time and who by their innovations forced a new manner of living on people belonging to an earlier state of culture; the nomad probably complained as much about the encroachment of enclosed fields on his pastures as does the peasant about the encroachments of industry.

---

acquires a functional justification thanks to the growth concept. Its ultimate results benefit even those who at first seem to be losers."

The changes to which such people must submit are part of the cost of progress, an illustration of the fact that not only the mass of men but, strictly speaking, every human being is led by the growth of civilization into a path that is not of his own choosing. If the majority were asked their opinion of all the changes involved in progress, they would probably want to prevent many of its necessary conditions and consequences and thus ultimately stop progress itself. And I have yet to learn of an instance when the deliberate vote of the majority (as distinguished from the decision of some governing elite) has decided on such sacrifices in the interest of a better future as is made by a free-market society. This does not mean, however, that the achievement of most things men actually want does not depend on the continuance of that progress which, if they could, they would probably stop by preventing the effects which do not meet with their immediate approval.

Not all the amenities that we can today provide for the few will sooner or later be available to all; with such amenities as personal services, it would be clearly impossible. They are among the advantages which the wealthy are deprived of by progress. But most of the gains of the few do, in the course of time, become available to the rest. Indeed, all our hopes for the reduction of present misery and poverty rest on this expectation. If we abandoned progress, we should also have to abandon all those social improvements that we now hope for. All the desired advances in education and health, the realization of our wish that at least a large proportion of the people should reach the goals for which they are striving, depend on the continuance of progress. We have only to remember that to prevent progress at the top would soon prevent it all the way down, in order to see that this result is really the last thing we want.

8. We have so far concerned ourselves mainly with our own country or with those countries which we consider to be members of our own civilization. But we must take into account the fact that the consequences of past progress— namely, world-wide extension of rapid and easy communication of knowledge and ambitions—have largely deprived us of the choice as to whether or not we want continued rapid progress. The new fact in our present position that forces us to push on is that the accomplishments of our civilization have become the object of desire and envy of all the rest of the world. Regardless of whether from some higher point of view our civilization is really better or not, we must recognize that its material results are demanded by practically all who have come to know them. Those people may not wish to adopt our entire civilization, but they certainly want to be able to pick and choose from it whatever suits them. We may regret, but cannot disregard, the fact that even where different civilizations are still preserved and dominate the lives of the majority, the leadership has fallen almost invariably into the hands of those

who have gone furthest in adopting the knowledge and technology of Western civilization.[17]

While superficially it may seem that two types of civilization are today competing for the allegiance of the people of the world, the fact is that the promise they offer to the masses, the advantages they hold out to them, are essentially the same. Though the free and the totalitarian countries both claim that their respective methods will provide more rapidly what those people want, the goal itself must seem to them the same. The chief difference is that only the totalitarians appear clearly to know how they want to achieve that result, while the free world has only its past achievements to show, being by its very nature unable to offer any detailed "plan" for further growth.

But if the material achievements of our civilization have created ambitions in others, they have also given them a new power to destroy it if what they believe is their due is not given them. With the knowledge of possibilities spreading faster than the material benefits, a great part of the people of the world are today dissatisfied as never before and are determined to take what they regard as their rights. They believe as much and as mistakenly as the poor in any one country that their goal can be achieved by a redistribution of already existing wealth, and they have been confirmed in this belief by Western teaching. As their strength grows, they will become able to extort such a redistribution if the increase in wealth that progress produces is not fast enough. Yet a redistribution that slows down the rate of advance of those in the lead must bring about a situation in which even more of the next improvement will have to come from redistribution, since less will be provided by economic growth.

The aspirations of the great mass of the world's population can today be satisfied only by rapid material progress. There can be little doubt that in their present mood a serious disappointment of their expectations would lead to grave international friction—indeed, it would probably lead to war. The peace of the world and, with it, civilization itself thus depend on continued progress at a fast rate. At this juncture we are therefore not only the creatures but the captives of progress; even if we wished to, we could not sit back and enjoy at leisure what we have achieved. Our task must be to continue to lead, to move ahead along the path which so many more are trying to tread in our

[17] Cf. on these effects in one of the most remote parts of the world John Clark, *Hunza: Lost Kingdom of the Himalayas* (New York: Funk and Wagnalls, 1956), p. 266: "Contact with the West, either directly or second-hand, has reached the outermost nomad, the deepest jungle village. More than a billion people have learned that we live happier lives, perform more interesting work, and enjoy greater physical comforts than they do. Their own cultures have not given them these things, and they are determined to possess them. Most Asians desire all of our advantages with as little change as possible in their own customs."

wake. At some future date when, after a long period of world-wide advance in material standards, the pipelines through which it spreads are so filled that, even when the vanguard slows down, those at the rear will for some time continue to move at an undiminished speed, we may again have it in our power to choose whether or not we want to go ahead at such a rate. But at this moment, when the greater part of mankind has only just awakened to the possibility of abolishing starvation, filth, and disease; when it has just been touched by the expanding wave of modern technology after centuries or millennia of relative stability; and as a first reaction has begun to increase in number at a frightening rate, even a small decline in our rate of advance might be fatal to us.

FOUR

FREEDOM, REASON, AND TRADITION

Nothing is more fertile in prodigies than the art of being free; but there is nothing more arduous than the apprenticeship of liberty. . . . Liberty . . . is generally established with difficulty in the midst of storms; it is perfected by civil discords; and its benefit cannot be appreciated until it is already old.

—A. de Tocqueville

1. Though freedom is not a state of nature but an artifact of civilization, it did not arise from design. The institutions of freedom, like everything freedom has created, were not established because people foresaw the benefits they would bring. But, once its advantages were recognized, men began to perfect and extend the rein of freedom and, for that purpose, to inquire how a free

The quotation at the head of the chapter is taken from Tocqueville, *Democracy in America*, vol. 1, chap. 14, pp. 246–47. [The French text, in full, reads: "On ne saurait trop le dire: il n'est rien de plus fécond en merveilles que l'art d'être libre; mais il n'y a rien de plus dur que l'apprentissage de la liberté. Il n'en est pas de même du despotisme. Le despotisme se présente souvent comme le réparateur de tous les maux soufferts; il est l'appui du bon droit, le soutien des opprimés et le fondateur de l'ordre. Les peuples s'endorment au sein de la prospérité momentanée qu'il fait naître; et lorsqu'ils se réveillent, ils sont misérables. La liberté, au contraire, naît d'ordinaire au milieu des orages, elle s'établit péniblement parmi les discordes civiles et ce n'est que quand elle est déjà vielle qu'on peut connaître ses bienfaits" (bk. 1, pt. 2, chap. 6). "De la démocratie en Amérique," in *Œuvres*, André Jardin, ed. Bibliothèque de la Pléiade (2 vols.; Paris: Éditions Gallimard, 1992), vol. 2, p. 275.—Ed.] Cf. also vol. 2, chap. 2, p. 96: "The advantages that freedom brings are shown only by the lapse of time, and it is always easy to mistake the cause in which they originate." ["Les biens que la liberté procure ne se montrent qu'à la longue, et il est toujours facile de méconnaître la cause qui les fait naître" (bk. 2, sec, 2, chap. 1, pp. 609–10). "De la démocratie en Amérique," in *Œuvres*, vol. 2, pp. 609–10.—Ed.] An earlier and slightly longer version of this chapter has appeared as "Freedom, Reason, and Tradition" in *Ethics*, 68 (1958): 229–45. See also David Hume, "The Rise and Progress of the Arts and Sciences," *Essays* [Essay 14], vol. 1, p. 185 [Liberty Fund edition, p. 124]: "To balance a large state or society, whether monarchical or republican, on general laws, is a work of so great difficulty, that no human genius, however comprehensive, is able, by the mere dint of reason and reflection, to effect it. The judgments of many must unite in this work: Experience must guide their labour. Time must bring it to perfection: and the feeling of inconveniencies must correct the mistakes, which they inevitably fall into, in their first trials and experiments" and "law, the source of all security and happiness, arises late in any government, and is the slow product of order and liberty." See also Cicero, *De re publica*, ii.1.2 (n. 19 below).

society worked. This development of a theory of liberty took place mainly in the eighteenth century. It began in two countries, England and France. The first of these knew liberty; the second did not.

As a result, we have had to the present day two different traditions in the theory of liberty:[1] one empirical and unsystematic, the other speculative and rationalistic[2]—the first based on an interpretation of traditions and institutions which had spontaneously grown up and were but imperfectly understood, the second aiming at the construction of a utopia, which has often been tried but never successfully. Nevertheless, it has been the rationalist, plausible, and apparently logical argument of the French tradition, with its flattering assumptions about the unlimited powers of human reason, that has progressively gained influence, while the less articulate and less explicit tradition of English freedom has been on the decline.

This distinction is obscured by the facts that what we have called the

[1] Tocqueville remarks somewhere: "Du dix-huitième siècle et de la révolution, étaient sortis deux fleuves: le premier conduisait les hommes aux institutions libres, tandis que le second les menant au pouvoir absolu." [The exact quotation reads: "Du dix-huitième siècle et de la révolution, comme d'une source commune, étaient sortis deux fleuves: le premier conduisait les hommes aux institutions libres, tandis que le second les menait au pouvoir absolu." ("From the eighteenth century and the Revolution, as from a common source, two streams issued. The first led men to free institutions, the second to absolute power.") The quotation appears in the "Discours de M. De Tocqueville Prononcé dan la Séance Publique du 21 avril 1842, en venant prendre séance à la place de M. le comte de Cessac," *Œuvres*, vol. 1, pp. 1208–09.—Ed.] Cf. the observation by Sir Thomas Erskine May, *Democracy in Europe: A History* (London: Longmans, Green, and Co., 1877), vol. 2, p. 334: "The history of the one [France], in modern times, is the history of Democracy, not of liberty: the history of the other [England] is the history of liberty, not of Democracy." See also Guido de Ruggiero, *The History of European Liberalism*, Robin George Collingwood, trans. (Oxford: Oxford University Press, 1927), esp. pp. 12, 71, and 81. [Ruggiero at one point notes that: "(English) Liberalism was now confronted by the new Liberalism of France; genuinely new, because instead of basing itself upon the privileged liberties of the Middle Ages, it arose from their ashes. It was far more akin in spirit to the absolute monarchy which had already begun to destroy the old feudal world and had given to its subjects the feeling of equality. The new Liberalism, like the monarchy, was egalitarian; but its egalitarianism was inspired and ennobled by a broader rationalistic consciousness attributing to all men one identical spiritual and human value. But the love of equality which gave its peculiar tone to the new freedom was so overwhelming that it ended by overthrowing and crushing it" (pp. 81–82). —Ed.] On the absence of a truly liberal tradition in France see Emile Faguet, *Le Liberalisme* (Paris: Société française d'imprimerie et de librairie, 1902), esp. p. 307, and Heinrich von Treitschke, *Die Freiheit* (1861) (Leipzig: Insel Bücherei, 1912), p. 12: "Daß die Franzosen trotz aller Begeisterung für die Freiheit doch immer nur die Gleichheit gekannt haben, nie die Freiheit." ["The French, despite all the excitement regarding liberty, have known only equality, never liberty."—Ed.]

[2] "Rationalism" and "rationalistic" will be used here throughout in the sense defined by Bernard Groethuysen in "Rationalism," *Encyclopedia of the Social Sciences*, vol. 13, p. 113, as a tendency "to regulate individual and social life in accordance with principles of reason and to eliminate as far as possible or to relegate to the background everything irrational." Cf. also Michael Oakeshott, "Rationalism in Politics," *Cambridge Journal*, 1 (1947): 81–98.

"French tradition" of liberty arose largely from an attempt to interpret British institutions and that the conceptions which other countries formed of British institutions were based mainly on their description by French writers.[3] The two traditions became finally confused when they merged in the liberal movement of the nineteenth century and when even leading British liberals drew as much on the French as on the British tradition.[4] It was, in the end, the victory of the Benthamite Philosophical Radicals over the Whigs in England that concealed the fundamental difference which in more recent years has reappeared as the conflict between liberal democracy and "social" or totalitarian democracy.[5]

This difference was better understood a hundred years ago than it is today. In the year of the European revolutions in which the two traditions merged, the contrast between "Anglican" and "Gallican" liberty was still clearly described by an eminent German American political philosopher. "Gallican Liberty," wrote Francis Lieber in 1848, "is sought in the *government*, and according to an Anglican point of view, it is looked for in a wrong place, where it cannot be found. Necessary consequences of the Gallican view are, that the French look for the highest degree of political civilization in *organization*, that is, in the highest degree of interference by public power. The question whether this interference be despotism or liberty is decided solely by the fact *who* interferes, and for the benefit of which class the interference takes place, while according to the Anglican view this interference would always be either absolutism or aristocracy, and the present dictatorship of the *ouvriers* would appear to us an uncompromising aristocracy of the *ouvriers*."[6]

---

[3] The author of the most detailed monograph on one of the first French economic theorists, Pierre de Boisguillebert (Hazel van Dyke Roberts, *Boisguilbert: Economist of the Reign of Louis XIV* [New York: Columbia University Press, 1935] has noted: "His positive theory may be said in a very real sense to have been simply a rationale of what he thought to be the English way of life, a way of life he would have the French adopt" (p. 327n).

[4] See Elie Halévy, *The Growth of Philosophic Radicalism* (London: Faber and Gwyer, 1928), pp. 17–18. See also Gerhard Ritter, *Vom sittlichen Problem der Macht* (Bern: A. Francke AG. Verlag, 1948), p. 132.

[5] Cf. Jacob Lieb Talmon, *The Origins of Totalitarian Democracy* (London: Secker and Warburg, 1952). Though Talmon does not identify "social" with "totalitarian" democracy, I cannot but agree with Hans Kelsen ("The Foundations of Democracy," *Ethics*, 66, part 2 [1955]: 95, n. 14) that "the antagonism which Talmon describes as tension between liberal and totalitarian democracy is in truth the antagonism between liberalism and socialism and not between two types of democracy."

[6] Francis Lieber, "Anglican and Gallican Liberty," originally published in a South Carolina newspaper in 1849 and reprinted in *The Miscellaneous Writings of Francis Lieber* (Philadelphia: J. B. Lippincott, 1881), vol. 2, pp. 382–83. See also vol. 2, p. 385: "The fact that Gallican liberty expects everything from organization, while Anglican liberty inclines to development, explains why we see in France so little improvement and expansion of institutions; but when improvement is attempted, a total abolition of the preceding state of things—a beginning *ab ovo*—a re-

Since this was written, the French tradition has everywhere progressively displaced the English.[7] To disentangle the two traditions it is necessary to look at the relatively pure forms in which they appeared in the eighteenth century. What we have called the "British tradition" was made explicit mainly by a group of Scottish moral philosophers led by David Hume, Adam Smith, and Adam Ferguson,[8] seconded by their English contemporaries Josiah Tucker, Edmund Burke, and William Paley, and drawing largely on a tradition rooted in the jurisprudence of the common law.[9] Opposed to them was the tradition of the French Enlightenment, deeply imbued with Cartesian rationalism: the Encyclopedists and Rousseau, the Physiocrats and Condorcet, are their best-known representatives. Of course, the division does not fully coincide with national boundaries. Frenchmen like Montesquieu and, later, Benjamin Con-

---

discussion of the first elementary principles." See also József Eötvös, *Der Einfluß der herrschenden Ideen des 19. Jahrhunderts auf den Staat* (2 vols.; Leipzig: F. A. Brockhaus, 1854), particularly vol. 1, p. 38, and James Mill, *Considerations on Representative Government* (London: Parker, Son, and Bourn, 1861), pp. 82–84.

[7] One of the reasons why the French notion of liberty was so attractive was offered by Friedrich Naumann in his previously cited treatise (*Das Ideal der Freiheit*, p. 16–17): He wrote: "Die Länder, wo der Sieg der Freiheit, das heißt in diesem Falle der gleichen Rechte (!) am vollkommensten ist, sind vom Standpunkt liberaler Romantik die langweiligsten, denn in ihnen gibt es keine Freiheitskämpfer mehr, höchstens noch einen gewissen pharisäischen Stolz denen gegenüber, die noch nicht so weit sind, und ein gewisses erhabenes Mitleid für die Opfer zurückgebliebener Zustände. So etwa erscheint bisweilen der englische Liberalismus." ["Those countries in which the victory of liberty, that is to say, equality of rights, was most complete, were, from the point of view of liberal romanticism, the most boring, since there were no longer any freedom fighters, while what remained, for the most part, was a certain Pharisaic pride towards those nations that had not yet advanced to this point and a species of pity for those people subject to these backward circumstances. This is, more or less, how English Liberalism appears."—Ed.]

One of the most amusing episodes of World War I was the dispute, which extended beyond the battlefield, between French and German intellectuals over the question of which country had discovered the secret of social organization. See Jean Labadié, ed., *L'Allemagne: A-t-elle le secret de l'organisation?* (Paris: Bibliothèque de l'Opinion, 1916). It would have been difficult for an Englishman to make this claim for his country. In this context, see the discussion about the role of "organization" during the Napoleonic era.

[8] An adequate account of this philosophy of growth which provided the intellectual foundations for a policy of freedom has yet to be written and cannot be attempted here. For a fuller appreciation of the Scottish-English school and its differences from the French rationalist tradition see Duncan Forbes, "Scientific Whiggism: Adam Smith and John Millar," *Cambridge Journal*, 7(1954): 643–70, and my own lecture, *Individualism: True and False* (Dublin: Hodges Figgis, 1946), reprinted in *Individualism and Economic Order* (Chicago: University of Chicago Press, 1948), pp. 1–32 (the latter particularly for the role played by Bernard Mandeville in this tradition which I am passing over here). [Now see *Studies on the Abuse and Decline of Reason*, pp. 46–74.—Ed.] For further reference see the earlier version of this article, "Freedom, Reason, and Tradition," in *Ethics*, pp. 229–45.

[9] See especially the work of Sir Mathew Hale, "Sir Mathew Hale's Criticism on Hobbes' Dialogue on the Common Law," reprinted as an appendix to William Searle Holdsworth, *A History of English Law* (London: Methuen, 1924), vol. 5, pp. 504–5. [While Holdsworth spells Hale's Christian name with one "t," Hale's biographer, Gilbert Burnet, shows it as "Matthew."—Ed.]

stant and, above all, Alexis de Tocqueville are probably nearer to what we have called the "British" than to the "French" tradition.[10] And, in Thomas Hobbes, Britain has provided at least one of the founders of the rationalist tradition, not to speak of the whole generation of enthusiasts for the French Revolution, like Godwin, Priestley, Price, and Paine, who (like Jefferson after his stay in France[11]) belong entirely to it.

2. Though these two groups are now commonly lumped together as the ancestors of modern liberalism, there is hardly a greater contrast imaginable than that between their respective conceptions of the evolution and functioning of a social order and the role played in it by liberty. The difference is directly traceable to the predominance of an essentially empiricist view of the world in England and a rationalist approach in France. The main contrast in the practical conclusions to which these approaches led has recently been well put, as follows: "One finds the essence of freedom in spontaneity and the absence of coercion, the other believes it to be realized only in the pursuit and attainment of an absolute collective purpose";[12] and "one stands for organic, slow, half-conscious growth, the other for doctrinaire deliberateness; one for trial and error procedure, the other for an enforced solely valid pattern."[13] It is the second view, as J. L. Talmon has shown in an important book from which this description is taken, that has become the origin of totalitarian democracy.

[10] Montesquieu, Constant, and Tocqueville were often regarded as Anglo-maniacs by their compatriots. Constant was partly educated in Scotland, and Tocqueville could say of himself that "So many of my thoughts and feelings are shared by the English that England has turned into a second native land of the mind for me." [The Simpson translation renders Tocqueville's French thus: "So many of my opinions and feelings are English, that England is to me almost a second country intellectually" (Tocqueville to Nassau Senior, Versailles, 27 July 1851, *Correspondence and Conversations of Alexis de Tocqueville and Naussau William Senior, from 1834 to 1959*, Mary Charlotte Mair Simpson, ed. and trans. [2 vols.; 2nd ed.; London: Henry S. King and Co., 1872], vol. 1, pp. 1, 264). Tocqueville's original reads: "J'ai d'ailleurs tant de sentiments et d'idées qui me sont communs avec les Anglais, que l'Angleterre est devenue pour moi comme une seconde patrie intellectuelle." Alexis de Tocqueville, *Œuvres complètes*. Tome 6: *Correspondance Anglaise*, 3 vols.; part 2: *Correspondance et Conversations d'Alexis de Tocqueville et Nassau William Senior* (Paris: Gallimard, 1991), p. 132.—Ed.] A fuller list of eminent French thinkers who belonged more to the evolutionary "British" than to the rationalistic "French" tradition would have to include the young Turgot and Etienne Bonnot de Condillac.

[11] On Jefferson's shift from the "British" to the "French" tradition as a result of his stay in France see the important work by Otto Vossler, *Die amerikanischen Revolutionsideale in ihrem Verhältnis zu den europäischen: untersucht an Thomas Jefferson* (Munich: Oldenbourg, 1929).

[12] Talmon, *Origins of Totalitarian Democracy*, p. 2.

[13] Talmon, *Origins of Totalitarian Democracy*, p. 71. Cf. also Lewis Mumford, *Faith for Living* (New York: Harcourt, Brace and Co., 1940), pp. 64–66, where a contrast is drawn between "ideal liberalism" and "pragmatic liberalism," and William Montgomery McGovern and David S. Collier, *Radicals and Conservatives* (Chicago: H. Regnery Co., 1958), pp. 9–20, where "conservative liberals" and "radical liberals" are distinguished. See also Carl Menger, *Untersuchungen*, p. 207, regarding "einseitigen rationalistischen Liberalismus," ["one-sided rationalistic Liberalism,"] of which he wrongly accuses Adam Smith.

The sweeping success of the political doctrines that stem from the French tradition is probably due to their great appeal to human pride and ambition. But we must not forget that the political conclusions of the two schools derive from different conceptions of how society works. In this respect the British philosophers laid the foundations of a profound and essentially valid theory, while the rationalist school was simply and completely wrong.

Those British philosophers have given us an interpretation of the growth of civilization that is still the indispensable foundation of the argument for liberty. They find the origin of institutions, not in contrivance or design, but in the survival of the successful. Their view is expressed in terms of how "nations stumble upon establishments which are indeed the result of human action but not the execution of any human design."[14] It stresses that what we call political order is much less the product of our ordering intelligence than is commonly imagined. As their immediate successors saw it, what Adam Smith and his contemporaries did was "to resolve almost all that has been ascribed to positive institution into the spontaneous and irresistible development of certain obvious principles,—and to show with how little contrivance or political wisdom the most complicated and apparently artificial schemes of policy might have been erected."[15]

This "anti-rationalistic insight into historical happenings that Adam Smith shares with Hume, Adam Ferguson, and others"[16] enabled them for the first time to comprehend how institutions and morals, language and law, have evolved by a process of cumulative growth and that it is only with and within this framework that human reason has grown and can successfully operate. Their argument is directed throughout against the Cartesian conception of an independently and antecedently existing human reason that invented these institutions and against the conception that civil society was formed by some wise original legislator or an original "social contract."[17] The latter idea of

---

[14] Ferguson, *An Essay on the History of Civil Society*, p. 187.

[15] [Francis Jeffrey], "Craig's Life of Millar," *Edinburgh Review*, 9 (1806): 84. Frederic William Maitland much later spoke similarly somewhere of "the stumbling forward in our empirical fashion, blundering into wisdom." [The quotation appears in Maitland's *Collected Papers of Frederic William Maitland: Dowling Professor of the Laws of England* (3 vols.; Cambridge: Cambridge University Press, 1911), in the section devoted to a discussion of "English Law Under Norman and Angevin," which forms a section of his essay on "The Outlines of English Legal History, 560–1600," vol. 2, p. 439.—Ed.]

[16] Forbes, "Scientific Whiggism: Adam Smith and John Millar," p. 654. The importance of the Scottish moral philosophers as forebears of cultural anthropology has been handsomely acknowledged by Edward Evan Evans-Pritchard, *Social Anthropology* (London: Cohen and West, 1951), pp. 23–25.

[17] Ludwig von Mises, *Socialism*, Jacques Kahane, trans. (new ed.; New Haven: Yale University Press, 1951), p. 43 [Liberty Fund edition, p. 33], writes with reference to the social contract: "Rationalism could find no other possible explanation after it had disposed of the old belief which traced social institutions back to divine sources or at least to the enlightenment which came to man through divine inspiration. Because it led to present conditions, people regarded

intelligent men coming together for deliberation about how to make the world anew is perhaps the most characteristic outcome of those design theories. It found its perfect expression when the leading theorist of the French Revolution, Abbé Sieyès, exhorted the revolutionary assembly "to act like men just emerging from the state of nature and coming together for the purpose of signing a Social Contract."[18]

The ancients understood the conditions of liberty better than that. Cicero quotes Cato as saying that the Roman constitution was superior to that of other states because it "was based upon the genius, not of one man, but of many: it was founded, not in one generation, but in a long period of several centuries and many ages of men. For, said he, there never has lived a man possessed of so great a genius that nothing could escape him, nor could the combined powers of all men living at one time possibly make all the necessary provisions for the future without the aid of actual experience and the test of time."[19] Neither republican Rome nor Athens—the two free nations of the ancient world—could thus serve as an example for the rationalists. For Descartes, the fountainhead of the rationalist tradition, it was indeed Sparta that provided the model; for her greatness "was due not the pre-eminence of each of its laws in particular . . . but to the circumstance that, originated by a single individual, they all tended to a single end."[20] And it was Sparta which became

the development of social life as absolutely purposeful and rational; how then could this development have come about except through conscious choice in recognition of the fact that it was purposeful and rational?"

[18] Quoted by Talmon, *Origins of Totalitarian Democracy*, p. 73.

[19] M. Tullius Cicero, *De re publica*, ii.1.2; cf. also ii.21.37 [wherein Cicero notes "Now we have further proof of the accuracy of Cato's statement that the foundation of our State was the work neither of one period nor of one man; for it is quite clear that every kind contributed many good and useful institutions."—Ed.] I am indebted to Prof. Bruno Leoni's lectures, now published as *Freedom and the Law* ([Princeton, NJ: D. van Nostrand, 1961], p. 89), for calling this source to my attention. Neratius, a later Roman jurist quoted in the *Corpus Iuris Civilis* [Samuel Parsons Scott, *The Civil Law, including the Twelve Tables, the Institutes of Gaius, the Rules of Ulpian, the Opinions of Paulus, the Enactments of Justinian, and the Constitutions of Leo* (17 vols. in 7; Cincinnati: Central Trust Co., 1932), vol. 2, p. 224], even went so far as to exhort lawyers: "Rationes eorum quae constituuntur inquiri non oportet, alioquin multa ex his quae certa sunt subvertuntur" ("We must avoid inquiring about the rationale of our institutions, since otherwise many that are certain would be overturned"). [The translation is Hayek's. The quotation appears in the *Digest*, 1.3.2. The original source is noted as Neratius, *Parchments*, book VI.—Ed.] Although in this respect the Greeks were somewhat more rationalistic, a similar conception of the growth of law is by no means absent. See, e.g., the Attic orator Antiphon, *On the Choreutes*, par. 2 (in *Minor Attic Orators*, Kenneth John. Maidment, ed. [Loeb Classical Library, 2 vols.; Cambridge, MA: Harvard University Press, 1941)], vol. 1, p. 247), where he speaks of laws having "the distinction of being the oldest in this country, . . . and that is the surest token of good laws, as time and experience show mankind what is imperfect."

[20] René Descartes, *A Discourse on the Method of Rightly Conducting One's Reason and of Seeking Truth in the Sciences* (Everyman ed.; London: Dent, 1912), pt. 2, p. 11. [The French reads: "Je crois que si Sparte a été autrefois très florissante, ce n'a pas été à cause de la bonté de chacune de ses lois

the ideal of liberty for Rousseau as well as for Robespierre and Saint-Just and for most of the later advocates of "social" or totalitarian democracy.[21]

Like the ancient, the modern British conceptions of liberty grew against the background of a comprehension, first achieved by the lawyers, of how institutions had developed. "There are many things specially in laws and governments," wrote Chief Justice Hale in the seventeenth century in a critique of Hobbes, "that mediately, remotely, and consequentially are reasonable to be approved, though the reason of the party does not presently or immediately and distinctly see its reasonableness. . . . Long experience makes more discoveries touching conveniences or inconveniences of laws than is possible for the wisest council of men at first to foresee. And that those amendments and supplements that through the various experiences of wise and knowing men have been applied to any law must needs be better suited to the convenience of laws, than the best invention of the most pregnant wits not aided by such a series and tract of experience. . . . This adds to the difficulty of a present fathoming of the reason of laws, because they are the production of long and iterated experience which, though it be commonly called the mistress of fools, yet certain it is the wisest expedient among mankind, and discovers those defects and supplies which no wit of man could either at once foresee or aptly remedy. . . . It is not necessary that the reasons of the institution should be evident unto us. It is sufficient that they are instituted laws that give a certainty to us, and it is reasonable to observe them though the particular reason of the institution appear not."[22]

---

en particulier . . . mais à cause que, n'ayant été inventées que par un seul, elles tendoient toutes à même fin."—Ed.]

[21] Cf. Talmon, *Origins of Totalitarian Democracy*, p. 142. [Talmon notes that "throughout the centuries of uninterrupted tyranny and crime, history knows only of one brief spell of liberty in a tiny corner of the earth—Sparta: 'brille comme un éclair dans les ténèbres immenses.' This is the key to the understanding of Robespierre and Saint-Just: Sparta as the ideal of liberty." —Ed.] On the influence of the Spartan ideal on Greek philosophy and especially on Plato and Aristotle see François Ollier, *Le Mirage spartiate: Étude sur l'idéalisation de Sparte dans l'antiquité grecque, de l'origine, jusqu'aux Cyniques* (Paris: E. de Boccard, 1933), and Sir Karl Raimund Popper, *The Open Society and Its Enemies* (London: G. Routledge and Co., 1945).

[22] "Sir Mathew Hale's "Criticism on Hobbes Dialogue on the Common Law," in Holdsworth, *A History of English Law*, vol. 5, pp. 504–5 (the spelling has been modernized). Holdsworth rightly points out the similarity of some of these arguments to those of Edmund Burke. [With reference to this passage in Hale, Holdsworth (vol. 5, p. 504, n. 1) quotes Burke's *Reflections on the Revolution in France* (London: Printed for J. Dodsley, in Pall-Mall, 1790, p. 90) (Liberty Fund edition, *Selected Works*, vol. 2, p. 153), to the effect that: "The science of government being therefore so practical in itself, and intended for such practical purposes, a matter which requires experience, and even more experience, than any person can gain in his whole life, however, sagacious and observing he may be, it is with infinite caution that any man ought to venture upon pulling down an edifice which has answered in any tolerable degree for ages the common purposes of society, or on building it up again, without having models and patterns of approved utility before his eyes."—Ed.] They are, of course, in effect an attempt to elaborate ideas of Sir Edward Coke (whom Hobbes had criticized), especially his famous conception of the "artificial reason." His

3. From these conceptions gradually grew a body of social theory that showed how, in the relations among men, complex and orderly and, in a very definite sense, purposive institutions might grow up which owed little to design, which were not invented but arose from the separate actions of many men who did not know what they were doing. This demonstration that something greater than man's individual mind may grow from men's fumbling efforts represented in some ways an even greater challenge to all design theories than even the later theory of biological evolution. For the first time it was shown that an evident order which was not the product of a designing human intelligence need not therefore be ascribed to the design of a higher, supernatural intelligence, but that there was a third possibility—the emergence of order as the result of adaptive evolution.[23]

Seventh Report (*The Reports of Edward Coke, Knt.: In thirteen parts,* John Henry Thomas and John Farquhar Fraser, eds. [13 parts in 6 vols.; London: J. Butterworth and Son, 1826] pt. 7, vol. 4, p. 6). [The quotation appears in "Calvin's Case, or the Case of the Postnati" (1608) Trinity Term, 6 James I.—Ed.] Coke explains as follows: "Our days upon earth are but a shadow in respect of the old ancient days and times past, wherein the laws have been by the wisdom of the most excellent men, in many succession of ages, by long and continual experience (the trial of light and truth) fined and refined, which no one man, (being of so short a time) albeit he had the wisdom of all the men in the world, in any one age could ever have effected or attained unto" [Liberty Fund edition, vol. 1, p. 173.]. Cf. also the legal proverb: "Per varios usus experientia legem fecit." [The phrase carries the following sense: Experience made law through diverse customs.—Ed.] See J. G. A. Pocock, *The Ancient Constitution and the Feudal Law* (New York: Cambridge University Press, 1957), as well as Sir John Davies, *Les Reports des Cases en Lay* (commonly cited as *Irish Reports* [London, 1612]), Preface: "As it is said of every Art and Science which is brought to perfection, *Per varios usus artem experiential fecit,* so may it properly be said of our Law *Per varios usus Legem experiential fecit.* Long experience, and many trials of what was best for the common good, did make the Common Law."

[23] A thorough examination of these problems from Bernard Mandeville's paradox to its first cogent expression by David Hume in his "Dialogues Concerning Natural Religion," (see *Treatise of Human Nature,* vol. 2, pp. 380–468) has yet to be undertaken. The best discussion of the character of this process of social growth known to me is still Carl Menger, *Untersuchungen,* bk. 3 [Das organische Verständnis der Socialerscheinungen] and app. 8 [Über den "organischen" Ursprung des Rechtes und das exacte Verständnis desselben], esp. pp. 163–65, 203–4n, and 208. Cf. also the discussion in Alexander Macbeath, *Experiments in Living: A Study of the Nature and Foundation of Ethics or Morals in the Light of Recent Work in Social Anthropology* (London: Macmillan, 1952), p. 120 and 120, n. 1, of "the principle laid down by Frazer [Sir James George Frazer, *Psyche's Task: A Discourse Concerning the Influence of Superstition on the Growth of Institutions* (London: Macmillan, 1909), p. 4] and endorsed by Malinowski and other anthropologists, that no institution will continue to survive unless it performs some useful function" and the remark added in a footnote: "But the function which it serves at a given time may not be that for the sake of which it was originally established"; and the following passage, in which Lord Acton indicates how he would have continued his brief sketches of freedom in antiquity and Christianity ("Freedom in Christianity," *History of Freedom,* p. 58 [Liberty Fund edition, *Essays in the History of Liberty,* vol. 1, p. 56]): "I should have wished . . . to relate by whom and in what connection, the true law of the formation of free States was recognised, and how that discovery, closely akin to those which, under the names of development, evolution, and continuity, have given a new and deeper method to other sciences, solved the ancient problem between stability and change, and determined the authority of tradi-

Since the emphasis we shall have to place on the role that selection plays in this process of social evolution today is likely to create the impression that we are borrowing the idea from biology, it is worth stressing that it was, in fact, the other way round: there can be little doubt that it was from the theories of social evolution that Darwin and his contemporaries derived the suggestion for their theories.[24] Indeed, one of those Scottish philosophers who first developed these ideas anticipated Darwin even in the biological field;[25] and the later application of these conceptions by the various "historical schools" in law and language rendered the idea that similarity of structure might be accounted for by a common origin,[26] a commonplace in the study of social

tion on the progress of thought; how that theory, which Sir James Mackintosh expressed by saying that Constitutions are not made, but grow; the theory that custom and the national qualities of the governed, and not the will of the government, are the makers of the law."

[24] I am not referring here to Darwin's acknowledged indebtedness to the population theories of Thomas Malthus (and, through him, of Richard Cantillon) but to the general atmosphere of an evolutionary philosophy which governed thought on social matters in the nineteenth century. Though this influence has occasionally been recognized (see, e.g., Henry Fairfield Osborn, *From the Greeks to Darwin: An Outline of the Development of the Evolution Idea* [New York: McMillan and Co., 1894], p. 87), it has never been systematically studied. I believe that such a study would show that most of the conceptual apparatus which Darwin employed lay ready at hand for him to use. One of the men through whom Scottish evolutionary thought reached Darwin was probably the Scottish geologist James Hutton.

[25] See Arthur Osborne Lovejoy, "Monboddo and Rousseau," *Modern Philology*, 30 (1933): 275–96, reprinted in *Essays in the History of Ideas* (Baltimore: Johns Hopkins University Press, 1948), pp. 38–61.

[26] It is perhaps significant that the first clearly to see this in the field of linguistics, Sir William Jones, was a lawyer by training and a prominent Whig by persuasion. Cf. his celebrated statement in the "Third Anniversary Discourse" delivered February 2, 1786, in *Asiatick Researches*, vol. 1, p. 422, and [as "The Third Anniversary Discourse, on the Hindus"] reprinted in *The Works of Sir William Jones* (13 vols.; London: Printed for John Stockdale, Piccadilly, and John Walker, Paternoster-Row, 1807), vol. 2, p. 34: "The *Sanscrit* language, whatever be its antiquity, is of a wonderful structure; more perfect than the Greek, more copious than the Latin, and more exquisitely refined than either, yet bearing to both of them a stronger affinity, both in the roots of verbs and in the forms of grammar, than could possibly have been produced by accident: so strong indeed, that no philologer could examine them all three, without believing them to have sprung from some common source, which, perhaps, no longer exists." The connection between speculation about language and that about political institutions is best shown by one of the most complete, though somewhat late, statements of the Whig doctrine by Dugald Stewart, *Lectures on Political Economy* (delivered 1809–10), printed in *The Collected Works of Dugald Stewart* (11 vols.; Edinburgh: T. Constable, 1854–60), vol. 9, pp. 422–24, and quoted at length in a note to the earlier version of this chapter in *Ethics*, 68 (1958): 243. It is of special importance because of Stewart's influence on the last group of Whigs, the *Edinburgh Review* circle. Is it an accident that in Germany her greatest philosopher of freedom, Wilhelm von Humboldt, was also one of her greatest theorists of language?

[Hayek's footnote in *Ethics*, quoting Stewart's *Lectures*, reads: "The English government (it is said) has been the gradual offspring of circumstances and events, and its different parts arose at different times; some of them from acts of the legislature prompted by emergencies, and some

phenomena long before it was applied to biology. It is unfortunate that at a later date the social sciences, instead of building on these beginnings in their own field, re-imported some of these ideas from biology and with them

---

of them from long established customs or usages, of which it is not always possible to trace the origin, so that no part of it is sanctioned by an authority paramount to that which gives force to every other law by which we are governed. It is pretended, therefore, that there are no fundamental or essential principles in our government, which fix a limit to the possibility of legislative encroachment, and to which an appeal could be made, if a particular law should appear to be hostile to the rights and liberties of the people. But surely the conclusion in this argument does not follow from the premises. For do we not every day speak of laws being *constitutional* or *unconstitutional;* and do not these words convey to men of plain understanding a very distinct and intelligible meaning, a meaning which no person can pretend to misapprehend, who is not disposed to cavil about expressions?

"It appears to me, that what we call the *constitution* differs from our other laws, not in its *origin*, but in the *importance of the subject to which it refers, and in the systematical connexion of its different principles*. It may, I think, be defined to be that form of government, and that mode of administering it, which is agreeable to the *general* spirit and tendency of our established laws and usages.

"According to this view of the subject, I apprehend that the constitution, *taken as a whole*, ought to modify every new institution which is introduced, so that it may accord with its general *spirit*; although every part of this constitution taken *separately*, arose from no higher authority than the common acts of our present legislature.

"To illustrate this proposition it may be proper to remark, that although the Constitution was the gradual result of circumstances which may be regarded as accidental and irregular, yet that the very mode of its formation necessarily produced a certain consistence and analogy in its different parts, so as to give to the whole a sort of systematic appearance. For unless every new institution which was successively introduced has possessed a certain reference or affinity to the laws and usages existing before, it could not possibly have been permanent in its operation. Wherever a Constitution has existed for ages, and men have enjoyed a tranquility under it, it is a proof that its great and fundamental principles are all animated by the same congenial spirit. In such a constitution, when any law contrary to the spirit of the rest is occasionally introduced, it soon falls into desuetude and oblivion; while those which accord in their general character and tendency, acquire additional stability from the influence of time and from the mutual support which they lend to each other. Of such a law we may say with propriety that it is *unconstitutional*, not because we dispute the authority from which it proceeds, but because it is contrary to the spirit and analogy of the laws which we have been accustomed to obey.

"Something similar to this obtains with respect to languages. *These*, as well as governments, are the gradual result of time and experience, and not of philosophical speculation: yet every language, in process of time, acquires a great deal of systematical beauty. When a new word, or a new combination of words, is introduced, it takes its raise from the same origin with every other expression which the language contains; the desire of an individual to communicate his own thoughts or feelings to others. But this consideration alone is not sufficient to justify the use of it. Before it is allowed by good writers or speakers to incorporate itself with those words which have the sanction of time in their favour, it must be shewn that it is not disagreeable to the general analogy of the language, otherwise it is soon laid aside as an innovation, revolting, anomalous, and *ungrammatical*. It is much in the same manner that we come to apply the epithet *unconstitutional* to a law.

"The zeal, therefore, which genuine patriots have always shewn for the maintenance of the Constitution, so far from being unreasonable, will be most strongly felt by the prudent and intel-

brought in such conceptions as "natural selection," "struggle for existence," and "survival of the fittest," which are not appropriate in their field; for in social evolution, the decisive factor is not the selection of the physical and inheritable properties of the individuals but the selection by imitation of successful institutions and habits. Though this operates also through the success of individuals and groups, what emerges is not an inheritable attribute of individuals, but ideas and skills—in short, the whole cultural inheritance which is passed on by learning and imitation.

4. A detailed comparison of the two traditions would require a separate book; here we can merely single out a few of the crucial points on which they differ.

While the rationalist tradition assumes that man was originally endowed with both the intellectual and the moral attributes that enabled him to fashion civilization deliberately, the evolutionists made it clear that civilization was the accumulated hard-earned result of trial and error; that it was the sum of experience, in part handed from generation to generation as explicit knowledge, but to a larger extent embodied in tools and institutions which had proved themselves superior—institutions whose significance we might discover by analysis but which will also serve men's ends without men's understanding them. The Scottish theorists were very much aware how delicate this artificial structure of civilization was which rested on man's more primitive and ferocious instincts being tamed and checked by institutions that he neither had designed nor could control. They were very far from holding such naïve views, later unjustly laid at the door of their liberalism, as the "natural goodness of man," the existence of a "natural harmony of interests," or the beneficent effects of "natural liberty" (even though they did sometimes use the last phrase). They knew that it required the artifices of institutions and traditions to reconcile the conflicts of interest. Their problem was how "that the *universal* Mover in human Nature, self-love, may receive such a Direction in this Case (as in all others) as to promote the Public Interest by those Efforts it shall make towards pursuing its own."[27] It was not "natural liberty" in any literal sense, but the institutions evolved to secure "life, liberty, and

---

ligent, because such men know that political wisdom is much more the result of experience than of speculation: and that when a Constitution has been matured by such slow steps as ours has been, in consequence of the struggle of able and enlightened individuals, jealous of their liberties, and anxious to preserve them, it may be considered as the result of the accumulated experience and wisdom of ages; possessing *on that very account* the strongest of all possible recommendations, an experimental proof of its excellence, of its fitness to perpetuate itself, and to promote the happiness of those who live under it."—Ed.]

[27] Josiah Tucker, "The Elements of Commerce and Theory of Taxes" (1755) in *Josiah Tucker: A Selection from his Economic and Political Writings*, Robert Livingston Schuyler, ed. (New York: Columbia University Press, 1931), p. 92.

property," which made those individual efforts beneficial.[28] Not Locke, nor Hume, nor Smith, nor Burke, could ever have argued, as Bentham did, that "every law is an evil for every law is an infraction of liberty."[29] Their argument was never a complete laissez faire argument, which, as the very words show, is also part of the French rationalist tradition and in its literal sense was never defended by any of the English classical economists.[30] They knew bet-

---

[28] That for Adam Smith in particular it was certainly not "natural liberty" in any literal sense on which the beneficial working of the economic system depended, but liberty under the law, is clearly expressed in *Wealth of Nations*, bk. 4, chap. 5, vol. 2, pp. 42–43 [Liberty Fund edition, vol. 1, p. 540]: "That security which the laws in Great Britain give to every man that he shall enjoy the fruits of his own labour, is alone sufficient to make any country flourish, notwithstanding these and twenty other absurd regulations of commerce: and this security was perfected by the revolution, much about the same time that the bounty was established. The natural effort of every individual to better his own condition, when suffered to exert itself with freedom and security, is so powerful a principle, that it is alone, and without any assistance, not only capable of carrying on the society to wealth and prosperity, but of surmounting a hundred impertinent obstructions with which the folly of human laws too often incumbers its operations." Cf. Colin Arthur Cooke, "Adam Smith and Jurisprudence," *Law Quarterly Review*, 51 (1935): 328: "The theory of political economy that emerges in the *Wealth of Nations* can be seen to be a consistent theory of law and legislation . . . the famous passage about the invisible hand rises up as the essence of Adam Smith's view of law"; and also the interesting discussion in Joseph Cropsey, *Polity and Economy: An Interpretation of the Principles of Adam Smith* (The Hague: M. Nijhoff, 1957). It is of some interest that Smith's general argument about the "invisible hand" "which leads man to promote an end which was no part of his intention" already appears in Montesquieu, *Spirit of the Laws*, bk. 3. chap. 7, vol. 1, p. 25 [French edition: vol. 2, p. 257], where he says that "thus each individual advances the public good, while he only thinks of promoting his own interest." ["Et il se trouve que chacun va au bien commun, croyant aller à ses intérêts particuliers."—Ed.] See also David Hume, "That Politics May Be Reduced to a Science," *Essays* [Essay 3], vol. 1, p. 99 [Liberty Fund edition, pp. 15–16]: "[But a] republican and free government would be an obvious absurdity, if the particular checks, and controuls, provided by the constitution, had really no influence, and made it not the interest, even of bad men, to act for the public good"; and Immanuel Kant, *Zum ewigen Frieden: Ein philosophischer Entwurf*, in *Werke*, vol. 6: *Schriften zur Anthropologie, Geschichsphilosophie, Politik und Pädagogik*, Wilhelm Weischedel, ed. (Wiesbaden: Insel-Verlag, 1956–64), pp. 223–24: "Aber nun kommt die Natur dem verehrten, aber zur Praxis ohnmächtigen allgemeinen, in der Vernunft gegründeten Willen, und zwar gerade durch jene selbstsüchtigen Neigungen, zu Hülfe, so, daß es nur auf eine gute Organisation des Staats ankommt (die allerdings im Vermögen der Menschen ist), jener ihre Kräfte so gegen einander zu richten, daß der Erfolg für die Vernunft so ausfällt, als wenn beide gar nicht da wären, und so der Mensch, wenn gleich nicht ein moralisch-guter Mensch, dennoch ein guter Bürger zu sein gezwungen wird." ["But precisely with these inclinations nature comes to the aid of the general will established on reason, which is revered even though impotent in practice. Thus it is only a question of a good organization of the state (which does lie in man's power), whereby the powers of each selfish inclination are so arranged in opposition that one moderates or destroys the ruinous effect of the other. The consequence for reason is the same as if none of them existed, and man is forced to be a good citizen even if not a morally good person."—Ed.]

[29] Jeremy Bentham, *Theory of Legislation* (5th ed.; London: Trübner, 1887), p. 48.

[30] See David Hutchison MacGregor, *Economic Thought and Policy* (Oxford: Oxford University Press, 1949), chap. 3, "The Laissez-Faire Doctrine," pp. 54–89, and Lionel Robbins, *The Theory of Economic Policy in English Classical Political Economy* (London: Macmillan, 1952), pp. 42–46.

ter than most of their later critics that it was not some sort of magic but the evolution of "well-constructed institutions," where the "rules and principles of contending interests and compromised advantages"[31] would be reconciled, that had successfully channeled individual efforts to socially beneficial aims. In fact, their argument was never antistate as such, or anarchistic, which is the logical outcome of the rationalistic laissez faire doctrine; it was an argument that accounted both for the proper functions of the state and for the limits of state action.

The difference is particularly conspicuous in the respective assumptions of the two schools concerning individual human nature. The rationalistic design theories were necessarily based on the assumption of the individual man's propensity for rational action and his natural intelligence and goodness. The evolutionary theory, on the contrary, showed how certain institutional arrangements would induce man to use his intelligence to the best effect and how institutions could be framed so that bad people could do least harm.[32] The antirationalist tradition is here closer to the Christian tradition of the fallibility and sinfulness of man, while the perfectionism of the rationalist is in irreconcilable conflict with it. Even such a celebrated figment as the "economic man" was not an original part of the British evolutionary tradition. It would be only a slight exaggeration to say that, in the view of those British philosophers,

---

[31] Edmund Burke, *Thoughts and Details on Scarcity*, in *Works*, vol. 7, p. 398 [Liberty Fund edition: *Miscellaneous Writings*, p. 73]. [The full quotation reads: "No slave were ever so beneficial to the master as a freeman that deals with him on an equal footing by convention, formed on the rules and principles of contending interests and compromised advantages."—Ed.]

[32] Cf., e.g., the contrast between David Hume, *Essays*, bk. 1, pp. 117–18, Essay 6: "On the Independency of Parliament" [Liberty Fund edition, p. 42]: "Political writers have established it as a maxim, that, in contriving any system of government, and fixing the several checks and controuls of the constitution, every man ought to be supposed a *knave*, and to have no other end, in all his actions, than private interest." (The reference is presumably to Niccolò Machiavelli, *Discorsi*, bk. 1, chap. 3 [*Discourses on the First Ten Books of Titus Livy*, in *The Works of the Famous Nicolas Machiavel, Citizen and Secretary of Florence* (3rd ed., carefully corrected; London: Printed for Thomas Wood for A. Churchill, 1720), p. 272], where Machiavelli notes that the lawgiver must assume for his purposes that all men are bad. [Machiavelli writes: "It is necessary to whoever will establish a government and prescribe laws to it to presuppose all men naturally bad." The Italian reads: "É necessario a chi dispone una republica, ed ordina leggi in quella, presupporre tutti gli uomini rei."—Ed.]

Cf. Richard Price, *Two Tracts on Civil Liberty, the War with America, and the Debts and Finances of the Kingdom* (2 vols. in 1; London: T. Caddell, 1778), p. 11: "Every man's will, if perfectly free from restraint, would carry him invariably to rectitude and virtue." [This work contains Price's *Observations on the Nature of Civil Liberty, the Principles of Government, and the Justice and Policy of the War with America. 8th ed., with Corrections and Additions, 1778. Additional Observations on the Nature and Value of Civil Liberty, and the War with America*, bound together and paginated separately. The quotation appears in *Additional Observations*, p. 11.—Ed.]

See also my *Individualism and Economic Order* (Chicago: University of Chicago Press, 1948), pp. 11–12. [*Collected Works* edition, vol. 13, p. 57.]

man was by nature lazy and indolent, improvident and wasteful, and that it was only by the force of circumstances that he could be made to behave economically or would learn carefully to adjust his means to his ends. The *homo oeconomicus* was explicitly introduced, with much else that belongs to the rationalist rather than to the evolutionary tradition, only by the younger Mill.[33]

5. The greatest difference between the two views, however, is in their respective ideas about the role of traditions and the value of all the other products of unconscious growth proceeding throughout the ages.[34] It would hardly

---

[33] See John Stuart Mill, "On the Definition of Political Economy; and on the Method of Investigation Proper to It," [Essay 5] in *Essays on Some Unsettled Questions of Political Economy* (London: J. W. Parker, 1844), pp. 120–64 [Liberty Fund edition, *Collected Works*, vol. 4, pp. 309–39].

[Joseph Persky ("The Ethology of Homo Economicus"), writing in the *Journal of Economic Perspectives*, 9 (1995): 221–31, maintains that "while John Stuart Mill is generally identified as the creator of economic man, he never actually used this designation in his own writings. But the term did emerge in reaction to Mill's work. In its first appearances in the late nineteenth century, 'economic man' carried a pejorative connotation reflecting the widespread hostility of the historical school toward Mill's theoretical abstractions. Economic man also raised the indignation of Victorian moralists shocked at the postulation of such blatant selfishness.

"For example, the earliest explicit naming of economic man that I have identified is in John Kells Ingram's *A History of Political Economy* (1888). Ingram, an advocate of a broad sociology in the tradition of Auguste Comte, took considerable pains to disparage John Stuart Mill's political economy, which 'dealt not with real but with imaginary men—"economic men" . . . conceived as simply "money-making animals"' (p. 218). Two years later, John Neville Keynes (1890) picked up (and singularized) the phrase in his much more extensive methodological treatment. Keynes' efforts, though considerably less hostile than Ingram's, still painted 'an "economic man" whose activities are determined solely by the desire for wealth' and ascribed the origins of this tightly drawn abstraction to John Stuart Mill" (p. 222). And, "The first use of the Latin 'homo œconomicus' I turned up is in Vilfredo Pareto's *Manual* (1906, pp. 12–14)."—Ed.]

[34] Ernest Renan, in an important essay ["M. De Sacy et l'école libérale"] on the principles and tendencies of the liberal school, first published in 1858 and later included in his *Essais de morale et de critique* (now in *Œuvres complètes*, Henriette Psichari, ed. [10 vols.; Paris: Calmann-Lévy, 1947], vol. 2, pp. 45–46) observes: "Le libéralisme, ayant la prétention de se fonder uniquement sur les principes de la raison, croit d'ordinaire n'avoir pas besoin de tradition. Là est son erreur . . . L'erreur de l'école libérale est d'avoir trop cru qu'il est facile de créer la liberté par la réflexion, et de n'avoir pas vu qu'un établissement n'est solide que quand il a des racines historiques . . . Elle ne vit pas que de tous ses efforts ne pouvait sortir qu'une bonne administration, mais jamais la liberté, puisque la liberté résulte d'un droit antérieur et supérieur à celui de l'État, et non d'une déclaration improvisée ou d'un raisonnement philosophique plus ou moins bien déduit." ["Liberalism, claiming as it does to be uniquely founded on the principles of reason, ordinarily holds that tradition need play no role. This is its error. . . . The liberal school errs in thoroughly embracing the view that it is easy to create a liberal regime solely through reflection, not seeing that its establishment has no solidity without historical roots. . . . Liberalism failed to see that all such efforts can only result in an efficient administration, but not in liberty, since liberty is the result of law that is both anterior to and superior to the State and not a determination of the moment or the result of philosophical reasoning that has been more or less deduced."—Ed.] Cf. also the observation by Ronald Buchanan McCallum in the Introduction to his edition of John Stuart Mill, *On Liberty and Considerations on Representative Government* (Oxford: B. Blackwell, 1946),

be unjust to say that the rationalistic approach is here opposed to almost all that is the distinct product of liberty and that gives liberty its value. Those who believe that all useful institutions are deliberate contrivances and who cannot conceive of anything serving a human purpose that has not been consciously designed are almost of necessity enemies of freedom. For them freedom means chaos.

To the empiricist evolutionary tradition, on the other hand, the value of freedom consists mainly in the opportunity it provides for the growth of the undesigned, and the beneficial functioning of a free society rests largely on the existence of such freely grown institutions. There probably never has existed a genuine belief in freedom, and there has certainly been no successful attempt to operate a free society, without a genuine reverence for grown institutions, for customs and habits and "all those securities of liberty which arise from regulation of long prescription and ancient ways."[35] Paradoxical as it may appear, it is probably true that a successful free society will always in a large measure be a tradition-bound society.[36]

This esteem for tradition and custom, of grown institutions, and of rules whose origins and rationale we do not know does not, of course, mean—as Thomas Jefferson believed with a characteristic rationalist misconception— that we "ascribe to the men of the preceding age a wisdom more than human, and . . . suppose what they did to be beyond amendment."[37] Far from assuming that those who created the institutions were wiser than we are, the evolutionary view is based on the insight that the result of the experimentation of many generations may embody more experience than any one man possesses.

6. We have already considered the various institutions and habits, tools and

---

p. xv: "While Mill admits the great power of custom, and within limits its uses, he is prepared to criticise all those rules which depend upon it and are not defended by reason. He remarks, 'People are accustomed to believe, and have been encouraged in the belief by some who aspire to the character of philosophers, that their feelings on subjects of this nature, are better than reasons and render reasons unnecessary.' This was that position which Mill, as a utilitarian rationalist, was bound never to accept. It was the 'sympathy-antipathy' principle which Bentham considered was the basis of all systems of other than the rationalist approach. Mill's primary contention as a political thinker is that all these unreasoning assumptions should be weighed and considered by the reflective and balanced judgment of thinking men."

[35] Joseph Butler, *The Works of Joseph Butler*, William Ewart Gladstone, ed. (2 vols.; Oxford: Clarendon Press, 1896), vol. 2, pp. 278. [The quotation in fact appears in Butler's "Sermon Preached Before the House of Lords, in the Abbey-Church of Westminster, on Friday, January 30, 1740–41. Being the Day Appointed to be Observed as the Day of Martyrdom of King Charles I" (Sermon III; sec. 15).—Ed.]

[36] Even Professor Herbert Butterfield, who understands this better than most people, finds it "one of the paradoxes of history" that "the name of England has come to be so closely associated with liberty on the one hand and tradition on the other hand" (*Liberty in the Modern World* [Toronto: Ryerson Press, 1952], p. 21).

[37] Thomas Jefferson, *The Works of Thomas Jefferson*, Paul Leicester Ford, ed. (12 vols.; New York: G. P. Putnam's Sons, 1904), vol. 12, p. 11.

methods of doing things, which have emerged from this process and constitute our inherited civilization. But we have yet to look at those rules of conduct which have grown as part of it, which are both a product and a condition of freedom. Of these conventions and customs of human intercourse, the moral rules are the most important but by no means the only significant ones. We understand one another and get along with one another, are able to act successfully on our plans, because, most of the time, members of our civilization conform to unconscious patterns of conduct, show a regularity in their actions that is not the result of commands or coercion, often not even of any conscious adherence to known rules, but of firmly established habits and traditions. The general observance of these conventions is a necessary condition of the orderliness of the world in which we live, of our being able to find our way in it, though we do not know their significance and may not even be consciously aware of their existence. In some instances it would be necessary, for the smooth running of society, to secure a similar uniformity by coercion, if such conventions or rules were not observed often enough. Coercion, then, may sometimes be avoidable only because a high degree of voluntary conformity exists, which means that voluntary conformity may be a condition of a beneficial working of freedom. It is indeed a truth, which all the great apostles of freedom outside the rationalistic school have never tired of emphasizing, that freedom has never worked without deeply ingrained moral beliefs and that coercion can be reduced to a minimum only where individuals can be expected as a rule to conform voluntarily to certain principles.[38]

There is an advantage in obedience to such rules not being coerced, not only because coercion as such is bad, but because it is, in fact, often desirable that rules should be observed only in most instances and that the individual should be able to transgress them when it seems to him worthwhile to incur the odium which this will cause. It is also important that the strength of the social pressure and of the force of habit which insures their observance is vari-

[38] See, e.g., Edmund Burke, *A Letter to a Member of the National Assembly*, in *Works*, vol. 6, p. 64 [Liberty Fund edition, *Further Reflections on the Revolution in France*, p. 69]: "Men are qualified for civil liberty, in exact proportion to their disposition to put moral chains upon their appetites; in proportion as their love of justice is above their rapacity; in proportion as their soundness and sobriety of understanding is above their vanity and presumption; in proportion as they are more disposed to listen to the council of the wise and good, in preference to the flattery of knaves." Also James Madison in the debates during the Virginia Ratifying Convention, June 20, 1788 (in *The Debates in the Several State Conventions on the Adoption of the Federal Constitution*, Jonathan Elliot, ed. [2nd ed.; 5 vols.; Philadelphia: J. B. Lippincott, 1863–91], vol. 2, p. 537): "To suppose that any form of government will secure liberty or happiness without any virtue in the people, is a chimerical idea." And Tocqueville, *Democracy in America*, vol. 1, p. 12: "Liberty cannot be established without morality, nor morality without faith" ["On ne peut établir le règne de la liberté sans celui des mœurs, ni fonder les mœurs sans les croyances." "Introduction," *Œuvres*, vol. 2, p. 13.—Ed.]; also vol. 2, p. 235: "No free communities ever existed without morals." ["On n'y a jamais eu de sociétés sans mœurs." *Œuvres*, vol. 2, p. 712.—Ed.]

able. It is this flexibility of voluntary rules which in the field of morals makes gradual evolution and spontaneous growth possible, which allows further experience to lead to modifications and improvements. Such an evolution is possible only with rules which are neither coercive nor deliberately imposed—rules which, though observing them is regarded as merit and though they will be observed by the majority, can be broken by individuals who feel that they have strong enough reasons to brave the censure of their fellows. Unlike any deliberately imposed coercive rules, which can be changed only discontinuously and for all at the same time, rules of this kind allow for gradual and experimental change. The existence of individuals and groups simultaneously observing partially different rules provides the opportunity for the selection of the more effective ones.

It is this submission to undesigned rules and conventions whose significance and importance we largely do not understand, this reverence for the traditional, that the rationalistic type of mind finds so uncongenial, though it is indispensable for the working of a free society. It has its foundation in the insight which David Hume stressed and which is of decisive importance for the antirationalist, evolutionary tradition—namely, that "the rules of morality are not the conclusions of our reason."[39] Like all other values, our morals are not a product but a presupposition of reason, part of the ends which the instrument of our intellect has been developed to serve. At any one stage of our evolution, the system of values into which we are born supplies the ends which our reason must serve. This givenness of the value framework implies that, although we must always strive to improve our institutions, we can never aim to remake them as a whole and that, in our efforts to improve them, we must take for granted much that we do not understand. We must always work inside a framework of both values and institutions which is not of our own making. In particular, we can never synthetically construct a new body

---

[39] Hume, *Treatise of Human Nature*, bk. 3, pt. 1, sec. 1 (vol. 2, p. 235), the paragraph headed "Moral Distinctions Not Deriv'd from Reason": "The rules of morality, therefore, are not conclusions of our reason." The same idea is already implied in the scholastic maxim, "Ratio est instrumentum non est judex." ["Reason is the tool, not the judge."—Ed.] Concerning Hume's evolutionary view of morals, I am glad to be able to quote a statement I should have been reluctant to make, for fear of reading more into Hume than is there, but which comes from an author who, I believe, does not look at Hume's work from my particular angle. In *The Structure of Freedom* (Stanford, CA: Stanford University Press, 1958), p. 33, Christian Bay writes: "Standards of morality and justice are what Hume calls 'artifacts'; they are neither divinely ordained, nor an integral part of original human nature, nor revealed by pure reason. They are an outcome of the practical experience of mankind, and the sole consideration in the slow test of time is the utility each moral rule can demonstrate toward promoting human welfare. Hume may be called a precursor of Darwin in the sphere of ethics. In effect, he proclaimed a doctrine of the survival of the fittest among human conventions—fittest not in terms of good teeth but in terms of maximum social utility."

of moral rules or make our obedience of the known rules dependent on our comprehension of the implications of this obedience in a given instance.

7. The rationalistic attitude to these problems is best seen in its views on what it calls "superstition."[40] I do not wish to underestimate the merit of the persistent and relentless fight of the eighteenth and nineteenth centuries against beliefs which are demonstrably false.[41] But we must remember that the extension of the concept of superstition to all beliefs which are not demonstrably true lacks the same justification and may often be harmful. That we ought not to believe anything which has been shown to be false does not mean that we ought to believe only what has been demonstrated to be true. There are good reasons why any person who wants to live and act successfully in society must accept many common beliefs, though the value of these reasons may have little to do with their demonstrable truth.[42] Such beliefs will also be based on some past experience but not on experience for which anyone can produce the evidence. The scientist, when asked to accept a generalization in his field, is of course entitled to ask for the evidence on which it is based. Many of the beliefs which in the past expressed the accumulated experience of the race have been disproved in this manner. This does not mean, however, that we can reach the stage where we can dispense with all beliefs for which such scientific evidence is lacking. Experience comes to man in many more forms than are commonly recognized by the professional experimenter or the seeker after explicit knowledge. We would destroy the foundations of

[40] Cf. Harry Burrows Acton, "Prejudice," *Revue internationale de philosophie*, 21(1952): 323–36, with the interesting demonstration of the similarity of the views of Hume and Burke; also the same author's address, "Tradition and Some Other Forms of Order," [The Presidential Address], *Proceedings of the Aristotelian Society*, n.s., 53 (1953): 1, especially the remark at the beginning that "liberals and collectivists join together against tradition when there is some 'superstition' to be attacked." See also Lionel Robbins, *The Theory of Economic Policy* (London: Macmillan, 1952), p. 196n.

[41] Perhaps even this is putting it too strongly. A hypothesis may well be demonstrably false and still, if some new conclusions follow from it which prove to be true, be better than no hypothesis at all. Such tentative, though partly erroneous, answers to important questions may be of the greatest significance for practical purposes, though the scientist dislikes them because they are apt to impede progress.

[42] Cf. Edward Sapir, *Selected Writings in Language, Culture, and Personality*, David Goodman Mandelbaum, ed. (Berkeley: University of California Press, 1949), pp. 558–59: "It is sometimes necessary to become conscious of the forms of social behavior in order to bring about a more serviceable adaptation to changed conditions, but I believe it can be laid down as a principle of far-reaching application that in the normal business of life it is useless and even mischievous for the individual to carry the conscious analysis of his cultural patterns around with him. That should be left to the student whose business it is to understand these patterns. A healthy unconsciousness of the forms of socialized behavior to which we are subject is as necessary to society as is the mind's ignorance, or better unawareness, of the workings of the viscera to the health of the body." See also p. 26.

much successful action if we disdained to rely on ways of doing things evolved by the process of trial and error simply because the reason for their adoption has not been handed down to us. The appropriateness of our conduct is not necessarily dependent on our knowing why it is so. Such understanding is one way of making our conduct appropriate, but not the only one. A sterilized world of beliefs, purged of all elements whose value could not be positively demonstrated, would probably be not less lethal than would an equivalent state in the biological sphere.

While this applies to all our values, it is most important in the case of moral rules of conduct. Next to language, they are perhaps the most important instance of an undesigned growth, of a set of rules which govern our lives but of which we can say neither why they are what they are nor what they do to us: we do not know what the consequences of observing them are for us as individuals and as a group. And it is against the demand for submission to such rules that the rationalistic spirit is in constant revolt. It insists on applying to them Descartes' principle which was "to reject as absolutely false all opinions in regard to which I could suppose the least ground for doubt."[43] The desire of the rationalist has always been for the deliberately constructed, synthetic system of morals, for the system in which, as Edmund Burke has described it, "the practice of all moral duties, and the foundations of society, rested upon their reasons made clear and demonstrative to every individual."[44] The rationalists of the eighteenth century, indeed, explicitly argued that, since they knew human nature, they "could easily find the morals which suited it."[45] They did not understand that what they called "human nature" is very largely the result of those moral conceptions which every individual learns with language and thinking.

[43] Descartes, *Discourse on Method*, pt. 4, p. 26. [The French reads: "que je rejetasse comme absolument faux tout ce en quoi je pourrois imaginer le moindre doute."—Ed.]

[44] Edmund Burke, *A Vindication of Natural Society*, Preface, in *Works*, vol. 1, p. 7 [Liberty Fund edition, p. 9].

[45] Paul Henri Thiry, Baron d'Holbach, *Système social, Ou Principes naturels de la morale et de la politique* (3 vols.; London [Rouen], 1773), vol. 1, p. 55, quoted in Talmon, *Origins of Totalitarian Democracy*, p. 270. [The full French statement reads: "En partant de l'homme lui-même on trouvera facilement la morale qui lui convient. Cette morale sera vraie, si l'on voit l'homme tel qu'il est . . . principes . . . evidents . . . capables d'être aussi rigoureusement démonstrés que l'arithmétique ou la géometrie."—Ed.] Similarly naïve statements are not difficult to find in the writings of contemporary psychologists. Burrus Frederic Skinner, e.g., in *Walden Two* (New York: Macmillan, 1948), p. 85, makes the hero of his utopia argue: "Why not experiment? The questions are simple enough. What's the best behavior for the individual so far as the group is concerned? And how can the individual be induced to behave in that way? Why not explore these questions in a scientific spirit?

"We could do just that in Walden Two. We had already worked out a code of conduct—subject, of course, to experimental modification. The code would keep things running smoothly if everybody lived up to it. Our job was to see that everybody did."

8. An interesting symptom of the growing influence of this rationalist conception is the increasing substitution, in all languages known to me, of the word "social" for the word "moral" or simply "good." It is instructive to consider briefly the significance of this.[46] When people speak of a "social conscience" as against mere "conscience," they are presumably referring to an awareness of the particular effects of our actions on other people, to an endeavor to be guided in conduct not merely by traditional rules but by explicit consideration of the particular consequences of the action in question. They are in effect saying that our action should be guided by a full understanding of the functioning of the social process and that it should be our aim, through conscious assessment of the concrete facts of the situation, to produce a foreseeable result which they describe as the "social good."

The curious thing is that this appeal to the "social" really involves a demand that individual intelligence, rather than rules evolved by society, should guide individual action—that men should dispense with the use of what could truly be called "social" (in the sense of being a product of the impersonal process of society) and should rely on their individual judgment of the particular case. The preference for "social considerations" over the adherence to moral rules is, therefore, ultimately the result of a contempt for what really is a social phenomenon and of a belief in the superior powers of individual human reason.

The answer to these rationalistic demands is, of course, that they require knowledge which exceeds the capacity of the individual human mind and that, in the attempt to comply with them, most men would become less useful members of society than they are while they pursue their own aims within the limits set by the rules of law and morals.

The rationalist argument here overlooks the point that, quite generally, the reliance on abstract rules is a device we have learned to use because our reason is insufficient to master the full detail of complex reality.[47] This is as true when we deliberately formulate an abstract rule for our individual guidance

---

[46] Cf. my article "Was ist und was heisst 'sozial'?" in *Masse und Demokratie*, Albert Hunold, ed. (Zurich: Erlenbach-Zurich: E. Rentsch, 1957), pp. 71–84, reprinted as "What is 'Social'?—What Does it Mean?" in *Studies in Philosophy, Politics, and Economics* (Chicago: University of Chicago Press, 1967), pp. 237–47. [An unauthorized translation of this essay appeared in *Freedom and Serfdom: An Anthology of Western Thought*, Albert Hunold, ed., Richard Henry Stevens, trans. (Dordrecht: D. Reidel, 1961), pp. 107–18. Hayek writes of this translation that "in parts (it) gravely misrepresented the meaning of the original."—Ed.] See also the attempted defense of the concept in Hermann Jahrreiss, *Freiheit und Sozialstaat* (Kölner Universitätsreden. No. 17; Krefeld, 1957), now reprinted in the same author's *Mensch und Staat. Rechtsphilosophische, staatsrechtliche und völkerrechtliche Grundfragen in unserer Zeit* (Cologne and Berlin: Carl Heymann, 1957), pp. 69–88.

[47] Cf. Tocqueville's emphasis on the fact that "general ideas are no proof of the strength, but rather of the insufficiency of the human intellect" ["Les idées générales n'attestent point la force de l'intelligence humaine, mais plutôt son insuffisance."—Ed.], *Democracy in America*, vol. 2, p. 13; *Œuvres*, vol. 2, p. 523.

as when we submit to the common rules of action which have been evolved by a social process.

We all know that, in the pursuit of our individual aims, we are not likely to be successful unless we lay down for ourselves some general rules to which we will adhere without reexamining their justification in every particular instance. In ordering our day, in doing disagreeable but necessary tasks at once, in refraining from certain stimulants, or in suppressing certain impulses, we frequently find it necessary to make such practices an unconscious habit, because we know that without this the rational grounds which make such behavior desirable would not be sufficiently effective to balance temporary desires and to make us do what we should wish to do from a long-term point of view. Though it sounds paradoxical to say that in order to make ourselves act rationally we often find it necessary to be guided by habit rather than reflection, or to say that to prevent ourselves from making the wrong decision we must deliberately reduce the range of choice before us, we all know that this is often necessary in practice if we are to achieve our long-range aims.

The same considerations apply even more where our conduct will directly affect not ourselves but others and where our primary concern, therefore, is to adjust our actions to the actions and expectations of others so that we avoid doing them unnecessary harm. Here it is unlikely that any individual would succeed in rationally constructing rules which would be more effective for their purpose than those which have been gradually evolved; and, even if he did, they could not really serve their purpose unless they were observed by all. We have thus no choice but to submit to rules whose rationale we often do not know, and to do so whether or not we can see that anything important depends on their being observed in the particular instance. The rules of morals are instrumental in the sense that they assist mainly in the achievement of other human values; however, since we only rarely can know what depends on their being followed in the particular instance, to observe them must be regarded as a value in itself, a sort of intermediate end which we must pursue without questioning its justification in the particular case.

9. These considerations, of course, do not prove that all the sets of moral beliefs which have grown up in a society will be beneficial. Just as a group may owe its rise to the morals which its members obey, and their values in consequence be ultimately imitated by the whole nation which the successful group has come to lead, so may a group or nation destroy itself by the moral beliefs to which it adheres. Only the eventual results can show whether the ideals which guide a group are beneficial or destructive. The fact that a society has come to regard the teaching of certain men as the embodiment of goodness is no proof that it might not be the society's undoing if their precepts were generally followed. It may well be that a nation may destroy itself by following

the teaching of what it regards as its best men, perhaps saintly figures unquestionably guided by the most unselfish ideals. There would be little danger of this in a society whose members were still free to choose their way of practical life, because in such a society such tendencies would be self-corrective: only the groups guided by "impractical" ideals would decline, and others, less moral by current standards, would take their place. But this will happen only in a free society in which such ideals are not enforced on all. Where all are made to serve the same ideals and where dissenters are not allowed to follow different ones, the rules can be proved inexpedient only by the decline of the whole nation guided by them.

The important question that arises here is whether the agreement of a majority on a moral rule is sufficient justification for enforcing it on a dissenting minority or whether this power ought not also to be limited by more general rules—in other words, whether ordinary legislation should be limited by general principles just as the moral rules of individual conduct preclude certain kinds of action, however good may be their purpose. There is as much need of moral rules in political as in individual action, and the consequences of successive collective decisions as well as those of individual decisions will be beneficial only if they are all in conformity with common principles.

Such moral rules for collective action are developed only with difficulty and very slowly. But this should be taken as an indication of their preciousness. The most important among the few principles of this kind that we have developed is individual freedom, which it is most appropriate to regard as a moral principle of political action. Like all moral principles, it demands that it be accepted as a value in itself, as a principle that must be respected without our asking whether the consequences in the particular instance will be beneficial. We shall not achieve the results we want if we do not accept it as a creed or presumption so strong that no considerations of expediency can be allowed to limit it.

The argument for liberty, in the last resort, is indeed an argument for principles and against expediency in collective action,[48] which, as we shall see, is equivalent to saying that only the judge and not the administrator may order coercion. When one of the intellectual leaders of nineteenth-century liber-

---

[48] It is often questioned today whether consistency is a virtue in social action. The desire for consistency is even sometimes represented as a rationalistic prejudice, and the judging of each case on its individual merits as the truly experimental or empiricist procedure. The truth is the exact opposite. The desire for consistency springs from the recognition of the inadequacy of our reason explicitly to comprehend all the implications of the individual case, while the supposedly pragmatic procedure is based on the claim that we can properly evaluate all the implications without reliance on those principles which tell us which particular facts we ought to take into account.

alism, Benjamin Constant, described liberalism as the *système de principes*,[49] he pointed to the heart of the matter. Not only is liberty a system under which all government action is guided by principles, but it is an ideal that will not be preserved unless it is itself accepted as an overriding principle governing all particular acts of legislation. Where no such fundamental rule is stubbornly adhered to as an ultimate ideal about which there must be no compromise for the sake of material advantages—as an ideal which, even though it may have to be temporarily infringed during a passing emergency, must form the basis of all permanent arrangements—freedom is almost certain to be destroyed by piecemeal encroachments. For in each particular instance it will be possible to promise concrete and tangible advantages as the result of a curtailment of freedom, while the benefits sacrificed will in their nature always be unknown and uncertain. If freedom were not treated as the supreme principle, the fact that the promises which a free society has to offer can always be only chances and not certainties, only opportunities and not definite gifts to particular individuals, would inevitably prove a fatal weakness and lead to its slow erosion.[50]

10. The reader will probably wonder by now what role there remains to be played by reason in the ordering of social affairs, if a policy of liberty demands so much refraining from deliberate control, so much acceptance of the undirected and spontaneously grown. The first answer is that, if it has become necessary to seek appropriate limits to the uses of reason here, to find these limits is itself a most important and difficult exercise of reason. Moreover, if our stress here has been necessarily on those limits, we have certainly not meant to imply thereby that reason has no important positive task. Reason undoubtedly is man's most precious possession. Our argument is intended to show merely that it is not all-powerful and that the belief that it can become its own master and control its own development may yet destroy it. What we have attempted is a defense of reason, against its abuse by those who do not understand the conditions of its effective functioning and continuous growth. It is an appeal to men to see that we must use our reason intelligently and that, in order to do so, we must preserve that indispensable matrix of the uncon-

---

[49] Benjamin Constant, "De l'arbitraire," in *Œuvres politiques de Benjamin Constant*, Charles Louandre, ed. (Paris: Charpentier et Cie., 1874), pp. 91–92.

[50] See Dicey, *Law and Public Opinion*, pp. 257–58: "The beneficial effect of State intervention, especially in the form of legislation, is direct, immediate, and, so to speak visible, whilst its evil effects are gradual and indirect, and lie out of sight.... Hence the majority of mankind must almost of necessity look with undue favour upon governmental intervention. This natural bias can be counteracted only by the existence in a given society ... of a presumption or prejudice in favour of individual liberty, that is, *laissez faire*" [Liberty Fund edition, p. 182]; and Carl Menger, *Untersuchungen*, p. 208, where he speaks of "Pragmatismus, der gegen die Absicht seiner Vertreter unausweichbar zum Sozialismus führt" ["pragmatism, that contrary to the intention of its representatives inexorably leads to socialism."—Ed.]; also see my essay, "Die Ursachen der ständigen Gefährdung der Freiheit," in *Ordo*, 12 (1961): 103–9.

trolled and non-rational which is the only environment wherein reason can grow and operate effectively.

The antirationalistic position here taken must not be confounded with irrationalism or any appeal to mysticism.[51] What is advocated here is not an abdication of reason but a rational examination of the field where reason is appropriately put in control. Part of this argument is that such an intelligent use of reason does not mean the use of deliberate reason in the maximum possible number of occasions. In opposition to the naïve rationalism which treats our present reason as an absolute, we must continue the efforts which David Hume commenced when he "turned against the enlightenment its own weapons" and undertook "to whittle down the claims of reason by the use of rational analysis."[52]

The first condition for such an intelligent use of reason in the ordering of human affairs is that we learn to understand what role it does in fact play and can play in the working of any society based on the co-operation of many separate minds. This means that, before we can try to remold society intelligently, we must understand its functioning; we must realize that, even when we believe that we understand it, we may be mistaken. What we must learn to understand is that human civilization has a life of its own, that all our efforts to improve things must operate within a working whole which we cannot entirely control, and the operation of whose forces we can hope merely to facilitate and assist so far as we understand them. Our attitude ought to be similar to that of the physician toward a living organism: like him, we have to deal with a self-maintaining whole which is kept going by forces which we cannot replace and which we must therefore use in all we try to achieve. What can be done to improve it must be done by working with these forces rather than against them.[53] In all our endeavor at improvement we must always work

---

[51] It must be admitted that after the tradition discussed was handed on by Burke to the French reactionaries and German romanticists, it was turned from an antirationalist position into an irrationalist faith and that much of it survived almost only in this form. But this abuse, for which Burke is partly responsible, should not be allowed to discredit what is valuable in the tradition, nor should it cause us to forget "how thorough a Whig [Burke] was to the last," as Frederic William Maitland (*Collected Papers*, vol. 1, p. 67) has rightly emphasized.

[52] Sheldon Sanford Wolin, "Hume and Conservatism," *American Political Science Review*, 48 (1954): 1001. [The quotation in full reads: "Hume was something more than the Enlightenment incarnate, for his significance is that he turned against the Enlightenment its own weapons. And herein lies his importance as a conservative thinker. His starting-point is to be found in *A Treatise of Human Nature* (1739–40) which bears the subtitle 'An attempt to introduce the experimental method of reasoning into moral subjects.' The first book illustrates Hume's tactic: to whittle down the claims of reason by the use of rational analysis."—Ed.] Cf. also Ernest Campbell Mossner, *Life of David Hume* (Oxford: Clarendon Press, 1954), p. 125: "In the Age of Reason, Hume set himself apart as a systematic anti-rationalist."

[53] See Dietrich Schindler, *Recht, Staat, Völkergemeinschaft: ausgewählte Schriften und Fragmente aus dem Nachlass* (Zurich: Schulthess and Co., 1948), p. 86: "Der Gesetzgeber gleicht eher dem Gärtner,

inside this given whole, aim at piecemeal, rather than total, construction,[54] and use at each stage the historical material at hand and improve details step by step rather than attempt to redesign the whole.

None of these conclusions are arguments against the use of reason, but only arguments against such uses as require any exclusive and coercive powers of government; not arguments against experimentation, but arguments against all exclusive, monopolistic power to experiment in a particular field—power which brooks no alternative and which lays a claim to the possession of superior wisdom—and against the consequent preclusion of solutions better than the ones to which those in power have committed themselves.

---

der mit dem vorhandenen Erdreich und mit den Wachstumsbedingungen der Pflanzen zu rechnen hat, als dem Maler, der seiner Phantasie freies Spiel läßt." ["The legislator more closely resembles a gardener, who has to assess the soil and the conditions necessary for his plants' growth, than a painter who gives free rein to his imagination."—Ed.]

[54] Sir Karl Raimund Popper, *The Open Society and Its Enemies* [1945 edition], passim.

FIVE

RESPONSIBILITY AND FREEDOM

It is doubtful that democracy could survive in a society organized on the principle of therapy rather than judgment, error rather than sin. If men are free and equal, they must be judged rather than hospitalized. —F. D. Wormuth

1. Liberty not only means that the individual has both the opportunity and the burden of choice; it also means that he must bear the consequences of his actions and will receive praise or blame for them. Liberty and responsibility are inseparable. A free society will not function or maintain itself unless its members regard it as right that each individual occupy the position that results from his action and accept it as due to his own action. Though it can offer to the individual only chances and though the outcome of his efforts will depend on innumerable accidents, it forcefully directs his attention to those circumstances that he can control as if they were the only ones that mattered. Since the individual is to be given the opportunity to make use of circumstances that may be known only to him and since, as a rule, nobody else can know whether he has made the best use of them or not, the presumption is that the outcome of his actions is determined by them, unless the contrary is quite obvious.

This belief in individual responsibility, which has always been strong when people firmly believed in individual freedom, has markedly declined, together with the esteem for freedom. Responsibility has become an unpopular concept, a word that experienced speakers or writers avoid because of the obvious boredom or animosity with which it is received by a generation that dislikes all moralizing. It often evokes the outright hostility of men who have been taught that it is nothing but circumstances over which they have no control that has determined their position in life or even their actions. This denial of responsibility is, however, commonly due to a fear of responsibility, a fear that necessarily becomes also a fear of freedom.[1] It is doubtless because the

The quotation at the head of the chapter is taken from Francis Dunham Wormuth, *The Origins of Modern Constitutionalism* (New York: Harper, 1949), pp. 212–13.

[1] This old truth has been succinctly expressed by George Bernard Shaw: "Liberty means responsibility. That is why most men dread it" (from "Maxims for Revolutionists" in *Man and Superman: A Comedy and a Philosophy* [Westminster: Archibald Constable, 1903], p. 229. [This

opportunity to build one's own life also means an unceasing task, a discipline that man must impose upon himself if he is to achieve his aims, that many people are afraid of liberty.

2. The concurrent decline in esteem for individual liberty and individual responsibility is in a great measure the result of an erroneous interpretation of the lessons of science. The older views were closely connected with a belief in the "freedom of the will," a conception that never did have a precise meaning but later seemed to have been deprived of foundation by modern science. The increasing belief that all natural phenomena are uniquely determined by antecedent events or subject to recognizable laws and that man himself should be seen as part of nature led to the conclusion that man's actions and the working of his mind must also be regarded as necessarily determined by external circumstances. The conception of universal determinism that dominated nineteenth-century science[2] was thus applied to the conduct of human beings, and this seemed to eliminate the spontaneity of human action. It had, of course, to be admitted that there was no more than a general presumption that human actions were also subject to natural law and that we actually did

---

and most subsequent editions contain, in addition to the play's text, the "Revolutionist's Handbook" and "Maxims for Revolutionists."—Ed.]). The theme has, of course, been treated fully in some of the novels of Fyodor Dostoevsky (especially in the Grand Inquisitor episode of *The Brothers Karamazov*), and there is not much that modern psychoanalysts and existentialist philosophers have been able to add to his psychological insight. But see Erich Fromm, *Escape from Freedom* (New York: Farrar and Rinehart, Inc., 1941; English edition entitled *The Fear of Freedom* [London: Routledge, 1942]); Marjorie Glicksman Grene, *Dreadful Freedom* (Chicago: University of Chicago Press, 1948); and Otto Veit, *Die Flucht vor der Freiheit: Versuch zur geschichtsphilosophischen Erhellung der Kulturkrise* (Frankfurt am Main: Vittorio Klostermann, 1947). The converse of the belief in individual responsibility and connected respect for the law which prevail in free societies is the sympathy with the lawbreaker which seems to develop regularly in unfree societies and which is so characteristic of nineteenth-century Russian literature.

[2] For a careful examination of the philosophical problems of general determinism see Karl Raimund Popper, *The Logic of Scientific Discovery—Postscript: After Twenty Years* (London, 1959) [Popper originally intended the Postscript to which Hayek refers as a series of appendices to the *Logik der Forschung (The Logic of Scientific Discovery)* to cover the period from 1934 to 1954. The postscript was set in galley proofs during the period 1956–57 and given the title *Postscript—After Twenty Years*; it circulated in this form for several years and is doubtless the work to which Hayek is referring. Sections of it were incorporated in the 1959 translation of Popper's book as a series of appendices (pp. 311–464). However, Popper continued to revise and expand his discussion and it was not until 1982 and 1983 that William W. Bartley III undertook the task of bringing this material together, which eventually appeared in three volumes: (1) *Realism and the Aim of Science* (Totowa, NJ: Rowman and Littlefield, 1983); (2) *The Open Universe: An Argument for Indeterminism* (Totowa, NJ: Rowman and Littlefield, 1982); and (3) *Quantum Theory and the Schism in Physics* (Totowa, NJ: Rowman and Littlefield, 1982).—Ed.]; cf. also my essay "Degrees of Explanation," *British Journal for the Philosophy of Science*, 6 (1955): 209–25; reprinted in *Studies in Philosophy, Politics, and Economics* (Chicago: University of Chicago Press, 1967), pp. 3–21. See also my "The Theory of Complex Phenomena," in *The Critical Approach: Essays in Honor of Karl R. Popper*, M. Bunge, ed. (New York: Free Press, 1964), pp. 332–49.[Also appears in *Studies in Philosophy, Politics, and Economics*, pp. 22–42.—Ed.]

not know how they were determined by particular circumstances except, perhaps, in the rarest of instances. But the admission that the working of man's mind must be believed, at least in principle, to obey uniform laws appeared to eliminate the role of an individual personality which is essential to the conception of freedom and responsibility.

The intellectual history of the last few generations gives us any number of instances of how this determinist picture of the world has shaken the foundation of the moral and political belief in freedom. And many scientifically educated people today would probably agree with the scientist who, when writing for the general public, admitted that freedom "is a very troublesome concept for the scientist to discuss, partly because he is not convinced that, in the last analysis, there is such a thing."[3] More recently, it is true, physicists have, it would seem with some relief, abandoned the thesis of universal determinism. It is doubtful, however, whether the newer conception of a merely statistical regularity of the world in any way affects the puzzle about the freedom of the will. For it would seem that the difficulties that people have had concerning the meaning of voluntary action and responsibility do not at all spring from any necessary consequence of the belief that human action is causally determined but are the result of an intellectual muddle, of drawing conclusions which do not follow from the premises.

It appears that the assertion that the will is free has as little meaning as its denial and that the whole issue is a phantom problem,[4] a dispute about

---

[3] Conrad Hal Waddington. *The Scientific Attitude* (Pelican Books; Harmondsworth: Penguin Books, 1941), p. 110. See also Burrhus Frederic Skinner, *Walden Two* (New York: Macmillan, 1948), p. 257: "I deny that freedom exists at all. I must deny it, or my program would be absurd. You can't have a science about a subject matter which leaps capriciously about." In addition, see Skinner's *Science and Human Behavior* (New York: Macmillan, 1953), which stands as the most extreme example of anti-liberal attitudes embraced by the modern "behavioral scientist."

[4] This was already clearly seen by John Locke (*An Essay Concerning Human Understanding* [London: Printed for Thomas Basset and sold by Edward Mory, 1690], bk. 2, chap. 14, sec. 14, p. 119, where he speaks of the "unreasonable because unintelligible Question, viz. *Whether Man's Will be free, or no?* For if I mistake not, it follows from what I have said, that the Question itself is altogether improper"), and even by Thomas Hobbes, *Leviathan; or, The Matter, Forme, and Power of a Commonwealth, Ecclesiasticall and Civil*, Michael Joseph Oakeshott, ed. (Oxford: B. Blackwell, 1946), pp. 137–38. For more recent discussions see Heinrich Gomperz, *Das Problem der Willensfreiheit* (Jena: Diederichs, 1907); Moritz Schlick, *Problems of Ethics*, David Rynin, trans. (New York: Prentice-Hall, 1939); Charles Dunbar Broad, *Determinism, Indeterminism, and Libertarianism: An Inaugural Lecture* (Cambridge: Cambridge University Press, 1934); Richard Merwyn Hare, *The Language of Morals* (Oxford: Clarendon Press, 1952); Herbert Lionel Adolphus Hart, "The Ascription of Responsibility and Rights," *Proceedings of the Aristotelian Society*, n.s., 49 (1949): 171–94, reprinted in *Logic and Language*, Anthony Flew, ed. (1st ser.; Oxford: Blackwell, 1951), pp. 145–66; Patrick Horace Nowell-Smith, "Freewill and Moral Responsibility," *Mind*, 17 (1948): 45–61, and the same author's *Ethics* (Pelican Books; London: Penguin Books, 1954); John David Mabbott, "Freewill and Punishment," in *Contemporary British Philosophy: Personal Statements, 3rd Series*, Howell David Lewis, ed. (London: Allen and Unwin, 1956), pp. 287–309; Charles

words in which the contestants have not made clear what an affirmative or a negative answer would imply. Surely, those who deny the freedom of the will deprive the word "free" of all its ordinary meaning, which describes action according to one's own will instead of another's; in order not to make a meaningless statement, they should offer some other definition, which, indeed, they never do.[5] Furthermore, the whole suggestion that "free" in any relevant or meaningful sense precludes the idea that action is necessarily determined by some factors proves on examination to be entirely unfounded.

The confusion becomes obvious when we examine the conclusion generally drawn by the two parties from their respective positions. The determinists usually argue that, because men's actions are completely determined by natural causes, there could be no justification for holding them responsible or praising or blaming their actions. The voluntarists, on the other hand, contend that, because there exists in man some agent standing outside the chain of cause and effect, this agent is the bearer of responsibility and the legitimate object of praise and blame. Now there can be little doubt that, so far as these practical conclusions are concerned, the voluntarists are more nearly right, while the determinists are merely confused. The peculiar fact about the dispute is, however, that in neither case do the conclusions follow from the alleged premises. As has often been shown, the conception of responsibility rests, in fact, on a determinist view,[6] while only the construction of a metaphysical "self" that stands outside the whole chain of cause and effect and

---

Arthur Campbell, "Is Free Will a Pseudo-Problem?" *Mind*, 60 (1951): 441–65; D. M. MacKay, "On Comparing the Brain with Machines" (British Association Symposium on Cybernetics), *Advancement of Science*, 10 (1954): 402–6, esp. 406; Sidney Hook, ed., *Determinism and Freedom in the Age of Modern Science: A Philosophical Symposium* [New York University Institute of Philosophy] (New York: New York University Press, 1958); Hans Kelsen, "Causality and Imputation," *Ethics*, 61 (1950–51): 1–11; Arthur Pap, "Determinism and Moral Responsibility," *Journal of Philosophy*, 43 (1946): 318–27; and Austin Marsden Farrer, *The Freedom of the Will: The Gifford Lectures Delivered in the University of Edinburgh, 1957* (London: Adam and Charles Black, 1958).

[5] Cf. David Hume, *An Enquiry Concerning Human Understanding*, in *Essays*, vol. 2, p. 78: "By liberty, then, we can only mean a power of acting or not acting, according to the determinations of the will." See also the discussion in my book, *The Sensory Order: An Inquiry into the Foundations of Theoretical Psychology* (Chicago: University of Chicago Press, 1952), secs. 8.93–8.94, p. 193. [A *Collected Works* edition is anticipated.—Ed.]

[6] Though this contention still has the appearance of a paradox, it goes back as far as David Hume and apparently even Aristotle. Hume stated explicitly (*Treatise of Human Nature* [bk. 2, pt. 3, sec. 2], vol. 2, p. 192): "'Tis only upon the principles of necessity, that a person acquires any merit or demerit from his actions, however the common opinion may incline to the contrary." On Aristotle see Yves Simon, *Traité du libre arbitre* (Liège: Sciences et lettres, 1951), pp. 93–99; and Carl Friedrich Heman, *Des Aristoteles Lehre von der Freiheit des menschlichen Willens* (Leipzig: Fues's R. Riesland, 1887), esp. pp. 168–94, quoted by Simon. For recent discussions see R. E. Hobart, "Free Will as Involving Determination and Inconceivable without It," *Mind*, 43 (1934): 1–27; and Philippa Foot, "Free Will Involving Determinism," *Philosophical Review*, 66 (1957): 439–50.

therefore could be treated as uninfluenced by praise or blame could justify man's exemption from responsibility.

3. It would be possible, of course, to construct, as illustration of an alleged determinist position, a bogey of an automaton that invariably responded to the events in its environment in the same predictable manner. This would correspond, however, to no position that has ever been seriously maintained even by the most extreme opponents of the "freedom of the will." Their contention is that the conduct of a person at any moment, his response to any set of external circumstances, will be determined by the joint effects of his inherited constitution and all his accumulated experience, with each new experience being interpreted in the light of earlier individual experience—a cumulative process which in each instance produces a unique and distinct personality. This personality operates as a sort of filter through which external events produce conduct which can be predicted with certainty only in exceptional circumstances. What the determinist position asserts is that those accumulated effects of heredity and past experience constitute the whole of the individual personality, that there is no other "self" or "I" whose disposition cannot be affected by external or material influences. This means that all those factors whose influence is sometimes inconsistently denied by those who deny the "freedom of the will," such as reasoning or argument, persuasion or censure, or the expectation of praise or blame, are really among the most important factors determining the personality and through it the particular action of the individual. It is just because there is no separate "self" that stands outside the chain of causation that there is also no "self" that we could not reasonably try to influence by reward or punishment.[7]

That we can, in fact, often influence people's conduct by education and example, rational persuasion, approval or disapproval, has probably never been seriously denied. The only question that can be legitimately asked is, therefore, to what extent particular persons in given circumstances are likely to be influenced in the desired direction by the knowledge that an action will raise or lower them in the esteem of their fellows or that they can expect reward or punishment for it.

Strictly speaking, it is nonsense to say, as is so often said, that "it is not a man's fault that he is as he is," for the aim of assigning responsibility is to

[7] The most extreme deterministic position tends to deny that the term "will" has any meaning (the word has indeed been banned from some kinds of superscientific psychology) or that there is such a thing as voluntary action. Yet even those who hold that position cannot avoid distinguishing between the kinds of actions that can be influenced by rational considerations and those that cannot. This is all that matters: Indeed, they will have to admit, what is in effect a *reductio ad absurdum* of their position, that whether a person does or does not believe in his capacity to form and carry out plans, which is what is popularly meant by his will being free or not, may make a great deal of difference to what he will do.

make him different from what he is or might be. If we say that a person is responsible for the consequences of an action, this is not a statement of fact or an assertion about causation. The statement would, of course, not be justifiable if nothing he "might" have done or omitted could have altered the result. But when we use words like "might" or "could" in this connection, we do not mean that at the moment of his decision something in him acted otherwise than was the necessary effect of causal laws in the given circumstances. Rather, the statement that a person is responsible for what he does aims at making his actions different from what they would be if he did not believe it to be true. We assign responsibility to a man, not in order to say that as he was he might have acted differently, but in order to make him different. If I have caused harm to somebody by negligence or forgetfulness, "which I could not help" in the circumstances, this does not exempt me from responsibility but should impress upon me more strongly than before the necessity of keeping the possibility of such consequences in mind.[8]

The only questions that can be legitimately raised, therefore, are whether the person upon whom we place responsibility for a particular action or its consequences is the kind of person who is accessible to normal motives (that is, whether he is what we call a responsible person) and whether in the given circumstances such a person can be expected to be influenced by the considerations and beliefs we want to impress upon him. As in most such problems, our ignorance of the particular circumstances will regularly be such that we will merely know that the expectation that they will be held responsible is likely, on the whole, to influence men in certain positions in a desirable direction. Our problem is generally not whether certain mental factors were operative on the occasion of a particular action but how certain considerations might be made as effective as possible in guiding action. This requires that the individual be praised or blamed, whether or not the expectation of this would in fact have made any difference to the action. Of the effect in the particular instance we may never be sure, but we believe that, in general, the knowledge that he will be held responsible will influence a person's conduct in a desirable direction. In this sense the assigning of responsibility does not involve the assertion of a fact. It is rather of the nature of a convention intended to make people observe certain rules. Whether a particular convention of this kind is effective may always be a debatable question. We shall rarely know more than that experience suggests that it is or is not, on the whole, effective.

[8] We still call a man's decision "free," though by the conditions we have created he is led to do what we want him to do, because these conditions do not uniquely determine his actions but merely make it more likely that anyone in his position will do what we approve. We try to "influence" but do not determine what he will do. What we often mean in this connection, as in many others, when we call his action "free," is simply that we do not know what has determined it, and not that it has not been determined by something.

Responsibility has become primarily a legal concept, because the law requires clear tests to decide when a person's actions create an obligation or make him liable to punishment. But it is, of course, no less a moral concept, a conception which underlies our view of a person's moral duties. In fact, its scope extends considerably beyond what we commonly consider as moral. Our whole attitude toward the working of our social order, our approval or disapproval of the manner in which it determines the relative position of different individuals, is closely tied up with our views about responsibility. The significance of the concept thus extends far beyond the sphere of coercion, and its greatest importance perhaps lies in its role in guiding man's free decisions. A free society probably demands more than any other that people be guided in their action by a sense of responsibility which extends beyond the duties exacted by the law and that general opinion approve of the individuals' being held responsible for both the success and the failure of their endeavors. When men are allowed to act as they see fit, they must also be held responsible for the results of their efforts.

4. The justification for assigning responsibility is thus the presumed effect of this practice on future action; it aims at teaching people what they ought to consider in comparable future situations. Though we leave people to decide for themselves because they are, as a rule, in the best position to know the circumstances surrounding their action, we are also concerned that conditions should permit them to use their knowledge to the best effect. If we allow men freedom because we presume them to be reasonable beings, we also must make it worth their while to act as reasonable beings by letting them bear the consequences of their decisions. This does not mean that a man will always be assumed to be the best judge of his interests; it means merely that we can never be sure who knows them better than he and that we wish to make full use of the capacities of all those who may have something to contribute to the common effort of making our environment serve human purposes.

The assigning of responsibility thus presupposes the capacity on men's part for rational action, and it aims at making them act more rationally than they would otherwise. It presupposes a certain minimum capacity in them for learning and foresight, for being guided by a knowledge of the consequences of their action. It is no objection to argue that reason in fact plays only a small part in determining human action, since the aim is to make that little go as far as possible. Rationality, in this connection, can mean no more than some degree of coherence and consistency in a person's action, some lasting influence of knowledge or insight which, once acquired, will affect his action at a later date and in different circumstances.

The complementarity of liberty and responsibility means that the argument for liberty can apply only to those who can be held responsible. It cannot apply to infants, idiots, or the insane. It presupposes that a person is capable of learning from experience and of guiding his actions by knowledge thus acquired; it is invalid for those who have not yet learned enough or are incapable of learning. A person whose actions are fully determined by the same unchangeable impulses uncontrolled by knowledge of the consequences or a genuine split personality, a schizophrenic, could in this sense not be held responsible, because his knowledge that he will be held responsible could not alter his actions. The same would apply to persons suffering from really uncontrollable urges, kleptomaniacs or dipsomaniacs, whom experience has proved not to be responsive to normal motives. But so long as we have reason to believe that a man's awareness that he will be held responsible is likely to influence his actions, it is necessary to treat him as responsible, whether or not in the particular instance this will have the desired effect. The assigning of responsibility is based, not on what we know to be true in the particular case, but on what we believe will be the probable effects of encouraging people to behave rationally and considerately. It is a device that society has developed to cope with our inability to look into other people's minds and, without resorting to coercion, to introduce order into our lives.

This is not the place to enter into a discussion of the special problem raised by all those who cannot be held responsible and to whom the argument for liberty therefore does not or cannot wholly apply. The important point is that being a free and responsible member of the community is a particular status that carries with it a burden as well as a privilege; and if freedom is to fulfill its aim, this status must not be granted at anybody's discretion but must automatically belong to all who satisfy certain objectively ascertainable tests (such as age), so long as the presumption that they possess the required minimum capacities is not clearly disproved. In personal relations the transition from tutelage to full responsibility may be gradual and indistinct, and those lighter forms of coercion which exist between individuals and with which the state should not interfere can be adjusted to degrees of responsibility. Politically and legally, however, the distinction must be sharp and definite and be determined by general and impersonal rules if freedom is to be effective. In our decisions as to whether a person is to be his own master or be subject to the will of another, we must regard him as being either responsible or not responsible, as either having or not having the right to act in a manner that may be unintelligible, unpredictable, or unwelcome to others. The fact that not all human beings can be given full liberty must not mean that the liberty of all should be subject to restrictions and regulations adjusted to individual conditions. The individualizing treatment of the juvenile court or the mental ward is the mark of unfreedom, of tutelage. Though in the intimate relations of private life we may adjust our conduct to the personality of our partners, in public life freedom requires that we be regarded as types, not as unique individuals, and treated on the presumption that normal motives and deterrents will be effective, whether this be true in the particular instance or not.

5. There is much confusion of the ideal that a person ought to be allowed to pursue his own aims with the belief that, if left free, he will or ought to pursue solely his selfish aims.[9] The freedom to pursue one's own aims is, however, as important for the most altruistic person, in whose scale of values the needs of other people occupy a very high place, as for any egotist. It is part of the ordinary nature of men (and perhaps still more of women) and one of the main conditions of their happiness that they make the welfare of other people their chief aim. To do so is part of the normal choice open to us and often the decision generally expected of us. By common opinion our chief concern in this respect should, of course, be the welfare of our family. But we also show our appreciation and approval of others by making them our friends and their aims ours. To choose our associates and generally those whose needs we make our concern is an essential part of freedom and of the moral conceptions of a free society.

General altruism, however, is a meaningless conception. Nobody can effectively care for other people as such; the responsibilities we can assume must always be particular, can concern only those about whom we know concrete facts and to whom either choice or special conditions have attached us. It is one of the fundamental rights and duties of a free man to decide what and whose needs appear to him most important.

The recognition that each person has his own scale of values which we ought to respect, even if we do not approve of it, is part of the conception of the value of the individual personality. How we value another person will necessarily depend on what his values are. But believing in freedom means that we do not regard ourselves as the ultimate judges of another person's values, that we do not feel entitled to prevent him from pursuing ends which we disapprove so long as he does not infringe the equally protected sphere of others.

A society that does not recognize that each individual has values of his own which he is entitled to follow can have no respect for the dignity of the individual and cannot really know freedom. But it is also true that in a free society an individual will be esteemed according to the manner in which he uses his freedom. Moral esteem would be meaningless without freedom: "If every action which is good or evil in [a] man of ripe years were to be under pittance and prescription and compulsion, what were virtue but a name, what praise could

---

[9] Cf. Thomas Nixon Carver, *Essays in Social Justice* (Cambridge, MA: Harvard University Press, 1922); [see especially Carver's introductory chapter, "What Is Justice?" (pp. 3–34) and chapter two, "Ultimate Basis of Social Conflict" (pp. 35–58)] and the first essay ["Individualism: True and False"] in my *Individualism and Economic Order* (Chicago: University of Chicago Press, 1948), pp. 1–32. [*Collected Works* edition, vol. 13, pp. 46–74.]

be due then to well-doing, what gramercy to be sober, just, or continent?"[10] Liberty is an opportunity for doing good, but this is so only when it is also an opportunity for doing wrong. The fact that a free society will function successfully only if the individuals are in some measure guided by common values is perhaps the reason why philosophers have sometimes defined freedom as action in conformity with moral rules. But this definition of freedom is a denial of that freedom with which we are concerned. The freedom of action

[10]John Milton, *Areopagitica* (Everyman ed.; London: J. M. Dent and Sons, 1927), p. 18 [Liberty Fund edition, p. 23]. The notion that moral worth required free action was already known in ancient Greece. See Euripides, *Heracleidae*, 551: "Frei verlasse ich das Leben, nicht gezwungen. Denn nur die freie Tat hat Wert." [Hayek's German translates as: "I give my life freely, not under compulsion. For only the free deed has value."—Ed.] The conception of moral merit depending on freedom was already emphasized by some of the Scholastic philosophers and again especially in the German "classical" literature (cf., e.g., Friedrich Schiller, *On the Aesthetic Education of Man: In A Series of Letters* [New Haven: Yale University Press, 1954], p. 74: "Man must have his freedom to be ready for morality." [While these words do not appear in Schiller's *On the Aesthetic Education of Man*, there is no question that Schiller believed that man's freedom and his moral disposition are intimately linked and that it is only when men are both physically and spiritually free that they can become fully moral. Consider: "(Man's) culture consists of two things: first, providing the receptive faculty with the most multifarious contacts with the world, and as regards feeling, pushing passivity to its fullest extent; secondly, securing for the determining faculty the fullest independence from the receptive, and as regards reason, pushing activity to its fullest extent. Where both qualities are united, Man will combine the greatest fullness of existence with the utmost self-dependence and freedom and instead of abandoning himself to the world he will rather draw it into himself with the whole infinity of its phenomena, and subject it to the unity of reason." (p. 69; "Seine Kultur wird also darin bestehen: erstlich: Dem empfangenden Vermögen die vielfältigsten Berührungen mit der Welt zu verschaffen und auf seiten des Gefühls die Passivität aufs Höchste zu treiben; zweitens dem bestimmenden Vermögen die höchste Unabhängigkeit von dem empfangenden zu erwerben und auf seiten der Vernunft die Aktivität aufs Höchste zu treiben. Wo beide Eigenschaften sich vereinigen, da wird der Mensch mit der höchsten Fülle von Dasein die höchste Selbständigkeit und Freiheit verbinden, und, anstatt sich an die Welt zu verlieren, diese vielmehr mit der ganzen Unendlichkeit ihrer Erscheinungen in sich ziehen und der Einheit seiner Vernunft unterwerfen." ("Uber die ästhetische Erziehung des Menschen" [Letter 13, *Sämtliche Werke in zehn Bänden*, vol. 8: *Philosophische Schriften*, Hans-Güther Thalheim, ed. (Berlin: Aufbau-Verlag, 2005), p. 345]); and "If in the dynamic state of rights man encounters man as force and restricts his activity, if in the ethical state of duties he opposes him with the majesty of the law and fetters his will, in the sphere of cultivated society, in the aesthetic state, he need appear to him only as shape, confront him only as an object of free play. To grant freedom by means of freedom is the fundamental law of this kingdom." (p. 137; "Wenn in dem dynamischen Staat der Rechte der Mensch dem Menschen als Kraft begegnet und sein Wirken beschränkt—wenn er sich ihm in dem ethischen Staat der Pflichten mit der Majestät des Gesetzes entgegenstellt und sein Wollen fesselt, so darf er ihm im Kreise des schönen Umgangs, in dem ästhetischen Staat, nur als Gestalt erscheinen, nur als Objekt des freien Spiels gegenüberstehen. Freiheit zu geben durch Freiheit ist das Grundgesetz dieses Reichs.") Letter 27; p. 406.)—Ed.] Also Alexis de Toccqueville, *Voyage en Angleterre et en Irlande de 1835*, in *Œuvres complètes*, Jacob Peter Mayer, ed. (18 vols.; Paris: Gallimard, 1951), vol. 5, pt. 2, p. 91: "qu'est-ce que la vertu, sinon le *choix libre* de ce qui est bien?" ["What is virtue, if not the free choice of what is good?"—Ed.]

that is the condition of moral merit includes the freedom to act wrongly: we praise or blame only when a person has the opportunity to choose, only when his observance of a rule is not enforced but merely enjoined.

That the sphere of individual freedom is also the sphere of individual responsibility does not mean that we are accountable for our actions to any particular persons. True, we may lay ourselves open to censure by others because we do what displeases them. But the chief reason why we should be held wholly responsible for our decisions is that this will direct our attention to those causes of events that depend on our actions. The main function of the belief in individual responsibility is to make us use our own knowledge and capacities to the full in achieving our ends.

6. The burden of choice that freedom imposes, the responsibility for one's own fate that a free society places on the individual, has under the conditions of the modern world become a main source of dissatisfaction. To a much greater degree than ever before, the success of a man will depend not on what special abilities he possesses in the abstract but on these abilities being put to the right use. In times of less specialization and less complex organization, when almost everybody could know most of the opportunities that existed, the problem of finding an opportunity for putting one's special skills and talents to good use was less difficult. As society and its complexity extend, the rewards a man can hope to earn come to depend more and more, not on the skill and capacity he may possess, but on their being put to the right use; and both the difficulty of discovering the best employment for one's capacities and the discrepancy between the rewards of men possessing the same technical skill or special ability will increase.

There is perhaps no more poignant grief than that arising from a sense of how useful one might have been to one's fellow men and of one's gifts having been wasted. That in a free society nobody has a duty to see that a man's talents are properly used, that nobody has a claim to an opportunity to use his special gifts, and that, unless he himself finds such opportunity, they are likely to be wasted, is perhaps the gravest reproach directed against a free system and the source of the bitterest resentment. The consciousness of possessing certain potential capacities naturally leads to the claim that it is somebody else's duty to use them.

The necessity of finding a sphere of usefulness, an appropriate job, ourselves is the hardest discipline that a free society imposes on us. It is, however, inseparable from freedom, since nobody can assure each man that his gifts will be properly used unless he has the power to coerce others to use them. Only by depriving somebody else of the choice as to who should serve him, whose capacities or which products he is to use, could we guarantee to any man that his gifts will be used in the manner he feels he deserves. It is of the essence of a free society that a man's value and remuneration depend not on capacity in the abstract but on success in turning it into concrete service which is useful to others who can reciprocate. And the chief aim of freedom is to provide both the opportunity and the inducement to insure the maximum use of the knowledge that an individual can acquire. What makes the individual unique in this respect is not his generic but his concrete knowledge, his knowledge of particular circumstances and conditions.

7. It must be recognized that the results of a free society in this respect are often in conflict with ethical views that are relics of an earlier type of society. There can be little question that, from the point of view of society, the art of turning one's capacity to good account, the skill of discovering the most effective use of one's gift, is perhaps the most useful of all; but too much resourcefulness of this kind is not uncommonly frowned upon, and an advantage gained over those of equal general capacity by a more successful exploitation of concrete circumstances is regarded as unfair. In many societies an "aristocratic" tradition that stems from the conditions of action in an organizational hierarchy with assigned tasks and duties, a tradition that has often been developed by people whose privileges have freed them from the necessity of giving others what they want, represents it as nobler to wait until one's gifts are discovered by others, while only religious or ethnic minorities in a hard struggle to rise have deliberately cultivated this kind of resourcefulness (best described by the German term *Findigkeit*)—and are generally disliked for that reason. Yet there can be no doubt that the discovery of a better use of things or of one's own capacities is one of the greatest contributions that an individual can make in our society to the welfare of his fellows and that it is by providing the maximum opportunity for this that a free society can become so much more prosperous than others. The successful use of this entrepreneurial capacity (and, in discovering the best use of our abilities, we are all entrepreneurs) is the most highly rewarded activity in a free society, while whoever leaves to others the task of finding some useful means of employing his capacities must be content with a smaller reward.

It is important to realize that we are not educating people for a free society if we train technicians who expect to be "used," who are incapable of finding their proper niche themselves, and who regard it as somebody else's responsibility to ensure the appropriate use of their ability or skill. However able a man may be in a particular field, the value of his services is necessarily low in a free society unless he also possesses the capacity of making his ability known to those who can derive the greatest benefit from it. Though it may offend our sense of justice to find that of two men who by equal effort have acquired the same specialized skill and knowledge, one may be a success and the other a failure, we must recognize that in a free society it is the use of particular opportunities that determines usefulness and must adjust our education and ethos accordingly. In a free society we are remunerated not for our skill but for using it rightly; and this must be so as long as we are free to choose our particular occupation and are not to be directed to it. True, it is almost never possible to determine what part of a successful career has been due to superior knowledge, ability, or effort and what part to fortunate accidents; but this in no way detracts from the importance of making it worthwhile for everybody to make the right choice.

How little this basic fact is understood is shown by such assertions, made not only by socialists, as that "every child has a natural 'right,' as citizen, not merely to 'life, liberty, and the pursuit of happiness,' but to that position in the social scale to which his talents entitle him."[11] In a free society a man's talents do not "entitle" him to any particular position. To claim that they do would mean that some agency has the right and power to place men in particular positions according to its judgment. All that a free society has to offer is an opportunity of searching for a suitable position, with all the attendant risk and uncertainty which such a search for a market for one's gifts must involve. There is no denying that in this respect a free society puts most individuals under a pressure which is often resented. But it is an illusion to think that one would be rid of such pressure in some other type of society; for the alternative to the pressure that responsibility for one's own fate brings is the far more invidious pressure of personal orders that one must obey.

It is often contended that the belief that a person is solely responsible for his own fate is held only by the successful. This in itself is not so unacceptable as its underlying suggestion, which is that people hold this belief because they have been successful. I, for one, am inclined to think that the connection is the other way round and that people often are successful because they hold this belief. Though a man's conviction that all he achieves is due solely to his exertions, skill, and intelligence may be largely false, it is apt to have the most beneficial effects on his energy and circumspection. And if the smug pride of the successful is often intolerable and offensive, the belief that success depends wholly on him is probably the pragmatically most effective incentive to successful action; whereas the more a man indulges in the propensity to blame others or circumstances for his failures, the more disgruntled and ineffective he tends to become.

8. The sense of responsibility has been weakened in modern times as much by overextending the range of an individual's responsibilities as by exculpating him from the actual consequences of his actions. Since we assign responsibility to the individual in order to influence his action, it should refer only to such effects of his conduct as it is humanly possible for him to foresee and to such as we can reasonably wish him to take into account in ordinary cir-

---

[11] Charles Anthony Raven Crosland, *The Future of Socialism* (London: Jonathan Cape, 1956), p. 208.

cumstances. To be effective, responsibility must be both definite and limited, adapted both emotionally and intellectually to human capacities. It is quite as destructive of any sense of responsibility to be taught that one is responsible for everything as to be taught that one cannot be held responsible for anything. Freedom demands that the responsibility of the individual extend only to what he can be presumed to judge, that his actions take into account effects which are within his range of foresight, and particularly that he be responsible only for his own actions (or those of persons under his care)—not for those of others who are equally free.

Responsibility, to be effective, must be individual responsibility. In a free society there cannot be any collective responsibility of members of a group as such, unless they have, by concerted action, all made themselves individually and severally responsible. A joint or divided responsibility may create for the individual the necessity of agreeing with others and thereby limit the powers of each. If the same concerns are made the responsibility of many without at the same time imposing a duty of joint and agreed action, the result is usually that nobody really accepts responsibility. As everybody's property in effect is nobody's property, so everybody's responsibility is nobody's responsibility.[12]

It is not to be denied that modern developments, especially the development of the large city, have destroyed much of the feeling of responsibility for local concerns which in the past led to much beneficial and spontaneous common action. The essential condition of responsibility is that it refer to circumstances that the individual can judge, to problems that, without too much strain of the imagination, man can make his own and whose solution he can, with good reason, consider his own concern rather than another's. Such a condition can hardly apply to life in the anonymous crowd of an industrial city. No longer is the individual generally the member of some small community with which he is intimately concerned and closely acquainted. While this has brought him some increase in independence, it has also deprived him of the security which the personal ties and the friendly interest of the neighbors provided. The increased demand for protection and security from the impersonal power of the state is no doubt largely the result of the disappearance of those smaller communities of interest and of the feeling of isolation of the

---

[12] Cf. also the observation by Johan Huizinga, *Incertitudes: Essai de diagnostic du mal dont suffre notre temps* (Paris: Librairie de Médici, 1939), p. 216: "Dans chaque groupe collectif une partie du jugement de l'individu est absorbée avec une partie de sa responsibilité par le mot d'ordre collectif. Le sentiment d'être tous ensemble responsables de tout, accroît dans le monde actuel le danger de l'irresponsabilité absolue de l'action des masses." ["In each group, a portion of one's judgment, and with it a part of one's responsibility, gets swallowed up in a series of catchwords. In today's world, the view that we are all responsible for each other results in the danger that all actions of the masses are completely lacking in responsibility."—Ed.]

individual who can no longer count on the personal interest and assistance of the other members of the local group.[13]

Much as we may regret the disappearance of those close communities of interest and their replacement by a wide-flung net of limited, impersonal, and temporary ties, we cannot expect the sense of responsibility for the known and familiar to be replaced by a similar feeling about the remote and the theoretically known. While we can feel genuine concern for the fate of our familiar neighbors and usually will know how to help when help is needed, we cannot feel in the same way about the thousands or millions of unfortunates whom we know to exist in the world but whose individual circumstances we do not know. However moved we may be by accounts of their misery, we cannot make the abstract knowledge of the numbers of suffering people guide our everyday action. If what we do is to be useful and effective, our objectives must be limited, adapted to the capacities of our mind and our compassions. To be constantly reminded of our "social" responsibilities to all the needy or unfortunate in our community, in our country, or in the world, must have the effect of attenuating our feelings until the distinctions between those responsibilities which call for our action and those which do not disappear. In order to be effective, then, responsibility must be so confined as to enable the individual to rely on his own concrete knowledge in deciding on the importance of the different tasks, to apply his moral principles to circumstances he knows, and to help to mitigate evils voluntarily.

[13] See David Riesman, *The Lonely Crowd: A Study of the Changing American Character* (New Haven: Yale University Press, 1950).

SIX

EQUALITY, VALUE, AND MERIT

I have no respect for the passion for equality, which seems to me merely ide-
alizing envy. —Oliver Wendell Holmes, Jr.

1. The great aim of the struggle for liberty has been equality before the law.
This equality under the rules which the state enforces may be supplemented
by a similar equality of the rules that men voluntarily obey in their relations
with one another. This extension of the principle of equality to the rules of
moral and social conduct is the chief expression of what is commonly called
the democratic spirit—and probably that aspect of it that does most to make
inoffensive the inequalities that liberty necessarily produces.

Equality of the general rules of law and conduct, however, is the only kind
of equality conducive to liberty and the only equality which we can secure
without destroying liberty. Not only has liberty nothing to do with any other
sort of equality, but it is even bound to produce inequality in many respects.[1]
This is the necessary result and part of the justification of individual liberty: if
the result of individual liberty did not demonstrate that some manners of living are more successful than others, much of the case for it would vanish.

It is neither because it assumes that people are in fact equal nor because
it attempts to make them equal that the argument for liberty demands that
government treat them equally. This argument not only recognizes that individuals are very different but in a great measure rests on that assumption. It
insists that these individual differences provide no justification for government
to treat them differently. And it objects to the differences in treatment by the

---

The quotation at the head of the chapter is taken from *The Holmes-Laski Letters: The Correspondence of Mr. Justice Holmes and Harold J. Laski, 1916–1935*, Mark DeWolfe Howe, ed. (Cambridge, MA: Harvard University Press, 1953), vol. 2, p. 942. A German translation of an earlier version of this chapter, "Gleichheit, Wert und Verdienst," [Equality, Value, and Merit] has
appeared in *Ordo: Jahrbuch für die Ordnung von Wirtschaft und Gesellschaft*, 10 (1958): 5–29.

[1] See Gerhard Leibholz, "Die Bedrohung der Freiheit durch die Macht der Gesetzgeber," in *Die Freiheit
der Persönlichkeit: eine Vortragsreihe*, Ludwig von Bertalanffy, ed. (Stuttgart: A. Kröner, 1958), p. 80:
"Freiheit erzeugt notwendig Ungleichheit und Gleichheit notwendig Unfreiheit." ["Freedom necessarily
creates inequality and equality necessarily creates unfreedom."—Ed.]

state that would be necessary if persons who are in fact very different were to be assured equal positions in life.

Modern advocates of a more far-reaching material equality usually deny that their demands are based on any assumption of the factual equality of all men.[2] It is nevertheless still widely believed that this is the main justification for such demands. Nothing, however, is more damaging to the demand for equal treatment than to base it on so obviously untrue an assumption as that of the factual equality of all men. To rest the case for equal treatment of national or racial minorities on the assertion that they do not differ from other men is implicitly to admit that factual inequality would justify unequal treatment; and the proof that some differences do, in fact, exist would not be long in forthcoming. It is of the essence of the demand for equality before the law that people should be treated alike in spite of the fact that they are different.

2. The boundless variety of human nature—the wide range of differences in individual capacities and potentialities—is one of the most distinctive facts about the human species. Its evolution has made it probably the most variable among all kinds of creatures. It has been well said that "biology, with variability as its cornerstone, confers on every human individual a unique set of attributes which give him a dignity he could not otherwise possess. Every newborn baby is an unknown quantity so far as potentialities are concerned because there are many thousands of unknown interrelated genes and gene patterns which contribute to his makeup. As a result of nature and nurture the newborn infant may become one of the greatest men or women ever to have lived. In every case he or she has the making of a distinctive individual. . . . If the differences are not very important, then freedom is not very important and the idea of individual worth is not very important."[3] The writer justly adds that the widely held uniformity theory of human nature, "which on the surface appears to accord with democracy . . . would in time undermine the very basic ideals of freedom and individual worth and render life as we know it meaningless."[4]

It has been the fashion in modern times to minimize the importance of congenital differences between men and to ascribe all the important differences to the influence of environment.[5] However important the latter may

---

[2] See, e.g., Richard Henry Tawney, *Equality* [Halley Stewart Lectures, 1929 (London: Allen and Unwin, 1931)], pp. 47–50.

[3] Roger John Williams, *Free and Unequal: The Biological Basis of Individual Liberty* (Austin: University of Texas Press, 1953), pp. 23 and 70; cf. also John Burdon Sanderson Haldane, *The Inequality of Man, and Other Essays* (London: Chatto and Windus, 1932), and Peter Brian Medawar, *The Uniqueness of the Individual* (London: Methuen, 1957).

[4] Williams, *Free and Unequal*, p. 152.

[5] See the description of this fashionable view in Horace Mever Kallen's article "Behaviorism," *Encyclopedia of the Social Sciences*, vol. 2, p. 498: "At birth human infants, regardless of their heredity, are as equal as Fords."

be, we must not overlook the fact that individuals are very different from the outset. The importance of individual differences would hardly be less if all people were brought up in very similar environments. As a statement of fact, it just is not true that "all men are born equal." We may continue to use this hallowed phrase to express the ideal that legally and morally all men ought to be treated alike. But if we want to understand what this ideal of equality can or should mean, the first requirement is that we free ourselves from the belief in factual equality.

From the fact that people are very different it follows that, if we treat them equally, the result must be inequality in their actual position,[6] and that the only way to place them in an equal position would be to treat them differently. Equality before the law and material equality are therefore not only different but are in conflict with each other; and we can achieve either the one or the other, but not both at the same time. The equality before the law which freedom requires leads to material inequality. Our argument will be that, though where the state must use coercion for other reasons, it should treat all people alike, the desire of making people more alike in their condition cannot be accepted in a free society as a justification for further and discriminatory coercion.

We do not object to equality as such. It merely happens to be the case that a demand for equality is the professed motive of most of those who desire to impose upon society a preconceived pattern of distribution. Our objection is against all attempts to impress upon society a deliberately chosen pattern of distribution, whether it be an order of equality or of inequality. We shall indeed see that many of those who demand an extension of equality do not really demand equality but a distribution that conforms more closely to human conceptions of individual merit and that their desires are as irreconcilable with freedom as the more strictly egalitarian demands.

If one objects to the use of coercion in order to bring about a more even or a more just distribution, this does not mean that one does not regard these as desirable. But if we wish to preserve a free society, it is essential that we recognize that the desirability of a particular object is not sufficient justification for the use of coercion. One may well feel attracted to a community in which there are no extreme contrasts between rich and poor and may welcome the fact that the general increase in wealth seems gradually to reduce those differences. I fully share these feelings and certainly regard the degree of social equality that the United States has achieved as wholly admirable.

[6] Cf. Plato, *Laws*, vii. 757a: "To unequals equals become unequal." [The Alfred Edward Taylor translation renders the passage as follows "Indeed, equal treatment of the unequal ends in inequality when not qualified by due proportion." *The Collected Dialogues of Plato, Including the Letters*, Edith Hamilton and Huntington Cairns, eds. (Bollingen Series; New York: Pantheon Books, 1961), pp. 1336–37.—Ed.]

There also seems no reason why these widely felt preferences should not guide policy in some respects. Wherever there is a legitimate need for government action and we have to choose between different methods of satisfying such a need, those that incidentally also reduce inequality may well be preferable. If, for example, in the law of intestate succession one kind of provision will be more conducive to equality than another, this may be a strong argument in its favor. It is a different matter, however, if it is demanded that, in order to produce substantive equality, we should abandon the basic postulate of a free society, namely, the limitation of all coercion by equal law. Against this we shall hold that economic inequality is not one of the evils which justify our resorting to discriminatory coercion or privilege as a remedy.

3. Our contention rests on two basic propositions which probably need only be stated to win fairly general assent. The first of them is an expression of the belief in a certain similarity of all human beings: it is the proposition that no man or group of men possesses the capacity to determine conclusively the potentialities of other human beings and that we should certainly never trust anyone invariably to exercise such a capacity. However great the differences between men may be, we have no ground for believing that they will ever be so great as to enable one man's mind in a particular instance to comprehend fully all that another responsible man's mind is capable of.

The second basic proposition is that the acquisition by any member of the community of additional capacities to do things which may be valuable must always be regarded as a gain for that community. It is true that particular people may be worse off because of the superior ability of some new competitor in their field; but any such additional ability in the community is likely to benefit the majority. This implies that the desirability of increasing the abilities and opportunities of any individual does not depend on whether the same can also be done for the others—provided, of course, that others are not thereby deprived of the opportunity of acquiring the same or other abilities which might have been accessible to them had they not been secured by that individual.

Egalitarians generally regard differently those differences in individual capacities which are inborn and those which are due to the influences of environment, or those which are the result of "nature" and those which are the result of "nurture." Neither, be it said at once, has anything to do with moral merit.[7] Though either may greatly affect the value which an individual has for his fellows, no more credit belongs to him for having been born with desirable

[7] Cf. Frank Hyneman Knight, *Freedom and Reform: Essays in Economics and Social Philosophy* (New York: Harper and Brothers, 1947), p. 151: "There is no visible reason why anyone is more or less entitled to the earnings of inherited personal capacities than to those of inherited property in any other form"; and the discussion in Wilhelm Röpke, *Mass und Mitte* (Erlenbach and Zurich: Eugen Rentsch, 1950), pp. 65–75.

qualities than for having grown up under favorable circumstances. The distinction between the two is important only because the former advantages are due to circumstances clearly beyond human control, while the latter are due to factors which we might be able to alter. The important question is whether there is a case for so changing our institutions as to eliminate as much as possible those advantages due to environment. Are we to agree that "all inequalities that rest on birth and inherited property ought to be abolished and none remain unless it is an effect of superior talent and industry?"[8]

The fact that certain advantages rest on human arrangements does not necessarily mean that we could provide the same advantages for all or that, if they are given to some, somebody else is thereby deprived of them. The most important factors to be considered in this connection are the family, inheritance, and education, and it is against the inequality which they produce that criticism is mainly directed. They are, however, not the only important factors of environment. Geographic conditions such as climate and landscape, not to speak of local and sectional differences in cultural and moral traditions, are scarcely less important. We can, however, consider here only the three factors whose effects are most commonly impugned.

So far as the family is concerned, there exists a curious contrast between the esteem most people profess for the institution and their dislike of the fact that being born into a particular family should confer on a person special advantages. It seems to be widely believed that, while useful qualities which a person acquires because of his native gifts under conditions which are the same for all are socially beneficial, the same qualities become somehow undesirable if they are the result of environmental advantages not available to others. Yet it is difficult to see why the same useful quality which is welcomed when it is the result of a person's natural endowment should be less valuable when it is the product of such circumstances as intelligent parents or a good home.

The value which most people attach to the institution of the family rests on the belief that, as a rule, parents can do more to prepare their children for a satisfactory life than anyone else. This means not only that the benefits which particular people derive from their family environment will be different but also that these benefits may operate cumulatively through several generations. What reason can there be for believing that a desirable quality in a person is less valuable to society if it has been the result of family background than if it has not? There is, indeed, good reason to think that there are some

[8] This is the position of Richard Henry Tawney as summarized by John Petrov Plamenatz, "Equality of Opportunity," in *Aspects of Human Equality*, from the Fifteenth Conference on Science, Philosophy, and Religion in Their Relation to the Democratic Way of Life, Columbia University, 1955, Lyman Bryson, ed. (New York: Distributed by Harper, 1956),p. 100. [Tawney explicates his views on equality at some length in his *Equality* (London: Allen and Unwin, 1931).—Ed.]

socially valuable qualities which will be rarely acquired in a single generation but which will generally be formed only by the continuous efforts of two or three. This means simply that there are parts of the cultural heritage of a society that are more effectively transmitted through the family.[9] Granted this, it would be unreasonable to deny that a society is likely to get a better elite if ascent is not limited to one generation, if individuals are not deliberately made to start from the same level, and if children are not deprived of the chance to benefit from the better education and material environment which their parents may be able to provide. To admit this is merely to recognize that belonging to a particular family is part of the individual personality, that society is made up as much of families as of individuals, and that the transmission of the heritage of civilization within the family is as important a tool in man's striving toward better things as is the heredity of beneficial physical attributes.

4. Many people who agree that the family is desirable as an instrument for the transmission of morals, tastes, and knowledge still question the desirability of the transmission of material property. Yet there can be little doubt that, in order that the former may be possible, some continuity of standards, of the external forms of life, is essential, and that this will be achieved only if it is possible to transmit not only immaterial but also material advantages. There is, of course, neither greater merit nor any greater injustice involved in some people being born to wealthy parents than there is in others being born to kind or intelligent parents. The fact is that it is no less of an advantage to the community if at least some children can start with the advantages which at any given time only wealthy homes can offer than if some children inherit great intelligence or are taught better morals at home.

We are not concerned here with the chief argument for private inheritance, namely, that it seems essential as a means to preserve the dispersal in the control of capital and as an inducement for its accumulation. Rather, our concern here is whether the fact that it confers unmerited benefits on some is a valid argument against the institution. It is unquestionably one of the institutional causes of inequality. In the present context we need not inquire whether liberty demands unlimited freedom of bequest. Our problem here is merely whether people ought to be free to pass on to children or others such material possessions as will cause substantial inequality.

---

[9] See William Graham Sumner, *Andrew Jackson* (Standard library ed.; Boston: Houghton Mifflin, 1899), pp. 24–25: "True honor, truthfulness, suppression of individual personal feeling, self-control and courtesy are inculcated best, if not exclusively, by the constant precept and example, in earliest childhood of highbred parents and relatives. There is nothing on earth which it costs more labor to produce than a highbred man. It is also indisputable that home discipline and training ingrain into the character of men the most solid and valuable elements and that, without such training, more civilization means better food and clothes rather than better men."

Once we agree that it is desirable to harness the natural instincts of parents to equip the new generation as well as they can, there seems no sensible ground for limiting this to non-material benefits. The family's function of passing on standards and traditions is closely tied up with the possibility of transmitting material goods. And it is difficult to see how it would serve the true interest of society to limit the gain in material conditions to one generation.

There is also another consideration which, though it may appear somewhat cynical, strongly suggests that if we wish to make the best use of the natural partiality of parents for their children, we ought not to preclude the transmission of property. It seems certain that among the many ways in which those who have gained power and influence might provide for their children, the bequest of a fortune is socially by far the cheapest. Without this outlet, these men would look for other ways of providing for their children, such as placing them in positions which might bring them the income and the prestige that a fortune would have done; and this would cause a waste of resources and an injustice much greater than is caused by the inheritance of property. Such is the case with all societies in which inheritance of property does not exist, including the Communist. Those who dislike the inequalities caused by inheritance should therefore recognize that, men being what they are, it is the least of evils, even from their point of view.

5. Though inheritance used to be the most widely criticized source of inequality, it is today probably no longer so. Egalitarian agitation now tends to concentrate on the unequal advantages due to differences in education. There is a growing tendency to express the desire to secure equality of conditions in the claim that the best education we have learned to provide for some should be made gratuitously available for all and that, if this is not possible, one should not be allowed to get a better education than the rest merely because one's parents are able to pay for it, but only those and all those who can pass a uniform test of ability should be admitted to the benefits of the limited resources of higher education.

The problem of educational policy raises too many issues to allow of their being discussed incidentally under the general heading of equality. We shall have to devote a separate chapter to them at the end of this book. For the present we shall only point out that enforced equality in this field can hardly avoid preventing some from getting the education they otherwise might. Whatever we might do, there is no way of preventing those advantages which only some can have, and which it is desirable that some should have, from going to people who neither individually merit them nor will make as good a use of them as some other person might have done. Such a problem cannot be satisfactorily solved by the exclusive and coercive powers of the state.

It is instructive at this point to glance briefly at the change that the ideal of equality has undergone in this field in modern times. A hundred years ago, at the height of the classical liberal movement, the demand was generally expressed by the phrase *la carrière ouverte aux talents*. It was a demand that all man-made obstacles to the rise of some should be removed, that all privileges of individuals should be abolished, and that what the state contributed to the chance of improving one's conditions should be the same for all. That so long as people were different and grew up in different families this could not assure an equal start was fairly generally accepted. It was understood that the duty of government was not to ensure that everybody had the same prospect of reaching a given position but merely to make available to all on equal terms those facilities which in their nature depended on government action. That the results were bound to be different, not only because the individuals were different, but also because only a small part of the relevant circumstances depended on government action, was taken for granted.

This conception that all should be allowed to try has been largely replaced by the altogether different conception that all must be assured an equal start and the same prospects. This means little less than that the government, instead of providing the same circumstances for all, should aim at controlling all conditions relevant to a particular individual's prospects and so adjust them to his capacities as to assure him of the same prospects as everybody else. Such deliberate adaptation of opportunities to individual aims and capacities would, of course, be the opposite of freedom. Nor could it be justified as a means of making the best use of all available knowledge except on the assumption that government knows best how individual capacities can be used.

When we inquire into the justification of these demands, we find that they rest on the discontent that the success of some people often produces in those that are less successful, or, to put it bluntly, on envy. The modern tendency to gratify this passion and to disguise it in the respectable garment of social justice is developing into a serious threat to freedom. Recently an attempt was made to base these demands on the argument that it ought to be the aim of politics to remove all sources of discontent.[10] This would, of course, necessarily mean that it is the responsibility of government to see that nobody is healthier or possesses a happier temperament, a better-suited spouse or more prospering children, than anybody else. If really all unfulfilled desires have a claim on the community, individual responsibility is at an end. However human, envy is certainly not one of the sources of discontent that a free society can eliminate. It is probably one of the essential conditions for the pres-

---

[10] Charles Anthony Raven Crosland, *The Future of Socialism* (London: Jonathan Cape, 1956), p. 205.

ervation of such a society that we do not countenance envy, not sanction its demands by camouflaging it as social justice, but treat it, in the words of John Stuart Mill, as "that most anti-social and odious of all passions."[11]

6. While most of the strictly egalitarian demands are based on nothing better than envy, we must recognize that much that on the surface appears as a demand for greater equality is in fact a demand for a juster distribution of the good things of this world and springs therefore from much more creditable motives. Most people will object not to the bare fact of inequality but to the fact that the differences in reward do not correspond to any recognizable differences in the merits of those who receive them. The answer commonly given to this is that a free society on the whole achieves this kind of justice.[12] This, however, is an indefensible contention if by justice is meant proportionality of reward to moral merit. Any attempt to found the case for

[11] John Stuart Mill, "On Liberty," in *On Liberty and Considerations on Representative Government*, Ronald Buchanan McCallum, ed. (Oxford: B. Blackwell, 1946), p. 70. See particularly Helmut Schoeck, *Der Neid: Eine Theorie der Gesellschaft* (Freiburg, Munich: Albers, 1966). [English translation by Michael Glenny and Betty Ross, published under the title *Envy: A Theory of Social Behavior* (New York: Harcourt, Brace and World, 1969.)—Ed.]

[12] Cf. Walter Bryce Gallie, "Liberal Morality and Socialist Morality," in *Philosophy, Politics, and Society*, Peter Laslett, ed. (Oxford: Blackwell, 1956), pp. 123–25. The author represents it as the essence of "liberal morality" that it claims that rewards are equal to merit in a free society. This was the position of some nineteenth-century liberals which often weakened their argument. A characteristic example is William Graham Sumner, *What Social Classes Owe to Each Other* (New York: Harper and Brothers, 1883), p. 164. [Hayek notes that this essay appears in *"Freeman,* vol. 6 (Los Angeles, n.d.), p. 141." The publication to which Hayek is referring is in fact vol. 4, no. 1 (n.d.) of a journal with that title and of very limited circulation, published irregularly by a group calling itself the Los Angeles Pamphleteers.—Ed.] Sumner argued that if all "have equal chances so far as chances are provided or limited by society," this will "produce inequal results—that is results which shall be proportioned to the merits of individuals." This is true only if "merit" is used in the sense in which we have used "value," without any moral connotations, but certainly not if it is meant to suggest proportionality to any endeavor to do the good or right thing, or to any subjective effort to conform to an ideal standard.

But, as we shall presently see, Mr. Gallie is right that, in the Aristotelian terms he uses, liberalism aims at commutative justice and socialism at distributive justice. But, like most socialists, he does not see that distributive justice is irreconcilable with freedom in the choice of one's activities: it is the justice of a hierarchic organization, not of a free society.

John Stuart Mill, *Principles of Political Economy, with Some of Their Applications to Social Philosophy*, vol. 2 of *The Collected Works of John Stuart Mill* (Toronto: University of Toronto Press, 1965), bk. 2, chap. 1, p. 210 [similarly, Liberty Fund edition]: "The proportioning of remuneration to work done is really just only in so far as the more or less of the work is a matter of choice: when it depends on natural differences of strength and capacity, this principle of remuneration is in itself an injustice: it gives to those who have; assigning most to those already most favoured by nature." See Gustav Radbruch, *Rechtsphilosophie* (5th ed.; Stuttgart: Koehler, 1956), e.g., p. 187: "Auch das sozialistische Gemeinwesen wird also ein Rechtsstaat sein, ein *Rechtsstaat* freilich, der statt von der ausgleichenden von der austeilenden Gerechtigkeit beherrscht wird." ["The socialist polity will therefore also be a state of law, a *Rechtsstaat* ruled by distributive instead of retributive justice."—Ed.]

freedom on this argument is very damaging to it, since it concedes that material rewards ought to be made to correspond to recognizable merit and then
opposes the conclusion that most people will draw from this by an assertion
which is untrue. The proper answer is that in a free system it is neither desirable nor practicable that material rewards should be made generally to correspond to what men recognize as merit and that it is an essential characteristic
of a free society that an individual's position should not necessarily depend on
the views that his fellows hold about the merit he has acquired.

This contention may appear at first so strange and even shocking that I
will ask the reader to suspend judgment until I have further explained the distinction between value and merit.[13] The difficulty in making the point clear
is due to the fact that the term "merit," which is the only one available to
describe what I mean, is also used in a wider and vaguer sense. It will be used
here exclusively to describe the attributes of conduct that make it deserving

---

[13] Although I believe that this distinction between merit and value is the same as that which
Aristotle and Thomas Aquinas had in mind when they distinguished "distributive justice" from
"commutative justice," I prefer not to tie up the discussion with all the difficulties and confusions which in the course of time have become associated with these traditional concepts. That
what we call here "reward according to merit" corresponds to the Aristotelian distributive justice seems clear. The difficult concept is that of "commutative justice," and to speak of justice
in this sense seems always to cause a little confusion. Cf. Max Salomon, *Der Begriff der Gerechtigkeit
bei Aristoteles: nebst einem Anhang über den Begriff des Tauschgeschäftes* (Leiden: Sijthoff, 1937); and for a
survey of the extensive literature Giorgio del Vecchio, *Die Gerechtigkeit* (2nd ed.; Basel: Verlag für
Recht und Gesellschaft, 1950).

Also see David Hume, *Enquiry Concerning the Principles of Morals*, in *Essays*, vol. 2, p. 187: "were
mankind to execute such a law [to assign the largest possessions to the most extensive virtue, and give
every one the power of doing good, proportioned to his inclination]; so great is the uncertainty of merit,
both from its natural obscurity, and from the self-conceit of each individual, that no determinate rule of conduct would ever result from it; and the total dissolution of society must be the immediate consequence";
Hugo Grotius, *The Jurisprudence of Holland*, Robert Warden Lee, trans. (Oxford: Clarendon Press, 1926),
vol. 1, p. 3: "Of the justice which has regard to right, narrowly understood, the kind which takes account
of merit is called 'distributive justice'; the other kind which gives heed to property is called 'commutative
justice'; the first commonly employs the rule of proportion, the second the rule of simple equality"; Adam
Smith, *The Theory of Moral Sentiments* (London: Printed for A Miller, 1759), pt. 2, sec. 1, pp. 141–69, "Of
the Sense of Merit and Demerit" [Liberty Fund edition, pp. 67–78]; Edwin Cannan, *The History of Local
Rates in England* (2nd ed.; London: P. S. King and Son, 1912), pp. 160–61: "the existing system proportions command over economic goods to the value of services rendered and property possessed. . . . As
against this established state of things, we find that many people, perhaps most people, have somewhere
in their minds two inconsistent and somewhat nebulous ideals . . . according to [the first], command over
economic goods ought to be in proportion to moral merit. . . . The second ideal is the communist one of
equal distribution"; Kenneth Ewart Boulding, *Principles of Economic Policy* (Englewood Cliffs, NJ: Prentice Hall, 1958), p. 85, remarks that "justice as a situation in which everybody gets what he deserves, may
be called the *merit standard*," and points out that "it would be a dangerous ethical fallacy to equate desert
with contribution." Also see Arthur William Hope Adkins, *Merit and Responsibility: A Study in Greek Values*
(Oxford: Clarendon Press, 1960), who, unfortunately, employs the term "merit" for what I call "value" and
"responsibility" for what I have called "merit."

of praise, that is, the moral character of the action and not the value of the achievement.[14]

As we have seen throughout our discussion, the value that the performance or capacity of a person has to his fellows has no necessary connection with its ascertainable merit in this sense. The inborn as well as the acquired gifts of a person clearly have a value to his fellows which does not depend on any credit due to him for possessing them. There is little a man can do to alter the fact that his special talents are very common or exceedingly rare. A good mind or a fine voice, a beautiful face or a skilful hand, and a ready wit or an attractive personality are in a large measure as independent of a person's efforts as the opportunities or the experiences he has had. In all these instances the value which a person's capacities or services have for us and for which he is recompensed has little relation to anything that we can call moral merit or deserts. Our problem is whether it is desirable that people should enjoy advantages in proportion to the benefits which their fellows derive from their activities or whether the distribution of these advantages should be based on other men's views of their merits.

Reward according to merit must in practice mean reward according to assessable merit, merit that other people can recognize and agree upon and not merit merely in the sight of some higher power. Assessable merit in this sense presupposes that we can ascertain that a man has done what some accepted rule of conduct demanded of him and that this has cost him some pain and effort. Whether this has been the case cannot be judged by the result: merit is not a matter of the objective outcome but of subjective effort. The attempt to achieve a valuable result may be highly meritorious but a complete failure, and full success may be entirely the result of accident and thus without merit. If we know that a man has done his best, we will often wish to see him rewarded irrespective of the result; and if we know that a most valuable achievement is almost entirely due to luck or favorable circumstances, we will give little credit to the author.

We may wish that we were able to draw this distinction in every instance. In fact, we can do so only rarely with any degree of assurance. It is possible only

---

[14] The terminological difficulties arise from the fact that we use the word merit also in an objective sense and will speak of the "merit" of an idea, a book, or a picture, irrespective of the merit acquired by the person who has created them. Sometimes the word is also used to describe what we regard as the "true" value of some achievement as distinguished from its market value. Yet even a human achievement which has the greatest value or merit in this sense is not necessarily proof of moral merit on the part of him to whom it is due. It seems that our use has the sanction of philosophical tradition. Cf., for instance, David Hume, *Treatise of Human Nature* [bk. 3, pt. 2, sec. 1], vol. 2, p. 252: "The external performance has no merit. We must look within to find the moral quality. . . . The ultimate object of our praise and approbation is the motive that produced them."

where we possess all the knowledge which was at the disposal of the acting person, including a knowledge of his skill and confidence, his state of mind and his feelings, his capacity for attention, his energy and persistence, etc. The possibility of a true judgment of merit thus depends on the presence of precisely those conditions whose general absence is the main argument for liberty. It is because we want people to use knowledge which we do not possess that we let them decide for themselves. But insofar as we want them to be free to use capacities and knowledge of facts which we do not have, we are not in a position to judge the merit of their achievements. To decide on merit presupposes that we can judge whether people have made such use of their opportunities as they ought to have made and how much effort of will or self-denial this has cost them; it presupposes also that we can distinguish between that part of their achievement which is due to circumstances within their control and that part which is not.

7. The incompatibility of reward according to merit with freedom to choose one's pursuit is most evident in those areas where the uncertainty of the outcome is particularly great and our individual estimates of the chances of various kinds of effort very different.[15] In those speculative efforts which we call "research" or "exploration," or in economic activities which we commonly describe as "speculation," we cannot expect to attract those best qualified for them unless we give the successful ones all the credit or gain, though many others may have striven as meritoriously. For the same reason that nobody can know beforehand who will be the successful ones, nobody can say who has earned greater merit. It would clearly not serve our purpose if we let all who have honestly striven share in the prize. Moreover, to do so would make it necessary that somebody have the right to decide who is to be allowed to strive for it. If in their pursuit of uncertain goals people are to use their own knowledge and capacities, they must be guided, not by what other people think they ought to do, but by the value others attach to the result at which they aim.

What is so obviously true about those undertakings which we commonly regard as risky is scarcely less true of any chosen object we decide to pursue. Any such decision is beset with uncertainty, and if the choice is to be as wise as it is humanly possible to make it, the alternative results anticipated must be labeled according to their value. If the remuneration did not correspond to

---

[15] Cf. the important essay by Armen Albert Alchian, "Uncertainty, Evolution, and Economic Theory," *Journal of Political Economy*, 58 (1950): 211–21, esp. 213–14, sec. 2, headed "Success Is Based on Results, Not Motivation." It probably is also no accident that the American economist who has done most to advance our understanding of a free society, Frank Hyneman Knight, began his professional career with a study of *Risk, Uncertainty, and Profit* (Boston: Houghton Mifflin Company, 1921). Cf. also Bertrand de Jouvenel, *Power: The Natural History of its Growth* (London: Hutchinson, 1948), p. 298. [There is a Liberty Fund edition of this work, released under the title *On Power*.]

the value that the product of a man's efforts has for his fellows, he would have no basis for deciding whether the pursuit of a given object is worth the effort and risk. He would necessarily have to be told what to do, and some other person's estimate of what was the best use of his capacities would have to determine both his duties and his remuneration.[16]

The fact is, of course, that we do not wish people to earn a maximum of merit but to achieve a maximum of usefulness at a minimum of pain and sacrifice and therefore a minimum of merit. Not only would it be impossible for us to reward all merit justly, but it would not even be desirable that people should aim chiefly at earning a maximum of merit. Any attempt to induce them to do this would necessarily result in people being rewarded differently for the same service. And it is only the value of the result that we can judge with any degree of confidence, not the different degrees of effort and care that it has cost different people to achieve it.

The prizes that a free society offers for the result serve to tell those who strive for them how much effort they are worth. However, the same prizes will go to all those who produce the same result, regardless of effort. What is true here of the remuneration for the same services rendered by different people is even more true of the relative remuneration for different services requiring different gifts and capacities: they will have little relation to merit. The market will generally offer for services of any kind the value they will have for those who benefit from them; but it will rarely be known whether it was necessary to offer so much in order to obtain these services, and often, no doubt, the community could have had them for much less. The pianist who was reported not long ago to have said that he would perform even if he had to pay for the privilege probably described the position of many who earn large incomes from activities which are also their chief pleasure.

8. Though most people regard as very natural the claim that nobody should be rewarded more than he deserves for his pain and effort, it is nevertheless based on a colossal presumption. It presumes that we are able to judge in every individual instance how well people use the different opportunities and talents given to them and how meritorious their achievements are in the light

---

[16] It is often maintained that justice requires that remuneration be proportional to the unpleasantness of the job and that for this reason the street cleaner or the sewage worker ought to be paid more than the doctor or office worker. This, indeed, would seem to be the consequence of the principle of remuneration according to merit (or "distributive justice"). In a market such a result would come about only if all people were equally skilful in all jobs so that those who could earn as much as others in the more pleasant occupations would have to be paid more to undertake the distasteful ones. In the actual world those unpleasant jobs provide those whose usefulness in the more attractive jobs is small an opportunity to earn more than they could elsewhere. That persons who have little to offer their fellows should be able to earn an income similar to that of the rest only at a much greater sacrifice is inevitable in any arrangement under which the individual is allowed to choose his own sphere of usefulness.

of all the circumstances which have made them possible. It presumes that some human beings are in a position to determine conclusively what a person is worth and are entitled to determine what he may achieve. It presumes, then, what the argument for liberty specifically rejects: that we can and do know all that guides a person's action.

A society in which the position of the individuals was made to correspond to human ideas of moral merit would therefore be the exact opposite of a free society. It would be a society in which people were rewarded for duty performed instead of for success, in which every move of every individual was guided by what other people thought he ought to do, and in which the individual was thus relieved of the responsibility and the risk of decision. But if nobody's knowledge is sufficient to guide all human action, there is also no human being who is competent to reward all efforts according to merit.

In our individual conduct we generally act on the assumption that it is the value of a person's performance and not his merit that determines our obligation to him. Whatever may be true in more intimate relations, in the ordinary business of life we do not feel that, because a man has rendered us a service at a great sacrifice, our debt to him is determined by this, so long as we could have had the same service provided with ease by somebody else. In our dealings with other men we feel that we are doing justice if we recompense value rendered with equal value, without inquiring what it might have cost the particular individual to supply us with these services. What determines our responsibility is the advantage we derive from what others offer us, not their merit in providing it. We also expect in our dealings with others to be remunerated not according to our subjective merit but according to what our services are worth to them. Indeed, so long as we think in terms of our relations to particular people, we are generally quite aware that the mark of the free man is to be dependent for his livelihood not on other people's views of his merit but solely on what he has to offer them. It is only when we think of our position or our income as determined by "society" as a whole that we demand reward according to merit.

Though moral value or merit is a species of value, not all value is moral value, and most of our judgments of value are not moral judgments. That this must be so in a free society is a point of cardinal importance; and the failure to distinguish between value and merit has been the source of serious confusion. We do not necessarily admire all activities whose product we value; and in most instances where we value what we get, we are in no position to assess the merit of those who have provided it for us. If a man's ability in a given field is more valuable after thirty years' work than it was earlier, this is independent of whether these thirty years were most profitable and enjoyable or whether they were a time of unceasing sacrifice and worry. If the pursuit of a hobby produces a special skill or an accidental invention turns out to be extremely useful to others, the fact that there is little merit in it does not make it any less valuable than if the result had been produced by painful effort.

This difference between value and merit is not peculiar to any one type of society—it would exist anywhere. We might, of course, attempt to make rewards correspond to merit instead of value, but we are not likely to succeed in this. In attempting it, we would destroy the incentives which enable people to decide for themselves what they should do. Moreover, it is more than doubtful whether even a fairly successful attempt to make rewards correspond to merit would produce a more attractive or even a tolerable social order. A society in which it was generally presumed that a high income was proof of merit and a low income of the lack of it, in which it was universally believed that position and remuneration corresponded to merit, in which there was no other road to success than the approval of one's conduct by the majority of one's fellows, would probably be much more unbearable to the unsuccessful ones than one in which it was frankly recognized that there was no necessary connection between merit and success.[17]

It would probably contribute more to human happiness if, instead of trying to make remuneration correspond to merit, we made clearer how uncertain is the connection between value and merit. We are probably all much too ready to ascribe personal merit where there is, in fact, only superior value. The possession by an individual or a group of a superior civilization or education certainly represents an important value and constitutes an asset for the community to which they belong; but it usually constitutes little merit. Popularity and esteem do not depend more on merit than does financial success. It is, in fact, largely because we are so used to assuming an often non-existent merit wherever we find value that we balk when, in particular instances, the discrepancy is too large to be ignored.

There is every reason why we ought to endeavor to honor special merit where it has gone without adequate reward. But the problem of rewarding

---

[17] Cf. Crosland, *The Future of Socialism*, p. 235: "Even if all the failures could be convinced that they had an equal chance, their discontent would still not be assuaged; indeed it might actually be intensified. When opportunities are known to be unequal, and the selection clearly biased towards wealth or lineage, people can comfort themselves for failure by saying that they never had a proper chance—the system was unfair, the scales too heavily weighted against them. But if the selection is obviously by merit, this source of comfort disappears, and failure induces a total sense of inferiority, with no excuse or consolation; and this, by a natural quirk of human nature, actually increases the envy and resentment at the success of others." Cf. also chap. 14 at n. 8 below. [Note 8 refers to several articles dealing with the notion of "Nulla poena sine lege" and its central importance to the rule of law.—Ed.] I have not yet seen Michael Dunlop Young, *The Rise of the Meritocracy, 1870–2023: An Essay on Education and Equality* (London: Thames and Hudson, 1958) which, judging from reviews, appears to bring out these problems very clearly. [The American edition carries the title *The Rise of the Meritocracy, 1870–2023: The New Elite of Our Social Revolution* (New York: Random House, 1959).—Ed.]

action of outstanding merit which we wish to be widely known as an example is different from that of the incentives on which the ordinary functioning of society rests. A free society produces institutions in which, for those who prefer it, a man's advancement depends on the judgment of some superior or of the majority of his fellows. Indeed, as organizations grow larger and more complex, the task of ascertaining the individual's contribution will become more difficult; and it will become increasingly necessary that, for many, merit in the eyes of the managers rather than the ascertainable value of the contribution should determine the rewards. So long as this does not produce a situation in which a single comprehensive scale of merit is imposed upon the whole society, so long as a multiplicity of organizations compete with one another in offering different prospects, this is not merely compatible with freedom but extends the range of choice open to the individual.

9. Justice, like liberty and coercion, is a concept which, for the sake of clarity, ought to be confined to the deliberate treatment of men by other men. It is an aspect of the intentional determination of those conditions of people's lives that are subject to such control. Insofar as we want the efforts of individuals to be guided by their own views about prospects and chances, the results of the individual's efforts are necessarily unpredictable, and the question as to whether the resulting distribution of incomes is just has no meaning.[18] Justice does require that those conditions of people's lives that are determined by government be provided equally for all. But equality of those conditions must lead to inequality of results. Neither the equal provision of particular public facilities nor the equal treatment of different partners in our voluntary dealings with one another will secure reward that is proportional to merit. Reward for merit is reward for obeying the wishes of others in what we do, not compensation for the benefits we have conferred upon them by doing what we thought best.

It is, in fact, one of the objections against attempts by government to fix income scales that the state must attempt to be just in all it does. Once the principle of reward according to merit is accepted as the just foundation for the distribution of incomes, justice would require that all who desire it should be rewarded according to that principle. Soon it would also be demanded that the same principle be applied to all and that incomes not in proportion to recognizable merit not be tolerated. Even an attempt merely to distinguish between those incomes or gains which are "earned" and those which are not

---

[18] See the interesting discussion in Robin George Collingwood, "Economics as a Philosophical Science," *International Journal of Ethics*, 36 (1926), who concludes (p. 174): "A just price, a just wage, a just rate of interest, is a contradiction in terms. The question what a person ought to get in return for his goods and labor is a question absolutely devoid of meaning. The only valid questions are what he *can* get in return for his goods or labor, and whether he ought to sell them at all."

will set up a principle which the state will have to try to apply but cannot in fact apply generally.[19] And every such attempt at deliberate control of some remunerations is bound to create further demands for new controls. The principle of distributive justice, once introduced, would not be fulfilled until the whole of society was organized in accordance with it. This would produce a kind of society which in all essential respects would be the opposite of a free society—a society in which authority decided what the individual was to do and how he was to do it.

10. In conclusion we must briefly look at another argument on which the demands for a more equal distribution are frequently based, though it is rarely explicitly stated. This is the contention that membership in a particular community or nation entitles the individual to a particular material standard that is determined by the general wealth of the group to which he belongs. This demand is in curious conflict with the desire to base distribution on personal merit. There is clearly no merit in being born into a particular community, and no argument of justice can be based on the accident of a particular individual's being born in one place rather than another. A relatively wealthy community in fact regularly confers advantages on its poorest members unknown to those born in poor communities. In a wealthy community the only justification its members can have for insisting on further advantages is that there is much private wealth that the government can confiscate and redistribute and that men who constantly see such wealth being enjoyed by others will have a stronger desire for it than those who know of it only abstractly, if at all.

There is no obvious reason why the joint efforts of the members of any group to ensure the maintenance of law and order and to organize the provision of certain services should give the members a claim to a particular share in the wealth of this group. Such claims would be especially difficult to defend where those who advanced them were unwilling to concede the same rights to those who did not belong to the same nation or community. The recognition of such claims on a national scale would in fact only create a new kind of collective (but not less exclusive) property right in the resources of the nation that could not be justified on the same grounds as individual property. Few people

---

[19] It is, of course, possible to give the distinction between "earned" and "unearned" incomes, gains, or increments a fairly precise legal meaning, but it then rapidly ceases to correspond to the moral distinction which provides its justification. Any serious attempt to apply the moral distinction in practice soon meets the same insuperable difficulties as any attempt to assess subjective merit. How little these difficulties are generally understood by philosophers (except in rare instances, as that quoted in the preceding note) is well illustrated by a discussion in Lizzie Susan Stebbing, *Thinking to Some Purpose* (Pelican Books; Harmondsworth, UK: Penguin Books, 1939), p. 184, in which, as an illustration of a distinction which is clear but not sharp, she chooses that between "legitimate" and "excess" profits and asserts: "The distinction is clear between 'excess profits' (or 'profiteering') and 'legitimate profits,' although it is not a sharp distinction."

would be prepared to recognize the justice of these demands on a world scale. And the bare fact that within a given nation the majority had the actual power to enforce such demands, while in the world as a whole it did not yet have it, would hardly make them more just.

There are good reasons why we should endeavor to use whatever political organization we have at our disposal to make provision for the weak or infirm or for the victims of unforeseeable disaster. It may well be true that the most effective method of providing against certain risks common to all citizens of a state is to give every citizen protection against those risks. The level on which such provisions against common risks can be made will necessarily depend on the general wealth of the community.

It is an entirely different matter, however, to suggest that those who are poor, merely in the sense that there are those in the same community who are richer, are entitled to a share in the wealth of the latter or that being born into a group that has reached a particular level of civilization and comfort confers a title to a share in all its benefits. The fact that all citizens have an interest in the common provision of some services is no justification for anyone's claiming as a right a share in all the benefits. It may set a standard for what some ought to be willing to give, but not for what anyone can demand.

National groups will become more and more exclusive as the acceptance of this view that we have been contending against spreads. Rather than admit people to the advantages that living in their country offers, a nation will prefer to keep them out altogether; for, once admitted, they will soon claim as a right a particular share in its wealth. The conception that citizenship or even residence in a country confers a claim to a particular standard of living is becoming a serious source of international friction. And since the only justification for applying the principle within a given country is that its government has the power to enforce it, we must not be surprised if we find the same principle being applied by force on an international scale. Once the right of the majority to the benefits that minorities enjoy is recognized on a national scale, there is no reason why this should stop at the boundaries of the existing states.

MAJORITY RULE

Though men be much governed by interest, yet even interest itself, and all human affairs, are entirely governed by opinion. —David Hume

1. Equality before the law leads to the demand that all men should also have the same share in making the law. This is the point where traditional liberalism and the democratic movement meet. Their main concerns are nevertheless different. Liberalism (in the European nineteenth-century meaning of the word, to which we shall adhere throughout this chapter) is concerned mainly with limiting the coercive powers of all government, whether democratic or not, whereas the dogmatic democrat knows only one limit to government—current majority opinion. The difference between the two ideals stands out most clearly if we name their opposites: for democracy it is authoritarian government; for liberalism it is totalitarianism. Neither of the two systems necessarily excludes the opposite of the other: a democracy may well wield totalitarian powers, and it is conceivable that an authoritarian government may act on liberal principles.[1]

The quotation at the head of the chapter is taken from David Hume, *Essays* ["Whether the British Government inclines more to Absolute Monarchy, or to a Republic" (Essay 9)], vol. 1, p. 125 [Liberty Fund edition, p. 51]. The idea apparently derives from the great debates of the preceding century. William Haller reprints as the Frontispiece to vol. 1 of the *Tracts on Liberty in the Puritan Revolution, 1638–1647* (3 vols.; New York: Columbia University Press, 1934), a broadside with an engraving by Wenceslas Hollar, dated 1641 and headed "The World Is Ruled and Governed by Opinion."

[1] On the origin of the conception of the "total' state and on the opposition of totalitarianism to liberalism, but not to democracy, see the early discussion in Heinz Otto Ziegler, *Autoritärer oder totaler Staat* [Reich und Staat in Geschichte und Gegenwart, no. 90] (Tübingen: Mohr, 1932), esp. pp. 6–14; cf. Franz Leopold Neumann, *The Democratic and the Authoritarian State: Essays in Political and Legal Theory* (Glencoe, IL: Free Press, 1957). The view of what throughout this chapter we shall call the "dogmatic democrats" may be clearly seen in Edwin Mims, Jr., *The Majority of the People* (New York: Modern Age Books, 1941), and Henry Steele Commager, *Majority Rule and Minority Rights* [James W. Richards Lectures in American History, the University of Virginia] (New York: Oxford University Press, 1943).

Like most terms in our field, the word "democracy" is also used in a wider and vaguer sense. But if it is used strictly to describe a method of government—namely, majority rule—it clearly refers to a problem different from that of liberalism. Liberalism is a doctrine about what the law ought to be, democracy a doctrine about the manner of determining what will be the law. Liberalism regards it as desirable that only what the majority accepts should in fact be law, but it does not believe that this is therefore necessarily good law. Its aim, indeed, is to persuade the majority to observe certain principles. It accepts majority rule as a method of deciding, but not as an authority for what the decision ought to be. To the doctrinaire democrat the fact that the majority wants something is sufficient ground for regarding it as good; for him the will of the majority determines not only what is law but what is good law.

About this difference between the liberal and the democratic ideal there exists widespread agreement.[2] There are, however, those who use the word

[2] Cf., e.g., José Ortega y Gasset, *Invertebrate Spain*, Mildred Adams, trans. (New York: W. W. Norton, 1937), p. 125: "Liberalism and Democracy happen to be two things which begin by having nothing to do with each other, and end by having, so far as tendencies are concerned, meanings that are mutually antagonistic. Democracy and Liberalism are two answers to two completely different questions.

"Democracy answers this question—'Who ought to exercise the public power?' The answer it gives is—the exercise of public power belongs to the citizens as a body.

"But this question does not touch on what should be the realm of the public power. It is solely concerned with determining to whom such power belongs. Democracy proposes that we all rule; that is, that we are sovereign in all social acts.

"Liberalism, on the other hand, answers this other question,—'regardless of who exercises the public power, what should its limits be?' The answer it gives—'Whether the public power is exercised by an autocrat or by the people, it cannot be absolute: the individual has rights which are over and above any interference by the state.'"

[Volume 2 of the *Obras Completas (Sobre la razón histórica)*, Paulino Garagorri, ed. (Madrid: Alianza 1979), shows this quotation as appearing not in *España Invertebrada* but rather in one of Ortega's articles that was published in *El Espectador* in 1927 entitled "Ideas de los Castillos: Liberalismo y Democracia." The Spanish reads:

"Liberalismo y democracia son dos cosas que empiezan por no tener nada que ver entre sí, y acaban por ser, en cuanto tendencias, de sentido antagónico.

"Democracia y liberalismo son dos respuestas a dos cuestiones de derecho político completamente distintas.

"La democracia responde a esta pregunta: ¿Quién debe ejercer el Poder público? La respuesta es: el ejercicio del Poder público corresponde a la colectividad de los ciudadanos.

"Pero en esa pregunta no se habla de qué extensión deba tener el Poder público. Se trata sólo de determinar el sujeto a quien el mando compete. La democracia propone que mandemos todos; es decir: que todos intervengamos soberanamente en los hechos sociales.

"El liberalismo, en cambio, responde a esta otra pregunta: ejerza quienquiera el Poder público, ¿cuáles deben ser los límites de éste? La respuesta suena así: el Poder

"liberty" in the sense of political liberty and are led by this to identify liberalism with democracy. For them the ideal of liberty can say nothing about what the aim of democratic action ought to be: every condition that democracy creates is, by definition, a condition of liberty. This seems, to say the least, a very confusing use of words.

While liberalism is one of those doctrines concerning the scope and purpose of government from which democracy has to choose, the latter, being a method, indicates nothing about the aims of government. Though "democratic" is often used today to describe particular aims of policy that happen to be popular, especially certain egalitarian ones, there is no necessary con-

---

público, ejérzalo un autócrata o el pueblo, no puede ser absoluto, sino que las personas tienen derechos previos a toda injerencia del Estado. Es, pues, la tendencia a limitar la intervención del Poder público." (pp. 416–17).—Ed.]

See also the same author's *The Revolt of the Masses* (London: Allen and Unwin, 1932), p. 83. No less emphatic, from the dogmatic democratic position, is Max Lerner, "Minority Rule and the Constitutional Tradition," in *The Constitution Reconsidered*, Conyers Read, ed. (New York: Columbia University Press, 1938), p. 199: "When I speak of *democracy* here, I want to distinguish it sharply from *liberalism*. There is no greater confusion in the layman's mind today than the tendency to identify the two." Cf. also Hans Kelsen, "Foundations of Democracy," *Ethics*, 66, no. 1, pt. 2 (1955): 3: "It is of importance to be aware that the principle of democracy and that of liberalism are not identical, that there exists even a certain antagonism between them." Also Ruth Fulton Benedict, "Primitive Freedom," *Atlantic Monthly*, 30 (1942): 760: "But being a democracy has not itself guaranteed the blessings of liberty."

One of the best historical accounts of the relation is to be found in Franz Schnabel, *Deutsche Geschichte im neunzehnten Jahrhundert*, Vol. 2: *Monarchie und Volkssouveränität* (4 vols.; Freiburg im Breisgau: Herder, 1933), p. 98: "Liberalismus und Demokratie waren also nicht sich ausschließende Gegensätze, sondern handelten von zwei verschiedenen Dingen: der Liberalismus sprach vom Umfang der staatlichen Wirksamkeit, die Demokratie vom Inhaber der staatlichen Souveränität." ["Liberalism and democracy were not, then, mutually exclusive nor opposites; rather they addressed two different things. Liberalism spoke to the extent of the government's potency while democracy had reference to those in whose hands the state's sovereignty rested."—Ed.] Cf. also Abbott Lawrence Lowell, "Democracy and Liberty," in *Essays on Government* (Boston: Houghton Mifflin, 1889), esp. pp. 50–117; Carl Schmitt, *Die geistesgeschichtliche Lage des heutigen Parlamentarismus* (Munich: Duncker und Humblot, 1926); Gustav Radbruch, *Rechtsphilosophie* (4th ed.; Stuttgart: K. F. Koehler, 1950), pp. 137ff., esp. p. 156–62; Benedetto Croce, "Liberalism as a Concept of Life," *Politics and Morals* (New York: Philosophical Library, 1945); and Leopold von Wiese, "Liberalismus und Demokratismus in ihren Zusammenhängen und Gegensätzen," *Zeitschrift für Politik*, 9 (1916): 407–25; Heinrich Ritter von Srbik, *Deutsche Einheit: Idee und Wirklichkeit vom Heiligen Reich bis Königgrätz* (4 vols.; Munich: F. Bruckmann KG, 1940), vol. 1, p. 245; Gerhard Ritter, *Vom sittlichen Problem der Macht* (Bern: A. Francke AG. Verlag, 1948), pp. 106 and 118; Peter Rossi, "Liberismo e regime parlamentare in Gaetano Mosca," *Giornale degli Economisti e Annali di Economia*, n.s., 8 (1949): 621–34; Werner Kägi, "Rechtsstaat und Demokratie: Antinomie und Synthese," in *Demokratie und Rechtsstaat: Festgabe zum 60. Geburtstag von Zaccaria Giacometti* (Zürich: Polygraphischer Verlag, 1953), pp. 107–42. A useful survey of some of the literature is Josef Thür, *Demokratie und Liberalismus in ihrem gegenseitigen Verhältnis* (dissertation; Bischofszell: Buchdruckerei L. Hildebrand, 1944). See also Konrad von Orelli, *Das Verhältnis von Demokratie und Gewaltenteilung und seine Wandlungen insbesondere im schweizerischen Bunde* (dissertation; Wädenswil: Villiger, 1947).

nection between democracy and any one view about how the powers of the majority ought to be used. In order to know what it is that we want others to accept, we need other criteria than the current opinion of the majority, which is an irrelevant factor in the process by which opinion is formed. It certainly provides no answer to the question of how a man ought to vote or of what is desirable—unless we assume, as many of the dogmatic democrats seem to assume, that a person's class position invariably teaches him to recognize his true interests and that therefore the vote of the majority always expresses the best interests of the majority.

2. The current undiscriminating use of the word "democratic" as a general term of praise is not without danger. It suggests that, because democracy is a good thing, it is always a gain for mankind if it is extended. This may sound self-evident, but it is nothing of the kind.

There are at least two respects in which it is almost always possible to extend democracy: the range of persons entitled to vote and the range of issues that are decided by democratic procedure. In neither respect can it be seriously contended that every possible extension is a gain or that the principle of democracy demands that it be indefinitely extended. Yet in the discussion of almost any particular issue the case for democracy is commonly presented as if the desirability of extending it as far as possible were indisputable.

That this is not so is implicitly admitted by practically everybody so far as the right to vote is concerned. It would be difficult on any democratic theory to regard every possible extension of the franchise as an improvement. We speak of universal adult suffrage, but the limits of suffrage are in fact largely determined by considerations of expediency. The usual age limit of twenty-one and the exclusion of criminals, resident foreigners, non-resident citizens, and the inhabitants of special regions or territories are generally accepted as reasonable. It is also by no means obvious that proportional representation is better because it seems more democratic.[3] It can scarcely be said that equality before the law necessarily requires that all adults should have the vote; the principle would operate if the same impersonal rule applied to all. If only persons over forty, or only income-earners, or only heads of households, or only literate persons were given the vote, this would scarcely be more of an infringement of the principle than the restrictions which are generally accepted. It is also possible for reasonable people to argue that the ideals of democracy would be better served if, say, all the servants of government or all recipients of public charity were excluded from the vote.[4] If in the Western

[3] See Ferdinand Aloys Hermens, *Democracy or Anarchy? A Study of Proportional Representation* (Notre Dame, IN: Review of Politics, Notre Dame University, 1941).

[4] It is useful to remember that in the oldest and most successful of European democracies, Switzerland, women are still excluded from the vote and apparently with the approval of the majority of them. It also seems possible that in primitive conditions only a suffrage confined, say,

world universal adult suffrage seems the best arrangement, this does not prove that it is required by some basic principle.

We should also remember that the right of the majority is usually recognized only within a given country and that what happens to be one country is not always a natural or obvious unit. We certainly do not regard it as right that the citizens of a large country should dominate those of a small adjoining country merely because they are more numerous. There is as little reason why the majority of the people who have joined for some purposes, be it as a nation or some supernational organization, should be regarded as entitled to extend the scope of their power as far as they please. The current theory of democracy suffers from the fact that it is usually developed with some ideal homogeneous community in view and then applied to the very imperfect and often arbitrary units which the existing states constitute.

These remarks are meant only to show that even the most dogmatic democrat can hardly claim that every extension of democracy is a good thing. However strong the general case for democracy, it is not an ultimate or absolute value and must be judged by what it will achieve. It is probably the best method of achieving certain ends, but not an end in itself.[5] Though there is a strong presumption in favor of the democratic method of deciding where it is obvious that some collective action is required, the problem of whether or not it is desirable to extend collective control must be decided on other grounds than the principle of democracy as such.

3. The democratic and the liberal traditions thus agree that whenever state action is required, and particularly whenever coercive rules have to be laid down, the decision ought to be made by the majority. They differ, however, on the scope of the state action that is to be guided by democratic decision. While the dogmatic democrat regards it as desirable that as many issues as possible be decided by majority vote, the liberal believes that there are definite limits to the range of questions which should be thus decided. The dogmatic democrat feels, in particular, that any current majority ought to have the right to decide what powers it has and how to exercise them, while the liberal regards it as important that the powers of any temporary majority be lim-

---

to landowners would produce a legislature sufficiently independent of the government to exercise effective control over it. [Women's suffrage in Switzerland was introduced at the cantonal level in 1971 and enshrined in the Swiss Constitution in 1985.—Ed.]

[5] Cf. Frederic William Maitland, *The Collected Papers of Frederic William Maitland, Downing Professor of the Laws of England* (3 vols.; Cambridge: Cambridge University Press, 1911), vol. 1, p. 84: "Those who took the road to democracy to be the road to freedom mistook temporary means for an ultimate end." Also Joseph Alois Schumpeter, *Capitalism, Socialism, and Democracy* (New York: Harper and Brothers, 1942), p. 242: "Democracy is a political *method*, that is to say, a certain type of institutional arrangement for arriving at political—legislative and administrative—decisions and hence incapable of being an end in itself, irrespective of what decisions it will produce under given historical conditions."

ited by long-term principles. To him it is not from a mere act of will of the momentary majority but from a wider agreement on common principles that a majority decision derives its authority.

The crucial conception of the doctrinaire democrat is that of popular sovereignty. This means to him that majority rule is unlimited and unlimitable. The ideal of democracy, originally intended to prevent all arbitrary power, thus becomes the justification for a new arbitrary power. Yet the authority of democratic decision rests on its being made by the majority of a community which is held together by certain beliefs common to most members; and it is necessary that the majority submit to these common principles even when it may be in its immediate interest to violate them. It is irrelevant that this view used to be expressed in terms of the "law of nature" or the "social contract," conceptions which have lost their appeal. The essential point remains: it is the acceptance of such common principles that makes a collection of people a community. And this common acceptance is the indispensable condition for a free society. A group of men normally become a society not by giving themselves laws but by obeying the same rules of conduct.[6] This means that the power of the majority is limited by those commonly held principles and that there is no legitimate power beyond them. Clearly, it is necessary for people to come to an agreement as to how necessary tasks are to be performed, and it is reasonable that this should be decided by the majority; but it is not obvious that this same majority must also be entitled to determine what it is competent to do. There is no reason why there should not be things which nobody has power to do. Lack of sufficient agreement on the need of certain uses of coercive power should mean that nobody can legitimately exercise it. If we recognize rights of minorities, this implies that the power of the majority ultimately derives from, and is limited by, the principles which the minorities also accept.

The principle that whatever government does should be agreed to by the

---

[6] Cf. Edward Adamson Hoebel, *The Law of Primitive Man: A Study in Comparative Legal Dynamics* (Cambridge, MA: Harvard University Press, 1954), p. 100, and Fritz Fleiner, *Tradition, Dogma, Entwicklung als aufbauende Kräfte der schweizerischen Demokratie* (Zurich: O. Füssli, 1933), reprinted in the author's *Ausgewählte Schriften und Reden* (Zurich: Polygraphischer Verlag, 1941), pp. 288–302; also Carl Menger, *Untersuchungen*, p. 277: "Das Volksrecht in seiner ursprünglichsten Form ist solcherart allerdings nicht das Ergebnis eines Vertrags oder einer auf die Sicherung des Gemeinwohls hinzielenden Reflexion. Es ist aber auch nicht, wie die historische Schule behauptet, mit dem Volke zugleich gegeben; es ist vielmehr älter, als die Erscheinung dieses letztern, ja es ist eines der stärksten Bindemittel, durch welches die Bevölkerung eines Territoriums zu einem Volke wird und zu einer staatlichen Organisation gelangt." ["National law in its most original form is thus, to be sure, not the result of a contract or a reflection aiming at the assurance of the common welfare. Nor is it, indeed, given with the nation, as the historical school asserts. Rather, it is older than the appearance of the latter. Indeed, it is one of the strongest ties by which the population of a territory becomes a nation and achieves state organization." (Carl Menger, *Investigations into the Method of the Social Sciences*, Francis J. Nock, trans. [Grove City, PA: Libertarian Press, Inc., 1996], p. 215.)—Ed.]

majority does not therefore necessarily require that the majority be morally entitled to do what it likes. There can clearly be no moral justification for any majority granting its members privileges by laying down rules which discriminate in their favor. Democracy is not necessarily unlimited government. Nor is a democratic government any less in need of built-in safeguards of individual liberty than any other. It was, indeed, at a comparatively late stage in the history of modern democracy that great demagogues began to argue that since the power was now in the hands of the people, there was no longer any need for limiting that power.[7] It is when it is contended that "in a democracy right is what the majority makes it to be"[8] that democracy degenerates into demagoguery.

4. If democracy is a means rather than an end, its limits must be determined in the light of the purpose we want it to serve. There are three chief arguments by which democracy can be justified, each of which may be regarded as conclusive. The first is that, whenever it is necessary that one of several conflicting opinions should prevail and when one would have to be made to prevail by force if need be, it is less wasteful to determine which has the stronger support by counting numbers than by fighting. Democracy is the only method of peaceful change that man has yet discovered.[9]

---

[7] Cf., e.g., Joseph Chamberlain's speech to the "Eighty" Club, April 28, 1885 (reported in the *Times* [London], April 29, 1885): "When government was represented only by the authority of the Crown and the views of a particular class, I can understand that it was the first duty of men who valued their freedom to restrict its authority and to limit its expenditure. But all that is changed. Now, government is the organized expression of the wishes and the wants of the people and under these circumstances let us cease to regard it with suspicion. Suspicion is the product of an older time, of circumstances which have long since disappeared. Now it is our business to extend its functions and to see in what way its operations can be usefully enlarged." [The Eighty Club comprised a group of liberal MPs who were first returned to Parliament in the 1880 election.—Ed.] But see John Stuart Mill, in 1848 already arguing against this view in *Principles*, bk. 5, chap. 11, sec. 3, p. 944 [Liberty Fund edition, *Collected Works*, vol. 3, pp. 944–45], and also in "On Liberty," in *On Liberty and Considerations on Representative Government*, Ronald Buchanan McCallum, ed. (Oxford: Blackwell, 1946), p. 3. See also the statement made by Thomas Jefferson noted in chap. 16, n. 79, below (Jefferson's draft of the Kentucky Resolutions, in Ethelbert Dudley Waterfield, *The Kentucky Resolutions of 1798: An Historical Study* [2nd ed.; New York: Putnam, 1894], pp. 157–58). Indeed, this idea can be traced back to Rousseau; see his *Du contrat social* [Bibliothèque Philosophique; Paris: Aubier, Editions Montaigne, 1943], bk. 1, chap. 7 ("Du Souverain", p. 106) who offers the view that when a people form a legislature with plenary powers "le puissance Souveraine n'a nul besoin de garant envers les sujets, parce qu'il est impossible que le corps veuille nuire à tous ses membres, et nous verrons ci-après qu'il ne peut nuire à aucun en particulière." ["the sovereign power need offer no guarantee to its subjects, because it is impossible for the body to wish to hurt all its members. And we shall later see that it cannot hurt any in particular."—Ed.]

[8] Herman Finer, *Road to Reaction* (Boston: Little, Brown and Co., 1945), p. 60.

[9] See James Fitzjames Stephen, *Liberty, Equality, Fraternity* (London: Smith, Elder, and Co., 1873), p. 27–28 [Liberty Fund edition, p. 21]: "We agree to try strength by counting heads instead of breaking heads. . . . It is not the wisest side which wins, but the one which for the time being shows its superior strength (of which no doubt wisdom is one element) by enlisting

The second argument, which historically has been the most important and which is still very important, though we can no longer be sure that it is always valid, is that democracy is an important safeguard of individual liberty. It was once said by a seventeenth-century writer that "the good of democracy is liberty, and the courage and industry which liberty begets."[10] This view recognizes, of course, that democracy is not yet liberty; it contends only that it is more likely than other forms of government to produce liberty. This view may be well founded so far as the prevention of coercion of individuals by other individuals is concerned: it can scarcely be to the advantage of a majority that some individuals should have the power arbitrarily to coerce others. But the protection of the individual against the collective action of the majority itself is another matter. Even here it can be argued that, since coercive power must in fact always be exercised by a few, it is less likely to be abused if the power entrusted to the few can always be revoked by those who have to submit to it. But if the prospects of individual liberty are better in a democracy than under other forms of government, this does not mean that they are certain. The prospects of liberty depend on whether or not the majority makes it its deliberate object. It would have little chance of surviving if we relied on the mere existence of democracy to preserve it.

---

the largest amount of active sympathy in its support. The minority gives way, not because it is convinced that it is wrong, but because it is convinced that it is a minority." Cf. also Ludwig von Mises, *Human Action* (New Haven: Yale University Press, 1949), p. 150 [Liberty Fund edition, vol. 1, p. 150]: "For the sake of domestic peace, liberalism aims at democratic government. Democracy is therefore not a revolutionary institution. On the contrary, it is the very means of preventing revolutions and civil wars. It provides a method for the peaceful adjustment of government to the will of the majority." Similarly, Sir Karl Raimund Popper, "Prediction and Prophecy and Their Significance for Social Theory," *Proceedings of the 10th International Congress of Philosophy, Amsterdam, August 11–18, 1948*, Evert Willem Beth, ed. (2 vols.; Amsterdam: North Holland Publishing Co., 1948), vol. 1, esp. p. 90: "I personally call the type of government which can be removed without violence 'democracy,' and the other 'tyranny.'" See also Learned Hand, "Democracy: Its Presumptions and Realities," *The Spirit of Liberty: Papers and Addresses of Learned Hand*, Irving Dillard, ed. (New York: Alfred A. Knopf, 1952), p. 98: "For abuse it as you will, it gives a bloodless measure of social forces—bloodless, have you thought of that?—a means of continuity, a principle of stability, a relief from the paralyzing terror of revolution."

[10] *An Exact Collection of All the Remonstrances, Declarations, Votes, Orders, Ordinances, Proclamations, Petitions, Messages, Answers, and Other Remarkable Passages between the King's Most Excellent Majesty, and His High Court of Parliament, Beginning at His Majesties Return from Scotland in December, 1641, and Continued until March the 21, 1643* (London: Printed for E. Husbands, T. Warren, R. Best, 1643), p. 320. [These words were uttered by none other than King Charles I in 1642. By the beginning of June 1642 most of the Royalist supporters in Parliament had returned to their home districts, at which point the members of the Parliamentary party who remained at Westminster took the occasion to draw up a petition to Charles I in the form of a series of demands that would have substantially circumscribed the King's powers. Known as the Nineteen Propositions, these proposals were passed by Parliament on June 1, 1642, and presented to the King, who responded on June 18. The response was in fact written by Sir John Culpeper and Lucius Cary, Viscount Falkland. The passage to which Hayek refers was almost certainly written by Culpeper.—Ed.]

The third argument rests on the effect which the existence of democratic institutions will have on the general level of understanding of public affairs. This seems to me the most powerful. It may well be true, as has been often maintained,[11] that, in any given state of affairs, government by some educated elite would be a more efficient and perhaps even a more just government than one chosen by majority vote. The crucial point, however, is that, in comparing the democratic form of government with others, we cannot take the understanding of the issues by the people at any time as a datum. It is the burden of the argument of Tocqueville's great work, *Democracy in America*, that democracy is the only effective method of educating the majority.[12] This is as true today as it was in his time. Democracy is, above all, a process of forming opinion. Its chief advantage lies not in its method of selecting those who govern but in the fact that, because a great part of the population takes an active part in the formation of opinion, a correspondingly wide range of persons is available from which to select. We may admit that democracy does not put power in the hands of the wisest and best informed and that at any given moment the decision of a government by an elite might be more beneficial to the whole; but this need not prevent us from still giving democracy the preference. It is in its dynamic, rather than in its static, aspects that the value of democracy proves itself. As is true of liberty, the benefits of democracy will show themselves only in the long run, while its more immediate achievements may well be inferior to those of other forms of government.

---

[11] How fascinated the rationalistic liberals were by the conception of a government in which political issues were decided not "by an appeal, either direct or indirect, to the judgment or will of an uninstructed mass, whether of gentlemen or of clowns, but by the deliberately formed opinions of a comparatively few, specially educated for the task," is well illustrated by John Stuart Mill's early essay on "Democracy and Government" from which this fragment is taken (*London Review*, 31 [(October) 1835]:85–129, reprinted in *Early Essays* [London: G. Bell and Sons, 1897], p. 384). [Mill's essay in the *London Review* is from a review of Tocqueville's *Democracy in America.*—Ed.] He goes on to point out that "of all governments, ancient or modern, the one by which this excellence is possessed in the most eminent degree, is the government of Prussia— a most powerfully and skillfully organized aristocracy of the most highly-educated men in the kingdom." Cf. also the passage in *On Liberty*, p. 9. With respect to the applicability of freedom and democracy to less civilized people, some of the old Whigs were considerably more liberal than the later radicals. Thomas Babington Macaulay, for example, says somewhere: "Many politicians of our time are in the habit of laying it down as a self-evident proposition, that no people ought to be free till they are fit to use their freedom. The maxim is worthy of the fool in the old story, who resolved not to go into the water till he had learned to swim. If men are to wait for liberty till they become wise and good in slavery, they may indeed have to wait forever." [The quotation is from Macaulay's essay on Milton, included in his *Critical and Historical Essays* (Everyman's Library; 2 vols.; London: J. M. Dent and Sons, 1907), vol. 2, p. 180.—Ed.]

[12] This seems also to explain the puzzling contrast between Tocqueville's persistent faultfinding with democracy on almost all particular points and the emphatic acceptance of the principle which is so characteristic of his work.

5. The conception that government should be guided by majority opinion makes sense only if that opinion is independent of government. The ideal of democracy rests on the belief that the view which will direct government emerges from an independent and spontaneous process.[13] It requires, therefore, the existence of a large sphere independent of majority control in which the opinions of the individuals are formed. There is widespread consensus that for this reason the case for democracy and the case for freedom of speech and discussion are inseparable.

The view, however, that democracy provides not merely a method of settling differences of opinion on the course of action to be adopted but also a standard for what opinion ought to be has already had far-reaching effects. It has, in particular, seriously confused the question of what is actually valid law and what ought to be the law. If democracy is to function, it is as important that the former can always be ascertained as that the latter can always be questioned. Majority decisions tell us what people want at the moment, but not what it would be in their interest to want if they were better informed; and, unless they could be changed by persuasion, they would be of no value. The argument for democracy presupposes that any minority opinion may become a majority one.

It would not be necessary to stress this if it were not for the fact that it is sometimes represented as the duty of the democrat, and particularly of the democratic intellectual, to accept the views and values of the majority. True, there is the convention that the view of the majority should prevail so far as collective action is concerned, but this does not in the least mean that one should not make every effort to alter it. One may have profound respect for that convention and yet very little for the wisdom of the majority. It is only because the majority opinion will always be opposed by some that our knowledge and understanding progress. In the process by which opinion is formed, it is very probable that, by the time any view becomes a majority view, it is no longer the best view: somebody will already have advanced beyond the point which the majority have reached.[14] It is because we do not yet know which of the many competing new opinions will prove itself the best that we wait until it has gained sufficient support.

The conception that the efforts of all should be directed by the opinion of

---

[13] See Kenneth Ewart Boulding, *The Organizational Revolution: A Study in the Ethics of Economic Organization* [Federal Council of the Churches of Christ in America] (New York: Harper and Bros., 1953), p. 250: "Increasingly, therefore, the state becomes an entity separate from its citizens even in democratic societies, making decisions of which they are not aware, maneuvering them into positions from which they cannot retreat, itself creating the public opinion on which its power ultimately rests, until the state is now in danger of becoming the greatest enemy of man instead of his wisest friend."

[14] Cf. the passage by Dicey, *Law and Public Opinion*, p. 33 [Liberty Fund edition, p. 25], quoted in n. 16 below.

the majority or that a society is better according as it conforms more to the standards of the majority is in fact a reversal of the principle by which civilization has grown. Its general adoption would probably mean the stagnation, if not the decay, of civilization. Advance consists in the few convincing the many. New views must appear somewhere before they can become majority views. There is no experience of society which is not first the experience of a few individuals. Nor is the process of forming majority opinion entirely, or even chiefly, a matter of discussion, as the overintellectualized conception would have it. There is some truth in the view that democracy is government by discussion, but this refers only to the last stage of the process by which the merits of alternative views and desires are tested. Though discussion is essential, it is not the main process by which people learn. Their views and desires are formed by individuals acting according to their own designs; and they profit from what others have learned in their individual experience. Unless some people know more than the rest and are in a better position to convince the rest, there would be little progress in opinion. It is because we normally do not know who knows best that we leave the decision to a process which we do not control. But it is always from a minority acting in ways different from what the majority would prescribe that the majority in the end learns to do better.

6. We have no ground for crediting majority decisions with that higher, superindividual wisdom which, in a certain sense, the products of spontaneous social growth may possess. The resolutions of a majority are not the place to look for such superior wisdom. They are bound, if anything, to be inferior to the decisions that the most intelligent members of the group will make after listening to all opinions: they will be the result of less careful thought and will generally represent a compromise that will not fully satisfy anybody. This will be even more true of the cumulative result emanating from the successive decisions of shifting majorities variously composed: the result will be the expression not of a coherent conception but of different and often conflicting motives and aims.

Such a process should not be confused with those spontaneous processes which free communities have learned to regard as the source of much that is better than individual wisdom can contrive. If by "social process" we mean the gradual evolution which produces better solutions than deliberate design, the imposition of the will of the majority can hardly be regarded as such. The latter differs radically from that free growth from which custom and institutions emerge, because its coercive, monopolistic, and exclusive character destroys the self-correcting forces which bring it about in a free society that mistaken efforts will be abandoned and the successful ones prevail. It also differs basically from the cumulative process by which law is formed by precedent, unless it is, as is true of judicial decisions, fused into a coherent whole by the fact that principles followed on earlier occasions are deliberately adhered to.

Moreover, majority decisions are peculiarly liable, if not guided by accepted common principles, to produce over-all results that nobody wanted. It often happens that a majority is forced by its own decisions to further actions that were neither contemplated nor desired. The belief that collective action can dispense with principles is largely an illusion, and the usual effect of its renouncing principles is that it is driven into a course by the unexpected implications of former decisions. The individual decision may have been intended only to deal with a particular situation. But it creates the expectation that wherever similar circumstances occur the government will take similar action. Thus principles which had never been intended to apply generally, which may be undesirable or nonsensical when applied generally, bring about future action that few would have desired in the first instance. A government that claims to be committed to no principles and to judge every problem on its merits usually finds itself having to observe principles not of its own choosing and being led into action that it had never contemplated. A phenomenon which is now familiar to us is that of governments which start out with the proud claim that they will deliberately control all affairs and soon find themselves beset at each step by the necessities created by their former actions. It is since governments have come to regard themselves as omnipotent that we now hear so much about the necessity or inevitability of their doing this or that which they know to be unwise.

7. If the politician or statesman has no choice but to adopt a certain course of action (or if his action is regarded as inevitable by the historian), this is because his or other people's opinion, not objective facts, allow him no alternative. It is only to people who are influenced by certain beliefs that anyone's response to given events may appear to be uniquely determined by circumstances. For the practical politician concerned with particular issues, these beliefs are indeed unalterable facts to all intents and purposes. It is almost necessary that he be unoriginal, that he fashion his program from opinions held by large numbers of people. The successful politician owes his power to the fact that he moves within the accepted framework of thought, that he thinks and talks conventionally. It would be almost a contradiction in terms for a politician to be a leader in the field of ideas. His task in a democracy is to find out what the opinions held by the largest number are, not to give currency to new opinions which may become the majority view in some distant future.

The state of opinion which governs a decision on political issues is always the result of a slow evolution, extending over long periods and proceeding at many different levels. New ideas start among a few and gradually spread until they become the possession of a majority who know little of their origin. In modern society this process involves a division of functions between those who are concerned mainly with the particular issues and those who are occupied with general ideas, with elaborating and reconciling the various principles of action which past experience has suggested. Our views both about what the consequences of our actions will be and about what we ought to aim at are mainly precepts that we have acquired as part of the inheritance of our society. These political and moral views, no less than our scientific beliefs, come to us from those who professionally handle abstract ideas. It is from them that both the ordinary man and the political leader obtain the fundamental conceptions that constitute the framework of their thought and guide them in their action.

The belief that in the long run it is ideas and therefore the men who give currency to new ideas that govern evolution, and the belief that the individual steps in that process should be governed by a set of coherent conceptions, have long formed a fundamental part of the liberal creed. It is impossible to study history without becoming aware of the "lesson given to mankind by every age, and always disregarded—to show that speculative philosophy, which to the superficial appears a thing so remote from the business of life and the outward interests of men, is in reality the thing on earth which most influences them, and in the long run overbears every other influence save those which it must itself obey."[15] Though this fact is perhaps even less under-

---

[15] John Stuart Mill, "Bentham," *London and Westminster Review*, 39 (August 1838): 327, reprinted in *Dissertations and Discussions Political, Philosophical, and Historical: Reprinted Chiefly from the Edinburgh and Westminster Reviews* (3rd ed.; 4 vols.; London: Longmans, Green, Reader, and Dyer, 1875), vol. 1, pp. 330–31 [Liberty Fund edition, *Collected Works*, vol. 10, p. 77]. [Mill's essay on Bentham has also been reprinted in *Early Essays by John Stuart Mill*, J. W. M. Gibbs, ed. (London: George Bell and Sons, 1897), pp. 327–28.—Ed.] The passage continues: "The writers of whom we speak [i.e., Bentham and Coleridge] have never been read by the multitude; except for the more slight of their works, their readers have been few: but they have been the teachers of the teachers; there is hardly to be found in England an individual of any importance in the world of mind, who (whatever opinions he may have afterwards adopted) did not first learn to think from one of these two; and though their influences have but begun to diffuse themselves through these intermediate channels over society at large, there is already scarcely a publication of any consequence addressed to the educated classes, which, if these persons had not existed, would not have been different from what it is." Cf. also the frequently quoted passage by Lord [John Maynard] Keynes, himself the most eminent example of such influence in our generation, in which he argues, at the end of *The General Theory of Employment, Interest, and Money* (London: Macmillan, 1936), pp. 383–84, that "the ideas of economists and political philosophers, both when they are right and when they are wrong, are more powerful than is commonly understood. Indeed the world is ruled by little else. Practical men, who believe themselves to be quite exempt from any intellectual influences, are usually the slaves of some defunct economist. Madmen in authority, who hear voices in the air, are distilling their frenzy from some academic scribbler of a few years back. I am sure that the power of vested interests is vastly exaggerated compared with the gradual encroachment of ideas. Not, indeed, immediately, but after a certain interval; for in the field

---

stood today than it was when John Stuart Mill wrote, there can be little doubt that it is true at all times, whether men recognize it or not. It is so little understood because the influence of the abstract thinker on the masses operates only indirectly. People rarely know or care whether the commonplace ideas of their day have come to them from Aristotle or Locke, Rousseau or Marx, or from some professor whose views were fashionable among the intellectuals twenty years ago. Most of them have never read the works or even heard the names of the authors whose conceptions and ideals have become part of their thinking.

So far as direct influence on current affairs is concerned, the influence of the political philosopher may be negligible. But when his ideas have become common property, through the work of historians and publicists, teachers and writers, and intellectuals generally, they effectively guide developments. This means not only that new ideas commonly begin to exercise their influence on political action only a generation or more after they have first been stated[16] but that, before the contributions of the speculative thinker can exercise such influence, they have to pass through a long process of selection and modification.

Changes in political and social beliefs necessarily proceed at any one time at many different levels. We must conceive of the process not as expanding over one plane but as filtering slowly downward from the top of a pyramid, where the higher levels represent greater generality and abstraction and not necessarily greater wisdom. As ideas spread downward, they also change their character. Those which are at any time still on a high level of generality will com-

---

of economic and political philosophy there are not many who are influenced by new theories after they are twenty-five or thirty years of age, so that the ideas which civil servants and politicians and even agitators apply to current events are not likely to be the newest. But, soon or late, it is ideas, not vested interests, which are dangerous for good or evil."

[16] The classical description of the manner in which ideas at a long interval affect policy is still that by Dicey, *Law and Public Opinion*, pp. 28ff. and esp. p. 33 [Liberty Fund edition, p. 25]: "The opinion which changes the law is in one sense the opinion of the time when the law is actually altered; in another sense it has often been in England the opinion prevalent some twenty or thirty years before that time; it has been as often as not in reality the opinion not of to-day but of yesterday.

"Legislative opinion must be the opinion of the day, because, when laws are altered, the alteration is of necessity carried into effect by legislators who act under the belief that the change is an amendment; but this law-making opinion is also the opinion of yesterday, because the beliefs which have at last gained such hold on the legislature as to produce an alteration in the law have generally been created by thinkers or writers, who exerted their influence long before the change in the law took place. Thus it may well happen that an innovation is carried through at a time when the teachers who supplied the arguments in its favour are in their graves, or even— and this is well worth noting—when in the world of speculation a movement has already set in against ideas which are exerting their full effect in the world of action and of legislation."

pete only with others of similar character, and only for the support of people interested in general conceptions. To the great majority these general conceptions will become known only in their application to concrete and particular issues. Which of these ideas will reach them and gain their support will be determined not by some single mind but by discussion proceeding on another level, among people who are concerned more with general ideas than with particular problems and who, in consequence, see the latter mainly in the light of general principles.

Except on rare occasions, such as constitutional conventions, the democratic process of discussion and majority decision is necessarily confined to part of the whole system of law and government. The piecemeal change which this involves will produce desirable and workable results only if it is guided by some general conception of the social order desired, some coherent image of the kind of world in which the people want to live. To achieve such an image is not a simple task, and even the specialist student can do no more than endeavor to see a little more clearly than his predecessors. The practical man concerned with the immediate problems of the day has neither the interest nor the tune to examine the interrelations of the different parts of the complex order of society. He merely chooses from among the possible orders that are offered him and finally accepts a political doctrine or set of principles elaborated and presented by others.

If people were not at most times led by some system of common ideas, neither a coherent policy nor even real discussion about particular issues would be possible. It is doubtful whether democracy can work in the long run if the great majority do not have in common at least a general conception of the type of society desired. But even if such a conception exists, it will not necessarily show itself in every majority decision. Groups do not always act in accordance with their best knowledge or obey moral rules that they recognize in the abstract any more than individuals do. It is only by appealing to such common principles, however, that we can hope to reach agreement by discussion, to settle conflict of interests by reasoning and argument rather than by brute force.

8. If opinion is to advance, the theorist who offers guidance must not regard himself as bound by majority opinion. The task of the political philosopher is different from that of the expert servant who carries out the will of the majority. Though he must not arrogate to himself the position of a "leader" who determines what people ought to think, it is his duty to show possibilities and consequences of common action, to offer comprehensive aims of policy as a whole which the majority have not yet thought of. It is only after such a comprehensive picture of the possible results of different policies has been presented that democracy can decide what it wants. If politics is the art of the

possible, political philosophy is the art of making politically possible the seemingly impossible.[17]

The political philosopher cannot discharge his task if he confines himself to questions of fact and is afraid of deciding between conflicting values. He cannot allow himself to be limited by the positivism of the scientist, which confines his functions to showing what is the case and forbids any discussion of what ought to be. If he does so, he will have to stop long before he has performed his most important function. In his effort to form a coherent picture he will often find that there are values which conflict with one another—a fact which most people are not aware of—and that he must choose which he should accept and which reject. Unless the political philosopher is prepared to defend values which seem right to him, he will never achieve that comprehensive outline which must then be judged as a whole.

In this task he will often serve democracy best by opposing the will of the majority. Only a complete misapprehension of the process by which opinion progresses would lead one to argue that in the sphere of opinion he ought to submit to majority views. To treat existing majority opinion as the standard for what majority opinion ought to be would make the whole process circular and stationary. There is, in fact, never so much reason for the political philosopher to suspect himself of failing in his task as when he finds that his opinions are very popular.[18] It is by insisting on considerations which the majority do not wish to take into account, by holding up principles which they regard as inconvenient and irksome, that he has to prove his worth. For intellectuals to bow to a belief merely because it is held by the majority is a betrayal not only of their peculiar mission but of the values of democracy itself.

The principles that plead for the self-limitation of the power of the majority are not proved wrong if democracy disregards them, nor is democracy proved undesirable if it often makes what the liberal must regard as the wrong decision. He simply believes that he has an argument which, when properly understood, will induce the majority to limit the exercise of its own powers

[17] Cf. Helmut Schoeck, "What Is Meant by 'Politically Impossible'?" *Pall Mall Quarterly*, 1 (1958): 48–53; see also Clarence Philbrook, "'Realism' in Policy Espousal," *American Economic Review*, 43 (1953): 846–59.

[18] Cf. Marshall's observation ("In Memoriam: Alfred Marshall," *Memorials of Alfred Marshall*, Arthur Cecil Pigou, ed. [London: Macmillan, 1925], p. 89) that "students of social science must fear popular approval: evil is with them when all men speak well of them. If there is any set of opinions by the advocacy of which a newspaper can increase its sale, then the student, who wishes to leave the world in general and his country in particular better than it would be if he had not been born, is bound to dwell on the limitations and defects and errors, if any, in that set of opinions: and never to advocate them unconditionally even in an *ad hoc* discussion. It is almost impossible for a student to be a true patriot and to have the reputation of being one in his own time."

and which he hopes it can be persuaded to accept as a guide when deciding on particular issues.

9. It is not the least part of this liberal argument that to disregard those limits will, in the long run, destroy not only prosperity and peace but democracy itself. The liberal believes that the limits which he wants democracy to impose upon itself are also the limits within which it can work effectively and within which the majority can truly direct and control the actions of government. So long as democracy constrains the individual only by general rules of its own making, it controls the power of coercion. If it attempts to direct them more specifically, it will soon find itself merely indicating the ends to be achieved while leaving to its expert servants the decision as to the manner in which they are to be achieved. And once it is generally accepted that majority decisions can merely indicate ends and that the pursuit of them is to be left to the discretion of the administrators, it will soon be believed also that almost any means to achieve those ends are legitimate.

The individual has little reason to fear any general laws which the majority may pass, but he has much reason to fear the rulers it may put over him to implement its directions. It is not the powers which democratic assemblies can effectively wield but the powers which they hand over to the administrators charged with the achievement of particular goals that constitute the danger to individual freedom today. Having agreed that the majority should prescribe rules which we will obey in pursuit of our individual aims, we find ourselves more and more subjected to the orders and the arbitrary will of its agents. Significantly enough, we find not only that most of the supporters of unlimited democracy soon become defenders of arbitrariness and of the view that we should trust experts to decide what is good for the community, but that the most enthusiastic supporters of such unlimited powers of the majority are often those very administrators who know best that, once such powers are assumed, it will be they and not the majority who will in fact exercise them. If anything has been demonstrated by modern experience in these matters, it is that, once wide coercive powers are given to governmental agencies for particular purposes, such powers cannot be effectively controlled by democratic assemblies. If the latter do not themselves determine the means to be employed, the decisions of their agents will be more or less arbitrary.

General considerations and recent experience both show that democracy will remain effective only so long as government in its coercive action confines itself to tasks that can be carried out democratically.[19] If democracy is a

---

[19] See the fuller discussion of these issues in chap. 5 [pp. 56–71] of my book *The Road to Serfdom* (Chicago, University of Chicago Press, 1944) [reprinted as vol. 2 of *The Collected Works of F. A. Hayek*, Bruce Caldwell, ed. (Chicago: University of Chicago Press, 2007), pp. 100–111] and in Walter Lippmann, *An Inquiry into the Principles of the Good Society* (Boston: Little, Brown and Co., 1937), esp. p. 267: "[The people] can govern only when they understand how a democracy *can*

means of preserving liberty, then individual liberty is no less an essential condition for the working of democracy. Though democracy is probably the best form of limited government, it becomes an absurdity if it turns into unlimited government. Those who profess that democracy is all-competent and support all that the majority wants at any given moment are working for its fall. The old liberal is in fact a much better friend of democracy than the dogmatic democrat, for he is concerned with preserving the conditions that make democracy workable. It is not "antidemocratic" to try to persuade the majority that there are limits beyond which its action ceases to be beneficial and that it should observe principles which are not of its own deliberate making. If it is to survive, democracy must recognize that it is not the fountainhead of justice and that it needs to acknowledge a conception of justice which does not necessarily manifest itself in the popular view on every particular issue. The danger is that we mistake a means of securing justice for justice itself. Those who endeavor to persuade majorities to recognize proper limits to their just power are therefore as necessary to the democratic process as those who constantly point to new goals for democratic action.

In Part II of this book we shall consider further those limits on government which seem to be the necessary condition for the workability of democracy and which the people of the West have developed under the name of the rule of law. Here we will merely add that there is little reason to expect that any people will succeed in successfully operating or preserving a democratic machinery of government unless they have first become familiar with the traditions of a government of law.

---

govern itself; that it can govern only by appointing representatives to adjudicate, enforce, and revise laws which declare the rights, duties, privileges, and immunities of persons, associations, communities, and the officials themselves, each in respect to all others.

"This is the constitution of a free state. Because democratic philosophers in the nineteenth century did not clearly see that the indispensable corollary of representative government is a particular mode of governing, they were perplexed by the supposed conflict between law and liberty, between social control and individual freedom. These conflicts do not exist where social control is achieved by a legal order in which reciprocal rights are enforced and adjusted. Thus in a free society the state does not administer the affairs of men. It administers justice among men who conduct their own affairs."

EIGHT

EMPLOYMENT AND INDEPENDENCE

Not for to hide it in a hedge,
Not for a train attendant,
But for the glorious privilege
Of being independent.

—Robert Burns

1. The ideals and principles restated in the preceding chapters were developed in a society which in important respects differed from ours. It was a society in which a relatively larger part of the people, and most of those who counted in forming opinion, were independent in the activities that gave them their livelihood.[1] How far, then, are those principles which operated in such a society still valid now, when most of us work as employed members of large organizations, using resources we do not own and acting largely on the instructions given by others? In particular, if the independents now constitute a so much smaller and less influential portion of society, have their contributions for this reason become less important, or are they still essential to the well-being of any free society?

Before we turn to the main issue, we must free ourselves from a myth concerning the growth of the employed class which, though believed in its crudest form only by Marxists, has gained wide enough acceptance to confuse opinion. This is the myth that the appearance of a propertyless proletariat is the

---

The quotation from Robert Burns at the head of the chapter is borrowed from Samuel Smiles, *Self Help: With Illustrations of Character and Conduct* (London: John Murray, 1859), where it is used similarly at the head of chap. 9, p. 215. [The quotation is from his "Epistle to a Young Friend," verse 7. In later editions of *Self Help*, it appears at the head of chap. 10.—Ed.]

[1] Cf. Charles Wright Mills, *White Collar: The American Middle Class* (New York: Oxford University Press, 1951), p. 63: "In the early nineteenth century, although there are no exact figures, probably four-fifths of the occupied population were self-employed enterprisers; by 1870, only about one-third, and in 1940, only about one-fifth were still in this old middle class." See also *White Collar*, p. 65, on the extent to which this development is largely an effect of the decreasing proportion of the agricultural population, which, however, does not alter its political significance.

result of a process of expropriation, in the course of which the masses were deprived of those possessions that formerly enabled them to earn their living independently. The facts tell a very different story. Until the rise of modern capitalism, the possibility for most people of establishing a family and of rearing children depended on the inheritance of a home and land and the necessary tools of production. What later enabled those who did not inherit land and tools from their parents to survive and multiply was the fact that it became practicable and profitable for the wealthy to use their capital in such a way as to give employment to large numbers. If "capitalism has created the proletariat," it has done so, then, by enabling large numbers to survive and procreate. In the Western world today, the effect of this process is, of course, no longer the increase in a proletariat in the old sense but the growth of a majority of employed who in many respects are alien and often inimical to much that constitutes the driving force of a free society.

The increase in population during the last two hundred years has been made up mostly of employed workers, urban and industrial. Though the technological change that has favored large-scale enterprise and helped to create the new large class of clerical workers has undoubtedly assisted this growth of the employed section of the population, the increasing number of propertyless that offered their services has probably in turn assisted the growth of large-scale organization.

The political significance of this development has been accentuated by the fact that, at the time when the dependent and propertyless were growing most rapidly in numbers, they were also given the franchise, from which most of them had been excluded. The result was that in probably all countries of the West the outlook of the great majority of the electorate came to be determined by the fact that they were in employed positions. Since it is now their opinion that largely governs policy, this produces measures that make the employed positions relatively more attractive and the independent ones ever less so. That the employed should thus use their political power is natural. The problem is whether it is in their long-term interest if society is thereby progressively turned into one great hierarchy of employment. Such a state seems to be the likely outcome unless the employed majority come to recognize that it would be in their interest to ensure the preservation of a substantial number of independents. For if they do not, we shall all find that our freedom has been affected, just as they will find that, without a great variety of employers to choose from, their position is not as it once was.

2. The problem is that many exercises of freedom are of little direct interest to the employed and that it is often not easy for them to see that their freedom depends on others' being able to make decisions which are not immediately relevant to their whole manner of life. Since they can and have to live with-

out making such decisions, they cannot see the need for them, and they attach little importance to opportunities for action which hardly ever occur in their lives. They regard as unnecessary many exercises of freedom which are essential to the independent if he is to perform his functions, and they hold views of deserts and appropriate remuneration entirely different from his. Freedom is thus seriously threatened today by the tendency of the employed majority to impose upon the rest their standards and views of life. It may indeed prove to be the most difficult task of all to persuade the employed masses that in the general interest of their society, and therefore in their own long-term interest, they should preserve such conditions as to enable a few to reach positions which to them appear unattainable or not worth the effort and risk.

If in the life of the employed certain exercises of liberty have little relevance, this does not mean that they are not free. Every choice made by a person as to his manner of life and way of earning a living means that, as a result, he will have little interest in doing certain things. A great many people will choose employment because it offers them better opportunities to live the kind of life they want than would any independent position. Even with those who do not especially want the relative security and absence of risk and responsibility that an employed position brings, the decisive factor is often not that independence is unattainable but that employment offers them a more satisfying activity and a larger income than they could earn as, say, independent tradesmen.

Freedom does not mean that we can have everything as we want it. In choosing a course of life we always must choose between complexes of advantages and disadvantages, and, once our choice is made, we must be prepared to accept certain disadvantages for the sake of the net benefit. Whoever desires the regular income for which he sells his labor must devote his working hours to the immediate tasks which are determined for him by others. To do the bidding of others is for the employed the condition of achieving his purpose. Yet, though he may find this at times highly irksome, in normal conditions he is not unfree in the sense of being coerced. True, the risk or sacrifice involved in giving up his job may often be so great as to make him continue in it, even though he intensely dislikes it. But this may be true of almost any other occupation to which a man has committed himself—certainly of many independent positions.

The essential fact is that in a competitive society the employed is not at the mercy of a particular employer, except in periods of extensive unemployment. The law wisely does not recognize contracts for the permanent sale of a person's labor and, in general, does not even enforce contracts for specific performance. Nobody can be coerced to continue to work under a particular boss, even if he has contracted to do so; and, in a normally operating competitive society, alternative employment will be available, even though it may often be less remunerative.[2]

That the freedom of the employed depends upon the existence of a great number and variety of employers is clear when we consider the situation that would exist if there were only one employer—namely, the state—and if taking employment were the only permitted means of livelihood. And a consistent application of socialist principles, however much it might be disguised by the delegation of the power of employment to nominally independent public corporations and the like, would necessarily lead to the presence of a single employer. Whether this employer acted directly or indirectly, he would clearly possess unlimited power to coerce the individual.

3. The freedom of the employed therefore depends on the existence of a group of persons whose position is different from theirs. Yet in a democracy in which they form the majority, it is their conception of life that can determine whether or not such a group can exist and fulfill its functions. The dominant conceptions will be those of the great majority, who are members of hierarchic organizations and who are largely unaware of the kind of problems and views that determine the relations between the separate units within which they work. The standards which such a majority develops may enable them to be effective members of society, but they cannot be applied to the whole of society if it is to remain free.

It is inevitable that the interests and values of the employed should differ somewhat from those of men who accept the risk and responsibility of organizing the use of resources. A man who works under direction for a fixed salary or wage may be as conscientious, industrious, and intelligent as one who must constantly choose between alternatives; but he can hardly be as inventive or as experimental simply because the range of choice in his work is more limited.[3] He is normally not expected to perform actions which cannot be

---

[2] It is important to remember that even those who, because of age or the specialized character of their abilities, individually cannot seriously contemplate a change in position are protected by the need of the employer to create working conditions which will secure him the necessary flow of new recruits.

[3] Cf. the interesting discussion of these problems in Ernst Bieri, "Kritische Gedanken zum Wohlfahrtsstaat," *Schweizer Monatshefte*, 35 (1956): esp. 575: "Die Zahl der *Unselbstständigerwerbenden* hat stark zugenommen, sowohl absolut wie prozentuell zu den Beschäftigten. Nun ist das Gefühl der Verantwortung für sich und die Zukunft bei den Selbstständigerwerbenden aus naheliegenden Gründen lebhafter entwickelt; sie müssen auf lange Sicht planen und haben auch die Möglichkeit, durch Geschick und Initiative für schlechtere Zeiten vorzusorgen. Die Unselbstständigerwerbenden hingegen, die in regelmäßigen Abständen ihren Lohn erhalten, haben ein anderes, [ein] statisches Lebensgefühl; sie planen selten auf lange Sicht, und erschrecken bei der geringsten Schwankung. Ihr Sinnen und Trachten ist auf *Stabilität und Sicherheit* gerichtet." ["The number of non-self-employed has sharply increased, both in absolute terms and as a percent-

THE CONSTITUTION OF LIBERTY

prescribed or which are not conventional. He cannot go beyond his allotted task even if he is capable of doing more. An assigned task is necessarily a limited task, confined to a given sphere and based on a predetermined division of labor.

The fact of being employed will affect more than a man's initiative and inventiveness. He has little knowledge of the responsibilities of those who control resources and who must concern themselves constantly with new arrangements and combinations; he is little acquainted with the attitudes and modes of life which the need for decisions concerning the use of property and income produces. For the independent there can be no sharp distinction between his private and his business life, as there is for the employed, who has sold part of his time for a fixed income. While, for the employed, work is largely a matter of fitting himself into a given framework during a certain number of hours, for the independent it is a question of shaping and reshaping a plan of life, of finding solutions for ever new problems. Especially do the employed and the independent differ in their views of what one can properly regard as income, what chances one ought to take, and what manner of life one should adopt that is most conducive to success.

The greatest difference between the two, however, will be found in their opinions of how appropriate remunerations for various services are to be determined. Whenever a person works under instruction and as a member of a large organization, the value of his individual services is difficult to ascertain. How faithfully and intelligently he has obeyed rules and instructions, how well he has fitted himself into the whole machinery, must be determined by the opinion of other people. Often he must be remunerated according to assessed merit, not according to result. If there is to be contentment within the organization, it is most important that remuneration be generally regarded as just, that it conform to known and intelligible rules, and that a human agency be responsible for every man's receiving what his fellows regard as being due to him.[4] However, this principle of rewarding a man according to what others think he deserves cannot apply to men who act on their own initiative.

4. When an employed majority determines legislation and policy, conditions will tend to be adapted to the standards of that group and become less favorable to the independent. The position of the former will, in consequence,

---

age of the workforce. Among the self-employed, a sense of responsibility for oneself and for the future is more strongly developed for the following reasons. They have to plan for the long term and the possibility of preparing for future difficulties through skill and initiative is thus open to them. In contrast, the non-self-employed, who receive their wages at regular intervals, have a different, more static sense of life. They rarely plan for the long term and are frightened by the slightest change. Their thoughts and their efforts are geared toward *stability and security*."—Ed.]

[4] Cf. the discussion in Chester Irving Barnard, *The Functions of the Executive* (Cambridge: Harvard University Press, 1938).

become steadily more attractive and its relative strength even greater. It may be that even the advantages which the large organization has today over the small are in part a result of policies that have made employed positions more attractive to many who in the past would have aimed at independence.

There can be little doubt, at any rate, that employment has become not only the actual but the preferred position of the majority of the population, who find that it gives them what they mainly want: an assured fixed income available for current expenditure, more or less automatic raises, and provision for old age. They are thus relieved of some of the responsibilities of economic life; and quite naturally they feel that economic misfortune, when it comes as a result of a decline or failure of the employing organization, is clearly not their fault but somebody else's. It is not surprising, then, that they should wish to have some higher tutelary power watch over the directing activities which they do not understand but on which their livelihood depends.

Where this class predominates, the conception of social justice becomes largely adjusted to its needs. This applies not only to legislation but also to institutions and business practices. Taxation comes to be based on a conception of income which is essentially that of the employee. The paternalistic provisions of the social services are tailored almost exclusively to his requirements. Even the standards and techniques of consumers' credit are primarily adjusted to them. And all that concerns the possession and employment of capital as part of making one's living comes to be treated as the special interest of a small privileged group which can justly be discriminated against.

To Americans this picture may still seem exaggerated, but to Europeans most of its features are all too familiar. The development in this direction is generally much accelerated, once the public servants become the most numerous and influential group among the employed, and the special privileges which they enjoy come to be demanded as a matter of right by all employees. Privileges such as security of tenure and automatic promotion by seniority that the public servant is given, not in his interest but in the interest of the public, then tend to be extended beyond this group. Also, it is even more true of government bureaucracy than of other large organizations that the specific value of an individual's services cannot be ascertained and that he must therefore be rewarded on the basis of assessable merit rather than result.[5] Such standards that prevail in the bureaucracy tend to spread, not least through the influence of public servants on legislation and on the new institutions catering to the needs of the employed.[6] In many European countries the bureaucracy

[5] On the connection between bureaucratic organization and practices and the impossibility of a profit-and-loss calculation see especially Ludwig von Mises, *Human Action* (New Haven: Yale University Press, 1949), pp. 300–307 [Liberty Fund edition, vol. 2, pp. 303–11].

[6] Lowell Mason, *The Language of Dissent* (Cleveland: World Publishing Co., 1959), particularly p. 19: "No one acquires a love of liberty working for government."

of the new social services in particular has become a very important political factor, the instrument as well as the creator of a new conception of need and merit, to whose standards the life of the people is increasingly subject.

5. The existence of a multiplicity of opportunities for employment ultimately depends on the existence of independent individuals who can take the initiative in the continuous process of re-forming and redirecting organizations. It might at first seem that multiplicity of opportunities could also be provided by numerous corporations run by salaried managers and owned by large numbers of shareholders and that men of substantial property would therefore be superfluous. But though corporations of this sort may be suited to well-established industries, it is very unlikely that competitive conditions could be maintained, or an ossification of the whole corporate structure be prevented, without the launching of new organizations for fresh ventures, where the propertied individual able to bear risks is still irreplaceable. And this superiority of individual over collective decisions is not confined to new ventures. However adequate the collective wisdom of a board may be in most instances, the outstanding success even of large and well-established corporations is often due to some single person who has achieved his position of independence and influence through the control of large means. However much the institution of the corporation may have obscured the simple distinction between the directing owner and the employee, the whole system of separate enterprises, offering both employees and consumers sufficient alternatives to deprive each organization from exercising coercive power, presupposes private ownership and individual decision as to the use of resources.[7]

6. The importance of the private owner of substantial property, however, does not rest simply on the fact that his existence is an essential condition for the preservation of the structure of competitive enterprise. The man of independent means is an even more important figure in a free society when he is not occupied with using his capital in the pursuit of material gain but uses it in the service of aims which bring no material return.[8] It is more in the support of aims which the mechanism of the market cannot adequately take care of than in preserving that market that the man of independent means has his indispensable role to play in any civilized society.[9]

---

[7] Cf. on all this Joseph Alois Schumpeter, *Capitalism, Socialism, and Democracy* (New York: Harper and Bros., 1942), p. 242, and the further discussion of the character of large organizations below, chap. 17, sec. 8.

[8] William Henry Beveridge, Baron Beveridge, *Power and Influence* (London: Hodder and Stoughton, 1955), p. 70. The Webbs "owed both things—time for thought and social contact with the powerful—to Beatrice's possession of £1,000 a year inherited from her father. Where will the next generation of reformers find their Webbs?"

[9] I wish I could command the eloquence with which I once heard the late Lord Keynes expatiate on the indispensable role that the man of independent means plays in any decent society.

Though the market mechanism is the most effective method for securing those services that can be priced, there are others of great importance that the market will not provide because they cannot be sold to the individual beneficiary. Economists have often given the impression that only what the public can be made to pay for is useful or have mentioned the exceptions only as an argument for the state's stepping in where the market has failed to provide whatever is desired. But, though the limitations of the market provide a legitimate argument for some kinds of government action, they certainly do not justify the argument that only the state should be able to provide such services. The very recognition that there are needs which the market does not satisfy should make it clear that the government ought not to be the only agency able to do things which do not pay, that there should be no monopoly here but as many independent centers as possible able to satisfy such needs.

The leadership of individuals or groups who can back their beliefs financially is particularly essential in the field of cultural amenities, in the fine arts, in education and research, in the preservation of natural beauty and historic treasures, and, above all, in the propagation of new ideas in politics, morals, and religion. If minority views are to have a chance to become majority views, it is necessary not only that men who are already highly esteemed by the majority should be able to initiate action but that representatives of all divergent views and tastes should be in a position to support with their means and their energy ideals which are not yet shared by the majority.

If we knew of no better way of providing such a group, there would exist a strong case for selecting at random one in a hundred, or one in a thousand, from the population at large and endowing them with fortunes sufficient for the pursuit of whatever they choose. So long as most tastes and opinions were represented and every type of interest given a chance, this might be well worth while, even if, of this fraction of the population, again only one in a

---

It came to me somewhat as a surprise that this should have come from the man who at an earlier date had welcomed the "euthanasia of the rentier." I would have been less surprised if I had known how acutely Keynes himself had felt that for the position to which he aspired the foundation of an independent fortune was necessary and how successful he had been in acquiring this fortune. As his biographer tells us, at the age of thirty-six, Keynes "was determined not to relapse into salaried drudgery. He must be financially independent. He felt that he had that in him which would justify such independence. He had many things to tell the nation. And he wanted a sufficiency." Thus he went deeply into speculation and, starting with practically nothing, made half a million pounds in twelve years (Sir Roy Forbes Harrod, *The Life of John Maynard Keynes* [London: Macmillan, 1951], p. 297. [Harrod notes that at the beginning of 1937, the year in which he turned 54, Keynes's assets, exclusive of his paintings and books, were valued at £506,450.—Ed.]). It ought not have surprised me, therefore, that at my attempt to draw him out on the subject he responded by an enthusiastic eulogy of the role played in the growth of civilization by the educated man of property; and I can only wish that this account, with the rich illustrations, had seen the light of print.

hundred or one in a thousand used the opportunity in a manner that in retrospect would appear beneficial. The selection through inheritance from parents, which in our society, in fact, produces such a situation, has at least the advantage (even if we do not take into account the probability of inherited ability) that those who are given the special opportunity will usually have been educated for it and will have grown up in an environment in which the material benefits of wealth have become familiar and, because they are taken for granted, have ceased to be the main source of satisfaction. The grosser pleasures in which the newly rich often indulge have usually no attraction for those who have inherited wealth. If there is any validity in the contention that the process of social ascent should sometimes extend through several generations, and if we admit that some people should not have to devote most of their energies to earning a living but should have the time and means to devote themselves to whatever purpose they choose, then we cannot deny that inheritance is probably the best means of selection known to us.

The point that is so frequently overlooked in this connection is that action by collective agreement is limited to instances where previous efforts have already created a common view, where opinion about what is desirable has become settled, and where the problem is that of choosing between possibilities already generally recognized, not that of discovering new possibilities. Public opinion, however, cannot decide in what direction efforts should be made to arouse public opinion, and neither government nor other existing organized groups should have the exclusive power to do so. But organized efforts have to be set in motion by a few individuals who possess the necessary resources themselves or who win the support of those that do; without such men, what are now the views of only a small minority may never have a chance of being adopted by the majority. What little leadership can be expected from the majority is shown by their inadequate support of the arts wherever they have replaced the wealthy patron. And this is even more true of those philanthropic or idealistic movements by which the moral values of the majority are changed.

We cannot attempt to recount here the long story of all good causes which came to be recognized only after lonely pioneers had devoted their lives and fortunes to arousing the public conscience, of their long campaigns until at last they gained support for the abolition of slavery, for penal and prison reform, for the prevention of cruelty to children or to animals, or for a more humane treatment of the insane. All these were for a long time the hopes of only a few idealists who strove to change the opinion of the overwhelming majority concerning certain accepted practices.

7. The successful performance of such a task by the wealthy is possible, however, only when the community as a whole does not regard it as the sole task of men possessing wealth to employ it profitably and to increase it, and

when the wealthy class consists not exclusively of men for whom the materially productive employment of their resources is their dominant interest. There must be, in other words, a tolerance for the existence of a group of idle rich—idle not in the sense that they do nothing useful but in the sense that their aims are not entirely governed by considerations of material gain. The fact that most people must earn their income does not make it less desirable that some should not have to do so, that a few be able to pursue aims which the rest do not appreciate. It would no doubt be offensive if, for that reason wealth were arbitrarily taken from some and given to others. There would also be little point if the majority were to grant the privilege, for they would select men whose aims they already approved. This would merely create another form of employment, or another form of reward for recognized merit, but not an opportunity to pursue aims that have not yet been generally accepted as desirable.

I have nothing but admiration for the moral tradition that frowns upon idleness where it means lack of purposeful occupation. But not working to earn an income does not necessarily mean idleness; nor is there any reason why an occupation that does not bring a material return should not be regarded as honorable. The fact that most of our needs can be supplied by the market and that this at the same time gives most men the opportunity of earning a living should not mean that no man ought to be allowed to devote all this energy to ends which bring no financial returns or that only the majority, or only organized groups, should be able to pursue such ends. That only a few can have the opportunity does not make it less desirable that some should have it.

It is doubtful whether a wealthy class whose ethos requires that at least every male member prove his usefulness by making more money can adequately justify its existence. However important the independent owner of property may be for the economic order of a free society, his importance is perhaps even greater in the fields of thought and opinion, of tastes and beliefs. There is something seriously lacking in a society in which all the intellectual, moral, and artistic leaders belong to the employed class, especially if most of them are in the employment of the government. Yet we are moving everywhere toward such a position. Though the freelance writer and artist and the professions of law and medicine still provide some independent leaders of opinion, the great majority of those who ought to provide such a lead—the learned in the sciences and humanities—are today in employed positions, in most countries in the employment of the state.[10] There has been a great change in this

---

[10] I certainly do not object to a due influence being exerted by the intellectual classes to which I myself belong, i.e., by the employed professor, journalist, or public servant. But I recognize that, being an employed group, they have their own professional bias which on some essential points is contrary to the requirements of a free society and which needs to be countered, or at

respect since the nineteenth century, when gentlemen-scholars like Darwin[11] and Macaulay, Grote and Lubbock, Motley and Henry Adams, Tocqueville and Schliemann, were public figures of great prominence and when even such a heterodox critic of society as Karl Marx could find a wealthy patron who enabled him to devote his life to the elaboration and propagation of doctrines which the majority of his contemporaries heartily detested.[12]

The almost complete disappearance of this class—and the absence of it in most parts of the United States—has produced a situation in which the propertied class, now almost exclusively a business group, lacks intellectual leadership and even a coherent and defensible philosophy of life. A wealthy class that is in part a leisured class will be interspersed with more than the average proportion of scholars and statesmen, literary figures and artists. It was through their intercourse in their own circle with such men who shared

---

least modified, by an approach from a different position, by the outlook of men who are not members of an organized hierarchy, whose position in life is independent of the popularity of the views which they express, and who can mix on equal terms with the wealthy and powerful. Occasionally in history this role has been performed by a landowning aristocracy (or the Virginia country gentlemen in the late eighteenth century). There is no need for hereditary privilege to create such a class, and the patrician families of many republican commercial cities have probably earned more credit in this respect than all the titled nobility. Yet, without a sprinkling of men who can devote their lives to whatever values they choose without having to justify their activities to superiors or customers and who are not dependent on rewards for recognized merits, some channels of evolution will be closed which have been very beneficial. If this "greatest of earthly blessings, independence" (as Edward Gibbon called it in his *Autobiography*, "as originally edited by Lord Sheffield [John Holroyd, Earl of Sheffield]," World Classics [London: Oxford University Press, 1950], p. 176) is a "privilege" in the sense that only few can possess it, it is no less desirable that some should enjoy it. We can only hope that this rare advantage is not meted out by human will but will fall by accident on a few lucky ones. [Gibbon actually refers to independence as "the first of earthly blessings."—Ed.]

[11] Charles Darwin himself was very much aware of this; see *The Descent of Man* (*The Origin of Species By Means of Natural Selection; or, The Preservation of Favored Races in the Struggle for Life* and *The Descent of Man and Selection in Relation to Sex* [New York: Modern Library, 1960]), p. 502: "The presence of a body of well-instructed men, who have not to labour for their daily bread, is important to a degree which cannot be over-estimated; as all highly intellectual work is carried on by them, and on such work material progress of all kinds mainly depends, not to mention other and higher advantages."

[12] On the important role that rich men have played in present-day America in spreading radical opinions see Milton Friedman, "Capitalism and Freedom," in *Essays on Individuality*, Felix Morley, ed. (Pittsburgh: University of Pennsylvania Press, 1958), p. 178 [Liberty Fund edition, p. 253] [Friedman's essay appeared in somewhat altered form under the title "The Relation Between Economic Freedom and Political Freedom," which forms chap. 1 of his *Capitalism and Freedom* (Chicago: University of Chicago Press, 1962), pp. 7–21.—Ed.]; cf. also Ludwig von Mises, *The Anti-capitalistic Mentality* (Princeton, NJ: Van Nostrand, 1956) [there is a Liberty Fund edition of this work]; and my essay, "The Intellectuals and Socialism," *University of Chicago Law Review*, 16 (1949): 417–33; reprinted in *Studies in Philosophy, Politics, and Economics* (Chicago: University of Chicago Press, 1967), pp. 178–94. [*Collected Works* edition, vol. 10, pp. 43–65.]

their style of life, that in the past the wealthy men of affairs were able to take part in the movement of ideas and in the discussions that shaped opinion. To the European observer, who cannot help being struck by the apparent helplessness of what in America is still sometimes regarded as its ruling class, it would seem that this is largely due to the fact that its traditions have prevented the growth of a leisured group within it, of a group that uses the independence which wealth gives for purposes other than those vulgarly called economic. This lack of a cultural elite within the propertied class, however, is also now apparent in Europe, where the combined effects of inflation and taxation have mostly destroyed the old and prevented the rise of a new leisured group.

8. It is undeniable that such a leisured group will produce a much larger proportion of *bons vivants* than of scholars and public servants and that the former will shock the public conscience by their conspicuous waste. But such waste is everywhere the price of freedom; and it would be difficult to maintain that the standard by which the consumption of the idlest of the idle rich is judged wasteful and objectionable is really different from that by which the consumption of the American masses will be judged wasteful by the Egyptian fellaheen or the Chinese coolie. Quantitatively, the wastes involved in the amusements of the rich are indeed insignificant compared with those involved in the similar and equally "unnecessary" amusements of the masses,[13] which divert much more from ends which may seem important on some ethical standards. It is merely the conspicuousness and the unfamiliar character of the wastes in the life of the idle rich that make them appear so particularly reprehensible.

It is also true that even when the lavish outlay of some men is most distasteful to the rest, we can scarcely ever be certain that in any particular instance even the most absurd experimentation in living will not produce generally beneficial results. It is not surprising that living on a new level of possibilities at first leads to much aimless display. I have no doubt, however—even though to say so is certain to provoke ridicule—that even the successful use of leisure needs pioneering and that we owe many of the now common forms of living to people who devoted all their time to the art of living[14] and that many of the toys and tools of sport that later became the instruments of recreation for the masses were invented by playboys.

Our evaluation of the usefulness of different activities has in this connection become curiously distorted by the ubiquity of the pecuniary standard.

[13] The expenditure on tobacco and drink alone of the population of the United States runs to about $120 per annum per each adult! [By 2003 the amount expended had increased to $415 per annum per adult.—Ed.]

[14] A study of the evolution of English domestic architecture and living habits has even led a distinguished Danish architect to assert that "in English culture idleness has been the root of all good" (Steen Eiler Rasmussen, *London, the Unique City* [New York: Macmillan, 1937], p. 294).

Surprisingly often, the same people who complain most loudly about the materialism of our civilization will admit of no other standard of usefulness of any service than that men should be willing to pay for it. Yet is it really so obvious that the tennis or golf professional is a more useful member of society than the wealthy amateurs who devoted their time to perfecting these games? Or that the paid curator of a public museum is more useful than a private collector? Before the reader answers these questions too hastily, I would ask him to consider whether there would ever have been golf or tennis professionals or museum curators if wealthy amateurs had not preceded them. Can we not hope that other new interests will still arise from the playful explorations of those who can indulge in them for the short span of a human life? It is only natural that the development of the art of living and of the non-materialistic values should have profited most from the activities of those who had no material worries.[15]

It is one of the great tragedies of our time that the masses have come to believe that they have reached their high standard of material welfare as a result of having pulled down the wealthy, and to fear that the preservation or emergence of such a class would deprive them of something they would otherwise get and which they regard as their due. We have seen why in a progressive society there is little reason to believe that the wealth which the few enjoy would exist at all if they were not allowed to enjoy it. It is neither taken from the rest nor withheld from them. It is the first sign of a new way of living begun by the advance guard. True, those who have this privilege of displaying possibilities which only the children or grandchildren of others will enjoy are not generally the most meritorious individuals but simply those who have been placed by chance in their envied position. But this fact is inseparable from the process of growth, which always goes further than any one man or group of men can foresee. To prevent some from enjoying certain advantages first may well prevent the rest of us from ever enjoying them. If through envy we make certain exceptional kinds of life impossible, we shall all in the end suffer material and spiritual impoverishment. Nor can we eliminate the unpleasant manifestations of individual success without destroying at the same time those forces which make advance possible. One may share to the full the distaste for the ostentation, the bad taste, and the wastefulness of many of the new rich and yet recognize that, if we were to prevent all that we disliked, the unforeseen good things that might be thus prevented would probably outweigh the bad. A world in which the majority could prevent the appearance of all that they did not like would be a stagnant and probably a declining world.

[15] Cf. Bertrand de Jouvenel, *The Ethics of Redistribution* (Cambridge: Cambridge University Press, 1951), esp. p. 80 [Liberty Fund edition, pp. 78–79].

PART II

FREEDOM AND THE LAW

At the first when some certain kind of regiment was once approved, it may be that nothing was then further thought upon for the manner of governing, but all permitted unto their wisdom and discretion which were to rule; till by experience they found this for all parts very inconvenient, so as the thing which they had devised for a remedy did but increase the sore which it should have cured. They saw that to live by one man's will became the cause of all men's misery. This constrained them to come unto laws, wherein all men might see their duties beforehand, and know the penalties of transgressing them. —Richard Hooker

This quotation is taken from Richard Hooker, *Of the Laws of Ecclesiastical Polity* (1593) (2 vols.; London: J. M. Dent, 1907),1, p. 192; the passage is instructive despite the rationalistic interpretation of historical development implied in it.

NINE

COERCION AND THE STATE

For that is an absolute villeinage from which an uncertain and indeterminate service is rendered, where it cannot be known in the evening what service is to be rendered in the morning, that is where a person is bound to whatever is enjoined to him. —Henry Bracton

1. Earlier in our discussion we provisionally defined freedom as the absence of coercion. But coercion is nearly as troublesome a concept as liberty itself, and for much the same reason: we do not clearly distinguish between what other men do to us and the effects on us of physical circumstances. As a matter of fact, English provides us with two different words to make the necessary distinction: while we can legitimately say that we have been compelled by circumstances to do this or that, we presuppose a human agent if we say that we have been coerced.

Coercion occurs when one man's actions are made to serve another man's will, not for his own but for the other's purpose. It is not that the coerced does not choose at all; if that were the case, we should not speak of his "acting." If my hand is guided by physical force to trace my signature or my finger pressed against the trigger of a gun, I have not acted. Such violence, which makes my

---

The quotation from Henry Bracton at the head of the chapter is borrowed from Michael Polanyi, *The Logic of Liberty: Reflections and Rejoinders* (London: Routledge and Kegan Paul, 1951), p. 158 [Liberty Fund edition (1998), p. 194]. [The quotation is from Henry Bracton's *De Legibus et Consuetudinibus Angliae* (*On the Laws and Customs of England*), George Edward Woodbine, ed. (4 vols.; Cambridge, MA: Published in association with the Selden Society by the Belknap Press of Harvard University Press, 1968–77), vol. 2, p. 89. The translation of Bracton's Latin original is that of Samuel Edmund Throne.—Ed.] The chief idea of the chapter has also been well expressed by Frederic William Maitland in his "Historical Sketch of Liberty and Equality as Ideals" (1875), in *Collected Papers of Frederic William Maitland, Downing Professor of the Laws of England* (3 vols.; Cambridge: Cambridge University Press, 1911), vol. 1, p. 80: "The exercise of power in ways which cannot be anticipated causes some of the greatest restraints, for restraint is most felt and therefore is greatest when it is least anticipated. We feel ourselves least free when we know that restraints may at any moment be placed on any of our actions, and yet we cannot anticipate these restraints. . . . Known general laws, however bad, interfere less with freedom than decisions based on no previously known rule." [Liberty Fund edition of the *Historical Sketch*, pp. 109–10.]

body someone else's physical tool, is, of course, as bad as coercion proper and must be prevented for the same reason. Coercion implies, however, that I still choose but that my mind is made someone else's tool, because the alternatives before me have been so manipulated that the conduct that the coercer wants me to choose becomes for me the least painful one.[1] Although coerced, it is still I who decide which is the least evil under the circumstances.[2]

Coercion clearly does not include all influences that men can exercise on the action of others. It does not even include all instances in which a person acts or threatens to act in a manner he knows will harm another person and will lead him to change his intentions. A person who blocks my path in the street and causes me to step aside, a person who has borrowed from the library the book I want, or even a person who drives me away by the unpleasant noises he produces cannot properly be said to coerce me. Coercion implies both the threat of inflicting harm and the intention thereby to bring about certain conduct.

Though the coerced still chooses, the alternatives are determined for him by the coercer so that he will choose what the coercer wants. He is not altogether deprived of the use of his capacities; but he is deprived of the possibility of using his knowledge for his own aims. The effective use of a person's intelligence and knowledge in the pursuit of his aims requires that he be able to foresee some of the conditions of his environment and adhere to a plan of action. Most human aims can be achieved only by a chain of connected actions, decided upon as a coherent whole and based on the assumption that the facts will be what they are expected to be. It is because, and insofar as, we can predict events, or at least know probabilities, that we can achieve anything. And though physical circumstances will often be unpredictable, they will not maliciously frustrate our aims. But if the facts which determine our plans are under the sole control of another, our actions will be similarly controlled.

Coercion thus is bad because it prevents a person from using his mental

---

[1] Cf. Frank Hyneman Knight, "Conflict of Values: Freedom and Justice," in *Goals of Economic Life*, Alfred Dudley Ward, ed. (New York: Harper and Bros., 1953), p. 208: "Coercion is 'arbitrary' manipulation by one of another's terms or alternatives of choice—and usually we should say an 'unjustified' interference." See also Robert Morrison MacIver, *Society: A Textbook of Sociology* (New York: Farrar and Rinehart, 1937), p. 342.

[2] Cf. the legal maxim "etsi coactus tamen voluit," deriving from *Corpus juris civilis, Digesta*, 50. 4. 21 [Samuel Parsons Scott, *The Civil Law, Including the Twelve Tables, the Institutes of Gaius, the Rules of Ulpian, the Opinions of Paulus, the Enactments of Justinian, and the Constitutions of Leo* (17 vols. in 7; Cincinnati: Central Trust Co., 1932), vol. 3/4, p. 65]. [The phrase translates as: "Although compelled, he nevertheless wished it." The original source is noted as Paulus, *On the Edict*, bk. 11.—Ed.] For a discussion of its significance see Ulrich von Lübtow, *Der Ediktstitel "Quod metus causa gestum erit"* (Greifswald: Bamberg, 1932), pp. 61–71. [The Latin phrase in the title of the book carries the meaning "When an act was performed because of fear."—Ed.]

powers to the full and consequently from making the greatest contribution that he is capable of to the community. Though the coerced will still do the best he can do for himself at any given moment, the only comprehensive design that his actions fit into is that of another mind.

2. Political philosophers have discussed power more often than they have coercion because political power usually means power to coerce.[3] But though the great men, from John Milton and Edmund Burke to Lord Acton and Jacob Burckhardt, who have represented power as the archevil,[4] were right

---

[3] Cf. Friedrich von Wieser, *Das Gesetz der Macht* (Vienna: Julius Springer, 1926); Bertrand Russell, *Power: A New Social Analysis* (London: Allen and Unwin, 1930); Guglielmo Ferrero, *The Principles of Power* (New York: G. P. Putnam's Sons, 1942) [This is the third volume of a trilogy. The first two volumes were originally published in Paris (Vol. 1: *The Gamble*, Vol. 2: *The Reconstruction of Europe*). The third appeared in New York because it could not be published on the Continent due to increased censorship.—Ed.]; Bertrand de Jouvenel, *Power: The Natural History of Its Growth* (London: Hutchinson, 1948) [The Liberty Fund reissued Jouvenel's book with a foreword by Denis William Brogan in 1993.—Ed.]; Gerhard Ritter, *Vom sittlichen Problem der Macht: Fünf Essays* (Bern: Francke, 1948); and the same author's *Machtstaat und Utopie: vom Streit um die Dämonie der Macht seit Machiavelli und Morus* (Munich: Oldenburg, 1940); Cyril John Radcliffe, Viscount Radcliffe of Werneth, *The Problem of Power* [Reith Lectures] (London: Secker and Warburg, 1952); and John Clark MacDermott, Baron MacDermott, *Protection from Power under English Law*, The Hamlyn Lectures (London: Stevens, 1957).

[4] The complaints about power as the archevil are as old as political thinking. Herodotus had already made Otanes say in his famous speech on democracy that "even the best of men raised to such a position [of irresponsible power] would be bound to change for the worst" (*Histories*, iii, 80); John Milton considers the possibility that "long continuance of Power may corrupt sincerest Men" ("The Ready and Easy Way to Establish a Free Commonwealth, and the Excellence thereof, Compared with the Inconveniences and Dangers of Readmitting Kingship in this Nation" [1660], in *Milton's Prose*, Malcolm William Wallace, ed. [World's Classics; London: Oxford University Press, 1925], p. 459 [Liberty Fund edition, p. 428]); Montesquieu asserts that "constant experience shows us that every man invested with power is apt to abuse it, and to carry his authority as far as it will go" ["Mais c'est une expérience éternelle que tout homme qui a du pouvoir est porté à en abuser; il va jusquà ce qu'il trouve des limites."—Ed.] (*Spirit of the Laws*, bk. 11, chap. 4, vol. 1, p. 150; French edition: vol. 2, p. 395); Immanuel Kant maintains that "the possession of power invariably debases the free judgment of reason" ["Der Besitz der Gewalt das freie Urteil der Vernunft unvermeidlich verdirbt." (*Zum ewigen Frieden: Ein philosophischer Entwurf* [1795], Karl Kehrbach, ed. [Leipzig: Philipp Reclam jun., 1881], p. 36.) The essay appears in English under the title *Perpetual Peace: A Philosophical Essay*.—Ed.]; Edmund Burke writes that "many of the greatest tyrants on [*sic*] the records of history have begun their reigns in the fairest manner. But the truth is, this unnatural power corrupts both the heart and the understanding" (*Thoughts on the Cause of Our Present Discontents*, in *Works*, II, p. 307 [Hayek is in error in locating the quotation in Burke's *Thoughts on the Cause of Our Present Discontents*. The quotation in fact appears in *A Vindication of Natural Society; or, A View of the Miseries and Evils Arising to Mankind from Every Species of Artificial Society* (3rd ed., with a new preface; Dublin: Printed by and for Sarah Cotter, 1766), p. 38; Liberty Fund edition, p. 46.—Ed.]); John Adams observes that "power is always abused when unlimited and unbalanced" (*Works: With a Life of the Author*, Charles Francis Adams, ed. [10 vols.; Boston: Charles C. Little and James Brown, 1851], vol. 6, p. 73), and that "absolute power intoxicates alike despots, monarchs, aristocrats, and democrats,

in what they meant, it is misleading to speak simply of power in this connection. It is not power as such—the capacity to achieve what one wants—that is bad, but only the power to coerce, to force other men to serve one's will by the threat of inflicting harm. There is no evil in the power wielded by the director of some great enterprise in which men have willingly united of their own will and for their own purposes. It is part of the strength of civilized society that, by such voluntary combination of effort under a unified direction, men can enormously increase their collective power.

It is not power in the sense of an extension of our capacities which corrupts, but the subjection of other human wills to ours, the use of other men against their will for our purposes. It is true that in human relations power and coercion dwell closely together, that great powers possessed by a few may enable them to coerce others, unless those powers are contained by a still greater power; but coercion is neither so necessary nor so common a consequence of power as is generally assumed. Neither the powers of a Henry Ford nor those of the Atomic Energy Commission, neither those of the General of the Salvation Army nor (at least until recently) those of the President of the United States, are powers to coerce particular people for the purposes they choose.

It would be less misleading if occasionally the terms "force" and "violence" were used instead of coercion, since the threat of force or violence is the most important form of coercion. But they are not synonymous with coercion, for the threat of physical force is not the only way in which coercion can be exercised. Similarly, "oppression," which is perhaps as much a true opposite of liberty as coercion, should refer only to a state of continuous acts of coercion.

3. Coercion should be carefully distinguished from the conditions or terms on which our fellow men are willing to render us specific services or bene-

---

and jacobins and *sans culottes*" (vol. 6, p. 477) [The first quotation appears in chap. 1 of Adams's "A Defence of the Constitutions of Government of the United States of America." The second is taken from Adams's Letters to John Taylor.—Ed.]; James Madison asserts [in his letter to Thomas Ritchie dated 18 December 1825] that "all power in human hands is liable to be abused" and [in an unsent letter to Thomas Lehre dated 2 August 1828] that "power, wherever lodged, is liable, more or less, to abuse" (*The Complete Madison: His Basic Writings*, Saul Kussiel Padover, ed. [New York: Harper, 1953], p. 46); Jacob Burckhardt never ceases to reiterate that power in itself is evil (*Force and Freedom: Reflections on History*, James Hastings Nichols, trans. [New York: Pantheon Books, 1943], e.g., p. 115 [Liberty Fund edition, p. 102]); and there is, of course, Lord Acton's maxim "power tends to corrupt, and absolute power corrupts absolutely" (*Historical Essays*, p. 504 [Liberty Fund edition, *Essays in the Study and Writing of History*, p. 383]). [Letter from Acton to Bishop Mandell Creighton (April 3,1887) regarding Acton's review of vols. 3 and 4 of Creighton's *History of the Papacy, The Italian Princes, 1464–1518*, contributed to the *English Historical Review* in 1887.—Ed.] See also Carl von Rotteck, "Absolutismus," in *Staatslexikon oder Encyklopädie der Staatswissenschaften*, Carl von Rotteck and Carl. T. Welcker, eds. (Altona: Hammrich, 1834), vol. 1, p. 155: "Es liegt in der unumschränkten Gewalt eine so schauerliche Macht der bösen Versuchung, daß nur die alleredelsten Menschen ihr widerstehen können." ["Absolute power contains within itself the awful temptation toward evil that only the most noble can resist."—Ed.]

fits. It is only in very exceptional circumstances that the sole control of a service or resource which is essential to us would confer upon another the power of true coercion. Life in society necessarily means that we are dependent for the satisfaction of most of our needs on the services of some of our fellows; in a free society these mutual services are voluntary, and each can determine to whom he wants to render services and on what terms. The benefits and opportunities which our fellows offer to us will be available only if we satisfy their conditions.

This is as true of social as of economic relations. If a hostess will invite me to her parties only if I conform to certain standards of conduct and dress, or my neighbor converse with me only if I observe conventional manners, this is certainly not coercion. Nor can it be legitimately called "coercion" if a producer or dealer refuses to supply me with what I want except at his price. This is certainly true in a competitive market, where I can turn to somebody else if the terms of the first offer do not suit me; and it is normally no less true when I face a monopolist. If, for instance, I would very much like to be painted by a famous artist and if he refuses to paint me for less than a very high fee, it would clearly be absurd to say that I am coerced. The same is true of any other commodity or service that I can do without. So long as the services of a particular person are not crucial to my existence or the preservation of what I most value, the conditions he exacts for rendering these services cannot properly be called "coercion."

A monopolist could exercise true coercion, however, if he were, say, the owner of a spring in an oasis. Let us say that other persons settled there on the assumption that water would always be available at a reasonable price and then found, perhaps because a second spring dried up, that they had no choice but to do whatever the owner of the spring demanded of them if they were to survive: here would be a clear case of coercion. One could conceive of a few other instances where a monopolist might control an essential commodity on which people were completely dependent. But unless a monopolist is in a position to withhold an indispensable supply, he cannot exercise coercion, however unpleasant his demands may be for those who rely on his services.

It is worth pointing out, in view of what we shall later have to say about the appropriate methods of curbing the coercive power of the state, that whenever there is a danger of a monopolist's acquiring coercive power, the most expedient and effective method of preventing this is probably to require him to treat all customers alike, i.e., to insist that his prices be the same for all and to prohibit all discrimination on his part. This is the same principle by which we have learned to curb the coercive power of the state.

The individual provider of employment cannot normally exercise coercion, any more than can the supplier of a particular commodity or service. So long as he can remove only one opportunity among many to earn a living, so long as he can do no more than cease to pay certain people who cannot hope to earn as much elsewhere as they had done under him, he cannot coerce, though he may cause pain. There are, undeniably, occasions when the condition of employment creates opportunity for true coercion. In periods of acute unemployment the threat of dismissal may be used to enforce actions other than those originally contracted for. And in conditions such as those in a mining town the manager may well exercise an entirely arbitrary and capricious tyranny over a man to whom he has taken a dislike. But such conditions, though not impossible, would, at the worst, be rare exceptions in a prosperous competitive society.

A complete monopoly of employment, such as would exist in a fully socialist state in which the government was the only employer and the owner of all the instruments of production, would possess unlimited powers of coercion. As Leon Trotsky discovered: "In a country where the sole employer is the State, opposition means death by slow starvation. The old principle, who does not work shall not eat, has been replaced by a new one: who does not obey shall not eat."[5]

Except in such instances of monopoly of an essential service, the mere power of withholding a benefit will not produce coercion. The use of such power by another may indeed alter the social landscape to which I have adapted my plans and make it necessary for me to reconsider all my decisions, perhaps to change my whole scheme of life and to worry about many things I had taken for granted. But, though the alternatives before me may be distressingly few and uncertain, and my new plans of a makeshift character, yet it is not some other will that guides my action. I may have to act under great pressure, but I cannot be said to act under coercion. Even if the threat of starvation to me and perhaps to my family impels me to accept a distasteful job at a very low wage, even if I am "at the mercy" of the only man willing to employ me, I am not coerced by him or anybody else. So long as the act that has placed me in my predicament is not aimed at making me do or not do specific things, so long as the intent of the act that harms me is not to make me serve another person's ends, its effect on my freedom is not different from that of any natural calamity—a fire or a flood that destroys my house or an accident that harms my health.

4. True coercion occurs when armed bands of conquerors make the subject people toil for them, when organized gangsters extort a levy for "protection," when the knower of an evil secret blackmails his victim, and, of course, when the state threatens to inflict punishment and to employ physical force to make us obey its commands. There are many degrees of coercion, from the extreme

[5] Leon Trotsky, *The Revolution Betrayed: What Is the Soviet Union and Where is it Going?* (Garden City, NY: Doubleday, Doran and Co., 1937), p. 283.

case of the dominance of the master over the slave or the tyrant over the subject, where the unlimited power of punishment exacts complete submission to the will of the master, to the instance of the single threat of inflicting an evil to which the threatened would prefer almost anything else.

Whether or not attempts to coerce a particular person will be successful depends in a large measure on that person's inner strength: the threat of assassination may have less power to turn one man from his aim than the threat of some minor inconvenience in the case of another. But while we may pity the weak or the very sensitive person whom a mere frown may "compel" to do what he would not do otherwise, we are concerned with coercion that is likely to affect the normal, average person. Though this will usually be some threat of bodily harm to his person or his dear ones, or of damage to a valuable or cherished possession, it need not consist of any use of force or violence. One may frustrate another's every attempt at spontaneous action by placing in his path an infinite variety of minor obstacles: guile and malice may well find the means of coercing the physically stronger. It is not impossible for a horde of cunning boys to drive an unpopular person out of town.

In some degree all close relationships between men, whether they are tied to one another by affection, economic necessity, or physical circumstances (such as on a ship or an expedition), provide opportunities for coercion. The conditions of personal domestic service, like all more intimate relations, undoubtedly offer opportunities for coercion of a peculiarly oppressive kind and are, in consequence, felt as restrictions on personal liberty. And a morose husband, a nagging wife, or a hysterical mother may make life intolerable unless their every mood is obeyed. But here society can do little to protect the individual beyond making such associations with others truly voluntary. Any attempt to regulate these intimate associations further would clearly involve such far-reaching restrictions on choice and conduct as to produce even greater coercion: if people are to be free to choose their associates and intimates, the coercion that arises from voluntary association cannot be the concern of government.

The reader may feel that we have devoted more space than is necessary to the distinction between what can be legitimately called "coercion" and what cannot and between the more severe forms of coercion, which we should prevent, and the lesser forms, which ought not to be the concern of authority. But, as in the case of liberty, a gradual extension of the concept has almost deprived it of value. Liberty can be so defined as to make it impossible of attainment. Similarly, coercion can be so defined as to make it an all-pervasive and unavoidable phenomenon.[6] We cannot prevent all harm that a person

---

[6] A characteristic instance of this which happened to come to my notice as I was writing occurs in a review by Bertram Francis Willcox, "*The Labor Policy of a Free Society* by Sylvester

may inflict upon another, or even all the milder forms of coercion to which life in close contact with other men exposes us; but this does not mean that we ought not to try to prevent all the more severe forms of coercion, or that we ought not to define liberty as the absence of such coercion.

5. Since coercion is the control of the essential data of an individual's action by another, it can be prevented only by enabling the individual to secure for himself some private sphere where he is protected against such interference. The assurance that he can count on certain facts not being deliberately shaped by another can be given to him only by some authority that has the necessary power. It is here that coercion of one individual by another can be prevented only by the threat of coercion.

The existence of such an assured free sphere seems to us so much a normal condition of life that we are tempted to define "coercion" by the use of such terms as "the interference with legitimate expectations," or "infringement of rights," or "arbitrary interference."[7] But in defining coercion we cannot take for granted the arrangements intended to prevent it. The "legitimacy" of one's expectations or the "rights" of the individual are the result of the recognition of such a private sphere. Coercion not only would exist but would be much more common if no such protected sphere existed. Only in a society that has already attempted to prevent coercion by some demarcation of a protected sphere can a concept like "arbitrary interference" have a definite meaning.

If the recognition of such individual spheres, however, is not itself to become an instrument of coercion, their range and content must not be determined by the deliberate assignment of particular things to particular men. If what was to be included in a man's private sphere were to be determined by the will of any man or group of men, this would simply transfer the power of coercion to that will. Nor would it be desirable to have the particular contents of a man's private sphere fixed once and for all. If people are to make the best use of their knowledge and capacities and foresight, it is desirable that they them-

---

Petro," *Industrial and Labor Relations Review*, 9 (1957–58): 273: In order to justify "peaceful economic coercion" by unions, the author argues that "peaceable competition, based on free choice, fairly reeks of coercion. A free seller of goods or services, by setting his price, coerces one who wants to buy—coerces him into paying, doing without, or going elsewhere. A free seller of goods or services, by setting a condition that no one may buy from him who buys from X, coerces one who wants to buy—coerces him into doing without, going elsewhere, or refraining from buying from X—and in the last case he coerces X as well." This abuse of the term "coercion" derives largely from John Rogers Commons (cf. his *Institutional Economics* [New York: Macmillan, 1934]), esp. pp. 336–37; see also Robert Lee Hale, "Coercion and Distribution in a Supposedly Noncoercive State," *Political Science Quarterly*, 38 (1923): 470–94, and his *Freedom through Law: Public Control of Private Governing Power* (New York: Columbia University Press, 1952).

[7] Cf. the passage by Frank Hyneman Knight, "Conflict of Values: Freedom and Justice," p. 208.

selves have some voice in the determination of what will be included in their personal protected sphere.

The solution that men have found for this problem rests on the recognition of general rules governing the conditions under which objects or circumstances become part of the protected sphere of a person or persons. The acceptance of such rules enables each member of a society to shape the content of his protected sphere and all members to recognize what belongs to their sphere and what does not.[8]

We must not think of this sphere as consisting exclusively, or even chiefly, of material things. Although to divide the material objects of our environment into what is mine and what is another's is the principal aim of the rules which delimit the spheres, they also secure for us many other "rights," such as security in certain uses of things or merely protection against interference with our actions.

6. The recognition of private or several[9] property is thus an essential condition for the prevention of coercion, though by no means the only one. We are rarely in a position to carry out a coherent plan of action unless we are certain of our exclusive control of some material objects; and where we do not control them, it is necessary that we know who does if we are to collaborate with others. The recognition of property is clearly the first step in the delimitation of the private sphere which protects us against coercion; and it has long been recognized that "a people averse to the institution of private property is without the first element of freedom"[10] and that "nobody is at liberty to attack several property and to say at the same time that he values civilization. The history of the two cannot be disentangled."[11] Modern anthropology confirms the fact that "private property appears very definitely on primitive levels" and that "the roots of property as a legal principle which determines the physical relationship between man and his environmental setting, natural or artificial, are the very prerequisite of any ordered action in the cultural sense."[12]

In modern society, however, the essential requisite for the protection of the

[8] On the role of property in the American tradition of liberty, see Paul Abraham Freund, *On Understanding the Supreme Court: A Series of Lectures Delivered under the Auspices of the Julius Rosenthal Foundation at Northwestern University School of Law, in April 1949* (3rd ed.; Boston: Little, Brown and Co., 1951), pp. 14ff.

[9] The expression "several property" used by Sir Henry Maine (*Village Communities in the East and West: Six Lectures Delivered at Oxford to which are added Other Lectures, Addresses, and Essays* [New York: H. Holt and Co., 1880], p. 230), is in many respects more appropriate than the more familiar one "private property," and we shall occasionally employ it in place of the latter.

[10] Acton, "Nationality," *History of Freedom*, p. 297 [Liberty Fund edition, *Essays in the History of Liberty*, p. 431].

[11] Sir Henry Maine, *Village Communities*, p. 230.

[12] Bronislaw Malinowski, *Freedom and Civilization* (New York: Roy Publishers, 1944), pp. 132–33.

individual against coercion is not that he possess property but that the material means which enable him to pursue any plan of action should not be all in the exclusive control of one other agent. It is one of the accomplishments of modern society that freedom may be enjoyed by a person with practically no property of his own (beyond personal belongings like clothing—and even these can be rented)[13] and that we can leave the care of the property that serves our needs largely to others. The important point is that the property should be sufficiently dispersed so that the individual is not dependent on particular persons who alone can provide him with what he needs or who alone can employ him.

That other people's property can be serviceable in the achievement of our aims is due mainly to the enforcibility of contracts. The whole network of rights created by contracts is as important a part of our own protected sphere, as much the basis of our plans, as any property of our own. The decisive condition for mutually advantageous collaboration between people, based on voluntary consent rather than coercion, is that there be many people who can serve one's needs so that nobody has to be dependent on specific persons for the essential conditions of life or the possibility of development in some direction. It is competition made possible by the dispersion of property that deprives the individual owners of particular things of all coercive powers.

In view of a common misunderstanding of a famous maxim,[14] it should be mentioned that we are independent of the will of those whose services

[13] I do not mean to suggest that this is a desirable form of existence. It is of some importance, however, that today a not inconsiderable portion of the men who largely influence public opinion, such as journalists and writers, often live for long periods with a minimum of personal possessions and that this undoubtedly affects their outlook. It seems that some people even have come to regard material possessions as an impediment rather than a help, so long as they have the income to buy what they need.

[14] Immanuel Kant, "Foundations of the Metaphysics of Morals," *Critique of Practical Reason and Other Writings in Moral Philosophy*, Lewis White Beck, ed. (Chicago: University of Chicago Press, 1949), p. 87: "Act so that you treat humanity, whether in your own person or in that of another, always as an end and never as a means only." ["Handle so, daß du die Menschheit sowohl in deiner Person als in der Person eines jeden andern jederzeit zugleich als Zweck, niemals bloß als Mittel brauchst." *Grundlegung zur Metaphysik der Sitten*, in *Kants Werke*, (Akademie Textausgabe; 9 vols.; Berlin: Walter de Gruyter, 1968), vol. 4, p. 429.—Ed.] So far as this means that no man should be made to do anything that serves only other people's purposes, it is just another way of saying that coercion should be avoided. But if the maxim is interpreted to mean that when we collaborate with other men, we should be guided not only by our own but also by their purposes, it soon comes into conflict with their freedom when we disagree with their ends. For an example of such an interpretation see John Maurice Clark, *The Ethical Basis of Economic Freedom* (Kazanjian Foundation Lecture; Westport, CT: C. K. Kazanjian Economics Foundation, 1955), p. 26, and the German literature discussed in the work quoted in the next note. [The two works cited in Mises's *Socialism* on the pages to which Hayek refers are: Friedrich Engels, *Ludwig Feuerbach und der Ausgang der klassischen deutschen Philosophie* (5th ed.; Stuttgart: J. H. W. Dietz, 1910), and Hermann Cohen, *Ethik des reinen Willens* (Berlin: B. Cassirer, 1904), pp. 303 et seq.—Ed.]

COERCION AND THE STATE

we need because they serve us for their own purposes and are normally little interested in the uses we make of their services. We should be very dependent on the beliefs of our fellows if they were prepared to sell their products to us only when they approved of our ends and not for their own advantage. It is largely because in the economic transactions of everyday life we are only impersonal means to our fellows, who help us for their own purposes, that we can count on such help from complete strangers and use it for whatever end we wish.[15]

The rules of property and contract are required to delimit the individual's private sphere wherever the resources or services needed for the pursuit of his aims are scarce and must, in consequence, be under the control of some man or another. But if this is true of most of the benefits we derive from men's efforts, it is not true of all. There are some kinds of services, such as sanitation or roads, which, once they are provided, are normally sufficient for all who want to use them. The provision of such services has long been a recognized field of public effort, and the right to share in them is an important part of the protected sphere of the individual. We need only remember the role that the assured "access to the King's highway" has played in history to see how important such rights may be for individual liberty.

We cannot enumerate here all the rights or protected interests which serve to secure to the legal person a known sphere of unimpeded action. But, since modern man has become a little insensitive on this point, it ought perhaps to be mentioned that the recognition of a protected individual sphere has in times of freedom normally included a right to privacy and secrecy, the conception that a man's house is his castle[16] and that nobody has a right even to take cognizance of his activities within it.

7. The character of those abstract and general rules that have been evolved to limit coercion both by other individuals and by the state will be the subject of the next chapter. Here we shall consider in a general way how that threat of coercion which is the only means whereby the state can prevent the coercion of one individual by another can be deprived of most of its harmful and objectionable character.

This threat of coercion has a very different effect from that of actual and unavoidable coercion, if it refers only to known circumstances which can be avoided by the potential object of coercion. The great majority of the threats

[15] Cf. Ludwig von Mises, *Socialism*, pp. 194 and 430–41 [Liberty Fund edition, pp. 171 and 388–389].

[16] In view of the often alleged lack of individual liberty in classical Greece, it deserves mention that in the Athens of the fifth century B.C. the sanctity of the private home was so fully recognized that even under the rule of the Thirty Tyrants a man "could save his life by staying at home" (see John Walter Jones, *The Law and Legal Theory of the Greeks: An Introduction* [Oxford: Clarendon Press, 1956], p. 91, with reference to Demosthenes xxiv, 52).

of coercion that a free society must employ are of this avoidable kind. Most of the rules that it enforces, particularly its private law, do not constrain private persons (as distinguished from the servants of the state) to perform specific actions. The sanctions of the law are designed only to prevent a person from doing certain things or to make him perform obligations that he has voluntarily incurred.

Provided that I know beforehand that if I place myself in a particular position, I shall be coerced and provided that I can avoid putting myself in such a position, I need never be coerced. At least insofar as the rules providing for coercion are not aimed at me personally but are so framed as to apply equally to all people in similar circumstances, they are no different from any of the natural obstacles that affect my plans. In that they tell me what will happen *if* I do this or that, the laws of the state have the same significance for me as the laws of nature; and I can use my knowledge of the laws of the state to achieve my own aims as I use my knowledge of the laws of nature.

8. Of course, in some respects the state uses coercion to make us perform particular actions. The most important of these are taxation and the various compulsory services, especially in the armed forces. Though these are not supposed to be avoidable, they are at least predictable and are enforced irrespective of how the individual would otherwise employ his energies; this deprives them largely of the evil nature of coercion. If the known necessity of paying a certain amount in taxes becomes the basis of all my plans, if a period of military service is a foreseeable part of my career, then I can follow a general plan of life of my own making and am as independent of the will of another person as men have learned to be in society. Though compulsory military service, while it lasts, undoubtedly involves severe coercion, and though a lifelong conscript could not be said ever to be free, a predictable limited period of military service certainly restricts the possibility of shaping one's own life less than would, for instance, a constant threat of arrest resorted to by an arbitrary power to ensure what it regards as good behavior.

The interference of the coercive power of government with our lives is most disturbing when it is neither avoidable nor predictable. Where such coercion is necessary even in a free society, as when we are called to serve on a jury or to act as special constables, we mitigate the effects by not allowing any person to possess arbitrary power of coercion. Instead, the decision as to who must serve is made to rest on fortuitous processes, such as the drawing of lots. These unpredictable acts of coercion, which follow from unpredictable events but conform to known rules, affect our lives as do other "acts of God," but do not subject us to the arbitrary will of another person.

9. Is the prevention of coercion the only justification for the use of the threat of coercion by the state? We can probably include all forms of violence under coercion or at least maintain that a successful prevention of coer-

cion will mean the prevention of all kinds of violence. There remains, however, one other kind of harmful action which it is generally thought desirable to prevent and which at first may seem distinct. This is fraud and deception. Yet, though it would be straining the meaning of words to call them "coercion," on examination it appears that the reasons why we want to prevent them are the same as those applying to coercion. Deception, like coercion, is a form of manipulating the data on which a person counts, in order to make him do what the deceiver wants him to do. Where it is successful, the deceived becomes in the same manner the unwilling tool, serving another man's ends without advancing his own. Though we have no single word to cover both, all we have said of coercion applies equally to fraud and deception.

With this correction, it seems that freedom demands no more than that coercion and violence, fraud and deception, be prevented, except for the use of coercion by government for the sole purpose of enforcing known rules intended to secure the best conditions under which the individual may give his activities a coherent, rational pattern.

The problem of the limit of coercion is not the same as that concerning the proper function of government. The coercive activities of government are by no means its only tasks. It is true that the non-coercive or purely service activities that government undertakes are usually financed by coercive means. The medieval state, which financed its activities mainly with the income from its property, might have provided services without resorting to coercion. Under modern conditions, however, it seems hardly practicable that government should provide such services as the care for the disabled or the infirm and the provision of roads or of information without relying on its coercive powers to finance them.

It is not to be expected that there will ever be complete unanimity on the desirability of the extent of such services, and it is at least not obvious that coercing people to contribute to the achievement of ends in which they are not interested can be morally justified. Up to a point, most of us find it expedient, however, to make such contributions on the understanding that we will in turn profit from similar contributions of others toward the realization of our own ends.

Outside the field of taxation, it is probably desirable that we should accept only the prevention of more severe coercion as the justification for the use of coercion by government. This criterion, perhaps, cannot be applied to each single legal rule, but only to the legal system as a whole. The protection of private property as a safeguard against coercion, for instance, may require special provisions that do not individually serve to reduce coercion but serve merely to insure that private property does not unnecessarily impede action that does not harm the owner. But the whole conception of interference or non-interference by the state rests on the assumption of a private sphere delimited by general rules enforced by the state; and the real issue is whether the state ought to confine its coercive action to enforcing these rules or go beyond this.

Attempts have often been made, notably by John Stuart Mill,[17] to define the private sphere that should be immune from coercion in terms of a distinction between actions that affect only the acting person and those which also affect others. But, as there is hardly any action that may not conceivably affect others, this distinction has not proved very useful. It is only by delimiting the protected sphere of each individual that the distinction becomes significant. Its aim cannot be to protect people against all actions by others that may be harmful to them[18] but only to keep certain of the data of their actions from the control of others. In determining where the boundaries of the protected sphere ought to be drawn, the important question is whether the actions of other people that we wish to see prevented would actually interfere with the reasonable expectations of the protected person.

In particular, the pleasure or pain that may be caused by the knowledge of other people's actions should never be regarded as a legitimate cause for coercion. The enforcement of religious conformity, for instance, was a legitimate object of government when people believed in the collective responsibility of the community toward some deity and it was thought that the sins of any member would be visited upon all. But where private practices cannot affect anybody but the voluntary adult actors, the mere dislike of what is being done by others, or even the knowledge that others harm themselves by what they do, provides no legitimate ground for coercion.[19]

We have seen that the opportunities of learning about new possibilities that the growth of civilization constantly offers provide one of the main arguments

---

[17] John Stuart Mill, "On Liberty," in *On Liberty and Considerations on Representative Government*, Ronald Buchanan McCallum, ed. (Oxford: Blackwell, 1946), chap. 4, pp. 66–83.

[18] Cf. Mill, *On Liberty*, p. 84: "In many cases, an individual, in pursuing a legitimate object, necessarily and therefore legitimately causes pain or loss to others, or intercepts a good which they had a reasonable hope of obtaining." Also the significant change from the misleading formulation of art. 4 in the French Declaration of the Rights of Man and of the Citizen of 1789, "La liberté consiste a pouvoir faire tout ce qui ne nuit pas à autrui," ["Liberty consists in the freedom to do everything not injurious to others."—Ed.] to the correct formulation of art. 6 of the Declaration of 1793: "La liberté est le pouvoir qui appartient à l'homme de faire tout ce que ne nuit pas aux droits d'autrui" ["Liberty is the power that man possesses to do whatever is not injurious to the rights of others."—Ed.].

[19] The most conspicuous instance of this in our society is that of the treatment of homosexuality. As Bertrand Russell has observed ("John Stuart Mill," *Proceedings of the British Academy*, 41 [1955]: 55): "If it were still believed, as it once was, that the toleration of such behaviour would expose the community to the fate of Sodom and Gomorrah, the community would have every right to intervene." But where such factual beliefs do not prevail, private practice among adults, however abhorrent it may be to the majority, is not a proper subject for coercive action for a state whose object is to minimize coercion.

for freedom; it would therefore make nonsense of the whole case for freedom if, because of the envy of others[20] or because of their dislike of anything that disturbs their ingrained habits of thought, we should be restrained from pursuing certain activities. While there is clearly a case for enforcing rules of conduct in public places, the bare fact that an action is disliked by some of those who learn about it cannot be a sufficient ground for prohibiting it.

Generally speaking, this means that the morality of action within the private sphere is not a proper object for coercive control by the state. Perhaps one of the most important characteristics that distinguish a free from an unfree society is indeed that, in matters of conduct that do not directly affect the protected sphere of others, the rules which are in fact observed by most are of a voluntary character and not enforced by coercion. Recent experience with totalitarian regimes has emphasized the importance of the principle "never [to] identify the cause of moral values with that of the State."[21] It is indeed probable that more harm and misery have been caused by men determined to use coercion to stamp out a moral evil than by men intent on doing evil.

10. Yet the fact that conduct within the private sphere is not a proper object for coercive action by the state does not necessarily mean that in a free society such conduct should also be exempt from the pressure of opinion or disapproval. A hundred years ago, in the stricter moral atmosphere of the Victorian era, when at the same time coercion by the state was at a minimum, John

---

[20] Charles Anthony Raven Crosland, *The Future of Socialism* (London: Jonathan Cape, 1956), p. 206.

[21] The statement quoted has been ascribed to Ignazio Silone. [The quotation comes from a speech made in Italian by Silone before the International PEN Club Conference held at Basle in 1947. It is reprinted, in a translation made by Eric Mossbacher, in "On the Place of the Intellect and the Pretensions of the Intellectual," *Horizon: A Review of Literature and Art*, 16 (December 1947): 323, reprinted in George Barnard de Huszar, ed, *The Intellectuals: A Controversial Portrait* (Glencoe, IL: The Free Press, 1960), p. 264.—Ed.] Cf. also Jacob Burckhardt, *Reflections on History*, p. 118 [Liberty Fund edition, p. 70]: "It is a degeneration, it is philosophical and bureaucratic arrogance, for the State to attempt to fulfil moral purposes directly, for only society can and may do that." See also Harold Stearns, *Liberalism in America: Its Origins, Its Temporary Collapse, Its Future* (New York: Boni and Liveright, 1919), p. 69: "Coercion for the sake of virtue is as repugnant as coercion for the sake of vice. If American liberals are unwilling to fight the principle of coercion in the case of the Prohibition Amendment simply because they personally are not much interested in whether the country is dry or not, then they are discredited the moment they fight coercion in those cases where they *are* interested." The typical socialist attitude on these problems is most explicitly stated in Robert Lowe Hall, *The Economic System in a Socialist State* (London: Macmillan, 1937), pp. 202–3, where it is argued (with regard to the duty of increasing the capital of the country) that "the fact that it is necessary to use such words as 'moral obligation' and 'duty' shows that there is no question of accurate calculation and that we are dealing with decisions which not only may be, but ought to be, taken by the community as a whole, that is to say with political decisions." For a conservative defense of the use of political power to enforce moral principles see Walter Berns, *Freedom, Virtue, and the First Amendment* (Baton Rouge: Louisiana State University Press, 1957).

213

Stuart Mill directed his heaviest attack against such "moral coercion."[22] In this he probably overstated the case for liberty. At any rate, it probably makes for greater clarity not to represent as coercion the pressure that public approval or disapproval exerts to secure obedience to moral rules and conventions.

We have already seen that coercion is, in the last resort, a matter of degree and that the coercion which the state must both prevent and threaten for the sake of liberty is only coercion in its more severe forms—the kind which, when threatened, may prevent a person of normal strength from pursuing an object important to him. Whether or not we wish to call coercion those milder forms of pressure that society applies to nonconformists, there can be little question that these moral rules and conventions that possess less binding power than the law have an important and even indispensable role to perform and probably do as much to facilitate life in society as do the strict rules of law. We know that they will be observed only generally and not universally, but this knowledge still provides useful guidance and reduces uncertainty. While the respect for such rules does not prevent people from occasionally behaving in a manner that is disapproved, it limits such behavior to instances in which it is fairly important to the person to disregard the rules. Sometimes these non-coercive rules may represent an experimental stage of what later in a modified form may grow into law. More often they will provide a flexible background of more or less unconscious habits which serve as a guide to most people's actions. On the whole, those conventions and norms of social intercourse and individual conduct do not constitute a serious infringement of individual liberty but secure a certain minimum of uniformity of conduct that assists individual efforts more than it impedes them.

[22] Mill, *On Liberty*, chap. 3, pp. 49–66.

TEN

LAW, COMMANDS, AND ORDER

Order is not a pressure imposed upon society from without, but an equilibrium which is set up from within. —J. Ortega y Gasset

1. "The rule whereby the indivisible border line is fixed within which the being and activity of each individual obtain a secure and free sphere is the law."[1] Thus one of the great legal scholars of the last century stated the basic

The quotation at the head of the chapter is taken from José Ortega y Gasset, *Mirabeau o El político* (1927), in *Obras completas* (Madrid: Revista de Occidente, 1947), vol. 3, p. 603: "Orden no es una presión que desde fuera se ejerce sobra la sociedad, sino un equilibrio que se suscita en su interior." Cf. John Corrie Carter, "The Ideal and the Actual in the Law," Annual address delivered at the *Thirteenth Annual Meeting of the American Bar Association* (Philadelphia: Dando Publishing Co., 1890), p. 21. [Reprinted from the *American Law Review*, 24 (1890): 768–69]: "Law is not a body of commands imposed upon society from without, either by an individual sovereign or superior, or by a sovereign body constituted by representatives of society itself. It exists at all times as one of the elements of society springing directly from habit and custom. It is therefore the unconscious creation of society, or in other words, a growth." Regarding Carter, who was influenced by Luther Stearns Cushing and Frederick Carl von Savigny, see M. J. Aronson, "The Juridical Evolutionism of James Coolidge Carter," *University of Toronto Law Journal*, 10 (1953): 1–53. The stress on the law being prior to the state, which is the organized effort to create and enforce it, goes back at least to David Hume (see his *Treatise of Human Nature*, bk. 3, pt. 2, vol. 2, pp. 252–333).

[1] Friedrich Karl von Savigny, *System des heutigen römischen Rechts* (Berlin: Veit und Comp., 1840), vol. 1, pp. 331–32. The passage quoted in translation is a condensation of two sentences which deserve to be quoted in their context: "Der Mensch steht inmitten der äussern Welt, und das wichtigste Element in dieser seiner Umgebung ist ihm die Berührung mit denen, die ihm gleich sind durch ihre Natur und Bestimmung. Sollen nun in solcher Berührung freie Wesen neben einander bestehen, sich gegenseitig fördernd, nicht hemmend, in ihrer Entwicklung, so ist dieses nur möglich durch Anerkennung einer unsichtbaren Grenze, innerhalb welcher das Dasein und die Wirksamkeit jedes Einzelnen einen sichern, freien Raum gewinne. Die Regel, wodurch jene Grenze und durch die dieser freie Raum bestimmt wird, ist das Recht. Damit ist zugleich die Verwandtschaft und die Verschiedenheit zwischen Recht und Sittlichkeit gegeben. Das Recht dient der Sittlichkeit, aber nicht indem es ihr Gebot vollzieht, sondern indem es die freie Entfaltung ihrer, jedem einzelnen Willen inwohnenden, Kraft sichert. Sein Dasein aber ist ein selbständiges, und darum ist es kein Widerspruch, wenn im einzelnen Fall die Möglichkeit unsittlicher Ausübung eines wirklich vorhandenen Rechts behauptet wird." (The spelling of this passage has been modernized.) ["We exist in the external world and the most important element in our surroundings is our contact with those who have similar natures and destinies. If these

conception of the law of liberty. This conception of the law which made it the basis of freedom has since been largely lost. It will be the chief aim of this chapter to recover and make more precise the conception of the law on which the ideal of freedom under the law was built and which made it possible to speak of the law as "the science of liberty."[2]

Life of man in society, or even of the social animals in groups, is made possible by the individuals acting according to certain rules.[3] With the growth of intelligence, these rules tend to develop from unconscious habits into explicit and articulated statements and at the same time to become more abstract and general. Our familiarity with the institutions of law prevents us from seeing how subtle and complex a device the delimitation of individual spheres by abstract rules is. If it had been deliberately designed, it would deserve to rank among the greatest of human inventions. But it has, of course, been as little invented by any one mind as language or money or most of the practices and conventions on which social life rests.[4]

A kind of delimitation of individual spheres by rules appears even in animal societies. A degree of order, preventing too frequent fights or interference with the search for food, etc., here arises often from the fact that the individual, as it strays farther from its lair, becomes less ready to fight. In consequence, when two individuals meet at some intermediate place, one of them will usually withdraw without an actual trial of strength. Thus a sphere belonging to each individual is determined, not by the demarcation of a concrete boundary, but by the observation of a rule—a rule, of course, that is not known as such by

---

contacts are of free beings, supporting and not hindering each other in our development, then we must recognize an invisible border line surrounding each one of us within which our essential nature and effectiveness finds a secure and unconstrained space. The arrangements by which the rules governing these boundaries and these spaces are determined is the law. Here too we see how law and morality are related and distinguished. The law serves morality, not in that it fulfills her commands, but rather in that it secures the free development of the moral power as it resides in each individual will. The existence of law, however, is independent of that of morality inasmuch as it is not a contradiction when, in any specific case, the immoral implementations of an existing law is claimed."—Ed.] See also John William Salmond, *Salmond on Jurisprudence*, Glanville Llewelyn Williams, ed. (11th ed.; London: Sweet and Maxwell, 1957), p. 63: "the rule of justice determines the sphere of individual liberty in the pursuit of individual welfare, so as to confine that liberty within the limits which are consistent with the general welfare of mankind."

[2] Charles Beudant, *Le Droit individuel et l'État: Introduction à l'étude du droit* (Paris: A. Rousseau, 1891), p. 5: "Le Droit, au sens le plus general du mot, est la science de la liberté." ["Law, in the most general sense of the term, is the science of liberty."—Ed.]

[3] A number of particularly insightful explanations about the role of rules in determining social structures can be found in the writings of Richard Stanley Peters, especially *The Concept of Motivation* (London: Routledge and Kegan Paul, 1958), as well as the book he wrote in conjunction with Stanley Isaac Benn, *Social Principles and the Democratic State* (London: Allen and Unwin, 1959).

[4] Cf. Carl Menger, *Untersuchungen*, app. 8, pp. 271–87.

the individual but that is honored in action. The illustration shows how even such unconscious habits will involve a sort of abstraction: a condition of such generality as that of distance from home will determine the response of any individual on meeting another. If we tried to define any of the more truly social habits that make possible the life of animals in groups, we should have to state many of them in terms of abstract rules.

That such abstract rules are regularly observed in action does not mean that they are known to the individual in the sense that it could communicate them. Abstraction occurs whenever an individual responds in the same manner to circumstances that have only some features in common.[5] Men generally act in accordance with abstract rules in this sense long before they can state them.[6] Even when they have acquired the power of conscious abstraction, their conscious thinking and acting are probably still guided by a great many such abstract rules which they obey without being able to formulate them. The fact that a rule is generally obeyed in action therefore does not mean that it does not still have to be discovered and formulated in words.

2. The nature of these abstract rules that we call "laws" in the strict sense is best shown by contrasting them with specific and particular commands. If we take the word "command" in its widest sense, the general rules governing human conduct might indeed also be regarded as commands. Laws and commands differ in the same way from statements of fact and therefore belong to the same logical category. But a general rule that everybody obeys, unlike a

[5] "Abstraction" does not appear only in the form of verbal statements. It manifests itself also in the way in which we respond similarly to any one of a class of events which in most respects may be very different from one another, and in the feelings which are evoked by these events and which guide our action, be it a sense of justice or of moral or aesthetic approval or disapproval. Also there are probably always more general principles governing our minds which we cannot formulate, yet which guide our thinking—laws of the structure of the mind which are too general to be formulated within that structure. Even when we speak of an abstract rule guiding decisions, we need not mean a rule expressed in words but merely one which could be so formulated. On all these problems compare my book, *The Sensory Order: An Inquiry into the Foundations of Theoretical Psychology* (Chicago: University of Chicago Press, 1952), and my article "Rules, Perception, and Intelligibility," *Proceedings of the British Academy*, 48 (1962): 321–44 [Reprinted in *Studies in Philosophy, Politics, and Economics*, pp.43–65.]; also Adam Ferguson, *An Essay on the History of Civil Society*, (London: A. Millar and T. Caddel, 1767), 38–46.

[6] Cf. Edward Sapir, *Selected Writings of Edward Sapir in Language, Culture, and Personality*, David Goodman Mandelbaum, ed. (Berkeley: University of California Press, 1949), p. 548: "It is easy for an Australian native, for instance, to say by what kinship term he calls so and so or whether or not he may undertake such and such relations with a given individual. It is exceedingly difficult for him to give a general rule of which these specific examples of behavior are but illustrations, though all the while he acts as though the rule were perfectly well known to him. *In a sense it is well known to him.* But this knowledge is not capable of conscious manipulation in terms of word symbols. It is, rather, a very delicately nuanced feeling of subtle relations, both experienced and possible."

command proper, does not necessarily presuppose a person who has issued it. It also differs from a command by its generality and abstractness.[7] The degree of this generality or abstractness ranges continuously from the order that tells a man to do a particular thing here and now to the instruction that, in such and such conditions, whatever he does will have to satisfy certain requirements. Law in its ideal form might be described as a "once-and-for-all" command that is directed to unknown people and that is abstracted from all particular circumstances of time and place and refers only to such conditions as may occur anywhere and at any time. It is advisable, however, not to confuse laws and commands, though we must recognize that laws shade gradually into commands as their content becomes more specific.

The important difference between the two concepts lies in the fact that, as we move from commands to laws, the source of the decision on what particular action is to be taken shifts progressively from the issuer of the command or law to the acting person. The ideal type of command determines uniquely the action to be performed and leaves those to whom it is addressed no chance to use their own knowledge or follow their own predilections. The action performed according to such commands serves exclusively the purposes of him who has issued it. The ideal type of law, on the other hand, provides merely additional information to be taken into account in the decision of the actor.

The manner in which the aims and the knowledge that guide a particular action are distributed between the authority and the performer is thus the most important distinction between general laws and specific commands. It can be illustrated by the different ways in which the chief of a primitive tribe, or the head of a household, may regulate the activities of his subordinates. At the one extreme will be the instance where he relies entirely on specific orders and his subjects are not allowed to act at all except as ordered. If the chief prescribes on every occasion every detail of the actions of his subordinates, they will be mere tools, without an opportunity of using their own knowledge and judgment, and all the aims pursued and all the knowledge utilized will be those of the chief. In most circumstances, however, it will better serve his purposes if he gives merely general instructions about the kinds of actions to be performed or the ends to be achieved at certain times, and leaves it to the different individuals to fill in the details according to circumstances—that is,

[7] The treatment of law as a species of command (deriving from Francis Bacon, Thomas Hobbes, and John Austin) was originally intended to stress the logical similarity of these two kinds of sentences as distinguished from, say, a statement of fact. It should not, however, obscure, as it has often done, the essential differences. Cf. Karl Olivecrona, *Law as Fact* (Copenhagen: E. Munksgaard, 1939), p. 43, where laws are described as "independent imperatives" which are "nobody's commands, though they have the form of language that is characteristic of a command"; also Richard Wollheim, "The Nature of Law," *Political Studies*, 2 (1954): 128–41.

according to their knowledge. Such general instructions will already constitute rules of a kind, and the action under them will be guided partly by the knowledge of the chief and partly by that of the acting persons. It will be the chief who decides what results are to be achieved, at what time, by whom, and perhaps by which means; but the particular manner in which they are brought about will be decided by the individuals responsible. The servants of a big household or the employees of a plant will thus be mostly occupied with the routine of carrying out standing orders, adapting them all the time to particular circumstances and only occasionally receiving specific commands.

In these circumstances the ends toward which all activity is directed are still those of the chief. He may, however, also allow members of the group to pursue, within certain limits, their own ends. This presupposes the designation of the means that each may use for his purposes. Such an allocation of means may take the form of the assignment of particular things or of times that the individual may use for his own ends. Such a listing of the rights of each individual can be altered only by specific orders of the chief. Or the sphere of free action of each individual may be determined and altered in accordance with general rules laid down in advance for longer periods, and such rules can make it possible for each individual by his own action (such as bartering with other members of the group or earning premiums offered by the head for merit) to alter or shape the sphere within which he can direct his action for his own purposes. Thus, from the delimitation of a private sphere by rules, a right like that of property will emerge.

3. A similar transition from specificity and concreteness to increasing generality and abstractness we also find in the evolution from the rules of custom to law in the modern sense. Compared with the laws of a society that cultivates individual freedom, the rules of conduct of a primitive society are relatively concrete. They not merely limit the range within which the individual can shape his own action but often prescribe specifically how he must proceed to achieve particular results, or what he must do at particular times and places. In them the expression of the factual knowledge that certain effects will be produced by a particular procedure and the demand that this procedure be followed in appropriate conditions are still undifferentiated. To give only one illustration: the rules which the Bantu observes when he moves between the fourteen huts of his village along strictly prescribed lines according to his age, sex, or status greatly restrict his choice.[8] Though he is not obeying another

---

[8] I have borrowed this illustration from José Ortega y Gasset, *Del imperio romano* (1940), in *Obras completas* (6 vols.; Madrid: Revista de Occidente, 1947), vol. 6, p. 76, who presumably derives it from some anthropologist. [Ortega writes: "El lector no sonreiría tan absolutamente si conociese un poco mejor la historia de la circulación humana, las angustias y luchas que ha ocasionado y si yo tuviese espacio libre para dibujar aquí un gráfico de las líneas rigurosamente prescritas que tiene que seguir hoy mismo el africano bantú para moverse, según su edad, sexo y condición,

man's will but impersonal custom, having to observe a ritual to reach a certain point restricts his choice of method more than is necessary to secure equal freedom to others.

The "compulsion of custom" becomes an obstacle only when the customary way of doing things is no longer the only way that the individual knows and when he can think of other ways of achieving a desirable object. It was largely with the growth of individual intelligence and the tendency to break away from the habitual manner of action that it became necessary to state explicitly or reformulate the rules and gradually to reduce the positive prescriptions to the essentially negative confinement to a range of actions that will not interfere with the similarly recognized spheres of others.

The transition from specific custom to law illustrates even better than the transition from command to law what, for lack of a better term, we have called the "abstract character" of true law.[9] Its general and abstract rules specify that in certain circumstances action must satisfy certain conditions; but all the many kinds of action that satisfy these conditions are permissible. The rules merely provide the framework within which the individual must move but within which the decisions are his. So far as his relations with other private persons are concerned, the prohibitions are almost entirely of a negative character, unless the person to whom they refer has himself, by his actions, created conditions from which positive obligations arise. They are instrumental, they are means put at his disposal, and they provide part of the data which, together with his knowledge of the particular circumstances of time and place, he can use as the basis for his decisions.

Since the laws determine only part of the conditions that the actions of the individual will have to satisfy, and apply to unknown people whenever certain conditions are present, irrespective of most of the facts of the particular situa-

---

entre las catorce chozas de su aldea." ("The reader would not smile so broadly were he better acquainted with the history of the movement of human beings, the anxieties and problems to which it has given rise and, had I sufficient space to describe it, the rigorously prescribed lines along which the African Bantu were today required to follow depending on his age, his sex, and his status, among the fourteen huts of his village.")—Ed.]

[9] If there were no danger of confusion with the other meanings of those terms, it would be preferable to speak of "formal" rather than of "abstract" laws, in the same sense as that in which the term "formal" is used in logical discussion. (Cf. Sir Karl Raimund Popper, *Logik der Forschung: Zur Erkenntnistheorie der modernen Naturwissenschaft* [Vienna: Julius Springer, 1935], pp. 85 and 29–32.) Unfortunately, "formal" is also applied to everything that is enacted by the legislature, while only if such an enactment takes the form of an abstract rule, such a law in the formal sense is a law also in the substantive or material sense. For example, when Max Weber, in *Max Weber on Law in Economy and Society*, Max Rheinstein, ed. (Cambridge, MA: Harvard University Press, 1954), pp. 226–29, speaks of "formal justice," he means justice determined by law, not merely in the formal but in the substantive sense. On this distinction in German and French constitutional law see chap. 14, n. 10, below.

tion, the lawgiver cannot foresee what will be their effect on particular people or for what purposes they will use them. When we call them "instrumental," we mean that in obeying them the individual still pursues his own and not the lawgiver's ends. Indeed, specific ends of action, being always particulars, should not enter into general rules. The law will prohibit killing another person or killing except under conditions so defined that they may occur at any time or place, but not the killing of particular individuals.

In observing such rules, we do not serve another person's end, nor can we properly be said to be subject to his will. My action can hardly be regarded as subject to the will of another person if I use his rules for my own purposes as I might use my knowledge of a law of nature, and if that person does not know of my existence or of the particular circumstances in which the rules will apply to me or of the effects they will have on my plans. At least in all those instances where the coercion threatened is avoidable, the law merely alters the means at my disposal and does not determine the ends I have to pursue. It would be ridiculous to say that I am obeying another's will in fulfilling a contract, when I could not have concluded it had there not been a recognized rule that promises must be kept, or in accepting the legal consequence of any other action that I have taken in full knowledge of the law.

The significance for the individual of the knowledge that certain rules will be universally applied is that, in consequence, the different objects and forms of action acquire for him new properties. He knows of man-made cause-and-effect relations which he can make use of for whatever purpose he wishes. The effects of these man-made laws on his actions are of precisely the same kind as those of the laws of nature: his knowledge of either enables him to foresee what will be the consequences of his actions, and it helps him to make plans with confidence. There is little difference between the knowledge that if he builds a bonfire on the floor of his living room his house will burn down, and the knowledge that if he sets his neighbor's house on fire he will find himself in jail. Like the laws of nature, the laws of the state provide fixed features in the environment in which he has to move; though they eliminate certain choices open to him, they do not, as a rule, limit the choice to some specific action that somebody else wants him to take.

4. The conception of freedom under the law that is the chief concern of this book rests on the contention that when we obey laws, in the sense of general abstract rules laid down irrespective of their application to us, we are not subject to another man's will and are therefore free. It is because the lawgiver does not know the particular cases to which his rules will apply, and it is because the judge who applies them has no choice in drawing the conclusions that follow from the existing body of rules and the particular facts of the case, that it can be said that laws and not men rule. Because the rule is laid down in ignorance of the particular case and no man's will decides the coercion used

to enforce it, the law is not arbitrary.[10] This, however, is true only if by "law" we mean the general rules that apply equally to everybody. This generality is probably the most important aspect of that attribute of law which we have called its "abstractness." As a true law should not name any particulars, so it should especially not single out any specific persons or group of persons.

The significance of a system in which all coercive action of government is confined to the execution of general abstract rules is often stated in the words of one of the great historians of the law; "The movement of the progressive societies has hitherto been a movement *from Status to Contract*."[11] The conception of status, of an assigned place that each individual occupies in society, corresponds, indeed, to a state in which the rules are not fully general but single out particular persons or groups and confer upon them special rights and duties. The emphasis on contract as the opposite of status is, however, a little misleading, as it singles out one, albeit the most important, of the instruments that the law supplies to the individual to shape his own position. The true contrast to a reign of status is the reign of general and equal laws, of the rules which are the same for all, or, we might say, of the rule of *leges* in the original meaning of the Latin word for laws—*leges* that is, as opposed to the *privi-leges*.

The requirement that the rules of true law be general does not mean that sometimes special rules may not apply to different classes of people if they refer to properties that only some people possess. There may be rules that can apply only to women or to the blind or to persons above a certain age. (In most such instances it would not even be necessary to name the class of people to whom the rule applies: only a woman, for example, can be raped or got with child.) Such distinctions will not be arbitrary, will not subject one group to the will of others, if they are equally recognized as justified by those inside and those outside the group. This does not mean that there must be unanimity as to the desirability of the distinction, but merely that individual

[10] Cf. George Cornewall Lewis, *An Essay on the Government of Dependencies* (London: John Murray, 1841), p. 16n.: "When a person voluntarily regulates his conduct according to a rule or maxim which he has previously announced his intention of conforming to, he is thought to deprive himself of *arbitrium*, free will, discretion, or *Willkür*, in the individual act. Hence when a government acts in an individual case, not in conformity with a pre-existing law or rule of conduct, laid down by itself, its act is said to be arbitrary." Also, (p. 24): "Every government, whether monarchical, aristocratical, or democratical, may be conducted arbitrarily, and not in accordance with general rules. There is not, and cannot be, anything in the form of any government, which will afford its subjects a legal security against an improper arbitrary exercise of the sovereign power. This security is to be found only in the influence of public opinion, and the other moral restraints which create the main difference in the goodness of supreme governments."

[11] Sir Henry Sumner Maine, *Ancient Law: Its Connection with the Early History of Society and Its Relation to Modern Ideas* (London: John Murray, 1861), p.141; cf. Ronald Harry Graveson, "The Movement from Status to Contract," *Modern Law Review*, 4 (1940–41): 261–72.

views will not depend on whether the individual is in the group or not. So long as, for instance, the distinction is favored by the majority both inside and outside the group, there is a strong presumption that it serves the ends of both. When, however, only those inside the group favor the distinction, it is clearly privilege; while if only those outside favor it, it is discrimination. What is privilege to some is, of course, always discrimination to the rest.

5. It is not to be denied that even general, abstract rules, equally applicable to all, may possibly constitute severe restrictions on liberty. But when we reflect on it, we see how very unlikely this is. The chief safeguard is that the rules must apply to those who lay them down and those who apply them— that is, to the government as well as the governed—and that nobody has the power to grant exceptions. If all that is prohibited and enjoined is prohibited and enjoined for all without exception (unless such exception follows from. another general rule) and if even authority has no special powers except that of enforcing the law, little that anybody may reasonably wish to do is likely to be prohibited. It is possible that a fanatical religious group will impose upon the rest restrictions which its members will be pleased to observe but which will be obstacles for others in the pursuit of important aims. But if it is true that religion has often provided the pretext for the establishing of rules felt to be extremely oppressive and that religious liberty is therefore regarded as very important for freedom, it is also significant that religious beliefs seem to be almost the only ground on which general rules seriously restrictive of liberty have ever been universally enforced. But how comparatively innocuous, even if irksome, are most such restrictions imposed on literally everybody, as, for instance, the Scottish Sabbath, compared with those that are likely to be imposed only on some! It is significant that most restrictions on what we regard as private affairs, such as sumptuary legislation, have usually been imposed only on selected groups of people or, as in the case of prohibition, were practicable only because the government reserved the right to grant exceptions.

It should also be remembered that, so far as men's actions toward other persons are concerned, freedom can never mean more than that they are restricted only by general rules. Since there is no kind of action that may not interfere with another person's protected sphere, neither speech, nor the press, nor the exercise of religion can be completely free. In all these fields (and, as we shall see later, in that of contract) freedom does mean and can mean only that what we may do is not dependent on the approval of any person or authority and is limited only by the same abstract rules that apply equally to all.

But if it is the law that makes us free, this is true only of the law in this sense of abstract general rule, or of what is called "the law in the material meaning," which differs from law in the merely formal sense by the character of the rules and not by their origin.[12] The "law" that is a specific command, an order that is called a "law" merely because it emanates from the legislative authority, is the chief instrument of oppression. The confusion of these two conceptions of law and the loss of the belief that laws can rule, that men in laying down and enforcing laws in the former sense are not enforcing their will, are among the chief causes of the decline of liberty, to which legal theory has contributed as much as political doctrine.

We shall have to return later to the manner in which modern legal theory has increasingly obscured these distinctions. Here we can only indicate the contrast between the two concepts of law by giving examples of the extreme positions taken on them. The classical view is expressed in Chief Justice John Marshall's famous statement: "Judicial power, as contradistinguished from the power of the laws, has no existence. Courts are the mere instruments of the law, and can will nothing."[13] Hold against this the most frequently quoted statement of a modern jurist, that has found the greatest favor among so-called progressives, namely, Justice Holmes's that "general propositions do not decide concrete cases."[14] The same position has been put by a contemporary political scientist thus: "The law cannot rule. Only men can exercise power over other men. To say that laws rule and not men may consequently signify that the fact is to be hidden that men rule over men."[15]

The fact is that, if "to rule" means to make men obey another's will, government has no such power to rule in a free society. The citizen as citizen cannot be ruled in this sense, cannot be ordered about, no matter what his position may be in the job he has chosen for his own purposes or while, in accordance with the law, he temporarily becomes the agent of government. He can be ruled, however, in the sense in which "to rule" means the enforcement of general rules, laid down irrespective of the particular case and equally applicable to all. For here no human decision will be required in the great majority of cases to which the rules apply; and even when a court has to determine how the general rules may be applied to a particular case, it is the implications of the whole system of accepted rules that decide, not the will of the court.

6. The rationale of securing to each individual a known range within which he can decide on his actions is to enable him to make the fullest use of his knowledge, especially of his concrete and often unique knowledge of the par-

---

[12] Cf. n. 9 above and the later discussion to which it refers.

[13] Chief Justice John Marshall in *Osborn v. Bank of United States*, 22 *U.S.* (9 *Wheaton*) 738, at 866 (1824).

[14] Oliver Wendell Holmes, Jr., *Lochner v. New York*, 198 *U.S.* 45, at 76 (1905).

[15] Franz Leopold Neumann, "The Concept of Political Freedom," *Columbia Law Review*, 53 (1953): 910, reprinted in his *The Democratic and the Authoritarian State: Essays in Political and Legal Theory* (Glencoe, IL: The Free Press, 1957), p. 169.

ticular circumstances of time and place.[16] The law tells him what facts he may count on and thereby extends the range within which he can predict the consequences of his actions. At the same time it tells him what possible consequences of his actions he must take into account or what he will be held responsible for. This means that what he is allowed or required to do must depend only on circumstances he can be presumed to know or be able to ascertain. No rule can be effective, or can leave him free to decide, that makes his range of free decisions dependent on remote consequences of his actions beyond his ability to foresee. Even of those effects which he might be presumed to foresee, the rules will single out some that he will have to take into account while allowing him to disregard others. In particular, such rules will not merely demand that he must not do anything that will damage others but will be—or should be—so expressed that, when applied to a particular situation, they will clearly decide which effects must be taken into account and which need not.

If the law thus serves to enable the individual to act effectively on his own knowledge and for this purpose adds to his knowledge, it also embodies knowledge, or the results of past experience, that are utilized so long as men act under these rules. In fact, the collaboration of individuals under common rules rests on a sort of division of knowledge,[17] where the individual must take account of particular circumstances but the law ensures that their action will be adapted to certain general or permanent characteristics of their society. This experience, embodied in the law, that individuals utilize by observing rules, is difficult to discuss, since it is ordinarily not known to them or to any one person. Most of these rules have never been deliberately invented but have grown through a gradual process of trial and error in which the experience of successive generations has helped to make them what they are. In most instances, therefore, nobody knows or has ever known all the reasons and considerations that have led to a rule being given a particular form. We must thus often endeavor to *discover* the functions that a rule actually serves. If we do not know the rationale of a particular rule, as is often the case, we

---

[16] Cf. Smith, *Wealth of Nations* [bk. 4, chap. 2], vol. 1, p. 421 [Liberty Fund edition, vol. 1, p. 456]: "What is the species of domestic industry which his capital can employ, and of which the produce is likely to be of the greatest value, every individual, it is evident, can, *in his local situation*, judge much better than any statesman or lawgiver can do for him." (Italics added.)

[17] Cf. Lionel Robbins, *The Theory of Economic Policy: Essays in Political and Legal Theory* (Glencoe, IL: The Free Press, 1957), p. 193: The classical liberal "proposes, as it were, a division of labor: the state shall prescribe what individuals shall not do, if they are not to get in each other's way, while the citizen shall be left free to do anything which is not so forbidden. To the one is assigned the task of establishing formal rules, to the other responsibility for the substance of specific action."

must try to understand what its general function or purpose is to be if we are to improve upon it by deliberate legislation.

Thus the rules under which the citizens act constitute an adaptation of the whole of society to its environment and to the general characteristics of its members. They serve, or should serve, to assist the individuals in forming plans of action that they will have a good chance of carrying through. The rules may have come to exist merely because, in a certain type of situation, friction is likely to arise among individuals about what each is entitled to do, which can be prevented only if there is a rule to tell each clearly what his rights are. Here it is necessary merely that some known rule cover the type of situation, and it may not matter greatly what its contents are.

There will, however, often be several possible rules which satisfy this requirement but which will not be equally satisfactory. What exactly is to be included in that bundle of rights that we call "property," especially where land is concerned, what other rights the protected sphere is to include, what contracts the state is to enforce, are all issues in which only experience will show what is the most expedient arrangement. There is nothing "natural" in any particular definition of rights of this kind, such as the Roman conception of property as a right to use or abuse an object as one pleases, which, however often repeated, is in fact hardly practicable in its strict form. But the main features of all somewhat more advanced legal orders are sufficiently similar to appear as mere elaborations of what David Hume called the "three fundamental laws of nature, *that of the stability of possession, of its transference by consent, and of the performance of promises.*"[18]

Our concern here cannot be, however, the particular content but only certain general attributes which these rules ought to possess in a free society. Since the lawgiver cannot foresee what use the persons affected will make of his rules, he can only aim to make them beneficial on the whole or in the majority of cases. But, as they operate through the expectations that they create, it is essential that they be always applied, irrespective of whether or not the con-

---

[18] David Hume, *Treatise of Human Nature* [bk. 3, pt. 2, sec. 6], (*Works*, vol. 2, p. 293); cf. also John Walter Jones, *Historical Introduction to the Theory of Law* (Oxford: Clarendon Press, 1940), p. 114: "In looking through the French Code and leaving out of account the law of the family, Duguit finds only three fundamental rules and no more—freedom of contract, the inviolability of property, and the duty to compensate another for damage due to one's fault. All the rest resolve themselves into subsidiary directions to some State agent or other." [Léon Duguit (1859–1928), noted French jurist and dean of the law school at Bordeaux. He was strongly opposed to the juridical theories of Georg Jellinek, whom he regarded as too "individualistic." Instead, he wished to incorporate the relationship of individuals to collectivities in legal thinking. More importantly, he rejected the notion that law was a creation of the State but posited the theory that it took its shape from the social needs of men.—Ed.]

sequences in a particular instance seem desirable.[19] That the legislator confines himself to general rules rather than particular commands is the consequence of his necessary ignorance of the special circumstances under which they apply; all he can do is to provide some firm data for the use of those who have to make plans for particular actions. But in fixing for them only some of the conditions of their actions, he can provide opportunities and chances, but never certainties so far as the results of their efforts are concerned.

The necessity of emphasizing that it is of the essence of the abstract rules of law that they will only be likely to be beneficial in most cases to which they apply and, in fact, are one of the means by which man has learned to cope

---

[19] Cf. David Hume, *Treatise of Human Nature*, bk. 2, pt. 2, secs. 2–6 (*Works*, vol. 2, pp. 258–300), which still contains perhaps the most satisfactory discussion of the problems considered here, esp. vol. 2, p. 269: "A single act of justice is frequently contrary to public interest; and were it to stand alone, without being follow'd by other acts, may, in itself, be very prejudicial to society. . . . Nor is every single act of justice, consider'd apart, more conducive to private interest than to public; . . . But however single acts of justice may be contrary, either to public or private interest, 'tis certain, that the whole plan or scheme is highly conducive, or indeed absolutely requisite, both to the support of society and the well-being of every individual. 'Tis impossible to separate the good from the ill. Property must be stable, and must be fix'd by general rules. Tho' in one instance the public be a sufferer, this momentary ill is amply compensated by the steady prosecution of the rule, and by the peace and order, which it establishes in society." See also Hume's *Enquiry Concerning the Principles of Morals*, in *Essays*, vol. 2, p. 273: "The benefit, resulting from [the social virtues of justice and fidelity] is not the consequence of every individual single act; but arises from the whole scheme or system, concurred in by the whole, or the greater part of the society. . . . The result of the individual acts is here, in many instances, directly opposite to that of the whole system of actions; and the former may be extremely hurtful, while the latter is, to the highest degree, advantageous. Riches, inherited from a parent, are, in a bad man's hand, the instrument of mischief. The right of succession may, in one instance, be hurtful. Its benefit arises only from the observance of the general rule; and it is sufficient, if compensation be thereby made for all the ills and inconveniencies, which flow from particular characters and situations." Also see the *Enquiry*, p. 274: "All the laws of nature, which regulate property, as well as all civil laws, are general, and regard alone some essential circumstances of the case, without taking into consideration the characters, situations, and connexions of the person concerned, or any particular consequences which may result from the determination of these laws, in any particular case which offers. They deprive, without scruple, a beneficent man of all his possessions, if acquired by mistake, without a good title; in order to bestow them on a selfish miser, who has already heaped up immense stores of superfluous riches. Public utility requires, that property should be regulated by general inflexible rules; and though such rules are adopted as best serve the same end of public utility, it is impossible for them to prevent all particular hardships, or make beneficial consequences result from every individual case. It is sufficient, if the whole plan or scheme be necessary to the support of civil society, and if the balance of good, in the main, do thereby preponderate much above that of evil." See my "The Legal and Political Philosophy of David Hume," *Il Politico*, 28 (1963): 691–704; reprinted in Friedrich August Hayek, *Studies in Philosophy, Politics, and Economics* (New York: Simon and Schuster, 1967), pp. 106–21. I would like in this connection to acknowledge my indebtedness to Sir Arnold Plant, who many years ago first drew my attention to the importance of Hume's discussion of these issues.

with his constitutional ignorance, has been imposed on us by certain rationalist interpretations of utilitarianism. It is true enough that the justification of any particular rule of law must be its usefulness—even though this usefulness may not be demonstrable by rational argument but known only because the rule has in practice proved itself more convenient than any other. But, generally speaking, only the rule as a whole must be so justified, not its every application.[20] The idea that each conflict, in law or in morals, should be so decided as would seem most expedient to somebody who could comprehend all the consequences of that decision involves the denial of the necessity of any rules. Only a society of omniscient individuals could give each person "complete liberty to weigh every particular action on general utilitarian grounds."[21] Such an "extreme" utilitarianism leads to absurdity; and only what has been called "restricted" utilitarianism has therefore any relevance to our problem. Yet few beliefs have been more destructive of the respect for the rules of law and of morals than the idea that a rule is binding only if the beneficial effect of observing it in the particular instance can be recognized.

The oldest form of this misconception has been associated with the (usually misquoted) formula "salus populi suprema lex esto" ("the welfare of the people ought to be—not 'is'—the highest law").[22] Correctly understood, it means that the end of the law ought to be the welfare of the people, that the general rules should be so designed as to serve it, but *not* that any conception of a particular social end should provide a justification for breaking those general rules. A specific end, a concrete result to be achieved, can never be a law.

7. The enemies of liberty have always based their arguments on the con-

---

[20] See John Stuart Mill, "On Liberty," in *On Liberty and Considerations on Representative Government*, Ronald Buchanan McCallum, ed. (Oxford: Blackwell, 1946), p. 68.

[21] See John Rawls, "Two Concepts of Rules," *Philosophical Review*, 64 (1955): 3–32; John Jamieson Carswell Smart, "Extreme and Restricted Utilitarianism," *Philosophical Quarterly*, 6 (1956): 344–54; Henry John McCloskey, "An Examination of Restricted Utilitarianism," *Philosophical Review*, 66 (1957): 466–85; James Opie Urmson, "The Interpretation of the Moral Philosophy of J. S. Mill," *Philosophical Quarterly*, 3 (1953): 33–39; John David Mabbott, "Interpretations of Mill's Utilitarianism," *Philosophical Quarterly*, 6 (1956): 115–20; and Stephen Edelston Toulmin, *An Examination of the Place of Reason in Ethics* (Cambridge: Cambridge University Press, 1950), esp. p. 161.

[22] John Selden in his *The Table Talk of John Selden* ([Oxford: Clarendon Press, 1892], p. 131) observes: "There is not anything in the world so much abused as this sentence, *Salus populi suprema lex esto*." [The phrase originates in Cicero *De Legibus*, bk. 3, chap. 3, sec. 8.—Ed.] Cf. Charles Howard McIlwain, *Constitutionalism: Ancient and Modern* (rev. ed.; Ithaca, NY: Cornell University Press, 1947), p. 149, n. 6 [Liberty Fund edition, p. 4 n. 6], and, on the general issue, Friedrich Meinecke, *Die Idee der Staatsräson in der neueren Geschichte* (Munich: R. Oldenburg, 1924), p. 265, now translated as *Machiavellism: the Doctrine of Raison d'état and its Place in Modern History*, Douglas Scott, trans. (London: Routledge and Kegan Paul, 1957); see also Mises, *Socialism*, p. 400 [Liberty Fund edition, p. 359].

tention that order in human affairs requires that some should give orders and others obey.[23] Much of the opposition to a system of freedom under general laws arises from the inability to conceive of an effective co-ordination of human activities without deliberate organization by a commanding intelligence. One of the achievements of economic theory has been to explain how such a mutual adjustment of the spontaneous activities of individuals is brought about by the market, provided that there is a known delimitation of the sphere of control of each individual. An understanding of that mechanism of mutual adjustment of individuals forms the most important part of the knowledge that ought to enter into the making of general rules limiting individual action.

The orderliness of social activity shows itself in the fact that the individual can carry out a consistent plan of action that, at almost every stage, rests on the expectation of certain contributions from his fellows. "That there is some kind of order, consistency and constancy, in social life is obvious. If there were not, none of us would be able to go about our affairs or satisfy our most elementary needs."[24] This orderliness cannot be the result of a unified direction if we want individuals to adjust their actions to the particular circumstances largely known only to them and never known in their totality to any one mind. Order with reference to society thus means essentially that individual action is guided by successful foresight, that people not only make effective use of their knowledge but can also foresee with a high degree of confidence what collaboration they can expect from others.[25]

---

[23] Cf., e.g., the opinion of James I, quoted by Francis Dunham Wormuth, *The Origins of Modern Constitutionalism* (New York: Harper, 1949), p. 51, that "order was dependent upon the relationship of command and obedience. All organization derived from superiority and subordination." [James makes this point in his "Triplici nodo, triplex cuneus. Or an apologie for the oath of allegiance. Against the two breves of pope pavlvs qvintvs, and the late letter of cardinall bellarmine to g. blackwel the arch-priest," in *The Political Works of James I* (reprinted from the edition of 1616), Charles Howard McIlwain, ed. (Cambridge, MA: Harvard University Press, 1918).—Ed.]

[24] I apologize to the author whose words I quote but whose name I have forgotten. I had noted the passage with a reference to Edward Evan Evans-Pritchard, *Social Anthropology* (London: Cohen and West, 1951), p. 19, but, though the same idea is expressed there, it is not in the words quoted. [The quotation that Hayek cannot place does indeed come from Evans-Pritchard's monograph *Social Anthropology* (Glencoe, IL: The Free Press, 1954), p. 49. The passage on p. 19, which expresses the same idea, reads: "It is evident that there must be uniformities and regularities in social life, that a society must have some sort of order, or its members could not live together."—Ed.]

[25] Cf. Hermann Jahrreiss, "Größe und Not der Gesetzgebung," in *Mensch und Staat: Rechtsphilosophische, staatsrechtliche und völkerrechtliche Grundfragen in unserer Zeit*, Hermann Jahrreiss, ed. (Cologne: C. Heymann, 1957), p. 22: "Sozial-Ordnung ist Sozial-Berechenbarkeit." ["Social order is social predictability."—Ed.]

Such an order involving an adjustment to circumstances, knowledge of which is dispersed among a great many people, cannot be established by central direction. It can arise only from the mutual adjustment of the elements and their response to the events that act immediately upon them. It is what M. Polanyi has called the spontaneous formation of a "polycentric order": "When order is achieved among human beings by allowing them to interact with each other on their own initiative—subject only to the laws which uniformly apply to all of them—we have a system of spontaneous order in society. We may then say that the efforts of these individuals are co-ordinated by exercising their individual initiative and that this self-co-ordination justifies this liberty on public grounds. The actions of such individuals are said to be free, for they are not determined by any *specific* command, whether of a superior or a public authority; the compulsion to which they are subject is impersonal and general."[26]

Though people more familiar with the manner in which men order physical objects often find the formation of such spontaneous orders difficult to comprehend, there are, of course, many instances in which we must similarly rely on the spontaneous adjustments of individual elements to produce a physical order. We could never produce a crystal or a complex organic compound if we had to place each individual molecule or atom in the appropriate place in relation to the others. We must rely on the fact that in certain conditions they will arrange themselves in a structure possessing certain characteristics. The use of these spontaneous forces, which in such instances is our only means of achieving the desired result, implies, then, that many features of the process creating the order will be beyond our control; we cannot, in other words, rely on these forces and at the same time make sure that particular atoms will occupy specific places in the resulting structure.

Similarly, we can produce the conditions for the formation of an order in society, but we cannot arrange the manner in which its elements will order themselves under appropriate conditions. In this sense the task of the lawgiver is not to set up a particular order but merely to create conditions in which an orderly arrangement can establish and ever renew itself. As in nature, to induce the establishment of such an order does not require that we be able to predict the behavior of the individual atom—that will depend on the unknown particular circumstances in which it finds itself. All that is required is a limited regularity in its behavior; and the purpose of the human laws we enforce is to secure such limited regularity as will make the formation of an order possible.

Where the elements of such an order are intelligent human beings whom

[26] Michael Polanyi, *The Logic of Liberty: Reflections and Rejoinders* (London: Routledge and Kegan Paul, 1951), p. 159 [Liberty Fund edition, p. 195].

we wish to use their individual capacities as successfully as possible in the pursuit of their own ends, the chief requirement for its establishment is that each know which of the circumstances in his environment he can count on. This need for protection against unpredictable interference is sometimes represented as peculiar to "bourgeois society."[27] But, unless by "bourgeois society" is meant any society in which free individuals co-operate under conditions of division of labor, such a view confines the need to far too few social arrangements. It is the essential condition of individual freedom, and to secure it is the main function of law.[28]

[27] Max Weber, *Theory of Social and Economic Organization: Being Part I of Wirtschaft und Gesellschaft*, Talcott Parsons, ed. (London: W. Hodge, 1947), p. 386, tends to treat the need for "calculability and reliability in the functioning of the legal order" as a peculiarity of "capitalism" or the "bourgeois phase" of society. This is correct only if these terms are regarded as descriptive of any free society based on the division of labor.

[28] Cf. Emil Brunner, *Justice and the Social Order* (New York: Harper, 1945), p. 22: "Law is order by foresight. With regard to human beings, that is the service it renders; it is also its burden and its danger. It offers protection from the arbitrary, it gives a feeling of reliability, of security, it takes from the future its ominous darkness."

ELEVEN

THE ORIGINS OF THE RULE OF LAW

The end of the law is, not to abolish or restrain, but to preserve and enlarge freedom. For in all the states of created beings capable of laws, where there is no law there is no freedom. For liberty is to be free from restraint and violence from others; which cannot be where there is no law: and is not, as we are told, a liberty for every man to do what he lists. (For who could be free when every other man's humour might domineer over him?) But a liberty to dispose, and order freely as he lists, his person, actions, possessions, and his whole property, within the allowance of those laws under which he is, and therein not to be the subject of the arbitrary will of another, but freely follow his own. —John Locke

1. Individual liberty in modern times can hardly be traced back farther than the England of the seventeenth century.[1] It appeared first, as it prob-

The quotation at the head of the chapter is taken from John Locke, *Second Treatise*, sec. 57, p. 29. The substance of this chapter as well as of chapters 13–16 have been used in my lectures *The Political Ideal of the Rule of Law*, National Bank of Egypt Fiftieth Anniversary Commemoration Lectures, (Cairo: National Bank of Egypt, 1955).

[1] The more I learn about the growth of these ideas, the more I am convinced of the important role which the example of the Dutch Republic played. But, though this influence is fairly clear in the later seventeenth and early eighteenth centuries, its earlier operation still needs investigation. In the meantime, see Sir George Norman Clark, "The Birth of the Dutch Republic" [The Raleigh Lecture on History], *Proceedings of the British Academy*, 32 (1946): 189–218; John Neville Figgis, *Studies of Political Thought from Gerson to Grotius 1414–1625* (Cambridge: Cambridge University Press, 1907), pp. 191, 198, 209; John Lothrop Motley, *The Rise of the Dutch Republic* (3 vols.; New York: Harper and Brothers, 1856); Pieter Geyl, "Liberty in Dutch History," *Delta: A Review of Arts, Life, and Thought in the Netherlands*, 1 (1958): 11–22; Pieter Geyl, *The Revolt of the Netherlands, 1555–1609* (London: Williams and Norgate Ltd., 1932); and John Selwyn Bromley and Ernest Heinrich Kossman, eds. *Britain and the Netherlands, Papers Delivered to the Oxford-Netherlands Historical Conference, 1959* (London: Chatto and Windus, 1960).

Ignorance also compels me to pass over the important discussions and the development of similar ideas in Renaissance Italy, especially in Florence. (For a brief discussion see the introduction to the notes to chap. 20.) Cf. also Rudolf von Albertini, *Das florentinische Staatsbewußtsein im Übergang von der Republik zum Prinzipat* (Bern: Francke, 1955), particularly p. 294, and Giovanni Battista Guarini, *Trattato della pubblica libertà* (ca. 1599), (Venice: Andreola, 1818). And I cannot speak with

ably always does, as a by-product of a struggle for power rather than as the result of deliberate aim. But it remained long enough for its benefits to be recognized. And for over two hundred years the preservation and perfection of individual liberty became the guiding ideal in that country, and its institutions and traditions the model for the civilized world.[2]

This does not mean that the heritage of the Middle Ages is irrelevant to modern liberty. But its significance is not quite what it is often thought to be. True, in many respects medieval man enjoyed more liberty than is now commonly believed. But there is little ground for thinking that the liberties of the English were then substantially greater than those of many Continental peoples.[3] But if men of the Middle Ages knew many liberties in the sense of

---

any competence about the interesting fact that the one great non-European civilization, that of China, appears to have developed, about the same time as the Greeks, legal conceptions surprisingly similar to those of Western civilization. According to Feng Youlan, *A History of Chinese Philosophy*. Vol. 1: *The Period of the Philosophers (from the Beginnings to Circa 100 B.C.)*, Derk Bodde, trans. (Peiping: H. Vetch, 1937), p. 312: "the great political tendency of the time [the seventh to third centuries B.C.] was a movement from feudal rule toward a government by rulers possessing absolute power; from government by customary morality (*li*), and by individuals, to government by law" (p. 321). The author quotes as evidence from the *Kuan-tzu*, a treatise attributed to Kuang Chung (ca. 715–645 B.C.), but probably composed in the third century B.C.: "When a state is governed by law, things will simply be done in their regular course. . . . If the law is not uniform, there will be misfortune for the holder of the state. . . . When ruler and minister, superior and inferior, noble and humble all obey the law, this is called having Great Good Government." He adds, however, that this is "an ideal which has never yet been actually attained in China" (p. 322). See also Herrlee Glessner Creel, "The Fa-chia: 'Legalists' or 'Administrators,'" in *Bulletin of the Institute of History and Philology*, Academia Sinica, 4 (1961): 607–36, and T'ung-Tsu Ch'ü [Tongzu Qu], *Law and Society in Traditional China* (Paris: Mouton, 1961), particularly pp. 242–44; Bertrand de Jouvenel, *On Power* [Liberty Fund edition available], maintains that the Chinese employed the terms "government of laws" and "government of men" 2,500 years ago.

[2] Cf. Montesquieu's remark in *The Spirit of the Laws* (vol. 1, p. 151; French edition: vol. 2, p. 396): "One nation there is also in the world that has for the direct end of its constitution political liberty." ["Il y a aussi une nation dans le monde qui a pour objet direct de sa constitution la liberté politique."—Ed.] See also Rudolph Henne, *Der englische Freiheitsbegriff* (dissertation; Zurich: R. Sauerländer, 1927). A careful study of the discovery of English liberty by the Continental people and of the influence of the English model on the Continent has yet to be made. Important early works are Guy Miège, *L'État présent de la Grande-Bretagne après son heureuse union en 1707, sous le règne glorieux d'Anne* (2 vols. in 1; Amsterdam: Chez les Wetsteins, 1708), also in an enlarged German edition as *Geist- und weltlicher Staat von Gross-Britannien und Irrland nach der gegenwärtigen Zeit* (Leipzig: Weidmanns, 1718); Paul de Rapin-Thoyras, *Dissertation sur les Whigs et les Torys, or an Historical Dissertation upon Whig and Tory*, John Ozell, trans. (London: Printed for E. Curll, 1717); and August Adolph Friedrich von Hennings, *Philosophische und statistische Geschichte des Ursprungs und des Fortgangs der Freyheit in Engeland nach Hume, Blackstone und andern Quellen ausgearbeitet* (Copenhagen: Proft, 1783).

[3] Cf. particularly Sir Frederick Pollock and Frederic William Maitland, *History of English Law Before the Time of Edward I* (2nd ed.; 2 vols.; Cambridge: Cambridge University Press, 1911); Robert von Keller, *Freiheitsgarantien für Person und Eigentum im Mittelalter: eine Studie zur Vorgeschichte moderner Verfassungsgrundrechte* (Heidelberg: C. Winter, 1933); Hans Planitz, "Zur Ideengeschichte der

---

privileges granted to estates or persons, they hardly knew liberty as a general condition of the people. In some respects the general conceptions that prevailed then about the nature and sources of law and order prevented the problem of liberty from arising in its modern form. Yet it might also be said that it was because England retained more of the common medieval ideal of the supremacy of law, which was destroyed elsewhere by the rise of absolutism, that she was able to initiate the modern growth of liberty.[4]

This medieval view, which is profoundly important as background for modern developments, though completely accepted perhaps only during the early Middle Ages, was that "the state cannot itself create or make law, and of course as little abolish or violate law, because this would mean to abolish justice itself, it would be absurd, a sin, a rebellion against God who alone creates

---

Grundrechte," in *Die Grundrechte und Grundpflichten der Reichsverfassung. Kommentar zum zweiten Teil der Reichsverfassung*, Hans Carl Nipperdey, ed. (3 vols.; Berlin: Verlag Reimar Hobbing, 1929–30), vol. 3, pp. 597–623, esp. 601; and Otto Friedrich von Gierke, *Johannes Althusius und die Entwicklung der naturrechtlichen Staatstheorien: zugleich ein Beitrag zur Geschichte der Rechtssystematik* (2nd ed.; Breslau: Verag Marcus, 1902).

[4] See Charles Howard McIlwain, "The English Common Law Barrier against Absolutism," *American Historical Review*, 49 (1934): 27. The extent to which even the most famous and later most influential clause of Magna Carta merely expressed ideas common to the period is shown by a decree of the Emperor Conrad II, dated May 28, 1037 (given in William Stubbs, *Germany in the Early Middle Ages, 476–1250*, Arthur Hassall, ed. [London: Longmans, Green, and Co., 1908], p. 147), which states: "No man shall be deprived of a fief . . . but by the laws of the empire and the judgment of his peers."

We cannot examine in any detail here the philosophical tradition handed down from the Middle Ages. But in some respects Lord Acton was not being altogether paradoxical when he described Thomas Aquinas as the first Whig (see "Freedom in Christianity," *History of Freedom*, p. 37 [Liberty Fund edition, p. 34], and cf. John Neville Figgis, *Studies of Political Thought from Gerson to Grotius*, p. 7). On Thomas Aquinas see Thomas Gilby, *Principality and Polity: Aquinas and the Rise of State Theory in the West* (London: Longmans, Green, and Co., 1958); and on his influence on early English political theory, especially Richard Hooker, see Sheldon Sandford Wolin, "Richard Hooker and English Conservatism," *Western Political Quarterly*, 6 (1953): 28–47. A fuller account would have to give special attention to Nicolas of Cusa in the thirteenth and Bartolus in the fourteenth centuries, who carried on the tradition. See particularly Nicholas of Cusa, *De concordantia catholica* (1514), Gerhard Kallen, ed. (4 vols.; Hamburg: Felix Meiner, 1963) [vol. 14 of *Opera omnia*], bk. 3, chap. 1, pp. 327–28; Marsilius of Padua, *Defensor Pacis*, Richard Scholtz, ed. (2 vols.; Hanover: Hahnsche Buchhandlung, 1933), vol. 1, Dictio 2, chap. 2, sec. 4, pp. 146–47); Franz Anton von Scharpff, *Der Cardinal und Bischof Nicolaus von Cusa als Reformator in Kirche, Reich und Philosophie des fünfzehnten Jahrhunderts* (Tübingen: Laupp, 1871), esp. p. 22; John Neville Figgis, "Bartolus and the Development of European Political Ideas," *Transactions of the Royal Historical Society*, n.s., 19 (1905): 147–68; and Cecil Nathan Sidney Woolf, *Bartolus of Sassoferato: His Position in the History of Medieval Political Thought* (Cambridge: Cambridge University Press, 1913); and, on the political theory of the period generally, Sir Robert Warrand Carlyle and Alexander James Carlyle, *A History of Medieval Political Theory in the West* (6 vols.; Edinburgh: Blackwood, 1903).

law."[5] For centuries it was recognized doctrine that kings or any other human authority could only declare or find the existing law, or modify abuses that had crept in, and not create law.[6] Only gradually, during the later Middle

[5] Cf. Otto Vossler, "Studien zur Erklärung der Menschenrechte," *Historische Zeitschrift*, 142 (1930): 518 ["Für das Mittelalter ist nicht der Staat souverän, sondern das Recht, die Gerechtigkeit . . . Der Staat ist nur die Schöpfung, der Diener des Rechts und der Gerechtigkeit, seine Aufgabe ist es, das Recht zu schützen und zu schirmen gegen das immer drohende Unrecht. Er kann aber nicht selbst Recht schaffen, setzen, ebensowenig natürlich Recht abschaffen oder verletzen, denn das hieße die Gerechtigkeit selbst abschaffen und verletzen, es wäre absurd und Sünde und wäre eine Auflehnung gegen Gott, der allein Recht schafft."—Ed.]; also Fritz Kern, *Kingship and Law in the Middle Ages*. Vol. 1: *The Divine Right of Kings and the Right of Resistance in the Early Middle Ages*. Vol. 2: *Law and Constitution in the Middle Ages: Studies*, Stanley Bertram Chrimes, trans. (Oxford: B. Blackwell, 1939); Edward Jenks, *Law and Politics in the Middle Ages: With a Synoptic Table of Sources* (London: J. Murray, 1898), pp. 24–25; Charles Howard McIlwain, *The High Court of Parliament and Its Supremacy: An Historical Essay on the Boundaries Between Legislation and Adjudication in England* (New Haven: Yale University Press, 1910); John Nevelle Figgis, *The Divine Right of Kings* (2nd ed., with three additional essays; Cambridge: Cambridge University Press, 1914); Charles Victor Langlois, *Le Règne de Philippe III, le Hardi* (Paris: Hachette et cie., 1887), p. 285; and, for a correction concerning the situation in the later Middle Ages, Theodore Frank Thomas Plucknett, *Statutes and Their Interpretation in the First Half of the Fourteenth Century* (Cambridge: Cambridge University Press, 1922), and *Legislation of Edward I* (Oxford: Clarendon Press, 1949). On the whole issue see John Wiedhofft Gough, *Fundamental Law in English Constitutional History* (Oxford: Clarendon Press, 1955).

[6] Cf. Bernhard Rehfeldt, *Die Wurzeln des Rechtes* [*Rechts*] (Berlin: Duncker und Humblot, 1951), p. 67: "Das Auftauchen des Phänomens der Gesetzgebung . . . bedeutet in der Menschheitsgeschichte die Erfindung der Kunst, Recht und Gesetz zu machen. Bis dahin hatte man ja geglaubt Recht nicht setzen, sondern nur anwenden zu können als etwas, das seit jeher war. An dieser Vorstellung gemessen ist die Erfindung der Gesetzgebung vielleicht die folgenschwerste, die je gemacht worden—folgenschwerer als die des Feuermachens oder des Schießpulvers—denn am stärksten von allen hat sie das Schicksal des Menschen in seine eigene Hand gelegt." ["The appearance of the phenomenon of legislation in the history of humanity marks the discovery of the art of determining right from wrong. Up to that point people believed that they were not able to create law but could only apply the rules that were already in place. Measured by this idea, the discovery of legislation is perhaps the most significant of all discoveries that have been made—more significant than the ability to make fire or gunpowder—because more than any other discovery, it placed man's destiny in his own hands."—Ed.]

Similarly in an as yet unpublished paper contributed to a symposium on "The Expansion of Society" organized by the Oriental Institute of the University of Chicago in December 1958, Max Rheinstein observes: "The notion that valid norms of conduct might be established by way of legislation was peculiar to later stages of Greek and Roman history; in western Europe it was dormant until the rediscovery of Roman law and the rise of absolute monarchy. The proposition that all law is the command of a sovereign is a postulate engendered by the democratic ideology of the French Revolution that all law had to emanate from the duly elected representatives of the people. It is not, however, a true description of reality, least of all in the countries of the Anglo-American Common Law." [Since Hayek wrote this, Rheinstein's article has been published. The symposium to which Hayek refers in fact carries a title substantially different from that given by him. The actual citation is: "Process and Change in the Cultural Spectrum

Ages, did the conception of deliberate creation of new law—legislation as we know it—come to be accepted. In England, Parliament thus developed from what had been mainly a law-finding body to a law-creating one. It was finally in the dispute about the authority to legislate in which the contending parties reproached each other for acting arbitrarily—acting, that is, not in accordance with recognized general laws—that the cause of individual freedom was inadvertently advanced. The new power of the highly organized national state which arose in the fifteenth and sixteenth centuries used legislation for the first time as an instrument of deliberate policy. For a while it seemed as if this new power would lead in England, as on the Continent, to absolute monarchy, which would destroy the medieval liberties.[7] The conception of limited government which arose from the English struggle of the seventeenth century was thus a new departure, dealing with new problems. If earlier English doctrine and the great medieval documents, from Magna Carta, the great "Constitutio Libertatis,"[8] downward, are significant in the development of the modern, it is because they served as weapons in that struggle.

Coincident with Expansion: Government and Law," in *City Invincible: A Symposium on Urbanization and Cultural Development in the Ancient Near East, held at the Oriental Institute of the University of Chicago, December 4–7, 1958*, Carl Hermann Kraeling and Robert McCormick Adams, eds. (Chicago: University of Chicago Press, 1960), pp. 405–18.—Ed.] It may be added that a philosopher trained in the German approach to the philosophy of right (John Austin) proved a necessary prerequisite to the success of legal positivism in England.

How profoundly the traditional view that laws are found and not made still influenced English opinion in the late eighteenth century is shown by Edmund Burke's statement in the *Tracts Relative to the Laws against Popery in Ireland*, in *Works*, vol. 9, pp. 352–53: "It would be hard to point to any errour more truly subversive of all the order and beauty, of all the peace and happiness, of human society, than the position, that any body of men have a right to make what Laws they please; or that Laws can derive any authority from their institution merely and independent of the quality of the subject matter. No arguments of policy, reason of State, or preservation of the Constitution, can be pleaded in favour of such a practice. . . . All human Laws are, properly speaking, only declaratory; they may alter the mode and application, but have no power over the substance of original justice." For other illustrations see Edward Samuel Corwin, *The "Higher Law" Background of American Constitutional Law* (Great Seal Books; Ithaca, NY: Cornell University Press, 1955), p. 6, n. 11, reprinted from the *Harvard Law Review*, 42 (1928–29): 153–54, n. 11; and in *Selected Essays on Constitutional Law*, Committee of the Association of American Law Schools and Douglas Blound Maggs, et al., eds. (5 vols. in 4; Chicago: Foundation Press, 1938), vol. 1, p. 5, n. 1 [Liberty Fund edition, p. 5, n. 2].

[7] Cf. Dicey, *Law of the Constitution*, p. 370 [Liberty Fund edition, p. 242]: "A lawyer, who regards the matter from an exclusively legal point of view, is tempted to assert that the real subject in dispute between statesmen such as Bacon and Wentworth on the one hand, and Coke or Eliot on the other, was whether a strong administration of the continental type should, or should not, be permanently established in England."

[8] This is how Henry Bracton describes Magna Carta in *De legibus et consuetudinus Angliae*, George Edward Woodbine, ed. (4 vols.; New Haven: Yale University Press, 1915–42), fol. 168b. [The reference to Magna Carta as "the constitution of liberty" occurs in vol. 3, p. 35 of this edition.—Ed.] On the consequences of what was in effect a seventeenth-century misinterpretation of

Yet if for our purposes we need not dwell longer on the medieval doctrine, we must look somewhat closer at the classical inheritance which was revived at the beginning of the modern period. It is important, not only because of the great influence it exercised on the political thought of the seventeenth century, but also because of the direct significance that the experience of the ancients has for our time.[9]

2. Though the influence of the classical tradition of the modern ideal of liberty is indisputable, its nature is often misunderstood. It has often been said that the ancients did not know liberty in the sense of individual liberty. This is true of many places and periods even in ancient Greece, but certainly not of Athens at the time of its greatness (or of late republican Rome); it may be true of the degenerate democracy of Plato's time, but surely not of those Athenians to whom Pericles said that "the freedom which we enjoy in our government extends also to our ordinary life [where], far from exercising a jealous surveillance over each other, we do not feel called upon to be angry with our neighbour for doing what he likes"[10] and whose soldiers, at the moment

---

Magna Carta see William Sharp McKechnie, *Magna Carta: A Commentary on the Great Charter of King John, With an Historical Introduction* (2nd ed., rev. and in part re-written; Glasgow: J. Maclehose and Sons, 1914), p. 133: "If the vague and inaccurate words of Coke have obscured the bearing of many chapters [of Magna Carta], and diffused false notions of the development of English Law, the service these very errors have done to the cause of constitutional progress is measureless." This view has since been expressed many times (see particularly Sir Herbert Butterfield, *The Englishman and His History* [Cambridge: Cambridge University Press, 1944], p. 7).

[9] Cf. Thomas Hobbes's description of how "one of the most frequent causes of it [the rebellious spirit of his period] is the reading of books of policy, and histories of the ancient Greeks and Romans" (p. 214) and that for this reason "there was never any thing so dearly bought, as these western parts have bought the learning of the Greek and Latin tongues" (*Leviathan; or, The Matter, Forme, and Power of a Commonwealth, Ecclesiasticall and Civil,* Michael Joseph Oakeshott, ed. [Oxford: B. Blackwell, 1946], p. 141). Hobbes shares this hostility towards the ancient classics with Francis Bacon, who wished to see the works of Aristotle banned. [But see p. 243, n. 29, below.—Ed.] See also Aubrey's remark that the roots of Milton's "zeal for the liberty of mankind" lay in his "being so conversant in Livy and the Roman authors, and the greatness he saw done by the Roman Commonwealth" (John Aubrey, "John Milton," *Aubrey's Brief Lives,* Oliver Lawson Dick, ed. [Ann Arbor: University of Michigan Press, 1957], p. 203). On the classical sources of the thought of Milton, Harrington, and Sidney see Zera Silver Fink, *The Classical Republicans: An Essay in the Recovery of a Pattern of Thought in Seventeenth Century England,* Northwestern University Studies in [the] Humanities, No. 9 (Evanston, IL: Northwestern University Press, 1945).

[10] Thucydides ii.37.2 (*Complete Writings: The Peloponnesian War,* translated by Richard Crawley, introduction by John Finley, Jr. [New York: Modern Library, 1951], p. 104.) The most convincing testimony is probably that of the enemies of the liberal democracy of Athens who reveal much when they complain, as Aristotle did (*Politics,* 1317b [bk. 6, chap. 1, sec. 7]), that "in such democracies each person lives as he likes." (Also see Plutarch, *Lycurgus,* 24.) The Greeks may have been the first to confuse personal and political freedom; but this does not mean that they did not know the former or did not esteem it. The Stoic philosophers, at any rate, preserved the original meaning and handed it on to later ages. Zeno, indeed, defined freedom as the "power of independent action, whereas slavery is privation of the same" (Diogenes Laertius, *Lives of Eminent Phi-*

of supreme danger during the Sicilian expedition, were reminded by their general that, above all, they were fighting for a country in which they had "unfettered discretion in it to all to live as they pleased."[11] What were the main characteristics of that freedom of the "freest of free countries," as Nicias called Athens on the same occasion, as seen both by the Greeks themselves and by Englishmen of the later Tudor and Stuart times?

The answer is suggested by a word which the Elizabethans borrowed from the Greeks but which has since gone out of use.[12] "Isonomia" was imported

---

losophers, vii.121, Robert Drew Hicks, trans. [Loeb Classical Library; London: W. Heinemann, 1925], vol. 2, p. 227). Philo of Alexandria, *Quod omnis probus liber sit* ["Every good man is free."—Ed.] 452.45 (*Works* [published in 10 volumes plus two supplementary volumes], F. A. Colson, trans. [Loeb Classical Library; London: W. Heinemann, 1941], vol. 9, p. 36), even offers a thoroughly modern conception of liberty under the law: *hosoi de meta nomou zōsin, eleutheroi* [The English reads: "All whose life is regulated by law are free."—Ed.]. Incidentally, he reports an inscription from Priene that reads: "there is nothing greater for Hellenic men than freedom" (vol. 9, 19, 13a). [This quotation does not appear in Philo's treatise "Quod Omnis Probus Liber Sit," certainly not in the form attributed. Philo does, however, write at some length on the importance of freedom to the Greeks. He notes that "this doctrine that freedom is glorious and honourable, slavery execrable and disgraceful, is attested by cities and nations, which are more ancient, more permanent, and, as far as mortals may be, immortal, and for immortals is a law of their being that their every word is true. The senates and national assemblies meet almost every day to discuss more than anything else how to confirm their freedom if they have it, or to acquire it if they have it not." (20.137–38; Loeb Classical Library, vol. 9, p. 89).—Ed.]; and Strabo in his *Geography* (H. L. Jones, ed.; Loeb Classical Library, vol. 5, p. 145 [10.4.16]) writes of the Cretans: "As for their constitution, which is described by Ephorus, it might suffice to tell in a way its most important provisions. The lawgiver, he says, seems to take it for granted that liberty is a state's greatest good, for this alone makes property belong specifically to those who acquire it, whereas in a condition of slavery everything belongs to the rulers and not to the ruled." See Eric Alfred Havelock, *The Liberal Temper in Greek Politics* (New Haven: Yale University Press, 1957). It is also no longer possible to deny the existence of freedom in ancient Athens by the assertion that its economic system was "based" on slavery, since recent research has clearly shown that it was comparatively unimportant; see William Linn Westermann, "Athenaeus and the Slaves of Athens," *Athenian Studies Presented to William Scott Ferguson* (London: H. Milford, Oxford University Press, 1940), pp. 451–70, and Arnold Hugh Martin Jones, "The Economic Basis of the Athenian Democracy," *Past and Present*, 1 (1952): 13–31, reprinted in *Athenian Democracy* (Oxford: B. Blackwell, 1957), pp. 3–20.

[11] Thucydides vii. 69 (p. 440). The misrepresentation of Greek liberty traces back to Thomas Hobbes and became widely known through Benjamin Constant, *De la liberté des anciens comparée à celle des modernes*, reprinted in *Cours de politique constitutionnelle; ou Collection des ouvrages publiés sur le gouvernement représentatif* (2 vols.; Paris: Guillaumin et cie., 1861), vol. 2, pp. 539–60, and Numa Denis Fustel de Coulanges, *La Cité antique* (Paris: Durand, 1864). About this whole discussion see Georg Jellinek, *Das Recht des modernen Staates*. Vol. 1: *Allgemeine Staatslehre* (2nd ed.; Berlin: O. Häring, 1905), pp. 285–305. It is difficult to understand how, as late as 1933, Harold Joseph Laski ("Liberty," *Encyclopedia of the Social Sciences*, vol. 9, p. 442) could still argue, with explicit reference to the Periclean period, that "in such an organic society the concept of individual liberty was virtually unknown."

[12] Cf. Johan Huizinga, *Wenn die Waffen schweigen: die Aussichten auf Genesung unserer Kultur* (Basel: Burg-Verlag, 1945), p. 95: "Man muss eigentlich bedauern, dass die Kulturen, die sich auf der

into England from Italy at the end of the sixteenth century as a word meaning "equality of laws to all manner of persons";[13] shortly afterward it was freely used by the translator of Livy in the Englished form "isonomy" to describe a state of equal laws for all and responsibility of the magistrates.[14] It continued in use during the seventeenth century[15] until "equality before the law," "government of law," or "rule of law" gradually displaced it.

The history of the concept in ancient Greece provides an interesting lesson because it probably represents the first instance of a cycle that civilizations seem to repeat. When it first appeared,[16] it described a state which Solon had earlier established in Athens when he gave the people "equal laws for the noble and the base"[17] and thereby gave them "not so much the control of

---

Grundlage der griechischen Antike aufbauten, nicht an Stelle des Wortes Demokratie jenes andere übernommen haben, das in Athen auf Grund der geschichtlichen Entwicklung besondere Achtung erweckte und ausserdem den hier wesentlichen Gedanken einer guten Regierungsform besonders rein zum Ausdruck brachte: das Wort 'Isonomia,' Gleichheit der Gesetze. Dies Wort hatte sogar einen unsterblichen Klang. . . . Aus dem Worte 'Isonomia' spricht weit deutlicher und unmittelbarer als aus 'Demokratia' das Ideal der Freiheit; auch ist die in der Bezeichnung 'Isonomia' enthaltene These nichts Unerfüllbares wie dies bei 'Demokatia' der Fall ist. Das wesentliche Prinzip des Rechtsstaates ist in diesem Wort bündig und klar wiedergegeben." ["It is unfortunate that the cultures that were to arise on the foundations of Greek antiquity appropriated the word 'democracy' rather than 'isonomia,' that other word employed in Athens that, for reasons of historical development, expressed in its purest form the essential notion of a good government, that is, equality before the law. The word 'isonomia' carries the sense of an ideal of freedom far more clearly and more directly than does 'democratia.' In addition, the term 'isonomia' does not suggest something that is ultimately unattainable, as does 'democratia.' The notion 'isonomia' best and most concisely reflects the essential principle of the *Rechtsstaat*.—Ed.]

[13] In the Italian dictionary by John Florio, *Worlde of Wordes, or Most Copious and Exact Dictionarie in Italian and English* (London: Printed by Arnold Hatfield for Edw. Blount, 1598), p. 195.

[14] Titus Livius, *Romane Historie* [also containing the *Breviaries* of Lucius Annaeus Florus], Philemon Holland, trans. (London: Printed by Adam Islip, 1600), pp. 114, 134, 1016.

[15] The *Oxford English Dictionary*, s.v. "Isonomy," gives instances of use in 1659 and 1684, each suggesting that the term was then in fairly common use. [The references are to: "1659 *Quaeries on Proposalls Officers Armie to Parlt.* 8 Every one pretending to equality and Isonomy, lifteth up and advanceth himself whilst he shoveth at, and thrusteth down others. 1684 tr. *Agrippa's Van. Arts* lv. 155 They who prefer a Popular State have dignifi'd it with the most agreeable and specious Title of Isonomie."—Ed.]

[16] The earliest preserved use of the word "isonomia" seems to be that by Alcmaeon about 500 B.C. (Hermann Diels, *Die Fragmente der Vorsokratiker: Griechisch und Deutsch* (4th ed.; 3 vols.; Berlin: Wiedmannsche Buchhandlung, 1922), vol. 1, p.136, Alkmaion, frag. 4). As the use is metaphorical, describing isonomy as a condition of physical health, it suggests that the term was well established by then. [The fragment to which Hayek refers is taken from the doxography of *Aëtius* (5.30.1) quoting Alkmaion and was later reconstructed by Diels.—Ed.]

[17] Ernst Diehl, *Anthologia lyrica Graeca* (3rd ed.; 3 vols.; Leipzig: Teubner, 1949–52), frag. 24, line 18, vol. 1, p. 45. [The passage is from Solon, frag. 24, line 18: "*thesmous d' homoiōs tōi kakōi te kagathōi.*"—Ed.] Cf. Erik Wolf, "Maß und Gerechtigkeit bei Solon," in *Gegenwartsprobleme des internationalen Rechtes und der Rechtsphilosophie: Festschrift für Rudolf Laun zu seinem 70. Geburtstag*, Demetrios S. Konstantopoulos and Hans Wehberg, eds. (Hamburg: Girardet, 1953), pp. 449–64; Kathleen

public policy, as the certainty of being governed legally in accordance with known rules."[18] Isonomy was contrasted with the arbitrary rule of tyrants and became a familiar expression in popular drinking songs celebrating the assassination of one of these tyrants.[19] The concept seems to be older than that of

---

Freeman, *The Work and Life of Solon: With a Translation of His Poems* (London: Milford, 1926); William John Woodhouse, *Solon, the Liberator: A Study of the Agrarian Problem in Attika in the Seventh Century* (London: Oxford University Press, 1938); and Karl Hönn, *Solon, Staatsmann und Weiser* (Vienna: L. W. Seidel, 1948), p. 107.

[18] Sir Ernest Barker, *Greek Political Theory: Plato and His Predecessors* (2nd ed.; London: Methuen, 1925), p. 44. [Barker footnotes the source of the statement as Sir Alfred Eckhard Zimmern, *The Greek Commonwealth: Politics and Economics in Fifth-Century Athens* (Oxford: Clarendon Press, 1911), pp. 130–31.—Ed.] Cf. Lord Acton, "Freedom in Antiquity," *History of Freedom*, p. 7 [Liberty Fund edition, *Essays in the History of Liberty*, p. 10], and Paul Vinogradoff, *Collected Papers of Paul Vinogradoff* (2 vols.; Oxford: Clarendon Press, 1928), vol. 2, pp. 41–42.

[19] Cf. Max Pohlenz, *Griechische Freiheit: Wesen und Werden eines Lebensideals* (Heidelberg: Quelle und Meyer, 1955); Georg Busolt, *Griechische Staatskunde*. Part 1 of *Allgemeine Darstellung des griechischen Staates* (3rd rev. ed.; Munich: Beck, 1920), p. 417–18; Jakob Aall Ottesen Larsen, "Cleisthenes and the Development of the Theory of Democracy at Athens," in *Essays in Political Theory Presented to George H. Sabine*, Milton Ridvas Konvitz and Arthur Edward Murphy, eds. (Ithaca, NY: Cornell University Press, 1948), pp. 1–16; *Pauly's Real-Encyclopädie der classischen Altertumswissenschaft*, August Friedrich Pauly, ed., Supplement 7, Georg Wissowa, ed. (Stuttgart: J. B. Metzler, 1940), s.v. "Isonomia," by Victor Ehrenberg (pp. 293–301); and Ehrenberg's articles "Origins of Democracy," *Historia: Zeitschrift für Alte Geschichte* [Wiesbaden] 1 (1950): 515–48, esp. 535, and "Das Harmodioslied," *Wiener Studien. Zeitschrift für klassische Philologie (Festschrift Albin Lesky)*, 69 (1956): 57–69; Gregory Vlastos, "Isonomia," *American Journal of Philology*, 74 (1953): 337–66; and John Walter Jones, *The Law and Legal Theory of the Greeks: An Introduction* (Oxford: Clarendon Press, 1956), chap. 4 ["Eunomia, Homonomia, Isonomia," pp. 73–92].

The Greek *skolion* mentioned in the text will be found in two versions in Diehl, *Anthologia lyrica Graeca*, vol. 2, *skolia* 10 (9) [vol. 2, pp. 184–85] and 13 (12) [p. 185]. A curious illustration of the appeal of these songs celebrating *isonomia* to late eighteenth-century English Whigs is the "Ode in Imitation of Callistratus" by Sir William Jones (whom we mentioned earlier as the link between the political views of the Whigs and the evolutionary tradition in linguistics; see *The Works of Sir William Jones* [13 vols.; London: Printed for J. Stockdale and J. Walker, 1807], vol. 4, p. 574), which is headed by the Greek text of the *skolion* and, after twenty lines in praise of Harmodios and Aristogiton, continues:

> "Then in *Athens* all was Peace;
> Equal Laws and Liberty:
> Nurse of Arts, and eye for *Greece*!
> People valiant, firm, and free!
> Not less glorious was thy deed,
> *Wentworth*, fix'd in Virtue's cause;
> Not less brilliant be thy meed,
> *Lenox*, friend to *Equal Laws*!
> High in Freedom's temple rais'd,
> See *Fitz Maurice* beaming stand,
> For collected Virtues prais'd,
> Wisdom's voice, and Valour's hand!
> Ne'er shall fate their eyelids close:

demokratia, and the demand for equal participation of all in the government appears to have been one of its consequences. To Herodotus it is still isonomy rather than democracy which is the "most beautiful of all names of a political order."[20] The term continued in use for some time after democracy had been achieved, at first in its justification and later, as has been said,[21] increasingly in order to disguise the character it assumed; for democratic government soon came to disregard that very equality before the law from which it had derived its justification. The Greeks clearly understood that the two ideals, though related, were not the same: Thucydides speaks without hesitation about an "isonomic oligarchy,"[22] and Plato even uses the term "isonomy" in deliberate contrast to democracy rather than in justification of it.[23] By the end of the fourth century it had come to be necessary to emphasize that "in a democracy the laws should be masters."[24]

Against this background certain famous passages in Aristotle, though he no longer uses the term "isonomia," appear as a vindication of that traditional ideal. In the *Politics* he stresses that "it is more proper that the law should govern than any one of the citizens," that the persons holding supreme power

---

They, in blooming regions blest,
   With *Harmodius* shall repose,
With *Aristogiton* rest."
[The verses refer to Harmodius, a youth, and his older lover, Aristogiton. The brother of the tyrant of Athens, Hipparchus, continued making advances towards Harmodius, publicly mocking the lovers when Harmodius refused to share his bed. Outraged, Aristogiton plotted the assassination both of Hipparchus and his tyrant brother Hippias. The plot failed but Hipparchus was killed while organizing a procession marking a festival. Harmodius was instantly killed by Hipparchus' bodyguard and Aristogiton was captured and tortured by Hippias. Rather than reveal the names of those involved in the plot, Aristogiton hurled insults at the tyrant, which so enraged him that he stabbed him to death. Their example was hailed by Athenians as a model of resistance to tyranny and as a model for young men.—Ed.]
Cf. also *Works,* vol. 4, p. 572, the "Ode in Imitation of Alcaeus," where Jones says with reference to the "Empress Sovereign Law":
   "Smit by her sacred frown
   The fiend *Discretion* like a vapour sinks."
[20] Herodotus *Histories* iii. 80; cf. also iii. 142, and v. 37.
[21] Busolt, *Allgemeine Darstellung des griechischen Staates,* p. 417, and Ehrenberg, in *Pauly,* Sup., s.v. "Isonomia," p. 299.
[22] Thucydides iii. 62.3–4 and contrast this use of the term in its legitimate sense with his reference to what he describes as its specious use, Thucydides iii. 82.8; cf. also Isokrates *Areopagiticus* vii. 20, and *Panathenaicus* xii. 178.
[23] Plato *Republic* viii. 557bc, 559d, 561e.
[24] Hyperides, *In Defence of Euxenippus* 5 (*Minor Attic Orators,* John Ormiston Burtt and Kenneth John Maidment, eds. [Loeb Classical Library; 2 vols.; Cambridge, MA: Harvard University Press, 1960], vol. 2, p. 468): "ὅπως ἐν δημοκρατίαι κύριοι οἱ νόμοι ἔσονται" ("*hopōs en demokratiai kurioi hoi nomoi esontai*"). The phrase about the law being king (*nomos basileus* ["the law as king"]) already occurs much earlier.

241

"should be appointed to be only guardians and the servants of the law," and that "he who would place the supreme power in mind, would place it in God and the laws."[25] He condemns the kind of government in which "the people govern and not the law" and in which "everything is determined by a majority vote and not by a law." Such a government is to him not that of a free state, "for, where government is not in the laws, then there is no free state, for the law ought to be supreme over all things." A government that "centers all power in the votes of the people cannot, properly speaking, be a democracy: for their decrees cannot be general in their extent."[26] If we add to this the following passage in the *Rhetoric*, we have indeed a fairly complete statement of the ideal of government by law:[27] "It is of great moment that well drawn laws should themselves define all the points they possibly can, and leave as few as possible to the decision of the judges, [for] the decision of the lawgiver is not particular but prospective and general, whereas members of the assembly and the jury find it their duty to decide on definite cases brought before them."[28]

[25] Aristotle, *Politics* 1287a [bk. 3, chap. 16, sec. 10]. The translation used, in preference to the more familiar renderings by Benjamin Jowett, is that by William Ellis, *The Politics of Aristotle: A Treatise on Government*, William Ellis, trans. (Everyman library; New York: Dutton, 1947).

[26] Aristotle, *Politics*, 1292a [bk. 4, chap. 4].

[27] How fundamental these conceptions remained for the Athenians is shown by a law to which Demosthenes refers in one of his orations (*Against Aristocrates* 86; cf. *Against Timocrates* 59) as a law "as good as ever law was." [The edition Hayek employed is Demosthenes, *Orations 21–26: Against Meidias. Against Androtion. Against Aristocrates. Against Timocrates. Against Aristogeiton 1 and 2*, James Herbert Vince, trans. (7 vols.; Loeb Classical Library; Cambridge, MA: Harvard University Press, 1935), vol. 3, pp. 275, 411.—Ed.] The Athenian who had introduced it had been of the opinion that, as every citizen had an equal share in civil rights, so everybody should have an equal share in the laws; and he had proposed, therefore, that "it should not be lawful to propose a law affecting any individual, unless the same applied to all Athenians." This became the law of Athens. We do not know when this happened—Demosthenes referred to it in 352 B.C. But it is interesting to see how, by that time, democracy had already become the primary concept superseding the older one of equality before the law. Although Demosthenes no longer uses the term "isonomia," his reference to the law is little more than a paraphrase of that old ideal. On the law in question cf. Justus Hermann Lipsius, *Das attische Recht und Rechtsverfahren* (3 vols. in 1; Leipzig: Reisland, 1905–15), vol. 1, p. 388, and Egon Weiss, *Griechisches Privatrecht auf rechtsvergleichender Grundlage. Vol. 1: Allgemeine Lehren* (Leipzig: F. Meiner, 1923), p. 93 (n. 186a); cf. also Arnold Hugh Martin Jones, "The Athenian Democracy and Its Critics," *Cambridge Historical Journal*, 9 (1953): 10, and reprinted in his *Athenian Democracy*, p. 52: "At no time was it legal [in Athens] to alter a law by a simple decree of the assembly. The mover of such a decree was liable to the famous 'indictment for illegal proceedings' which, if upheld by the courts, . . . exposed the mover to heavy penalties."

[28] Aristotle, *Rhetoric* 1354ab [bk. 1, chap. 1] in *The Works of Aristotle*, William Rhys Roberts, trans., William David Ross, ed., vol. 11 (Oxford: Clarendon Press, 1924), [p. 2]. I do not quote in the text the passage from *Politics* 1317b.5 [bk. 6, chap. 1, sec. 8] where Aristotle mentions as a condition of liberty that "no magistrate should be allowed any discretionary power but in a few instances, and of no consequence to public business," because it occurs in a context where he does not express his own opinion but cites the views of others. An important statement of his

There is clear evidence that the modern use of the phrase "government by laws and not by men" derives directly from this statement of Aristotle. Thomas Hobbes believed that it was just "another error of Aristotle's politics, that in a well-ordered commonwealth not men should govern, but the laws,"[29] whereupon James Harrington retorted that the "art whereby a civil society of men is instituted and preserved upon the foundation of common right or interest . . . [is], to follow Aristotle and Livy, the empire of laws, not of men."[30]

3. In the course of the seventeenth century the influence of Latin writers largely replaced the direct influence of the Greeks. We should therefore take a brief look at the tradition derived from the Roman Republic. The famous Laws of the Twelve Tables, reputedly drawn up in conscious imitation of Solon's laws, form the foundation of its liberty. The first of the public laws in them provides that "no privileges, or statutes, shall be enacted in favour of private persons, to the injury of others contrary to the law common to all citizens, and which individuals, no matter of what rank, have a right to make use of."[31] This was the basic conception under which there

---

views on judicial discretion is to be found in *Nicomachean Ethics* 1137b.5 [bk. 5, chap. 10] where he argues that the judge should fill a gap in the law "by ruling as the lawgiver himself would rule were he there present, and would have provided by law had he foreseen the case would arise"— thus anticipating a famous clause of the Swiss Civil Code.

[29] Hobbes, *Leviathan*, p. 448. It is characteristic that Francis Bacon started with this animosity against Aristotle, whose books he wished to see banned. See the introduction to Francis Bacon, *Instauratio Magna*. [The edition to which Hayek is referring is most likely *Francisici Baconi Baronus de Verulamio . . . opera omnia* (4 vols.; London: R. Gosling, 1730), with an introduction by Bacon's contemporary and friend, the Rev. Dr. William Rawley. If so, Hayek is in error in suggesting that Bacon wished to ban the work of Aristotle. Rawley writes: "Though there was bred in Mr. Bacon so early a dislike of the physiology of Aristotle, yet he did not despise him with that pride and haughtiness, with which youth is wont to be puffed up. He had a just esteem of that great master in learning, and greater than that of Aristotle himself expressed towards the philosophers that went before him. For he endeavoured (some say) to stifle all their labours, designing to himself an universal monarchy over opinions, as his patron Alexander did over men" (vol. 1, p. 20).—Ed.]

[30] James Harrington, *The Common-wealth of Oceana* (London: Printed by J. Streater for Livewell Chapman, and are to be sold at his shop, 1656), p. 2. The phrase occurs soon afterward in a passage in *The Leveller* of 1659, quoted by Gough, *Fundamental Law in English Constitutional History*, p. 137. [*The Leveller; or, the Principles and Maxims Concerning Government and Religion, Which are Asserted by those that are commonly called Levellers* (London: Printed, for Thomas Brewster, at the Three Bibles, at the West-End of Pauls, 1659), p. 5, which maintains that "they assert it as Fundamental, that the Government of England ought to be by Laws, and not by Men."—Ed.]

[31] See Samuel Parsons Scott, *The Civil Law, Including the Twelve Tables, the Institutes of Gaius, the Rules of Ulpian, the Opinions of Paulus, the Enactments of Justinian, and the Constitutions of Leo* (17 vols. in 7; Cincinnati: Central Trust Co., 1932), vol. 1, p. 73 [Table 9, 'Concerning Public Law,' Law 1].

On the whole of this section see, in addition to the works of Theodor Mommsen [particularly *The History of Rome*, William Purdie Dickson, trans. (new ed.; 4 vols.; New York: Charles Scribner's Sons, 1885), bk. 2, chap. 8.—Ed.]; Chaim Wirszubski, *Libertas as a Political Idea at Rome*

was gradually formed, by a process very similar to that by which the common law grew,[32] the first fully developed system of private law—in spirit very different from the later Justinian code, which determined the legal thinking of the Continent.

This spirit of the laws of free Rome has been transmitted to us mainly in the works of the historians and orators of the period, who once more became influential during the Latin Renaissance of the seventeenth century. Livy—whose translator made people familiar with the term "isonomia" (which Livy himself did not use) and who supplied Harrington with the distinction between the government of law and the government of men[33]— Tacitus and, above all, Cicero became the chief authors through whom the classical tradition spread. Cicero indeed became the main authority for modern liberalism,[34] and we owe to him many of the most effective formulations of freedom under the law.[35] To him is due the conception of general rules or

during the Late Republic and Early Principate (Cambridge: Cambridge University Press, 1950); and Ulrich von Lübtow, Blüte und Verfall der römischen Freiheit: Betrachtungen zur Kultur- und Verfassungsgeschichte des Abendlandes (Berlin: Blaschker 1953), which came to my knowledge only after the text was completed.

[32] See William Warwick Buckland and Arnold Duncan McNair, Baron McNair, Roman Law and Common Law: A Comparison in Outline (Cambridge: Cambridge University Press, 1936).

[33] Titus Livius, Ab Urbe Condita ii.1.1: "imperia legum potentiora quam hominum." ["The commands of the laws (are) more powerful than the commands of men."—Ed.] The Latin phrase is quoted (inexactly) by Algernon Sidney (in Discourses Concerning Government, in The Works of Algernon Sydney, Thomas Hollis, ed., with additions and corrections by Joseph Robertson (new ed.; London: Printed for W. Strahan Iun. for T. Becket and Co. and T. Cadell in the Strand, T. Davies in Russel Street, and T. Evans in King Street, 1772), p. 10 [Liberty Fund edition of the Discourses, p. 17]. See also John Adams, Works: With a Life of the Author, Charles Francis Adams, ed. (10 vols.; Boston: Charles C. Little and James Brown, 1851), vol. 4, p. 403. In Holland's translation of Livy of 1600 [The Romane Historie, Written by T. Livius of Padua (also containing the Breviaries of Lucus Annaeus Florus), Philemon Holland, trans. (London: Printed by Adam Islip, 1600), p. 44] these words are rendered as "the authoritie and rule of laws, more powerfull and mightie than those of men." The words I have italicized provide the earliest instance known to me in which "rule" is used in the sense of "government" or "dominion."

[34] Cf. Walter Rüegg, Cicero und der Humanismus: formale Untersuchungen über Petrarca und Erasmus (Zurich: Rheinverlag, 1946), and George Holland Sabine and Stanley Barney Smith, "Introduction," to Marcus Tullius Cicero, On the Commonwealth (Columbus: Ohio State University Press, 1929), pp. 74–99. On Cicero's influence on David Hume in particular see David Hume, My Own Life, in Essays, vol. 1, p. 2 [Liberty Fund edition, p. xxxiii], and John Laird, Hume's Philosophy of Human Nature (London: Methuen and Co., Ltd., 1932), pp. 241–43, who speaks of "the Ciceronian flavour of Hume's ethical thinking." [Hume writes: "I found an unsurmountable aversion to everything but the pursuits of philosophy and general learning; and while I fancied I was poring upon Voet and Vinnius, Cicero and Virgil were the authors I was secretly devouring." Johannes Voet was an eminent eighteenth-century Dutch legal theorist, who attempted to systematize Roman-Dutch civil law; Arnoldus Vinnius (1588–1657) was also a Dutch legal theorist and a contemporary of Grotius.—Ed.]

[35] Marcus Tullius Cicero, De Domo Sua, 13.33 (Loeb edition, pp. 172–73), where he speaks of "the peculiar mark of a free community—the right, I mean, in accordance with which it is unlawful for any

leges legum, which govern legislation,[36] the conception that we obey the law in order to be free,[37] and the conception that the judge ought to be merely the mouth through whom the law speaks.[38] No other author shows more clearly that during the classical period of Roman law it was fully understood that there is no conflict between law and freedom and that freedom is dependent

---

abatement of civil privilege or private property to be made without a verdict of the senate, of people, or of the courts constituted to deal with each type of offense."

[36] Marcus Tullius Cicero, *De legibus* ii.7.18. ["Leges legum" translates literally as "laws in the legal style."—Ed.] These "higher laws" were recognized by the Romans, who inscribed in their statutes a provision stating that they were not intended to abrogate what was sacrosanct or *jus* (see Corwin, *"Higher Law" Background,* pp. 12–18 [*Harvard Law Review,* 42 (1928–29): 157–64; *Selected Essays,* vol. 1, pp. 8–14; Liberty Fund edition, pp. 11–17], and the literature there quoted).

[37] Marcus Tullius Cicero, *Pro Cluentio* 53.146: "omnes legum servi sumus ut liberi esse possimus." [Cicero writes: "Legum ministri magistratus, legum interpretes iudices, legum denique idcirco omnes servi sumus, ut liberi esse possimus." ("The magistrates who administer the law, the jurors who interpret it—all of us in short—obey the law to the end that we may be free.")—Ed.] Cf. Montesquieu, *Spirit of the Laws* [bk. 26, chap. 20 (vol. 2, p. 76); French edition, vol. 2, p. 772]: "Liberty consists, principally in not being forced to do a thing where the laws do not oblige: people are in this state only as they are governed by civil laws; and because they live under those civil laws they are free." ["La liberté consiste principalement à ne pouvoir être forcé à faire une chose que la loi n'ordonne pas; et on n'est dans cet état que parce qu'on est gouverné par des lois civiles: nous sommes donc libres, parce que nous vivons sous les lois civiles."]

Voltaire, *Pensées sur le gouvernement* (1752) in *Œuvres complètes,* Louis Moland, ed. (52 vols.; Paris: Garnier frères, 1877–85), vol. 23, p. 526: "La liberté consiste à ne dependre que de lois." ["Liberty consists of depending only upon the law."] Jean Jacques Rousseau, *Lettres écrites de la Montagne,* Letter 8, in *The Political Writings of Jean Jacques Rousseau,* Charles Edwyn Vaughan, ed., edited from the Original Manuscripts and Authentic Editions (2 vols.; Cambridge: Cambridge University Press, 1915), vol. 2, p. 235. "There is no liberty without laws, nor where someone is above the laws; even in the state of nature, man is free only because of the natural law, which enjoins everyone." [The original French reads: "Il n'y a donc point de liberté sans Loix, ni où quelqu'un est au dessus des Loix: dans l'état même de nature l'homme n'est libre qu'à la faveur de la Loi naturelle qui commande à tous." "Lettres Écrites de la Montagne," (Huitième Lettre), *Œuvres Complètes,* Bernard Gagnebin and Marcel Raymond, eds. Bibliothèque de la Pléiade (5 vols.; Paris: Éditions Gallimard, 1964), vol. 3, p. 842.]

[38] Marcus Tullius Cicero, *De legibus* iii.122: "Magistratum legem esse loquentem." ["The magistrate is the law speaking."—Ed.] Cf. Sir Edward Coke ["Seventh Report," in *The Reports of Edward Coke, Knt.: In Thirteen Parts,* John Henry Thomas and John Farquhar Fraser, eds. (13 parts in 6 vols.; London: J. Butterworth and Son, 1826), pt. 7, 6 (vol. 4, p. 6); Liberty Fund edition, vol. 1, p. 174] in Calvin's Case (as quoted in chapter 4, note 18); "Judex est lex loquens," ["The judge is the spoken law."—Ed.] and the eighteenth-century legal maxim, "Rex nihil alius est quam lex agens" ["The king is nothing other than the law in action."—Ed.]; also Montesquieu, *Spirit of the Laws,* bk. 11, chap. 6 (vol. 1, p. 159; French edition: vol. 2, p. 404) "The national judges are no more than the mouth that pronounces the word of the law, mere passive beings, incapable of moderating either its force or rigor." ["Mais les juges de la nation ne sont, comme nous avons dit, que la bouche qui prononce les paroles de la loi; des êtres inanimés qui n'en peuvent modérer ni la force ni la rigueur"—Ed.] The phrase was still repeated in the United States by Chief Justice John Marshall (*Osborn v. Bank of United States,* 22 *U.S.* [9, *Wheaton*] 738 at 866), when he spoke of judges as "the mere mouthpieces of the law" and "capable of willing nothing." [In fact, what Marshall wrote was: "Courts are the mere instruments of the law, and can will nothing."—Ed.]

upon certain attributes of the law, its generality and certainty, and the restrictions it places on the discretion of authority.

This classical period was also a period of complete economic freedom, to which Rome largely owed its prosperity and power.[39] From the second century AD, however, state socialism advanced rapidly.[40] In this development the freedom which equality before the law had created was progressively destroyed as demands for another kind of equality arose. During the later empire the strict law was weakened as, in the interest of a new social policy, the state increased its control over economic life. The outcome of this process, which culminated under Constantine, was, in the words of a distinguished student of Roman law, that "the absolute empire proclaimed together with the principle of equity the authority of the imperial will unfettered by the barrier of law. Justinian with his learned professors brought this process to its conclusion."[41] Thereafter, for a thousand years, the conception that legislation should serve to protect the freedom of the individual was lost. And when the art of legislation was rediscovered, it was the code of Justinian with its conception of a prince who stood above the law[42] that served as the model on the Continent.

4. In England, however, the wide influence which the classical authors enjoyed during the reign of Elizabeth helped to prepare the way for a differ-

---

[39] See Michael Ivanovitch Rostovtzeff, *Gesellschaft und Wirtschaft im römischen Kaiserreich*, Lothar Wickert, trans. (2 vols.; Leipzig: Quelle und Meyer, 1931), vol. 1, pp. 49 and 140.

[40] Cf. Friedrich Oertel, "The Economic Life of the Empire," in *Cambridge Ancient History*. Vol. 12: *The Imperial Crisis and Recovery, A.D. 193–324* (Cambridge: Cambridge University Press, 1939), pp. 232–81, esp. 270ff., and the "Appendix" to Robert von Pöhlmann, *Geschichte der sozialen Frage und des Sozialismus in der antiken Welt* (3rd ed.; 2 vols.; Munich: C. H. Beck, 1925), vol. 2, pp. 511–85; also von Lubtow, *Blüte und Verfall der römischen Freiheit*, pp. 87–107; Michael Ivanovitch Rostovtzeff, "The Decay of the Ancient World and Its Economic Explanation," *Economic History Review*, 2 (1930): 196–214; Tenney Frank, "Epilogue: The Economic Decay of the Roman World," in *Economic Survey of Ancient Rome* (6 vols.; Baltimore: Johns Hopkins Press, 1933–40), vol. 5, pp. 296–304; Henry Joseph Haskell, *The New Deal in Old Rome: How Government in the Ancient World Tried to Deal with Modern Problems* (New York: A. Knopf, 1939); and Luigi Roberto Einaudi, "Greatness and Decline of Planned Economy in the Hellenistic World," *Kyklos* 2 (1948) [part 1, pp. 193–210; part 2, pp. 289–316], reprinted as *Greatness and Decline of Planned Economy in the Hellenistic World* (Berne: A. Francke, 1950).

[41] Fritz Pringsheim, "Jus aequum und jus strictum," *Zeitschrift der Savigny-Stiftung für Rechtsgeschichte, Romanistische Abteilung* 42 (1921): 668. [The original German reads: "Das absolute Kaisertum verkündet mit der aequitas zugleich die von der Schranke des jus befreite Autorität des kaiserlichen Willens. Justinian mit seinen gelehrten Professoren bringt die Entwicklung zum Abschlusse."—Ed.] Cf. also the same author's *Hohe und Ende der Römischen Jurisprudenz: Vortrag gehalten bei der Freiburger wissenschaftlichen Gesellschaft am 3. Dezember 1932* (Freiburg in Baden: Speyer und Kaerner, 1933).

[42] See Adhémar Esmein, "La Maxime *Princeps legibus solutus est* dans l'ancien droit public français," *Essays in Legal History Read Before the International Congress of Historical Studies Held in London in 1913*, Sir Paul Vinogradoff, ed. (London: Oxford University Press, 1913), pp. 201–14.

ent development. Soon after her death the great struggle between king and Parliament began, from which emerged as a by-product the liberty of the individual. It is significant that the disputes began largely over issues of economic policy very similar to those which we again face today. To the nineteenth-century historian the measures of James I and Charles I which provoked the conflict might have seemed antiquated issues without topical interest. To us the problems caused by the attempts of the kings to set up industrial monopolies have a familiar ring: Charles I even attempted to nationalize the coal industry and was dissuaded from this only by being told that this might cause a rebellion.[43]

Ever since a court had laid down in the famous Case of Monopolies[44] that the grant of exclusive rights to produce any article was "against the common law and the liberty of the subject," the demand for equal laws for all citizens became the main weapon of Parliament in its opposition to the king's aims. Englishmen then understood better than they do today that the control of production always means the creation of privilege: that Peter is given permission to do what Paul is not allowed to do.

It was another kind of economic regulation, however, that occasioned the first great statement of the basic principle. The Petition of Grievances of 1610 was provoked by new regulations issued by the king for building in London and prohibiting the making of starch from wheat. This celebrated plea of the House of Commons states that, among all the traditional rights of British subjects, "there is none which they have accounted more dear and precious than this, to be guided and governed by the certain rule of law, which giveth to the head and the members that which of right belongeth to them, and not by any uncertain and arbitrary form of government. . . . Out of this

---

[43] Cf. John Ulric Nef, *Industry and Government in France and England: 1540–1640* (Philadelphia: American Philosophical Society, 1940), p. 114. An interesting account of how later "the freedom of the Press thus came to England all but incidentally to the elimination of a commercial monopoly" is given by Maurice William Cranston, *John Locke, a Biography* (London: Longmans, 1957), p 387.

[44] *Darcy v. Allein* [also spelled "Allen"] ("The Case of Monopolies") 11 Co. Rep. 84 b, 77 Eng. Rep. 1260 (1603); Moore 671, 72 Eng. Rep. 830 (1603); Noy 173, 74 Eng. Rep. 1131 (1603). [The case also appears in the Liberty Fund edition, vol. 1, pp. 394–404.] [The phrase "against the common law because it was against the liberty of the subject" appears—in law French—in *Davenant v. Hurdis* and is quoted in English by Coke in *Darcy v. Allen* (77 Eng. Rep. 1263).—Ed.] The principle seems to have been stated first four years earlier in *Davenant v. Hurdis* [("The Merchant Tailors' Case") Moore 576, 72 Eng. Rep. 769 (King's Bench 1599)], when it was said that "prescription of such nature, to induce sole trade or traffic to a company or person, and to exclude all others is against the law." See William Lewis Letwin, "The English Common Law Concerning Monopolies," *University of Chicago Law Review*, 21 (1953–54): 355–85, and the two articles by Donald Owen Wagner, "Coke and the Rise of Economic Liberalism," *Economic History Review*, 6 (1935–36): 30–44, and "The Common Law and Free Enterprise: An Early Case of Monopoly," *Economic History Review*, 7 (1936–37): 217–20.

root has grown the indubitable right of the people of this kingdom, not to be made subject to any punishments that shall extend to their lives, lands, bodies, or goods, other than such as are ordained by the common laws of this land, or the statutes made by their common consent in parliament."[45]

It was, finally, in the discussion occasioned by the Statute of Monopolies of 1624 that Sir Edward Coke, the great fountain of Whig principles, developed his interpretation of Magna Carta that became one of the cornerstones of the new doctrine. In the second part of his *Institutes of the Laws of England*, soon to be printed by order of the House of Commons, he not only contended (with reference to the Case of Monopolies) that "if a grant be made to any man to have the sole making of cards, or the sole dealing with any other trade, that grant is against the liberty and freedom of the subject, that before did, or lawfully might have used that trade, and consequently against this Great Charter";[46] but he went beyond such opposition to the royal prerogative to warn Parliament itself "to leave all causes to be measured by the golden and straight metewand of the law, and not to the incertain and crooked cord of discretion."[47]

Out of the extensive and continuous discussion of these issues during the Civil War, there gradually emerged all the political ideals which were thenceforth to govern English political evolution. We cannot attempt here to trace their evolution in the debates and pamphlet literature of the period, whose extraordinary wealth of ideas has come to be seen only since their re-publication in recent times.[48] We can only list the main ideas that appeared more and

[45] Great Britain, Public Record Office, *Calendar of State Papers, Domestic Series, of the Reign of James I* [Preserved in the State Paper Department of Her Majesty's Public Record Office], Mary Anne Everett Green, ed. (5 vols.; London: Longman, Brown, Green, Longmans, and Roberts, 1857–72), vol. 5, July 7, 1610. [*The Calendar of State Papers* does not generally include the full text of the documents to which it refers, but rather to documents held in the British National Archives. The citation should presumably therefore be to the original document, details of which should be available from the National Archives. A transcript of the petition can be found in *Proceedings in Parliament, 1610*. Vol. 2: *House of Commons*, Elizabeth Read Foster, ed. (New Haven: Yale University Press, 1966), pp. 257–71. The passage quoted is located at p. 258.—Ed.]

[46] Sir Edward Coke, *The Second Part of the Institutes of the Laws of England. Containing the Exposition of Many Ancient and Modern Statutes* (London: Printed for E. and R. Brooke, 1797), p. 47 [Liberty Fund edition, vol. 1, p. 851]. [The quotation can also be found in *The Golden Passage in the Great Charter of England, Called Magna Carta; or, the Charter of English Liberties Granted by King John to His Subjects in the 17th Year of his Reign in Running-Mead* (London: Printed for the use of the London Association, 1776), p. 10.—Ed.]

[47] Sir Edward Coke, *The Second Part of the Institutes.* [Hayek is in error in ascribing this quotation to the Second Part of Coke's Institutes. It is, in fact, to be found in the *Fourth Part of the Institutes of the Laws of England, Concerning the Jurisdiction of Courts* (London: Printed for E. and R. Brooke, 1797), pp. 40–41; Liberty Fund edition, vol. 1, p. 1143.—Ed.]

[48] See Sir William Clarke, *The Clarke Papers: Selections from the Papers of William Clarke, Secretary to the Council of the Army, 1647–1649, and to General Monck and the Commanders of the Army in Scotland,*

more frequently until, by the time of the Restoration, they had become part of an established tradition and, after the Glorious Revolution of 1688, part of the doctrine of the victorious party.

The great event that became for later generations the symbol of the permanent achievements of the Civil War was the abolition in 1641 of the prerogative courts and especially the Star Chamber which had become, in F. W. Maitland's often quoted words, "a court of politicians enforcing a policy, not a court of judges administering the law."[49] At almost the same time an effort was made for the first time to secure the independence of the judges.[50] In the debates of the following twenty years the central issue became increasingly the prevention of arbitrary action of government. Though the two meanings of "arbitrary" were long confused, it came to be recognized, as Parliament began to act as arbitrarily as the king,[51] that whether or not an action was arbitrary depended not on the source of the authority but on whether it was in conformity with pre-existing general principles of law.[52] The points most frequently emphasized were that there must be no punishment without a previously existing law providing for it,[53] that all statutes should have only prospective and not retrospective operation,[54] and that the discretion of all mag-

---

1651–1660, Charles Harding Firth, ed. (4 vols.; London: Printed for the Camden Society, 1891–1901); George Peabody Gooch, *English Democratic Ideas in the Seventeenth Century* (Cambridge: Cambridge University Press, 1898); Theodore Calvin Pease, *The Leveller Movement: A Study in the History and Political Theory of the English Civil War* (Washington, DC: American Historical Association, 1916); William Haller, ed., *Tracts on Liberty in the Puritan Revolution, 1638–1647* (3 vols.; New York: Columbia University Press, 1934); Arthur Sutherland Pigott Woodhouse, ed., *Puritanism and Liberty: Being the Army Debates (1647–9) from the Clarke Manuscripts, with Supplementary Documents* (London: J. M. Dent and Sons, 1938); William Haller and Godfrey Davies, eds., *The Leveller Tracts: 1647–1653* (New York: Columbia University Press in cooperation with the Henry E. Huntington Library and Art Gallery, 1944); Don Marion Wolfe, *Leveller Manifestoes of the Puritan Revolution* (New York: T. Nelson and Sons, 1944); William Haller, *Liberty and Reformation in the Puritan Revolution* (New York: Columbia University Press, 1955); Perez Zagorin, *A History of Political Thought in the English Revolution* (London: Routledge and Paul, 1954).

[49] Frederic William Maitland, *The Constitutional History of England: A Course of Lectures* (Cambridge: Cambridge University Press, 1909), p. 263.

[50] Cf. Charles Howard McIlwain, "The Tenure of English Judges," in *Constitutionalism and the Changing World: Collected Papers* (Cambridge: Cambridge University Press, 1939), p. 300.

[51] See Gough, *Fundamental Law in English Constitutional History*, pp. 76ff. and 159.

[52] Samuel Rawson Gardiner, *History of the Great Civil War: 1642–1649* (new ed.; 4 vols.; London: Longmans, Green, and Co., 1898), vol. 3, pp. 392–94.

[53] This is one of the main topics of the recorded part of the Army Debates (see Arthur Sutherland Pigott Woodhouse, ed., *Puritanism and Liberty: Being the Army Debates (1647–49) from the Clarke Manuscripts, With Supplementary Documents* [London: J. M. Dent and Sons, 1938], pp. 336, 345, 354–55, and 472).

[54] This recurring phrase apparently derives from Sir Edward Coke, *The Second Part of the Institute*, p. 292: "Nova constitutio futuris formam imponere debet, non praeteritis." ["A new law ought to regulate what is to follow, not the past." The quotation carries the meaning that any

istrates should be strictly circumscribed by law.[55] Throughout, the governing idea was that the law should be king or, as one of the polemical tracts of the period expressed it, *Lex, Rex*.[56]

Gradually, two crucial conceptions emerged as to how these basic ideals should be safeguarded: the idea of a written constitution[57] and the principle of the separation of powers.[58] When in January, 1660, just before the Resto-

new law that is made ought to affect future transactions, not past ones. The quotation appears in chap. 4 of the *Second Part of the Institutes* marked "Merton," which is not included in the Liberty Fund edition.—Ed.]

[55] See Woodhouse, *Puritanism and Liberty*, pp. 154ff. and 353ff.

[56] Samuel Rutherford, *Lex, Rex: The Law and the Prince: A Dispute for the Just Prerogative of King and People* (London: Printed for John Field, 1644); excerpts are given in Woodhouse, *Puritanism and Liberty*, pp. 199, 212. The phrase of the title goes back to the ancient Greek *nomos basileus*. The issue of law versus arbitrariness was not used only by the Roundheads; it also appears frequently in the Royalist argument, and Charles I [in his *King Charls, his Speech Made upon the Scaffold at Whitehall-Gate, Immediately before his Execution, on Tuesday the 30 of Jan. 1648. With a Relation of the Maner of His Going to Execution* (London: Printed by P. Cole, 1649), p. 6] could assert that "Their Liberty and their Freedom consists in having of government those Laws, by which their Life and their Goods may be most their own: It is not for having share in Government."

[57] See Samuel Rawson Gardiner, *The Constitutional Documents of the Puritan Revolution, 1625–1660* (3rd ed. rev.; Oxford: Clarendon Press, 1906). Much the best brief account is now to be found in Francis Dunham Wormuth, *The Origins of Modern Constitutionalism* (New York: Harper, 1949); see also Walther Rothschild, *Der Gedanke der geschriebenen Verfassung in der englischen Revolution* (Tübingen: J. C. B. Mohr, 1903); Margaret Atwood Judson, *The Crisis of the Constitution: An Essay in Constitutional and Political Thought in England, 1603–1945* (New Brunswick, NJ: Rutgers University Press, 1949); and the work by Gough, *Fundamental Law in English Constitutional History*; also cf. Oliver Cromwell, *Oliver Cromwell's Letters and Speeches*, Thomas Carlyle, ed. (2nd ed. enlarged; 3 vols.; London: Chapman and Hall, 1846), vol. 3, p. 67 [Speech delivered before the First Protectorate Parliament, 12 September 1654]: "In every Government there must be somewhat [*sic*] fundamental, somewhat like a *Magna Carta*, which must be standing, be unalterable."

[58] The idea of the separation of powers seems first to have appeared in 1645 in a pamphlet by John Lilburne (see Pease, *The Leveller Movement*, p. 114) [The pamphlet to which Hayek refers is entitled *England's Birth-right Justified*.—Ed.], and soon after that it occurs frequently, for instance in John Milton's *Eikonoklastes* (1649), in *The Prose Works, With a Preface, Preliminary Remarks, and Notes*, James Augustus St. John, ed. (5 vols.; London: H. J. Bohn, 1884), vol. 1, p. 363: "In all wise nations the legislative power, and the judicial execution of that power, have been most commonly distinct, and in several hands; but yet the former supreme, the other subordinate"; and in John Sadler, *Rights of the Kingdom* (1649), quoted in Wormuth, *The Origins of Modern Constitutionalism*, p. 61: "It may be much disputed, that the legislative, judicial, and executive power should be in distinct subjects by the law of nature." [The original source is Anonymous (John Sadler), *Rights of the Kingdom; or, Customs of our Ancestors: Touching the Duty, Power, Election, or Succession of our Kings and Parliaments* (London: Printed by Richard Bishop, 1649), p. 92.—Ed.] The idea was very fully elaborated by George Lawson, *An Examination of the Political Part of Mr. Hobbs, His Leviathan* (London: Printed by R. White for Francis Tyton, 1657). (See A. H. Maclean, "George Lawson and John Locke," *Cambridge Historical Journal* 9 [1947]: 69–78). Additional references will be found in Wormuth, *Origins of Modern Constitutionalism*, pp. 59–72, and, for the later development, pp. 191–206. One particularly useful guide to the literature of the eighteenth-century English Whigs is the work of Caroline Robbins, *The Eighteenth Century Commonwealthmen* (Cambridge, MA: Harvard University Press, 1959).

ration, a last attempt was made in the "Declaration of Parliament Assembled at Westminster" to state in a formal document the essential principles of a constitution, this striking passage was included: "There being nothing more essential to the freedom of a state, than that the people should be governed by the laws, and that justice be administered by such only as are account-able for mal-administration, it is hereby further declared that all proceedings touching the lives, liberties and estates of all the free people of this common-wealth, shall be according to the laws of the land, and that the Parliament will not meddle with ordinary administration, or the executive part of the law: it being the principal part of this, as it hath been of all former Parliaments, to provide, for the freedom of the people against arbitrariness in government."[59] If thereafter the principle of the separation of powers was perhaps not quite "an accepted principle of constitutional law,"[60] it at least remained part of the governing political doctrine.

5. All these ideas were to exercise a decisive influence during the next hun-dred years, not only in England but also in America and on the Continent, in the summarized form they were given after the final expulsion of the Stuarts in 1688. Though at the time perhaps some other works were equally and per-haps even more influential,[61] John Locke's *Second Treatise on Civil Government* is so outstanding in its lasting effects that we must confine our attention to it.

---

[59] Wormuth, *Origins of Modern Constitutionalism*, p. 71.

[60] Ibid., p.72.

[61] The two main authors whom a fuller account would mainly have to consider are Algernon Sidney and Gilbert Burnet. The chief points relevant to us in Sidney's *Discourses concerning Gov-ernment* (first published in 1698) are that "liberty solely consists in an independency upon the will of another" which connects with the maxim "potentiora erant legum quam hominum impe-ria" (*Works*, p. 10 [Liberty Fund edition, p. 17]), that "laws that aim at the public good make no distinction of persons" (*Works*, p. 150 [Liberty Fund edition, p. 150]), that laws are made "because nations will be governed by rule, and not arbitrarily" (*Works*, p. 338 [Liberty Fund edition, p. 392]), and that laws "ought to aim at perpetuity" (*Works*, p. 492 [Liberty Fund edi-tion, p. 559]). Of Gilbert Burnet's numerous writings, see particularly his anonymously pub-lished *Enquiry into the Measures of Submission to the Supreme Authority and of the Grounds upon which it may be Lawful or Necessary for Subjects to Defend Their Religion, Lives, and Liberties* (London, 1688); quoted in the *Harleian Miscellany; or, A Collection of Scarce, Curious, and Entertaining Pamphlets and Tracts*, Wil-liam Oldys, ed. (12 vols.; London: Printed for R. Dutton, 1808–11), vol. 9, p. 204: "The plea for liberty always proves itself, unless it appears that it is given up, or limited by any special agree-ment. . . . In the management of this civil society, great distinction is to be made between the power of making laws for the regulating the conduct of it, and the power of executing those laws; the supreme authority must still be supposed to be lodged with those who have the legis-lative power reserved to them; but not with those who have only the executive, which is plainly a trust when it is separated from the legislative power." Also vol. 9, pp. 205–6: "The measures of power, and, by consequence, of obedience, must be taken from the express laws of any state, or body of men, from the oaths that they swear; or from immemorial prescription, and a long possession, which both give a title, and, in a long tract of time, make a bad one become good; since prescription, when it passes the memory of man, and is not disputed by any other pre-tender, gives, by the common sense of all men, a just and good title. So, upon the whole matter,

Locke's work has come to be known mainly as a comprehensive philosophical justification of the Glorious Revolution;[62] and it is mostly in his wider speculations about the philosophical foundations of government that his original contribution lies. Opinions may differ about their value. The aspect of his work which was at least as important at the time and which mainly concerns us here, however, is his codification of the victorious political doctrine, of the practical principles which, it was agreed, should thenceforth control the powers of government.[63]

While in his philosophical discussion Locke's concern is with the source which makes power legitimate and with the aim of government in general, the practical problem with which he is concerned is how power, whoever exercises it, can be prevented from becoming arbitrary: "Freedom of men under

---

the degrees of all civil authority, are to be taken either from express laws, immemorial customs, or from particular oaths, which the subjects swear to their princes; this being still to be laid down for a principle, that, in all the disputes between power and liberty, power must always be proved, but liberty proves itself; the one being founded upon positive law, and the other upon the law of nature." Vol. 9, p. 209: "The chief design of our whole law, and all the several rules of our constitution, is to secure and maintain our liberty." It was to this tract that a contemporary Continental discoverer of English liberty such as Guy Miège (*L'État présent de la Grande-Bretagne*, pp. 512–13), primarily referred to in his writings: Miège contended that "no subjects in the world enjoyed so many fundamental and inheritable liberties as the people of England" and that "their state was therefore most happy and preferable to that of all European subjects." [Hayek is here quoting from the German translation of 1718: *Geist- und weltlicher Staat von Groß-Britannien und Irrland nach der gegenwärtigen Zeit*, Johann Bernhard Heinzelmann, trans. (Leipzig: Verlag Moritz George Weidmanns, 1718), pp. 512–13. The German reads: "keine Unterthanen in der Welt, die so viel *fundamentale* und erbliche Freyheiten genießen, wie das Volck in England" and "sein Stand (sey) glückseelig und er allen Europäischen Unterthanen hierin . . . vorzuziehen."—Ed.]

[62] This may still be said even though it now appears that the *Treatise* was drafted before the revolution of 1688. (See Cranston, *John Locke: A Biography*, p. 326, and especially Peter Laslett's introductory essay in John Locke, *Two Treatises of Government: A Critical Edition*, Peter Laslett, ed. [Cambridge: Cambridge University Press, 1964], which we are here quoting.)

[63] Cf. John Wiedhofft Gough, *John Locke's Political Philosophy: Eight Studies* (Oxford: Clarendon Press, 1950). The extent to which Locke in dealing with the points here discussed merely summarized views long expressed by lawyers of the period still deserves study. Especially important in this connection is Sir Mathew Hale, who, in a manuscript reply to Hobbes which was written about 1673 and which Locke is likely to have known (see Aubrey's letter to Locke quoted in Cranston, *John Locke: A Biography*, p. 152), argued that "to avoid that great uncertainty in the application of reason by particular persons to particular instances; and so to the end that men might understand by what rule and measure to live and possess; and might not be under the unknown arbitrary uncertain reason of particular persons, has been the prime reason, that the wiser sort of the world have in all ages agreed upon some certain laws and rules and methods of administration of common justice, and these to be as particular and certain as could be well thought of"("Sir Mathew Hale's Criticisms on Hobbes's Dialogue of the Common Law," reprinted as an appendix to William Searle Holdsworth, *A History of English Law* [London: Methuen, 1924], vol. 5, p. 503). See also John Greville Agard Pocock, *The Ancient Constitution and the Feudal Law* (New York: Cambridge University Press, 1957).

government is to have a standing rule to live by, common to every one of that society, and made by the legislative power erected in it; a liberty to follow my own will in all things, where that rule prescribes not: and not to be subject to the inconstant, uncertain, arbitrary will of another man."[64] It is against the "irregular and uncertain exercise of the power"[65] that the argument is mainly directed: the important point is that "whoever has the legislative or supreme power of any commonwealth is bound to govern by established standing laws promulgated and known to the people, and not by extemporary decrees; by indifferent and upright judges, who are to decide controversies by those laws; and to employ the forces of the community at home only in the execution of such laws."[66] Even the legislature has no "absolute arbitrary power,"[67] "cannot assume to itself a power to rule by extemporary arbitrary decrees, but is bound to dispense justice, and decide the rights of the subject by promulgated standing laws, and known authorized judges,"[68] while the "supreme executor of the law . . . has no will, no power, but that of law."[69] Locke is loath to recognize any sovereign power, and the *Treatise* has been described as an assault upon the very idea of sovereignty.[70] The main practical safeguard against the abuse of authority proposed by him is the separation of powers, which he expounds somewhat less clearly and in a less familiar form than did some of his predecessors.[71] His main concern is how to limit the discretion of "him that has the executive power,"[72] but he has no special safeguards to offer. Yet his ultimate aim throughout is what today is often called the "taming of power": the end why men "choose and authorize a legislative is that there may be laws made, and rules set, as guards and fences to the properties of all the members of society, to limit the power and moderate the dominion of every part and member of the society."[73]

6. It is a long way from the acceptance of an ideal by public opinion to its full realization in policy; and perhaps the ideal of the rule of law had not yet

[64] John Locke, *Second Treatise*, sec. 22, p. 13.

[65] Ibid., sec. 127, p. 63.

[66] Ibid., sec. 131, p. 64.

[67] Ibid., sec. 137, p. 69.

[68] Ibid., sec. 136, p. 68.

[69] Ibid., sec. 151, p.75.

[70] See John Neville Figgis, *The Divine Rights of Kings* (2nd ed., with three additional essays; Cambridge: Cambridge University Press, 1914), p. 242; William Searle Holdsworth, *Some Lessons from Our Legal History* (New York: Macmillan, 1928), pp. 126–27; and Charles Edwyn Vaughan, *Studies in the History of Political Philosophy before and after Rousseau* (2 vols.; Manchester: Manchester University Press, 1939), vol. 1, p. 134.

[71] John Locke, *Second Treatise*, chap. 13, pp. 74–79. Compare n. 58, above, on the separation of powers.

[72] John Locke, *Second Treatise*, sec. 159, p. 80.

[73] John Locke, *Second Treatise*, sec. 222, p. 107.

been completely put into practice when the process was reversed two hundred years later. At any rate, the main period of consolidation, during which it progressively penetrated everyday practice, was the first half of the eighteenth century.[74] From the final confirmation of the independence of the judges in the Act of Settlement of 1701,[75] through the occasion when the last bill of attainder ever passed by Parliament in 1706 led not only to a final restatement of all the arguments against such arbitrary action of the legislature[76] but also to a reaffirmation of the principle of the separation of powers,[77] the period is one of slow but steady extension of most of the principles for which the Englishmen of the seventeenth century had fought.

A few significant events of the period may be briefly mentioned, such as the occasion when a member of the House of Commons (at a time when Dr. Johnson was reporting the debates) restated the basic doctrine of *nulla poena sine lege*, which even now is sometimes alleged not to be part of English law:[78]

[74] Cf. George Macaulay Trevelyan, *English Social History: A Survey of Six Centuries, Chaucer to Queen Victoria* (London: Longmans, Green, and Co., 1942), pp. 245 and 350ff., esp. 351: "The specific work of the earlier Hanoverian epoch was the establishment of the rule of law; and that law, with all its grave faults, was at least a law of freedom. On that solid foundation all our subsequent reforms were built."

[75] On the significance of this event see particularly Holdsworth, *History of English Law*, vol. 10, esp. p. 647: "As the result of all these consequences of the independence of the courts, the doctrine of the rule or supremacy of the law was established in its modern form, and became perhaps the most distinctive, and certainly the most salutary, of all the characteristics of English constitutional law."

[76] Its influence was revived in the nineteenth century by the dramatic account given of the episode in Thomas Babington Macaulay, Baron Macaulay, *History of England from the Accession of James II* (Everyman ed.; 4 vols.; London: J. M. Dent, 1953), chap. 22, vol. 4, pp. 272–92. [The events described concern the attainting and execution of Sir John Fenwick in 1696. The last bill of attainder was in fact enacted by Parliament in 1798 against Lord Edward Fitzgerald for his participation in the Irish Rebellion of that year. Bills of attainder were finally abolished in Great Britain in 1870.—Ed.]

[77] Cf. also Daniel Defoe, *The History of the Kentish Petition* (London, 1701), and his so-called *Legion's Memorial* (1701) ["A Memorial from the Gentlemen, Freeholders, and Inhabitants of the Counties of ———, in Behalf of Themselves and Many Thousands of the Good People of England"] in *The Works of Daniel Defoe* (3 vols.; London: John Clements, 1843), vol. 3, p. 5 [no continuous pagination; p. 5 of the pamphlet in question], where he writes that "Englishmen are no more to be slaves to Parliaments, than to Kings." See on this also McIlwain, *Constitutionalism: Ancient and Modern: A Constitutional Interpretation* (rev. ed.; Ithaca, NY: Cornell University Press, 1947), p. 150, n. 6 [Liberty Fund edition, p. 5, n. 6].

[78] Cf., for instance, Sir Alfred Denning, Baron Denning, *Freedom under the Law* (London: Steven, 1949), p. 41, where he says with respect to the Continental doctrine *Nullum crimen, nulla poena sine lege*: "In this country, however, the common law has not limited itself in that way. It is not contained in a code but in the breast of the judges, who enunciate and develop the principles needed to deal with any new situations which arise." See also Stefan Glaser, "Nullum crimen nulla poena sine lege," *Journal of Comparative Legislation and International Law*, 3rd ser., 24 (1942): 29–41. In the form quoted, the Latin maxim dates only from the end of the eighteenth century (see chap. 13, n. 22, below), but there was current in eighteenth-century England the

"That where there is no law there is no transgression, is a maxim not only established by universal consent, but in itself evident and undeniable; and it is, Sir, surely no less certain that where there is no transgression there can be no punishment."[79] Another is the occasion when Lord Camden in the Wilkes case made it clear that courts are concerned only with general rules and not with the particular aims of government or, as his position is sometimes interpreted, that public policy is not an argument in a court of law.[80] In other respects progress was more slow, and it is probably true that, from the point of view of the poorest, the ideal of equality before the law long remained a somewhat doubtful fact. But if the process of reforming the laws in the spirit of those ideals was slow, the principles themselves ceased to be a matter of dispute: they were no longer a party view but had come to be fully accepted by the Tories.[81] In some respects, however, evolution moved away rather than toward the ideal. The principle of the separation of powers in particular, though regarded throughout the century as the most distinctive feature of the British constitution,[82] became less and less a fact as modern cabinet government developed. And Parliament with its claim to unlimited power was soon to depart from yet another of the principles.

7. The second half of the eighteenth century produced the coherent expo-

similar expression: "Ubi non est lex ibi non est transgressio." ["Where there is no law, there is no transgression."—Ed.]

[79] Samuel Johnson, *The Works of Samuel Johnson, LL.D.* (14 vols.; London: Printed for J. Buckland [vols. 12–14 printed by J. Stockdale], 1787), vols. 12 and 13 published separately as *Debates in Parliament*, vol. 12, p. 22, reporting a speech of Mr. Campbell in the Corn Bill Debate of the House of Commons on November 26, 1740. [The debate on the corn bill reported by Johnson was held on November 25, 1740, not November 26.—Ed.]. Cf. Edward Lippincott McAdam, *Dr. Johnson and the English Law* (Syracuse, NY: Syracuse University Press, 1951), p. 17. Also see Donald Johnson Greene, *The Politics of Samuel Johnson* (New Haven: Yale University Press, 1960).

[80] Thus Lord Camden's opinion is sometimes quoted. The only statement of his expressing substantially the same view that I can find occurs in *Entick v. Carrington* (1765), in Thomas Bayly Howell, *A Complete Collection of State Trials and Proceedings for High Treason and Other Crimes and Misdemeanors from the Earliest Period [1163] to the Present Time [1820]* (34 vols.; London: T. C. Hansard for Longman, Hurst, Rees, Orme, and Brown, 1809–28), vol. 19: *A.D. 1753–1771* (1813), p. 1073: "With respect to the argument of state necessity, or a distinction that has been aimed at between states offences and others, the common law does not understand that kind of reasoning, nor do our books take notice of any such distinctions."

[81] What finally decided this incorporation into Tory doctrine was probably Henry Saint-John Bolingbroke, Letter 10 (1734) in *A Dissertation upon Parties in Several Letters to Caleb d'Anvers* (5th ed., carefully revised and corrected; London: Printed for R. Francklin, 1739), p. 111, with its acceptance of the contrast between a "government by constitution" and a "government by will."

[82] Cf. Holdsworth, *A History of English Law*, vol. 10, p. 713: "If a lawyer, a statesman, or a political philosopher of the eighteenth century had been asked what was, in his opinion, the most distinctive feature of the British constitution, he would have replied that its most distinctive feature was the separation of the powers of the different organs of government." Yet even at the time that Montesquieu popularized the conception on the Continent, it was true of the actual situation in England only to a limited degree.

sitions of the ideals which largely determined the climate of opinion for the next hundred years. As is so often the case, it was less the systematic expositions by political philosophers and lawyers than the interpretations of events by the historians that carried these ideas to the public. The most influential among them was David Hume, who in his works again and again stressed the crucial points[83] and of whom it has justly been said that for him the real meaning of the history of England was the evolution from a "government of will to a government of law."[84] At least one characteristic passage from his *History of England* deserves to be quoted. With reference to the abolition of the Star Chamber he writes: "No government, at that time, appeared in the world, nor is perhaps to be found in the records of any history, which subsisted without the mixture of some arbitrary authority, committed to some magistrate; and it might reasonably, beforehand, appear doubtful, whether human society could ever arrive at that state of perfection, as to support itself with no other control, than the general and rigid maxims of law and equity. But the parliament justly thought, that the King was too eminent a magistrate to be trusted with discretionary power, which he might so easily turn to the destruction of liberty. And in the event it has been found, that, though some inconve-

---

[83] In addition to the passage quoted later on in the text, see particularly David Hume, "Of the Origin of Government," vol. 1, p. 117 [Liberty Fund edition, p. 41]; "Of Civil Liberty," vol. 1, p.161 [Liberty Fund edition, p. 94]; "Of the Rise and Progress of the Arts and Sciences, vol. 1, p.178 [Liberty Fund edition, p. 116] in *Essays*, where he argues: "All general laws are attended with inconveniencies, when applied to particular cases; and it requires great penetration and experience, both to perceive that these inconveniencies are fewer than what results from full discretionary powers in every magistrate; and also to discern what general laws are, upon the whole, attended with fewest inconveniencies. This is a matter of so great difficulty, that men have made some advances, even in the sublime arts of poetry and eloquence, where a rapidity of genius and imagination assist their progress, before they arrived at any great refinement in their municipal laws, where frequent trial and diligent observation can alone direct their improvements." Cf. also *Enquiry Concerning the Principles of Morals, Essays II*, pp. 179–96, 256, and 272–78. [The sections of the *Enquiry* to which Hayek refers are: sec. 2, "Of Justice" (pp. 179–96), and app. 3: "Some farther Considerations with regard to Justice" (pp. 272–78).—Ed.] As Hume is often represented as a Tory, it deserves notice that he himself stated that "my views of things are more conformable to Whig principles; my representations of persons to Tory prejudices" (quoted in Ernest Campbell Mossner, *Life of David Hume* [Oxford: Clarendon Press, 1954], p. 311; see also *Life*, p. 179, where Hume is described as a "'Revolution Whig,' though not of the dogmatic variety"). Thomas Carlyle, "Boswell's Life of Johnson," *Critical and Miscellaneous Essays* (5 vols.; London: Chapman and Hall, Ltd., 1899), vol. 3, p. 133, even calls Hume "the father of all succeeding Whigs." See also David Hume, "Liberty of the Press," *Essays* [Essay 2], vol. 1, p. 96 [Liberty Fund edition, p. 12]: "As the republican part of the government prevails in England, though with a great mixture of monarchy, it is obliged, for its own preservation, to maintain a watchful *jealousy* over the magistrates, to remove all discretionary powers, and to secure every one's life and fortune by general and inflexible laws. No action must be deemed a crime but what the law has plainly determined to be such."

[84] Friedrich Meinecke, *Die Entstehung des Historismus* (2 vols.; Munich and Berlin: R. Oldenbourg, 1936), vol. 1, p. 234.

niencies arise from the maxim of adhering strictly to law, yet the advantages so much overbalance them, as should render the English forever grateful to the memory of their ancestors, who, after repeated contests, at last established that noble principle."[85]

Later in the century these ideals are more often taken for granted than explicitly stated, and the modern reader has to infer them when he wants to understand what men like Adam Smith[86] and his contemporaries meant

---

[85] David Hume, *History of England from the Invasion of Julius Caesar to the Revolution of 1688* (6 vols.; new ed. corr.; London: Printed for A. Miller, 1762), vol. 5, p. 280 [Liberty Fund edition, vol. 5, p. 329].

[86] For the manner in which Adam Smith accepts the separation of powers and its justification as a matter of course see *Wealth of Nations* [bk. 5, chap. 1, pt. 2], vol. 2, pp. 213–14 [Liberty Fund edition, vol. 2, pp. 708–23]. An earlier incidental reference to these problems (*Wealth of Nations*, vol. 2, p. 201) [Liberty Fund edition, vol. 2, p. 707], in which Smith briefly explains that in England "the public safety does not require, that the sovereign is trusted with any discretionary power," even for suppressing "the rudest, the most groundless, and the most licentious remonstrances," because he is "secured by a well-regulated army" has provided the occasion for an important discussion of this unique situation by one of the acutest foreign students of the British Constitution: Jean Louis de Lolme in his *Constitution of England; or, An Account of the English Government* [1794] (new ed., corr.; London: G. G. and J. Robinson, 1800), represents it as "the most characteristic circumstance in the English government, and the most pointed proof that can be given of the true freedom which is the consequence of its frame" (p. 441) [Liberty Fund edition, p. 295] ["le plus particulière la manière dont l'Angleterre est gouvernée, et est la preuve la plus convaincante de la liberté réelle qui resulte de tous son gouvernement." *Constitution d'Angleterre*, vol. 2, p.178.—Ed.], that in England "all the individual's actions are supposed to be lawful, till that law is pointed out which make them to be otherwise" (p. 436) [Liberty Fund edition, p. 292] ["Toutes les actions de l'individu passent pour légitimes jusqu'à ce qu'on nomme la loi que leur donne une autre dénomination." *Constitution d'Angleterre, ou état du gouvernement anglois* (2 vols.; London: G. Robinson, J. Murray, 1785), vol. 2, p. 174.—Ed.]. He then goes on to say: "The foundation of that law principle, or doctrine, which confines the exertion of the power of the government to such cases only as are expressed by a law in being" (p. 439) [Liberty Fund edition, p. 294] ["Le fondement de cette maxime du droit, qui borne l'exercice du pouvoir suprême aux cas seuls exprimés par une loi écrite." *Constitution d'Angleterre*, vol. 2, p. 176.—Ed.] and which, though tracing back to Magna Carta, was put into actual force only by the abolition of the Star Chamber, with the result that "it has appeared by the event, that the very extraordinary restriction upon the governing authority we are alluding to, and its execution, are no more than what the intrinsic situation of things, and the strength of the constitution, can bear" (p. 440) [Liberty Fund edition, pp. 294–95] ["Il parut par l'événement que cette restriction même qui paroit singulière quant à l'autorité suprême et ses fonctions, n'est que ce que les choses en elles-mêmes et la force de la constitution, peuvent supporter." *Constitution d'Angleterre*, vol. 2, p. 178.—Ed.]. (Note how this passage is evidently influenced by the exposition of Hume quoted in the text.)

Many similar statements from the period could be quoted, but two particularly characteristic ones must suffice. The first is from John Wilkes's *The North Briton* 64 ([Saturday], September 3, 1768) [p. 1]; quoted by Sir Carleton Kemp Allen, *Law and Orders: An Inquiry into the Nature and Scope of Delegated Legislation and Executive Powers in England* (London: Stevens, 1945), pp. 5–6: "In a *free government*, these three powers ever have been, at least ever ought to be, kept separate: because, were all the three, or any two of them, to be united in the same person, the liberties of the

by "liberty." Only occasionally, as in Blackstone's *Commentaries*, do we find endeavors to elaborate particular points, such as the significance of the independence of the judges and of the separation of powers,[87] or to clarify the meaning of "law" by its definition as "a rule; not a transient sudden order from a superior or concerning a particular person; but something permanent, uniform and universal."[88]

Many of the best-known expressions of those ideals are, of course, to be found in the familiar passages of Edmund Burke.[89] But probably the fullest statement of the doctrine of the rule of law occurs in the work of William Paley, the "great codifier of thought in an age of codification."[90] It deserves quoting at some length: "The first maxim of a free state," he writes, "is, that the laws be made by one set of men, and administered by another; in other words; that the legislative and the judicial characters be kept separate. When

---

people would be, from that moment, ruined. For instance, were the *legislative* and *executive powers* united in the same magistrate, or in the same body of magistrates, there could be no such thing as liberty, inasmuch as there would be great reason to fear lest the same monarch, or senate, should enact tyrannical laws in order to execute them in a tyrannical manner. Nor could there, it is evident, be such a thing as liberty, were the *judiciary power* united either to the *legislative* or to the *executive*. In the former case, the life and liberty of the subject would be necessarily exposed to the most imminent danger, because then the same person would be both judge and legislator. In the latter, the condition of the subject would be no less deplorable, for the very same person might pass a cruel sentence in order, perhaps, to execute it with still greater cruelty."

The second passage occurs in Junius [William Petty-Fitzmaurice, Earl of Shelburne], *The Letters of Junius*, Charles Warren Everett, ed. (London: Faber and Gwyer, 1927), Letter 47, dated May 25, 1771, p. 208: "The government of England is a government of law. We betray ourselves, we contradict the spirit of our laws, and we shake the whole system of English jurisprudence, whenever we intrust a discretionary power over the life, liberty, or fortune of the subject, to any man or set of men whatsoever upon a presumption that it will not be abused."

[87] Sir William Blackstone, *Commentaries on the Laws of England* (4 vols.; Oxford: Clarendon Press, 1765), vol. 1, p. 259: "In this distinct and separate existence of the judicial power in a peculiar body of men, nominated indeed, but not removable at pleasure, by the Crown, consists one main preservative of public liberty; which cannot subsist long in any state, unless the administration of common justice be in some degree separated both from the legislative and also from the executive power. Were it joined with the legislative, the life, liberty, and property of the subject would be in the hands of arbitrary judges, whose decisions would be then regulated only by their own opinions, and not by any fundamental principles of law; which, though legislatures may depart from them, yet judges are bound to observe."

[88] Sir William Blackstone, *Commentaries on the Laws of England*, p. 44.

[89] See particularly Edmund Burke, *Speech on the Motion Made in the House of Commons, the 7th of February, 1771, Relative to the Middlesex Elections*, in *Works*, vol. 10, pp. 63–71.

[90] Sir Ernest Barker, *Traditions of Civility: Eight Essays* (Cambridge: Cambridge University Press, 1948), p. 216. Note also the interesting account at pp. 245 and 248 of the same work. regarding Albert Venn Dicey's admiration for Paley. [William Paley (1743–1805); His *Principles of Moral and Political Philosophy* (1785), was based on his Cambridge lectures of 1766–76. The work reflects the beginnings of the transformation of Whiggism into what later became liberal doctrine.—Ed.]

these offices are united in the same person or assembly, particular laws are made for particular cases, springing oftentimes from partial motives, and directed to private ends: whilst they are kept separate, general laws are made by one body of men, without foreseeing whom they may affect; and, when made, must be applied by the other, let them affect whom they will. . . . When the parties and the interests to be affected by the law were known, the inclinations of the law makers would inevitably attach on one side or the other; and where there were neither any fixed rules to regulate their determinations, nor any superior power to control their proceedings, these inclinations would interfere with the integrity of public justice. The consequence of which must be, that the subjects of such a constitution would live either without any constant laws, that is, without any known pre-established rules of adjudication whatever; or under laws made for particular cases and particular persons, and partaking of the contradictions and iniquity of the motives to which they owed their origin.

"Which dangers, by the division of the legislative and judicial functions, are in this country effectually provided against. Parliament knows not the individuals upon whom its acts will operate; it has no cases or parties before it; no private designs to serve: consequently, its resolutions will be suggested by the considerations of universal effects and tendencies, which always produces impartial, and commonly advantageous regulations."[91]

8. With the end of the eighteenth century, England's major contributions to the development of the principles of freedom come to a close. Though Macaulay did once more for the nineteenth century what Hume had done for the eighteenth,[92] and though the Whig intelligentsia of the *Edinburgh Review* and economists in the Smithian tradition, like J. R. MacCulloch and N. W. Senior, continued to think of liberty in classical terms, there was little further development. The new liberalism that gradually displaced Whiggism came more and more under the influence of the rationalist tendencies of the philosophical radicals and the French tradition. Bentham and his Utilitarians did

---

[91] William Paley, *The Principles of Moral and Political Philosophy* (1785) (London: Printed for T. Tegg, 1824), p. 308.

[92] Macaulay's success in making the achievement of the constitutional struggles of the past once more a living possession of every educated Englishman is now rarely remembered. But see "The Literary Historian," in the *Times Literary Supplement*, January 16, 1953, p. 40, col. 5: "He did for our history what Livy did for the history of Rome; and he did it better." Cf. also Lord Acton's remark, *Historical Essays*, p. 482, that Macaulay "had done more than any writer in the literature of the world for the propagation of the Liberal faith, and he was not only the greatest, but the most representative Englishman then [1856] living." [Liberty Fund edition, *Essays in the History of Liberty*, p. 170. Acton's comments originally appear in his review of *A History of England, 1837–1880* by the Rev. J. Franck Bright, originally published in the *English Historical Review*, vol. 3 (1888).—Ed.]

much to destroy the beliefs[93] which England had in part preserved from the Middle Ages, by their scornful treatment of most of what until then had been the most admired features of the British constitution. And they introduced into Britain what had so far been entirely absent—the desire to remake the whole of her law and institutions on rational principles.

The lack of understanding of the traditional principles of English liberty on the part of the men guided by the ideals of the French Revolution is clearly illustrated by one of the early apostles of that revolution in England, Dr. Richard Price. As early as 1778 he argued: "Liberty. Therefore, is too imperfectly defined when it is said to be 'a Government Of LAWS and not by MEN.' If the laws are made by one man, or a junto of men in a state, and not by common CONSENT, a government by them is not different from Slavery."[94] Eight years later he was able to display a commendatory letter from Turgot: "How comes it that you are almost the first of the writers of your country, who has given a just idea of liberty, and shown the falsity of the notion so frequently repeated by almost all Republican Writers, 'that liberty consists in being subject only to the laws?'"[95] From then onward, the essentially French concept of political liberty was indeed progressively to displace the English ideal of individual liberty, until it could be said that "in Great Britain, which, little more than a century ago, repudiated the ideas on which the French Revolution was based, and led the resistance to Napoleon, those ideas have triumphed."[96] Though in Britain most of the achievements of the seventeenth century were preserved beyond the nineteenth, we must look elsewhere for the further development of the ideals underlying them.

[93] In some respects even the Benthamites could not but build on and improve the old tradition which they did so much to destroy. This applies certainly to John Austin's efforts to provide sharp distinctions between true general "laws" and "occasional or particular commands" (see Austin's *Lectures on Jurisprudence; or, The Philosophy of Positive Law* [Lecture One], Robert Campbell, ed. [5th ed. rev.; 2 vols.; London: J. Murray, 1885]; vol. 1, p. 92).

[94] Richard Price, *Two Tracts on Civil Liberty: The War with America and the Debts and Finances of the Kingdom* (2 vols. in 1; London: T. Cadell, 1778), p. 7. [In fact, Price first wrote these words in his *Observations on the Nature of Civil Liberty, the Principles of Government, and the Justice and Policy of the War with America* (London: T. Cadell, 1776), which appeared two years earlier than the eighth edition of these *Observations*, which appeared in the *Two Tracts*.—Ed.]

[95] Richard Price, *Observations on the Importance of the American Revolution and the Means of Making It a Benefit to the World, to Which is Added a Letter from M. Turgot* [dated March 22, 1778] (London: T. Caddell, 1785), p.111. [The French reads: "Comment se fait-il que vous soyez presque le premier parmi vos écrivains qui ayez donné des notions justes de la liberté, et qui ayez fait sentir la fausseté de cette notion rebattue par presque tous les écrivains les plus républicains, que la liberté consiste à n'être soumis qu'aux loix, comme si un homme opprimé par une loi injuste étoit libre."—Ed.]

[96] William Searle Holdsworth, *A History of English Law*, vol. 10, p. 23.

TWELVE

THE AMERICAN CONTRIBUTION: CONSTITUTIONALISM

Europe seemed incapable of becoming the home of free States. It was from America that the plain ideas that men ought to mind their own business, and that the nation is responsible to Heaven for the acts of State—ideas long locked in the breast of solitary thinkers, and hidden among Latin folios— burst forth like a conqueror upon the world they were destined to transform, under the title of the Rights of Man. —Lord Acton

1. "When in 1767 this modernised British Parliament, committed by now to the principle of parliamentary sovereignty unlimited and unlimitable, issued a declaration that a parliamentary majority could pass any law it saw fit, it was greeted with an out-cry of horror in the colonies. James Otis and Sam Adams in Massachusetts, Patrick Henry in Virginia, and other colonial leaders along the seaboard screamed 'Treason!' and 'Magna Carta!' Such a doctrine, they insisted, demolished the essence of all their British ancestors had fought for, took the very savor out of that fine Anglo-Saxon liberty for which the sages and patriots of England had died."[1] Thus one of the modern American enthusiasts for the unlimited power of the majority describes the beginning of the movement that led to a new attempt to secure the liberty of the individual.

The movement in the beginning was based entirely on the traditional conceptions of the liberties of Englishmen. Edmund Burke and other English sympathizers were not the only ones who spoke of the colonists as "not only devoted to liberty, but to liberty according to English ideas, and on English principles";[2] the colonists themselves had long held this

The quotation at the head of the chapter is taken from Lord Acton, "Freedom in Christianity," *History of Freedom*, p. 55 [Liberty Fund edition, *Essays on the History of Liberty*, p. 49].

[1] Edwin Mims, Jr., *The Majority of the People* (New York: Modern Age Books, 1941), p. 71.

[2] Edmund Burke, "Speech on Conciliation with America" (1775), in *Works*, vol. 3, p. 49 [Liberty Fund edition, *Selected Works*, vol. 1, p. 237]. The predominant influence of English ideals on the American Revolution seems even more striking to the Continental European student than to contemporary American historians; cf. particularly Otto Vossler, *Die amerikanischen Revolutionsideale in ihrem Verhältnis zu den europäischen: untersucht an Thomas Jefferson* [Beiheft 17 to the *Historische Zeitschrift*] (Munich: Oldenbourg, 1929); but see also Charles Howard McIlwain, *The*

view.[3] They felt that they were upholding the principles of the Whig revolution of 1688;[4] and as "Whig statesmen toast[ed] General Washington, rejoiced that America had resisted, and insist[ed] on the acknowledgment of independence,"[5] so the colonists toasted William Pitt and the Whig statesmen who supported them.[6]

In England, after the complete victory of Parliament, the conception that no power should be arbitrary and that all power should be limited by higher law tended to be forgotten. But the colonists had brought these ideas with them and now turned them against Parliament. They objected not only that they were not represented in that Parliament but even more that it recognized no limits whatever to its powers. With this application of the principle of legal limitation of power by higher principles to Parliament itself, the ini-

---

American Revolution: A Constitutional Interpretation (New York: Macmillan, 1923), esp. pp. 148–59 and 181–93.

[3] Cf., e.g., the reply given by the Massachusetts House of Representatives to Governor Sir Francis Bernard on June 19,1769 (quoted by Andrew Cunningham McLaughlin, *A Constitutional History of the United States* [New York: D. Appleton-Century Co., 1935], p. 67, from *Speeches of the Governors of Massachusetts, 1765–1775; and the Answers of the House of Representatives to the same; with Their Resolutions and Addresses for that Period, and Other Public Papers Relating to the Dispute between This Country and Great Britain which Led to the Independence of the United States*, Alden Bradford, ed. [Boston: Printed for Russell and Gardner, 1818], p.173): "no time can better be employed, than in the preservation of the rights derived from the British constitution, and insisting upon points, which, though your Excellency may consider them as nonessential, we esteem its best bulwarks. No treasure can be better expended, than in securing that true old English liberty, which gives a relish to every other enjoyment."

[4] Cf. Anonymous [Arthur Lee], *The Political Detection; or, the Treachery and Tyranny of Administration Both at Home and Abroad; Displayed in a Series of Letters Signed Junius Americanus* (London: Printed by J. and W. Oliver, 1770), pp. 73–74. "In principle, this dispute is essentially the same with that which subsisted in the last Century between the people of this Country and Charles the First. . . . The King and the House of Commons may differ in name, but unlimited power makes them in effect the same, except that it is infinitely more to be dreaded in *many* than in *one*"; and Edmund Burke, *An Appeal from the New to the Old Whigs* (1791), in *Works*, vol. 6, p. 123 [Liberty Fund edition, *Further Reflections*, p. 107], where he speaks of the Americans standing at the time of the Revolution "in the same relation to England, as England did to King James the Second, in 1688." On the whole issue see George Herbert Guttridge, *English Whiggism and the American Revolution* (Berkeley: University of California Press, 1942).

[5] Lord Acton, "The Rise of the Whigs," *Lectures on Modern History*, John Neville Figgis and Reginald Vere Laurence, eds. (London: Macmillan, 1906), p. 217 [Liberty Fund edition, *Essays in the History of Liberty*, p. 107]. [The actual quotation reads: "The charter of Rhode Island is worth more than the British Constitution, and Whig statesmen toast General Washington, rejoice that America has resisted, and insist on the acknowledgement of independence."—Ed.]

[6] See Clinton Rossiter, *Seedtime of the Republic: The Origin of the American Principle of Political Liberty* (New York: Harcourt, Brace, 1953), p. 360, where he quotes from the *Newport Mercury* of May 19, 1766, a toast of "A Son of Liberty in Bristol County, Mass.": "Our toast in general is,—*Magna Charta*, the *British Constitution*,—PITT and Liberty forever!" [The quotation does not appear in Rossiter's book. However, the original quotation does indeed appear, on p. 3, of the *Newport Mercury* of May 12 to May 19, 1766.—Ed.]

tiative in the further development of the ideal of free government passed to the Americans.

They were singularly fortunate, as perhaps no other people has been in a similar situation, in having among their leaders a number of profound students of political philosophy. It is a remarkable fact that when in many other respects the new country was still so very backward, it could be said that "it is in political science only that America occupies the first rank. There are six Americans on a level with the foremost Europeans, with Smith and Turgot, Mill and Humboldt."[7] They were, moreover, men as much steeped in the classical tradition as any of the English thinkers of the preceding century had been and were fully acquainted with the ideas of the latter.[8]

2. Until the final break, the claims and arguments advanced by the colonists in the conflict with the mother country were based entirely on the rights and privileges to which they regarded themselves entitled as British subjects. It was only when they discovered that the British constitution, in whose principles they had firmly believed, had little substance and could not be successfully appealed to against the claims of Parliament, that they concluded that the missing foundation had to be supplied.[9] They regarded it as fundamental doctrine that a "fixed constitution"[10] was essential to any free government

[7] Acton, "James Bryce's *The American Commonwealth*," *History of Freedom*, p. 578 [Liberty Fund edition, *Essays in the History of Liberty*, p. 398].

[8] See Charles Frederic Mullett, *Fundamental Law and the American Revolution, 1760–1776* (dissertation; New York: Columbia University, 1933), pp. 13–78, quoting Randolph Greenfield Adams, *Political Ideas of the American Revolution: Britannic-American Contributions to the Problem of Imperial Organization, 1765–1775* (3rd ed.; New York: Barnes and Noble, 1958) [esp. pp. 193–99.—Ed.], who notes that Jefferson referred to the works from Aristotle to Locke as "elementary books" for Americans of the eighteenth century.

[9] An excellent brief summary of the influence of these ideas is given in Robert Arthur Humphreys, "The Rule of Law and the American Revolution," *Law Quarterly Review*, 53 (1937): 80–98. See also John Walter Jones, "Acquired and Guaranteed Rights," in *Cambridge Legal Essays Written in Honour of and Presented to Doctor* [Henry] *Bond, Professor* [William Warwick] *Buckland, and Professor* [Courtney Stanhope] *Kenny*, Sir Percy Henry Winfield and Arnold Duncan McNair, Baron McNair, eds. (Cambridge: W. Heffer and Sons Ltd., 1926), pp. 223–42; Charles Frederic Mullett, *Fundamental Law and the American Revolution, 1760–1776* (New York: Columbia University Press, 1933) [Also issued in the form of a Ph.D. thesis, which, apparently, was Hayek's source]; and Alice Mary Baldwin, *The New England Clergy and the American Revolution* (Durham, NC: Duke University Press, 1928); and cf. Lord Acton's remark, "Freedom in Christianity," *History of Freedom*, p. 56 [Liberty Fund edition, pp. 49–50], that the Americans "did more; for having subjected all civil authorities to the popular will, they surrounded the popular will with restrictions that the British legislature would not endure."

[10] The expression "fixed constitution," constantly used by James Otis and Samuel Adams, apparently derives from Emer de Vattel, *Law of Nations; or, the Principles of Natural Law* (new ed., rev., corr., and enriched with many valuable notes; London: Printed for G. G. and J. Robinson London, 1797) [bk. 1, chap. 3, sec. 34], p. 11 [Liberty Fund edition, p. 95]. [The term "fixed constitution" appears neither in French nor in the early English translations of Vattel's

and that a constitution meant limited government.[11] From their own history
they had become familiar with written documents which defined and circumscribed the powers of government such as the Mayflower compact and the
colonial charters.[12]

---

work. However, in bk. 1, chap. 3, sec. 34, vol. 1, p. 37, of the 1758 French edition (*Le Droit des
Gens, ou Principes de la Loi Naturelle* [2 vols.; London (probably Paris), 1758]), Vattel remarks that
"la Constitution de l'état doit être stable." ("For the constitution of the state ought to possess
stability.")—Ed.] The best-known statement of the conceptions discussed in the text occurs in
the "Massachusetts Circular Letter of February 11, 1768 [the author of which was Samuel
Adams—Ed.] (quoted in William MacDonald, *Documentary Source Book of American History, 1606–
1926* [3rd ed., rev. and enl.; New York: Macmillan, 1929], pp. 146–50), the most significant
paragraph of which is as follows: "The House have humbly represented to the ministry, their
own sentiments, that His Majesty's high court of Parliament is the supreme legislative power
over the whole empire: that in all free states the constitution is fixed, and as the supreme legislative derives its power and authority from the constitution, it cannot overleap the bounds of
it, without destroying its own foundation; that the constitution ascertains and limits both sovereignty and allegiance, and, therefore, his Majesty's American subjects, who acknowledge themselves bound by the ties of allegiance, have an equitable claim to the full enjoyment of the [fun-
damental rules of the British constitution; that it is an essential, unalterable] right, in nature,
engrafted into the British constitution, as a fundamental law, and ever held sacred and irrevocable by the subjects within the realm, that what a man has honestly acquired is absolutely his
own, which he may freely give, but cannot be taken from him without his consent; that the
American subjects may, therefore, exclusive of any consideration of charter rights, with a decent
firmness, adapted to the character of free men and subjects, assert this natural and constitutional right."
    [11] The phrase most commonly used was "limited constitution," into which form the idea of a
constitution limiting the powers of government had been contracted. See especially Alexander
Hamilton, James Madison, and John Jay, *The Federalist, or the New Constitution*, Alexander Hamilton, "The Judiciary Department" (No. 78), Max Beloff, Baron Beloff, ed. (Oxford: B. Blackwell,
1948), p. 397 [Liberty Fund edition, p. 403], where Hamilton gives the following definition: "By
a limited constitution, I understand one which contains certain specified exceptions to the legislative authority; such, for instance, as that it shall pass no bills of attainder, no *ex post facto* laws,
and the like. . . . Limitations of this kind can be preserved in practice no other way than through
the medium of the courts of justice; whose duty it must be to declare all acts contrary to the
manifest tenor of the constitution void. Without this, all the reservations of particular rights or
privileges would amount to nothing." The term "limited constitution" as applied to Greece and Rome
already appears in David Hume, *History of England: From the Invasion of Julius Caesar to the Revolution
of 1688* (new ed.; 6 vols.; London: A. Millar, 1762), vol. 5, p. 14 [Liberty Fund edition, pp. 18–19].
    [12] Cf. Jones, "Acquired and Guaranteed Rights," pp. 229ff.: "By the time of the dispute with
the Mother Country the colonists were therefore well acquainted with two ideas more or less
strange to the general trend of English legal thought—the doctrine of the rights of man, and
the possibility or even necessity (for they were now struggling against a Parliament) of limiting
legislative power by a written constitution."
    For the whole of the following discussion I am indebted mainly to two American authors,
Charles Howard McIlwain and Edwin Samuel Corwin, whose chief works may be listed here
instead of many detailed references:
    Charles Howard McIlwain, *The High Court of Parliament and Its Supremacy: An Historical Essay
on the Boundaries Between Legislation and Adjudication in England* (New Haven: Yale University Press,

Their experience had also taught them that any constitution that allocated and distributed the different powers thereby necessarily limited the powers of any authority. A constitution might conceivably confine itself to procedural matters and merely determine the source of all authority. But they would hardly have called "constitution" a document which merely said that whatever such and such a body or person says shall be law. They perceived that, once such a document assigned specific powers to different authorities, it would also limit their powers not only in regard to the subjects or the aims to be pursued but also with regard to the methods to be employed. To the colonists, freedom meant that government should have powers only for such action as was explicitly required by law, so that nobody should possess any arbitrary power.[13]

The conception of a constitution thus became closely connected with the conception of representative government, in which the powers of the representative body were strictly circumscribed by the document that conferred upon it particular powers. The formula that all power derives from the people referred not so much to the recurrent election of representatives as to the fact that the people, organized as a constitution-making body, had the exclusive

---

1910); *The American Revolution: A Constitutional Interpretation* (New York: Macmillan, 1923); "The English Common Law, Barrier against Absolutism," *American Historical Review* 49 (1943): 23–31; *Constitutionalism and the Changing World: Collected Papers* (Cambridge: Cambridge University Press, 1939) [chap. 10, "The Transfer of the Charter to New England and Its Significance in American Constitutional History," (pp. 231–43), and chap. 11, "The Fundamental Law behind the Constitution of the United States," (pp. 244–58)]; *Constitutionalism, Ancient and Modern: A Constitutional Interpretation* (rev. ed.; Ithaca, NY: Cornell University Press, 1947), esp. pp. 1–22 [Liberty Fund edition, pp. 22–38].

Edwin Samuel Corwin, *The Doctrine of Judicial Review: Its Legal and Historical Basis, and Other Essays* (Princeton, NJ: Princeton University Press, 1914); *The Constitution and What It Means Today* (1920) (11th ed.; Princeton, NJ: Princeton University Press, 1954); "The Progress of Constitutional Theory between the Declaration of Independence and the Meeting of the Philadelphia Convention," *American Historical Review*, 30 (1925): 511–36; "Judicial Review in Action," *University of Pennsylvania Law Review*, 74 (1926): 639–71; *The "Higher Law" Background of American Constitutional Law* (Ithaca, NY: Great Seal Books, Cornell University Press, 1955), first published in the *Harvard Law Review*, 42 (1929): 149–85 and 365–409, and reprinted in *Selected Essays on Constitutional Law*, Committee of the Association of American Law Schools and Douglas Blound Maggs, et al. eds. (5 vols. in 4; Chicago: Foundation Press, 1938), vol. 1, pp. 1–67 [A Liberty Fund edition is available.]; *Liberty Against Government: The Rise, Flowering, and Decline of a Famous Juridical Concept* (Baton Rouge: Louisiana State University Press, 1948); and his edition of *The Constitution of the United States: Analysis and Interpretation; Annotation of Cases Decided by the Supreme Court of the United States to June 30, 1952* (Washington, DC: Government Printing Office, 1953). Several of the articles mentioned and some still to be quoted are conveniently collected in vol. 1 of the *Selected Essays on Constitutional Law*. See also Charles Lund Black, *The People and the Court: Judicial Review in a Democracy* (New York: Macmillan, 1960).

[13] Cf. Humphreys, "The Rule of Law and the American Revolution, p. 90: "The very definition of liberty was freedom from arbitrary rule."

right to determine the powers of the representative legislature.[14] The constitution was thus conceived as a protection of the people against all arbitrary action, on the part of the legislative as well as the other branches of government.

A constitution which in such manner is to limit government must contain what in effect are substantive rules, besides provisions regulating the derivation of authority. It must lay down general principles which are to govern the acts of the appointed legislature. The idea of a constitution, therefore, involves not only the idea of hierarchy of authority or power but also that of a hierarchy of rules or laws, where those possessing a higher degree of generality and proceeding from a superior authority control the contents of the more specific laws that are passed by a delegated authority.

3. The conception of a higher law governing current legislation is a very old one. In the eighteenth century it was usually conceived as the law of God, or that of Nature, or that of Reason. But the idea of making this higher law explicit and enforceable by putting it on paper, though not entirely new, was for the first time put into practice by the Revolutionary colonists. The individual colonies, in fact, made the first experiments in codifying this higher law with a wider popular basis than ordinary legislation. But the model that was profoundly to influence the rest of the world was the federal Constitution.

The fundamental distinction between a constitution and ordinary laws is similar to that between laws in general and their application by the courts to a particular case: as in deciding concrete cases the judge is bound by general rules, so the legislature in making particular laws is bound by the more general principles of the constitution. The justification for these distinctions is also similar in both cases: as a judicial decision is regarded as just only if it is in conformity with a general law, so particular laws are regarded as just only if they conform to more general principles. And as we want to prevent the judge from infringing the law for some particular reason, so we also want to prevent the legislature from infringing certain general principles for the sake of temporary and immediate aims.

We have already discussed the reason for this need in another connection.[15] It is that all men in the pursuit of immediate aims are apt—or, because of the limitation of their intellect, in fact bound—to violate rules of conduct which they would nevertheless wish to see generally observed. Because of the restricted capacity of our minds, our immediate purposes will always loom large, and we will tend to sacrifice long-term advantages to them. In individ-

---

[14] On the derived character of the power of all representative assemblies in the process of constitution-making see particularly McLaughlin, *Constitutional History*, p. 109.

[15] See chap. 4, sec. 8, and chap. 7, sec. 6, above; and cf., on the whole subject, David Hume, *Treatise of Human Nature* [bk. 3, pt. 2, sec. 7], vol. 2, pp. 300–304.

ual as in social conduct we can therefore approach a measure of rationality or consistency in making particular decisions only by submitting to general principles, irrespective of momentary needs. Legislation can no more dispense with guidance by principles than any other human activity if it is to take account of effects in the aggregate.

A legislature, like an individual, will be more reluctant to take certain measures for an important immediate aim if this requires the explicit repudiation of principles formally announced. To break a particular obligation or a promise is a different matter from explicitly stating that contracts or promises may be broken whenever such and such general conditions occur. Making a law retroactive or by law conferring privileges or imposing punishments on individuals is a different matter from rescinding the principle that this should never be done. And a legislature's infringing rights of property or the freedom of speech in order to achieve some great objective is quite a different thing from its having to state the general conditions under which such rights can be infringed.[16]

The stating of those conditions under which such actions by the legislature are legitimate would probably have beneficial effects, even if only the legislature itself were required to state them, much as the judge is required to state the principles on which he proceeds. But it will clearly be more effective if only another body has the power to modify these basic principles, especially if the procedure of this body is lengthy and thus allows time for the importance of the particular objective that has given rise to the demand for modification to be seen in the proper proportion. It is worth noting here that, in general, constitutional conventions or similar bodies set up to lay down the most general principles of government are regarded as competent to do only this, and not to pass any particular laws.[17]

[16] This provision is explicitly recognized in art. 19, par. 1, of the Basic Law (*Grundgesetz*) of the Federal Republic of Germany, noteworthy in that it requires that laws that infringe a basic right not only must be "general and not solely applicable to an individual case" but that it name the basic law which is being infringed, citing the specific article. [The provision reads: "Insofar as under this Basic Law a basic right may be restricted by or pursuant to a law, the law must apply generally and not solely to an individual case. Furthermore the law must name the basic right, indicating the Article."—Ed.]

[17] Cf. Zaccaria Giacometti, *Allgemeine Lehren des rechtsstaatlichen Verwaltungsrechts: Allgemeines Verwaltungsrecht des Rechtsstaates* (Zürich: Polygraphischer Verlag, 1960), vol. 1, p. 24, n. 4. See John Lilburne's *Legal Fundamental Liberties* (partially reprinted in *Puritanism and Liberty*, Arthur Sutherland Pigott Woodhouse, ed. [Chicago: University of Chicago Press, 1951], p. 344), where, in providing for what we would call a constitutional convention, he explicitly stipulated that "those persons ought not to exercise any legislative power, but only to draw up the foundations of a just government, and to propound them to the well-affected people in every County, to be agreed to: Which agreement ought to be above law; and therefore the bounds, limits, and extent of the people's legislative deputies in parliament, contained in the Agreement, [ought] to be drawn up into a formal contract to be mutually signed." [Woodhouse's source is Lilburne's *Legal Fundamental Liberties of the People of England, Revived, Asserted, and Vindicated; or an Epistle, Written the 8th of*

The expression an "appeal from the people drunk to the people sober," which is often used in this connection, stresses only one aspect of a much wider problem and, by the levity of its phrasing, has probably done more to veil than to clarify the very important issues involved. The problem is not merely one of giving time for passions to cool, though this on occasion may be very important, as that of taking into account man's general inability to consider explicitly all the probable effects of a particular measure and his dependence on generalizations or principles if he is to fit his individual decisions into a coherent whole. It is "impossible for men to consult their interest in so effectual a manner, as by an universal and inflexible observance of rules of justice."[18]

It need hardly be pointed out that a constitutional system does not involve an absolute limitation of the will of the people but merely a subordination of immediate objectives to long-term ones. In effect this means a limitation of the means available to a temporary majority for the achievement of particular objectives by general principles laid down by another majority for a long period in advance. Or, to put it differently, it means that the agreement to submit to the will of the temporary majority on particular issues is based on the understanding that this majority will abide by more general principles laid down beforehand by a more comprehensive body.

This division of authority implies more than may at first be apparent. It implies a recognition of limits to the power of deliberate reason and a preference for reliance on proved principles over *ad hoc* solutions; furthermore, it implies that the hierarchy of rules does not necessarily end with the explicitly stated rules of constitutional law. Like the forces governing the individual mind, the forces making for social order are a multilevel affair; and even constitutions are based on, or presuppose, an underlying agreement on more

---

June 1649 (2nd ed., corrected and amended; London: "Reprinted in the grand year of Hipocritical and abominable Dissimulation," 1649), p. 34.—Ed.] Significant in this connection is also the resolution of the Concord, Massachusetts, town meeting of October 21, 1776 (reprinted in *Sources and Documents Illustrating the American Revolution, 1764–1788, and the Formulation of the Federal Constitution*, Samuel Eliot Morison, ed. (Oxford: Clarendon Press, 1923), p. 177), which declared that the legislative was no proper body to form a constitution, "first, because we conceive that a Constitution in its proper idea intends a system of principles established to secure the subject in the possession of enjoyment of their rights and privileges against any encroachment of the governing part. Second, because the same body that forms a Constitution have of consequence a power to alter it. Third, because a Constitution alterable by the Supreme Legislative is no security at all to the subject against any encroachment of the governing part on any, or on all the rights and privileges." It was, of course, largely the wish to prevent the ultimate authority from concerning itself with particulars, much more than its technical impracticability, that led the fathers of the American Constitution unanimously to reject direct democracy of the kind that had existed in ancient Greece.

[18] David Hume, *Treatise of Human Nature* [bk. 3, pt. 2, sec. 7], vol. 2, p. 300; cf. also p. 301.

fundamental principles—principles which may never have been explicitly expressed, yet which make possible and precede the consent and the written fundamental laws. We must not believe that, because we have learned to make laws deliberately, all laws must be deliberately made by some human agency.[19] Rather, a group of men can form a society capable of making laws because they already share common beliefs which make discussion and persuasion possible and to which the articulated rules must conform in order to be accepted as legitimate.[20]

From this it follows that no person or body of persons has complete freedom to impose upon the rest whatever laws it likes. The contrary view that underlies the Hobbesian conception of sovereignty[21] (and the legal positivism deriving from it) springs from a false rationalism that conceives of an autonomous and self-determining reason and overlooks the fact that all rational thought moves within a non-rational framework of beliefs and institutions. Constitutionalism means that all power rests on the understanding that it will be exercised according to commonly accepted principles, that the persons on whom power is conferred are selected because it is thought that they are most likely to do what is right, not in order that whatever they do should be right. It rests, in the last resort, on the understanding that power is ultimately not a physical fact but a state of opinion which makes people obey.[22]

Only a demagogue can represent as "antidemocratic" the limitations which long-term decisions and the general principles held by the people impose upon the power of temporary majorities. These limitations were conceived to protect the people against those to whom they must give power, and they are the only means by which the people can determine the general character of the order under which they will live. It is inevitable that, by accepting general principles, they will tie their hands as far as particular issues are concerned. For only by refraining from measures which they would not wish to be used on themselves can the members of a majority forestall the adoption of such measures when they are in a minority. A commitment to long-term principles, in fact, gives the people more control over the general nature of the political order than they would possess if its character were to be determined solely by successive decisions of particular issues. A free society certainly needs permanent means of restricting the powers of government, no matter what the par-

---

[19] Cf. chap. 4, above, especially nn. 5 and 8.

[20] On the conception of legitimacy cf. Guglielmo Ferrero, *The Principles of Power: The Great Political Crises of History*, Theodore R. Jaeckel, trans. (New York: G. P. Putnam's Sons, 1942), esp. pp. 131–276.

[21] This is not true of the original concept of sovereignty as introduced by Jean Bodin. Cf. McIlwain, *Constitutionalism and the Changing World*, chap. 2.

[22] As has been stressed by David Hume and a long line of theorists down to Friedrich von Wieser and his fullest elaboration of the idea in *Das Gesetz der Macht* (Vienna: Julius Springer, 1926).

ticular objective of the moment may be. And the Constitution which the new American nation was to give itself was definitely meant not merely as a regulation of the derivation of power but as a constitution of liberty, a constitution that would protect the individual against all arbitrary coercion.

4. The eleven years between the Declaration of Independence and the framing of the federal Constitution were a period of experimentation by the thirteen new states with the principles of constitutionalism. In some respects their individual constitutions show more clearly than the final Constitution of the Union how much the limitation of all governmental power was the object of constitutionalism. This appears, above all, from the prominent position that was everywhere given to inviolable individual rights, which were listed either as part of these constitutional documents or as separate Bills of Rights.[23] Though many of them were no more than restatements of the rights which the colonists had in fact enjoyed,[24] or thought they had always been entitled to, and most of the others were formulated hastily with reference to issues currently under dispute, they show clearly what constitutionalism meant to the Americans. In one place or another they anticipate most of the principles that were to inspire the federal Constitution.[25] The principal concern of all was, as the Bill of Rights preceding the constitution of Massachusetts of 1780 expressed it, that the government should be "a government of laws and not of men."[26]

The most famous of these Bills of Rights, that of Virginia, which was drafted and adopted before the Declaration of Independence and modeled on English and colonial precedents, largely served as the prototype not only for those of the other states but also for the French Declaration of the Rights of Men and

[23] See Roscoe Pound, *The Development of Constitutional Guarantees of Liberty* (New Haven: Yale University Press, 1957). There exists an important German literature on the origin of the Bills of Rights, of which the following may be mentioned here: Georg Jellinek, *Die Erklärung der Menschen- und Bürgerrechte. Ein Beitrag zur modernen Verfassungsgeschichte*, Walter Jellinek, ed. (3rd ed.; Munich and Leipzig: Duncker und Humblot, 1919), pp. iii–xiv, which contains a survey of the discussions since the first publication of the work in 1895; Richard Karl Schmidt, "Die Vorgeschichte der geschriebenen Verfassung," in *Festgabe für Otto Mayer: Zum siebzigsten Geburtstag dargebracht von Freunden, Verehrern und Schülern. 29. März 1916*, Otto Mayer, ed. (Leipzig: F, Meiner, 1916), pp. 81–191; Justus Hashagen, "Zur Entstehungsgeschichte der nordamerikanischen Erklärungen der Menschenrechte," *Zeitschrift für die gesamte Staatswissenschaft*, 78 (1924): 461–95; Gustav Adolf Salander, *Vom Werden der Menschenrechte: ein Beitrag zur modernen Verfassungsgeschichte unter Zugrundelegung der virginischen Erklärung der Rechte von 12. Juni 1776* (Leipzig: T. Weicher, 1926); Otto Vossler, "Studien zur Erklärung der Menschenrechte," *Historische Zeitschrift*, 142 (1930): 516–45.

[24] William Clarence Webster, "A Comparative Study of the State Constitutions of the American Revolution," *Annals of the American Academy of Political and Social Science*, 9 (1897): 415.

[25] Webster, "Comparative Study of State Constitutions," p. 418.

[26] Constitution of Massachusetts (March 2, 1780): part 1, art. 30. Though this clause does not yet appear in the original draft by John Adams, it is entirely in the spirit of his thinking.

Citizens of 1789 and, through that, for all similar European documents.[27] In substance, the various Bills of Rights of the American states and their main provisions are now familiar to everybody.[28] Some of these provisions, however, which occur only occasionally, deserve mention, such as the prohibition of retroactive laws, which occurs in four of the state Bills of Rights, or that of "perpetuities and monopolies," which occurs in two.[29] Also important is the emphatic manner in which in some of the constitutions the principle of the separation of powers is laid down[30]—no less so because in practice this was honored more in the breach than in the observance. Another recurring feature which to present readers will appear to be no more than a rhetorical flourish but to the men of the time was very important is the appeal to "the fundamental principles of a free government" which several of the constitutions contain[31] and the repeated reminder that "a frequent recurrency to fundamental principles is absolutely necessary to preserve the blessing of liberty."[32]

---

[27] For a discussion of the relationship see the works cited in n. 23 above.

[28] Cf. Webster, "Comparative Study of State Constitutions," p. 386: "Each of these instruments declared that no one should be deprived of his liberty except by law or by judgment of his peers; that every one, when prosecuted, should be entitled to a copy of the indictment brought against him, as well as to the right of procuring counsel and evidence; and that no one should be compelled to give evidence against himself. They all carefully guarded the right of trial by jury; guaranteed freedom of the press and free elections; forbade general warrants and standing armies in time of peace, forbade the granting of titles of nobility, hereditary honors and exclusive privileges. All of these instruments, except those of Virginia and Maryland, guaranteed the rights of assembly, petition, and instruction of representatives. All except those of Pennsylvania and Vermont forbade the requirement of excessive bail, the imposition of excessive fines, the infliction of unusual punishments, the suspension of laws by any other authority than the legislature, and taxation without representation."

[29] Constitution of North Carolina, art. 23. Cf. Constitution of Maryland, "Declaration of Rights," art. 41: "That monopolies are odious, contrary to the spirit of a free government and the principles of commerce, and ought not to be suffered." [Art. 23 of the Declaration of Rights of the Constitution of North Carolina of December 18, 1776, reads: "That perpetuities and monopolies are contrary to the genius of a free State, and ought not to be allowed." The provision of the Declaration of Rights of Maryland's Constitution of November 11, 1776, that Hayek quotes is actually art. 39.—Ed.]

[30] See especially the Constitution of Massachusetts (1780), part 1, "Declaration of Rights," art. 30: "In the government of this Commonwealth, the legislative department shall never exercise the executive and judicial powers, or either of them; the executive shall never exercise the legislative and judicial powers, or either of them; . . . to the end it may be a government of laws, and not of men."

[31] Constitution of Massachusetts (1780), part 1, art. 24. [The text of the article reads: "Laws made to punish for actions done before the existence of such laws, and which have not been declared crimes by preceding laws, are unjust, oppressive, and inconsistent with the fundamental principles of a free government."—Ed.]

[32] The phrase occurs first in the draft of the Virginia Declaration of Rights of May 1776, by George Mason (see Kate Mason Rowland, *The Life of George Mason, 1725–1792* (2 vols.; New

It is true that many of these admirable principles remained largely theory and that the state legislatures soon came as near to claiming omnipotence as the British Parliament had done. Indeed, "under most of the revolutionary constitutions the legislature was truly omnipotent and the executive correspondingly weak. Nearly all of these instruments conferred upon the former body practically unlimited power. In six constitutions there was nothing whatever to prevent the legislature amending the constitution by ordinary legislative process."[33] Even where this was not so, the legislatures often highhandedly disregarded the text of the constitution and still more those unwritten rights of the citizens which these constitutions had been intended to protect. But the development of explicit safeguards against such abuses required time. The main lesson of the period of Confederation was that the mere writing down

---

York: G. P. Putnam's Sons, 1892), vol. 1, pp. 435ff., and then as sec. 15 of the declaration as adopted. [Some two years following its passage by the Virginia Convention, Mason prepared a copy of the first draft of the Declaration from memory. The provision to which Hayek refers, art. 13, reads almost identically to its final passage on June 12, 1776. The phrase, as it occurs in Mason's first draft of May 20–26, 1776, remains essentially unchanged in the Committee's draft of May 27. It reads "That no free Government, or the Blessings of Liberty can be preserved by any People, but by a firm adherence to Justice, Moderation, Temperance, Frugality, and Virtue and by frequent Recurrence to fundamental Principles."—Ed.]

See also the Constitution of New Hampshire, art. 16 [art. 16 of the New Hampshire Constitution of June 2, 1784, reads: "A frequent recurrence to the fundamental principles of the constitution, and a constant adherence to justice, moderation, temperance, industry, frugality, and all the social virtues, are indispensably necessary to preserve the blessings of liberty and good government."—Ed.]; and that of Vermont, art. 16 [chap. 1, art. 16 of the Vermont Constitution of July 8, 1777, reads: "That frequent recurrence to fundamental principles, and a firm adherence to justice, moderation, temperance, industry and frugality, are absolutely necessary to preserve the blessings of liberty, and keep government free."—Ed.].

(Since there seems to exist no collection of the state constitutions in force in 1787, I am using *The Constitutions of All the United States, According to the Latest Amendments: To Which are Prefixed, the Declaration of Independence and the Federal Constitution* (Lexington, KY: Printed and sold by Thomas T. Skillman, 1817), which does not in all instances give the dates of the texts printed. In consequence, some of the references given in this and in the last few notes may refer to amendments later than the federal Constitution.) [In fact, all of Hayek's references to the various provisions of these early state constitutions were enacted before passage of the United States Constitution.—Ed.] On the origin of this clause see Gerald Stourzh's forthcoming book, *The Pursuit of Greatness.* [Professor Stourzh did not publish a work with this title. However, he was kind enough to explain Hayek's footnote. He writes: "*The Pursuit of Greatness* was the title of the first draft of my book which became *Alexander Hamilton and the Idea of Republican Government* (finally published in 1970). 'The Pursuit of Greatness' remains as the title to the last chapter, chap. 5, of the Hamilton book." The passage Hayek referred to, can be found in chap. 1, on pp. 34 to 37, of *Alexander Hamilton and the Idea of Republican Government.*—Ed.] See also David Hume, "Idea of a Perfect Commonwealth," *Essays* [Essay 16], vol. 1, p. 482 [Liberty Fund edition, p. 516]: "A government, says Machiavel, must often be brought back to its original principles."

[33] Webster, "A Comparative Study of State Constitutions," p. 398.

on paper of a constitution changed little unless explicit machinery was provided to enforce it.[34]

5. Much is sometimes made of the fact that the American Constitution is the product of design and that, for the first time in modern history, a people deliberately constructed the kind of government under which they wished to live. The Americans themselves were very conscious of the unique nature of their undertaking, and in a sense it is true that they were guided by a spirit of rationalism, a desire for deliberate construction and pragmatic procedure closer to what we have called the "French tradition" than to the "British."[35] This attitude was often strengthened by a general suspicion of tradition and an exuberant pride in the fact that the new structure was entirely of their own making. It was more justified here than in many similar instances, yet still essentially mistaken. It is remarkable how different from any clearly foreseen structure is the frame of government which ultimately emerged, how much of the outcome was due to historical accident or the application of inherited principles to a new situation. What new discoveries the federal Constitution contained either resulted from the application of traditional principles to particular problems or emerged as only dimly perceived consequences of general ideas.

When the Federal Convention, charged "to render the constitution of the federal government more adequate to the exigencies of the Union," met at Philadelphia in May, 1787, the leaders of the federalist movement found themselves confronted by two problems. While everybody agreed that the powers of the confederation were insufficient and must be strengthened, the

[34] Cf. James Madison at the end of *The Federalist* ["These Departments Should Not Be So Far Separated as to Have No Constitutional Control Over Each Other," (No. 48)], p. 256 [Liberty Fund edition, p. 260]: "A mere demarcation on parchment of the constitutional limits of the several departments, is not a sufficient guard against those encroachments which lead to a tyrannical concentration of all the powers of government in the same hands."

[35] John Jay is quoted by Michael Joseph Oakeshott ("Rationalism in Politics," *Cambridge Journal*, 1 [1947]: 151) as saying in 1777: "The Americans are the first people whom Heaven has favoured with an opportunity of deliberating upon, and choosing the forms of government under which they should live. All other constitutions have derived their existence from violence or accidental circumstances, and are therefore probably more distant from their perfection." [The quotation is taken from *The Correspondence and Public Papers of John Jay*, Henry Phelps Johnston, ed. (4 vols.; New York: P. Putnam's Sons, 1890), vol. 4, p. 365.—Ed.] But compare John Dickinson's emphatic statement in the Philadelphia Convention (of August 13, 1787, quoted in *The Records of the Federal Convention of 1787*, Max Farrand, ed. [New Haven: Yale University Press, 1911], vol. 2, p. 278): "Experience must be our only guide. Reason may mislead us. It was not Reason that discovered the singular and admirable mechanism of the English Constitution. It was not Reason that discovered . . . the odd and in the eye of those who are governed by reason, the absurd mode of trial by Jury. Accidents probably produced these discoveries, and experience has given a sanction to them. This is then our guide."

main concern was still to limit the powers of government as such, and not the least motive in seeking reform was to curb the arrogation of powers by the state legislatures.[36] The experience of the first decade of independence had merely somewhat shifted the emphasis from protection against arbitrary government to the creation of one effective common government. But it had also provided new grounds for suspecting the use of power by the state legislatures. It was scarcely foreseen that the solution of the first problem would also provide the answer to the second and that the transference of some essential powers to a central government, while leaving the rest to the separate states, would also set an effective limit on all government. Apparently it was from Madison that "came the idea that the problem of producing adequate safeguards for private rights and adequate powers for national government was in the end the same problem, inasmuch as a strengthened national government could be a make-weight against the swollen prerogatives of state legislatures."[37] Thus the great discovery was made of which Lord Acton later

[36] James Madison in the Philadelphia Convention mentioned as the chief objects of national government, "the necessity of providing more effectively for the security of private rights and the steady dispensation of justice. Interference with these were evils which had more, perhaps, than anything else produced this convention" (June 6, 1787, in *Records of the Federal Convention*, Max Farrand, ed., vol. 1, p. 134). Cf. also the famous passage quoted by Madison in the *Federalist* ["These Departments Should Not Be So Far Separated as to Have No Constitutional Control Over Each Other," (No. 48), pp. 254–55, from Thomas Jefferson's *Notes on the State of Virginia* in *Writings*, Merrill Daniel Peterson, ed., Library of America (New York: Literary Classics of the United States, 1984), pp. 245–46]: "All the powers of government, legislative, executive, and judiciary, result to the legislative body. The concentrating these in the same hands, is precisely the definition of despotic government. It will be no alleviation that these powers will be exercised by a plurality of hands, and not by a single one. One hundred and seventy-three despots would surely be as oppressive as one. Let those who doubt it, turn their eyes on the republic of Venice. As little will it avail us, that they are chosen by ourselves. An *elective despotism* was not the government we fought for; but one which should not only be founded on free principles, but in which the powers of government should be so divided and balanced among several bodies of magistracy, as that no one could transcend their legal limits, without being effectually checked and restrained by the others. . . . [The branches other than the legislature] have accordingly, in many instances *decided rights*, which should have been left to *judiciary controversy*, and *the direction of the executive, during the whole time of their session, is becoming habitual and familiar.*"—R. A. Humphreys' conclusion ("The Rule of Law and the American Revolution," p. 98) is true, therefore, even of Jefferson, the idol of the latter doctrinaire democrats: "Such was the republic which the authors of the Federal Constitution tried to build. They were concerned not to make America safe for democracy, but to make democracy safe for America. From Lord Chief Justice Coke to the Supreme Court of the United States is a long way, but a clear one. The controlling rule of law which the seventeenth century set above King or Parliament, which the Puritans exalted in matter both civil and ecclesiastical, which the philosophers saw as the governing principle of the universe, which the colonists invoked against the absolutism of Parliament, this 'was now made the essential principle of federation.'"

[37] Edward Samuel Corwin, "The Progress of Constitutional Theory between the Declaration of Independence and the Meeting of the Philadelphia Convention," *American Historical Review*,

said: "Of all checks on democracy, federalism has been the most efficacious and the most congenial. . . . The federal system limits and restrains the sovereign power by dividing it, and by assigning to Government only certain defined rights. It is the only method of curbing not only the majority but the power of the whole people, and it affords the strongest basis for a second chamber, which has been found essential security for freedom in every genuine democracy."[38]

The reason why a division of powers between different authorities always reduces the power that anybody can exercise is not always understood. It is not merely that the separate authorities will, through mutual jealousy, prevent one another from exceeding their authority. More important is the fact that certain kinds of coercion require the joint and co-ordinated use of different powers or the employment of several means, and, if these means are in separate hands, nobody can exercise those kinds of coercion. The most familiar illustration is provided by many kinds of economic control which can be effective only if the authority exercising them can also control the movement of men and goods across the frontiers of its territory. If it lacks that power, though it has the power to control internal events, it cannot pursue policies which require the joint use of both. Federal government is thus in a very definite sense limited government.[39]

The other chief feature of the Constitution relevant here is its provision guaranteeing individual rights. The reasons why it was at first decided not to include a Bill of Rights in the Constitution and the considerations which later persuaded even those who had at first opposed the decision are equally significant. The argument against inclusion was explicitly stated by Alexander Hamilton in the *Federalist:* "[Bills of rights are] not only unnecessary in the proposed constitution, but would even be dangerous. They would contain various exceptions to powers not granted, and on this very account would afford a colourable pretext to claim more than were granted. For why declare that things shall not be done which there is no power to do? Why, for instance, should it be said, that the liberty of the press shall not be restrained, when no power is given by which restrictions may be imposed? I will not contend that such a provision would confer a regulating power; but it is evident that

---

30 (1925): 536; the passage continues: "It remained for the Constitutional Convention, however, while it accepted Madison's main idea, to apply it through the agency of judicial review. Nor can it be doubted that this determination was assisted by a growing comprehension in the Convention of the *doctrine* of judicial review."

[38] Lord Acton, "Sir Erskine May's *Democracy in Europe*," *History of Freedom*, p. 98 [Liberty Fund edition, *Essays in the History of Liberty*, p. 84].

[39] Cf. my essay on "The Economic Conditions of Inter-State Federalism," *New Commonwealth Quarterly*, 5 (1939): 131–49, reprinted in Hayek, *Individualism and Economic Order* (Chicago: University of Chicago Press, 1948), pp. 255–72.

it would furnish, to men disposed to usurp, a plausible pretence for claiming that power. They might urge with a semblance of reason that the constitution ought not to be charged with the absurdity of providing against the abuse of an authority, which was not given, and that the provision against restraining the liberty of the press afforded a clear implication, that a right to prescribe proper regulations concerning it, was intended to be vested in the national government. This may serve as a specimen of the numerous handles which would be given to the doctrine of constructive powers, by the indulgence of an injudicious zeal for bills of rights."[40]

The basic objection thus was that the Constitution was intended to protect a range of individual rights much wider than any document could exhaustively enumerate and that any explicit enumeration of some was likely to be interpreted to mean that the rest were not protected.[41] Experience has shown that there was good reason to fear that no bill of rights could fully state all the rights implied in "the general principles which are common to our political institutions"[42] and that to single out some would seem to imply that the others were not protected. On the other hand, it was soon recognized that the Constitution was bound to confer on government powers which might be used to infringe individual rights if these were not specially protected and that, since some such rights had already been mentioned in the body of the Constitution, a fuller catalogue might with advantage be added. "A bill of rights," it was

---

[40] "Certain General and Miscellaneous Objections to the Constitution Considered and Answered" (No. 84), *The Federalist*, pp. 439–40 [Liberty Fund edition, pp. 445–46].

[41] An even clearer statement of this view than in the passage by Hamilton quoted in the text is that by James Wilson in the debate on the Constitution in the Pennsylvania convention (*The Debates in the Several State Conventions on the Adoption of the Federal Constitution, as Recommended by the General Convention at Philadelphia in 1787*, Jonathan Elliot, ed. [5 vols.; 2nd ed., with considerable additions; Philadelphia: J. B. Lippincott and Co., 1836–59], vol. 2, p. 436): He described a bill of rights as "highly imprudent" because "in all societies, there are many powers and rights which cannot be particularly enumerated. A bill of rights annexed to a constitution is an *enumeration of the powers* reserved. If we attempt an enumeration, everything that is not enumerated is presumed to be given." James Madison, however, seems from the beginning to have held the view which ultimately prevailed. In an important letter to Jefferson, dated October 27, 1788 (quoted here from *The Complete Madison: His Basic Writings*, Saul Kussiel Padover, ed. [New York: Harper, 1953], p. 253), too long to reproduce here in full, he wrote: "My own opinion has always been in favor of a bill of rights; provided it be so framed as not to imply powers not meant to be included in the enumeration. . . . The invasion of private rights is *chiefly* to be apprehended, not from acts of Government contrary to the sense of its constituents, but from acts in which the Government is the mere instrument of the major number of the Constituents. This is a truth of great importance but not yet sufficiently attended to. . . . What use then it may be asked can a bill of rights serve in popular Governments? . . . The political truths declared in that solemn manner acquire by degrees the character of fundamental maxims of free Government, and as they become incorporated with the national sentiment, counteract the impulses of interest and passion. . . ."

[42] John Marshall in *Fletcher v. Peck*, 10 *U.S.* (6, *Cranch*) 87 at 139 (1810).

later said, "is important, and may often be indispensable, whenever it operates, as a qualification upon powers actually granted by the people to the government. This is the real ground of all the bills of rights in the parent country, in the colonial constitutions and laws, and in the state constitutions," and "A bill of rights is an important protection against unjust and oppressive conduct on the part of the people themselves."[43]

The danger so clearly seen at the time was guarded against by the careful proviso (in the Ninth Amendment) that "the enumeration of certain rights in this Constitution shall not be construed to deny or disparage others retained by the people"—a provision whose meaning was later completely forgotten.[44]

We must at least briefly mention another feature of the American Constitution, lest it appear that the admiration that the protagonists of liberty have always felt for the Constitution[45] necessarily extends to this aspect also, particularly as it is a product of the same tradition. The doctrine of the separation of powers led to the formation of a presidential republic in which the chief executive derives his power directly from the people and, in consequence, may belong to a different party from that which controls the legislature. We shall see later that the interpretation of the doctrine on which this arrangement rests is by no means required by the aim it serves. It is difficult to see the expediency of erecting this particular obstacle to the efficiency of the executive, and one may well feel that the other excellencies of the American Constitution would show themselves to greater advantage if they were not combined with that feature.

6. If we consider that the aim of the Constitution was largely to restrain legislatures, it becomes evident that arrangements had to be made for applying such restraints in the way that other laws are applied—namely, through courts of justice. It is therefore not surprising that a careful historian finds

---

[43] Joseph Story, *Commentaries on the Constitution of the United States, With a Preliminary Review of the Constitutional History of the Colonies and States, Before the Adoption of the Constitution* (Boston: Hilliard, Gray, and Co., 1833), vol. 3, pp. 718, 720.

[44] Cf. Leslie Wallace Dunbar, "James Madison and the Ninth Amendment," *Virginia Law Review*, 42 (1956): 627–45. It is significant that even the leading authority on the American Constitution misquotes in a well-known essay (Edward S. Corwin, "The 'Higher Law' Background of American Constitutional Law" [1955 reprint], p. 5 [Liberty Fund edition, p. 4]) the text of the Ninth Amendment and reprints the misquotation twenty-five years later, apparently because nobody had noticed the substitution of a phrase of six words for one of eleven in the authentic text!

[45] This admiration was widely shared by nineteenth-century liberals such as W. E. Gladstone, who once described the American Constitution as "the most wonderful work ever struck off at a given time by the brain and purpose of men." [The quotation reads: "As the British Constitution is the most subtle organism which has proceeded from progressive history, so the American Constitution is the most wonderful work ever struck off at a given time by the brain and purpose of man." William Ewart Gladstone, "Kin Beyond Sea," *North American Review*, 264 (September–October 1878): 185.—Ed.]

that "judicial review, instead of being an American invention, is as old as constitutional law itself, and without it constitutionalism would never have been attained."[46] In view of the character of the movement that led to the design of a written constitution, it must indeed seem curious that the need for courts which could declare laws unconstitutional should ever have been questioned.[47] The important fact, at any rate, is that to some of the drafters of the Constitution judicial review was a necessary and self-evident part of a constitution, that when occasion arose to defend their conception in the early discussions after its adoption, they were explicit enough in their statements;[48] and that through a decision of the Supreme Court it soon became the law of the land. It had already been applied by the state courts with respect to the state constitutions (in a few instances even before the adoption of the federal Con-

[46] McIlwain, *Constitutionalism and the Changing World*, p. 278 [The quotation in fact reads: "Judicial review, instead of being an American invention, is really as old as constitutionalism itself, and without its constitutionalism could never have been maintained."—Ed.]; cf. Edward S. Corwin, "Basic Doctrine of American Constitutional Law," in the *Michigan Law Review*, 12 (February 1914): 252; reprinted in *Selected Essays on Constitutional Law*, vol. 1, p. 105: "The history of judicial review is, in other words, the history of constitutional limitations." See also Gottfried Dietze, "America and Europe: Decline and Emergence of Judicial Review," *Virginia Law Review*, 44 (1958): 1233–72.

[47] All the arguments supporting the denial have recently been marshaled in detail in William Winslow Crosskey, *Politics and the Constitution in the History of the United States* (2 vols.; Chicago: University of Chicago Press, 1953).

[48] See mainly *The Federalist*, Alexander Hamilton, "The Judiciary Department" (No. 78), p. 399 [Liberty Fund edition, p. 405]: "Whenever a particular statute contravenes the constitution it will be the duty of the judicial tribunals to adhere to the latter, and disregard the former"; also James Madison, *Debates and Proceedings in the Congress* [*Annals of Congress*], 1st Congress, 1st Session, Senate: June 8, 1789, vol. 1, p. 457, where he declares that the courts would "consider themselves in a peculiar manner the guardians of those rights; they will be an impenetrable bulwark against every assumption of power in the Legislative or Executive: they will be naturally led to resist every encroachment upon rights expressly stipulated for in the Constitution by the declaration of rights," and his later statement in a letter to George Thompson, dated June 30, 1825 (quoted in *The Complete Madison*, p. 344): "No doctrine can be sound that releases a Legislature from the controul of a constitution. The latter is as much a law to the former, as the acts of the former are to individuals and although always liable to be altered by the people who formed it, is not alterable by any other authority; certainly not by those chosen by the people to carry it into effect. This is so vital a principle, and has been so justly the pride of our popular Government, that a denial of it cannot possibly last long or spread far." Further, Senator Mason's and Gouverneur Morris's statements in the congressional discussion of the repeal of the judiciary act of 1801 quoted in McLaughlin, *Constitutional History of the United States*, p. 291, and James Wilson's Lectures delivered in 1792 to students of the University of Pennsylvania (*The Works of James Wilson, Associate Justice of the Supreme Court of the United States and Professor Law in the College of Philadelphia: Being His Public Discourses Upon Jurisprudence and the Political Science, Including Lectures as Professor of Law, 1790–92*, James DeWitt Andrews, ed. [2 vols.; Chicago: Callaghan and Co., 1896], vol. 1, p.417) in which he presents judicial review as "the necessary result of the distribution of power, made, by the constitution, between the legislative and the judicial departments."

stitution[49]), although none of the state constitutions had explicitly provided for it, and it seemed obvious that the federal courts should have the same power where the federal Constitution was concerned. The opinion in *Marbury v. Madison*, in which Chief Justice Marshall established the principle, is justly famous also for the masterly manner in which it summed up the rationale of a written constitution.[50]

It has often been pointed out that for fifty-four years after that decision the Supreme Court found no further occasion to reassert this power. But it must be remarked that the corresponding power was frequently used during the period by the state courts and that the non-use of it by the Supreme Court would be significant only if it could be shown that it did not use it in cases where it ought to have used it.[51] Moreover, there can be no question that it was in this very period that the whole doctrine of the Constitution on which judicial review was based was most fully developed. There appeared during these years a unique literature on the legal guaranties of individual liberty which deserves a place in the history of liberty next to the great English debates of the seventeenth and eighteenth centuries. In a fuller exposition the contributions of James Wilson, John Marshall, Joseph Story, James Kent, and Daniel

---

[49] Even the most critical recent survey by Crosskey, *Politics and the Constitution in the History of the United States*, vol. 2, p. 943, sums up the situation by saying that "some evidence has been found, that the basic notion of judicial review had some acceptance in America, in the Colonial period."

[50] *Marbury v. Madison*, 5 *U.S.* (1 *Cranch*) 137 (1803); only a few passages from this famous decision can be quoted here: "The Government of the United States has been emphatically termed a government of laws, and not of men. It will certainly cease to deserve this high appellation if the laws furnish no remedy for the violation of a vested legal right. . . . The question, whether an Act, repugnant to the constitution can become the law of the land, is a question deeply interesting to the United States, but, happily, not of an intricacy proportioned to its interest. It seems only necessary to recognize certain principles supposed to have been long and well established, to decide it. . . . The powers of the legislature are defined and limited; and that those limits may not be mistaken or forgotten, the constitution is written. To what purpose are powers limited, and to what purpose is that limitation committed to writing, if these limits may, at any time, be passed by those intended to be restrained? The distinction between a government with limited and unlimited powers is abolished if those limits do not confine the persons on whom they are imposed and if Acts prohibited and Acts allowed are of equal obligation. . . . It is emphatically the province and duty of the judicial department to say what the law is. Those who apply the rule to particular cases must of necessity expound and interpret that rule. If two laws conflict with each other, the courts must decide on the operation of each."

[51] Cf. Robert Houghwout Jackson, *The Struggle for Judicial Supremacy: A Study of a Crisis in American Power Politics* (New York: Alfred A. Knopf, 1941), pp. 36–37, where he suggests that "this may have been the result not merely of judicial abstinence but of the fact that there was little Congressional legislation at least that would offend conservative minds: *Laissez faire*, to some degree, was the philosophy of the legislature, as it was of the Court. It is partly this fact which obscured the potentialities of *Marbury v. Madison* and even more of *Dred Scott*" [*Dred Scott v. Sanford*, 19 *Howard* 393 (March 1857)].

Webster would deserve careful consideration. The later reaction against their doctrines has somewhat obscured the great influence which this generation of jurists had on the evolution of the American political tradition.[52]

We can consider here only one other development of constitutional doctrine during this period. It is the increasing recognition that a constitutional system based on the separation of powers presupposed a clear distinction between laws proper and those other enactments of the legislature which are not general rules. We find in discussions of the period constant references to the conception of "general laws, formed upon deliberation, under the influence of no resentment, and without knowing upon whom they will operate."[53] There was much discussion of the undesirability of "special" as distinguished from "general" acts.[54] Judicial decisions repeatedly stressed that laws proper ought to be "general public laws equally binding upon every member of the community under similar circumstances."[55] Various attempts were made to

[52] On the great influence of legal thought on American politics during the period see particularly Tocqueville, *Democracy in America* [bk. 1, sec. 2, chap. 16], vol. 1, pp. 272–80 [French edition, vol. 2, pp. 303–10]. Few facts are more indicative of the change of atmosphere than the decline of the reputation of men like Daniel Webster, whose effective statements of constitutional theory were once considered classic but are now largely forgotten. See particularly his arguments in the Dartmouth Case [*The Trustees of Dartmouth College v. Woodward*, 17 *U.S.* 518; 4 *Wheat*; 4 *L. Ed.* 629 (February 1819)] and in *Luther v. Borden* [*Rachel Luther et al. v. Luther M. Borden et al.*, 48 *U.S.* 1; 12 *L. Ed.* 581; 7 *How.* 1 (January 1849)] in *The Writings and Speeches of Daniel Webster*, Edward Everett, ed. (18 vols.; National ed.; Boston: Little, Brown, 1903), vols. 10 and 11, esp. vol. 10, p. 219: "By the law of the land is most clearly intended the general law; a law which hears before it condemns; which proceeds upon inquiry, and renders judgment only after trial. The meaning is, that every citizen shall hold his life, liberty, property, and immunities under the protection of the general rules which govern society. Everything which may pass under the form of an enactment is not therefore to be considered the law of the land." Also Webster, vol. 10, p. 232, where he stresses that the people "have most wisely, chosen to take the risk of occasional inconvenience from the want of power, in order that there might be a settled limit to its exercise, and a permanent security against its abuse." See also Webster, vol. 11, p. 224: "I have said that it is one principle of the American system, that the people limit their governments, National and State. They do so, but it is another principle, equally true and certain, and, according to my judgment of things, equally important, that the people often *limit themselves*. They set bounds to their own power. They have chosen to secure the institutions which they establish against the sudden impulses of mere majorities. All our institutions teem with instances of this. It was their great conservative principle, in constituting forms of government, that they should secure what they had established against hasty changes by simple majorities."
[53] *Ex parte Bollman* and *Ex parte Swartwout* 8 *U.S. Reports* 75 (4 Cranch 750); 2 *L. Ed.* 554 (February 1807) at 127.
[54] See Corwin, "The Basic Doctrine of American Constitutional Law," p. 258 [reprinted in *Selected Essays on Constitutional Law*, vol. 1, p. 111], as quoted in n. 46 above.
[55] See Corwin, "The Basic Doctrine of American Constitutional Law," p. 259 [reprinted in *Selected Essays on Constitutional Law*, p. 112]. [The statement is not Corwin's but forms part of the decision in a case heard before the Tennessee Supreme Court, *Vanzant v. Waddell* (2 Yerg. [10 Tenn.] 259 [1829]) that is quoted by Corwin. The Court there held that the legislature was

embody this distinction in state constitutions,[56] until it came to be regarded as one of the chief limitations upon legislation. This, together with the explicit prohibition of retroactive laws by the federal Constitution (somewhat unaccountably restricted to criminal law by an early decision of the Supreme Court),[57] indicate how constitutional rules were meant to control substantive legislation.

7. When in the middle of the century the Supreme Court again found occasion to reassert its power of examining the constitutionality of congressional legislation, the existence of that power was hardly questioned. The problem had become rather one of the nature of the substantive limitations which the Constitution or constitutional principles imposed upon legislation. For a time judicial decisions appealed freely to the "essential nature of all free governments" and the "fundamental principles of civilization." But gradually, as the ideal of popular sovereignty grew in influence, what the opponents of an explicit enumeration of protected rights had feared happened: it became accepted doctrine that the courts are not at liberty "to declare an act void, because in their opinion it is opposed to a *spirit* supposed to pervade the constitution *but not expressed in words*."[58] The meaning of the Ninth Amendment was forgotten and seems to have remained forgotten ever since.[59]

Thus bound to the explicit provisions of the Constitution, the judges of the Supreme Court in the second half of the century found themselves in a somewhat peculiar position when they encountered uses of legislative power which, they felt, it had been the intention of the Constitution to prevent but which the Constitution did not explicitly prohibit. In fact, they at first deprived themselves of one weapon which the Fourteenth Amendment might have provided. The prohibition that "no state shall make or enforce any law which shall abridge the privileges or immunities of citizens of the United

---

created to enact "general public law equally binding upon every member of the community . . . under similar circumstances." (Ellipses part of Corwin's quote.)—Ed.]

[56] See the constitutions of *Arkansas* (1874), art. 5, sec. 25; *Georgia* (1877), art. 1, sec. 4, par. 1 [Identical language appears in the 1945 Constitution (art. 1, sec. 4, par. 1) and the 1976 Constitution (art. 1, sec. 4, par. 7), while there are similar provisions in the 1968 Constitution (art. 1, sec. 26) and in art. 3, sec. 6, par. 4 of the Georgia Constitution of 1983.—Ed.]; *Kansas* (July, 1859), art. 2, sec. 17; *Michigan* (1863), art. 4, sec. 29 [A similar provision appears in the Michigan Constitution of 1908 (art. 5, sec. 30).—Ed.]; and *Ohio* (1851), sec. 2, art. 26. For a discussion of this feature see Hermann von Mangoldt, *Rechtsstaatsgedanke und Regierungsformen in den Vereinigten Staaten von Amerika: Die geistigen Grundlagen des amerikanischen Verfassungsrechts* (Essen: Essener Verlagsanstalt, 1938), pp. 315–18, esp. 316.

[57] *Calder v. Bull*, 3 U.S. (3 *Dall*) 386, 388 (1798); cf. Corwin, "The Basic Doctrine of American Constitutional Law," pp. 248–58 [reprinted in *Selected Essays on Constitutional Law*, pp. 102–11].

[58] Thomas McIntyre Cooley, *A Treatise on Constitutional Limitations Which Rest Upon the Legislative Power of the States of the American Union* (1st ed.; Boston: Little, Brown, and Co., 1868), p. 171. [The phrase "but not expressed in words" italicized by Hayek.—Ed.]

[59] Cf. Jackson, *The Supreme Court in the American System of Government*, p. 74.

States" was, within five years, reduced to a "practical nullity" by a decision of the Court.[60] But the continuation of the same clause, "nor shall any State deprive any person of life, liberty, or property, without due process of law; nor deny to any person within its jurisdiction the equal protection of the laws," was to achieve altogether unforeseen importance.

The "due process" provision of this amendment repeats with explicit reference to state legislation what the Fifth Amendment had already provided and several state constitutions similarly stated. In general, the Supreme Court had interpreted the earlier provision according to what was undoubtedly its original meaning of "due process for the enforcement of law." But in the last quarter of the century, when it had, on the one hand, become unquestioned doctrine that only the letter of the Constitution could justify the Court's declaring a law unconstitutional, and when, on the other hand, it was faced with more and more legislation which seemed contrary to the spirit of the Constitution, it clutched at that straw and interpreted the procedural as a substantive rule. The "due process" clauses of the Fifth and Fourteenth Amendments were the only ones in the Constitution that mentioned property. During the next fifty years they thus became the foundation on which the Court built a body of law concerning not only individual liberties but government control of economic life, including the use of police power and of taxation.[61]

The results of this peculiar and partly accidental historical development do not provide enough of a general lesson to justify any further consideration here of the intricate issues of present American constitutional law which they raise. Few people will regard as satisfactory the situation that has emerged. Under so vague an authority the Court was inevitably led to adjudicate, not on whether a particular law went beyond the specific powers conferred on

---

[60] The "Slaughter House Cases," 83 *U.S.* (16 *Wallace*) 36 (1873). Cf. Edward S. Corwin, *Liberty against Government*, p. 122. [In the Slaughterhouse Cases, the Court held that the original intent of the Fourteenth Amendment was to guarantee the freedom of black slaves that had been freed by virtue of the Thirteenth Amendment. While the Fourteenth Amendment was not to be construed as referring solely to black slaves the Amendment's scope did not cover the issues raised in this case, that is, that the slaughterhouse operators who had been barred from engaging in their trade were deprived of their property without due process of law. The Court ruled that it was necessary to draw a distinction between United States citizenship and the citizenship of a state and that the Amendment did not seek to deprive the state of its legal jurisdiction over the civil rights of its citizens. It was therefore held that the restraints placed by the state of Louisiana on slaughterhouse operators did not deprive them of their property without "due process" nor of the "equal protection of the laws."—Ed.]

[61] In E. S. Corwin's standard annotated edition of the Constitution of the United States (1953), 215 out of 1,237 pages are devoted to the jurisdiction on the Fourteenth Amendment as against 136 pages devoted to the "commerce clause"! [In the 2002 edition of the annotated edition, the difference in the number of pages devoted to commentary on these two sections increased; analysis of the commerce clause occupies 113 pages while 379 pages are devoted to the Fourteenth Amendment.—Ed.]

the legislatures, or whether legislation infringed general principles, written or unwritten, which the Constitution had been intended to uphold, but whether the ends for which the legislature used its powers were desirable. The problem became one of whether the purposes for which powers were exercised were "reasonable"[62] or, in other words, whether the need in the particular instance was great enough to justify the use of certain powers, though in other instances there might be justification. The Court was clearly overstepping its proper judicial functions and arrogating what amounted to legislative powers. This finally led to conflicts with public opinion and the Executive in which the authority of the Court suffered somewhat.

8. Though to most Americans this is still familiar recent history, we cannot altogether ignore here the climax of the struggle between the Executive and the Supreme Court, which from the time of the first Roosevelt and the anti-Court campaign of the progressives under the elder La Follette had been a standing feature of the American scene. The conflict of 1937, while it induced the Court to retreat from its more extreme position, also led to a reaffirmation of the fundamental principles of the American tradition which is of lasting significance.

When the most severe economic depression of modern times was at its peak, the American presidency came to be occupied by one of those extraordinary figures whom Walter Bagehot had in mind when he wrote: "some man of genius, of attractive voice and limited mind, who declaims and insists, not only that the special improvement is a good thing in itself, but the best of all things, and the root of all other good things."[63] Fully convinced that he knew best what was needed, Franklin D. Roosevelt conceived it as the function of democracy in times of crisis to give unlimited powers to the man it trusted, even if this meant that it thereby "forged new instruments of power which in some hands would be dangerous."[64]

---

[62] Cf. the comment in Ernest Freund, *Standards of American Legislation: An Estimate of Restrictive and Constructive Factors* (Chicago: University of Chicago Press, 1917), p. 211: "The only criterion that is suggested is that of reasonableness. From the point of view of legal science it would be difficult to conceive of anything more unsatisfactory."

[63] Walter Bagehot, "The Metaphysical Basis of Toleration," (1874) in *The Works and Life of Walter Bagehot*, Mrs. Russell Barrington, ed. (London: Longman, Green, and Co., 1915), vol. 6, pp. 232–33.

[64] Quoted by Dorothy Thompson, *Essentials of Democracy: The American Scene* [the first of three "Town Hall Pamphlets" published under the title "Essentials of Democracy," on the basis of lectures delivered by Dorothy Thompson at Town Hall] (New York: The Town Hall, 1938), p. 21. [Dorothy Thompson, a prominent political commentator and columnist for the *New York Herald Tribune*, is here paraphrasing Roosevelt. In actuality, in the course of his Annual Message to Congress of January 3, 1936, Roosevelt made the following remarks: "Our resplendent economic autocracy does not want to return to that individualism of which they prate, even though the advantages under that system went to the ruthless and the strong. They realize that in thirty-four

THE CONSTITUTION OF LIBERTY

It was inevitable that this attitude, which regarded almost any means as legitimate if the ends were desirable, should soon lead to a head-on clash with a Supreme Court which for half a century had habitually judged on the "reasonableness" of legislation. It is probably true that in its most spectacular decision, when the Court unanimously struck down the National Recovery Administration Act, it not only saved the country from an ill-conceived measure but also acted within its constitutional rights. But thereafter its small conservative majority proceeded to annul, on much more questionable grounds, one after another of the measures of the President until he became convinced that his only chance of carrying them out was to restrict the powers or alter the personnel of the Court. It was over what became known as the "Court Packing Bill" that the struggle came to a head. The re-election of the President by an unprecedented majority in 1936, however, which sufficiently strengthened his position to attempt this, also seems to have persuaded the Court that the President's program had wide approval. When, in consequence, the Court withdrew from its more extreme position and not only reversed itself on some of the central issues but in effect abandoned the use of the due process clause as a substantive limit on legislation, the President was deprived of his strongest arguments. In the end his measure was completely defeated in the Senate, where his party held the overwhelming majority, and his prestige suffered a serious blow at the moment when he had reached the pinnacle of his popularity.

It is mainly because of the brilliant restatement of the traditional role of the Court in the report of the Senate Judiciary Committee that this episode forms a fitting conclusion to this survey of the American contribution to the ideal of freedom under the law. Only a few of the most characteristic passages from that document can be quoted here. Its statement of the principles starts from the presumption that the preservation of the American constitutional system is "immeasurably more important . . . than the immediate adoption of any legislation however beneficial." It declares "for the continuation and perpetuation of government and rule by law; as distinguished from government and rule by men, and in this we are but re-asserting the principles basic to the Constitution of the United States." And it goes on to state: "If the Court of last resort is to be made to respond to a prevalent sentiment of a current hour, politically imposed, that Court must ultimately become subservient to the pressure of public opinion of the hour, which might at the moment embrace mob passion abhorrent to a more calm, lasting, consideration. . . .

---

months we have built up new instruments of public power. In the hands of a people's Government this power is wholesome and proper. But in the hands of political puppets of an economic autocracy such power would provide shackles for the liberties of the people." (reported in the *Washington Post*, January 4, 1936, p. 4, cols. 5–6).—Ed.]

No finer or more durable philosophy of free government is to be found in all the writings and practices of great statesmen than may be found in the decisions of the Supreme Court when dealing with great problems of free government touching human rights."[65]

No greater tribute has ever been paid by a legislature to the very Court which limited its powers. And nobody in the United States who remembers this event can doubt that it expressed the feelings of the great majority of the population.[66]

9. Incredibly successful as the American experiment in constitutionalism has been—and I know of no other written constitution which has lasted half as long—it is still an experiment in a new way of ordering government, and we must not regard it as containing all wisdom in this field. The main features of the American Constitution crystallized at so early a stage in the understanding of the meaning of a constitution, and so little use has been made of the amending power to embody in the written document the lessons learned, that in some respects the unwritten parts of the Constitution are more instructive than its text. For the purposes of this study, at any rate, the general principles underlying it are more important than any of its particular features.

The chief point is that in the United States it has been established that the legislature is bound by general rules; that it must deal with particular problems in such a manner that the underlying principle can also be applied in other cases; and that, if it infringes a principle hitherto observed, though perhaps

---

[65] *Reorganization of the Federal Judiciary: Adverse Report from the [Senate] Committee on the Judiciary Submitted to Accompany S. 1392* (75th Congress, 1st Session; Senate Report 711, June 7, 1937), pp. 8, 15, 19, and 20. Cf. also p. 19: "The courts are not perfect, nor are the judges. The Congress is not perfect, nor are Senators and Representatives. The Executive is not perfect. These branches of government and the office under them are filled by human beings who for the most part strive to live up to the dignity and idealism of a system that was designed to achieve the greatest possible measure of justice and freedom for all the people. We shall destroy the system when we reduce it to the imperfect standards of the men who operate it. We shall strengthen it and ourselves, we shall make justice and liberty for all men more certain when, by patience and self-restraint, we maintain it on the high plane on which it was conceived.

"Inconvenience and even delay in the enactment of legislation is not a heavy price to pay for our system. Constitutional democracy moves forward with certainty rather than with speed. The safety and the permanence of the progressive march of our civilization are far more important to us and to those who are to come after us than the enactment now of any particular law. The Constitution of the United States provides ample opportunity for the expression of the popular will to bring about such reforms and changes as the people may deem essential to their present and future welfare. It is the people's charter of the powers granted those who govern them."

[66] I shall not easily forget how this feeling was expressed by the taxi driver in Philadelphia in whose cab we heard the radio announcement of President Roosevelt's sudden death. I believe he spoke for the great majority of the people when he concluded a deeply felt eulogy of the President with the words: "But he ought not to have tampered with the Supreme Court, he should never have done *that*!" The shock had evidently gone very deep.

never explicitly stated, it must acknowledge this fact and must submit to an elaborate process in order to ascertain whether the basic beliefs of the people really have changed. Judicial review is not an absolute obstacle to change, and the worst it can do is to delay the process and make it necessary for the constitution-making body to repudiate or reaffirm the principle at issue.

The practice of restraining government's pursuit of immediate aims by general principles is partly a precaution against drift; for this, judicial review requires as its complement the normal use of something like the referendum, an appeal to the people at large, to decide on the question of general principle. Furthermore, a government which can apply coercion to the individual citizen only in accordance with pre-established long-term general rules but not for specific, temporary ends is not compatible with every kind of economic order. If coercion is to be used only in the manner provided for in the general rules, it becomes impossible for government to undertake certain tasks. Thus it is true that, "stripped of all its husks, liberalism is constitutionalism, 'a government of laws and not of men'"[67] if by "liberalism" we mean what it still meant in the United States during the Supreme Court struggle of 1937, when the "liberalism" of the defenders of the Court was attacked as minority thinking.[68] In this sense Americans have been able to defend freedom by defending their Constitution. We shall presently see how on the European Continent in the early nineteenth century the liberal movement, inspired by the American example, came to regard as its principal aim the establishment of constitutionalism and the rule of law.

[67] C. H. McIlwain, *Constitutionalism and the Changing World* (New York: Macmillan, 1939), p. 286; cf. also Franz Leopold Neumann, *The Democratic and the Authoritarian State: Essays in Political and Legal Theory* (Glencoe, IL: The Free Press, 1957), p. 31.

[68] See Max Lerner, "Minority Rule and the Constitutional Tradition," in *The Constitution Reconsidered*, Conyers Read, ed. (New York: Columbia University Press, 1938), pp. 199ff.

THIRTEEN

LIBERALISM AND ADMINISTRATION:
THE *RECHTSSTAAT*

How can there be a definite limit to the supreme power if an indefinite general happiness, left to its judgment, is to be its aim? Are the princes to be the fathers of the people, however great be the danger that they will also become its despots? —G. H. von Berg

The quotation at the head of the chapter is taken from Günther Heinrich von Berg, *Handbuch des teutschen Policeyrechtes* [i.e., deutschen Polizeirechts] (7 vols.; Hanover: Hahn, 1799–1804), vol. 2, p. 3. The German text is: "Wo bleibt eine bestimmte Grenze der höchsten Gewalt, wenn eine unbestimmte, ihrem eigenen Urtheile überlassene allgemeine Glückseligkeit ihr Ziel sein soll? Sollen die Fürsten Väter des Volks seyn, so gross auch die Gefahr ist, dass sie seine Despoten seyn werden?" See also Johann Christoph, Freiherr von Aretin (continued by Carl von Rotteck), *Staatsrecht der konstitutionellen Monarchie: Ein Handbuch für Geschäftsmänner, studirende Jünglinge und gebildete Bürger* (2 vols.; Altenburg: Literatur-Comptoir, 1824–27), vol. 2, p. 179: "Die Rechtsherrschaft vom Staate verlangen, heißt ihn verpflichten, die Rechte jedes Einzelnen zu schützen und zu achten, die Wohlfahrt von ihm verlangen, heißt ihn auffordern, die Rechte der Einzelnen zu verletzen, weil die Mittel, wodurch die Größe, die Macht, der Ruhm, der Wohlstand einer Nation befördert werden soll, in der Regel von der Art sind, daß jene Rechte dadurch beeinträchtigt werden." ["To demand that the state institute the rule of law means that it is obliged to protect and respect the rights of the individual. To demand that the state provide for its citizens' welfare is to ask that it abuse the rights of the individual, inasmuch as the promotion of the size, power, glory, and prosperity of a nation impairs these rights."—Ed.] All of this seems to be rooted in Immanuel Kant, *Sämmtliche Werke*, Gustav Hartenstein, ed. (8 vols.; Leipzig: Leopold Voss, 1868), "Vom Verhältniss der Theorie zur Praxis im Staatsrecht" ["On the Relationship of Theory to Practice in Public Law"], vol. 6, p. 327; "Von dem Kampf des guten Princips mit dem bösen und die Gründung eines Reichs Gottes auf Erden" ["Struggle between the Good and the Evil Principle and Founding the Kingdom of God"], vol. 6, pp. 220–29; and "Metaphysische Anfangsgründe der Rechtslehre" ["Metaphysical Elements of the Theory of Law"], vol. 7, p. 130.

How little the problems have changed in a century and a half is shown when we compare this with the observation by Alfred Wilhelm von Martin, *Ordnung und Freiheit. Materialien und Reflexionen zu Grundfragen des Soziallebens* (Frankfurt am Main: Josef Knecht, 1956), p. 177: "Denn es kann auch bei aller revolutionär-demokratischen Ideologie-keinen weiterreichenden Freibrief fur die Macht geben, als wenn sie lediglich an den (jeder jeweiligen 'Generallinie' nachgebenden) Kautschukbegriff des Gemeinwohls gebunden ist, der unter dem Deckmantel des Moralischen, jeder politischen Beliebigkeit freie Bahn gibt." ["All revolutionary-democratic ideology notwithstanding, there can be no more wide-ranging license for power than when it is solely bound to the elastic notion (which invariably yields to whatever happens to be the 'general line'

1. In most countries of the European Continent, two hundred years of absolute government had, by the middle of the eighteenth century, destroyed the
traditions of liberty. Though some of the earlier conceptions had been handed
on and developed by the theorists of the law of nature, the main impetus for
a revival came from across the Channel. But, as the new movement grew, it
encountered a situation different from that which existed in America at the
time or which had existed in England a hundred years earlier.

This new factor was the powerful centralized administrative machinery
which absolutism had built, a body of professional administrators who had
become the main rulers of the people. This bureaucracy concerned itself
much more with the welfare and the needs of the people than the limited government of the Anglo-Saxon world either could or was expected to do. Thus,
at an early stage of their movement, the Continental liberals had to face problems which in England and in the United States appeared only much later
and so gradually that there was little occasion for systematic discussion.

The great aim of the movement against arbitrary power was, from the
beginning, the establishment of the rule of law. Not only those interpreters of
English institutions—chief of whom was Montesquieu—represented a government of law as the essence of liberty; even Rousseau, who became the
main source of a different and opposed tradition, felt that "the great problem
in politics, that I compare to squaring the circle in geometry, [is] to find a form
of government which places the law above men."[1] His ambivalent concept

---

of the moment) of the general good, which under cover of morality, gives free reign to political
arbitrariness."—Ed.]

For reference to an earlier publication of the substance of this and the three following chapters see the note at the beginning of chapter 11.

[1] Jean Jacques Rousseau, *Lettre à Mirabeau* [from Rousseau to Mirabeau, Trye, 26 July 1767], in
Œuvres complètes de J. J. Rousseau; Avec des éclairissements et des notes historiques (2nd ed.; 25 vols.; Paris:
Baudouin frères, 1826), vol. 24, p. 175. [The full quotation in French reads: "Le grand problème
en politique, que je compare à celui de la quadrature du cercle en géométrie, et à celui des longi-
tudes en astronomie: *Trouver une forme de gouvernement qui mette la loi au-dessus de l'homme.*"—Ed.] Cf.
also the passage from his *Lettres écrites de la montagne* (no. 8), in *The Political Writings of Jean Jacques
Rousseau*, Charles Edwyn Vaughan, ed., from the Original Manuscripts and Authentic Editions
(2 vols.; Cambridge: Cambridge University Press, 1915), vol. 2, p. 235, quoted above in n. 37,
chap. 11 ["There is no liberty without laws, nor where someone is above the laws; even in the
state of nature, man is free only because of the natural law, which enjoins everyone." (The original French reads: "Il n'y a donc point de liberté sans Loix, ni où quelqu'un est au dessus des
Loix: dans l'état même de nature l'homme n'est libre qu'à la faveur de la Loi naturelle qui commande à tous." "Lettres Écrites de la Montagne," [Huitième Lettre], *Œuvres Complètes*, Bernard
Gagnebin and Marcel Raymond, eds. Bibliothèque de la Pléiade [5 vols.; Paris: Éditions Gallimard, 1964], vol. 3, p. 842).—Ed.], and the discussion in Hans Nef, "Jean Jacques Rousseau
und die Idee des Rechtsstaates," *Schweizer Beiträge zur allgemeinen Geschichte / Études suisse d'histoire
générale / Studi svizzeri di storia generale*, 5 (1947): 167–85. Cesare Bonesana, Marchese di Beccaria,

of the "general will" also led to important elaborations on the conception of the rule of law. It was to be general not only in the sense of being the will of all but also in intent: "When I say that the object of laws is always general, I mean that the law always considers the subject in the round and actions in the abstract and never any individual man or one particular action. For instance, a law may provide that there shall be privileges, but it must not name the persons who are to enjoy them: the law may create several classes of citizens and even designate the qualifications which will give entry into each class; but it must not nominate for admission such and such persons; it may establish a royal government with a hereditary succession, but it must not select the king or nominate a royal family; in a word, anything that relates to a named individual is outside the scope of legislative authority."[2]

2. The revolution of 1789 was therefore universally welcomed, to quote the memorable phrase of the historian Michelet, as "l'avènement de la loi."[3] As

---

Dei Delitti e delle Pene edizione rivista, corretta, e disposta secondo l'ordine della traduzione francese approuato dall'autore coll'aggiunta del commentario alla detta opera di Mr. de Voltaire tradotto da celebre autore [An Essay on Crimes and Punishments] (London [Venice]: Presso la Società dei Filosofi, 1774). First published anonymously in 1764 in Italy, Beccaria notes that the "legislatore" or the "sovrano" can only institute "leggi generali, chi obblighino tutti i membri" ["general laws that are equally applicable to all."—Ed.] and holds that legislation must be interpreted syllogistically. "In ogni delitto si deve fare dal giudice un sillogismo perfetto; la maggiore dev'essere la legge generale, la minore l'azione conforme o no alla legge, la conseguenza la libertà o la pena" (p. 9). ["In every criminal cause the judge should reason syllogistically. The major should be the general law; the minor, the conformity of the action, or its opposition to the laws; the conclusion, liberty, or punishment."—Ed.]

[2] Jean Jacques Rousseau, *Du contrat social* [bk. 2, chap. 6], in *Œuvres complètes de J. J. Rousseau; Avec des éclairissements et des notes historiques* (2nd ed.; 25 vols.; Paris: Baudouin frères, 1826), vol. 6, p. 72. [The original reads: "Quand je dis que l'objet des loix est toujours général, j'entends que la loi considère les sujets en corps et les actions comme abstraites, jamais un homme comme individu ni une action particulière. Ainsi la loi peut bien statuer qu'il y aura des privilèges, mais elle n'en peut donner nommément à personne; la loi peut faire plusieurs Classes de Citoyens, assigner même les qualités qui donneront droit à ces classes, mais elle ne peut nommer tels et tels pour y être admis; elle peut établir un Gouvernement royal et une succession héréditaire, mais elle ne peut élire un roi ni nommer une famille royale; en un mot toute fonction qui se rapporte à un objet individuel n'appartient point à la puissance législative."—Ed.]

[3] [The phrase carries the meaning "the advent of the law."—Ed.] Jules Michelet, *Histoire de la révolution française* (5 vols.; Paris: Chamerot, 1847–50), vol. 1, p. xxiii. See also François-Auguste-Marie-Alexis Mignet, *Histoire de la Révolution française, depuis 1789 jusqu'en 1814* (2 vols.; Paris: Didot, 1824), p. 2. [In writing of the old regime, Mignet notes: "Le peuple ne possèdait aucun droit, la royauté n'avait pas de limites et la France était livrée à la confusion de l'arbitraire ministériel, des régimes particuliers et des privilèges des corps. A cet ordre abusif la révolution en a substitué un plus conforme à la justice et plus approprié à nos temps. Elle a remplacé l'arbitraire par la loi [et] le privilège par l'égalité." ("The people possessed no rights, the Crown was unrestrained, and France had submitted to the confusion of ministerial arbitrariness, perverse administration, and the privileges of authority. To this abusive order the Revolution

A. V. Dicey wrote later: "The Bastille was the outward and visible sign of law-less power. Its fall was felt, and felt truly, to herald in for the rest of Europe that rule of law which already existed in England."[4] The celebrated "Décla-ration des droits de l'homme et du citoyen," with its guaranties of individual rights and the assertion of the principle of the separation of powers, which it represented as an essential part of any constitution, aimed at the establish-ment of a strict reign of law.[5] And the early efforts at constitution-making are full of painstaking and often even pedantic endeavors to spell out the basic conceptions of a government of laws.[6]

However much the Revolution was originally inspired by the ideal of the rule of law,[7] it is doubtful whether it really enhanced its progress. The fact that the ideal of popular sovereignty gained a victory at the same time as the ideal of the rule of law made the latter soon recede into the background. Other aspirations rapidly emerged which were difficult to reconcile with it.[8] Perhaps

---

substituted one more in conformity with justice and more appropriate to our time. It replaced the arbitrary with law and privilege with equality.")—Ed.]

[4] Albert Venn Dicey, *Introduction to the Study of the Law of the Constitution* (1st ed.; London: Macmillan, 1885), p. 177 [Liberty Fund edition, p. 113]. The first edition of Dicey's book was published under the title *Lectures Introductory to the Study of the Law of the Constitution* and appeared in 1885.

[5] See point 16 of the *Déclaration des droits d l'homme et du citoyen*, of August 26, 1789: "Toute société dans laquelle la garantie des droits n'est assurée, ni la séparation des pouvoirs détermi-née, n'a point de Constitution." ["A society in which the observance of the law is not assured, nor the separation of powers defined, has no constitution whatever."—Ed.]

[6] Especially the writings and various constitutional drafts of Jean-Antoine-Nicholas de Caritat, Marquis de Condorcet are concerned with such fundamental distinctions which go right to the heart of the matter as that between true laws in the sense of general rules and mere orders. See particularly the "Projet girondin" in *Archives parlementaires de 1787 à 1860: Recueil complet des débats législatifs et politiques des chambres françaises* [imprimé par ordre du Corps législatif sous la direc-tion de Jérome Mavidal and Émile Laurent, ed. Series 1 (1787–99), vol. 58 (Paris, 1900; vols. 52–70 (September 20, 1792–August 10, 1793)]: 1st series, vol. 58, title 7, sec. 2, arts. 1–7, vol. 58, pp. 617–18; and Condorcet, *Œuvres de Condorcet*, Arthur Condorcet O'Connor and François Arago, eds. (12 vols.; Paris: Firmin Didot frères, 1847–49), vol. 12, pp. 356–58 and 367. [The pages Hayek cites are part of Condorcet's "Exposition des Principes et des Motifs du Plan de Constitution," pp. 335–415.—Ed.] See also the passage quoted without reference by Joseph Hippolyte Jean Baptiste Barthélemy, *Le Rôle du pouvoir exécutif dans les républiques modernes* (Paris: Giard et Brière, 1906), p. 489. See also Alfred Stern, "Condorcet und der girondistische Verfas-sungsentwurf von 1793," *Historische Zeitschrift*, 141 (1930): 479–96.

[7] Cf. Jean Ray, "La Révolution française et la pensée juridique: l'idée du règne de la loi," *Revue philosophique*, 128 (1939): 364–425; and Jean Belin, *La Logique d'une idée-force: l'idée d'utilité sociale et la Révolution française* (7 vols.; Paris: Hermann and Cie., 1939).

[8] Cf. Ray, "La Révolution française," p. 372. It is of some interest that one of the clearest statements of the English conception of liberty occurs in a work published in Geneva in 1792 by Jean-Joseph Mounier in protest against the abuse of the word "liberty" during the French Revo-lution. It bears the significant title *Recherches sur les causes qui ont empêché les François de devenir libres, et sur les moyens qui leur restent pour acquérir la liberté*, and its first chapter, headed "Quels sont les car-

no violent revolution is likely to increase the respect for the law. A Lafayette might appeal to the "reign of law" against the "reign of the clubs," but he would do so in vain. The general effect of "the revolutionary spirit" is probably best described in the words which the chief author of the French civil code used when submitting it to the legislature: "This ardent resolve to sacrifice violently all rights to a revolutionary aim and no longer to admit any other consideration than an indefinable and changeable notion of what the state interest demands."[9]

The decisive factor which made the efforts of the Revolution toward the enhancement of individual liberty so abortive was that it created the belief that, since at last all power had been placed in the hands of the people, all safeguards against the abuse of this power had become unnecessary. It was thought that the arrival of democracy would automatically prevent the arbi-

---

actères de la liberté?" begins: "Les citoyens sont libres, lorsqu'ils ne peuvent être constraints ou empêchés dans leurs actions ou dans le jouissance de leurs biens et de leur industrie, si ce n'est en vertu des loix antérieures, établies pour l'intérêt public, et jamais d'après l'autorité d'aucun homme, quels que soient son rang et son pouvoir.

"Pour qu'un peuple jouisse de la liberté, les lois, qui sont les actes plus essentiels de la puissance souveraine, doivent être dictées par des vues générales, et non par des motifs d'intérêt particulier; elles ne doivent jamais avoir un effet rétroactif, ni se rapporter à [des circonstances passés, ou à] certaines personnes."

["Citizens are free inasmuch as they cannot be constrained or obstructed in their actions or in the enjoyment of their possessions and their industry unless by laws previously enunciated, established in the public interest, and never as a consequence of the authority of one man, regardless of his rank or power.

"For a people blessed with liberty, the laws, which are crucial to the sovereign power, must be determined by the general good and not those of particular interests. They must never have retroactive effect, nor have reference to prior circumstances or to particular persons."—Ed.] Mounier is fully aware that what he is defending is the English concept of liberty, and on the next page he explicitly says: "Sureté, propriété, disent les Anglois, quand ils veulent caractériser la liberté civile ou personele. Cette définition est en effet très exacte: tous les avantages que la liberté procure sont exprimés dans ces deux mots." ["'Security,' 'Property,' say the English, when they wish to characterize personal or civil liberty. This definition is especially accurate; all of the advantages liberty allows are expressed in these two words."—Ed.] On Mounier and generally on the initial influence and gradual receding of the English example in the course of the French Revolution see Gabriel Bonno, *La Constitution britannique devant l'opinion française de Montesquieu à Bonaparte* (Paris: H. Champion, 1931), esp. chap. 6 ["La période révolutionnaire"], pp. 191–272.

[9] Jean Portalis in an address on the occasion of the submission of the third draft of the French civil code to the Council of the Five Hundred in 1796, quoted in P. Antoine Fenet, *Recueil complet des travaux préparatoires du code civil, suivi d'une édition de ce code, à laquelle sont ajoutés les lois, décrets et ordonnances formant le complément de la législation civile de la France, et ou se trouvent indiqués, sous chaque article séparément, tous les passages du recueil qui s'y rattachent* (15 vols.; Paris: Ducessois, 1827), vol. 1, pp. 464–67. [The French reads: "L'esprit révolutionnaire se glisse dans toutes. Nous appelons *esprit révolutionnaire*, le désir exalté de sacrifier violemment tous les droits à un but politique, et de ne plus admettre d'autre considération que celle d'un mystérieux et variable intérêt d'état." Jean Etienne Marie Portalis (1746–1807) drew up the Code Napoléon.—Ed.]

trary use of power. The elected representatives of the people, however, soon proved much more anxious that the executive organs should fully serve their aims than that the individual should be protected against the power of the executive. Though in many respects the French Revolution was inspired by the American, it never achieved what had been the chief result of the other— a constitution which puts limits to the powers of legislation.[10] Moreover, from the beginning of the Revolution, the basic principles of equality before the law were threatened by the new demands of the precursors of modern social-ism, who demanded an *égalité de fait* instead of a mere *égalité de droit*.

3. The one thing which the Revolution did not touch and which, as Tocque-ville has so well shown,[11] survived all the vicissitudes of the following decades was the power of the administrative authorities. Indeed, the extreme interpre-tation of the principle of the separation of powers that had gained acceptance in France served to strengthen the powers of the administration. It was used largely to protect the administrative authorities against any interference by the courts and thus to strengthen, rather than to limit, the power of the state.

The Napoleonic regime which followed the Revolution was necessarily more concerned with increasing the efficiency and power of the administra-tive machine than with securing the liberty of the individual. Against this ten-dency, liberty under the law, which once more became the watchword dur-

---

[10] For an account of how France failed ever to achieve a real constitution in the American sense and how this gradually led to a decline of the rule of law see Louis Auguste Paul Rougier, *La France à la recherche d'une constitution* (Paris: Recueil Sirey, 1952).

[11] In addition to Alexis de Tocqueville, *L'ancien régime* (1856), Melville Watson Patterson, trans. (Oxford: B. Blackwell, 1952), bk. 2, particularly chap. 2 ["Administrative Centralization an institution of the 'Old Order' and not, as some have said, the Work of the Revolution and the Empire" (pp. 37–46)] and chap. 4 ["Administrative Justice and Indemnity of Officials were Institutions of the 'Old Order' of Society" (pp. 58–62)], see particularly the *Recollections of Alexis de Tocqueville*, Alexander Teixeira de Mattos, trans. (London: H. Henry, 1896), p. 238: "When, therefore, people assert that nothing is safe from revolutions, I tell them they are wrong, and that centralization is one of those things. In France there is only one thing we can't set up: that is, a free government; and only one institution we can't destroy: that is, centralization. How could it ever perish? The enemies of government love it, and those who govern cherish it. The latter perceive, it is true, from time to time that it exposes them to sudden and irremediable disasters; but this does not disgust them with it. The pleasure it procures them of interfering with every one and holding everything in their hands atones to them for its dangers." ["Lors donc qu'on prétend qu'il n'y a rien parmi nous qui soit à l'abri des révolutions, je dis qu'on trompe, et que la centralisation s'y trouve. En France, il n'y a guère qu'une seule chose qu'on ne puisse faire: c'est un gouvernement libre, et qu'une seule institution qu'on ne puisse détruire: la centralisa-tion. Comment pourrait-elle périr? Les ennemis des gouvernements l'aiment et les gouvernants la chérissent. Ceux-ci s'aperçoivent, il est vrai, de temps à autre, qu'elle les expose à des désastres soudains et irrémédiables, mais cela ne les en dégoûte point. Le plaisir qu'elle leur procure de se mêler de tout et de tenir chacun dans leurs mains leur fait supporter ses périls." *Souvenirs d'Alexis de Tocqueville*, Luc Monnier, ed. (nouv. ed. Paris: Gallimard, 1942), pp.163–64.—Ed.]

ing the short interval of the July Monarchy, could make little headway.[12] The republic found little occasion to make any systematic attempts to protect the individual against the arbitrary power of the executive. It was, in fact, largely the situation which prevailed in France during the greater part of the nineteenth century that gave "administrative law" the bad name it has had so long in the Anglo-Saxon world.

It is true that there gradually evolved within the administrative machine a new power which increasingly assumed the function of limiting the discretionary powers of administrative agencies. The Conseil d'État, originally created merely to assure that the intentions of the legislature were carried out faithfully, has in modern times developed in a way which, as Anglo-Saxon students have recently discovered with some surprise,[13] gives the citizen more protection against discretionary action by administrative authorities than is available in contemporary England. These French developments have attracted much more attention than the similar evolution that took place in Germany at the same time. Here the continuance of monarchic institutions never allowed a naïve confidence in the automatic efficacy of democratic control to cloud the issue. Systematic discussion of the problems therefore produced an elaborate theory of the control of administration which, though its practi-

---

[12] King Louis Philippe himself is reported to have said in a speech to the National Guard [quoted in an essay by Hugues Félicité Robert de Lamennais in *L'Avenir* of May 23, 1831, reprinted in *Troisièmes mélanges* (Paris: P. Daubrée et Cailleux,1835), p. 266]: "La liberté ne consiste que dans le règne des lois. Que chacun ne puisse pas être tenu de faire autre chose que ce que la loi exige de lui, et qu'il puisse faire tout ce que la loi n'interdit pas, telle est la liberté: C'est vouloir la détruire que de vouloir autre chose." ["Liberty consists solely in the rule of law. That no one may be held to do other than what the law demands of him and that he may act in any manner not prohibited by law, therein lies one's liberty. To desire other than this is tantamount to destroying it."—Ed.] A fuller account of French developments during this period would have to give considerable space to some of the leading political thinkers and statesmen of the period, such as Benjamin Constant, Guizot, and the group of "doctrinaires," who developed a theory of *garantisme*, a system of checks designed to protect the rights of the individual against the encroachment of the state. On them, see Guido de Ruggiero, *The History of European Liberalism*, Robin George Collinwood, trans. (London: Oxford University Press, 1927); Luis Díez el Corral, *El Liberalismo doctrinario* (Madrid: Instituto de estudios políticos, 1945). On the doctrinal development of French administrative law and jurisdiction during the period compare particularly Achille-Léon-Victor, Duc de Broglie, "De la jurisdiction administrative," in *Écrits et discours* (3 vols.; Paris: Didier et cie, 1863), vol. 1, pp. 249–331; and Louis-Marie de Lahaye, Vicomte de Cormenin, *Questions de droit administratif* (2 vols.; Paris: M. Ridler, 1822). Regarding Tocqueville's intense interest in bringing bureaucratic decisions under judicial control as a essential condition for liberty, see especially Jack Lively, *The Social and Political Thought of Alexis de Tocqueville* (Oxford: Clarendon Press, 1962), pp. 166–82.

[13] See Bernard Schwartz, *French Administrative Law and the Common-Law World* (New York: New York University Press, 1954); Charles John Hamson, *Executive Discretion and Judicial Control: An Aspect of the French Conseil d'État* (London: Stevens, 1954); and Marguerite A. Sieghart, *Government by Decree* (London: Stevens, 1950).

cal political influence was of short duration, profoundly affected Continental legal thought.[14] And as it was against this German form of the rule of law that the new legal theories were mainly developed which have since conquered the world and everywhere undermined the rule of law, it is important to know a little more about it.

4. In view of the reputation which Prussia acquired in the nineteenth century, it may surprise the reader to learn that the beginning of the German movement for a government of law is to be found in that country.[15] In some

[14] On the importance of the German theoretical developments cf. Paul Alexéef, "L'État— le droit—et le pouvoir discrétionnaire des autorités publiques," *Revue internationale de la théorie du droit*, 3 (1928–29): 216; Charles Howard McIlwain, *Constitutionalism and the Changing World: Collected Papers* (Cambridge: Cambridge University Press, 1939), p. 270; and Léon Duguit, *Manuel de droit constitutionnel, théorie générale de l'état, le droit de l'état, les libertés publiques, organisation politique* (3rd ed.; Paris: Fontenoing and Cie., 1918), which is a good example of how one of the Continental treatises on constitutional law most widely known in the Anglo-Saxon world derives its argument at least as much from German as from French predecessors.

[15] See esp. Hermann Conrad, *Rechtsstaatliche Bestrebungen im Absolutismus Preußens und Österreichs am Ende des 18. Jahrhunderts* [Arbeitsgemeinschaft für Forschung des Landes Nordrhein-Westfalen, bk. 95] (Cologne: Westdeutscher Verlag, 1961), and the earlier studies by the same author mentioned there. Cf. the perceptive observation in Abbott Lawrence Lowell, *Governments and Parties in Continental Europe* (2 vols.; New York: Houghton, Mifflin, 1896), vol. 2, p. 86: "In Prussia, the bureaucracy was so ordered as to furnish a better protection of individual rights and a firmer maintenance of law. But this broke down with the spread of French ideas after 1848, when the antagonistic interests in the state, taking advantage of the parliamentary system, abused the administrative power and introduced a veritable party tyranny." [This quotation does not seem to appear in Lowell's book, although he does discuss the relationship of the Prussian bureaucracy at some length. At one point he writes: "Notwithstanding the excellent organization of the bureaucracy, its enormous power could hardly be endured without restraint exercised by the administrative courts. Before the present century the elaborate system of administrative appeals, and the permanence of traditions that prevailed in the bureaucracy, many of whom were learned in the law, preserved the great uniformity in the administration, and furnished a real guarantee against arbitrary conduct on the part of officials. But with the spread of new ideas after the French Revolution, a marked change took place. The sharp distinction drawn between justice and administration deprived administrative procedure of its judicial character, and made the decisions of the officials turn less on law and more on expediency." (vol. 1, p. 294); and again: "The present constitution of Prussia (1896), which dates from January 31, 1850, was granted by the King after the revolutionary movement of 1848 had begun to subside, and is far less democratic than the Liberals would have liked. In some ways it is even less liberal than the text would lead one to suppose; for although it contains quite an elaborate bill of rights, Professor Gneist spoke of it as a *lex imperfecta*, owing to the absence of machinery for giving effect to its provisions. It purports, for example, to guarantee the liberty of instruction; but as no statute has been passed to carry this out, the previous laws remain in force, whereby no school can be opened without permission from the government. Again, it declares that the right to assemble without arms, except in the open air, shall be free; but in fact notice of every meeting held to discuss public affairs must be given to the police, who have a right to be present, and a very extensive power of breaking it up. The result of such a state of things is that neither the parliament nor the citizens have sufficient means of defending their rights; and although the recent increase

respects, however, the rule of enlightened despotism of the eighteenth century had been surprisingly modern there—indeed, one might say almost liberal, so far as legal and administrative principles were concerned. It was by no means a meaningless assertion when Frederick II described himself as the first servant of the state.[16] The tradition, deriving mainly from the great theorists of the law of nature and partly from Western sources, during the later part of the eighteenth century was greatly strengthened by the influence of the moral and legal theories of the philosopher Immanuel Kant.

German writers usually place Kant's theories at the beginning of their accounts of the movement toward the *Rechtsstaat*. Though this probably exaggerates the originality of his legal philosophy,[17] he undoubtedly gave those ideas the form in which they exerted the greatest influence in Germany. His chief contribution is indeed a general theory of morals which made the principle of the rule of law appear as a special application of a more general principle. His celebrated "categorical imperative," the rule that man should always "act only on that maxim whereby thou canst at the same time will that

---

of local self-government and the establishment of administrative justice have done something towards remedying this defect, personal and political liberty are still far from enjoying the same protection as in Anglo-Saxon countries. The constitution was clearly not intended as a restraint on legislation, for it can be changed by simple majority vote of both chambers, sanctioned by the King" (vol. 1, pp. 286–87).—Ed.]

[16] The conception of the power of law that prevailed in eighteenth-century Prussia is well illustrated by an anecdote known to every German child. Frederick II is said to have been annoyed by an old windmill standing close to his palace of Sans-Souci, impairing the view, and, after various unsuccessful attempts at buying it from the owner, is said to have threatened him with eviction; to which the miller is supposed to have answered: "We still have courts of justice in Prussia" ("Es gibt noch ein Kammergericht in Berlin!" is the phrase usually quoted). For the facts, or rather absence of factual basis in the legend, see Reinhold Koser, *Geschichte Friedrichs des Großen* (4th ed.; 4 vols.; Stuttgart: Cotta, 1912–14), vol. 3, pp. 413ff. The story suggests limits to kingly power which at the time probably existed in no other country on the Continent and which I am not sure apply today to the heads of democratic states: a hint to their town planners would quickly lead to the forcible removal of such an eyesore—although, of course, solely in the public interest and not to please anybody's whim! [The actual quote, as Koser has it, is "Es gibt noch Richter in Berlin!"—Ed.]

[17] For Immanuel Kant's legal philosophy see particularly his *Die Metaphysik der Sitten* (1785). Vol. 1: *Anfangsgründe der Rechtslehre*, part 2: "Das Staatsrecht," secs. 45–49. See also Kant's two essays "Über den Gemeinspruch: Das mag in der Theorie richtig sein, taugt aber nicht für die Praxis" (1793) and "Zum ewigen Frieden" (1795). [For an English translation of these works, see: Immanuel Kant, *Practical Philosophy*, Mary J. Gregory, ed. and trans. (Cambridge: Cambridge University Press, 1999), which contains the *Groundwork of the Metaphysics of Morals* (*Grundlegung zur Metaphysik der Sitten*) and the two essays to which Hayek refers: (1) "On the Common Saying: That May Be Correct in Theory, but It Is of No Use in Practice" (1793) and (2) "Toward Perpetual Peace" (1795).—Ed.] Cf. Werner Haensel, *Kants Lehre von Widerstandsrecht. Ein Beitrag zur Systematik der Kantischen Rechtsphilosophie* [Kant-Studien No. 60] (Berlin: Pan-Verlag Rolf Heise, 1926), and Friedrich Darmstädter, *Die Grenzen der Wirksamkeit des Rechtsstaates. Eine Untersuchung zur gegenwärtigen Krise des liberalen Staatsgedankens* (Heidelberg: C. Winter, 1930).

it should become universal law,"[18] is in fact an extension to the general field of ethics of the basic idea underlying the rule of law. It provides, as does the rule of law, merely one criterion to which particular rules must conform in order to be just.[19] But in emphasizing the necessity of the general and abstract character of all rules if such rules are to guide a free individual, the conception proved of the greatest importance in preparing the ground for the legal developments.

This is not the place for a full treatment of the influence of Kantian philosophy on constitutional developments.[20] We shall mention here merely the

[18] Immanuel Kant, *Fundamental Principles of Morals*, A. D. Lindsay, trans., p. 421. [The "Exhaustive Bibliography of English Translations of Kant" lists no translation by Lindsay of the *Grundlegung zur Metaphysik der Sitten* (variously translated as the *Fundamental Principles of the Metaphysics of Morals*, the *Foundations of the Metaphysics of Morals*, and the *Groundwork of the Metaphysics of Morals*). The standard translation, and the one to which Hayek is probably referring, is by Thomas Kingsmill Abbott made in 1873 and reprinted numerous times. Abbott's translation of the categorical imperative reads: "I am never to act otherwise than so that I could also will that my maxim should become a universal law." (*Kant's Theory of Ethics or Practical Philosophy: Comprising: 1. Fundamental Principles of the Metaphysics of Morals; 2. Dialectic and Methodology of Practical Reason; 3. On the Radical Evil in Human Nature*, Thomas Kingsmill Abbott, trans. [4th rev. ed.; London: Longmans, Green, Reader, and Dyer, 1889], p. 18.) The categorical imperative is further discussed in Kant's *Kritik der praktischen Vernunft* (1788), translated by Thomas Kingmill Abbott in 1873 as the *Critical Examination of Practical Reason* and published as part 2 of *Kant's Theory of Ethics or Practical Philosophy* (pp. 87–262).—Ed.]

It is in agreement with this transfer of the concept of the rule of law to the field of morals when for Kant the conception of freedom as depending only on the law becomes "independence of anything other than the moral law alone." [The full quotation reads: "We should also see not merely the possibility, but even the necessity, of the moral law as the supreme law of rational beings, to whom we attribute freedom of causality of their will; because both concepts are so inseparably united that we might define practical freedom as independence of the will on anything but the moral law." The German reads: "Wenn man die Möglichkeit der Freiheit einer wirkenden Ursache einsähe, man auch nicht etwa bloß die Möglichkeit, sondern gar die Notwendigkeit des moralischen Gesetzes als obersten praktischen Gesetzes vernünftiger Wesen, denen man Freiheit der Causalität ihres Willens beilegt, einsehen würde: weil beide Begriffe so unzertrennlich sind, daß man praktische Freiheit auch durch Unabhängigkeit des Willens von jedem anderen, ausser allein dem moralischen Gesetze, definieren könnte." (*Kritik der praktischen Vernunft*, in *Kants Werke* [Akademie Textausgabe; 9 vols.; Berlin: Walter de Gruyter, 1968], vol. 5, p. 93).—Ed.]

[19] Cf. Karl Menger, *Moral, Wille und Weltgestaltung. Grundlegung zur Logik der Sitten* (Vienna: J. Springer, 1934), pp.13–17.

[20] A fuller account would have to consider particularly the early work of the philosopher Johann Gottlieb Fichte, *Grundlage des Naturrechts nach Principien der Wissenschaftslehre* (1796). Vol. 3 of *Sämmtliche Werke*, Immanuel Hermann Fichte, ed. (8 vols.; Berlin: Veit, 1845), and the writings of the poet Friedrich Schiller [See his *Werke und Briefe*, Klaus Harro Hilzinger, ed. (12 vols.; Frankfurt: Deutscher Klassiker Verlag, 1988–2004).] who did probably as much as any man to spread liberal ideas in Germany. See Erich Eyck, "Freiheit und Demokratie, 1848–1948," in Accademia Nazionale dei Lincei (Fondazione Alessandro Volta), *Convegno di scienze morali, storiche e filologiche. 4–10 ottobre 1948* [Tema: Il 1848 Nella Storia d'Europa] (Rome: Accademia Nazionale dei Lincei, 1949), p. 31. On these and the other German classics see Gustav Falter, *Staatsideale unserer Klassiker* (Leipzig:

extraordinary essay of the young Wilhelm von Humboldt on *The Sphere and Duties of Government*,[21] which, in expounding the Kantian view, not only gave currency to the much used phrase "the certainty of legal freedom" but in some respects also became the prototype for an extreme position; that is, he not merely limited all the coercive action of the state to the execution of previously announced general laws but represented the enforcement of the law as the *only* legitimate function of the state. This is not necessarily implied in the conception of individual liberty, which leaves open the question of what other non-coercive functions the state may undertake. It was due mainly to Humboldt's influence that these different conceptions were frequently confused by the later advocates of the *Rechtsstaat*.

5. Of the legal developments in the Prussia of the eighteenth century, two became so important later that we must look at them more closely. One is the effective initiation by Frederick II, through his civil code of 1751,[22] of that movement for the codification of all the laws which spread rapidly and achieved its best-known results in the Napoleonic codes of 1800–1810. This whole movement must be regarded as one of the most important aspects of the endeavor on the Continent to establish the rule of law, for it determined to a large extent both its general character and the general direction of the advances that were made, at least in theory, beyond the stage reached in the common-law countries.

The possession of even the most perfectly drawn-up legal code does not, of course, insure that certainty which the rule of law demands; and it therefore provides no substitute for a deeply rooted tradition. This, however, should

---

C. L. Hirschfeld, 1911), and Wilhelm Metzger, *Gesellschaft, Recht und Staat in der Ethik des deutschen Idealismus mit einer Einleitung: Prolegomena zu einer Theorie und Geschichte der sozialen Werte* (Heidelberg: C. Winter, 1917). I am, however, under the impression that nobody seems to recognize the central role played by Christian Garve, who was an authority on Hume, Smith, Ferguson, Paley, and Burke, who translated Aristotle and Cicero, was a friend of Schiller, and exchanged letters with Kant and Gentz.

[21] Wilhelm von Humboldt, *Ideen zu einem Versuch, die Gränzen der Wirksamkeit des Staats zu bestimmen* (Breslau: E. Trewendt, 1851). [The English translation was published under the title *The Sphere and Duties of Government*, Joseph Coulthard, Jr., trans. (London: John Chapman, 1854).—Ed.] Only part of this work was published soon after its composition in 1792, and the whole appeared only in the posthumous edition quoted, rapidly followed by an English translation, when it profoundly affected not only John Stuart Mill but also Édouard Laboulaye in France. See the latter's *L'État et ses limites: suivi d'essais politiques* (Paris: Charpentier, 1863). [The phrase used by Humboldt is "Gewißheit der gesetzmäßigen Freiheit." See chap. 9, "On Security," in *Über die Grenzen der Wirksamkeit des Staates* (Nuremberg: Verlag Hans Carl, 1946), p. 132. There is a Liberty Fund edition of this essay published under the title *The Limits of State Action*.—Ed.]

[22] It had been preceded by a Swedish code in 1734 and an even earlier Danish code. [*The Encyclopedia Britannica* notes that the Prussian code (*Code Frédéric*), published by Frederick the Great in 1751, "was intended to take the place of Roman, common Saxon, and other foreign subsidiary laws and statutes." Earlier, in 1683, Christian V promulgated a civil code for Denmark, which was later extended to Norway and Iceland. In 1734, the Swedish Parliament approved a new enactment for the Realm of Sweden, actually a collection of codes.—Ed.]

not obscure the fact that there seems to exist at least a prima facie conflict between the ideal of the rule of law and a system of case law. The extent to which under an established system of case law the judge actually creates law may not be greater than under a system of codified law. But the explicit recognition that jurisdiction as well as legislation is the source of law, though in accord with the evolutionary theory underlying the British tradition, tends to obscure the distinction between the creation and the application of law. And it is a question whether the much praised flexibility of the common law, which has been favorable to the evolution of the rule of law so long as that was the accepted political ideal, may not also mean less resistance to the tendencies undermining it, once that vigilance which is needed to keep liberty alive disappears.

At least there can be no doubt that the efforts at codification led to the explicit formulation of some of the general principles underlying the rule of law. The most important event of this kind was the formal recognition of the principle "nullum crimen, nulla poena sine lege,"[23] which was first incorporated into the Austrian penal code of 1787[24] and, after its inclusion in the French Declaration of the Rights of Man, was embodied in the majority of Continental codes.

The most distinctive contribution of eighteenth-century Prussia to the realization of the rule of law lay, however, in the field of the control of public administration. While in France the literal application of the ideal of the separation of powers had led to an exemption of administrative action from judicial control, the Prussian development proceeded in the opposite direction. The guiding ideal which profoundly affected the liberal movement of the nineteenth century was that all exercise of administrative power over the person or property of the citizen should be made subject to judicial review. The most far-reaching experiment in this direction—a law of 1797 which applied

[23] The principle seems to have been first stated in this form by Paul Johann Anselm Feuerbach, *Lehrbuch des gemeinen in Deutschland gültigen peinlichen Rechts* (Giessen: G. H. Heyer, 1801), p. 20. But see chap. 11, n. 78, above.

[24] "Art. 8: "La loi ne doit établir que des peines strictement et évidemment nécessaire, et nul ne peut être puni qu'en vertu d'une loi établie et promulguée antérieurement au délit, et légalement appliquée." [Hayek is here quoting not the Austrian criminal code of 1787 but art. 8 of the Declaration of the Rights of Man and of the Citizen of 1789. It reads: "The law shall provide for such punishments only as are strictly and obviously necessary, and no one shall suffer punishment except it be legally inflicted in virtue of a law passed and promulgated before the commission of the offense." The Austrian Criminal Code of 1787, promulgated by the Emperor Joseph II and known as the Josephine Code, provides that "no action contrary to law, shall be considered as criminal, but such as shall have been determined by the present criminal code" and that "punishment follows a criminal offense discovered and proved. It cannot be decreed by a judge, appointed to discharge the functions of criminal jurisdiction" (Articles 1 and 10). See *The Emperor's New Code of Criminal Laws, Published at Vienna, the 15th of January 1787*, translated from the German by an officer (London: Printed for G. G. J. And J. Robinson, 1787), sec. 1, p. 1; sec. 10, p. 6.—Ed.]

only to the new eastern provinces of Prussia but was conceived as a model to be generally followed—went so far as to subject all disputes between the administrative authorities and private citizens to the jurisdiction of the ordinary courts.[25] This was to provide one of the chief prototypes in the discussion on the *Rechtsstaat* during the next eighty years.

6. It was on this basis that in the early part of the nineteenth century the theoretical conception of the state of law, the *Rechtsstaat*, was systematically developed[26] and became, together with the ideal of constitutionalism, the

[25] Cf. Edgar Loening, *Gerichte und Verwaltungsbehörden in Brandenburg-Preußen: Ein Beitrag zur preußischen Rechts- und Verfassungsgeschichte* (Halle: Waisenhaus, 1914), and particularly the extensive review article on this work by Otto Hintze, "Preußens Entwicklung zum *Rechtsstaat*," in *Geist und Epochen der preußichen Geschichte* (Leipzig: Koehler and Amelang, 1943) [chap. 4], pp.105–71.

[26] We cannot enter here into a further examination of the earlier history of this German concept and especially of the interesting question of how far it may have derived from Jean Bodin's conception of a "droit gouvernement." On the more specific German sources see Otto Friedrich von Gierke, *Johannes Althusius und die Entwicklung der naturrechtlichen Staatstheorien: zugleich ein Beitrag zur Geschichte der Rechtssystematik* (2nd ed.; Breslau: W. Koebner, 1880). According to Carl Schmitt, "Was bedeutet der Streit um den, *Rechtsstaat?*" *Zeitschrift für die gesamte Staatswissenschaft*, 95 (1935): 190, the term *Rechtsstaat* appears for the first time in Adam Heinrich Müller (*Elemente der Staatskunst: Öffentliche Vorlesungen vor Sr. Durchlaucht dem Prinzen Bernhard von Sachsen-Weimar und einer Versammlung von Staatsmännern und Diplomaten, im Winter von 1808 auf 1809, zu Dresden, gehalten* [Berlin: Sander, 1809]) with reference to "a truly organic legal system." Later, however, this sense was seldom meant.

The word *Rechtsstaat* seems to appear for the first time, but hardly yet with its later meaning, in Karl Teodor Welcker, *Die letzten Gründe von Recht, Staat und Strafe: Philosophisch und nach den Gesetzen der merkwürdigsten Völker rechtshistorisch entwickelt* (Giessen: Heyer, 1813), where three types of government are distinguished: despotism, theocracy, and *Rechtsstaat*. On the history of the conception see Reimund Asanger, *Beiträge zur Lehre vom Rechtsstaat im 19. Jahrhundert* (unpublished doctoral dissertation; Westfälische Wilhelms-Universität, Münster, 1938). The best account of the role of the ideal in the German liberal movement is to be found in Franz Schnabel, *Deutsche Geschichte im neunzehnten Jahrhundert* (4 vols.; Freiburg im Breisgau: Herder, 1933–59), vol. 2, pp. 99–109. See also Thomas Ellwein, *Das Erbe der Monarchie in der deutschen Staatskrise: Zur Geschichte des Verfassungsstaates in Deutschland* (Munich: Isar, 1954).

It is probably no accident that the beginning of the theoretical movement that led to the development of the ideal of the *Rechtsstaat* came from Hanover, which, through its kings, had had more contact with England than the rest of Germany. See Franz Rosin, *Gesetz und Verordnung: Gesetz und Verordnung nach badischem Staatsrecht* (Freiburger Abhandlungen aus dem Gebiet des öffentlichen Rechts, Heft 18, dissertation; Karlsruhe, G. Braun, 1911), p. 30–47, who refers particularly to Justi and Justus Möser and shows how Freiherr vom Stein founded this tradition. See also Hermann Christern, *Friedrich Christoph Dahlmanns politische Entwicklung bis 1848: ein Beitrag zur Geschichte des deutschen Liberalismus* (Leipzig: Haessel, 1921). During the later part of the eighteenth century there appeared here a group of distinguished political theorists who built on the English Whig tradition; among them E. Brandes, A. W. Rehberg, and later F. C. Dahlmann were the most important in spreading English constitutional ideas in Germany. [Ernest Brandes (1768–1810), August Wilhelm Rehberg (1757–1836), and Frederick C. Dahlmann (1785–1860), known as Hanoverian Whigs, who traced the origins of English constitutionalism to Anglo-Saxon institutions and rejected the notion that Norman political notions served as the basis of English liberty.—Ed.] See on these men Hermann Christern, *Deutscher Ständestaat und englischer Parlamentarismus am Ende des 18. Jahrhunderts* (Munich: C. H. Beck'sche Verlagsbuchhandlung, 1939). For

main goal of the new liberal movement.[27] Whether it was mainly because, by
the time the German movement had started, the American precedent was

our present purposes the most important figure of the group is, however, Günther Heinrich
von Berg, whose work was quoted at the beginning of this chapter (see esp. the *Handbuch*, vol. 1,
pp. 158–60 and vol. 2, pp. 1–4 and 12–17). The influence of his work is described in Gustav
Marchet, *Studien über die Entwickelung der Verwaltungslehre in Deutschland von der zweiten Hälfte des 17. bis
zum Ende des 18. Jahrhunderts* (Munich: R. Oldenbourg, 1885), pp. 419–28.

The scholar who later did most to propagate the theory of the *Rechtsstaat*, Robert von Mohl,
had been a close student of the American Constitution; see his *Das Bundes-Staatsrecht der Vereinigten
Staaten von Nord-Amerika* (Stuttgart: J. G. Cotta, 1824), which appears to have earned him a considerable reputation in the United States and led to his being asked to review Judge Story's *Commentaries* ("German Criticism of Mr. Justice Story's *Commentaries on the Constitution of the United
States*," in the *American Jurist and Law Magazine*, 14 (October 1835): 330–45). The main works in
which he elaborated the theory of the *Rechtsstaat* include his *Staatsrecht des Königreiches Württem-
berg* (2 vols.; Tübingen: H. Laupp, 1829–31), in which he embraces Welcker's distinction between
despotism, theocracy, and a constitutional state, while adding a fourth type, the patriarchal state (see vol.
1, pp. 6–9), in the course of which he gives what is probably the most accurate definition of the constitutional state found in German literature, a state in which "the citizen is apprised of any changes in the
purpose or conditions of every law not by virtue of the arbitrary commands of a higher human or spiritual
power, but only through laws equally applicable to all (p. 182). See also Mohl's *Das Recht der Steuerverwilligung nach den Grundsätzen der württembergischen Verfassung, mit Rücksicht auf entgegenstehende
Bestimmungen des deutschen Bundes* (Stuttgart: Liesching, 1836), which contains one of the earliest dif-
ferentiations between substantive and formal law. [The author of this work is, in fact, Paul Achatius Pfizer.—Ed.] Further, see Mohl's *Die Polizei-Wissenschaft nach den Grundsätzen des Rechtsstaates*
(3 vols.; Tübingen: Laupp, 1832–34) and *Die Geschichte und Literatur der Staatswissenschaften* (3 vols.;
Erlangen: Ferdinand Enke, 1855–58). The best-known formulation of the conception of the
Rechtsstaat as it ultimately emerged is that by one of the conservative theorists of the period,
Friedrich Julius Stahl. In *Die Philosophie des Rechts*. Vol. 2: *Rechts- und Staatslehre*, part 2 (1837) (5th
ed.; 2 vols. in 3; Tübingen and Leipzig: J. C. B. Mohr, 1878), pp. 137–38), he defines it as follows (p. 352): "The State should be a State of law, this is the watchword and, in truth, also the
tendency of recent times. It should exactly and irrevocably determine and secure the *directions*
and the *limits* of its activity and the free sphere of the citizen, and not enforce on its own behalf
or directly any moral ideas beyond the sphere of law. This is the conception of the *Rechtsstaat*
and not that the state should confine itself to administering the law and pursue no administrative purpose or *only* protect the rights of the individual. It says nothing about the *content* or *aim*
of the state but defines only the manner and method of achieving them." [The original German reads: "Der Staat soll *Rechtsstaat* seyn, das ist die Losung und ist auch in Wahrheit der Ent-
wickelungstrieb der neueren Zeit. Er soll die Bahnen und Gränzen seiner Wirksamkeit wie die
freie Sphäre seiner Bürger in der Weise des Rechts genau bestimmen und unverbrüchlich sichern und soll die sittlichen Ideen von Staats wegen also direkt, nicht weiter verwirklichen (erz-
wingen), als es der Rechtssphäre angehört, d.i. nur bis zur nothwendigsten Umzäunung. Dieß
ist der Begriff des *Rechtsstaates*, nicht etwa daß der Staat bloß die Rechtsordnung handhabe
ohne administrative Zwecke, oder vollends bloß die Rechte der Einzelnen schütze, er bedeutet überhaupt nicht Ziel und Inhalt des Staates, sondern nur Art und Charakter, dieselben zu
verwirklichen."—Ed.] (The last sentences are aimed at the extreme position represented, for example, by Wilhelm von Humboldt.)

[27] Cf., e.g., Paul Achatius Pfizer, "Liberal, Liberalismus," *Staats-Lexicon oder Enzyklopädie der
Staatswissenschaften*, Karl Wenceslaus von Rotteck and Karl Theodor Welcker, eds. (new ed.;
12 vols.; Altona: J. F. Hammerich, 1845–48), vol. 8, p. 534. "Noch mächtiger und unbesieg-

already better known and understood than it had been at the time of the French Revolution, or because the German development proceeded within the framework of a constitutional monarchy rather than that of a republic and was therefore less subject to the illusion that the problems would be automatically solved by the advent of democracy, it was here that the limitation of all government by a constitution, and particularly the limitation of all administrative activity by law enforceable by courts, became the central aim of the liberal movement.

Much of the argument of the German theorists of the time was indeed explicitly directed against "administrative jurisdiction" in the sense in which this term was still accepted in France—that is, against the quasi-judicial bodies inside the administrative machinery which were primarily intended to watch over the execution of the law rather than to protect the liberty of the individual. The doctrine, as one of the chief justices of a south German state expressed it, that "whenever a question arises whether any private rights are well founded or have been violated by official action, the matter must be decided by ordinary courts,"[28] enjoyed fairly rapid progress. When the Frankfort parliament of 1848 attempted to draft a constitution for all Germany, it inserted into it a clause that all "administrative justice" (as then understood) was to cease, and all violations of private rights were to be adjudicated by courts of justice.[29]

---

barer muss aber der Liberalismus dann erscheinen, wenn man sich überzeugt, dass er nichts Anderes ist als der auf einer gewissen Stufe menschlicher Entwickelung nothwendige Übergang des Naturstaats in den *Rechtsstaat.*" ["Liberalism must seem even more powerful, more invincible, when one is convinced that it constitutes nothing more than the transition, required at a particular stage of human history, from the state of nature to a state of law."—Ed.]

[28] Ludwig Minnigerode, *Beitrag zur Beanwortung der Frage: Was ist Justiz- und was ist Administrativ-Sache?* (Darmstadt: Meyer, 1835), p. 8. [The German reads: "So oft Streit entsteht oder die Frage ist, ob der vorkommende Fall unter ein vorhandenes allgemeines oder spezielles Gesetz subsumiert werden müsse oder nicht,—muß die Justizbehörde entscheiden."—Ed.] See also Paul Achatius Pfizer's work *Das Recht der Steuerverwilligung,* where, as remarked in n. 27, he points out of the difference between material and formal laws.

[29] It deserves notice that there was a significant difference of opinion between south Germany, where French influences predominated, and north Germany, where a combination of old Germanic tradition and the influence of the theorists of the law of nature and of the English example seems to have been stronger. In particular, the group of south German lawyers who, in the political encyclopedia quoted above (n. 27), provided the most influential handbook of the liberal movement, were distinctly more influenced by Frenchmen like Benjamin Constant and François Pierre Guillaume Guizot than by any other source. On the importance of the *Staatslexikon* see Hans Zehntner, *Das Staatslexicon von Rotteck und Welcker: eine Studie zur Geschichte des deutschen Frühliberalismus* (List Studien, No. 3; Jena: G. Fischer, 1924), and on the predominantly French influences on south German liberalism see Artur Fickert, *Montesquieus und Rousseaus Einfluss auf den vormärzlichen Liberalismus Badens* (Leipziger historische Abhandlungen, vol. 37; Leipzig: Quelle und Meyer, 1914). Cf. Theodor Wilhelm, *Die englische Verfassung und der vormärzliche deutsche Liberalismus: eine Darstellung und Kritik des Verfassungsbildes der liberalen Führer* (Stuttgart: W. Kohlham-

The hope, however, that the achievement of constitutional monarchy by the individual German states would effectively realize the ideal of the rule of law was soon disappointed. The new constitutions did little in that direction, and it was soon discovered that, though "the constitution had been given, the *Rechtsstaat* proclaimed, in fact the police state continued. Who was to be the guardian of public law and its individualistic principle of fundamental rights? Nobody else than that very administration against whose drive for expansion and activity those fundamental laws had been meant to protect."[30] It was, in fact, during the next twenty years that Prussia acquired the reputation of a police state, that in the Prussian parliament the great battles over the principle of the *Rechtsstaat* had to be fought,[31] and that the final solution of the problem took form. For some time the ideal remained, at least in northern Germany, of intrusting the control of the lawfulness of the acts of administration to the ordinary courts. This conception of the *Rechtsstaat*, usually referred to later as "justicialism,"[32] was soon to be superseded by a different conception, advanced mainly by a student of English administrative practice, Rudolf von Gneist.[33]

7. There are two different reasons why it may be contended that ordinary jurisdiction and the judicial control of administrative action should be kept separate. Though both considerations contributed to the ultimate establishment of a system of administrative courts in Germany and though they are

---

mer, 1928). The difference in the tradition manifested itself later in the fact that, while in Prussia judicial review was extended, at least in principle, to questions on which the administrative agencies possessed discretionary powers, in south Germany such questions were explicitly excluded from judicial review.

[30] Gerhard Anschütz, "Verwaltungsrecht," in *Systematische Rechtswissenschaft*, Rudolf Stammler, ed. (Kultur der Gegenwart, vol. 2, no. 7; Leipzig and Berlin: B. G. Taeubner, 1906), p. 352. [The German reads: "Die Verfassung war gegeben, der *Rechtsstaat* proklamiert, der Polizeistaat dauerte fort. Denn wer war der Hüter des neuen öffentlichen Rechtes, seiner individualistischen Grundsätze und Grundrechte? Niemand anderes als die Verwaltung selbst, eben sie, gegen deren Expansions- und Betätigungsdrang jene Grundsätze gegeben, jene Grundrechte verliehen worden waren."—Ed.]

[31] See Eduard Lasker, "Polizeigewalt und Rechtsschutz in Preußen," *Deutsche Jahrbucher für Politik und Literatur*, 1 (1861): 27–48; reprinted in Eduard Lasker, *Zur Verfassungsgeschichte Preußens* (Leipzig: F. A. Brockhaus, 1874), pp. 179–212. The essay is significant also for showing how far the English example guided north German developments.

[32] The representative work stating this view is Otto Bähr, *Der Rechtsstaat: Eine publicistische Skizze* (Cassel: Wigand, 1864).

[33] Heinrich Rudolf von Gneist, *Der Rechtsstaat* (Berlin: Julius Springer, 1872), and especially the second and enlarged edition of the same work, *Der Rechtsstaat und die Verwaltungsgerichte in Deutschland* (2nd ed., enlarged; Berlin: Julius Springer, 1879). The significance which was attached to Gneist's work at the time may be gathered from the title of an anonymous pamphlet of the period: *H. Prof. Gneist, oder der Retter der Gesellschaft durch den "Rechtsstaat"* (Berlin: Schoppmeyer, 1873).

frequently confused, they aim at quite different and even incompatible ends, and thus should be kept clearly distinct.

One argument is that the kind of problems which are raised by disputes over administrative acts requires a knowledge both of branches of law and of fact which the ordinary judge, trained mainly in private or criminal law, cannot be expected to possess. It is a strong and probably a conclusive argument, but it does not support a greater separation between the courts adjudging private and those adjudging administrative disputes than often exists between courts dealing with matters of private law, commercial law, and criminal law, respectively. Administrative courts separated from ordinary courts only in this sense could still be as independent of government as the latter and be concerned only with the administration of the law, that is, with the application of a body of pre-existing rules.

Separate administrative courts, however, may also be thought necessary on the altogether different ground that disputes about the lawfulness of an administrative act cannot be decided on as a pure matter of law, since they always involve issues of governmental policy or expediency. Courts established separately for this reason will always be concerned with the aims of the government of the moment and cannot be fully independent: they must be part of the administrative apparatus and be subject to direction at least by its executive head. Their purpose will be not so much to protect the individual against encroachments on his private sphere by governmental agencies as to make sure that this does not happen against the intentions and instructions of the government. They will be a device to insure that the subordinate agencies carry out the will of the government (including that of the legislature) rather than a means of protecting the individual.

The distinction between these tasks can be drawn neatly and unambiguously only where there exists a body of detailed legal rules for guiding and limiting the actions of the administration. It inevitably becomes blurred if administrative courts are created at a time when the formulation of such rules is a task yet to be attempted by legislation and jurisdiction. In such a situation one of the necessary tasks of these courts will be to formulate as legal norms what, so far, have been merely internal rules of the administration; and in doing so they will find it very difficult to distinguish between those internal rules which possess a general character and those which express merely specific aims of current policy.

This very situation existed in Germany in the 1860s and 1870s when an attempt was finally made to translate into practice the long-cherished ideal of the *Rechtsstaat*. The argument which in the end defeated the long-maintained argument for "justicialism" was that it would be impracticable to leave to ordinary judges not specially trained for it the task of handling the intricate issues which would arise from disputes over administrative acts. As a consequence, separate new administrative courts were created, which were meant to be completely independent courts, concerned exclusively with questions of law; and it was hoped that in the course of time they would assume a strictly judicial control over all administrative action. To the men who devised the system, especially to its main architect, Rudolf von Gneist, and to most of the later German administrative lawyers, this creation of a system of separate administrative courts therefore appeared as the crowning piece of the *Rechtsstaat*, the definite achievement of the rule of law.[34] The fact that there were still left open a large number of loopholes for what in effect were arbitrary administrative decisions appeared merely as minor and temporary defects, made inevitable by the then existing conditions. They believed that, if the administrative apparatus was to continue to function, it had for a time to be given wide discretion until a definite body of rules for its actions had been laid down.

Thus, though organizationally the establishment of independent administrative courts seemed to be the final stage of the institutional arrangement designed to secure the rule of law, the most difficult task still lay in the future. The superposition of an apparatus of judicial control over a firmly entrenched bureaucratic machinery could become effective only if the task of rule-making was continued in the spirit in which the whole system had been conceived. Actually, however, the completion of the structure designed to serve the ideal of the rule of law more or less coincided with the abandonment of the ideal. Just as the new device was introduced, there commenced a major reversal of intellectual trends; the conceptions of liberalism, with the *Rechtsstaat* as its main goal, were abandoned. It was in the 1870s and 1880s, when that system of administrative courts received its final shape in the German states (and also in France), that the new movement toward state socialism and the welfare state began to gather force. There was, in consequence, little willingness to implement the conception of limited government which the new institutions had been designed to serve by gradually legislating away the discretionary powers still possessed by the administration. Indeed, the tendency now was to widen those loopholes in the newly created system by explicitly exempting from judicial review the discretionary powers required by the new tasks of government.

Thus the German achievement proved to be more considerable in theory than in practice. But its significance must not be underrated. The Germans were the last people that the liberal tide reached before it began to recede. But they were the ones who most systematically explored and digested all the

---

[34] See, for example, Gustav Radbruch, *Einführung in die Rechtswissenschaft* (2nd ed.; Leipzig: Quelle und Meyer, 1913); Fritz Fleiner, *Institutionen des deutschen Verwaltungsrechts* (8th ed.; Tübingen: Mohr, 1928), and Ernst Forsthoff, *Lehrbuch des Verwaltungsrechts*. Vol. 1: *Allgemeiner Teil* (Munich: C. H. Beck, 1950), p 394 [see chap. 7, "Der Rechtsschutz in Verwaltungssachen," pp. 386–420].

experience of the West and deliberately applied its lessons to the problems of the modern administrative state. The conception of the *Rechtsstaat* which they developed is the direct result of the old ideal of the rule of law, where an elaborate administrative apparatus rather than a monarch or a legislature was the chief agency to be restrained.[35] Even though the new conceptions which they developed never took firm root, they represent in some respects the last stage in a continuous development and are perhaps better adapted to the problems of our time than many of the older institutions. As it is the power of the professional administrator that is now the main threat to individual liberty, the institutions developed in Germany for the purpose of keeping him in check deserve more careful examination than they have been given.

8. One of the reasons why these German developments did not receive much attention was that, toward the end of the last century, conditions that prevailed there and elsewhere on the Continent showed a strong contrast between theory and practice. In principle the ideal of the rule of law had long been recognized, and, though the effectiveness of the one important institutional advance—the administrative courts—was somewhat limited, it constituted an important contribution to the solution of new problems. But, in the short time that the new experiment was given to develop its new possibilities, some of the features of former conditions never quite disappeared; and the advance toward a welfare state, which began on the Continent much earlier than in England or in the United States, soon introduced new features which could hardly be reconciled with the ideal of government under the law.

The result was that, even immediately preceding the first World War, when the political structure of the Continental and the Anglo-Saxon countries had become most similar, an Englishman or an American who observed the daily practice in France or Germany would still feel that the situation was

[35] It is certainly not correct to maintain with regard to the earlier phase of this German development, as did Franz Leopold Neumann, "The Concept of Political Freedom," *Columbia Law Review*, 53 (1953): 910; reprinted in the same author's *The Democratic and Authoritarian State: Essays in Political and Legal Theory* (Glencoe, IL: The Free Press, 1957), p. 169 (also the conflicting statement in the latter vol., p. 22), that "the English rule of law and the German *Rechtsstaat* doctrines have nothing in common." This may be true of the emasculated concept of the merely "formal" *Rechtsstaat* which became dominant at the end of the century, but not of the ideals which inspired the liberal movement of the first half of the century or of the theoretical conceptions which guided the reform of administrative jurisdiction in Prussia. Rudolph von Gneist, in particular, quite deliberately made the English position his model (and was, incidentally, the author of an important treatise on English "administrative law," a fact which ought to have prevented A. V. Dicey, if he had known of it, from so completely misunderstanding the use of the term on the Continent). The German translation of "rule of law," *Herrschaft des Gesetzes*, was in fact frequently used in place of *Rechtsstaat*. [The treatise on administrative law by Gneist to which Hayek is referring is *Das englische Verwaltungsrecht mit Einschluss des Heeres, der Gerichte und der Kirche*. Vol 1: *Geschichte des englischen Verwaltungsrechts*; Vol 2: *Das heutige englische Verwaltungsrecht* (2 vols.; Berlin: Julius Springer, 1867).—Ed.]

very far from reflecting the rule of law. The differences between the powers and the conduct of the police in London and those in Berlin—to mention an often quoted example—seemed nearly as great as ever. And though signs of developments similar to those which had already taken place on the Continent began to appear in the West, an acute American observer could still describe the basic difference at the end of the nineteenth century as follows: "In some cases, it is true, [even in England] an officer of the [local] board is given by statute power to make regulations. The Local Government Board (in Great Britain) and our boards of health furnish examples of this; but such cases are exceptional, and most Anglo-Saxons feel that this power is in its nature arbitrary, and ought not to be extended any further than is absolutely necessary."[36]

It was in this atmosphere that in England A. V. Dicey, in a work that has become a classic,[37] restated the traditional conception of the rule of law in a manner that governed all later discussion and proceeded to contrast it with the situation on the Continent. The picture he drew was, however, somewhat misleading. Starting from the accepted and undeniable proposition that the rule of law prevailed only imperfectly on the Continent and perceiving that this was somehow connected with the fact that administrative coercion was still in a great measure exempt from judicial review, he made the possibility of a review of administrative acts by the ordinary courts his chief test. He appears to have known only the French system of administrative jurisdiction (and even that rather imperfectly)[38] and to have been practically ignorant of German developments. With regard to the French system, his severe strictures may then have been somewhat justified, although even at that time the Conseil d'État had already initiated a development which, as a modern observer has suggested, "might in time succeed in bringing all discretionary powers of the administration . . . within the range of judicial control."[39] But they were certainly inapplicable to the *principle* of the German administrative courts; these had been constituted from the beginning as independent judicial bodies with the purposes of securing that rule of law which Dicey was so anxious to preserve.

It is true that in 1885, when Dicey published his famous *Lectures Introductory to the Study of the Law of the Constitution*, the German administrative courts were only just taking shape, and the French system had only recently received its definitive form. Nevertheless, the "fundamental mistake" of Dicey, "so fundamental that it is difficult to understand or excuse in a writer of his

---

[36] Lowell, *Governments and Parties in Continental Europe*, vol. 1, p. 44.

[37] Dicey, *Law of the Constitution*, originally delivered as lectures in 1884.

[38] Dicey later became at least partly aware of his error. See his article *"Droit Administratif* in Modern French Law," *Law Quarterly Review*, 17 (1901): 302–18.

[39] Sieghart, *Government by Decree*, p. 221.

eminence,"[40] has had the most unfortunate consequences. The very idea of separate administrative courts—and even the term "administrative law"—came to be regarded in England (and to a lesser extent in the United States) as the denial of the rule of law. Thus, by his attempt to vindicate the rule of law as he saw it, Dicey in effect blocked the development which would have offered the best chance of preserving it. He could not stop the growth in the Anglo-Saxon world of an administrative apparatus similar to that which existed on the Continent. But he did contribute much to prevent or delay the growth of institutions which could subject the new bureaucratic machinery to effective control.

---

[40] Sir Carleton Kemp Allen, *Law and Orders: An Inquiry into the Nature and Scope of Delegated Legislation and Executive Powers in England* (London: Stevens, 1945), p. 28.

FOURTEEN

THE SAFEGUARDS OF INDIVIDUAL LIBERTY

At this little gap every man's liberty may in time go out. —John Selden

1. It is time to try to pull together the various historical strands and to state systematically the essential conditions of liberty under the law. Mankind has learned from long and painful experience that the law of liberty must possess certain attributes.[1] What are they?

The quotation at the head of the chapter is taken from John Selden's speech in the "Proceedings in Parliament Relating to the Liberty of the Subject, 1627–1628," in Thomas Bayly Howell, *A Complete Collection of State Trials and Proceedings for High Treason and Other Crimes and Misdemeanors from the Earliest Period to the Year 1783* (34 vols.; London: T. C. Hansard, 1816–28), vol. 3, p. 170. [The debate took place regarding the Proceedings on Habeas Corpus brought by Sir Thomas Darnel, Sir John Corbet, Sir Walter Earl, Sir John Heveningham, and Sir Edmund Hampton, November 1627, at the Court of King's Bench in Westminster.—Ed.]

[1] The recent discussions of the meaning of the rule of law are very numerous, and we can list here merely some of the more significant ones: Sir Carleton Kemp Allen, *Law and Orders: An Inquiry into the Nature and Scope of Delegated Legislation and Executive Powers in England* (London: Stevens, 1945), esp. pp. 274–75; Sir Ernest Barker, "The 'Rule of Law,'" *Political Quarterly*, 1 (1914): 117–40; reprinted in Ernest Barker, *Church, State, and Study: Essays* (London: Methuen, 1930), pp. 171–92; Hale Leigh Bellot, "The Rule of Law," *Quarterly Review*, 246 (1926): 346–65; Robin George Collingwood, *The New Leviathan; or, Man, Society, Civilization, and Barbarism* (Oxford: Clarendon Press, 1942), chap. 39 ["Law and Order"], pp. 326–32; John Dickinson, *Administrative Justice and the Supremacy of Law in the United States* (Cambridge, MA: Harvard University Press, 1927); Carl Joachim Friedrich, *Constitutional Government and Democracy: Theory and Practice in Europe and America* (Boston: Little, Brown and Co., 1941); Frank Johnson Goodnow, *Politics and Administration: A Study in Government* (New York: Macmillan, 1900); Arthur Norman Holcombe, *The Foundations of the Modern Commonwealth* (New York: Harper and Brothers, 1923), chap. 11, pp. 436–79; Harry W. Jones, "The Rule of Law and the Welfare State," *Columbia Law Review*, 58 (1958): 143–56; Walter Lippman, *An Inquiry into the Principles of the Good Society* (Boston: Little, Brown and Co., 1937); Horace Harmon Lurton, "A Government of Law or a Government of Men," *North American Review*, 193 (1911): 1–25; Charles Howard McIlwain, "Government by Law," *Foreign Affairs: An American Quarterly Review*, 14 (1935–36): 185–98; reprinted in his *Constitutionalism and the Changing World* (Cambridge: Cambridge University Press, 1939), pp. 266–82; Franz Leopold Neumann, *The Democratic and the Authoritarian State: Essays in Political and Legal Theory* (Glencoe, IL: The Free Press, 1957); James Roland Pennock, *Administration and the Rule of Law* (New York: Farrer and Rinehart, 1941); Roscoe Pound, *Encyclopedia of the Social Sciences*, vol. 13 (1934), pp. 463–66, s.v. "Rule of Law," and "The Rule of Law and the Modern Social Welfare State," *Vanderbilt Law*

THE SAFEGUARDS OF INDIVIDUAL LIBERTY

The first point that must be stressed is that, because the rule of law means that government must never coerce an individual except in the enforcement

Review, 7 (1953): 1–34; Francis Graham Wilson, *The Elements of Modern Politics: An Introduction to Political Science* (New York: McGraw-Hill, 1936); cf. also Inns of Court Conservative and Unionist Society, *Rule of Law: A Study* (London: Conservative Political Centre, 1955).

Maxime Leroy, *La Loi: Essai sur la théorie de l'autorité dans la démocratie* (Paris: V. Giard and E. Brière, 1908); Albert Picot, *L'État fondé sur le droit et le droit pénal* (Basel: Helbling and Lichtenhahn, 1944), pp. 201a–8a of the *Actes de la Société Suisse des Juristes / Verhandlungen des Schweizerischen Juristenvereins / Atti della Società svizzera dei Giuristi*; Marcel Waline, *L'Individualisme et le droit* (2nd ed.; Paris: Éditions Domat Montchrestien, 1949).

The conduct of Carl Schmitt under the Hitler regime does not alter the fact that, of the modern German writings on the subject, his are still among the most learned and perceptive; see particularly his *Verfassungslehre* (Munich: Duncker und Humblot, 1928) and *Der Hüter der Verfassung* (Tübingen: Mohr, 1931). Similarly important for the pre-Nazi state of thought are Hermann Heller, *Rechtsstaat oder Diktatur?* (Tübingen: Mohr, 1930) and *Staatslehre* (Leiden: A. W. Sijthoff, 1934), and Friedrich Darmstädter, *Die Grenzen der Wirksamkeit des Rechtsstaates: Eine Untersuchung zur gegenwärtigen Krise des liberalen Staatsgedankens* (Heidelberg: C. Winter, 1930) and *Rechtsstaat oder Machtstaat?* (Berlin: Rothschild, 1932). Cf. John Hamilton Hallowell, *The Decline of Liberal Ideology: With Particular Reference to German Politco-Legal Thought* (Berkeley: University of California Press, 1943). Of the German postwar literature see particularly Franz Böhm, "Freiheitsordnung und soziale Frage," in *Grundsatzfragen der Wirtschaftsordnung: Vortragszyklus [veranstaltet von der Wirtschafts- und Sozialwissenschaftlichen Fakultät der Freien Universität Berlin Sommersemester 1953, Wirtschaftswissenschaftliche Abhandlungen*, vol. 2] (Berlin: Duncker und Humblot, 1954), pp. 71–95; Christian-Friedrich Menger, *Der Begriff des sozialen Rechtsstaates im Bonner Grundgesetz* (Tübingen: J. C. B. Mohr, 1953); Richard Lange, *Der Rechtsstaat als Zentralbegriff der neuesten Strafrechtsentwicklung* (Tübingen: Mohr, 1952); Hermann Wandersleb, ed., *Recht, Staat, Wirtschaft; Schriftenreihe des Innenministers des Landes Nordrhein-Westfalen für staatswissenschaftliche Fortbildung* (4 vols.; vols. 1–2, Stuttgart: Kohlhammer; vols. 3–4, Düsseldorf: L. Swann, 1949–53); and René Marcic, *Vom Gesetzesstaat zum Richterstaat* (Vienna: Springer, 1957).

Of special importance, mainly on the relation between democracy and the *Rechtsstaat*, is the extensive Swiss literature in this field, largely under the influence of Fritz Fleiner and his disciple and successor, Zaccaria Giacometti. Beginning with Fleiner's *Schweizerisches Bundesstaatsrecht* (Tübingen: Mohr, 1923; new ed. by Zaccaria Giacometti [Zurich: Polygraphischer Verlag, 1949]) and his *Institutionen des deutschen Verwaltungsrechts* (8th ed.; Tübingen: Mohr, 1928), see Giacometti's *Die Verfassungsgerichtsbarkeit des schweizerischen Bundesgerichtes (die staatsrechtliche Beschwerde)* (Zurich: Polygraphischer Verlag, 1933), and the volume dedicated to him under the title. *Demokratie und Rechtsstaat: Festgabe zum 60. Geburtstag von Zaccaria Giacometti* (Zurich: Polygraphischer Verlag, 1953), especially the contribution by Werner Kägi ["Rechtsstaat und Demokratie (Antinomie und Synthese)," pp. 107–42]; Richard Bäumlin, *Die rechtsstaatliche Demokratie: eine Untersuchung der gegenseitigen Beziehungen von Demokratie und Rechtsstaat* (Zurich: Polygraphischer Verlag, 1954); Rudolph Heinrich Grossmann, *Die staats- und rechtsideologischen Grundlagen der Verfassungsgerichtsbarkeit in den Vereinigten Staaten von Amerika und in der Schweiz. Eine Studie in amerikanischem und schweizerischem Staats- und Rechtsdenken* (dissertation; Zurich: Schulthess, 1948); Werner Kägi, *Die Verfassung als rechtliche Grundordnung des Staates: Untersuchungen über die Entwicklungstendenzen im modernen Verfassungsrecht* (Zurich: Polygraphischer Verlag, 1945); "Demokratie, Gleichheit und Egalitarismus," in *Die Schweiz: Ein nationales Jahrbuch* [vol. 25] (Bern: Jahrbuch Verlag, 1954), pp. 36–45; and esp. "Rechtsfragen der Volksinitiative auf Partialrevision," in *Verhandlungen des Schweizerischen Juristenvereins*, bk. 4 (Basel, 1956); Max Imboden, *Der Schutz vor staatlicher Willkür* (Zürich: Polygraphischer Verlag, 1945); and Max Imboden, *Das Gesetz als Garantie rechtsstaatlicher Verwaltung* (Basel: Helbing,

of a known rule,[2] it constitutes a limitation on the powers of all government, including the powers of the legislature. It is a doctrine concerning what the law ought to be, concerning the general attributes that particular laws should possess. This is important because today the conception of the rule of law is sometimes confused with the requirement of mere legality in all government action. The rule of law, of course, presupposes complete legality, but this is not enough: if a law gave the government unlimited power to act as it pleased, all its actions would be legal, but it would certainly not be under the rule of law. The rule of law, therefore, is also more than constitutionalism: it requires that all laws conform to certain principles.

From the fact that the rule of law is a limitation upon all legislation, it follows that it cannot itself be a law in the same sense as the laws passed by the legislator. Constitutional provisions may make infringements of the rule of law more difficult. They may help to prevent inadvertent infringements by

---

1954); Andreas Brunner, *Rechtsstaat gegen Totalstaat* (dissertation; 2 vols.; Zürich: Polygraphischer Verlag, 1948); and Juristische Fakultäten der schweizerischen Universitäten, ed., *Die Freiheit des Bürgers im schweizerischen Recht: Festgabe zur Hundertjahrfeier der Bundesverfassung / La liberté du citoyen en droit suisse: recueil du centenaire de la constitution fédérale publié par la Faculté de Droit des Universités suisses*, by various authors (Zurich: Polygraphischer Verlag, 1948).

Cf. also Carel Henrik Frederik Polak, *Ordening en Rechtsstaat* [Accepted by the Rijksuniversiteit te Leiden, 12 October 1951] (Zwolle: W. E. J. Tjeenk Willink, 1951); Luís Legaz y Lacambra, "El Estado de derecho," *Revista de administración pública*, 2 (1951): 13–34 [Published in Madrid by the Instituto de Estudios Políticos]; Felice Battaglia, "Stato etico e Stato di diritto," *Rivista internazionale di filosofia di diritto* 17 (1937): 237–87; and International Commission of Jurists, *Report of the International Congress of Jurists, held June 13–20, 1955, at Athens* (The Hague: International Commission of Jurists, 1956).

[2] A clear recent statement of this basic principle of a truly liberal system occurs in Neumann, *The Democratic and the Authoritarian State*, p. 31: "It is the most important and perhaps the decisive demand of liberalism that interference with the rights reserved to the individual is not permitted on the basis of individual but only on the basis of general laws"; and p. 166: "The liberal legal tradition rests, therefore, upon a very simple statement: individual rights may be interfered with by the state only if the state can prove its claim by reference to a general law which regulates an indeterminate number of future cases; this excludes retroactive legislation and demands a separation of legislative from judicial functions." Cf. also the quotation in n. 12 to chapter 13, above. The seemingly slight shift in emphasis which, with the rise of legal positivism, made this doctrine ineffective comes out clearly if we compare two characteristic statements from the latter part of the last century. Adhémar Esmein, (*Éléments de droit constitutionnel français et comparé* (1896), Henry Nézard, ed. [7th ed., rev.; 2 vols.; Paris: L. Tenin, 1921], vol. 1, p. 22), sees the essence of liberty in the limitation of authority by the existence of "des règles fixes, connues d'avance, qui, dans le cas donné, *dicteront* au souverain sa décision" ["fixed rules, known in advance, which, in any given case, *will determine* the sovereign's decision."—Ed.] [Italics added by Hayek.]

However, for Georg Jellinek, *System der subjektiven öffentlichen Rechte* (Freiburg: J. C. B. Mohr, 1892), p. 98, "alle Freiheit ist einfach Freiheit von gesetzwidrigem Zwange." ["All freedom is nothing more than freedom from unlawful coercion."—Ed.] In the first statement only such coercion is permissible as the law requires, in the second all coercion which the law does not forbid!

routine legislation.[3] But the ultimate legislator can never limit his own powers by law, because he can always abrogate any law he has made.[4] The rule of law is therefore not a rule of the law, but a rule concerning what the law ought to be, a meta-legal doctrine or a political ideal.[5] It will be effective only in so far as the legislator feels bound by it. In a democracy this means that it will not prevail unless it forms part of the moral tradition of the community, a common ideal shared and unquestioningly accepted by the majority.[6]

It is this fact that makes so very ominous the persistent attacks on the principle of the rule of law. The danger is all the greater because many of the applications of the rule of law are also ideals which we can hope to approach very closely but can never fully realize. If the ideal of the rule of law is a firm element of public opinion, legislation and jurisdiction will tend to approach it more and more closely. But if it is represented as an impracticable and even undesirable ideal and people cease to strive for its realization, it will rapidly disappear. Such a society will quickly relapse into a state of arbitrary tyranny. This is what has been threatening during the last two or three generations throughout the Western world.

It is equally important to remember that the rule of law restricts govern-

---

[3] Heinrich Stoll, "Rechtsstaatsidee und Privatrechtslehre," *Jherings Jahrbücher für die Dogmatik des bürgerlichen Rechts*, 76 (1925): esp. 193–204. [*Jhering* is an alternative spelling of *Ihering.*—Ed.]

[4] Cf. Francis Bacon's statement: "For a supreme and absolute power cannot conclude itself, neither can that which is in its nature revocable be made fixed" (quoted by Charles Howard McIlwain, *The High Court of Parliament* [New Haven: Yale University Press, 1910]. [Bacon's much-quoted statement does not appear in McIlwain's treatise, despite his devoting an extensive chapter to "The Political History of Parliamentary Supremacy" (pp. 336–93). It is, however, quoted by Dicey in his *Law of the Constitution*, p. 62, n. 2 (Liberty Fund edition, p. 21, n. 39). The quotation originates in Bacon's *History of King Henry VII from The Works of Francis Bacon, Baron Verulam, Viscount St. Albans, and Lord High Chancellor of England* (4 vols.; Printed by R. Gosling, 1730), vol. 3, p. 463.—Ed.]

[5] See Georg Jellinek, *Die rechtliche Natur der Staatenverträge: Ein Beitrag zur juristischen Construction des Völkerrechts* (Vienna: A. Hölder, 1880), pp. 2–3, and Hans Kelsen, *Hauptprobleme der Staatsrechtslehre entwickelt aus der Lehre vom Rechtssatze* (Tübingen: J. C. B. Mohr, 1911), pp. 50ff; cf. Benedikt Winckler, *Soltquellensis Principiorum juris libri quinque, in quibus genuina iuris, tam Naturalis quam Positivi, principia, firmissima Iurisprudentiae fundamenta ostenduntur, ejusque summus finis ob oculos ponitur, & Divina autoritas probatur* (Leipzig: Imprimebat Laurentius Cober, 1615): "In tota jurisprudentia nihil est quod minus legaliter tractari possit quam ipsa principia." ["In all jurisprudence, nothing is less able to be investigated according to the law than the first principles themselves." Rather than having referred to the 1615 edition, which is extremely rare, Hayek is almost certain to have consulted Winckler's essay in the reprint included in Carl von Kallenborn, *Die Vorläufer des Hugo Grotius* (Abtheilung II: Kritische Ausgabe der Autoren) (Leipzig: Verlag von Gustav Mayer, 1848), pp. 45–148. The quotation appears on p. 50.—Ed.]

[6] Cf. Fritz Fleiner, *Ausgewählte Schriften und Reden* (Zurich: Polygraphischer Verlag, 1941). This larger work contains Fleiner's essay *Tradition, Dogma, Entwicklung als aufbauende Kräfte der schweizerischen Demokratie*, pp. 288–302, and Léon Duguit, *Traité de droit constitutionnel* (2nd ed.; 5 vols.; Paris: E. de Boccard, 1921–25), vol. 1, *La règle de droit—Le problème de L'État*, pp. 408–9.

ment only in its coercive activities.[7] These will never be the only functions of government. Even in order to enforce the law, the government requires an apparatus of personal and material resources which it must administer. And there are whole fields of governmental activity, such as foreign policy, where the problem of coercion of the citizens does not normally arise. We shall have to return to this distinction between the coercive and the non-coercive activities of government. For the moment, all that is important is that the rule of law is concerned only with the former.

The chief means of coercion at the disposal of government is punishment. Under the rule of law, government can infringe a person's protected private sphere only as punishment for breaking an announced general rule. The principle "nullum crimen, nulla poena sine lege"[8] is therefore the most important consequence of the ideal. But clear and definite as this statement may at first seem, it raises a host of difficulties if we ask what precisely is meant by "law." Certainly the principle would not be satisfied if the law merely said that whoever disobeys the orders of some official will be punished in a specified manner. Yet even in the freest countries the law often seems to provide for such acts of coercion. There probably exists no country where a person will not on certain occasions, such as when he disobeys a policeman, become liable to punishment for "an act done to the public mischief" or for "disturbing the public order" or for "obstructing the police." We shall therefore not fully understand even this crucial part of the doctrine without examining the whole complex of principles which together make possible the rule of law.

2. We have seen earlier that the ideal of the rule of law presupposes a very definite conception of what is meant by law and that not every enactment

---

[7] It seems to be a misunderstanding of this point that makes Lionel Robbins ("Freedom and Order," in *Economics and Public Policy*, Arthur Smithies, ed. [Washington, DC: Brookings Institution, 1955], p.153) fear that to suggest "a conception of government that is too limited to the execution of known laws, to the exclusion of functions of initiative and discretion that cannot without distortion be left out of the picture," is to oversimplify our position and expose it to ridicule.

[8] Cf. Stefan Glaser "Nullum crimen sine lege," *Journal of Comparative Legislation and International Law*, 3rd ser., 24 (1942): 29–41; Heinrich Balthassar Gerland, "Nulla poena sine lege," in *Die Grundrechte und Grundpflichten der Reichsverfassung: Kommentar zum zweiten Teil der Reichsverfassung*, Carl Nipperdey, ed. (3 vols.; Berlin: Hobbing, 1929), vol. 1, pp. 368–86; Jerome Hall, "Nulla poena sine lege," *Yale Law Journal*, 47 (1937–38): 165–93; Léon Julliot de La Morandière, *De la règle "nulla poena sine lege"* (doctoral dissertation; Paris: L. Larose et L. Tenin, 1910); Adolf Schottländer, *Die geschichtliche Entwicklung des Satzes: Nulla poena sine lege* (Strafrechtliche Abhandlungen, vol. 132; Breslau: Schletter, 1911); and Orio Giacchi, "Precedenti canonistici del principio 'Nullum crimen sine proevia lege poenali,'" in *Studi in onore di Francesco Scaduto* (2 vols.; Florence: Casa editrice poligrafia universitaria del dott. C. Cya, 1936), vol. 1, pp. 433–49. On the position of the principle as the primary condition of the rule of law see Dicey, *Law of the Constitution*, p. 187 [Liberty Fund edition, p. 110].

of the legislative authority is a law in this sense.[9] In current practice, everything is called "law" which has been resolved in the appropriate manner by a legislative authority. But of these laws in the formal sense of the word,[10] only some—today usually only a very small proportion—are substantive (or "material") laws regulating the relations between private persons or between

[9] See particularly Carl Schmitt, *Unabhängigkeit der Richter, Gleichheit vor dem Gesetz und Gewährleistung des Privateigentums nach der Weimarer Verfassung: Ein Rechtsgutachten zu den Gesetzentwürfen über die Vermögensauseinandersetzung mit den frührer regierenden Fürstenhäusern* (Berlin: Walter de Gruyter, 1926), and Carl Schmitt, *Verfassungslehre* (Munich and Leipzig: Duncker und Humblot, 1928).

[10] On this distinction see Paul Laband, *Das Staatsrecht des deutschen Reiches* (5th ed.; 4 vols.; Tübingen: J. C. B. Mohr, 1911–14), vol. 2, pp. 54–56; Ernst Seligmann, *Der Begriff des Gesetzes im materiellen und formellen Sinne* (Berlin: Guttentag, 1886); Albert Haenel, *Studien zum deutschen Staatsrechte*. Vol. 2: *Die organisatorische Entwicklung der deutschen Reichsverfassung. Gesetz im formellen und materiellen Sinne* (2 vols.; Leipzig: Verlag H. Haessel, 1873–88); and, for a discussion of the subsequent development and current state of German teaching, Karl Zeidler, *Maßnahmegesetz und "klassiches" Gesetz: Eine Kritik* (Karlruhe: C. F. Müller, 1961); Ernest Wolfgang Böckenförde, *Gesetz und gesetzgebende Gewalt: Von den Anfängen der deutschen Staatsrechtslehre bis zur Höhe des staatsrechslichen Positivismus* (Tübingen: Mohr Siebeck, 1958); Hans Werner Kopp, *Inhalt und Form der Gesetze als ein Problem der Rechtstheorie; mit vergleichender Berücksichtigung der Schweiz, Deutschlands, Frankreichs, Grossbritanniens und der USA.* (dissertation; 2 vols.; Zürich: Polygraphischer Verlag, 1958); and especially Konrad Huber, *Rechtsgesetz und Maßnahmegesetz: eine Studie zum rechtsstaatlichen Gesetzesbegriff* (dissertation; Berlin: Duncker und Humblot, 1963); Léon Duguit, *Traité de droit constitutionnel.* Vol. 1, pp. 539–50; and Raymond Carré de Malberg, *La Loi: Expression de la volonté générale: étude sur le concept de la loi dans la constitution de 1875* (Paris: Sirey, 1931).

Of great importance in this connection is also a series of cases in American constitutional law, of which only two can be quoted here. The best-known statement is probably that by Justice [Stanley] Mathews in *Hurtado v. California*, 110 *U.S.* 516, at 535 (1884): "It is not every act, legislative in form, that is law. Law is something more than mere will exerted as an act of power. It must be not a special rule for a particular person or a particular case, but, in the language of Mr. Webster, in his familiar definition, 'the general law, a law which hears before it condemns, which proceeds upon inquiry, and renders judgment only after trial,' so 'that every citizen shall hold his life, liberty, property and immunities under the protection of the general rules which govern society,' and thus excluding as not due process of law, acts of attainder, bills of pains and penalties, acts of confiscation, acts reversing judgments and acts directly transferring one man's estate to another, legislative judgments and decrees, and other similar special, partial and arbitrary exertions of power under the form of legislation. Arbitrary power, enforcing its edicts to the injury of the persons and property of its subjects, is not law, whether manifested as the decree of a personal monarch or of an impersonal multitude. And the limitations imposed by our constitutional law upon the action of the governments, both State and national, are essential to the preservation of public and private rights, notwithstanding the representative character of our political institutions. The enforcement of these limitations by judicial process is the device of self-governing communities to protect the rights of individuals and minorities, as well against the power of numbers, as against the violence of public agents transcending the limits of lawful authority, even when acting in the name and wielding the force of government." Cf. the more recent statement in *State v. Boloff*, 138 Or 568, at 611; 646 4 P2d 326; 7 P2d 775 (1932): "A legislative act creates a rule for all: it is not an order or command to some individual; it is permanent, not transient. A law is universal in its application; not a sudden order to and concerning a particular person."

313

such persons and the state. The great majority of the so-called laws are rather instructions issued by the state to its servants concerning the manner in which they are to direct the apparatus of government and the means which are at their disposal. Today it is everywhere the task of the same legislature to direct the use of these means and to lay down the rules which the ordinary citizen must observe. This, though the established practice, is not a necessary state of affairs. I cannot help wondering whether it might not be desirable to prevent the two types of decisions from being confused[11] by entrusting the task of laying down general rules and the task of issuing orders to the administration to distinct representative bodies and by subjecting their decisions to independent judicial review so that neither will overstep its bounds. Though we may wish both kinds of decisions to be controlled democratically, this need not mean that they should be in the hands of the same assembly.[12]

---

[11] See Walter Bagehot, *The English Constitution* (1867) in *The Works and Life of Walter Bagehot*, [Mrs.] Russell Barrington, ed. (London: Longman, Green, and Co., 1915), vol. 5, pp. 254–55: "An immense mass, indeed, of the legislation is not, in the proper language of jurisprudence, legislation at all. A law is a general command applicable to many cases. The 'special acts' which crowd the statute book and weary Parliamentary committees are applicable to one case only. They do not lay down rules according to which railways shall be made, they enact that such and such a railway shall be made from this place to that place, and they have no bearing upon any other transaction." Today this tendency has gone so far that an eminent English judge has been led to ask: "Have we not come to a time when we must find another name for statute law than Law itself? Para-law, perhaps: or even sub-laws" (Cyril John Radcliffe, Viscount Radcliffe of Werneth, *Law and the Democratic State: Being the Presidential Address of the Right Hon. Lord Radcliffe, President of the Holdsworth Club of the Faculty of Law in the University of Birmingham, 1954–1955* [Holdsworth lecture] [Birmingham: Holdsworth Club of the University of Birmingham, 1955], p. 4. Cf. also Hermann Jahrreiss, *Freiheit and Sozialstaat* (Kölner Universitätreden No. 17; Krefeld: Scherpe, 1957); reprinted in *Mensch und Staat: Rechtsphilosophische, staatsrechtliche und völkerrechtliche Grundfragen in unserer Zeit* (Cologne: C. Heymann, 1957), p. 15: "Wir sollten es uns einmal überlegen, ob wir nicht hinfort unter diesem ehrwürdigen Namen 'Gesetz' nur solche Normen setzen und Stafdrohungen nur hinter solche Normen stellen sollten, die dem Jedermann '*das* Gesetz' zu werden vermögen. Sie, nur sie, seien 'Gesetze'! Alle übrigen Regelungen—die technischen Details zu solchen echten Gesetzen oder selbständige Vorschriften ephemeren Charakters—sollten äußerlich abgesondert unter einem anderen Namen, als etwa 'Anordnungen' ergehen und allenfalls Sanktionen nicht strafrechtlichen Charakters vorsehen, auch wenn die Legislative sie beschließt." ["We should give serious consideration, from this point forward, whether under the honored name of 'law' we should place those norms and attach penalties only to those rules that can be universalized. They, and only they, are true laws! All other regulations—the technical details that are associated with true laws or instructions of a fleeting character—should be clearly separated and labeled differently, and perhaps called 'directions.' In any case, they should not be accompanied by sanctions of the character of the penal code, even were they established by the legislature."—Ed.]

[12] It is interesting to speculate what the development would have been if at the time when the House of Commons successfully claimed the exclusive control over expenditure and thereby in effect the control of administration, the House of Lords had succeeded in achieving exclusive power of laying down general laws including the principles on which the private individual

The present arrangements help to obscure the fact that, though government has to administer means which have been put at its disposal (including the services of all those whom it has hired to carry out its instructions), this does not mean that it should similarly administer the efforts of private citizens. What distinguishes a free from an unfree society is that in the former each individual has a recognized private sphere clearly distinct from the public sphere, and the private individual cannot be ordered about but is expected to obey only the rules which are equally applicable to all. It used to be the boast of free men that, so long as they kept within the bounds of the known law, there was no need to ask anybody's permission or to obey anybody's orders. It is doubtful whether any of us can make this claim today.

The general, abstract rules, which are laws in the substantive sense, are, as we have seen, essentially long-term measures, referring to yet unknown cases and containing no references to particular persons, places, or objects. Such laws must always be prospective, never retrospective, in their effect. That this should be so is a principle, almost universally accepted but not always put into legal form; it is a good example of those meta-legal rules which must be observed if the rule of law is to remain effective.

3. The second chief attribute which must be required of true laws is that they be known and certain.[13] The importance which the certainty of the law has for the smooth and efficient running of a free society can hardly be exaggerated. There is probably no single factor which has contributed more to the prosperity of the West than the relative certainty of the law which has prevailed here.[14] This is not altered by the fact that complete certainty of the law is an ideal which we must try to approach but which we can never perfectly attain. It has become the fashion to belittle the extent to which such certainty has in fact been achieved, and there are understandable reasons why lawyers, concerned mainly with litigation, are apt to do so. They have normally

---

could be taxed. A division of competence of the two legislative chambers on this principle has never been tried but may be well worth consideration.

[13] See Sir Henry William Rawson Wade, "The Concept of Legal Certainty: A Preliminary Skirmish," *Modern Law Review*, 4 (1941): 183–99; Hermann Jahrreiss, *Berechenbarkeit und Recht* (Leipzig: T. Weicher, 1927); Carl August Emge, *Sicherheit und Gerechtigkeit: Ihre gemeinsame meta-juristische Wurzel* (Berlin: Akademie der Wissenschaften in Kommission bei W. De Guyter, 1940); and Paul Roubier, *Théorie générale du droit: histoire des doctrines juridiques et philosophie des valeurs sociales* (Paris: Recueil Sirey, 1946), esp. pp. 267–79. See also Luis Recaséns Siches, "Human Life, Society, and Law: Fundamentals of the Philosophy of Law," in *Latin American Legal Philosophy*, Luis Recaséns Siches, et al., eds. (Cambridge, MA: Harvard University Press, 1948), pp. 7–341.

[14] Cf. George Godfrey Phillips, "Notes: The Rule of Law," *Journal of Comparative Legislation*, 16 (1934): 302–4, and the literature there quoted. See, however, Montesquieu, *Spirit of the Laws*, bk. 6, chap. 2, and the extensive discussion in Max Weber, *Max Weber on Law in Economy and Society*, Max Rheinstein, ed. (Cambridge, MA: Harvard University Press, 1954); also Neumann, *The Democratic and the Authoritarian State*, p. 40.

to deal with cases in which the outcome is uncertain. But the degree of the certainty of the law must be judged by the disputes which do not lead to litigation because the outcome is practically certain as soon as the legal position is examined. It is the cases that never come before the courts, not those that do, that are the measure of the certainty of the law. The modern tendency to exaggerate this uncertainty is part of the campaign against the rule of law, which we shall examine later.[15]

The essential point is that the decisions of the courts can be predicted, not that all the rules which determine them can be stated in words. To insist that the actions of the courts be in accordance with pre-existing rules is not to insist that all these rules be explicit, that they be written down beforehand in so many words. To insist on the latter would, indeed, be to strive for an unattainable ideal. There are "rules" which can never be put into explicit form. Many of these will be recognizable only because they lead to consistent and predictable decisions and will be known to those whom they guide as, at most, manifestations of a "sense of justice."[16] Psychologically, legal reasoning does not, of course, consist of explicit syllogisms, and the major premises will often not be explicit.[17] Many of the general principles on which the conclusions depend will be only implicit in the body of formulated law and will have to be discovered by the courts. This, however, is not a peculiarity of legal reasoning. Probably all generalizations that we can formulate depend on still higher generalizations which we do not explicitly know but which nevertheless govern the working of our minds. Though we will always try to discover those more general principles on which our decisions rest, this is probably by its nature an unending process that can never be completed.

4. The third requirement of true law is equality. It is as important, but much more difficult, to define than the others. That any law should apply equally to all means more than that it should be general in the sense we have defined. A law may be perfectly general in referring only to formal characteristics of the persons involved[18] and yet make different provisions for different classes

---

[15] It is a curious fact that the same people who stress the uncertainty of the law most often at the same time represent the prediction of judicial decisions as the sole aim of legal science. If the law were as uncertain as these authors sometimes suggest, there would exist, on their own showing, no legal science whatsoever.

[16] Cf. Roscoe Pound, "Why Law Day?" *Harvard Law School Bulletin*, 10 (1958): 4: "The vital, the enduring part of the law, is in principles—starting points for reasoning, not in rules. Principles remain relatively constant or develop along constant lines. Rules have relatively short lives. They do not develop; they are repealed and are superseded by other rules."

[17] See Edward Hirsch Levi, *An Introduction to Legal Reasoning* (Chicago: University of Chicago Press, 1949); reprinted from *The University of Chicago Law Review*, 15 (1948): 501–74.

[18] Cf. René Brunet, *Le Principe d'egalité en droit français* (Doctoral dissertation, Université de Paris Faculté de Droit; Paris: F. Alcan, 1910); Max Friedrich Rümelin, *Die Gleichheit von dem Gesetz: Rede gehalten bei der akademischen Preisverteilung am 6. November 1928* (Tübingen: Mohr, 1928); Otto

of people. Some such classification, even within the group of fully responsible citizens, is clearly inevitable. But classification in abstract terms can always be carried to the point at which, in fact, the class singled out consists only of particular known persons or even a single individual.[19] It must be admitted that, in spite of many ingenious attempts to solve this problem, no entirely satisfactory criterion has been found that would always tell us what kind of classification is compatible with equality before the law. To say, as has so often been said, that the law must not make irrelevant distinctions or that it must not discriminate between persons for reasons which have no connection with the purpose of the law[20] is little more than evading the issue.

Mainzer, *Gleichheit vor dem Gesetz, Gerechtigkeit und Recht: Entwickelt an der Frage: welche Gewalten bindet der Gleichheitssatz in Art. 109 I RV?* (Berlin: J. Springer, 1929); Erich Kaufmann, Hans Nawiasky, Albert Hensel, and Ottmar Bühler, *Die Gleichheit vor dem Gesetz im Sinne des Art. 109 der Reichsverfassung; Der Einfluss des Steurrechts auf die Begriffsbildung des öffentlichen Rechts* (Veröffentlichungen der Vereinigung deutscher Staatsrechtslehrer, No. 33; Berlin: Walter de Gruyter, 1927); Gerhard Leibholz, *Die Gleichheit vor dem Gesetz: eine Studie auf rechtsvergleichender und rechstphilosophischer Grundlage* (Berlin: O. Liebmann, 1925); Hans Nef, *Gleichheit und Gerechtigkeit* (Zurich: Polygraphischer Verlag, 1941); Hans Peter Ipsen, "Gleichheit," in *Die Grundrechte: Handbuch der Theorie und Praxis der Grundrechte,* Franz Leopold Neumann, Hans Carl Nipperdey, and Ulrich Scheuner, eds. (5 vols. in 7; Berlin: Duncker und Humblot, 1954), vol. 2, pp. 111–98; and Eduardo Luis Llorens, *La Igualdad ante la Ley* (Murcia: Instituto de estudios políticos de la Universidad de Murcia, 1934).

[19] A good illustration from another field of how a non-discrimination rule can be evaded by provisions formulated in general terms (given by Gottfried Haberler, *The Theory of International Trade with its Applications to Commercial Policy* [London: W. Dodge and Co., 1936], p. 339) is the German customs tariff of 1902 (still in force in 1936), which, to avoid a most-favored-nations obligation, provided for a special rate of duty for "brown or dappled cows reared at a level of at least 300 meters above the sea and passing at least one month in every summer at a height of at least 800 meters."

[20] Cf. art. 4 of the Swiss Federal Constitution: "Die Verschiedenheiten, die der Gesetzgeber aufstellt, müssen sachlich begründet sein, d. h. auf vernünftigen und ausschlaggebenden Erwägungen in der Natur der Sache beruhen derart, dass der Gesetzgeber nur durch solche Unterscheidungen dem inneren Zweck der Ordnung der betreffenden Lebensverhältnisse." [The English reads: "The distinctions that the legislator specifies must be grounded in fact; that is, they must rest on reasonable and essential aspects of the matter before him such that only by making such distinctions would the legislator do justice to the intrinsic purpose of regulating the circumstances in question." The quotation is not a transcription of Art. 4 of the Federal Constitution, as amended to 1 July 1953 and in place at the time *The Constitution of Liberty* was written. Art. 4 reads: "Alle Schweizer sind vor dem Gesetz gleich. Es gibt in der Schweiz keine Untertanenverhältnisse, keine Vorrechte des Ortes, der Geburt, der Familie oder Personen." ("All Swiss are equal before the Law. In Switzerland there is neither subjection or privilege of locality, birth, family, or person.") See Christopher Hughes, trans., *The Federal Constitution of Switzerland* (Oxford: Clarendon Press, 1954), pp. 6–7, 173. Hayek's quotation is contained in *Die Gleichheit vor dem Gesetz,* Erich Kaufmann, et al., eds (Berlin: Walter de Gruyter, 1927), p. 10, which itself gives a quotation from Ulrich Lampert, *Das schweizerische Bundesstaatsrecht* (Zürich: Orell Füssli, 1918). For a bibliographical listing of works concerning this section of the Swiss Constitution see Zaccaria Giacometti, *Schweizerisches Bundesstaatsrecht* (Zurich: Polygraphischer Verlag, 1949), p. 401.—Ed.]

Yet, though equality before the law may thus be one of the ideals that indicate the direction without fully determining the goal and may therefore always remain beyond our reach, it is not meaningless. We have already mentioned one important requirement that must be satisfied, namely, that those inside any group singled out acknowledge the legitimacy of the distinction as well as those outside it. As important in practice is that we ask whether we can or cannot foresee how a law will affect particular people. The ideal of equality of the law is aimed at equally improving the chances of yet unknown people but incompatible with benefiting or harming known persons in a predictable manner.

It is sometimes said that, in addition to being general and equal, the law of the rule of law must also be just. But though there can be no doubt that, in order to be effective, it must be accepted as just by most people, it is doubtful whether we possess any other formal criteria of justice than generality and equality—unless, that is, we can test the law for conformity with more general rules which, though perhaps unwritten, are generally accepted, once they have been formulated. But, so far as its compatibility with a reign of freedom is concerned, we have no test for a law that confines itself to regulating the relations between different persons and does not interfere with the purely private concerns of an individual, other than its generality and equality. It is true that such "a law may be bad and unjust; but its general and abstract formulation reduces this danger to a minimum. The protective character of the law, its very *raison d'être*, are to be found in its generality."[21]

If it is often not recognized that general and equal laws provide the most effective protection against infringement of individual liberty, this is due mainly to the habit of tacitly exempting the state and its agents from them and of assuming that the government has the power to grant exemptions to individuals. The ideal of the rule of law requires that the state either enforce the law upon others—and that this be its only monopoly—or act under the same law and therefore be limited in the same manner as any private person.[22] It is this fact that all rules apply equally to all, including those who govern, which makes it improbable that any oppressive rules will be adopted.

[21] Léon Duguit, *Manuel de droit constitutionnel, théorie générale de l'état, le droit de l'état, les libertés publiques, organisation politique* (3rd ed.; Paris: Fontenoing and Cie., 1918), p. 96. ["La loi peut être mauvaise, injuste; mais étant formulée par voie générale et abstraite, ce danger se trouve réduit au minimum. Ainsi encore le caractère protecteur de la loi, sa raison d'être elle-même se trouvent dans sa généralité."—Ed.]

[22] It would lead too far here to raise the question of whether the distinct attributes which Continental law attaches to "public" as distinct from "private" law are compatible with freedom under the law in the Anglo-Saxon sense. Though such a classification may be useful for some purposes, it has served to give the law which regulates the relations between the individual and the state a different character from that which regulates the relations between individuals, while it seems of the essence of the rule of law that this character ought to be the same in both fields.

5. It would be humanly impossible to separate effectively the laying-down of new general rules and their application to particular cases unless these functions were performed by different persons or bodies. This part at least of the doctrine of the separation of powers[23] must therefore be regarded as an integral part of the rule of law. Rules must not be made with particular cases in mind, nor must particular cases be decided in the light of anything but the general rule—though this rule may not yet have been explicitly formulated and therefore have to be discovered. This requires independent judges who are not concerned with any temporary ends of government. The main point is that the two functions must be performed separately by two co-ordinated bodies before it can be determined whether coercion is to be used in a particular case.

A much more difficult question is whether, under a strict application of the rule of law, the executive (or the administration) should be regarded as a distinct and separate power in this sense, co-ordinated on equal terms with the other two. There are, of course, areas where the administration must be free to act as it sees fit. Under the rule of law, however, this does not apply to coercive powers over the citizen. The principle of the separation of powers must not be interpreted to mean that in its dealing with the private citizen the administration is not always subject to the rules laid down by the legislature and applied by independent courts. The assertion of such a power is the very antithesis of the rule of law. Though under any workable system the administration must undoubtedly have powers which cannot be controlled by independent courts, "Administrative Powers over Person and Property" cannot be among them. The rule of law requires that the executive in its coercive action be bound by rules which prescribe not only when and where it may use coercion but also in what manner it may do so. The only way in which this can be ensured is to make all its actions of this kind subject to judicial review.

Whether the rules by which the administration is bound should be laid down by the general legislature or whether this function may be delegated

---

[23] See William Searle Holdsworth's review of the 9th edition of Dicey's *Introduction to the Study of the Law of the Constitution*, in *Law Quarterly Review*, 55 (1939): 587–88, which contains one of the latest authoritative statements in England of the traditional conception of the rule of law. It deserves quotation at length, but we will reproduce only one paragraph here: "The rule of law is as valuable a principle today as it has ever been. For it means that the Courts can see to it that the powers of officials, and official bodies of persons entrusted with government, are not exceeded and are not abused, and that the rights of citizens are determined in accordance with the law enacted and unenacted. In so far as the jurisdiction of the Courts is ousted, and officials or official bodies of persons are given a purely administrative discretion, the rule of law is abrogated. It is not abrogated if these officials or official bodies are given a judicial or quasi-judicial discretion, although the machinery through which the rule is applied is not that of the Courts." Cf. also Arthur Thomas Vanderbilt, *The Doctrine of the Separation of Powers and Its Present-Day Significance* (Lincoln: University of Nebraska Press, 1953).

to another body is, however, a matter of political expediency.[24] This does not bear directly on the principle of the rule of law, but rather on the question of the democratic control of government. So far as the principle of the rule of law is concerned, there is no objection to delegation of legislation as such. Clearly, the delegation of the power of making rules to local legislative bodies, such as provincial assemblies or municipal councils, is unobjectionable from every point of view. Even the delegation of this power to some non-elective authority need not be contrary to the rule of law, so long as such authority is bound to announce these rules prior to their application and then can be made to adhere to them. The trouble with the widespread use of delegation in modern times is not that the power of making general rules is delegated but that administrative authorities are, in effect, given power to wield coercion without rule, as no general rules can be formulated which will unambiguously guide the exercise of such power. What is often called "delegation of lawmaking power" is often not delegation of the power to make rules—which might be undemocratic or politically unwise—but delegation of the authority to give to any decision the force of law, so that, like an act of the legislature, it must be unquestioningly accepted by the courts.

6. This brings us to what in modern times has become the crucial issue, namely the legal limits of administrative discretion. Here is "the little gap at which in time every man's liberty may go out."[25]

The discussion of this problem has been obscured by a confusion over the meaning of the term "discretion." We use the word first with regard to the power of the judge to interpret the law. But authority to interpret a rule is not discretion in the sense relevant to us. The task of the judge is to discover the implications contained in the spirit of the whole system of valid rules of law or to express as a general rule, when necessary, what was not explicitly stated previously in a court of law or by the legislator. That this task of interpretation is not one in which the judge has discretion in the sense of authority to follow his own will to pursue particular concrete aims appears from the fact that his interpretation of the law can be, and as a rule is, made subject to review by a higher court. Whether or not the substance of a decision is subject to review by another such body that needs to know only the existing rules and the facts of the case is probably the best test as to whether a decision is bound

---

[24] See Sir Cecil Thomas Carr, *Delegated Legislation: Three Lectures* (Cambridge: Cambridge University Press, 1921); Allen, *Law and Orders*, esp. pp. 114–15; and the studies by various authors collected in *Die Übertragung rechtsetzender Gewalt im Rechtsstaat*, Walter E. Genzer and Wolfgang Einbeck, eds. (Frankfurt: Institut zur Förderung öffentlicher Angelegenheiten, 1952).

[25] Hans Huber, "Niedergang des Rechts und Krise des Rechtsstaates," in *Demokratie und Rechtsstaat: Festgabe zum 60. Geburtstag von Zaccaria Giacometti*, p. 66, writes similarly of the concept of discretion as a "Trojan horse in constitutional, administrative law."

by rule or left to the discretion of the judge's authority. A particular interpretation of the law may be subject to dispute, and it may sometimes be impossible to arrive at a fully convincing conclusion; but this does not alter the fact that the dispute must be settled by an appeal to the rules and not by a simple act of will.

Discretion in a different and for our purposes equally irrelevant sense is a problem which concerns the relation between principal and agent throughout the whole hierarchy of government. At every level, from the relation between the sovereign legislature and the heads of the administrative departments down the successive steps in the bureaucratic organization, the problem arises as to what part of the authority of government as a whole should be delegated to a specific office or official. Since this assignment of particular tasks to particular authorities is decided by law, the question of what an individual agency is entitled to do, what parts of the powers of government it is allowed to exercise, is often also referred to as a problem of discretion. It is evident that not all the acts of government can be bound by fixed rules and that at every stage of the governmental hierarchy considerable discretion must be granted to the subordinate agencies. So long as the government administers its own resources, there are strong arguments for giving it as much discretion as any business management would require in similar circumstances. As Dicey has pointed out, "in the management of its own business, properly so called, the government will be found to need that freedom of action, necessarily possessed by every private person in the management of his own personal concerns."[26] It may well be that legislative bodies are often overzealous in limiting the discretion of the administrative agencies and unnecessarily hamper their efficiency. This may be unavoidable to some degree; and it is probably necessary that bureaucratic organizations should be bound by rule to a greater extent than business concerns, as they lack that test of efficiency which profits provide in commercial affairs.[27]

The problem of discretionary powers as it directly affects the rule of law is not a problem of the limitation of the powers of particular agents of government but of the limitation of the powers of the government as a whole. It is a problem of the scope of administration in general. Nobody disputes the fact that, in order to make efficient use of the means at its disposal, the government must exercise a great deal of discretion. But, to repeat, under the rule of

---

[26] Albert Venn Dicey, "The Development of Administrative Law in England," *Law Quarterly Review*, 31 (1915): 150. [The full quotation reads: "When the State undertakes the management of business properly so called, and business which hitherto has been carried on by each individual citizen simply with a view to his own interest, the Government, or in the language of English law, the servants of the Crown, will be found to need that freedom of action necessarily possessed by every private person in the management of his own personal concerns."—Ed.]

[27] See Ludwig von Mises, *Bureaucracy* (New Haven: Yale University Press, 1944).

law the private citizen and his property are not an object of administration by the government, not a means to be used for its purposes. It is only when the administration interferes with the private sphere of the citizen that the problem of discretion becomes relevant to us; and the principle of the rule of law, in effect, means that the administrative authorities should have no discretionary powers in this respect.

In acting under the rule of law the administrative agencies will often have to exercise discretion as the judge exercises discretion in interpreting the law. This, however, is a discretionary power which can and must be controlled by the possibility of a review of the substance of the decision by an independent court. This means that the decision must be deducible from the rules of law and from those circumstances to which the law refers and which can be known to the parties concerned. The decision must not be affected by any special knowledge possessed by the government or by its momentary purposes and the particular values it attaches to different concrete aims, including the preferences it may have concerning the effects on different people.[28]

At this point the reader who wants to understand how liberty in the modern world may be preserved must be prepared to consider a seemingly fine point of law, the crucial importance of which is often not appreciated. While in all civilized countries there exists some provision for an appeal to courts against administrative decisions, this often refers only to the question as to whether an authority had a right to do what it did. We have already seen, however, that

---

[28] See Ernest Freund, *Administrative Powers Over Persons and Property: A Comparative Survey* (Chicago: University of Chicago Press, 1928), pp. 71 [Hayek is here referring to chap. 6 of Freund's book, entitled "Administrative Discretion," pp. 71–103—Ed.]; Ralph Follen Fuchs, "Concepts and Policies in Anglo-American Administrative Law Theory," *Yale Law Journal*, 47 (1938): 538–76; Robert M. Cooper, "Administrative Justice and the Role of Discretion," *Yale Law Journal*, 47 (1938): 577–602; Morris Raphael Cohen, "Rule versus Discretion," *Journal of Philosophy, Psychology and Scientific Methods*, 11(1914): 208–15; reprinted in Morris Raphael Cohen, *Law and the Social Order: Essays in Legal Philosophy* (New York: Harcourt, Brace and Co., 1933), pp. 259–67; Fritz Morstein Marx, "Comparative Administrative Law: A Note on Review of Discretion," *University of Pennsylvania Law Review*, 87 (1938–39): 954–78; G. E. Treves, "Administrative Discretion and Judicial Control," *Modern Law Review*, 10 (1947): 276–91; Rudolf von Laun, *Das freie Ermessen und seine Grenzen* (Leipzig: Deuticke, 1910); Paul Oertmann, *Die staatsbürgerliche Freiheit und das freie Ermessen der Behörden* [Vortrag gehalten in der Gehe- Stiftung zu Dresden, am 18. November 1911] (Leipzig: B. G. Teubner, 1912); Friedrich Tezner, *Das freie Ermessen der Verwaltungsbehörden. Kritisch-systematisch erörtert auf Grund der österreichischen verwaltungsgerichtlichen Rechtsprechung* (Leipzig and Vienna: F. Deuticke, 1924); Christian-Friedrich Menger, *System des verwaltungsrechtlichen Rechtsschutzes: eine verwaltungsgerichtliche und prozeßvergleichende Studie* (Tübingen: Mohr, 1954); and Paul Alexéef, "L'État–le droit–et le pouvoir discrétionnaire des autorités publiques," *Revue internationale de la théorie du droit*, 3 (1928–29): 195–219. Also Oskar Adolf Germann, "Zur Problematik der Ermessensentschiede" in *Festgabe zum siebzigsten Geburtstag von Erwin Ruck*, Juristische Fakultät der Universität Basel, ed. (Basel: Helbing und Lichenhahn, 1952), pp. 173–96; and Horst Ehmke, *"Ermessen" und "unbestimmter Rechtsbegriff" im Verwaltungsrecht* [Recht und Staat, No. 230/231] (Tübingen: J. C. B. Mohr, 1960).

if the law said that everything a certain authority did was legal, it could not be restrained by a court from doing anything. What is required under the rule of law is that a court should have the power to decide whether the law provided for a particular action that an authority has taken. In other words, in all instances where administrative action interferes with the private sphere of the individual, the courts must have the power to decide not only whether a particular action was *infra vires* or *ultra vires* but whether the substance of the administrative decision was such as the law demanded. It is only if this is the case that administrative discretion is precluded.

This requirement clearly does not apply to the administrative authority which tries to achieve particular results with the means at its disposal.[29] It is, however, of the essence of the rule of law that the private citizen and his property should not in this sense be means at the disposal of government. Where coercion is to be used only in accordance with general rules, the justification of every particular act of coercion must derive from such a rule. To ensure this, there must be some authority which is concerned only with the rules and not with any temporary aims of government and which has the right to say not only whether another authority had the right to act as it did but whether what it did was required by the law.

7. The distinction with which we are now concerned is sometimes discussed in terms of the contrast between legislation and policy. If the latter term is appropriately defined, we will indeed be able to express our main point by saying that coercion is admissible only when it conforms to general laws and not when it is a means of achieving particular objects of current policy. This manner of stating it is, however, somewhat misleading, because the term "policy" is also used in a wider sense, in which all legislation falls under it. In this sense legislation is the chief instrument of long-term policy, and all that is done in applying the law is to carry out a policy that has been determined in advance.

A further source of confusion is the fact that within law itself the expression "public policy" is commonly used to describe certain pervading general principles which are often not laid down as written rules but are understood to qualify the validity of more specific rules.[30] When it is said that it is the policy of the law to protect good faith, to preserve public order, or not to recognize

---

[29] Cf. the observation by Edgar Bodenheimer in his instructive discussion of the relation between law and administration in *Jurisprudence* (New York: McGraw-Hill, 1940), p. 95: "Law is mainly concerned with rights; administration is mainly concerned with results. Law is conducive to liberty and security, while administration promotes efficiency and quick decision."

[30] On this see Dennis Lloyd, Baron Lloyd of Hampstead, *Public Policy: A Comparative Study of English and French Law* (London: University of London Press, 1953); also Hans Heinz Todsen, *Der Gesichtspunkt der Public Policy im englischen Recht unter besonderer Berücksichtigung der Lehre von den "contracts in restraint of trade"* (Hamburg: P. Evert Verlag, 1937).

contracts for immoral purposes, this refers to rules, but rules which are stated in terms of some permanent end of government rather than in terms of rules of conduct. It means that, within the limits of the powers given to it, the government must so act that that end will be achieved. The reason why the term "policy" is used in such instances appears to be that it is felt that to specify the end to be achieved is in conflict with the conception of law as an abstract rule. Though such reasoning may explain the practice, it is clearly one which is not without danger.

Policy is rightly contrasted with legislation when it means the pursuit by government of the concrete, ever changing aims of the day. It is with the execution of policy in this sense that administration proper is largely concerned. Its task is the direction and allocation of resources put at the disposal of government in the service of the constantly changing needs of the community. All the services which the government provides for the citizen, from national defense to upkeep of roads, from sanitary safeguards to the policing of the streets,[31] are necessarily of this kind. For these tasks it is allowed definite means and its own paid servants, and it will constantly have to decide on the next urgent task and the means to be used. The tendency of the professional administrators concerned with these tasks is inevitably to draw everything they can into the service of the public aims they are pursuing. It is largely as a protection of the private citizen against this tendency of an ever growing administrative machinery to engulf the private sphere that the rule of law is so important today. It means in the last resort that the agencies entrusted with such special tasks cannot wield for their purpose any sovereign powers (no *Hoheitsrechte*, as the Germans call it) but must confine themselves to the means specially granted to them.

8. Under a reign of freedom the free sphere of the individual includes all action not explicitly restricted by a general law. We have seen that it was found especially necessary to protect against infringement by authority some of the more important private rights, and also how apprehension was felt that such an explicit enumeration of some might be interpreted to mean that only they enjoyed the special protection of the constitution. These fears have proved to be only too well founded. On the whole, however, experience seems to confirm the argument that, in spite of the inevitable incompleteness of any bill of rights, such a bill affords an important protection for certain rights known to be easily endangered. Today we must be particularly aware that, as a result of technological change, which constantly creates new potential threats to indi-

---

[31] What the English call "police" sometimes refers to the German "Politik" and sometimes to "Polizei." The medical services police were in fact not police in the modern sense and the police science of the early nineteenth century was simply administrative science.

vidual liberty, no list of protected rights can be regarded as exhaustive.[32] In an age of radio and television, the problem of free access to information is no longer a problem of the freedom of the press. In an age when drugs or psychological techniques can be used to control a person's actions, the problem of free control over one's body is no longer a matter of protection against physical restraint. The problem of the freedom of movement takes on a new significance when foreign travel has become impossible for those to whom the authorities of their own country are not willing to issue a passport.

The problem assumes the greatest importance when we consider that we are probably only at the threshold of an age in which the technological possibilities of mind control are likely to grow rapidly and what may appear at first as innocuous or beneficial powers over the personality of the individual will be at the disposal of government. The greatest threats to human freedom probably still lie in the future. The day may not be far off when authority, by adding appropriate drugs to our water supply or by some other similar device, will be able to elate or depress, stimulate or paralyze, the minds of whole populations for its own purposes.[33] If bills of rights are to remain in any way meaningful, it must be recognized early that their intention was certainly to protect the individual against all vital infringements of his liberty and that therefore they must be presumed to contain a general clause protecting against government's interference those immunities which individuals in fact have enjoyed in the past.

In the last resort these legal guaranties of certain fundamental rights are no more than part of the safeguards of individual liberty which constitutionalism provides, and they cannot give greater security against legislative infringements of liberty than the constitutions themselves. As we have seen, they can do no more than give protection against hasty and improvident action of current legislation and cannot prevent any suppression of rights by the deliberate action of the ultimate legislator. The only safeguard against this is clear awareness of the dangers on the part of public opinion. Such provisions are important mainly because they impress upon the public mind the value of

---

[32] Zaccaria Giacometti, *Die Freiheitsrechtskataloge als Kodifikation der Freiheit* [Festrede des Rektors gehalten an der 122. Stiftungsfeier der Universität Zürich am 29. April 1955. Jahresbericht 1954/55] (Zurich: Orell Füssli, 1955); cf. also Maurice Hauriou, *Précis de droit constitutionnel* (2nd ed.; Paris: Librairie du Recueil Sirey, 1929), p. 625; and Felice Battaglia, *Le Carte dei diritti [dalla Magna Charta alla Carta di San Francisco]* (2nd ed.; Florence: Sansoni, 1946).

[33] For a none too pessimistic account of the horrors that may be in store for us see Aldous Huxley, *Brave New World: A Novel* (London: Chatto and Windus, 1932), and *Brave New World Revisited* (New York: Harper, 1958); and, even more alarming, because not intended as a warning but expounding a "scientific" ideal, Burrhus Frederic Skinner, *Walden Two* (New York: Macmillan, 1948).

these individual rights and make them part of a political creed which the people will defend even when they do not fully understand its significance.

9. We have up to this point represented those guaranties of individual freedom as if they were absolute rights which could never be infringed. In actual fact they cannot mean more than that the normal running of society is based on them and that any departure from them requires special justification. Even the most fundamental principles of a free society, however, may have to be temporarily sacrificed when, but only when, it is a question of preserving liberty in the long run, as in the case of war. Concerning the need of such emergency powers of government in such instances (and of safeguards against their abuse) there exists widespread agreement.

It is not the occasional necessity of withdrawing some of the civil liberties by a suspension of habeas corpus or the proclamation of a stage of siege that we need to consider further, but the conditions under which the particular rights of individuals or groups may occasionally be infringed in the public interest. That even such fundamental rights as freedom of speech may have to be curtailed in situations of "clear and present danger," or that the government may have to exercise the right of eminent domain for the compulsory purchase of land, can hardly be disputed. But if the rule of law is to be preserved, it is necessary that such actions be confined to exceptional cases defined by rule, so that their justification does not rest on the arbitrary decision of any authority but can be reviewed by an independent court; and, second, it is necessary that the individuals affected be not harmed by the disappointment of their legitimate expectations but be fully indemnified for any damage they suffer as a result of such action.

The principle of "no expropriation without just compensation" has always been recognized wherever the rule of law has prevailed. It is, however, not always recognized that this is an integral and indispensable element of the principle of the supremacy of the law. Justice requires it; but what is more important is that it is our chief assurance that those necessary infringements of the private sphere will be allowed only in instances where the public gain is clearly greater than the harm done by the disappointment of normal individual expectations. The chief purpose of the requirement of full compensation is indeed to act as a curb on such infringements of the private sphere and to provide a means of ascertaining whether the particular purpose is important enough to justify an exception to the principle on which the normal working of society rests. In view of the difficulty of estimating the often intangible advantages of public action and of the notorious tendency of the expert administrator to overestimate the importance of the particular goal of the moment, it would even seem desirable that the private owner should always have the benefit of the doubt and that compensation should be fixed as high as possible without opening the door to outright abuse. This means, after all, no more than that the public gain must clearly and substantially exceed the loss if an exception to the normal rule is to be allowed.

10. We have now concluded the enumeration of the essential factors which together make up the rule of law, without considering those procedural safeguards such as habeas corpus, trial by jury, and so on, which, in the Anglo-Saxon countries, appear to most people as the chief foundations of their liberty.[34] English and American readers will probably feel that I have put the cart before the horse and concentrated on minor features while leaving out what is fundamental. This has been quite deliberate.

I do not wish in any way to disparage the importance of these procedural safeguards. Their value for the preservation of liberty can hardly be overstated. But while their importance is generally recognized, it is not understood that they presuppose for their effectiveness the acceptance of the rule of law as here defined and that, without it, all procedural safeguards would be valueless. True, it is probably the reverence for these procedural safeguards that has enabled the English-speaking world to preserve the medieval conception of the rule of law over men. Yet this is no proof that liberty will be preserved if the basic belief in the existence of abstract rules of law which bind all authority in their action is shaken. Judicial forms are intended to insure that decisions will be made according to rules and not according to the relative desirability of particular ends or values. All the rules of judicial procedure, all the principles intended to protect the individual and to secure impartiality of justice, presuppose that every dispute between individuals or between individuals and the state can be decided by the application of general law. They are designed to make the law prevail, but they are powerless to protect justice where the law deliberately leaves the decision to the discretion of authority. It is only where the law decides—and this means only where independent courts have the last word—that the procedural safeguards are safeguards of liberty.

I have here concentrated on the fundamental conception of law which the traditional institutions presuppose because the belief that adherence to the external forms of judicial procedure will preserve the rule of law seems to me the greatest threat to its preservation. I do not question, but rather wish to emphasize, that the belief in the rule of law and the reverence for the forms of justice belong together and that neither will be effective without the other. But it is the first which is chiefly threatened today; and it is the illusion that it will be preserved by scrupulous observation of the forms of justice that is one

---

[34] Cf. Arthur Thomas Vanderbilt, "The Role of Procedure in the Protection of Freedom," in *Conference on Freedom and the Law, May 7, 1953; Fiftieth Anniversary Celebration*, Thurman Arnold Wesley, ed. [University of Chicago Law School Conference Series, 13] (Chicago: University of Chicago Law School, 1953), pp. 64–73; also Mr. Justice Frankfurter's often quoted statement: "The history of liberty has largely been the history of observance of procedural safeguards," *McNabb v. United States* 318 *U.S.* 332, at 347 (1943).

of the chief causes of this threat. "Society is not going to be saved by import-ing the forms and rules of judicial procedure into places where they do not naturally belong."[35] To use the trappings of judicial form where the essential conditions for a judicial decision are absent, or to give judges power to decide issues which cannot be decided by the application of rules, can have no effect but to destroy the respect for them even where they deserve it.

[35] Cyril John Radcliffe, Viscount Radcliffe of Werneth, *Holdsworth Club of Law and the Demo-cratic State*, p. 16; also, "Have we not come to a time when we must find another name for stat-ute law than Law itself? Para-law, perhaps: or even sub-law" (p. 4). On the situation in Amer-ica see the important article by Robert Green McCloskey, "American Political Thought and the Study of Politics," *American Political Science Review*, 51 (1957), esp. the observation on p. 126 about the manifestation by American courts of "a pervasive concern for procedural niceties coupled with broad tolerance of substantive inhibitions on freedom. . . . The American concern for pro-cedural rights runs more deeply and steadily than the concern for substantive liberty. Indeed, so far as it goes the evidence implies that freedom in the obvious sense of liberty to think and speak and act unhindered holds no very favored place in the American hierarchy of political values." But there seems to be an increasing awareness of this danger, well expressed by Allen Keith-Lucas, *Decisions about People in Need: A Study of Administrative Responsiveness in Public Assistance* (Chapel Hill: University of North Carolina Press, 1957), p. 156: "To rely on procedure alone to produce justice is the fallacy of modern liberalism. It has made possible the legality of totalitar-ian regimes such as Hitler's."

FIFTEEN

ECONOMIC POLICY AND THE RULE OF LAW

The House of Representatives . . . can make no law which will not have its full operation on themselves and their friends, as well as the great mass of the society. This [circumstance] has always been deemed one of the strongest bonds by which human policy can connect the rulers and the people together. It creates between them that communion of interest, and sympathy of sentiments, of which few governments have furnished examples; but without which every government degenerates into tyranny. —James Madison

1. The classical argument for freedom in economic affairs rests on the tacit postulate that the rule of law should govern policy in this as in all other spheres. We cannot understand the nature of the opposition of men like Adam Smith or John Stuart Mill to government "intervention" unless we see it against this background. Their position was therefore often misunderstood by those who were not familiar with that basic conception; and confusion arose in England and America as soon as the conception of the rule of law ceased to be assumed by every reader. Freedom of economic activity had meant freedom under the law, not the absence of all government action. The "interference" or "intervention" of government which those writers opposed as a matter of principle therefore meant only the infringement of that private sphere which the general rules of law were intended to protect. They did not mean that government should never concern itself with any economic matters. But they did mean that there were certain kinds of governmental measures which should be precluded on principle and which could not be justified on any grounds of expediency.

To Adam Smith and his immediate successors the enforcement of the ordinary rules of common law would certainly not have appeared as government interference; nor would they ordinarily have applied this term to an alter-

The quotation at the head of the chapter is taken from James Madison, "The Alleged Tendency of the Plan to Elevate the Few at the Expense of the Many Considered in Connection with Representation" (No. 57), in Alexander Hamilton, James Madison, and John Jay, *The Federalist, or the New Constitution*, Max Beloff, Baron Beloff, ed. (Oxford: B. Blackwell, 1948), p. 294 [Liberty Fund edition, p. 297].

ation of these rules or the passing of a new rule by the legislature so long
as it was intended to apply equally to all people for an indefinite period of
time. Though they perhaps never explicitly said so, interference meant to
them the exercise of the coercive power of government which was not regular
enforcement of the general law and which was designed to achieve some specific purpose.[1] The important criterion was not the aim pursued, however,
but the method employed. There is perhaps no aim which they would not
have regarded as legitimate if it was clear that the people wanted it; but they
excluded as generally inadmissible in a free society the method of specific
orders and prohibitions. Only indirectly, by depriving government of some
means by which alone it might be able to attain certain ends, may this principle deprive government of the power to pursue those ends.

The later economists bear a good share of the responsibility for the confusion on these matters.[2] True, there are good reasons why all governmen-

---

[1] Cf. Ludwig von Mises, *Kritik des Interventionismus: Untersuchungen zur Wirtschaftspolitik und
Wirtschaftsideologie der Gegenwart* (Jena: G. Fischer, 1929), p. 6: "Der Eingriff ist ein von einer
gesellschaftlichen Gewalt ausgehender *isolierter Befehl*, der die Eigentümer der Produktionsmittel und die Unternehmer zwingt, die Produktionsmittel anders zu verwenden, als sie es sonst tun
würden." ["Intervention is a *limited order* by a social authority forcing the owners of the means of
production and entrepreneurs to employ their means in a different manner than they otherwise
would." (*A Critique of Interventionism*, Hans F. Sennholz, trans. [Irvington-on-Hudson, NY: Foundation for Economic Education, 1996], p. 20; Hayek's italics; the entire sentence is emphasized
in the original).—Ed.] See also the distinction between *produktionspolitische* and *preispolitische Ein-
griffe* elaborated later in the same work. John Stuart Mill, "On Liberty," in *On Liberty and Considerations on Representative Government*, Ronald Buchanan McCallum, ed. (Oxford: B. Blackwell, 1946),
p. 85, even argues that "the so-called doctrine of Free Trade . . . rests on grounds different from,
though equally solid with, the principle of individual liberty asserted in this Essay. Restrictions
on trade, or on production for purposes of trade, are indeed restraints; and all restraint, *qua*
restraint, is an evil: but the restraints in question affect only that part of conduct which society is
competent to restrain, and are wrong solely because they do not really produce the results which
it is desired to produce by them. As the principle of individual liberty is not involved in the doctrine of Free Trade, so neither is it in most of the questions which arise respecting the limit of
that doctrine; as, for example, what amount of public control is admissible for the prevention
of fraud by adulteration; how far sanitary precautions, or arrangements to protect work-people
employed in dangerous occupations, should be enforced on employers."

[2] As the examination of measures of policy for their expediency is one of the chief tasks of
the economists, it is not surprising that they should have lost sight of the more general criterion.
John Stuart Mill, by admitting (*On Liberty*, p. 8) that "there is, in fact, no recognized principle by
which the propriety of government interference is customarily tested," had already given the
impression that it was all a matter of expediency. And his contemporary, Nassau William Senior,
usually regarded as much more orthodox, explicitly said so at about the same time: "The only
rational foundation of government, the only foundation of a right to govern and a correlative
duty to obey, is expediency—the general benefit of the community" (quoted in Lionel Robbins,
The Theory of Economic Policy in English Classical Political Economy [London: Macmillan, 1952], p. 45).
[Senior's comments appear in his Oxford lectures of 1847–52, Course 1, Lecture 6, "The Power
of Government to alter the degree in which wealth is Desirable." The citation appears in Mar-

tal concern with economic matters is suspect and why, in particular, there is a strong presumption against government's actively participating in economic efforts. But these arguments are quite different from the general argument for economic freedom. They rest on the fact that the great majority of governmental measures which have been advocated in this field are, in fact, inexpedient, either because they will fail or because their costs will outweigh the advantages. This means that, so long as they are compatible with the rule of law, they cannot be rejected out of hand as government intervention but must be examined in each instance from the viewpoint of expediency. The habitual appeal to the principle of non-interference in the fight against all ill-considered or harmful measures has had the effect of blurring the fundamental distinction between the kinds of measures which are and those which are not compatible with a free system. And the opponents of free enterprise have been only too ready to help this confusion by insisting that the desirability or undesirability of a particular measure could never be a matter of principle but is always one of expediency.

In other words, it is the character rather than the volume of government activity that is important. A functioning market economy presupposes certain activities on the part of the state; there are some other such activities by which its functioning will be assisted; and it can tolerate many more, provided that they are of the kind which is _compatible_ with a functioning market. But there are those which run counter to the very principle on which a free system rests and which must therefore be altogether excluded if such a system is to work. In consequence, a government that is comparatively inactive but does the wrong things may do much more to cripple the forces of a market economy than one that is more concerned with economic affairs but confines itself to actions which _assist_ the spontaneous forces of the economy.

It is the purpose of this chapter to show that the rule of law provides the criterion which enables us to distinguish between those measures which are and those which are not compatible with a free system. Those that are may be examined further on the grounds of expediency. Many such measures will, of course, still be undesirable or even harmful. But those that are not must be rejected even if they provide an effective, or perhaps the only effective, means to a desirable end. We shall see that the observation of the rule of law is a necessary, but not yet a sufficient, condition for the satisfactory working of a free economy. But the important point is that all coercive action of government must be unambiguously determined by a permanent legal framework which

ian Bowley, *Nassau Senior and Classical Economics* (New York: Octagon Books, Inc., 1967), p. 265. —Ed.] Yet both these men unquestionably took it for granted that interference with the protected sphere of the individual was permissible only where it was provided for by the general rules of law and never on mere grounds of expediency.

enables the individual to plan with a degree of confidence and which reduces human uncertainty as much as possible.

2. Let us consider, first, the distinction between the coercive measures of government and those pure service activities where coercion does not enter or does so only because of the need of financing them by taxation.[3] In so far as the government merely undertakes to supply services which otherwise would not be supplied at all (usually because it is not possible to confine the benefits to those prepared to pay for them), the only question which arises is whether the benefits are worth the cost. Of course, if the government claimed for itself the exclusive right to provide particular services, they would cease to be strictly non-coercive. In general, a free society demands not only that the government have the monopoly of coercion but that it have the monopoly only of coercion and that in all other respects it operate on the same terms as everybody else.

A great many of the activities which governments have universally undertaken in this field and which fall within the limits described are those which facilitate the acquisition of reliable knowledge about facts of general significance.[4] The most important function of this kind is the provision of a reliable and efficient monetary system. Others scarcely less important are the setting of standards of weights and measures; the providing of information gathered from surveying, land registration, statistics, etc.; and the support, if not also the organization, of some kind of education.

All these activities of government are part of its effort to provide a favorable framework for individual decisions; they supply means which individuals can use for their own purposes. Many other services of a more material kind fall into the same category. Though government must not use its power of coercion to reserve for itself activities which have nothing to do with the enforcement of the general rules of law, there is no violation of principle in its engaging in all sorts of activities on the same terms as the citizens. If in the majority of fields there is no good reason why it should do so, there are fields in which the desirability of government action can hardly be questioned.

To this latter group belong all those services which are clearly desirable

---

[3] The distinction is the same as that which Mill, (*Principles*, bk. 5, chap. 11, sec. 1, p. 942 [Liberty Fund edition, *Collected* Works, vol. 2, p. 937]) draws between "authoritative" and "unauthoritative" government interference. It is a distinction of great importance, and the fact that all government activity has been assumed more and more to be necessarily of the "authoritative" character is one of the chief causes of the objectionable developments of modern times. I do not here adopt Mill's terms because it seems to me inexpedient to call his "unauthoritative" activities of government "interference." This term is better confined to infringements of the protected private sphere, which can be done only "authoritatively."

[4] See again the careful treatment of this in Mill, *Principles*, bk. 5, chap. 11, sec. 3, pp. 944–45 [Liberty Fund edition, *Collected Works*, vol. 2, pp. 938–39].

but which will not be provided by competitive enterprise because it would be either impossible or difficult to charge the individual beneficiary for them. Such are most sanitary and health services, often the construction and maintenance of roads, and many of the amenities provided by municipalities for the inhabitants of cities. Included also are the activities which Adam Smith described as "those public works, which, though they may be in the highest degree advantageous to a great society, are, however, of such a nature, that the profit could never repay the expense to any individual or small number of individuals."[5] And there are many other kinds of activity in which the government may legitimately wish to engage, in order perhaps to maintain secrecy in military preparations or to encourage the advancement of knowledge in certain fields.[6] But though government may at any moment be best qualified to take the lead in such fields, this provides no justification for assuming that this will always be so and therefore for giving it exclusive responsibility. In most instances, moreover, it is by no means necessary that government engage in the actual management of such activities; the services in question can generally be provided, and more effectively provided, by the government's assuming some or all of the financial responsibility but leaving the conduct of the affairs to independent and in some measure competitive agencies.

There is considerable justification for the distrust with which business looks on all state enterprise. There is great difficulty in ensuring that such enterprise will be conducted on the same terms as private enterprise; and it is only if this condition is satisfied that it is not objectionable in principle. So long as government uses any of its coercive powers, and particularly its power of taxation, in order to assist its enterprises, it can always turn their position into one of actual monopoly. To prevent this, it would be necessary that any spe-

---

[5] A. Smith, *Wealth of Nations*, bk. 5, chap. 1, pt. 2, vol. 2, p. 214 [Liberty Fund edition, vol. 2, p. 723]; cf. also the argument in favor of local, as against central, government taking charge of public works, ibid., p. 222 [Liberty Fund edition, vol. 2, p.730].

[6] There is, finally, the theoretically interesting, though in practice not very significant, situation in which, though certain services can be supplied by competitive private effort, either not all the cost involved or not all the benefits rendered would enter the calculations of the market and for this reason it may seem desirable to impose special charges on, or offer special grants to all who engage in those activities. These instances may perhaps be included among the measures by which government may assist the direction of private production, not by specific intervention, but by acting according to general rules.

That these cases are not of great practical significance, not because such situations may not often occur, but because it is rarely possible to ascertain the magnitude of such "divergences between the marginal social net product and the private social net product," is now admitted by the author who has done more than anybody else to draw attention to them: see Arthur Cecil Pigou, "Some Aspects of the Welfare State," *Diogenes*, 7 (1954): 6: "It must be confessed, however, that we seldom know enough to decide in what fields and to what extent the State, on account of [the gaps between private and public costs] could usefully interfere with individual freedom of choice."

cial advantages, including subsidies which government gives to its own enterprises in any field, should also be made available to competing private agencies. There is no need to emphasize that it would be exceedingly difficult for government to satisfy these conditions and that the general presumption against state enterprise is thereby considerably strengthened. But this does not mean that all state enterprise must be excluded from a free system. Certainly it ought to be kept within narrow limits; it may become a real danger to liberty if too large a section of economic activity comes to be subject to the direct control of the state. But what is objectionable here is not state enterprise as such but state monopoly.

3. Furthermore, a free system does not exclude on principle all those general regulations of economic activity which can be laid down in the form of general rules specifying conditions which everybody who engages in a certain activity must satisfy. They include, in particular, all regulations governing the techniques of production. We are not concerned here with the question of whether such regulations will be wise, which they probably will be only in exceptional cases. They will always limit the scope of experimentation and thereby obstruct what may be useful developments. They will normally raise the cost of production or, what amounts to the same thing, reduce over-all productivity. But if this effect on cost is fully taken into account and it is still thought worthwhile to incur the cost to achieve a given end, there is little more to be said about it.[7] The economist will remain suspicious and hold that there is a strong presumption against such measures because their over-all cost is almost always underestimated and because one disadvantage in particular—namely, the prevention of new developments—can never be fully taken into account. But if, for instance, the production and sale of phosphorus matches is generally prohibited for reasons of health or permitted only if certain precautions are taken, or if night work is generally prohibited, the appropriateness of such measures must be judged by comparing the over-all costs with the gain; it cannot be conclusively determined by appeal to a general principle. This is true of most of the wide field of regulations known as "factory legislation."

It is often maintained today that these or similar tasks which are generally acknowledged to be proper functions of government could not be adequately performed if the administrative authorities were not given wide discretionary powers and all coercion were limited by the rule of law. There is little reason to fear this. If the law cannot always name the particular measures which the authorities may adopt in a particular situation, it can be so framed as to enable any impartial court to decide whether the measures adopted were necessary to achieve the general effect aimed at by the law. Though the variety

---

[7] See Ludwig von Mises, *Kritik des Interventionismus*, p. 6.

of circumstances in which the authorities may have to act cannot be foreseen, the manner in which they will have to act, once a certain situation has arisen, can be made predictable to a high degree. The destroying of a farmer's cattle in order to stop the spreading of a contagious disease, the tearing down of houses to prevent the spreading of a fire, the prohibition of an infected well, the requirement of protective measures in the transmission of high-tension electricity, and the enforcement of safety regulations in buildings undoubtedly demand that the authorities be given some discretion in applying general rules. But this need not be a discretion unlimited by general rules or of the kind which need to be exempt from judicial review.

We are so used to such measures being referred to as evidence of the necessity of conferring discretionary powers that it comes somewhat as a surprise that, as recently as thirty years ago, an eminent student of administrative law could still point out that "health and safety statutes are, generally speaking, by no means conspicuous for the use of discretionary powers; on the contrary, in much of that legislation such powers are conspicuously absent. . . . Thus British factory legislation has found it possible to rely practically altogether on general rules (though to a large extent framed by administrative regulation) . . . many building codes are framed with a minimum of administrative discretion, practically all regulation being limited to requirements capable of standardization. . . . In all these cases the consideration of flexibility yielded to the higher consideration of certainty of private right, without any apparent sacrifice of public interest."[8]

In all such instances the decisions are derived from general rules and not from particular preferences which guide the government of the moment or from any opinion as to how particular people ought to be situated. The coercive powers of government still serve general and timeless purposes, not specific ends. It must not make any distinctions between different people. The discretion conferred on it is a limited discretion in that the agent is to apply the sense of a general rule. That this rule cannot be made completely unambiguous in its application is a consequence of human imperfection. The problem, nevertheless, is one of applying a rule, which is shown by the fact that an independent judge, who in no way represents the particular wishes or values of the government or of the majority of the moment, will be able to decide not only whether the authority had a right to act at all but also whether it was required by law to do exactly what it did.

The point at issue here has nothing to do with the question of whether the regulations justifying the actions of government are uniform for the whole country or whether they have been laid down by a democratically elected as-

---

[8] Ernest Freund, *Administrative Powers Over Persons and Property: A Comparative Survey* (Chicago: University of Chicago Press, 1928), p. 98.

sembly. There is clearly need for some regulations to be passed by local ordinances, and many of them, such as building codes, will necessarily be only in form and never in substance the product of majority decisions. The important question again concerns not the origin but the limits of the powers conferred. Regulations drawn up by the administrative authority itself but duly published in advance and strictly adhered to will be more in conformity with the rule of law than will vague discretionary powers conferred on the administrative organs by legislative action.

Though there have always been pleas on the ground of administrative convenience that these strict limits should be relaxed, this is certainly not a necessary requirement for the achievement of the aims we have considered so far. It was only after the rule of law had been breached for other aims that its preservation no longer seemed to outweigh considerations of administrative efficiency.

4. We must now turn to the kinds of governmental measures which the rule of law excludes in principle because they cannot be achieved by merely enforcing general rules but, of necessity, involve arbitrary discrimination between persons. The most important among them are decisions as to who is to be allowed to provide different services or commodities, at what prices or in what quantities—in other words, measures designed to control the access to different trades and occupations, the terms of sale, and the amounts to be produced or sold.

So far as the entry into different occupations is concerned, our principle does not necessarily exclude the possible advisability in some instances of permitting it only to those who possess certain ascertainable qualifications. The restriction of coercion to the enforcement of general rules requires, however, that any one possessing these qualifications have an enforceable claim to such permission and that the grant of the permission depend only on his satisfying the conditions laid down as a general rule and not on any particular circumstances (such as "local need") which would have to be determined by the discretion of the licensing authority. Even the need for such controls could probably be rendered unnecessary in most instances by merely preventing people from pretending to qualifications which they do not possess, that is, by applying the general rules preventing fraud and deception. For this purpose the protection of certain designations or titles expressing such qualifications might well be sufficient (it is by no means evident that even in the case of doctors this would not be preferable to the requirement of a license to practice). But it is probably undeniable that in some instances, such as where the sale of poisons or firearms is involved, it is both desirable and unobjectionable that only persons satisfying certain intellectual and moral qualities should be allowed to practice such trade. So long as everybody possessing the necessary qualifications has the right to practice the occupation in question and, if necessary, can have his claim examined and enforced by an independent court, the basic principle is satisfied.[9]

There are several reasons why all direct control of prices by government is irreconcilable with a functioning free system, whether the government actually fixes prices or merely lays down rules by which the permissible prices are to be determined. In the first place, it is impossible to fix prices according to long-term rules which will effectively guide production. Appropriate prices depend on circumstances which are constantly changing and must be continually adjusted to them. On the other hand, prices which are not fixed outright but determined by some rule (such as that they must be in a certain relation to cost) will not be the same for all sellers and, for this reason, will prevent the market from functioning. A still more important consideration is that, with prices different from those that would form on a free market, demand and supply will not be equal, and if the price control is to be effective, some method must be found for deciding who is to be allowed to buy or sell. This would necessarily be discretionary and must consist of *ad hoc* decisions that discriminate between persons on essentially arbitrary grounds. As experience has amply confirmed, price controls can be made effective only by quantitative controls, by decisions on the part of authority as to how much particular persons or firms are to be allowed to buy or sell. And the exercise of all controls of quantities must, of necessity, be discretionary, determined not by rule but by the judgment of authority concerning the relative importance of particular ends.

It is thus not because the economic interests with which such measures interfere are more important than others that price and quantity controls must be altogether excluded in a free system, but because this kind of controls cannot be exercised according to rule but must in their very nature be discretionary and arbitrary. To grant such powers to authority means in effect to give it power arbitrarily to determine what is to be produced, by whom, and for whom.

5. Strictly speaking, then, there are two reasons why all controls of prices and quantities are incompatible with a free system: one is that all such controls must be arbitrary, and the other is that it is impossible to exercise them in such a manner as to allow the market to function adequately. A free system can adapt itself to almost any set of data, almost any general prohibition or regulation, so long as the adjusting mechanism itself is kept functioning. And

[9] On the issue of licensing see Walter Gellhorn, *Individual Freedom and Governmental Restraints* (Baton Rouge: Louisiana State University Press, 1956), esp. chap. 3, pp. 105–51). I would not have treated this matter so lightly if the final text of this chapter had not been completed before I knew this work. I believe few foreign observers and probably not many Americans are aware how far this practice has been carried in the United States in recent years—so far, indeed, that it must now appear as one of the real threats to the future of American economic development.

it is mainly changes in prices that bring about the necessary adjustments. This means that, for it to function properly, it is not sufficient that the rules of law under which it operates be general rules, but their content must be such that the market will work tolerably well. The case for a free system is not that any system will work satisfactorily where coercion is confined by general rules, but that under it such rules can be given a form that will enable it to work. If there is to be an efficient adjustment of the different activities in the market, certain minimum requirements must be met; the more important of these are, as we have seen, the prevention of violence and fraud, the protection of property and the enforcement of contracts, and the recognition of equal rights of all individuals to produce in whatever quantities and sell at whatever prices they choose. Even when these basic conditions have been satisfied, the efficiency of the system will still depend on the particular content of the rules. But if they are not satisfied, government will have to achieve by direct orders what individual decisions guided by price movements will.

The relation between the character of the legal order and the functioning of the market system has received comparatively little study, and most of the work in this field has been done by men who were critical of the competitive order[10] rather than by its supporters. The latter have usually been content to state the minimal requirements for the functioning of the market which we have just mentioned. A general statement of these conditions, however, raises almost as many questions as the answers it provides. How well the market will function depends on the character of the particular rules. The decision to rely on voluntary contracts as the main instrument for organizing the relations between individuals does not determine what the specific content of the law of contract ought to be; and the recognition of the right of private property does not determine what exactly should be the content of this right in order that the market mechanism will work as effectively and beneficially as possible. Though the principle of private property raises comparatively few problems so far as movable things are concerned, it does raise exceedingly difficult ones where property in land is concerned. The effect which the use of any one piece of land often has on neighboring land clearly makes it undesirable to give the owner unlimited power to use or abuse his property as he likes.

But, while it is to be regretted that economists have on the whole contributed little to the solution of these problems, there are some good reasons for this. General speculation about the character of a social order cannot produce much more than equally general statements of the principles that the

[10] See particularly John Rogers Commons, *The Legal Foundations of Capitalism* (New York: Macmillan, 1924); Walton Hale Hamilton and Douglass Adair, *The Power to Govern: The Constitution— Then and Now* (New York: W. W. Norton, 1937); and John Maurice Clark, *Social Control of Business* (2nd ed.; New York: Whittlesey House, McGraw-Hill, 1939); and cf. on this school, Abram Lincoln Harris, *Economics and Social Reform* (New York: Harper, 1958).

legal order must follow. The application in detail of these general principles must be left largely to experience and gradual evolution. It presupposes concern with concrete cases, which is more the province of the lawyer than of the economist. At any rate, it is probably because the task of gradually amending our legal system to make it more conducive to the smooth working of competition is such a slow process that it has had little appeal for those who seek an outlet for their creative imagination and are impatient to draw up blueprints for further development.

6. There is still another point we must consider a little more closely. Since the time of Herbert Spencer[11] it has become customary to discuss many aspects of our problem under the heading of "freedom of contract." And for a period of time this point of view played an important role in American jurisdiction.[12] There is indeed a sense in which freedom of contract is an important part of individual freedom. But the phrase also gives rise to misconceptions. In the first place, the question is not what contracts individuals will be allowed to make but rather what contracts the state will enforce. No modern state has tried to enforce all contracts, nor is it desirable that it should. Contracts for criminal or immoral purposes, gambling contracts, contracts in restraint of trade, contracts permanently binding the services of a person, or even some contracts for specific performances are not enforced.

Freedom of contract, like freedom in all other fields, really means that the permissibility of a particular act depends only on general rules and not on its specific approval by authority. It means that the validity and enforcibility of a contract must depend only on those general, equal, and known rules by which all other legal rights are determined, and not on the approval of its particular content by an agency of the government. This does not exclude the possibility of the law's recognizing only those contracts which satisfy certain general conditions or of the state's laying down rules for the interpretation of contracts which will supplement the explicitly agreed terms. The existence of such recognized standard forms of contract which, so long as no contrary terms are stipulated, will be presumed to be part of the agreement often greatly facilitates private dealings.

A much more difficult question is whether the law should ever provide for obligations arising out of a contract which may be contrary to the intentions of both parties, as, for example, in the case of liability for industrial accidents irrespective of negligence. But even this is probably more a question of expe-

[11] See especially Herbert Spencer, *Justice: Being Part IV of the Principles of Ethics* (Authorized ed.; London: D. Appleton and Co., 1891) [Liberty Fund edition, *Principles of Ethics*, vol. 2, pp. 19–279]; and cf. Thomas Hill Green, "Lecture on 'Liberal Legislation and Freedom of Contract,'" [1880] in *Works of T. H. Green* (3 vols.; London: Longmans, Green, and Co., 1888), vol. 3: *Miscellanies and Memoir* [1885–88], pp. 365–86.

[12] Cf. Roscoe Pound, "Liberty of Contract," *Yale Law Journal*, 18 (1908–09): 454–87.

diency than of principle. The enforcibility of contracts is a tool which the law provides for us, and what consequences will follow upon concluding a contract is for the law to say. So long as these consequences can be predicted from a general rule and the individual is free to use the available types of contracts for his own purposes, the essential conditions of the rule of law are satisfied.

7. The range and variety of government action that is, at least in principle, reconcilable with a free system is thus considerable. The old formulae of laissez faire or non-intervention do not provide us with an adequate criterion for distinguishing between what is and what is not admissible in a free system. There is ample scope for experimentation and improvement within that permanent legal framework which makes it possible for a free society to operate most efficiently. We can probably at no point be certain that we have already found the best arrangements or institutions that will make the market economy work as beneficially as it could. It is true that after the essential conditions of a free system have been established, all further institutional improvements are bound to be slow and gradual. But the continuous growth of wealth and technological knowledge which such a system makes possible will constantly suggest new ways in which government might render services to its citizens and bring such possibilities within the range of the practicable.

Why, then, has there been such persistent pressure to do away with those limitations upon government that were erected for the protection of individual liberty? And if there is so much scope for improvement within the rule of law, why have the reformers striven so constantly to weaken and undermine it? The answer is that during the last few generations certain new aims of policy have emerged which cannot be achieved within the limits of the rule of law. A government which cannot use coercion except in the enforcement of general rules has no power to achieve particular aims that require means other than those explicitly entrusted to its care and, in particular, cannot determine the material position of particular people or enforce distributive or "social" justice. In order to achieve such aims, it would have to pursue a policy which is best described—since the word "planning" is so ambiguous—by the French word *dirigisme*, that is, a policy which determines for what specific purposes particular means are to be used.

This, however, is precisely what a government bound by the rule of law cannot do. If the government is to determine how particular people ought to be situated, it must be in a position to determine also the direction of individual efforts. We need not repeat here the reasons why, if government treats different people equally, the results will be unequal, or why, if it allows people to make what use they like of the capacities and means at their disposal, the consequences for the individuals will be unpredictable. The restrictions which the rule of law imposes upon government thus preclude all those measures which would be necessary to insure that individuals will be rewarded according to another's conception of merit or desert rather than according to the value that their services have for their fellows or, what amounts to the same thing, it precludes the pursuit of distributive, as opposed to commutative, justice. Distributive justice requires an allocation of all resources by a central authority; it requires that people be told what to do and what ends to serve. Where distributive justice is the goal, the decisions as to what the different individuals must be made to do cannot be derived from general rules but must be made in the light of the particular aims and knowledge of the planning authority. As we have seen before, when the opinion of the community decides what different people shall receive, the same authority must also decide what they shall do.

This conflict between the ideal of freedom and the desire to "correct" the distribution of incomes so as to make it more "just" is usually not clearly recognized. But those who pursue distributive justice will in practice find themselves obstructed at every move by the rule of law. They must, from the very nature of their aim, favor discriminatory and discretionary action. But, as they are usually not aware that their aim and the rule of law are in principle incompatible, they begin by circumventing or disregarding in individual cases a principle which they often would wish to see preserved in general. But the ultimate result of their efforts will necessarily be, not a modification of the existing order, but its complete abandonment and its replacement by an altogether different system—the command economy.

While it is certainly not true that such a centrally planned system would be more efficient than one based on a free market, it is true that only a centrally directed system could attempt to ensure that the different individuals would receive what someone thought they deserved on moral grounds. Within the limits set by the rule of law, a great deal can be done to make the market work more effectively and smoothly; but, within these limits, what people now regard as distributive justice can never be achieved. We shall have to examine the problems which have arisen in some of the most important fields of contemporary policy as a result of the pursuit of distributive justice. Before we do so, however, we must consider the intellectual movements which have done so much during the last two or three generations to discredit the rule of law and which, by disparaging this ideal, have seriously undermined the resistance to a revival of arbitrary government.

SIXTEEN

THE DECLINE OF THE LAW

> The dogma, that absolute power may, by the hypothesis of a popular origin, be as legitimate as constitutional freedom, began . . . to darken the air.
>
> —Lord Acton

1. Earlier in our discussion we devoted more attention than is usual to developments in Germany, partly because it was in that country that the theory, if not the practice, of the rule of law was developed furthest, and partly because it was necessary to understand the reaction against it which commenced there. As is true of so much of socialist doctrine, the legal theories which undermined the rule of law originated in Germany and spread from there to the rest of the world.

The interval between the victory of liberalism and the turn toward socialism or a kind of welfare state was shorter in Germany than elsewhere. The institutions meant to secure the rule of law had scarcely been completed before a change in opinion prevented their serving the aims for which they had been created. Political circumstances and developments which were purely intellectual combined to accelerate a development which proceeded more slowly in other countries. The fact that the unification of the country had at last been achieved by the artifice of statesmanship rather than by gradual evolution strengthened the belief that deliberate design should remodel society according to a preconceived pattern. The social and political ambitions which this situation encouraged were strongly supported by philosophical trends then current in Germany.

The demand that government should enforce not merely "formal" but "substantive" (i.e., "distributive" or "social") justice had been advanced recurrently since the French Revolution. Toward the end of the nineteenth century these ideas had already profoundly affected legal doctrine. By 1890 a

---

The quotation at the head of the chapter is taken from Lord Acton, "Sir Erskine May's *Democracy in Europe*," *History of Freedom*, p. 78 [Liberty Fund edition, *Essays in the History of Liberty*, p. 68]. The title of the chapter is borrowed from Georges Ripert, *Le Déclin du droit* (Paris: Pichon and Durand-Auzias, 1949).

leading socialist theorist of the law could thus express what was increasingly becoming the dominant doctrine: "By treating in a perfectly equal manner all citizens regardless of their personal qualities and economic position, and by allowing unlimited competition between them, it came about that the production of goods was increased without limit; but the poor and weak had only a small share in that output. The new economic and social legislation therefore attempts to protect the weak against the strong and to secure for them a moderate share in the good things of life. This is because today it is understood that there is no greater injustice than to treat as equal what is in fact unequal!"[1] And there was Anatole France, who scoffed at "the majestic equality of the law that forbids the rich as well as the poor to sleep under bridges, to beg in the streets and to steal bread."[2] This famous phrase has been repeated countless times by well-meaning but unthinking people who did not understand that they were undermining the foundations of all impartial justice.

[1] Anton Menger, *Das bürgerliche Recht und die besitzlosen Volksklassen* (1890) (3rd ed.; Tübingen: H. Laupp, 1904), p. 30. [The original German reads: "Indem man nun alle Staatsbürger ohne Rücksicht auf ihre persönlichen Eigenschaften und auf ihre wirtschaftliche Lage völlig gleich behandelte und zwischen ihnen einen zügellosen Wettbewerb zuliess, bewirkte man zwar, dass die Gütererzeugung ins unendliche stieg, zugleich aber auch, dass die Armen und Schwachen an den gesteigerten Gütermengen nur einen sehr geringen Anteil hatten. Daher die neue wirtschaftliche und Sozialgesetzgebung, welche bestrebt ist, den Schwachen gegen den Starken zu schützen und ihm an den Gütern des Lebens wenigstens einen bescheidenen Anteil zu sichern. Man weiss eben heute, dass es keine grössere Ungleichheit gibt, als das Ungleiche gleich zu behandeln."—Ed.] The full consequences of this conception are worked out in that author's later book, *Neue Staatslehre* (Jena: Gustav Fischer, 1903). About the same time the great German criminologist, Franz Eduard von Liszt could already comment (*Strafrechtliche Aufsätze und Vorträge*. Vol. 2: *1892 bis 1904* [2 vols.; Berlin: J. Guttentag, 1905], p. 60): "Das heranwachsende sozialistische Geschlecht, das die gemeinsamen Interessen schärfer betont als seine Vorgänger, für dessen Ohren das Wort 'Freiheit' einen archaistischen Klang gewonnen hat, rüttelt an diesen Grundlagen." ["The coming socialist generation, which emphasizes common interests with greater force than did its predecessors and for whose ears the word 'freedom' has an archaic ring, is buffeting the foundations (of justice)."—Ed.] The infiltration of the same ideas into England is well illustrated by David George Ritchie, *Natural Rights: A Criticism of Some Political and Ethical Conceptions* (1894) (3rd ed.; London: Allen and Unwin, 1916), p. 258: "The claim of equality, in its widest sense, means the demand for equal opportunity—the *carrière ouverte aux talents*. The result of such equality of opportunity will clearly be the very reverse of equality of social condition, if the law allows the transmission of property from parent to child, or even the accumulation of wealth by individuals. And thus, as has often been pointed out, the effect of the nearly complete triumph of the principles of 1789—the abolition of legal restrictions on free competition—has been to accentuate the difference between wealth and poverty. Equality in political rights, along with great inequalities in social condition, has laid bare 'the social question'; which is no longer concealed, as it formerly was, behind the struggle for equality before the law and for equality in political rights."

[2] Anatole France, *Le Lys rouge* (Paris: Calmann-Lévy, 1894), p. 118. [The original reads: "La majestueuse égalité des lois, qui interdit au riche comme au pauvre de coucher sous les ponts, de mendier dans les rues et de voler du pain."—Ed.]

2. The ascendancy of these political views was greatly assisted by the increasing influence of various theoretical conceptions which had arisen earlier in the century and which, though in many respects strongly opposed to one another, had in common the dislike of any limitation of authority by rules of law and shared the desire to give the organized forces of government greater power to shape social relations deliberately according to some ideal of social justice. The four chief movements which operated in this direction were, in descending order of importance, legal positivism, historicism, the "free law" school, and the school of "jurisprudence of interest." We shall only briefly consider the last three before we turn to the first, which must detain us a little longer.

The tradition which only later became known as "jurisprudence of interest" was a form of sociological approach somewhat similar to the "legal realism" of contemporary America. At least in its more radical forms it wanted to get away from the kind of logical construction which is involved in the decision of disputes by the application of strict rules of law and to replace it by a direct assessment of the particular "interests" at stake in the concrete case.[3] The "free law" school was in a way a parallel movement concerned mainly with criminal law. Its objective was to free the judge as far as possible from the shackles of fixed rules and permit him to decide individual cases mainly on the basis of his "sense of justice." It has often been pointed out how much the latter in particular prepared the way for the arbitrariness of the totalitarian state.[4]

Historicism, which must be precisely defined so that it may be sharply distinguished from the great historical schools (in jurisprudence and elsewhere)

[3] The tradition traces back to the later work of Rudolph von Ihering (1818–1882). [Von Ihering's most important works were probably *The Spirit of the Roman Laws* (1852–65), originally published in German under the title *Geist des römischen Rechts auf den verschieden Stufen seiner Entwicklung* (4 vols.; Leipzig: Breitkopf und Härtel, 1852–65); *The Struggle for Law* (1879), translated from the 5th German ed. of *Der Kampf um's Recht* (Vienna: Manz, 1877); and *Law as a Means to an End*. Vol. 1: 1877; Vol. 2: 1883, which was a translation of the first volume of the 4th ed. of Ihering's *Der Zweck im Recht* (Leipzig: Breitkopf und Härtel, 1904–05). These works underscored Ihering's theory that self-interest was of crucial importance in shaping the law and that the process by which legal rules were maintained was self-regulating.—Ed.] For the modern development see the essays collected in *The Jurisprudence of Interests: Selected Writings of Max Rümelin*, Magdalena Schoch, ed. (Twentieth Century Legal Philosophy Series, vol. 2; Cambridge, MA: Harvard University Press, 1948).

[4] See, e.g., Fritz Fleiner, *Ausgewählte Schriften und Reden* (Zurich: Polygraphischer Verlag, 1941), p. 438: "Dieser Umschwung [zum totalitären Staat] ist vorbereitet worden durch gewisse Richtungen innerhalb der deutschen Rechtswissenschaft (z.B. die sogenannte Freirechtsschule), die geglaubt haben, dem Rechte zu dienen, indem sie die Gesetzestreue durchbrachen." ["This change (this transformation toward the totalitarian state) was adumbrated by certain tendencies that marked German jurisprudence (e.g., the so-called school of free-law) that held that it was possible to serve the law by violating its integrity." (Interpolation Hayek's.)—Ed.]

that preceded it,[5] was a school that claimed to recognize necessary laws of historical development and to be able to derive from such insight knowledge of what institutions were appropriate to the existing situation. This view led to an extreme relativism which claimed, not that we are the product of our own time and bound in a large measure by the views and ideas we have inherited, but that we can transcend those limitations and explicitly recognize how our present views are determined by circumstances and use this knowledge to remake our institutions in a manner appropriate to our time.[6] Such a view would naturally lead to a rejection of all rules that cannot be rationally justified or have not been deliberately designed to achieve a specific purpose. In this respect historicism supports what we shall presently see is the main contention of legal positivism.[7]

3. The doctrines of legal positivism have been developed in direct opposition to a tradition which, though it has for two thousand years provided the framework within which our central problems have been mainly discussed, we have not explicitly considered. This is the conception of a law of nature, which to many still offers the answer to our most important question. We have so far deliberately avoided discussing our problems with reference to this conception because the numerous schools which go under this name hold really different theories and an attempt to sort them out would require a separate book.[8] But we must at least recognize here that these different schools of the law of nature have one point in common, which is that they address themselves to the same problem. What underlies the great conflict between the

---

[5] About the character of this historicism see Menger, *Untersuchungen*, and Sir Karl Raimund Popper, *The Poverty of Historicism* (London: Routledge and Kegan Paul, 1957).

[6] Cf. my *The Counter-Revolution of Science: Studies in the Abuse of Reason* (Glencoe, IL: Free Press, 1952), pt. 1, chap. 7 ["The Historicism of the Scientific Approach," pp. 64–79; *Collected Works* edition, vol. 13, pp. 126–41].

[7] On the connection between historicism and legal positivism cf. Hermann Heller, "Bemerkungen zur staats- und rechtstheoretischen Problematik der Gegenwart," *Archiv für öffentliches Recht*, 16 (1929): 336.

[8] The best brief survey of the different "natural-law" traditions that I know of is Alessandro Passerin d'Entrèves, *Natural Law: An Introduction to Legal Philosophy* (Hutchinson's University Library; London: Hutchinson, 1951). [This book is the outcome of eight lectures delivered at the University of Chicago in April 1948.—Ed.] It may also be briefly mentioned here that modern legal positivism derives largely from Thomas Hobbes and René Descartes, the two [The 1971 German edition reads: "three" and includes "Francis Bacon."—Ed.] men against whose rationalistic interpretation of society the evolutionary, empiricist, or "Whig" theology was developed, and that positivism gained its present-day ascendancy largely because of the influence of Hegel and Marx. For Marx's position, see the discussion of individual rights in the Introduction to his *Kritik der Hegelschen Rechtsphilosophie*, in Karl Marx and Friedrich Engels, *Historisch-kritische Gesamtausgabe, Werke, Schriften, Briefe*, David Borisovic Rjazanov [David Borisovic Gol'dendach], ed. (11 vols.; Berlin: Marx-Engels Archiv, Marx-Engels Verlag, 1927–32), vol. 1, pt. 1.

defenders of natural law and the legal positivists is that, while the former recognize the existence of that problem, the latter deny that it exists at all, or at least that it has a legitimate place within the province of jurisprudence.

What all the schools of natural law agree upon is the existence of rules which are not of the deliberate making of any lawgiver. They agree that all positive law derives its validity from some rules that have not in this sense been made by men but which can be "found" and that these rules provide both the criterion for the justice of positive law and the ground for men's obedience to it. Whether they seek the answer in divine inspiration or in the inherent powers of human reason, or in principles which are not themselves part of human reason but constitute non-rational factors that govern the working of the human intellect, or whether they conceive of the natural law as permanent and immutable or as variable in content, they all seek to answer a question which positivism does not recognize. For the latter, law by definition consists exclusively of deliberate commands of a human will.

For this reason, legal positivism from the very beginning could have no sympathy with and no use for those meta-legal principles which underlie the ideal of the rule of law or the *Rechtsstaat* in the original meaning of this concept, for those principles which imply a limitation upon the power of legislation. In no other country did this positivism gain such undisputed sway in the second half of the last century as it did in Germany. It was consequently here that the ideal of the rule of law was first deprived of real content. The substantive conception of the *Rechtsstaat*, which required that the rules of law possess definite properties, was displaced by a purely formal concept which required merely that all action of the state be authorized by the legislature. In short, a "law" was that which merely stated that whatever a certain authority did should be legal. The problem thus became one of mere legality.[9] By the turn of the century it had become accepted doctrine that the "individualist" ideal of the substantive *Rechtsstaat* was a thing of the past, "vanquished by the creative powers of national and social ideas."[10] Or, as an authority on administrative law described the situation shortly before the outbreak of the first World War: "We have returned to the principles of the police state [!] to such an extent that we again recognize the idea of a *Kulturstaat*. The only difference

[9] Cf. Hermann Heller, *Rechtsstaat oder Diktatur?* (Tübingen: Mohr, 1930); John Hamilton Hallowell, *The Decline of Liberalism as an Ideology, with Particular Reference to German Politico-legal Thought* (Berkeley: University of California Press, 1943); and *The Moral Foundation of Democracy* (Chicago: University of Chicago Press, 1954), chap. 4, "Democracy and Liberalism," pp. 68–88, esp. p. 73.

[10] Richard Thoma, "Rechtsstaatsidee und Verwaltungstrechtswissenschaft," in *Jahrbuch des offentlichen Rechts der Gegenwart*, 4 (1910): 199. [The German reads: "Diese individualistische Rechtsstaatsidee hat in der Tat ihre Rolle ausgespielt. Die schöpferische Kräfte der nationalen und der sozialen Ideen haben sie überwunden. Es wird das häufig betont und niemand zweifelt daran."—Ed.]

is in the means. On the basis of laws the modern state permits itself everything, much more than the police state did. Thus, in the course of the nineteenth century, the term *Rechtsstaat* was given a new meaning. We understand by it a state whose whole activity takes place on the basis of laws and in legal form. On the purpose of the state and the limits of its competence the term *Rechtsstaat* in its present-day meaning says nothing."[11]

It was, however, only after the first World War that these doctrines were given their most effective form and began to exert a great influence which extended far beyond the limits of Germany. This new formulation, known as the "pure theory of law" and expounded by Professor H. Kelsen,[12] signaled the definite eclipse of all traditions of limited government. His teaching was avidly taken up by all those reformers who had found the traditional limitations an irritating obstacle to their ambitions and who wanted to sweep away all restrictions on the power of the majority. Kelsen himself had early observed how the "fundamentally irretrievable liberty of the individual . . . gradually recedes into the background and the liberty of the social collective occupies the front of the stage"[13] and that this change in the conception of

---

[11] Edmund Bernatzik, *Die Ausgestaltung des Nationalgefühls im 19. Jahrhundert. Rechtsstaat und Kulturstaat: Zwei Vorträge gehalten in der Vereinigung für staatswissenschaftliche Fortbildung in Cöln im April 1912* (Hanover: Helwing, 1912), p. 56. [The German reads: "Wir Heutigen kehren zu den Principien des Polizeistaates insofern zurück, als wir seine Kulturstaatsidee wieden anerkennen. Der einzige Unterschied liegt in den rechlichen Mitteln. Auf Grund von Gesetzen gestattet sich der heutige Staat alles noch viel mehr als der Polizeistaat. Und so gelangte man im Laufe des 19. Jahrhunderts zu einer neuen Bedeutung des Ausdruckes 'Rechtsstaat.' Man verstand jetzt darunter einen Staat, dessen ganze Tätigkeit sich auf Grund von Gesetzen in rechtlichen Formen abspielt. Über den Staatszweck und die Grenzen der staatlichen Kompetenz sagt das Wort 'Rechtsstaat' in seiner heutigen Bedeutung gar nichts mehr aus und in dieser neuen Bedeutung steht daher das Wort auch nicht mehr in einem Gegensatz zum Kulturstaat."—Ed.]. Cf. also the same author's "Polizei und Kulturpflege," in *Systematische Rechtswissenschaft* (Berlin: Teubner, 1906) [pt. 2, sec. 8 of *Die Kultur der Gegenwart. Ihre Entwicklung und ihre Ziele*, edited by Paul Hinneberg], pp. 387–426.

[12] The victory of legal positivism had been secured earlier, mainly through the relentless efforts of Carl Bergbohm, *Jurisprudenz und Rechtsphilosophie: kritische Abhandlungen* (Leipzig: Duncker und Humblot, 1892), but it was in the form given to it by Hans Kelsen that it achieved a widely accepted and consistent philosophical basis. We shall here quote mainly from Kelsen's *Allgemeine Staatslehre* (Berlin: Julius Springer, 1925), but the reader will find most of the essential ideas restated in his *General Theory of Law and State*, Anders Wedberg, trans. (Twentieth Century Legal Philosophy Series; Cambridge, MA: Harvard University Press, 1945), which also contains a translation of an important lecture on *Die philosophischen Grundlagen der Naturrechtslehre und des Rechtspositivismus* (Charlottenburg: Verlag Rolf Heise, 1928). [An English translation of Kelsen's *Die philosophischen Grundlagen* appears on pp. 391–446 of his *General Theory of Law and State*.—Ed.]

[13] Hans Kelsen, *Vom Wesen und Wert der Demokratie* (Tübingen: J. C. B. Mohr, 1920), p.10 [The German reads: "die im Grunde genommen unrettbare Freiheit des Individuums tritt allmählich in den Hintergrund und die Freiheit des sozialen Kollektivums in den Vordergrund."—Ed.]. The phrase "im Grunde unrettbare Freiheit des Individuums" ["the fundamentally irretrievable

---

THE CONSTITUTION OF LIBERTY

freedom meant an "emancipation of democratism from liberalism,"[14] which he evidently welcomed. The basic conception of his system is the identification of the state and the legal order. Thus the *Rechtsstaat* becomes an extremely formal concept and an attribute of all states,[15] even a despotic one.[16] There are no possible limits to the power of the legislator,[17] and there are no "so-called fundamental liberties";[18] and any attempt to deny to an arbitrary despotism the character of a legal order represents "nothing but the naïveté

---

freedom of the individual"—Ed.] becomes in the second edition of 1929 "im Grunde unmögliche Freiheit des Individuums" ["the in fact impossible freedom of the individual"—Ed.] (*Von Wesen und Wert der Demokatie* [2nd ed.; Tübingen: J. C. B. Mohr, 1929], p. 11).

[14] "Loslösung des Demokratismus von Liberalismus," Hans Kelsen, *Vom Wesen und Wert der Demokratie*, p. 10.

[15] Hans Kelsen, *Allgemeine Staatslehre*, p. 91. Cf. also his *Hauptprobleme der Staatsrechtslehre: entwickelt aus der Lehre vom Rechtssatze* (2nd ed.; Tübingen: J. C. B. Mohr, 1923), p. 249, where his approach leads him consistently to assert that "a wrong of the state must under all circumstances be a contradiction in terms." ["Ein Unrecht des Staates muß unter allen Umständen ein Widerspruch in sich selbst sein."—Ed.]

[16] Hans Kelsen, *Allgemeine Staatslehre*, p. 335; the relevant passages read in translation: "Entirely meaningless is the assertion that under a despotism there exists no order of law [*Rechtsordnung*], [that there] the arbitrary will of the despot reigns. . . . The despotically governed state also represents some order of human behavior. This order is the order of law. To deny to it the name of an order of law is nothing but naïveté and presumption deriving from natural-law thinking. . . . What is interpreted as arbitrary will is merely the legal possibility of the autocrat's taking on himself every decision, determining unconditionally the activities of subordinate organs and rescinding or altering at any time norms once announced, either generally or for a particular case. Such a condition is a condition of law even when it is felt to be disadvantageous. It has also its good aspects. The demand for dictatorship not uncommon in the modern *Rechtsstaat* shows this very clearly." ["Vollends sinnlos ist die Behauptung, daß in der Despotie keine Rechtsordnung bestehe, sondern Willkür des Despoten herrsche. . . . stellt doch auch der despotisch regierte Staat irgendeine Ordnung menschlichen Verhaltens dar, weil ja ohne eine solche Ordnung überhaupt kein Staat, ja überhaupt keine Gemeinschaft möglich, kein Mensch als Herrscher, König, Fürst qualifizierbar wäre. Diese Ordnung ist eben die Rechtsordnung. Ihr den Charakter des Rechts absprechen, ist nur eine naturrechtliche Naivität oder Überhebung. . . . Was als Willkür gedeutet wird, ist nur die rechtliche Möglichkeit des Autokraten, jede Entscheidung an sich zu ziehen, die Tätigkeit der untergeordneten Organe bedingungslos zu bestimmen und einmal gesetzte Normen jederzeit mit allgemeiner oder nur besonderer Geltung aufzuheben oder abzuändern. Ein solcher Zustand ist ein Rechtzustand, auch wenn er als nachteilig empfunden wird. Doch hat er auch seine guten Seiten. Der im modernen *Rechtsstaat* gar nicht seltene Ruf nach Diktatur zeigt dies ganz deutlich."—Ed.] That this passage still represents the author's views is explicitly acknowledged by him in his essay "Foundations of Democracy," *Ethics*, no. 1, pt. 2, 66 (1955):100, n. 13; see also an earlier version of the same argument, entitled "Democracy and Socialism," in *Conference of Jurisprudence and Politics*, Scott Buchanan, ed. (Chicago: University of Chicago Law School, 1955), pp. 63–87.

[17] Hans Kelsen, *Allgemeine Staatslehre*, p. 14.

[18] Hans Kelsen, *Allgemeine Staatslehre*, pp. 154ff. [the phrase is "die sogenannten Freiheitsrechte."—Ed.]

and presumption of natural-law thinking."[19] Every effort is made not only to obscure the fundamental distinction between true laws in the substantive sense of abstract, general rules and laws in the merely formal sense (including all acts of a legislature) but also to render indistinguishable from them the orders of any authority, no matter what they are, by including them all in the vague term "norm."[20] Even the distinction between jurisdiction and administrative acts is practically obliterated. In short, every single tenet of the traditional conception of the rule of law is represented as a metaphysical superstition.

This logically most consistent version of legal positivism illustrates the ideas which by the 1920s had come to dominate German thinking and were rapidly spreading to the rest of the world. At the end of that decade they had so completely conquered Germany that "to be found guilty of adherence to natural law theories [was] a kind of social disgrace."[21] The possibilities which this state of opinion created for an unlimited dictatorship were already clearly seen by acute observers at the time Hitler was trying to gain power. In 1930 a German legal scholar, in a detailed study of the effects of the "efforts to realize the socialist State, the opposite of the *Rechtsstaat*,"[22] was able to point out that these "doctrinal developments have already removed all obstacles to the disappearance of the *Rechtsstaat*, and opened the doors to the victory of the fascist and bolshevist will of the State."[23] The increasing concern over these developments which Hitler was finally to complete was given expression by more than one speaker at a congress of German constitutional lawyers.[24]

---

[19] Hans Kelsen, *Allgemeine Staatslehre*, p. 335. [The original quotation reads: "Ihr den Charakter des Rechts absprechen, ist nur eine naturrechtliche Naivität oder Überhehung."—Ed.]

[20] Hans Kelsen, *Allgemeine Staatslehre*, pp. 231–35ff.; cf. the same author's *General Theory of Law and State*, p. 38.

[21] Erich Voegelin, "Kelsen's Pure Theory of Law," *Political Science Quarterly*, 42 (1927): 269.

[22] Friedrich Darmstädter, *Die Grenzen der Wirksamkeit des Rechtsstaates. Eine Untersuchung zur gegenwärtigen Krise des liberalen Staatsgedankens* (Heidelberg: Carl Winters, 1930), passim. (On socialism see esp. pp. 48–51.) Cf. Hallowell, *The Decline of Liberalism as an Ideology* and *The Moral Foundations of Democracy*. On the further development under the Nazis see Franz Leopold Neumann, *Behemoth: The Structure and Practice of National Socialism, 1933–1944* (2nd ed.; New York: Oxford University Press, 1944), and Aurel Kolnai, *The War Against the West* (New York: Viking Press, 1938), pp. 299–310.

[23] Darmstädter, *Die Grenzen der Wirksamkeit des Rechtsstaates*, p. 95. [The German reads: "Tendenz das Wesen des Rechtsstaates im Staatsbegriff schlechthin untergehen zu lassen, . . . dem Siege und der Alleingeltung des faschistischen und bolschewistischen Staatswollens . . . derart von der Staatslehre her ein grundsätzliches Hindernis nicht mehr engegen [stellt]."—Ed.]

[24] Heinrich Triepel, Comment on "Die Reform des Wahlrechts" (pp. 194–98), and Gerhard Leibholz, "Die Wahlrechtsreform und ihre Grundlagen" (pp. 159–90), in *Entwicklung und Reform des Beamtenrechts. Die Reform des Wahlrechts*, Hans Gerber, ed. (Series title: Veröffentlichungen der Vereinigung der Deutschen Staatsrechtslehrer: Vol. 7; Berlin: Walter de Gruyter, 1932).

But it was too late. The antilibertarian forces had learned too well the positivist doctrine that the state must not be bound by law. In Hitler Germany and in Fascist Italy, as well as in Russia, it came to be believed that under the rule of law the state was "unfree,"[25] a "prisoner of the law,"[26] and that, in order to act "justly," it must be released from the fetters of abstract rules.[27] A "free" state was to be one that could treat its subjects as it pleased.

4. The inseparability of personal freedom from the rule of law is shown most clearly by the absolute denial of the latter, even in theory, in the country where modern despotism has been carried furthest. The history of the development of legal theory in Russia during the early stages of communism, when the ideals of socialism were still taken seriously and the problem of the role of law in such a system was extensively discussed, is very instructive.

[25] Aleksandr Leonidovitch Malitzki, quoted by Boris Mirkin-Getzewitsch, *Die rechtstheoretischen Grundlagen des Sowjetstaates* (Leipzig: Franz Deuticke, 1929), p. 117. [Translated from the French by Rita Willfort, *La théorie générale de l'état soviétique* (Paris: Marcel Giard, 1928).] [The quotation to which Hayek is referring reads: "'Die Lehre vom *Rechtsstaat* sagt die Sowjettheorie, 'ist in ihren Grundzügen eine Doktrin vom unfreien Staat.'" ("The rule of law, according to Soviet theory, has as its fundamental principle the doctrine of the unfree state.")—Ed.] Cf., however, a similar discussion in Rudolph von Ihering, *Law as a Means to an End*, Isaac Husik, trans. (Boston: Boston Book Co., 1913), pp. 314–15: "Exclusive domination of the law is synonymous with the resignation on the part of society, of the free use of its hands. Society would give herself up with bound hands to rigid necessity, standing helpless in the presence of all circumstances and requirements of life which were not provided for in the law, or for which the latter was found to be inadequate. We derive from this the maxim that the State must not limit its own power of spontaneous self-activity by law any more than is absolutely necessary—rather too little in this direction than too much. It is a wrong belief that the interest or the security of right and of political freedom requires the greatest possible limitation of the government by the law. This is based upon the strange notion [!] that force is an evil which must be combated to the utmost. But in reality it is a good, in which, however, as in every good, it is necessary, in order to make possible its wholesome use, to take the possibility of its abuse into the bargain." Cf. Otto Friedrich von Gierke, *Johannes Althusius und die Entwicklung der naturrechtlichen Staatstheorien: zugleich ein Beitrag zur Geschichte der Rechtssystematik* (Breslau: W. Koebner, 1880), p. 304, in which he remarks about the theory of the *Rechtsstaat* put forward by Kant and Humboldt: "Dieser *Rechtsstaat* wäre, wenn seine Verwirklichung überhaupt denkbar gewesen wäre, mit der vollen Unfreiheit und Ohnmacht der Staatsgewalt erkauft worden." ["The *Rechtsstaat* could have been purchased only at the cost of the total impotence and incapacity of the state, were it even conceivable."—Ed.]

[26] Giacomo Perticone, "Quelques aspects de la crise du droit public en Italie," *Revue internationale de la théorie du droit / Internationale Zeitschrift für Theorie des Rechts*, 5 (1931–32): 2. [The full French quotation reads: "En se passant de toute l'évolution de la pensée juridique, on a cru pouvoir considérer l'État de droit comme l'État prisonnier du droit, incapable, par conséquent, de mouvement, de volonté, de puissance; un État aboulique, neutre, et ce qui s'ensuit." ("During the whole of the evolution of juridical thought, one was led to the conclusion that a regime of law was one in which the State was a prisoner of the law, and as a consequence incapable of action, of will, of power, a State indecisive, emasculated, and all that which follows.")—Ed.]

[27] See Carl Schmitt, "Was bedeutet der Streit um den '*Rechtsstaat*,'" *Zeitschrift für die gesamte Staatswissenschaft* [*Journal of Institutional and Theoretical Economics*] (Tübingen), 95 (1935): 190.

In their ruthless logic the arguments advanced in these discussions show the nature of the problem more clearly than does the position taken by Western socialists, who usually try to have the best of both worlds.

The Russian legal theorists deliberately continued in a direction which, they recognized, had long been established in western Europe. As one of them put it, the conception of law itself was generally disappearing, and "the center of gravity was shifting more and more from the passing of general norms to individual decisions and instructions which regulate, assist, and co-ordinate activities of administration."[28] Or, as another contended at the same time, "since it is impossible to distinguish between laws and administrative regulations, this contrast is a mere fiction of bourgeois theory and practice."[29] The best description of these developments we owe to a non-Communist Russian scholar, who observed that "what distinguishes the Soviet system from all other despotic government is that . . . it represents an attempt to found the state on *principles* which are the opposite of those of the rule of law . . . [and it] has evolved a *theory* which exempts the rulers from every obligation or limitation."[30] Or, as a Communist theorist expressed it, "the fundamental principle of our legislation and our private law, which the bourgeois theorist will never recognize is: everything is prohibited which is not specifically permitted."[31]

[28] R. Archipov, *Law in the State* (in Russian), quoted in Boris Mirkin-Getzewitsch, *Die rechtstheoretischen Grundlagen des Sowjetstaates*, p. 108–9. [The German reads: "Ein Sowjetjurist behauptet, daß 'der Schwerpunkt sich mehr und mehr von der Erlassung genereller Normen zur Setzung individueller Akte und Instruktionen verschiebe, welche die Tätigkeit der Verwaltung regeln, fördern und koordinieren."—Ed.]

[29] Peter Ivanovitch Stuchka, *Uchenie o gosudarstve proletariata i krest'ianstva i ego konstitutsii: SSSR / RSFSR [Theory of the State of the Proletarians and Peasants and Its Constitution]* (5th ed.; Moscow: Gos. izd-vo, 1926), quoted in Boris Mirkin-Getzewitsch, *Die rechtstheoretischen Grundlagen des Sowjetstaates*, p. 70ff. [The French translation of the Russian text (Petr Ivanovitch Stoutchka, *La théorie de l'État prolétarien et paysan et ses constitutions* [5th ed.; Moscow, 1926], p. 194) reads: "Dans l'impossibilité où l'on est de distinguer où finit la loi et où commence l'ordonnance administrative, cette opposition n'est qu'une pure fiction de la science et la pratique bourgeoise."—Ed.]

[30] Mirkin-Getzewitsch, *Die rechtstheoretischen Grundlagen des Sowjetstaates*, p. 107. [The German reads: "Aber was gerade das Sowjetsystem von sämtlichen übrigen despotischen Staatsformen der Gegenwart und Vergangenheit unterscheidet, ist, daß es nicht nur die faktische Gewalt kennt, die tatsächliche Ungesetzlichkeit, sondern daß es außerdem auf einer sozialen Basis von ungeheurer Ausdehnung einen Versuch dastellt, den Staat auf Grundsätzen zu begründen, die denen eines Rechtsstaates entgegengesetzt sind. . . . Der Sowjetstaat hingegen hat eine Theorie ausgearbeitet, die Herrschenden von jeder Verpflichtung, von jeder Beschränkung ausnimmt."—Ed.]

[31] Malitzki, quoted by Mirkin-Getzewitsch, *Die rechtstheoretischen Grundlagen des Sowjetstaates*, p. 89. [The full quotation reads: "Hieraus folgt der fundamentale Grundsatz unserer Gesetzgebung und unseres Zivilrechtes, den die bürgerlichen Theorien niemals anerkennen werden: Alles, was nicht speziell erlaubt worden ist, ist verboten," denn "'entgegen der europäischen Doktrin erklären wir, daß Subjekt der Gewalt, Quelle des Rechtes nicht der Einzelne, sondern der Staat

Finally, the Communist attacks came to be directed at the conception of law itself. In 1927 the president of the Soviet Supreme Court explained in an official handbook of private law: "Communism means not the victory of socialist law, but the victory of socialism over any law, since with the abolition of classes with antagonistic interests, law will disappear altogether."[32]

The reasons for this stage of the development were most clearly explained by the legal theorist E. Pashukanis, whose work for a time attracted much attention both inside and outside Russia but who later fell into disgrace and disappeared.[33] He wrote: "To the administrative technical direction by subordination to a general economic plan corresponds the method of direct, technologically determined direction in the shape of programs for production and distribution. The gradual victory of this tendency means the gradual extinction of law as such."[34] In short: "As, in a socialist community, there was no

---

ist." ("From this follows that the fundamental principle of our legislation and our private law, which bourgeois theories will never recognize, is: everything that is not specifically permitted is prohibited" because "in contrast to European teaching, we hold that the subject of power and the source of law is not the individual but the state.")—Ed.] It has to be admitted, however, that this principle is also to be found in Aristotle, *Nicomachean Ethics*, 1138a.1 [bk. 5, chap. 11]: "Whatever [the law] does not bid it forbids."

[32] Quoted by Vladimir Gsovski, *Soviet Civil Law: Private Rights and Their Background Under the Soviet Regime; Comparative Survey and Translation of the Civil Code, Code of Domestic Relations, Judiciary Act, Code of Civil Procedure, Laws on Nationality, Corporations, Patents, Copyright, Collective Farms, Labor, and Related Laws* (2 vols.; Ann Arbor: University of Michigan Law School, 1948–49), vol. 1, p. 170; quoted in Peter Ivanovitch Stuchka, *Entsiklopediia gosudarstva i prava* [*Encyclopedia of State and Law*] (3 vols.; Moscow: Izd-vo Kommunisticheskoi Akademii, 1925–27), p. 1593.

[33] Concerning Pashukanis's fate, Roscoe Pound observes in his *Administrative Law: Its Growth, Procedure, and Significance* (Pittsburgh: University of Pittsburgh Press, 1942), p. 127: "The Professor [Evgenii Bronislavovich Pashukanis] is not with us now. With the setting up of a plan by the present government in Russia, a change of doctrine was called for and he did not move fast enough in his teaching to conform to the doctrinal exigencies of the new order. If there had been law instead of only administrative orders it might have been possible for him to lose his job without losing his life."

[34] Evgenii Bronislavovich Pashukanis, *Allgemeine Rechtslehre und Marxismus: Versuch einer Kritik der juristischen Grundbegriffe*, trans. from the 2nd Russian edition by Edith Hajós (Vienna: Verlag für Literatur und Politik, 1929), p. 117. [The German reads: "Die verwaltungstechnische Leitung durch Unterwerfung unter einen allgemeinen Wirtschaftsplan ist analog der Methode der direkten technologisch bestimmten Leitung in der Gestaltung der Programme für die Produktion und Verteilung. Der allmähliche Sieg dieser Tendenz bedeutet die allmähliche Aufgabe des Rechts als solchem."—Ed.] An English translation of this and of a later work by Pashukanis has been published in *Soviet Legal Philosophy*, Hugh Webster Badd, trans., Introduction by John Newbold Hazard (Cambridge, MA: Harvard University Press, 1951). For discussions, see Hans Kelsen, *The Communist Theory of Law* (New York: Praeger, 1955); Rudolph Schlesinger, *Soviet Legal Theory: Its Social Background and Development* (2nd ed.; London: Routledge and Kegan Paul, 1951); Lon Luvois Fuller, "Pashukanis and Vyshinsky: A Study in the Development of Marxian Legal Theory," *Michigan Law Review*, 47 (1948–49): 1157–66; and Samuel Dobrin, "Soviet Jurisprudence and Socialism," *Law Quarterly Review*, 52 (1936): 402–24.

scope for autonomous private legal relations, but only for regulation in the interest of the community, all law was converted into administration; all fixed rules into discretion and utility."[35]

5. In England developments away from the rule of law had started early but for a long time remained confined to the sphere of practice and received little theoretical attention. Though, by 1915, Dicey could observe that "the ancient veneration for the rule of law has in England suffered during the last thirty years a marked decline,"[36] the increasingly frequent infringements of the principle attracted little notice. Even when in a 1929 book called *The New Despotism*[37] appeared, in which Lord Justice Hewart pointed out how little in accord with the rule of law was the situation which had developed, it achieved a *succès de scandale* but could do little to change the complacent belief that the liberties of Englishmen were safely protected by that tradition. The book was treated as a mere reactionary pamphlet, and the venom which was directed at it[38] is difficult to understand a quarter of a century later, when not only liberal organs like the *Economist*[39] but also socialist authors[40] have come to speak of the danger in the same terms. The book did indeed lead to the appointment of an official "Committee on Ministers' Powers"; but its Report,[41] while mildly reasserting Dicey's doctrines, tended on the whole to minimize the dan-

---

[35] This summary of Pashukanis's argument is taken from Wolfgang Gaston Friedmann, *Law and Social Change in Contemporary Britain* (London: Stevens and Sons, 1951), p. 154.

[36] Dicey, *Law of the Constitution* (8th ed.), p. xxxviii. [Liberty Fund edition, p. lv. The 8th ed. of Dicey's book appeared in 1915.]

[37] Gordon Hewart, Baron Hewart, *The New Despotism* (London: Ernest Benn Ltd., 1929).

[38] Characteristic of the treatment which that well justified warning received even in the United States is the following comment by Professor (now Justice) Felix Frankfurter, published in 1938: "As late as 1929 Lord Hewart attempted to give fresh life to the moribund unrealities of Dicey by garnishing them with alarm. Unfortunately, the eloquent journalism of this book carried the imprimatur of the Lord Chief Justice. His extravagant charges demanded authoritative disposition and they received it" (foreword to "Current Developments in Administrative Law," *Yale Law Journal*, 47 [1938]: 517). [Lord Hewart called attention to the dangers inherent in the increasingly common practice of Parliament delegating their powers to administrative tribunals, thus subverting Parliamentary government.—Ed.]

[39] "What is the Public Interest?" *Economist*, June 19, 1954, p. 952: "The 'new despotism,' in short, is not an exaggeration, it is a reality. It is a despotism that is practised by the most conscientious, incorruptible and industrious tyrants that the world has ever seen."

[40] Richard Howard Stafford Crossman, *Socialism and the New Despotism* [Fabian Tracts, No. 298] (London: Fabian Society, 1956).

[41] Committee on Ministers' Powers, *Report Presented by the Lord High Chancellor to Parliament by Command of His Majesty, April 1932* [the Donoughmore Report], chaired from 30 October 1929 to 2 May 1931 by the Rt. Hon. The Earl of Donoughmore. Cmd. 4060 (London: His Majesty's Stationery Office, 1932); see also the Committee on Ministers' Powers, *Memoranda Submitted by Government Departments in Reply to Questionnaire of November 1929 and Minutes of Evidence* (2 vols.; London: His Majesty's Stationery Office, 1932).

gers. Its main effect was that it made the opposition to the rule of law articulate and evoked an extensive literature which outlined an antirule-of-law doctrine which has since come to be accepted by many besides socialists.

This movement was led by a group[42] of socialist lawyers and political scientists gathered around the late Professor Harold J. Laski. The attack was opened by Dr. (now Sir Ivor) Jennings in reviews of the *Report* and the *Documents* on which the latter was based.[43] Completely accepting the newly fashionable positivist doctrine, he argued that the conception of the rule of law, in the sense in which it was used in that Report, means that "equality before the law, the ordinary law of the land, administered by the ordinary courts . . . taken literally . . . is just nonsense."[44] This rule of law, he contended, "is either common to all nations or does not exist."[45] Though he had to concede that "the fixity and certainty of the law have been part of the English tradition for centuries," he did so only with evident impatience at the fact that this tradition was "but reluctantly breaking down."[46] For the belief shared by "most of the members of the Committee, and most of the witnesses . . . that there was a clear distinction between the functions of a judge and the functions of an administrator,"[47] Dr. Jennings had only scorn.

He later expounded these views in a widely used textbook, in which he expressly denied that "the rule of law and discretionary powers are contradictory"[48] or that there is any opposition "between 'regular law' and 'administrative powers.'"[49] The principle in Dicey's sense, namely, that public authorities ought not to have wide discretionary powers, was "a rule of action for Whigs and may be ignored by others."[50] Though Dr. Jennings recognized that "to a constitutional lawyer of 1870, or even 1880, it might have seemed that the British Constitution was essentially based on the individualist rule of law, and that the British State was the *Rechtsstaat* of individualist political and

---

[42] For the description of Harold Joseph Laski, Sir Ivor Jennings, William Alexander Robson, and Herman Finer as members of the same group see William Ivor Jennings, "Administrative Law and Administrative Jurisdiction," *Journal of Comparative Legislation and International Law*, 3rd ser., 20 (1938): 103.

[43] Sir William Ivor Jennings, "The Report on Ministers' Powers," *Public Administration* (London), 10 (1932): 333–51, and Book Review ["Official Ministers' Powers"], 11 (1933): 109–14.

[44] Jennings, "Report on Ministers' Powers," p. 342.

[45] Ibid., p. 343.

[46] Ibid., p. 345.

[47] Ibid., p. 345. [The quotation actually appears in Jenning's review of "Official Ministers' Powers," *Public Administration*, 11 (1933): 111.—Ed.]

[48] Sir William Ivor Jennings, *The Law of the Constitution* (4th ed.; London: University of London Press, 1952), p. 54.

[49] Ibid., p. 291.

[50] Ibid., p. 292.

legal theory,"[51] this meant to him merely that "the Constitution frowned on 'discretionary' powers, unless they were exercised by judges. When Dicey said that Englishmen 'are ruled by the law, and by the law alone' he meant that 'Englishmen are ruled by judges, and by judges alone.' That would have been an exaggeration, but it was good individualism."[52] That it was a necessary consequence of the ideal of liberty under the law that only experts in the law and no other experts, and especially no administrators concerned with particular aims, should be entitled to order coercive action seems not to have occurred to the author.

It should be added that further experience appears to have led Sir Ivor to modify his views considerably. He begins and concludes a recent popular book[53] with sections in praise of the rule of law and even gives a somewhat idealized picture of the degree to which it still prevails in Britain. But this change did not come before his attacks had had a wide effect. In a popular *Vocabulary of Politics*,[54] for instance, which had appeared in the same series only a year before the book just mentioned, we find it argued that "it is therefore odd that there should be a prevalent view that the Rule of Law is something which some people have but other people do not have, like motor cars and telephones. What does it mean, then, to be without the Rule of Law? Is it to have no laws at all?" I fear this question correctly represents the position of most of the younger generation, grown up under the exclusive influence of positivist teaching.

Equally important and influential has been the treatment of the rule of law in a widely used treatise on administrative law by another member of the same group, Professor W. A. Robson. His discussion combines a commendable zeal for regularizing the chaotic state of the control over administrative action with an interpretation of the task of administrative tribunals which, if applied, would make them entirely ineffective as a means of protecting individual liberty. He aims explicitly at accelerating the "break-away from that Rule of Law which the late Professor A. V. Dicey regarded as an essential feature of the English constitutional system."[55] The argument commences with an attack on "that antique and rickety chariot," the "legendary separation of powers."[56] The whole distinction between law and policy is to him "utterly

---

[51] Ibid., p. 294.

[52] Ibid.

[53] Sir William Ivor Jennings, *The Queen's Government* (Pelican Books; London: Penguin Books, 1954), pp. 9–13.

[54] Thomas Dewar Weldon, *The Vocabulary of Politics* (Pelican Books; London: Penguin Books, 1953), p. 68.

[55] William Alexander Robson, *Justice and Administrative Law* (3rd ed.; London: Stevens, 1951), p. xi.

[56] Ibid., p. 16.

false,"[57] and the conception that the judge is not concerned with governmental ends but with the administration of justice a matter for ridicule. He even represents as one of the main advantages of administrative tribunals that they "can enforce a policy unhampered by rules of law and judicial precedents. . . . Of all the characteristics of administrative law, none is more advantageous, when rightly used for the public good, than the power of the tribunal to decide the cases coming before it with the avowed object of furthering a policy of social improvement in some particular field; and of adapting their attitude towards the controversy so as to fit the needs of that policy."[58]

Few other discussions of these problems show as clearly how reactionary many of the "progressive" ideas of our time really are! It is therefore not too surprising that such a view as Professor Robson's has rapidly found favor with the conservatives and that a recent Conservative party pamphlet on the Rule of Law echoes him in commending administrative tribunals for the fact that "flexible and unbound by rules of law or precedent, they can be of real assistance to their Minister in carrying out his policy."[59] This acceptance of socialist doctrine by the conservatives is perhaps the most alarming feature of the development. It has gone so far that it could be said of a conservative symposium on *Liberty in the Modern State:*[60] "So far have we travelled from the conception of the Englishman protected by the courts from the risks of oppression by the Government or its servants that no one of the contributors suggests that it would now be possible for us to go back to that nineteenth century ideal."[61]

Where these views can lead to is shown by the more indiscreet statements of some of the less-well-known members of that group of socialist lawyers. One commences an essay on *The Planned State and the Rule of Law* by "redefining" the rule of law.[62] It emerges from the mauling as "whatever parliament as the supreme lawgiver makes it."[63] This enables the author "to assert

[57] Ibid., p. 433.

[58] Ibid., pp. 572–73.

[59] Inns of Court, Conservative and Unionist Society, *Rule of Law: A Study* (London: Conservative Political Centre, 1955), p. 30.

[60] Conservative Political Centre, *Liberty in the Modern State: Eight Oxford Lectures* (London: Conservative Political Centre, 1957).

[61] *Times Literary Supplement,* March 1, 1957 [Review of *Liberty in the Modern State: Eight Oxford Lectures*], p. 123. In this respect some socialists show greater concern than is noticeable in the official conservative position. Mr. R. H. S. Crossman, in the pamphlet quoted in n. 40 above (*Socialism and the New Despotism,* p. 19), looks forward to the next step "to reform the Judiciary, so that it can regain the traditional function of defending individual rights against encroachment."

[62] Wolfgang Gaston Friedmann, *Law and Social Change in Contemporary Britain* (London: Stevens and Sons, 1951), pp. 277–310. One of the essays in this collection, *The Planned State and the Rule of Law,* was published separately several years earlier (Melbourne: Melbourne University Press, 1948).

[63] Friedmann, *Law and Social Change in Contemporary Britain,* p. 284.

with confidence that the incompatibility of planning with the rule of law [first suggested by socialist authors!] is a myth sustainable only by prejudice or ignorance."[64] Another member of the same group even finds it possible to reply to the question as to whether, if Hitler had obtained power in a constitutional manner, the rule of law would still have prevailed in Nazi Germany: "The answer is Yes; the majority would be right: the Rule of Law would be in operation, *if* the majority *voted* him into power. The majority might be unwise, and it might be wicked, but the Rule of Law would prevail. For in a democracy right is what the majority makes it to be."[65] Here we have the most fatal confusion of our time expressed in the most uncompromising terms.

It is not surprising, then, that under the influence of such conceptions there has been in Great Britain during the last two or three decades a rapid growth of very imperfectly checked powers of administrative agencies over the private life and property of the citizen.[66] The new social and economic legislation has conferred ever increasing discretionary powers on those bodies and has provided only occasional and highly defective remedies in the form of a medley of tribunals of committees for appeal. In extreme instances the law has even gone so far as to give administrative agencies the power to determine "the general principles" whereby what amounted to expropriation could

---

[64] Ibid., p. 310. It is curious that the contention that the rule of law and socialism are incompatible, which had long been maintained by socialist authors, should have aroused so much indignation among them when it was turned against socialism. Long before I had emphasized the point in *The Road to Serfdom*, Karl Mannheim, *Man and Society in an Age of Reconstruction: Studies in Modern Social Structure* (London: K. Paul, Trench, Trubner and Co., 1940), p. 180, had summed up the result of a long discussion in the statement that "recent studies in the sociology of law once more confirm that the fundamental principle of formal law by which every case must be judged according to general rational precepts, which have as few exceptions as possible and are based on logical subsumption, obtains only for the liberal-competitive phase of capitalism." Cf. also Franz Leopold Neumann, *The Democratic and the Authoritarian State: Essays in Political and Legal Theory* (Glencoe, IL: The Free Press, 1957), p. 50, and Max Horkheimer, "Bemerkung zur philosophischen Anthropologie," *Zeitschrift für Sozialforschung*, 4 (1935): esp. 14: "The economic basis of the significance of promises becomes less important from day to day, because to an increasing extent economic life is characterised not by contract but by command and obedience." [The original reads: "Die ökonomische Grundlage für die Bedeutung von Versprechungen wird daher schmäler von Tag zu Tag. Denn nicht mehr der Vertrag, sondern Befehlsgewalt und Gehorsam kennzeichnen jetzt in steigendem Maß den inneren Verkehr."—Ed.]

[65] Herman Finer, *The Road to Reaction* (Boston: Little, Brown and Co., 1945), p. 60.

[66] Cf. Winston Spencer Churchill, "The Conservative Case for a New Parliament," [Party Political Broadcast XI] *Listener*, February 19, 1948, p. 302: "I am told that 300 officials have the power to make new regulations, apart altogether from Parliament, carrying with them the penalty of imprisonment for crimes hitherto, unknown to the law." [Churchill further notes: "A rate of war-time taxation has been maintained in a manner which has hampered and baffled enterprise and recovery in every walk of life; 700,000 more officials, all hard-working decent men and women but producing nothing themselves, have settled down upon us to administer 25,000 regulations never enforced before in time of peace" (p. 302).—Ed.]

be applied,[67] the executive authority then refusing to tie itself down by any firm rules.[68] Only lately, and especially after a flagrant instance of highhanded bureaucratic action was brought to the attention of the public by the persistent efforts of a wealthy and public spirited man,[69] has the disquiet over these developments long felt by a few informed observers spread to wider circles and produced the first signs of a reaction, to which we shall refer later.

6. It is somewhat surprising to find that in many respects developments in this direction have gone hardly less far in the United States. In fact, both the modern trends in legal theory and the conceptions of the "expert adminis-

[67] Town and Country Planning Act (1947) [10 and 11 Geo. 6, chap. 51] sec. 70, subsec. (3), provides that "regulations made under this Act with the consent of the Treasury may prescribe general principles to be followed by the Central Land Board in determining . . . whether any and if so what development charge is to be paid" (p. 84 of the act). It was under this provision that the Minister of Town and Country Planning was able unexpectedly to issue a regulation under which the development charges were normally "not to be less" than the whole additional value of the land which was due to the permission for a particular development. [The Central Land Board was established by the Town and Country Planning Act of 1947, among whose duties was to assess and levy charges on new developments of land. When planning permission was granted for any development, a charge was payable on the enhanced value of the land. In cases of default the Board could issue an order for payment, together with a penalty, enforceable as a land charge, subject to appeal to one of the county courts or the High Court. Under the bill no development was permitted to take place without consent and where permission to develop was refused, there was no right to compensation.—Ed.]

[68] Central Land Board, *Practice Notes (First Series): Being Notes on Development Charges Under the Town and Country Planning Act, 1947* (London: His Majesty's Stationery Office, 1949), Preface [pp. ii–iii]. It is explained there that the Notes "are meant to describe principles and working rules in accordance with which any applicant can confidently assume his case will be dealt, unless either he shows good cause for different treatment, or the Board informs him that for special reasons the normal rules do not apply." It is further explained that "a general working rule must always be variable if it does not fit a particular case" and that the board "have no doubt that from time to time we shall vary our policy." For further discussion of this measure see chap. 22, sec. 6, below.

[69] Cf. the official report of the Minister of Agriculture and Fisheries, *Public Inquiry Ordered by the Minister of Agriculture into the Disposal of Land at Crichel Down* (London: History Majesty's Stationery Office, 1954) [Cmd. 9176]; and cf. also the less-known but nearly as instructive case of *Odlum v. Stratton* (1946), before Mr. Justice Atkinson, King's Bench Division, a report of the proceedings of which has been printed by the *Wiltshire Gazette* [*Odlum v. Stratton: Verbatim Report of the Proceedings in the High Court of Justice, King Bench Division, before Mr. Justice Atkinson* (Devizes, Wiltshire: Wilshire Gazette, 1946)]. [The case was the subject of comment on ministerial discretion by Lord Simon of Glaisdale in the House of Lords on 26 February 1996. Lord Simon remarked: "(*Odlum v. Stratton*) was a libel action in which the professional competence of a farmer was in question. A series of reports on his competence was in the hands of the Ministry of Agriculture. The Ministry claimed that it was immune from disclosure except for two documents. Those two documents told against the plaintiff. He wanted to see the others, but those were the only two for which immunity was waived. The judge had no doubt at all, nor do I think would anyone reading a transcript have had any doubt, that the documents were divulged precisely with the objective of discrediting the plaintiff" (*Hansard, Lords*, column 1265–66).—Ed.]

trator" without legal training have had an even greater influence here than in Great Britain; it may even be said that the British socialist lawyers we have just considered have usually found their inspiration more often in American than in British legal philosophers. The circumstances which have brought this about are little understood even in the United States and deserve to be better known.

The United States is, in fact, unique in that the stimulation received from European reform movements early crystallized into what came to be known significantly as the "public administration movement." It played a role somewhat similar to that of the Fabian movement in Britain[70] or of the "socialists of the chair" movement in Germany. With efficiency in government as its watchword, it was skilfully designed to enlist the support of the business community for basically socialist ends. The members of this movement, generally with the sympathetic support of the "progressives," directed their heaviest attack against the traditional safeguards of individual liberty, such as the rule of law, constitutional restraints, judicial review, and the conception of a "fundamental law." It was characteristic of these "experts in administration" that they were equally antagonistic to (and commonly largely ignorant of) both law and economics.[71] In their efforts to create a "science" of administration, they were guided by a rather naïve conception of "scientific" procedure and showed all the contempt for tradition and principles characteristic of the extreme rationalist. It was they who did most to popularize the idea that "liberty for liberty's sake is clearly a meaningless notion: it must be liberty to do and enjoy something. If more people are buying automobiles and taking vacations, there is more liberty."[72]

It was mainly because of their efforts that Continental European conceptions of administrative powers were introduced into the United States rather earlier than into England. Thus, as early as 1921, one of the most distinguished American students of jurisprudence could speak of "a tendency away from courts and law and a reversion to justice without law in the form of revival of executive and even of legislative justice and reliance upon arbitrary governmental power."[73] A few years later a standard work on administrative

---

[70] See Dwight Waldo, *The Administrative State: A Study of the Political Theory of American Public Administration* (New York: Ronald Press Co., 1948), p. 70, n. 13; cf. also pp. 5, 15, and 40 of the same work.

[71] See Ibid., p. 79: "If any person is to count for less than one in the New Order it is the Lawyer!"

[72] Ibid., p. 73.

[73] Roscoe Pound, *The Spirit of the Common Law* (Boston: Marshall Jones Co., 1921), p. 72; cf. also Charles Howard McIlwain, *Constitutionalism and the Changing World: Collected Papers* (Cambridge: Cambridge University Press, 1939), p. 261: "Slowly but surely we are drifting toward the totalitarian state, and strange to say many if not most of the idealists are either enthusiastic about it or unconcerned."

law could already represent it as accepted doctrine that "every public officer has, marked out for him by law, a certain area of 'jurisdiction.' Within the boundaries of that area he can act freely according to his own discretion, and the courts will respect his action as final and not inquire into its rightfulness. But if he oversteps those bounds, then the court will intervene. In this form, the law of court review of the acts of public officers becomes simply a branch of the law of *ultra vires*. The only question before the courts is one of jurisdiction, and the court has no control of the officer's exercise of discretion within that jurisdiction."[74]

The reaction against the tradition of stringent control of the courts over not only administrative but also legislative action had, in fact, commenced some time before the first World War. As an issue of practical politics it became important for the first time in Senator La Follette's campaign for the presidency in 1924, when he made the curbing of the power of the courts an important part of his platform.[75] It is mainly because of this tradition which the Senator established that, in the United States more than elsewhere, the progressives have become the main advocates of the extension of the discretionary powers of the administrative agency. By the end of the 1930s, this characteristic of the American progressives had become so marked that even European socialists, when "first faced with the dispute between the American liberals and the American conservatives concerning the questions of administrative law and administrative discretion," were inclined "to warn them against the inherent dangers of the rise of administrative discretion, and to tell them that we [i.e., the European socialists] could vouch for the truth of the stand of the American conservative."[76] But they were soon mollified when they discovered how greatly this attitude of the progressives facilitated the gradual and unnoticed movement of the American system toward socialism.

The conflict referred to above reached its height, of course, during the Roosevelt era, but the way had already been prepared for the developments of that time by the intellectual trends of the preceding decade. The 1920s and

[74] John Dickinson, *Administrative Justice and the Supremacy of Law in the United States* (Cambridge: Harvard University Press, 1927), p. 41.

[75] Cf. Robert Marion La Follette, *The Political Philosophy of Robert M. La Follette as Revealed in His Speeches and Writings*, Ellen Torelle, ed. (Madison, WI: Robert M. La Follette Co., 1920), esp. pp. 179–81. [Art. 14 of the La Follette Progressive Republican Platform of 1920 reads: "We denounce the alarming usurpation of legislative power, by the federal courts, as subversive of democracy, and we favor such amendments to the constitution, and thereupon, the enactment of such statutes as may be necessary, to provide for the election of all federal judges, for fixed terms not exceeding ten years, by direct vote of the people" (p. 419).—Ed.]

[76] Alexander Haim Pekelis, "Administrative Discretion and the Law of Rule," *Law and Social Action: Selected Essays of Alexander H. Pekelis*, Milton Ridvas Konvitz, ed. (Ithaca, NY: Cornell University Press, 1950), p. 88; cf. Also Hans Kelsen, "Foundations of Democracy," *Ethics*, no. 1, pt. 2, 66 (1955): 77ff.

early 1930s had seen a flood of antirule-of-law literature which had considerable influence on the later developments. We can mention here only two characteristic examples. One of the most active of those who led the frontal attack on the American tradition of a "government of law and not of men" was Professor Charles G. Haines, who not only represented the traditional ideal as an illusion[77] but seriously pleaded that "the American people should establish governments on a theory of trust in men in public affairs."[78] To realize how completely this is in conflict with the whole conception underlying the American Constitution, one need merely remember Thomas Jefferson's statement that "free government is founded in jealousy, not in confidence; it is jealousy and not confidence which prescribes limited constitutions, to bind those we are obliged to trust with power . . . our Constitution has accordingly fixed the limits to which, and no further, our confidence may go. . . . In questions of power, then, let no more be heard of confidence in man, but bind him down from mischief by the chains of the Constitution."[79]

Perhaps even more characteristic of the intellectual tendencies of the time is a work by the late justice Jerome Frank, called *Law and the Modern Mind*, which, when it first appeared in 1930, enjoyed a success which for the reader of today is not quite easy to understand. It constitutes a violent attack on the whole ideal of the certainty of the law, which the author ridicules as the product of "a childish need for an authoritative father."[80] Basing itself on psychoanalytic theory, the work supplied just the kind of justification for a contempt for the traditional ideals that a generation unwilling to accept any limitation on collective action wanted. It was the young men brought up on such ideas who became the ready instruments of the paternalistic policies of the New Deal.

Toward the end of the 1930s there was increasing uneasiness over these developments, which led to the appointment of a committee of investigation, the U.S. Attorney General's Committee on Administrative Procedure, whose task was similar to that of the British committee of ten years earlier. But this, too, even more than the British committee, tended in its Majority Report[81] to

[77] Charles Grove Haines, *A Government of Laws or a Government of Men: Judicial or Legislative Supremacy* (Berkeley: University of California Press, 1929), p. 37.

[78] Ibid., p. 18.

[79] Thomas Jefferson, "Draft of the Kentucky Resolution of 1789," in Ethelbert Dudley Warfield, *The Kentucky Resolutions of 1798* (2nd ed.; New York: Putman, 1894), pp. 157–58.

[80] Jerome Frank, *Law and the Modern Mind* (New York: Brentano's, 1930), p. 21. More than a quarter of a century after the publication of this book, Thurman Wesley Arnold, in the *University of Chicago Law Review* ["Judge Jerome Frank," 24 (1957): 635], could say of it that "more than any other it cleared the way for a new set of conceptions and ideals with respect to the relationship of the citizen to his government."

[81] Dean Acheson, chairman, *Administrative Procedure in Government Agencies: Final Report of the Committee on Administrative Procedure* (Washington, DC: Government Printing Office, 1941). [The

represent what was happening as both inevitable and harmless. The general tenor of the report is best described in the words of Dean Roscoe Pound: "Even if quite unintended, the majority are moving in the line of administrative absolutism which is a phase of the rising absolutism throughout the world. Ideas of the disappearance of law, of a society in which there will be no law, or only one law, namely that there are no laws but only administrative orders; doctrines that there are no such things as rights and that laws are only threats of exercise of state force, rules and principles being nothing but superstition and pious wish, a teaching that separation of powers is an outmoded eighteenth century fashion of thought, that the common law doctrine of the supremacy of law had been outgrown, and expounding of a public law which is to be a 'subordinating law,' subordinating the interests of the individual to those of the public official and allowing the latter to identify one side of a controversy with the public interest and so give it a greater value and ignore the others: and finally a theory that law is whatever is done officially and so whatever is done officially is law and beyond criticism by lawyers—such is the setting in which the proposals of the majority must be seen."[82]

7. Fortunately, there are clear signs in many countries of a reaction against these developments of the last two generations. They are perhaps most conspicuous in the countries that have gone through the experience of totalitarian regimes and have learned the dangers of relaxing the limits on the powers of the state. Even among those socialists who not long ago had nothing but ridicule for the traditional safeguards of individual liberty, a much more respectful attitude can be observed. Few men have so frankly expressed this change of view as the distinguished dean of socialist legal philosophers, the late Gustav Radbruch, who in one of his last works said: "Though democ-

---

Federal Administrative Procedure Act of 1946 was an outgrowth of the Final Report of the Attorney General's committee on Administrative Procedure in Government Agencies, which was established in response to the immense number of administrative agencies created under the New Deal. The issues that the committee confronted were extremely contentious. So much of private conduct had been made subject to administrative regulation since 1934 and there were so few checks on the arbitrary power of administrators that many feared that the United States was on the verge of being reconstructed into a centrally planned state. To assuage them, Roosevelt requested his attorney general, Frank Murray, to strike a committee. The FAPA of 1946, which had authority over both independent agencies and those falling within the executive branch, governed the way regulations could be proposed and enacted and provided for judicial review of its decisions.—Ed.]

[82] Roscoe Pound, "Administrative Procedure Legislation for the 'Minority Report,'" *American Bar Association Journal*, 27 (1941): 678. On the present situation see Bernard Schwartz, "Administrative Justice and Its Place in the Legal Order," *New York University Law Review*, 30 (1955): 1390–1417; and Walter Gellhorn, *Individual Freedom and Governmental Restraints* (Baton Rouge: Louisiana State University Press, 1956), esp. the remark on pp. 18–19, that "some of the former upholders of the administrative process [including the author] now feel that what were mainly imaginary dangers have become real—and frightening."

racy is certainly a praiseworthy value, the *Rechtsstaat* is like the daily bread, the water we drink and the air we breathe; and the greatest merit of democracy is that it alone is adapted to preserve the *Rechtsstaat*."[83] That democracy does not in fact necessarily or invariably do so is only too clear from Radbruch's description of developments in Germany. It would probably be truer to say that democracy will not exist long unless it preserves the rule of law.

The advance of the principle of judicial review since the war and the revival of the interest in the theories of natural law in Germany are other symptoms of the same tendencies.[84] In other Continental countries similar movements are under way. In France, G. Ripert has made a significant contribution with his study of *The Decline of Law*, in which he rightly concludes that "above all, we must put the blame on the jurists. It was they who for half a century undermined the conception of individual rights without being aware that they thereby delivered these rights to the omnipotence of the political state. Some of them wished to prove themselves progressive, while others believed that they were rediscovering traditional doctrine which the liberal individualism of the nineteenth century had obliterated. Scholars often show

---

[83] Gustav Radbruch, *Rechtsphilosophie* (4th ed.; Stuttgart: K. F. Koehler, 1950), p 357. [The English quotation appears in the original German as: "Demokratie ist gewiß ein preiswertes Gut, *Rechtsstaat* aber ist wie das tägliche Brot, wie Wasser zum Trinken und wie Luft zum Atmen, und das Beste an der Demokratie gerade dieses, daß nur sie geeignet ist, den *Rechtsstaat* zu sichern." (p. 357)—Ed.] See also the significant comments in this work on the role which legal positivism has played in destroying the belief in the *Rechtsstaat*, esp. p. 335: "Dieses Auffassung vom Gesetz und seiner Geltung (wir nennen sie die positivistische Lehre) hat die Juristen wie das Volk wehrlos gemacht gegen noch so willkürliche, noch so grausame, noch so verbrecherische Gesetze. Sie setzt letzten Endes das Recht der Macht gleich, nur wo die Macht ist, ist das Recht"; and p. 352: "Der Positivismus hat in der Tat mit seiner Überzeugung 'Gesetz ist Gesetz' den deutschen Juristenstand wehrlos gemacht gegen Gesetze willkürlichen und verbrecherischen Inhalts. Dabei ist der Positivismus gar nicht in der Lage, aus eigener Kraft die Geltung von Gesetzen zu begründen. Er glaubt die Geltung eines Gesetzes schon damit erwiesen zu haben, daß es die Macht besessen hat, sich durchzusetzen." ["This understanding of the law and of its merits (which we call positivist theory) has made legal theorists as well as the great mass of people defenseless against laws that are arbitrary, cruel, and criminal. Ultimately this view equates law with power; that is, only where power resides is there law" (p. 335). "In fact, positivism, with its claim that 'all law is law' has rendered the German legal profession defenseless against arbitrary and criminal laws. At the same time, it is impossible for positivism on its own to justify the validity of a law. For it believes that a law's validity has been proved by the power to assert itself" (p. 352).—Ed.] It is thus not too much of an exaggeration when Emil Brunner, *Justice and the Social Order* (New York: Harper, 1945), p. 7, maintains that "the totalitarian state is simply and solely legal positivism in political practice."

[84] See Gottfried Dietze, "America and Europe: Decline and Emergence of Judicial Review," *Virginia Law Review*, 44 (1958): 1233–72, and, concerning the revival of natural law, Helmut Coing, *Grundzüge der Rechtsphilosophie* (Berlin: Walter de Gruyter, 1950); Heinrich Mitteis, *Über das Naturrecht* (Berlin: Akademie-Verlag, 1948); Klaus Ritter, *Zwischen Naturrecht und Rechtspositivismus: Eine rrkenntnistheoretische Auseinandersetzung mit den neueren Versuchen zur Wiederherstellung einer Rechtsmetaphysik* (Witten-Ruhr: Luther-Verlag, 1956).

a certain single-mindedness which prevents them from seeing the practical conclusions which others will draw from their disinterested doctrines."[85]

There has been no lack of similar warning voices[86] in Great Britain, and the first outcome of the increasing apprehension has been a renewed tendency in recent legislation to restore the courts of law as the final authority in administrative disputes. Encouraging signs are also to be found in a recent report of a committee of inquiry into procedure for appeals to other than ordinary courts.[87] In it the committee not only made important suggestions for eliminating the numerous anomalies and defects of the existing system but also admirably reaffirmed the basic distinction between "what is judicial, its antithesis being what is administrative, and the notion of what is according to the rule of law, its antithesis being what is arbitrary." It then went on to state: "The rule of law stands for the view that decisions should be made by known principles or laws. In general such decisions will be predictable, and the citizen will know where he is."[88] But there still remains in Britain a "considerable field of administration in which no special tribunal or enquiry is provided"[89] (which problem was outside the terms of reference of the committee) and where the conditions remain as unsatisfactory as ever and the citizen in effect is still at the mercy of an arbitrary administrative decision. If the process of erosion of the rule of law is to be halted, there seems to be urgent need for some in-

[85] Georges Ripert, *Le Déclin du droit* (Paris: Pichon and Durand-Auzias, 1949), p. 192. [The French reads: "Il nous faut tout d'abord faire le procès des juristes. Ce sont eux qui depuis un demi-siècle ont affaibli la notion de droit individuel sans avoir conscience qu'ils livraient ainsi ces droits à toute puissance de l'État politique. Les uns étaient désireux de se classer parmi les hommes de progrès. Les autres croyaient retrouver une doctrine traditionnelle étouffée par l'individualisme libéral du xixe siècle. Les hommes de science ont souvent une certaine candeur qui ne leur permet pas d'apercevoir les conséquences pratiques que d'autres tireront de leurs doctrines désintéressées."—Ed.] Cf. also Paul Roubier, *Théorie générale du droit: histoire des doctrines juridiques et philosophie des valeurs sociales* (Paris: Recueil Sirey, 1946); Louis Auguste Paul Rougier, *La France à la recherche d'une constitution* (Paris: Recueil Sirey, 1952).

[86] See Sir Carleton Kemp Allen, *Law and Orders: An Inquiry into the Nature and Scope of Delegated Legislation and Executive Powers in England* (London, 1945); George Williams Keeton, *The Passing of Parliament* (London: E. Benn, 1952); Charles John Hamson, *Executive Discretion and Judicial Control: An Aspect of the Conseil d'État* (London: Stevens, 1954); Cyril John Radcliffe, Viscount Radcliffe of Werneth, *Law and the Democratic State: Being the Presidential Address of the Right Hon. Lord Radcliffe, President of the Holdsworth Club of the Faculty of Law in the University of Birmingham, 1954–1955* [Holdsworth lecture] (Birmingham: Holdsworth Club of the University of Birmingham, 1955); and Geoffrey Marshall, "The Recent Development of English Administrative Law," *Il Politico*, 24 (December 1959): 637–45.

[87] Committee on Administrative Tribunals and Enquiries, *Report of the Committee on Administrative Tribunals, Presented by the Lord High Chancellor to Parliament by Command of Her Majesty* [the Franks Report], chaired by Sir Oliver Franks, Baron Franks of Headington. Cmd. 218 (London: Her Majesty's Stationery Office, 1957), p. 8, par. 37.

[88] Ibid., p. 6, pars.27, 29.

[89] Ibid., p 28, par. 120.

dependent court to which appeal lies in all such cases, as has been proposed from several quarters.[90]

Finally, we might mention, as an effort on an international scale, the "Act of Athens" adopted in June, 1955, at a congress of the International Commission of Jurists, in which the importance of the rule of law is strongly reaffirmed.[91]

It can hardly be said, however, that the widespread desire to revive an old tradition is accompanied by a clear awareness of what this would involve[92] or that people would be prepared to uphold the principles of this tradition even when they are obstacles in the most direct and obvious route to some desired aim. These principles which not long ago seemed commonplaces hardly worth restating and which perhaps even today will seem more obvi-

[90] See Inns of Court, Conservative and Unionist Society, *Rule of Law: A Study* (mentioned in note 59 above), and William Alexander Robson, *Justice and Administrative Law* (3rd ed.; London: Stevens, 1951). On similar recommendations of the Hoover Commission in the United States see the Symposium on the "Hoover Commission and Task Force Reports on Legal Services and Procedure," *New York University Law Review*, 30, no. 7 (1955): 1267–1417.

[91] The International Commission of Jurists at The Hague (now at Geneva) convened at Athens in June 1955, and adopted a resolution which solemnly declared: "1. The State is subject to the law. 2. Governments should respect the rights of the individual under the Rule of Law and provide effective means for their enforcement. 3. Judges should be guided by the Rule of Law, protect and enforce it without fear or favor and resist any encroachments by governments or political parties on their independence as judges. 4. Lawyers of the world should preserve the independence of their profession, assert the rights of the individual under the Rule of Law and insist that every accused is afforded a fair trial." (See the *Report of the International Congress of Jurists, Held June 13–20, 1955, at Athens* [The Hague: International Commission of Jurists, 1956], p. 9.) [These four "resolutions" do not, in fact, form part of the formal resolutions of the Congress but, rather, were adopted by the International Commission of Jurists as "fundamental principles of justice . . . essential to a lasting peace throughout the world."—Ed.]

Unfortunately, since then the International Commission of Jurists (in its "Declaration of Delhi" of January 10, 1959) decided to introduce a "new" and "dynamic" conception of the Rule of Law which included the establishment of "social, economic, educational and cultural conditions under which [the individual's] aspirations and dignity may be realized." However desirable these objectives might be, extending the notion of the Rule of Law to include these goals can only lead to making the term worthless and can only accelerate the repudiation of those constraints that the Rule of Law places on the actions of the state should these limitations stand in the way of pursuing certain social ends. Cf. "The Declaration of Delhi," *Newsletter of the International Commission of Jurists*, no. 6 (March–April 1959): 1.

[92] It is no exaggeration when one student of jurisprudence (Julius Stone, *The Province and Function of Law: Law as Logic, Justice, and Social Control; A Study in Jurisprudence* [Cambridge, MA: Harvard University Press, 1950], p. 261) asserts that the restoration of the rule of law as here defined "would strictly require the reversal of legislative measures which all democratic legislatures seem to have found essential in the last half century." The fact that democratic legislatures have done this does not, of course, prove that it was wise or even that it was essential to resort to this kind of measure in order to achieve what they wanted to achieve, and still less that they ought not to reverse their decisions if they recognize that they produce unforeseen and undesirable consequences.

ous to the layman than to the contemporary lawyer have been so forgotten that a detailed account of both their history and their character seemed necessary. It is only on this basis that we can attempt in the next part to examine in more detail the different ways in which the various modern aspirations of economic and social policy can or cannot be achieved within the framework of a free society.

PART III

FREEDOM IN THE WELFARE STATE

Above this race of men stands an immense and tutelary power, which takes upon itself alone to secure their gratifications and to watch over their fate. That power is absolute, minute, regular, provident, and mild. It would be like the authority of a parent if, like that authority, its object was to prepare men for manhood; but it seeks, on the contrary, to keep them in perpetual childhood: it is well content that the people should rejoice, provided they think of nothing but rejoicing. For their happiness such a government willingly labors, but it chooses to be the sole agent and the only arbiter of that happiness; it provides for their security, foresees and supplies their necessities, facilitates their pleasures, manages their principal concerns, directs their industry, regulates the descent of property, and subdivides their inheritances; what remains, but to spare them all care of thinking and all the trouble of living?

—Alexis de Tocqueville

This quotation is taken from Tocqueville, *Democracy in America*, vol. 2, p. 318. [The French reads: "Au-dessus de ceux-là s'élève un pouvoir immense et tutélaire, qui se charge seul d'assurer leur jouissance et de veiller sur leur sort. Il est absolu, détaillé, régulier, prévoyant et doux. Il ressemblerait à la puissance paternelle si, comme elle, il avait pour objet de préparer les hommes à l'âge viril; mais il ne cherche, au contraire, qu'à les fixer irrévocablement dans l'enfance; il aime que les citoyens se réjouissent, pourvu qu'ils ne songent qu'à se réjouir. Il travaille volontiers à leur bonheur; mais il veut en être l'unique agent et le seul arbitre; il pourvoit à leur sécurité, prévoit et assure leurs besoins, facilite leur plaisirs, conduit leurs principales affaires, dirige leur industrie, règle leurs successions, devise leurs héritages; que ne peut-il leur ôter entièrement le trouble de penser et la peine de vivre?" (bk. 2, sec. 4, pt. 6; vol. 2, p. 837).—Ed.] The three paragraphs which follow, or indeed the whole of chapter 6 of book 4, from which it is taken, would deserve quotation as a prologue to the following discussion.

SEVENTEEN

THE DECLINE OF SOCIALISM AND THE RISE OF THE WELFARE STATE

Experience should teach us to be most on our guard to protect liberty when the Government's purposes are beneficent. Men born to freedom are naturally alert to repel invasion of their liberty by evil-minded rulers. The greatest dangers to liberty lurk in insidious encroachment by men of zeal, well meaning but without understanding. —Louis Brandeis

1. Efforts toward social reform, for something like a century, have been inspired mainly by the ideals of socialism—during part of this period even in countries like the United States which never has had a socialist party of importance. Over the course of these hundred years socialism captured a large part of the intellectual leaders and came to be widely regarded as the ultimate goal toward which society was inevitably moving. This development reached its peak after the second World War, when Britain plunged into her socialist experiment. This seems to have marked the high tide of the socialist advance. Future historians will probably regard the period from the revolution of 1848 to about 1948 as the century of European socialism.

During this period socialism had a fairly precise meaning and a definite program. The common aim of all socialist movements was the nationalization of the "means of production, distribution, and exchange," so that all economic activity might be directed according to a comprehensive plan toward some ideal of social justice. The various socialist schools differed mainly in the political methods by which they intended to bring about the reorganization of society. Marxism and Fabianism differed in that the former was revolutionary and the latter gradualist; but their conceptions of the new society they hoped to create were basically the same. Socialism meant the common ownership of the means of production and their "employment for use, not for profit."

The quotation at the head of the chapter is taken from the dissenting opinion of Mr. Justice Louis Brandeis in *Olmstead v. United States* 277 U.S. 438, at 479 (1927). Also see Jeremy Bentham, *Deontology; or, The Science of Morality: In Which the Harmony and Co-incidence of Duty and Self-interest, Virtue and Felicity, Prudence and Benevolence, are Explained and Exemplified* (2 vols.; London: Rees, Orme, Browne, Green, and Longman, 1834), vol. 2, p. 289: "Despotism never takes a worse shape than when it comes in the guise of benevolence."

The great change that has occurred during the last decade is that social-ism in this strict sense of a particular method of achieving social justice has collapsed. It has not merely lost its intellectual appeal; it has also been aban-doned by the masses so unmistakably that socialist parties everywhere are searching for a new program that will insure the active support of their fol-lowers.[1] They have not abandoned their ultimate aim, their ideal of social justice. But the methods by which they had hoped to achieve this and for which the name "socialism" had been coined have been discredited. No doubt the name will be transferred to whatever new program the existing socialist parties will adopt. But socialism in the old definite sense is now dead in the Western world.

Though such a sweeping statement will still cause some surprise, a survey of the stream of disillusionist literature from socialist sources in all countries and the discussions inside the socialist parties amply confirm it.[2] To those who watch merely the developments inside a single country, the decline of social-ism may still seem no more than a temporary setback, the reaction to political

---

[1] The most lively discussion of these problems is going on in Britain. See particularly Richard Howard Stafford Crossman, ed., *New Fabian Essays* (London: Turnstile Press, 1952); and Socialist Union, *Socialism: A New Statement of Principles* (London: Lincolns-Prager, 1952). Crossman has him-self written, in "Communication: On Political Neuroses," *Encounter*, 3 (May 1954): 66, that socialism today is viewed by most European socialist leaders as a "Utopian myth . . . often remote from the realities of day to day politics." Also, George Douglas Howard Cole, *Is This Socialism?* [*New Statesman* pamphlet] (London: New Statesman and Nation, 1954); Hugh Todd Naylor Gaitskell, *Recent Developments in British Socialist Thinking* (London: Cooperative Union, Southern Section Education Council, 1956); Socialist Union, ed., *Twentieth Century Socialism: The Economy of Tomorrow* (Harmondsworth, Middlesex: Penguin Books, 1956); Charles Anthony Raven Crosland, *The Future of Socialism* (Lon-don: Jonathan Cape, 1956); Richard Howard Stafford Crossman, *Socialism and the New Despotism* [Fabian Tracts, No. 298] (London: Fabian Society, 1956); Douglas Jay, *Socialism and the New So-ciety* (London: Longmans, 1962); Roy Jenkins, *The Labour Case* (Harmondsworth, Middlesex: Penguin, 1959); Reuben Kelf-Cohen, *Nationalisation in Britain: The End of a Dogma* (London: Macmillan, 1958); and the discussions carried on in the journals *Socialist Commentary* and the *New Statesman*. A useful survey of these debates is Thomas Wilson, "Changing Tendencies in Socialist Thought," *Lloyds Bank Review* (July 1956): 1–21. Illuminating comments on the British experiment by foreign observers are Bertrand de Jouvenel, *Problèmes de l'Angleterre socialiste: ou, L'échec d'une expérience* (Paris: La table ronde, 1947); Clare Elmer Griffin, *Britain: A Case Study for Americans* (Ann Arbor: Uni-versity of Michigan Press, 1950); David McCord Wright, *Post-War West German and United King-dom Recovery* (Washington, DC: American Enterprise Association, 1957); and Johannes Messner, *Das englische Experiment des Sozialismus: auf Grund ökonomischer Tatsachen und sozialistischer Selbstzeugnisse dargestellt* (Innsbruck: Tyrolia, 1954).

[2] For the Continental developments see particularly Joseph Buttinger, *In the Twilight of Social-ism: A History of the Revolutionary Socialists of Austria*, Elizabeth Bruce Ashton, trans. (New York: F. A. Praeger, 1953); Karl Bednarik, *The Young Worker of Today: A New Type*, Renée Tupholme, trans. (London: Faber and Faber, 1955); Fritz Klenner, *Das Unbehagen in der Demokratie: ein Beitrag zu Gegenwartsproblemen der Arbeiterbewegung* (Vienna: Wiener Volksbuchhandlung, 1956). A similar change in attitude among American socialists is shown by Norman Thomas, *Democratic Socialism: A New Appraisal* (New York: League for Industrial Democracy, 1953).

defeat. But the international character and the similarity of the developments in the different countries leave no doubt that it is more than that. If, fifteen years ago, doctrinaire socialism appeared as the main danger to liberty, today it would be tilting at windmills to direct one's argument against it. Most of the arguments that were directed at socialism proper can now be heard from within the socialist movements as arguments for a change of program.

2. The reasons for this change are manifold. So far as the socialist school which at one time was most influential is concerned, the example of the "greatest social experiment" of our time was decisive: Marxism was killed in the Western world by the example of Russia. But for a long time comparatively few intellectuals comprehended that what had happened in Russia was the necessary outcome of the systematic application of the traditional socialist program. Today, however, it is an effective argument, even within socialist circles, to ask: "If you want one hundred per cent socialism, what's wrong with the Soviet Union?"[3] But the experience of that country has in general discredited only the Marxist brand of socialism. The widespread disillusionment with the basic methods of socialism is due to more direct experiences.

The chief factors contributing to the disillusionment were probably three: the increasing recognition that a socialist organization of production would be not more but much less productive than private enterprise; an even clearer recognition that, instead of leading to what had been conceived as greater social justice, it would mean a new arbitrary and more inescapable order of rank than ever before; and the realization that, instead of the promised greater freedom, it would mean the appearance of a new despotism.

The first to be disappointed were those labor unions which found that, when they had to deal with the state instead of a private employer, their power was greatly reduced. But the individuals also soon discovered that to be confronted everywhere by the authority of the state was no improvement upon their position in a competitive society. This happened at a time when the general rise in the standard of living of the working class (especially of the manual workers) destroyed the conception of a distinct proletarian class and, with it, the class-consciousness of the workers—creating in most of Europe a situation similar to that which in the United States had always prevented the growth of an organized socialist movement.[4] In the countries that had experienced a totalitarian regime there also took place a strong individualist reaction among the younger generation, who became deeply distrustful of all collective activities and suspicious of all authority.[5]

---

[3] Crossman, *Socialism and the New Despotism*, p. 4. Crossman's essay contains a description of a discussion at a Fabian Summer School at Oxford in 1955.

[4] Crosland, *The Future of Socialism*, and Bednarik, *The Young Worker of Today: A New Type*.

[5] See especially Klenner, *Das Unbehagen in der Demokratie*, pp. 66ff.

Perhaps the most important factor in the disillusionment of socialist intellectuals has been the growing apprehension among them that socialism would mean the extinction of individual liberty. Though the contention that socialism and individual liberty were mutually exclusive had been indignantly rejected by them when advanced by an opponent,[6] it made a deep impression when stated in powerful literary form by one from their own midst.[7] More recently the situation has been very frankly described by one of the leading intellectuals of the British Labour Party. Mr. R. H. S. Crossman, in a pamphlet entitled *Socialism and the New Despotism*, records how "more and more serious-minded people are having second thoughts about what once seemed to them the obvious advantages of central planning and the extension of State ownership";[8] and he continues to explain that "the discovery that the Labour Government's 'Socialism' meant the establishment of a number of vast, bureaucratic public corporations,"[9] of "a vast centralised State bureaucracy [which] constitutes a grave potential threat to social democracy,"[10] had created a situation in which "the main task of Socialists to-day is to convince the nation that its liberties are threatened by this new feudalism."[11]

3. But, though the characteristic methods of collectivist socialism have few defenders left in the West, its ultimate aims have lost little of their attraction. While the socialists no longer have a clear-cut plan as to how their goals are to be achieved, they still wish to manipulate the economy so that the distribution of incomes will be made to conform to their conception of social justice.

---

[6] As was made clear by the quotation from Karl Mannheim that I placed at the head of the chapter on "Planning and the Rule of Law" (in *The Road to Serfdom* [Chicago: University of Chicago Press, 1944], chap. 6, pp. 72–87, reprinted as vol. 2 of *The Collected Works of F. A. Hayek*, Bruce Caldwell, ed. [Chicago: University of Chicago Press, 2007], pp. 112–23) and repeated in note 64, chap. 16, above.

[7] Especially George Orwell, *Nineteen Eighty-four: A Novel* (London: Secker and Warburg, 1949); cf. also his review of *The Road to Serfdom*, "Grounds for Dismay," in the (London) *Observer*, April 9, 1944, p. 3. [Orwell's review is more easily accessible in "Review: *The Road to Serfdom* by F. A. Hayek, and *The Mirror of the Past* by Konni Zilliacus," in *The Collected Essays, Journalism, and Letters of George Orwell*, Sonia Orwell and Ian Angus, eds. (4 vols.; New York: Harcourt, Brace and World, Inc., 1968), vol. 3, pp. 117–18.—Ed.]

[8] Crossman, *Socialism and the New Despotism*, p. 1.

[9] Ibid., p. 1.

[10] Ibid., p. 6.

[11] Ibid., p. 13. These apprehensions have clearly also affected the latest official statement of the British Labour party on these issues (see Labour Party [Great Britain], *Personal Freedom: Labour's Policy for the Individual and Society* [London: Labour Party, 1956]). But, though this pamphlet deals with most of the crucial issues and shows how much the problems we have discussed have forced themselves into the foreground under a socialist regime even in a country with liberal traditions, it is, a curiously contradictory document. It not only repeats the phrase that "freedom with gross inequalities is hardly worth having" (p. 7) but even expressly reasserts the basic thesis of administrative despotism that "a minister must remain free to take different decisions in cases which are exactly similar" (p. 26).

The most important outcome of the socialist epoch, however, has been the destruction of the traditional limitations upon the powers of the state. So long as socialism aimed at a complete reorganization of society on new principles, it treated the principles of the existing system as mere encumbrances to be swept away. But now that it no longer has any distinctive principles of its own, it can only present its new ambitions without any clear picture of the means. As a result, we approach the new tasks set by the ambition of modern man as un-principled, in the original meaning of this word, as never before.

What is significant is that, in consequence, though socialism has been generally abandoned as a goal to be deliberately striven for, it is by no means certain that we shall not still establish it, albeit unintentionally. The reformers who confine themselves to whatever methods appear to be the most effective for their particular purposes and pay no attention to what is necessary to preserve an effective market mechanism are likely to be led to impose more and more central control over economic decisions (though private property may be preserved in name) until we get that very system of central planning which few now consciously wish to see established. Furthermore, many of the old socialists have discovered that we have already drifted so far in the direction of a redistributive state that it now appears much easier to push further in that direction than to press for the somewhat discredited socialization of the means of production. They seem to have recognized that by increasing governmental control of what nominally remains private industry, they can more easily achieve that redistribution of incomes that had been the real aim of the more spectacular policy of expropriation.

It is sometimes regarded as unfair, as blind conservative prejudice, to criticize those socialist leaders who have so frankly abandoned the more obviously totalitarian forms of "hot" socialism, for having now turned to a "cold" socialism which in effect may not be very different from the former. We are in danger, however, unless we succeed in distinguishing those of the new ambitions which can be achieved in a free society from those which require for their realization the methods of totalitarian collectivism.

4. Unlike socialism, the conception of the welfare state[12] has no precise

---

[12] The term "welfare state" is comparatively new in the English language and was probably still unknown twenty-five years ago. Since the German *Wohlfahrtsstaat* has been in use in that country for a long time and the thing it describes was first developed in Germany, the English term probably derives from the German. It deserves mention that the German term, from the beginning, was employed to describe a variant of the conception of the police state (*Polizeistaat*)—apparently first by nineteenth-century historians to describe the more favorable aspects of eighteenth-century government. The modern conception of the welfare state was first fully developed by the German academic *Sozialpolitiker*, or "socialists of the chair," from about 1870 onward and was first put into practice by Bismarck. [The term "socialists of the chair" (*Kathedersozialisten* or *Sozialpolitiker*) has reference to those German professors whose sympathies were with the German Historical School, that is, those who regarded history as the

meaning. The phrase is sometimes used to describe any state that "concerns" itself in any manner with problems other than those of the maintenance of law and order. But, though a few theorists have demanded that the activities of government should be limited to the maintenance of law and order, such a stand cannot be justified by the principle of liberty. Only the coercive measures of government need be strictly limited. We have already seen (in chap. 15) that there is undeniably a wide field for non-coercive activities of government and that there is a clear need for financing them by taxation.

Indeed, no government in modern times has ever confined itself to the "individualist minimum" which has occasionally been described,[13] nor has such confinement of governmental activity been advocated by the "orthodox" classical economists.[14] All modern governments have made provision for the indigent, unfortunate, and disabled and have concerned themselves with questions of health and the dissemination of knowledge. There is no reason why the volume of these pure service activities should not increase with the general growth of wealth. There are common needs that can be satisfied only by collective action and which can be thus provided for without restricting individual liberty. It can hardly be denied that, as we grow richer, that minimum of sustenance which the community has always provided for those not able to look after themselves, and which can be provided outside the market, will gradually rise, or that government may, usefully and without doing any harm, assist or even lead in such endeavors. There is little reason why the government should not also play some role, or even take the initiative, in such areas as social insurance and education, or temporarily subsidize certain experimental developments. Our problem here is not so much the aims as the methods of government action.

---

sole basis upon which conclusions in the field of economics could be reached and who questioned the emphasis orthodox economics placed on the production of wealth rather than its distribution.—Ed.]

The similar developments in England contemplated by the Fabians and by theorists like Arthur Cecil Pigou and Leonard Trelawney Hobhouse and put into practice by Lloyd George and Lord William Beveridge were, at least in their beginnings, strongly influenced by the German example. The acceptance of the term "welfare state" was assisted by the fact that the theoretical foundations that Pigou and his school had provided were known as "welfare economics."

By the time F. D. Roosevelt followed in the footsteps of Bismarck and Lloyd George, the ground had been similarly well prepared in the United States, and the use made since 1937 by the Supreme Court of the "general welfare" clause of the Constitution naturally led to the adoption of the term "welfare state" already in use elsewhere. [The Supreme Court's rulings in May 1937 upholding the constitutionality of the Social Security Act by reference to the "general welfare" clause were *Helvering v. Davis* (301 *U.S.* 619); *Steward Machine Company v. Davis* (301 *U.S.* 548); and *Carmichael v. Southern Coal and Coke Co.* (201 *U.S.* 495).—Ed.]

[13] Cf., e.g., Henry Sidgwick, *The Elements of Politics* (London: Macmillan, 1891), chap. 4 "Individualism and Individualistic Minimum," pp. 40–61.

[14] See on this particularly Lionel Robbins, *The Theory of Economic Policy in English Classical Political Economy* (London: Macmillan, 1952).

References are often made to those modest and innocent aims of governmental activity to show how unreasonable is any opposition to the welfare state as such. But, once the rigid position that government should not concern itself at all with such matters is abandoned—a position which is defensible but has little to do with freedom—the defenders of liberty commonly discover that the program of the welfare state comprises a great deal more that is represented as equally legitimate and unobjectionable. If, for instance, they admit that they have no objection to pure-food laws, this is taken to imply that they should not object to any government activity directed toward a desirable end. Those who attempt to delimit the functions of government in terms of aims rather than methods thus regularly find themselves in the position of having to oppose state action which appears to have only desirable consequences or of having to admit that they have no general rule on which to base their objections to measures which, though effective for particular purposes, would in their aggregate effect destroy a free society. Though the position that the state should have nothing to do with matters not related to the maintenance of law and order may seem logical so long as we think of the state solely as a coercive apparatus, we must recognize that, as a service agency, it may assist without harm in the achievement of desirable aims which perhaps could not be achieved otherwise. The reason why many of the new welfare activities of government are a threat to freedom, then, is that, though they are presented as mere service activities, they really constitute an exercise of the coercive powers of government and rest on its claiming exclusive rights in certain fields.

5. The current situation has greatly altered the task of the defender of liberty and made it much more difficult. So long as the danger came from socialism of the frankly collectivist kind, it was possible to argue that the tenets of the socialists were simply false: that socialism would not achieve what the socialists wanted and that it would produce other consequences which they would not like. We cannot argue similarly against the welfare state, for this term does not designate a definite system. What goes under that name is a conglomerate of so many diverse and even contradictory elements that, while some of them may make a free society more attractive, others are incompatible with it or may at least constitute potential threats to its existence.

We shall see that some of the aims of the welfare state can be realized without detriment to individual liberty, though not necessarily by the methods which seem the most obvious and are therefore most popular; that others can be similarly achieved to a certain extent, though only at a cost much greater than people imagine or would be willing to bear, or only slowly and gradually as wealth increases; and that, finally, there are others—and they are those particularly dear to the hearts of the socialists—that cannot be realized in a society that wants to preserve personal freedom.

There are all kinds of public amenities which it may be in the interest of all members of the community to provide by common effort, such as parks and museums, theaters and facilities for sports—though there are strong reasons why they should be provided by local rather than national authorities. There is then the important issue of security, of protection against risks common to all, where government can often either reduce these risks or assist people to provide against them. Here, however, an important distinction has to be drawn between two conceptions of security: a limited security which can be achieved for all and which is, therefore, no privilege, and absolute security, which in a free society cannot be achieved for all. The first of these is security against severe physical privation, the assurance of a given minimum of sustenance for all; and the second is the assurance of a given standard of life, which is determined by comparing the standard enjoyed by a person or a group with that of others. The distinction, then, is that between the security of an equal minimum income for all and the security of a particular income that a person is thought to deserve.[15] The latter is closely related to the third main ambition that inspires the welfare state: the desire to use the powers of government to insure a more even or more just distribution of goods. Insofar as this means that the coercive powers of government are to be used to insure that particular people get particular things, it requires a kind of discrimination between, and an unequal treatment of, different people which is irreconcilable with a free society. This is the kind of welfare state that aims at "social justice" and becomes "primarily a redistributor of income."[16] It is bound to lead back to socialism and its coercive and essentially arbitrary methods.

6. Though *some* of the aims of the welfare state can be achieved *only* by methods inimical to liberty, *all* its aims *may* be pursued by such methods. The chief danger today is that, once an aim of government is accepted as legitimate, it is then assumed that even means contrary to the principles of freedom may be legitimately employed. The unfortunate fact is that, in the majority of fields, the most effective, certain, and speedy way of reaching a given end will seem to be to direct all available resources toward the now visible solution. To the ambitious and impatient reformer, filled with indignation at a particular evil, nothing short of the complete abolition of that evil by the quickest and most direct means will seem adequate. If every person now suffering from unemployment, ill health, or inadequate provision for his old age is at once to be relieved of his cares, nothing short of an all-comprehensive and compulsory scheme will suffice. But if, in our impatience to solve such problems

[15] The preceding sentences are deliberately repeated, with only small alterations, from my book *The Road to Serfdom*, chap. 9, pp. 119–20, where this subject is treated at greater length. [*Collected Works* edition, pp. 147–48.]

[16] Alvin Harvey Hansen, "The Task of Promoting Economic Growth and Stability," address to the National Planning Association, February 26, 1956 (mimeographed). [While this address does not appear to have ever seen print, similar sentiments are contained in Hansen's *Economic Issues of the 1960s* (New York: McGraw-Hill, 1960), passim, esp. chaps. 5 and 6, pp. 43–68.—Ed.]

immediately, we give government exclusive and monopolistic powers, we may find that we have been shortsighted. If the quickest way to a now visible solution becomes the only permissible one and all alternative experimentation is precluded, and if what now seems the best method of satisfying a need is made the sole starting point for all future development, we may perhaps reach our present goal sooner, but we shall probably at the same time prevent the emergence of more effective alternative solutions. It is often those who are most anxious to use our existing knowledge and powers to the full that do most to impair the future growth of knowledge by the methods they use. The controlled single-channel development toward which impatience and administrative convenience have frequently inclined the reformer and which, especially in the field of social insurance, has become characteristic of the modern welfare state may well become the chief obstacle to future improvement.

If government wants not merely to facilitate the attainment of certain standards by the individuals but to make certain that everybody attains them, it can do so only by depriving individuals of any choice in the matter. Thus the welfare state becomes a household state in which a paternalistic power controls most of the income of the community and allocates it to individuals in the forms and quantities which it thinks they need or deserve.

In many fields persuasive arguments based on considerations of efficiency and economy can be advanced in favor of the state's taking sole charge of a particular service; but when the state does so, the result is usually not only that those advantages soon prove illusory but that the character of the services becomes entirely different from that which they would have had if they had been provided by competing agencies. If, instead of administering limited resources put under its control for a specific service, government uses its coercive powers to insure that men are given what some expert thinks they need; if people thus can no longer exercise any choice in some of the most important matters of their lives, such as health, employment, housing, and provision for old age, but must accept the decisions made for them by appointed authority on the basis of its evaluation of their need; if certain services become the exclusive domain of the state, and whole professions—be it medicine, education, or insurance—come to exist only as unitary bureaucratic hierarchies, it will no longer be competitive experimentation but solely the decisions of authority that will determine what men shall get.[17]

---

[17] Cf. John Stuart Mill, "On Liberty," in *On Liberty and Considerations on Representative Government*, Ronald Buchanan McCallum, ed. (Oxford: B. Blackwell, 1946), pp. 99–100: "If the roads, the railways, the banks, the insurance offices, the great joint stock companies, the universities, and the public charities, were all of them branches of the government; if, in addition, the municipal corporations and local boards, with all that now devolves on them, became departments of the central administration; if the employees of all these different enterprises were appointed and paid by the government, and looked to the government for every rise in life; not all the freedom

The same reasons that generally make the impatient reformer wish to organize such services in the form of government monopolies lead him also to believe that the authorities in charge should be given wide discretionary powers over the individual. If the objective were merely to improve opportunities for all by supplying certain specific services according to a rule, this could be attained on essentially business lines. But we could then never be sure that the results for all individuals would be precisely what we wanted. If each individual is to be affected in some particular way, nothing short of the individualizing, paternalistic treatment by a discretionary authority with powers of discriminating between persons will do.

It is sheer illusion to think that when certain needs of the citizen have become the exclusive concern of a single bureaucratic machine, democratic control of that machine can then effectively guard the liberty of the citizen. So far as the preservation of personal liberty is concerned, the division of labor between a legislature which merely says that this or that should be done[18] and an administrative apparatus which is given exclusive power to carry out these instructions is the most dangerous arrangement possible. All experience confirms what is "clear enough from American as well as from English experience, that the zeal of administrative agencies to achieve the immediate end they see before them leads them to see their function out of focus and to assume that constitutional limitations and guaranteed individual rights must give way before their zealous efforts to achieve what they see as a paramount purpose of government."[19]

It would scarcely be an exaggeration to say that the greatest danger to liberty today comes from the men who are most needed and most powerful in modern government, namely, the efficient expert administrators exclusively concerned with what they regard as the public good. Though theorists may still talk about the democratic control of these activities, all who have direct experience in this matter agree that (as one recent English writer put it) "if the Minister's control . . . has become a myth, the control of Parliament is and always has been the merest fairy-tale."[20] It is inevitable that this sort of admin-

---

of the press and popular constitution of the legislature would make this or any other country free otherwise than in name. And the evil would be greater, the more efficiently and scientifically the administrative machinery was constructed—the more skilful the arrangements for obtaining the best qualified hands and heads with which to work it."

[18] Cf. Thomas Humphrey Marshall, *Citizenship and Social Class, and Other Essays* (Cambridge: Cambridge University Press, 1950), p. 59: "So we find that legislation . . . acquires more and more the character of a declaration of policy that it is hoped to put into effect some day."

[19] Roscoe Pound, "The Rise of the Service State and Its Consequences," in *The Welfare State and the National Welfare: A Symposium on Some of the Threatening Tendencies of our Times*, Sheldon Glueck, ed. (Cambridge, MA: Addison-Wesley Press, 1952), p. 226.

[20] Peter Wiles, "Property and Equality," in *The Unservile State: Essays in Liberty and Welfare*, George Watson, ed. (London: Allen and Unwin, 1957), p. 107. Cf. also the statement in the Inns

istration of the welfare of the people should become a self-willed and uncontrollable apparatus before which the individual is helpless, and which becomes increasingly invested with all the *mystique* of sovereign authority—the *Hoheitsverwaltung* or *Herrschaftsstaat* of the German tradition that used to be so unfamiliar to Anglo-Saxons that the strange term "hegemonic"[21] had to be coined to render its meaning.

7. It is not the aim of the following chapters to expound a complete program of economic policy for a free society. We shall be concerned mainly with those comparatively new aspirations whose place in a free society is still uncertain, concerning which our various positions are still floundering between extremes, and where the need for principles which will help us to sort out the good from the bad is most urgent. The problems we shall select are chiefly those which seem particularly important if we are to rescue some of the more modest and legitimate aims from the discredit which over-ambitious attempts may well bring to all actions of the welfare state.

There are many parts of government activity which are of the highest importance for the preservation of a free society but which we cannot examine satisfactorily here. First of all, we shall have to leave aside the whole complex of problems which arise from international relations—not only because any serious attempt to consider these issues would unduly expand this book but also because an adequate treatment would require philosophical foundations other than those we have been able to provide. Satisfactory solutions to these problems will probably not be found as long as we have to accept as the ultimate units of international order the historically given entities known as sovereign nations. And to what groups we should entrust the various powers of government if we had the choice is far too difficult a question to answer briefly. The moral foundations for a rule of law on an international scale seem to be completely lacking still, and we should probably lose whatever advantages it brings within the nation if today we were to entrust any of the new powers of government to supra-national agencies. I will merely say that only makeshift solutions to problems of international relations seem possible so long as we have yet to learn how to limit the powers of all government effectively and how to divide these powers between the tiers of authority. It should also be said that

---

of Court Conservative and Unionist Society, *Rule of Law: A Study* (London: Conservative Political Centre, 1955), p. 20, and endorsed by the Franks Committee (Committee on Administrative Tribunals and Enquiries), *Report of the Committee on Administrative Tribunals and Enquiries, Presented by the Lord High Chancellor to Parliament by Command of Her Majesty*, chaired by Sir Oliver Franks, Cmd. 218 (London: Her Majesty's Stationery Office, 1957), p. 60, par. 273, that "whatever the theoretical validity of this argument, those of us who are Members of Parliament have no hesitation in saying that it bears little relation to reality. Parliament has neither the time nor the knowledge to supervise the Minister and call him to account for his administrative decisions."

[21] See Ludwig von Mises, *Human Action*, pp. 195–99 [Liberty Fund edition, vol. 4, p. 196].

modern developments in national policies have made the international problems very much more difficult than they would have been in the nineteenth century.[22] I wish to add here my opinion that, until the protection of individual freedom is much more firmly secured than it is now, the creation of a world state probably would be a greater danger to the future of civilization than even war.[23]

Hardly less important than the problems of international relations is that of centralization versus decentralization of governmental functions. In spite of its traditional connection with most of the problems we shall be discussing, we shall not be able to consider it systematically. While it has always been characteristic of those favoring an increase in governmental powers to support maximum concentration of these powers, those mainly concerned with individual liberty have generally advocated decentralization. There are strong reasons why action by local authorities generally offers the next best solution where private initiative cannot be relied upon to provide certain services and where some sort of collective action is therefore needed; for it has many of the advantages of private enterprise and fewer of the dangers of the coercive action of government. Competition between local authorities or between larger units within an area where there is freedom of movement provides in a large measure that opportunity for experimentation with alternative methods which will secure most of the advantages of free growth. Though the majority of individuals may never contemplate a change of residence, there will usually be enough people, especially among the young and more enterprising, to make it necessary for the local authorities to provide as good services at as reasonable costs as their competitors.[24] It is usually the authoritarian planner who, in the interest of uniformity, governmental efficiency, and administrative convenience, supports the centralist tendencies and in this receives the strong support of the poorer majorities, who wish to be able to tap the resources of the wealthier regions.

8. There are several other important problems of economic policy that we can mention only in passing. Nobody will deny that economic stability and the prevention of major depressions depends in part on government action.

[22] Cf. Lionel Robbins, *Economic Planning and International Order* (London: Macmillan, 1937).

[23] Cf. Walter Fred Berns, "The Case against World Government," *Readings in World Politics*, Robert Allen Goldwin, ed. (3rd ed.; 3 vols.; Chicago: American Foundation for Political Education, 1955), vol. 3, pp. 62–75.

[24] Cf. George Joseph Stigler, "The Tenable Range of Functions of Local Government (unpublished lecture, 1957) [mimeographed]. [The article which Hayek appears to have seen only in mimeographed form has since appeared in print. See Stigler, "The Tenable Range of Functions of Local Government," *Federal Expenditure Policy for Economic Growth and Stability* (Papers Submitted by Panelists Appearing Before the Subcommittee on Fiscal Policy; 35th Congress, 1st Session; Washington, DC: Joint Economic Committee, 1957), pp. 213–219.—Ed.]

We shall have to consider this problem under the subjects of employment and monetary policy. But a systematic survey would lead us into highly technical and controversial issues of economic theory, where the position I should have to take as the result of my specialized work in this field would be largely independent of the principles discussed in the present book.

Similarly, the subsidization of particular efforts out of funds raised by taxation, which we shall have to consider in connection with housing, agriculture, and education, raises problems of a more general nature. We cannot dismiss them simply by maintaining that no government subsidies should ever be given, since in some unquestioned fields of government activity, such as defense, it is probably often the best and least dangerous method of stimulating necessary developments and is often to be preferred to the government's taking over completely. Probably the only general principle that can be laid down with respect to subsidies is that they can never be justified in terms of the interest of the immediate beneficiary (whether it be the provider of the subsidized service or its consumer) but only in terms of the general benefits which may be enjoyed by all citizens—i.e., the general welfare in the true sense. Subsidies are a legitimate tool of policy, not as a means of income redistribution, but only as a means of using the market to provide services which cannot be confined to those who individually pay for them.

The most conspicuous gap in the following survey is probably the omission of any systematic discussion of enterprise monopoly. The subject was excluded after careful consideration mainly because it seemed not to possess the importance commonly attached to it.[25] For liberals antimonopoly policy has usually been the main object of their reformatory zeal. I believe I have myself in the past used the tactical argument that we cannot hope to curb the coercive powers of labor unions unless we at the same time attack enterprise monopoly. I have, however, become convinced that it would be disingenuous to represent the existing monopolies in the field of labor and those in the field of enterprise as being of the same kind. This does not mean that I share the position of some authors[26] who hold that enterprise monopoly is in some respects beneficial and desirable. I still feel, as I did fifteen years ago,[27] that it may be a good thing if the monopolist is treated as a sort of whipping boy of economic policy; and I recognize that, in the United States, legislation has succeeded in creating a climate of opinion unfavorable to monopoly. So far

[25] See the encyclopedic treatment of these problems by my friend Fritz Machlup, *The Political Economy of Monopoly: Business, Labor, and Government Policies* (Baltimore: Johns Hopkins Press, 1952).

[26] See notably Joseph Alois Schumpeter, *Capitalism, Socialism, and Democracy* (New York: Harper and Brothers, 1942), chap. 7 ["The Process of Creative Destruction,"], pp. 81–86.

[27] *The Road to Serfdom*, chap. 4 ["The Inevitability of Planning,"], pp. 43–55. [*Collected Works* edition, pp. 91–99].

as the enforcement of general rules (such as that of non-discrimination) can curb monopolistic powers, such action is all to the good. But what can be done effectively in this field must take the form of that gradual improvement of our law of corporations, patents, and taxation, on which little that is useful can be said briefly. I have become increasingly skeptical, however, about the beneficial character of any discretionary action of government against particular monopolies, and I am seriously alarmed at the arbitrary nature of all policy aimed at limiting the size of individual enterprises. And when policy creates a state of affairs in which, as is true of some enterprises in the United States, large firms are afraid to compete by lowering prices because this may expose them to antitrust action, it becomes an absurdity.

Current policy fails to recognize that it is not monopoly as such, or bigness, but only obstacles to entry into an industry or trade and certain other monopolistic practices that are harmful. Monopoly is certainly undesirable, but only in the same sense in which scarcity is undesirable; in neither case does this mean that we can avoid it.[28] It is one of the unpleasant facts of life that certain capacities (and also certain advantages and traditions of particular organizations) cannot be duplicated, as it is a fact that certain goods are scarce. It does not make sense to disregard this fact and to attempt to create conditions "as if" competition were effective. The law cannot effectively prohibit states of affairs but only kinds of action. All we can hope for is that, whenever the possibility of competition again appears, nobody will be prevented from taking advantage of it. Where monopoly rests on man-made obstacles to entry into a market, there is every case for removing them. There is also a strong case for prohibiting price discrimination so far as is possible by the application of general rules. But the record of governments in this field is so deplorable

[28] Cf. Frank Hyneman Knight, "Conflict of Values: Freedom and Justice," in *Goals of Economic Life*, Alfred Dudley Ward, ed. (New York: Harper and Brothers, 1953), pp. 224–25: "The public has most exaggerated ideas of the scope of monopoly as really bad and remediable, and talk of 'abolishing' it is merely ignorant or irresponsible. There is no clear line between legitimate and necessary profit and the monopoly gain that presents a problem for action. Every doctor or artist of repute has a monopoly, and monopolies are deliberately granted by law to encourage invention and other creative activities. And, finally, most monopolies work in the same ways as 'patents,' etc., and are temporary and largely balanced by losses. Moreover, by far the worst monopolist restrictions are those organized by wage earners and farmers with the connivance or direct aid of government and with public approval." Cf. also the earlier statement by the same author in his review "The Meaning of Freedom," *Ethics*, 52 (1941–42): 103: "It is needful to state that the role of 'monopoly' in actual economic life is enormously exaggerated in the popular mind and also that a large part of the monopoly which is real, and especially the worst part, is due to the activities of government. In general (and especially in the United States under the New Deal), these have been very largely such as to promote, if not directly to create, monopoly rather than to create or to enforce the conditions of market competition. What competition actually means is simply the freedom of the individual to 'deal' with any and all other individuals and to select the best terms as judged by himself, among those offered."

that it is astounding that anyone should still expect that giving governments discretionary powers will do anything but increase those obstacles. It has been the experience of all countries that discretionary powers in the treatment of monopoly are soon used to distinguish between "good" and "bad" monopolies and that authority soon becomes more concerned with protecting the supposedly good than with preventing the bad. I doubt whether there are any "good" monopolies that deserve protection. But there will always be inevitable monopolies whose transitory and temporary character is often turned into a permanent one by the solicitude of government.

But, though very little is to be hoped for from any specific government action against enterprise monopoly, the situation is different where governments have deliberately fostered the growth of monopoly and even failed to perform the primary function of government—the prevention of coercion, by granting exceptions from the general rules of law—as they have been doing for a long time in the field of labor. It is unfortunate that in a democracy, after a period in which measures in favor of a particular group have been popular, the argument against privilege becomes an argument against the groups that in recent times have enjoyed the special favor of the public because they were thought to need and deserve special help. There can be no question, however, that the basic principles of the rule of law have nowhere in recent times been so generally violated and with such serious consequences as in the case of labor unions. Policy with respect to them will therefore be the first major problem that we shall consider.

EIGHTEEN

LABOR UNIONS AND EMPLOYMENT

> Government, long hostile to other monopolies, suddenly sponsored and promoted widespread labor monopolies, which democracy cannot endure, cannot control without destroying, and perhaps cannot destroy without destroying itself. —Henry C. Simons

1. Public policy concerning labor unions has, in little more than a century, moved from one extreme to the other. From a state in which little the unions could do was legal if they were not prohibited altogether, we have now reached a state where they have become uniquely privileged institutions to which the general rules of law do not apply. They have become the only important instance in which governments signally fail in their prime function—the prevention of coercion and violence.

This development has been greatly assisted by the fact that unions were at first able to appeal to the general principles of liberty[1] and then retain the support of the liberals long after all discrimination against them had ceased and they had acquired exceptional privileges. In few other areas are progressives so little willing to consider the reasonableness of any particular measure

---

The quotation at the head of the chapter is taken from Henry Calvert Simons, "Hansen on Fiscal Policy," *Journal of Political Economy*, 50 (1942): 171; reprinted in *Economic Policy for a Free Society* (Chicago: University of Chicago Press, 1948), p. 193.

[1] Including the most "orthodox" political economists, who invariably supported freedom of association. See particularly the discussion in John Ramsay McCulloch, *Treatise on the Circumstances Which Determine the Rate of Wages and the Condition of the Labouring Classes* (London: Longman, Brown, Green, and Longmans, 1851), pp. 79–89, with its stress on *voluntary* association. [McCulloch at one point notes: "A voluntary combination among workmen is certainly in no respect injurious to any of the rights of their masters. It is a contradiction to pretend that masters have any right or title to the services of free workmen in the event of the latter not choosing to accept the price offered them for their labour. And as the existence of a combination to procure a rise in wages shows that they have not so chosen, and is proof of the want of all concord and agreement between the parties, so it is also a proof that the workmen are fairly entitled to enter into it; and that, however injurious their proceedings may be to themselves, they do not encroach on the privileges or rights of others."—Ed.] For a comprehensive statement of the classical liberal attitude toward the legal problems involved see Ludwig Bamberger, *Die Arbeiterfrage unter dem Gesichtspunkte des Vereinsrechtes* (Stuttgart: J. G. Cotta, 1873).

but generally ask only whether it is "for or against unions" or, as it is usually put, "for or against labor."[2] Yet the briefest glance at the history of the unions should suggest that the reasonable position must lie somewhere between the extremes which mark their evolution.

Most people, however, have so little realization of what has happened that they still support the aspirations of the unions in the belief that they are struggling for "freedom of association," when this term has in fact lost its meaning and the real issue has become the freedom of the individual to join or not to join a union. The existing confusion is due in part to the rapidity with which the character of the problem has changed; in many countries voluntary associations of workers had only just become legal when they began to use coercion to force unwilling workers into membership and to keep non-members out of employment. Most people probably still believe that a "labor dispute" normally means a disagreement about remuneration and the conditions of employment, while as often as not its sole cause is an attempt on the part of the unions to force unwilling workers to join.

The acquisition of privilege by the unions has nowhere been as spectacular as in Britain, where the Trade Dispute Act of 1906 conferred "upon a trade union a freedom from civil liability for the commission of even the most heinous wrong by the union or its servant, and in short confer[red] upon every trade union a privilege and protection not possessed by any other person or body of persons, whether corporate or incorporate."[3] Similar friendly legis-

---

[2] Characteristic is the description of the "liberal" attitude to unions in Charles Wright Mills, *The New Men of Power: America's Labor Leaders* (New York: Harcourt, Brace, 1948), p. 21. "In many liberal minds there seems to be an undercurrent that whispers: 'I will not criticize the unions and their leaders. There I draw the line.' This, they must feel distinguishes them from the bulk of the Republican Party and the right-wing Democrats; this keeps them leftward and socially pure."

[3] Dicey, "Introduction," *Law and Opinion* (2nd edition), pp. xlv–xlvii [Liberty Fund edition, pp. 373–74]. He continues to say that the law "makes a trade union a privileged body exempted from the ordinary law of the land. No such privileged body has ever before been deliberately created by an English Parliament [and that] it stimulates among workmen the fatal delusion that workmen should aim at the attainment, not of equality, but of privilege." Cf. also the comment on the same law, thirty years later, by Joseph Alois Schumpeter, *Capitalism, Socialism, and Democracy* (New York: Harper and Brothers, 1942), p. 321, n. 4: "It is difficult, at the present time, to realize how this measure must have struck people who still believed in a state and in a legal system that centered in the institution of private property. For in relaxing the law of conspiracy in respect to peaceful picketing—which practically amounted to legalization of trade-union action implying the threat of force—and in exempting trade-union funds from liability in action for damages *for torts*—which practically amounted to enacting that trade unions could do not wrong— this measure in fact resigned to the trade unions part of the authority of the state and granted to them a position of privilege which the formal extension of the exemption to employers' unions was powerless to affect." Still more recently the Lord Chief Justice of Northern Ireland said of the same act (John Clark MacDermott, Baron MacDermott, *Protection from Power under English Law*. The Hamlyn Lectures. [London: Stevens, 1957], p. 174): "In short, it put trade unionism

lation helped the unions in the United States, where first the Clayton Act of 1914 exempted them from the antimonopoly provisions of the Sherman Act; the Norris-LaGuardia Act of 1932 "went a long way to establish practically complete immunity of labor organizations for torts";[4] and, finally, the Supreme Court in a crucial decision sustained "the claim of a union to the right to deny participation in the economic world to an employer."[5] More or less the same situation had gradually come to exist in most European countries by the 1920s, "less through explicit legislative permission than by the tacit toleration by authorities and courts."[6] Everywhere the legalization of unions was interpreted as a legalization of their main purpose and as recognition of their right to do whatever seemed necessary to achieve this purpose—namely, monopoly. More and more they came to be treated not as a group which was pursuing a legitimate selfish aim and which, like every other interest, must be kept in check by competing interests possessed of equal rights, but as a group whose aim—the exhaustive and comprehensive organization of all labor—must be supported for the good of the public.[7]

Although flagrant abuses of their powers by the unions have often shocked public opinion in recent times and uncritical pro-union sentiment is on the wane, the public has certainly not yet become aware that the existing legal position is fundamentally wrong and that the whole basis of our free society is gravely threatened by the powers arrogated by the unions. We shall not be concerned here with those criminal abuses of union power that have lately attracted much attention in the United States, although they are not entirely

---

in the same privileged position which the Crown enjoyed until ten years ago in respect of wrongful acts committed on its behalf."

[4] Roscoe Pound, *Legal Immunities of Labor Unions* (Washington, DC: American Enterprise Association, 1957), p. 23, reprinted in Edward Hastings Chamberlin, et al., *Labor Unions and Public Policy* (Washington, DC: American Enterprise Institute for Public Policy Research, 1958).

[5] *Hunt v. Crumboch* 325 *U.S.* 821, at 831 (1944) (Mr. Justice Robert Jackson's dissent).

[6] Ludwig von Mises, *Die Gemeinwirtschaft. Untersuchungen über den Sozialismus* (2nd ed.; Jena: Verlag von Gustav Fischer, 1932), p. 447. [The extended German quotation reads: "Es genügt festzustellen, daß sie es in den letzten Jahrzehnten überall errungen haben, weniger durch ausdrückliche gesetzliche Zustimmung als durch stillschweigende Duldung der Behörden und Gerichte." ("It is sufficient to say that in the last decades it has been established everywhere, less by explicit legislative sanction than by the tacit toleration of public authority and the law.") (*Socialism*, Jacques Kahane, trans. [London: Jonathan Cape, 1936]).—Ed.]

[7] Few liberal sympathizers of the trade unions would dare to express the obvious truth which a courageous woman from within the British labor movement frankly stated, namely, that "it is in fact the business of a Union to be anti-social: the members would have a just grievance if their officials and committees ceased to put sectional interests first" (Barbara Wootton, *Freedom under Planning* [London: Allen and Unwin, 1945], p. 97). On the flagrant abuses of union power in the United States, which I shall not further consider here, see Sylvester Petro, *Power Unlimited: The Corruption of Union Leadership; A Report on the McClellan Committee Hearings* (New York: Ronald Press, 1959).

unconnected with the privileges that unions legally enjoy. Our concern will be solely with those powers that unions today generally possess, either with the explicit permission of the law or at least with the tacit toleration of the law-enforcing authorities. Our argument will not be directed against labor unions as such; nor will it be confined to the practices that are now widely recognized as abuses. But we shall direct our attention to some of their powers which are now widely accepted as legitimate, if not as their "sacred rights." The case against these is strengthened rather than weakened by the fact that unions have often shown much restraint in exercising them. It is precisely because, in the existing legal situation, unions could do infinitely more harm than they do, and because we owe it to the moderation and good sense of many union leaders, that the situation is not much worse that we cannot afford to allow the present state of affairs to continue.[8]

---

[8] In this chapter, more than in almost any other, I shall be able to draw upon a body of opinion that is gradually forming among an increasing number of thoughtful students of these matters—men who in background and interest are at least as sympathetic to the true concerns of the workers as those who in the past have been championing the privileges of the unions. See particularly William Harold Hutt, *The Theory of Collective Bargaining: A History, Analysis and Criticism of the Principal Theories Which Have Sought to Explain the Effects of Trade Unions and Employers Associations Upon the Distribution of the Product of Industry* (London: P. S. King, 1930), and his *Economists and the Public: A Study of Competition and Opinion* (London: Jonathan Cape, 1936); Henry Calvert Simons, "Some Reflections on Syndicalism," *Journal of Political Economy*, 52 (1944): 1–25, reprinted in his *Economic Policy for a Free Society* (Chicago: University of Chicago Press, 1948), pp. 121–59; John Thomas Dunlop, *Wage Determination under Trade Unions* (New York: Macmillan, 1944); Chamber of Commerce, *Economic Institute on Wage Determination and the Economics of Liberalism*, Joseph H. Ball, moderator [Addresses delivered at an Economic Institute on Wage Determination and Economic Liberalism, held at the Chamber of Commerce, January 11, 1947] (Washington, DC: Chamber of Commerce of the United States, 1947), especially the contributions of Jacob Viner ("The Role of Costs in a System of Economic Liberalism," pp. 15–33) and Fritz Machlup ("Monopolistic Wage Determination as a Part of the General Problem of Monopoly," pp. 49–82); Leo Wolman, *Industry-wide Bargaining* (Irvington-on-Hudson, NY: Foundation for Economic Education, 1948); Charles Edward Lindblom, *Unions and Capitalism* (New Haven: Yale University Press, 1949), cf. the reviews of this book by Aaron Director ("Book Review of *Unions and Capitalism*," *University of Chicago Law Review*, 18 [1950]: 164–67), by John Thomas Dunlop ("Review of *Unions and Capitalism*," *American Economic Review*, 40 [1950]: 463–68), and by Albert Rees ("Labor Unions and the Price System," *Journal of Political Economy*, 58 [1950]: 254–63); David McCord Wright, ed., *The Impact of the Union: Eight Economic Theorists Evaluate the Labor Union Movement* [Institute on the Structure of the Labor Market held at the American University, May 12–13, 1950] (New York: Harcourt, Brace, 1951), especially the contributions of Milton Friedman ("Some Comments on the Significance of Labor Unions for Economic Policy," pp. 204–34) and Gottfried Haberler ("Wage Policy, Employment, and Economic Stability," pp. 34–62); Fritz Machlup, *The Political Economy of Monopoly: Business, Labor, and Government Policies* (Baltimore: Johns Hopkins Press, 1952); Donald Randall Richberg, *Labor Union Monopoly: A Clear and Present Danger* (Chicago: H. Regnery Co., 1957); Sylvester Petro, *The Labor Policy of a Free Society* (New York: Ronald Press, 1957); Benjamin Charles Roberts, *Trade Unions in a Free Society* (London: Institute of Economic Affairs, 1959); and John Davenport's two articles, "Labor Unions in the Free So-

2. It cannot be stressed enough that the coercion which unions have been permitted to exercise contrary to all principles of freedom under the law is primarily the coercion of fellow workers. Whatever true coercive power unions may be able to wield over employers is a consequence of this primary power of coercing other workers; the coercion of employers would lose most of its objectionable character if unions were deprived of this power to exact unwilling support. Neither the right of voluntary agreement between workers nor even their right to withhold their services in concert is in question. It should be said, however, that the latter—the right to strike—though a normal right, can hardly be regarded as an inalienable right. There are good reasons why in certain employments it should be part of the terms of employment that the worker should renounce this right; i.e., such employments should involve long-term obligations on the part of the workers, and any concerted attempts to break such contracts should be illegal.

It is true that any union effectively controlling all potential workers of a firm or industry can exercise almost unlimited pressure on the employer and that, particularly where a great amount of capital has been invested in specialized equipment, such a union can practically expropriate the owner and command nearly the whole return of his enterprise.[9] The decisive point, however, is that this will never be in the interest of all workers—except in the unlikely

ciety," *Fortune*, April 1959, pp. 132–34, 204, 206, 211–12; "Labor and the Law," *Fortune*, May 1959, pp. 142–43, 237–38, 240, 242, 246.

See also Edward Hastings Chamberlin, *The Economic Analysis of Labor Union Power* (Washington: American Enterprise Institute for Public Policy Research, 1958); Philip D. Bradley, *Involuntary Participation in Unionism* (Washington, DC: American Enterprise Institute for Public Policy Research, 1956); and Gerard Denis Reilly, *States Rights and the Law of Labor Relations* (Washington, DC: American Enterprise Institute for Public Policy Research, 1955). These three articles, together with Roscoe Pound, *Legal Immunities of Labor Unions* (see n. 4, above) are reprinted in Edward Hastings Chamberlin, et al., *Labor Unions and Public Policy* (Washington: American Enterprise Institute for Public Policy Research, 1958).

On general wage theory and the limits of the powers of the unions see also John Richard Hicks, *The Theory of Wages* (London: Macmillan, 1932), Richard von Strigl, *Angewandte Lohntheorie: Untersuchungen über die wirtschaftlichen Grundlagen der Sozialpolitik* (Leipzig: F. Deuticke, 1926), and Dunlop, *Wage Determination under Trade Unions* (cited above).

[9] See particularly the works by Henry Calvert Simons ["Some Reflections on Syndicalism," *Journal of Political Economy*, 52 (1944): 1–25, reprinted in his *Economic Policy for a Free Society* (Chicago: University of Chicago Press, 1948), pp. 121–59] and William Harold Hutt [*The Theory of Collective Bargaining: A History, Analysis, and Criticism of the Principal Theories Which Have Sought to Explain the Effects of Trade Unions and Employers Associations Upon the Distribution of the Product of Industry* (London: P. S. King, 1930); and *Economists and the Public: A Study of Competition and Opinion* (London: Jonathan Cape, 1936) cited in n. 8 above]. Whatever limited validity the old argument about the necessity of "equalizing bargaining power" by the formation of unions may ever have had, has certainly been destroyed by the modern development of the increasing size and specificity of the employers' investment, on the one hand, and the increasing mobility of labor (made possible by the automobile), on the other.

case where the total gain from such action is equally shared among them, irrespective of whether they are employed or not—and that, therefore, the union can achieve this only by coercing some workers against their interest to support such a concerted move.

The reason for this is that workers can raise real wages above the level that would prevail on a free market only by limiting the supply, that is, by withholding part of labor. The interest of those who will get employment at the higher wage will therefore always be opposed to the interest of those who, in consequence, will find employment only in the less highly paid jobs or who will not be employed at all.

The fact that unions will ordinarily first make the employer agree to a certain wage and then see to it that nobody will be employed for less makes little difference. Wage fixing is quite as effective a means as any other of keeping out those who could be employed only at a lower wage. The essential point is that the employer will agree to the wage only when he knows that the union has the power to keep out others.[10] As a general rule, wage fixing (whether by unions or by authority) will make wages higher than they would otherwise be only if they are also higher than the wage at which all willing workers can be employed.

Though unions may still often act on a contrary belief, there can now be no doubt that they cannot in the long run increase real wages for all wishing to work above the level that would establish itself in a free market—though they may well push up the level of money wages, with consequences that will occupy us later. Their success in raising real wages beyond that point, if it is to be more than temporary, can benefit only a particular group at the expense of others. It will therefore serve only a sectional interest even when it obtains the support of all. This means that strictly voluntary unions, because their wage policy would not be in the interest of all workers, could not long receive the support of all. Unions that had no power to coerce outsiders would thus not be strong enough to force up wages above the level at which all seeking work could be employed, that is, the level that would establish itself in a truly free market for labor in general.

But, while the real wages of all the employed can be raised by union action only at the price of unemployment, unions in particular industries or crafts may well raise the wages of their members by forcing others to stay in less-well-paid occupations. How great a distortion of the wage structure this in fact causes is difficult to say. If one remembers, however, that some unions find it expedient to use violence in order to prevent any influx into their trade and that others are able to charge high premiums for admission (or even to

[10] This must be emphasized especially against the argument of Lindblom in *Unions and Capitalism*.

reserve jobs in the trade for children of present members), there can be little doubt that this distortion is considerable. It is important to note that such policies can be employed successfully only in relatively prosperous and highly paid occupations and that they will therefore result in the exploitation of the relatively poor by the better-off. Even though within the scope of any one union its actions may tend to reduce differences in remuneration, there can be little doubt that, so far as relative wages in major industries and trades are concerned, unions today are largely responsible for an inequality which has no function and is entirely the result of privilege.[11] This means that their activities necessarily reduce the productivity of labor all around and therefore also the general level of real wages; because, if union action succeeds in reducing the number of workers in the highly paid jobs and in increasing the number of those who have to stay in the less remunerative ones, the result must be that the over-all average will be lower. It is, in fact, more than likely that, in countries where unions are very strong, the general level of real wages is lower than it would otherwise be.[12] This is certainly true of most countries of Europe, where union policy is strengthened by the general use of restrictive practices of a "make-work" character.

If many still accept as an obvious and undeniable fact that the general wage level has risen as fast as it has done because of the efforts of the unions, they do so in spite of these unambiguous conclusions of theoretical analysis—and in spite of empirical evidence to the contrary. Real wages have often risen much faster when unions were weak than when they were strong; furthermore, even the rise in particular trades or industries where labor was not organized has frequently been much faster than in highly organized and equally prosperous industries.[13] The common impression to the contrary is due partly to the fact that wage gains, which are today mostly obtained in union negotiations, are for that reason regarded as obtainable only in this manner[14] and even more to the fact that, as we shall presently see, union activity does in fact

[11] Chamberlin, *The Economic Analysis of Labor Union Power*, pp. 4–5, rightly stresses that "there can be no doubt that one effect of trade union policy . . . is to diminish still further the real income of the really low income groups, including not only the low income wage receivers but also such other elements of society as 'self-employed' and small business men."

[12] Cf. Fritz Machlup in "Monopolistic Wage Determination as a Part of the General Problem of Monopoly" and *The Political Economy of Monopoly: Business, Labor, and Government*.

[13] A conspicuous example of this in recent times is the case of the notoriously unorganized domestic servants whose average annual wages (as pointed out by Milton Friedman in "Some Comments on the Significance of Labor Unions for Economic Policy," David McCord Wright, ed., *The Impact of the Union: Eight Economic Theorists Evaluate the Labor Union Movement*, p. 224) in the United States in 1947 were 2.72 times as high as they had been in 1939, while at the end of the same period the wages of the comprehensively organized steel workers had risen only to 1.98 times the initial level.

[14] Cf. Bradley, *Involuntary Participation in Unionism*.

bring about a continuous rise in money wages exceeding the increase in real wages. Such increase in money wages is possible without producing general unemployment only because it is regularly made ineffective by inflation— indeed, it must be if full employment is to be maintained.

3. If unions have in fact achieved much less by their wage policy than is generally believed, their activities in this field are nevertheless economically very harmful and politically exceedingly dangerous. They are using their power in a manner which tends to make the market system ineffective and which, at the same time, gives them a control of the direction of economic activity that would be dangerous in the hands of government but is intolerable if exercised by a particular group. They do so through their influence on the relative wages of different groups of workers and through their constant upward pressure on the level of money wages, with its inevitable inflationary consequences.

The effect on relative wages is usually greater uniformity and rigidity of wages within any one union-controlled group and greater and non-functional differences in wages between different groups. This is accompanied by a restriction of the mobility of labor, of which the former is either an effect or a cause. We need say no more about the fact that this may benefit particular groups but can only lower the productivity and therefore the incomes of the workers in general. Nor need we stress here the fact that the greater stability of the wages of particular groups which unions may secure is likely to involve greater instability of employment. What is important is that the accidental differences in union power of the different trades and industries will produce not only gross inequalities in remuneration among the workers which have no economic justification but uneconomic disparities in the development of different industries. Socially important industries, such as building, will be greatly hampered in their development and will conspicuously fail to satisfy urgent needs simply because their character offers the unions special opportunities for coercive monopolistic practices.[15] Because unions are most powerful where capital investments are heaviest, they tend to become a deterrent to investment—at present probably second only to taxation. Finally, it is often union monopoly in collusion with enterprise that becomes one of the chief foundations of monopolistic control of the industry concerned.

The chief danger presented by the current development of unionism is that, by establishing effective monopolies in the supply of the different kinds of labor, the unions will prevent competition from acting as an effective regulator of the allocation of all resources. But if competition becomes ineffective as a means of such regulation, some other means will have to be adopted in

---

[15] Cf. Stephen Paul Sobotka, "Union Influence on Wages: The Construction Industry," *Journal of Political Economy*, 61 (1953): 127–43.

its place. The only alternative to the market, however, is direction by authority. Such direction clearly cannot be left in the hands of particular unions with sectional interests, nor can it be adequately performed by a unified organization of all labor, which would thereby become not merely the strongest power in the state but a power completely controlling the state. Unionism as it is now tends, however, to produce that very system of over-all socialist planning which few unions want and which, indeed, it is in their best interest to avoid.

4. The unions cannot achieve their principal aims unless they obtain complete control of the supply of the type of labor with which they are concerned; and, since it is not in the interest of all workers to submit to such control, some of them must be induced to act against their own interest. This may be done to some extent through merely psychological and moral pressure, encouraging the erroneous belief that the unions benefit all workers. Where they succeed in creating a general feeling that every worker ought, in the interest of his class, to support union action, coercion comes to be accepted as a legitimate means of making a recalcitrant worker do his duty. Here the unions have relied on a most effective tool, namely, the myth that it is due to their efforts that the standard of living of the working class has risen as fast as it has done and that only through their continued efforts will wages continue to increase as fast as possible—a myth in the assiduous cultivation of which the unions have usually been actively assisted by their opponents. A departure from such a condition can come only from a truer insight into the facts, and whether this will be achieved depends on how effectively economists do their job of enlightening public opinion.

But though this kind of moral pressure exerted by the unions may be very powerful, it would scarcely be sufficient to give them the power to do real harm. Union leaders apparently agree with the students of this aspect of unionism that much stronger forms of coercion are needed if the unions are to achieve their aims. It is the techniques of coercion that unions have developed for the purpose of making membership in effect compulsory, what they call their "organizational activities" (or, in the United States, "union security"—a curious euphemism) that give them real power. Because the power of truly voluntary unions will be restricted to what are common interests of all workers, they have come to direct their chief efforts to the forcing of dissenters to obey their will.

They could never have been successful in this without the support of a misguided public opinion and the active aid of government. Unfortunately, they have to a large extent succeeded in persuading the public that complete unionization is not only legitimate but important to public policy. To say that the workers have a right to form unions, however, is not to say that the unions have a right to exist independently of the will of the individual workers. Far from being a public calamity, it would indeed be a highly desirable state of affairs if the workers should not feel it necessary to form unions. Yet the fact that it is a natural aim of the unions to induce all workers to join them has been so interpreted as to mean that the unions ought to be entitled to do whatever seems necessary to achieve this aim. Similarly, the fact that it is legitimate for unions to try to secure higher wages has been interpreted to mean that they must also be allowed to do whatever seems necessary to succeed in their effort. In particular, because striking has been accepted as a legitimate weapon of unions, it has come to be believed that they must be allowed to do whatever seems necessary to make a strike successful. In general, the legalization of unions has come to mean that whatever methods they regard as indispensable for their purposes are also to be treated as legal.

The present coercive powers of unions thus rest chiefly on the use of methods which would not be tolerated for any other purpose and which are opposed to the protection of the individual's private sphere. In the first place, the unions rely—to a much greater extent than is commonly recognized— on the use of the picket line as an instrument of intimidation. That even so-called "peaceful" picketing in numbers is severely coercive and the condoning of it constitutes a privilege conceded because of its presumed legitimate aim is shown by the fact that it can be and is used by persons who themselves are not workers to force others to form a union which they will control, and that it can also be used for purely political purposes or to give vent to animosity against an unpopular person. The aura of legitimacy conferred upon it because the aims are often approved cannot alter the fact that it represents a kind of organized pressure upon individuals which in a free society no private agency should be permitted to exercise.

Next to the toleration of picketing, the chief factor which enables unions to coerce individual workers is the sanction by both legislation and jurisdiction of the closed or union shop and its varieties. These constitute contracts in restraint of trade, and only their exemption from the ordinary rules of law has made them legitimate objects of the "organizational activities" of the unions. Legislation has frequently gone so far as to require not only that a contract concluded by the representatives of the majority of the workers of a plant or industry be available to any worker who wishes to take advantage of it, but that it apply to all employees, even if they should individually wish and be able to obtain a different combination of advantages.[16] We must also regard as

[16] It would be difficult to exaggerate the extent to which unions prevent the experimentation with, and gradual introduction of, new arrangements that might be in the mutual interest of employers and employees. For example, it is not at all unlikely that in some industries it would be in the interest of both to agree on "guaranteed annual wages" if unions permitted individuals to make a sacrifice in the amount of wages in return for a greater degree of security.

inadmissible methods of coercion all secondary strikes and boycotts which are used not as an instrument of wage bargaining but solely as a means of forcing other workers to fall in with union policies.

Most of these coercive tactics of the unions can be practiced, moreover, only because the law has exempted groups of workers from the ordinary responsibility of joint action, either by allowing them to avoid formal incorporation or by explicitly exempting their organizations from the general rules applying to corporate bodies. There is no need to consider separately various other aspects of contemporary union policies such as, to mention one, industry-wide or nation-wide bargaining. Their practicability rests on the practices already mentioned, and they would almost certainly disappear if the basic coercive power of the unions were removed.[17]

5. It can hardly be denied that raising wages by the use of coercion is today the main aim of unions. Even if this were their sole aim, legal prohibition of unions would however, not be justifiable. In a free society much that is undesirable has to be tolerated if it cannot be prevented without discriminatory legislation. But the control of wages is even now not the only function of the unions; and they are undoubtedly capable of rendering services which are not only unobjectionable but definitely useful. If their only purpose were to force up wages by coercive action, they would probably disappear if deprived of coercive power. But unions have other useful functions to perform, and, though it would be contrary to all our principles even to consider the possibility of prohibiting them altogether, it is desirable to show explicitly why there is no economic ground for such action and why, as truly voluntary and non-coercive organizations, they may have important services to render. It is in fact more than probable that unions will fully develop their potential usefulness only after they have been diverted from their present antisocial aims by an effective prevention of the use of coercion.[18]

---

[17] To illustrate the nature of much contemporary wage bargaining in the United States, Edward Hastings Chamberlin, in his essay *The Economic Analysis of Labor Union Power*, pp. 40–41, uses an analogy which I cannot better: "Some perspective may be had on what is involved by imagining an application of the techniques of the labor market in some other field. If A is bargaining with B over the sale of his house, and if A were given the privileges of a modern labor union, he would be able (1) to conspire with all other owners of houses not to make any alternative offers to B, using violence or the threat of violence if necessary to prevent them, (2) to deprive B himself of access to any alternative offers, (3) to surround the house of B and cut off all deliveries of food (except by parcel post), (4) to stop all movement from B's house, so that if he were for instance a doctor he could not sell his services and make a living, and (5) to institute a boycott of B's business. All of these privileges, if he were capable of carrying them out, would no doubt strengthen A's position. But they would not be regarded by anyone as part of 'bargaining'—unless A were a labor union."

[18] Cf. Petro, *The Labor Policy of a Free Society*, p. 51: "Unions can and do serve useful purposes, and they have only barely scratched the surface of their potential utility to employees. When

Unions without coercive powers would probably play a useful and important role even in the process of wage determination. In the first place, there is often a choice to be made between wage increases, on the one hand, and, on the other, alternative benefits which the employer could provide at the same cost but which he can provide only if all or most of the workers are willing to accept them in preference to additional pay. There is also the fact that the relative position of the individual on the wage scale is often nearly as important to him as his absolute position. In any hierarchical organization it is important that the differentials between the remuneration for the different jobs and the rules of promotion are felt to be just by the majority.[19] The most effective way of securing consent is probably to have the general scheme agreed to in collective negotiations in which all the different interests are represented. Even from the employer's point of view it would be difficult to conceive of any other way of reconciling all the different considerations that in a large organization have to be taken into account in arriving at a satisfactory wage structure. An agreed set of standard terms, available to all who wish to take advantage of them, though not excluding special arrangements in individual cases, seems to be required by the needs of large-scale organizations.

The same is true to an even greater extent of all the general problems relating to conditions of work other than individual remuneration, those problems which truly concern all employees and which, in the mutual interest of workers and employers, should be regulated in a manner that takes account of as many desires as possible. A large organization must in a great measure be governed by rules, and such rules are likely to operate most effectively if drawn up with the participation of the workers.[20] Because a contract between employers and employees regulates not only relations between them but also relations between the various groups of employees, it is often expedient to

---

they really get to work on the job of serving employees instead of making such bad names for themselves as they do in coercing and abusing employees, they will have much less difficulty than they presently have in securing and keeping new members. As matters now stand, union insistence upon the closed shop amounts to an admission that unions are really not performing their functions very well."

[19] Cf. Chester Irving Barnard, "Functions and Pathology of Status Systems in Formal Organizations," in *Industry and Society*, William Foote Whyte, ed. (New York: McGraw-Hill, 1946), pp. 46–83; reprinted in Chester Irving Barnard, *Organization and Management: Selected Papers* (Cambridge, MA: Harvard University Press, 1949), pp. 207–44.

[20] Cf. Sumner Huber Slichter, *Trade Unions in a Free Society* [Revision of a paper prepared for a bicentennial conference on the evolution of social institutions at Princeton University, October 8, 1946] (Cambridge, MA: Harvard University Press, 1947), p. 12, where it is argued that such rules "introduce into industry the equivalent of civil rights, and they greatly enlarge the range of human activities which are governed by rule or law rather than by whim or caprice." See also Alvin Ward Gouldner, *Patterns of Industrial Bureaucracy* (Glencoe, IL: Free Press, 1954), esp. the discussion of "rule by rule," in chap. 9, "About the Functions of Bureaucratic Rules," pp. 157–80.

give it the character of a multilateral agreement and to provide in certain respects, as in grievance procedure, for a degree of self-government among the employees.

There is, finally, the oldest and most beneficial activity of the unions, in which as "friendly societies" they undertake to assist members in providing against the peculiar risks of their trade. This is a function which must in every respect be regarded as a highly desirable form of self-help, albeit one which is gradually being taken over by the welfare state. We shall leave the question open, however, as to whether any of the above arguments justify unions of a larger scale than that of the plant or corporation.

An entirely different matter, which we can mention here only in passing, is the claim of unions to participation in the conduct of business. Under the name of "industrial democracy" or, more recently, under that of "co-determination," this has acquired considerable popularity, especially in Germany and to a lesser degree in Britain. It represents a curious recrudescence of the ideas of the syndicalist branch of nineteenth-century socialism, the least-thought-out and most impractical form of that doctrine. Though these ideas have a certain superficial appeal, they reveal inherent contradictions when examined. A plant or industry cannot be conducted in the interest of some permanent distinct body of workers if it is at the same time to serve the interests of the consumers. Moreover, effective participation in the direction of an enterprise is a full-time job, and anybody so engaged soon ceases to have the outlook and interest of an employee. It is not only from the point of view of the employers, therefore, that such a plan should be rejected; there are very good reasons why in the United States union leaders have emphatically refused to assume any responsibility in the conduct of business. For a fuller examination of this problem we must, however, refer the reader to the careful studies, now available, of all its implications.[21]

6. Though it may be impossible to protect the individual against all union coercion so long as general opinion regards it as legitimate, most students of the subject agree that comparatively few and, as they may seem at first, minor changes in law and jurisdiction would suffice to produce far-reaching and probably decisive changes in the existing situation.[22] The mere withdrawal of the special privileges either explicitly granted to the unions or arrogated by them with the toleration of the courts would seem enough to deprive them

---

[21] See particularly Franz Böhm, "Das wirtschaftliche Mitbestimmungsrecht der Arbeiter im Betrieb," *Ordo*, 4 (1951): 21–250, and Goetz Antony Briefs, *Zwischen Kapitalismus und Syndikalismus: die Gewerkschaften am Scheideweg* (Bern: A. Francke, 1952).

[22] See the essays by Jacob Viner, "The Role of Costs in a System of Economic Liberalism"; Gottfried Haberler, "Wage Policy, Employment, and Economic Stability;" Milton Friedman, "Some Comments on the Significance of Labor Unions for Economic Policy;" and the book by Sylvester Petro, *The Labor Policy of a Free Society*.

of the more serious coercive powers which they now exercise and to channel their legitimate selfish interests so that they would be socially beneficial.

The essential requirement is that true freedom of association be assured and that coercion be treated as equally illegitimate whether employed for or against organization, by the employer or by the employees. The principle that the end does not justify the means and that the aims of the unions do not justify their exemption from the general rules of law should be strictly applied. Today this means, in the first place, that all picketing in numbers should be prohibited, since it is not only the chief and regular cause of violence but even in its most peaceful forms is a means of coercion. Next, the unions should not be permitted to keep non-members out of any employment. This means that closed- and union-shop contracts (including such varieties as the "maintenance of membership" and "preferential hiring" clauses) must be treated as contracts in restraint of trade and denied the protection of the law. They differ in no respect from the "yellow-dog contract" which prohibits the individual worker from joining a union and which is commonly prohibited by the law.

The invalidating of all such contracts would, by removing the chief objects of secondary strikes and boycotts, make these and similar forms of pressure largely ineffective. It would be necessary, however, also to rescind all legal provisions which make contracts concluded with the representatives of the majority of workers of a plant or industry binding on all employees and to deprive all organized groups of any right of concluding contracts binding on men who have not voluntarily delegated this authority to them.[23] Finally, the responsibility for organized and concerted action in conflict with contractual obligations or the general law must be firmly placed on those in whose hands the decision lies, irrespective of the particular form of organized action adopted.

It would not be a valid objection to maintain that any legislation making certain types of contracts invalid would be contrary to the principle of freedom of contract. We have seen before (in chap. 15) that this principle can never mean that all contracts will be legally binding and enforceable. It means merely that all contracts must be judged according to the same general rules and that no authority should be given discretionary power to allow or disallow particular contracts. Among the contracts to which the law ought to deny validity are contracts in restraint of trade. Closed- and union-shop contracts fall clearly into this category. If legislation, jurisdiction, and the tolerance of executive agencies had not created privileges for the unions, the need for special legislation concerning them would probably not have arisen in

---

[23] Such contracts binding on third parties are equally as objectionable in this field as is the forcing of price-maintenance agreements on non-signers by "fair-trade" laws.

common-law countries. That there is such a need is a matter for regret, and the believer in liberty will regard any legislation of this kind with misgivings. But, once special privileges have become part of the law of the land, they can be removed only by special legislation. Though there ought to be no need for special "right-to-work laws," it is difficult to deny that the situation created in the United States by legislation and by the decisions of the Supreme Court may make special legislation the only practicable way of restoring the principles of freedom.[24]

The specific measures which would be required in any given country to reinstate the principles of free association in the field of labor will depend on the situation created by its individual development. The situation in the United States is of special interest, for here legislation and the decisions of the Supreme Court have probably gone further than elsewhere[25] in legalizing union coercion and very far in conferring discretionary and essentially irresponsible powers on administrative authority. But for further details we must refer the reader to the important study by Professor Petro on *The Labor Policy of the Free Society*,[26] in which the reforms required are fully described.

Though all the changes needed to restrain the harmful powers of the unions involve no more than that they be made to submit to the same general principles of law that apply to everybody else, there can be no doubt that the existing unions will resist them with all their power. They know that the achievement of what they at present desire depends on that very coercive power which will have to be restrained if a free society is to be preserved. Yet the situation is not hopeless. There are developments under way which sooner or later will prove to the unions that the existing state cannot last. They will find that, of the alternative courses of further development open to them, submitting to the general principle that prevents all coercion will be greatly preferable in the long run to continuing their present policy; for the latter is bound to lead to one of two unfortunate consequences.

7. While labor unions cannot in the long run substantially alter the level of real wages that all workers can earn and are, in fact, more likely to lower than to raise them, the same is not true of the level of money wages. With

---

[24] Such legislation, to be consistent with our principles, should not go beyond declaring certain contracts invalid, which is sufficient for removing all pretext for action to obtain them. It should not, as the title of the "right-to-work laws" may suggest, give individuals a claim to a particular job, or even (as some of the laws in force in certain American states do) confer a right to damages for having been denied a particular job, when the denial is not illegal on other grounds. The objections against such provisions are the same as those which apply to "fair employment practices" laws.

[25] See Arthur Lenhoff, "The Problem of Compulsory Unionism in Europe," *American Journal of Comparative Law*, 5 (1956): 18–43.

[26] See Sylvester Petro, *The Labor Policy of a Free Society*, esp. pp. 235ff. and 282.

respect to them, the effect of union action will depend on the principles governing monetary policy. What with the doctrines that are now widely accepted and the policies accordingly expected from the monetary authorities, there can be little doubt that current union policies must lead to continuous and progressive inflation. The chief reason for this is that the dominant "full-employment" doctrines explicitly relieve the unions of the responsibility for any unemployment and place the duty of preserving full employment on the monetary and fiscal authorities. The only way in which the latter can prevent union policy from producing unemployment is, however, to counter through inflation whatever excessive rises in real wages unions tend to cause.

In order to understand the situation into which we have been led, it will be necessary to take a brief look at the intellectual sources of the full-employment policy of the "Keynesian" type. The development of Lord Keynes's theories started from the correct insight that the regular cause of extensive unemployment is real wages that are too high. The next step consisted in the proposition that a direct lowering of money wages could be brought about only by a struggle so painful and prolonged that it could not be contemplated. Hence he concluded that real wages must be lowered by the process of lowering the value of money. This is really the reasoning underlying the whole "full-employment" policy, now so widely accepted.[27] If labor insists on a level of money wages too high to allow of full employment, the supply of money must be so increased as to raise prices to a level where the real value of the prevailing money wages is no longer greater than the productivity of the workers seeking employment. In practice, this necessarily means that each separate union, in its attempt to overtake the value of money, will never cease to insist on further increases in money wages and that the aggregate effort of the unions will thus bring about progressive inflation.

This would follow even if individual unions did no more than prevent any reduction in the money wages of any particular group. Where unions make such wage reductions impracticable and wages have generally become, as the economists put it, "rigid downward," all the changes in relative wages of the different groups made necessary by the constantly changing conditions must be brought about by raising all money wages except those of the group whose relative real wages must fall. Moreover, the general rise in money wages and the resulting increase in the cost of living will generally lead to attempts, even on the part of the latter group, to push up money wages, and several rounds of successive wage increases will be required before any readjustment of rela-

---

[27] See the articles by Gottfried Haberler, "Creeping Inflation Resulting from Wage Increases in Excess of Productivity" (vol. 1, pp. 137–46), and myself, "Inflation Resulting from Downward Inflexibility of Wages" (vol. 1, pp. 147–52), in Committee for Economic Development, *Problems of United States Economic Development* (2 vols.; New York: Committee for Economic Development, 1958).

tive wages is produced. Since the need for adjustment of relative wages occurs all the time, this process alone produces the wage-price spiral that has prevailed since the second World War, that is, since full-employment policies became generally accepted.[28]

The process is sometimes described as though wage increases directly produced inflation. This is not correct. If the supply of money and credit were not expanded, the wage increases would rapidly lead to unemployment. But under the influence of a doctrine that represents it as the duty of the monetary authorities to provide enough money to secure full employment at any given wage level, it is politically inevitable that each round of wage increases should lead to further inflation.[29] Or it is inevitable until the rise of prices becomes sufficiently marked and prolonged to cause serious public alarm. Efforts will then be made to apply the monetary brakes. But, because by that time the economy will have become geared to the expectation of further inflation and much of the existing employment will depend on continued monetary expansion, the attempt to stop it will rapidly produce substantial unemployment. This will bring a renewed and irresistible pressure for more inflation. And, with ever bigger doses of inflation, it may be possible for quite a long time to prevent the appearance of the unemployment which the wage pressure would otherwise cause. To the public at large it will seem as if progressive inflation were the direct consequence of union wage policy rather than of an attempt to cure its consequences.

Though this race between wages and inflation is likely to go on for some time, it cannot go on indefinitely without people coming to realize that it must somehow be stopped. A monetary policy that would break the coercive powers of the unions by producing extensive and protracted unemployment must be excluded, for it would be politically and socially fatal. But if we do not succeed in time in curbing union power at its source, the unions will soon be faced with a demand for measures that will be much more distasteful to the individual workers, if not the union leaders, than the submission of the unions to the rule of law: the clamor will soon be either for the fixing of wages by government or for the complete abolition of the unions.

---

[28] Cf. Arthur Joseph Brown, *The Great Inflation, 1939–1951* (London: Oxford University Press, 1955).

[29] See John Richard Hicks, "Economic Foundations of Wage Policy," *Economic Journal*, 65 (1955): esp. 391: "The world we now live in is one in which the monetary system has become relatively elastic, so that it can accommodate itself to changes in wages, rather than the other way about. Instead of actual wages having to adjust themselves to an equilibrium level, monetary policy adjusts the equilibrium level of money wages so as to make it conform to the actual level. It is hardly an exaggeration to say that instead of being on a Gold Standard, we are on a Labour Standard." But see also the same author's later article, "The Instability of Wages," *Three Banks Review*, 31 (September 1956): 3–19.

8. In the field of labor, as in any other field, the elimination of the market as a steering mechanism would necessitate the replacement of it by a system of administrative direction. In order to approach even remotely the ordering function of the market, such direction would have to co-ordinate the whole economy and therefore, in the last resort, have to come from a single central authority. And though such an authority might at first concern itself only with the allocation and remuneration of labor, its policy would necessarily lead to the transformation of the whole of society into a centrally planned and administered system, with all its economic and political consequences.

In those countries in which inflationary tendencies have operated for some time, we can observe increasingly frequent demands for an "over-all wage policy." In the countries where these tendencies have been most pronounced, notably in Great Britain, it appears to have become accepted doctrine among the intellectual leaders of the Left that wages should generally be determined by a "unified policy," which ultimately means that government must do the determining.[30] If the market were thus irretrievably deprived of its function, there would be no efficient way of distributing labor throughout the industries, regions, and trades, other than having wages determined by authority. Step by step, through setting up an official conciliation and arbitration machinery with compulsory powers, and through the creation of wage boards, we are moving toward a situation in which wages will be determined by what must be essentially arbitrary decisions of authority.

All this is no more than the inevitable outcome of the present policies of labor unions, who are led by the desire to see wages determined by some conception of "justice" rather than by the forces of the market. But in no workable system could any group of people be allowed to enforce by the threat of violence what it believes it should have. And when not merely a few privileged groups but most of the important sections of labor have become effectively organized for coercive action, to allow each to act independently would not only produce the opposite of justice but result in economic chaos. When we can no longer depend on the impersonal determination of wages by the

---

[30] See William Henry Beveridge, *Full Employment in a Free Society* (London: Allen and Unwin, 1944); Margaret F. W. Joseph and Nicholas Kaldor, *Economic Reconstruction after the War* (Handbooks for discussion groups, no. 5; London: Published for the Association for Education in Citizenship by the English Universities Press, 1942); Barbara Wootton, *The Social Foundations of Wage Policy: A Study of Contemporary British Wage and Salary Structure* (London: Allen and Unwin, 1955); and, on the present state of the discussion, Sir Daniel Thompson Jack, "Is a Wage Policy Desirable and Practicable?" *Economic Journal*, 67 (1957): 585–90. It seems that some of the supporters of this development imagine that this wage policy will be conducted by "labor," which presumably means by joint action of all unions. This seems neither a probable nor a practicable arrangement. Many groups of workers would rightly object to their relative wages being determined by a majority vote of all workers, and a government permitting such an arrangement would in effect transfer all control of economic policy to the labor unions.

market, the only way we can retain a viable economic system is to have them determined authoritatively by government. Such determination must be arbitrary, because there are no objective standards of justice that could be applied.[31] As is true of all other prices or services, the wage rates that are compatible with an open opportunity for all to seek employment do not correspond to any assessable merit or any independent standard of justice but must depend on conditions which nobody can control.

Once government undertakes to determine the whole wage structure and is thereby forced to control employment and production, there will be a far greater destruction of the present powers of the unions than their submission to the rule of equal law would involve. Under such a system the unions will have only the choice between becoming the willing instrument of governmental policy and being incorporated into the machinery of government, on the one hand, and being totally abolished, on the other. The former alternative is more likely to be chosen, since it would enable the existing union bureaucracy to retain their position and some of their personal power. But to the workers it would mean complete subjection to the control by a corporative state. The situation in most countries leaves us no choice but to await some such outcome or to retrace our steps. The present position of the unions cannot last, for they can function only in a market economy which they are doing their best to destroy.

9. The problem of labor unions constitutes both a good test of our principles and an instructive illustration of the consequences if they are infringed. Having failed in their duty of preventing private coercion, governments are now driven everywhere to exceed their proper function in order to correct the results of that failure and are thereby led into tasks which they can perform only by being as arbitrary as the unions. So long as the powers that the unions have been allowed to acquire are regarded as unassailable, there is no way to

---

[31] See, e.g., Barbara Wootton, *Freedom under Planning*, p. 101: "The continual use of terms like 'fair,' however, is quite subjective: no commonly accepted ethical pattern can be implied. The wretched arbitrator, who is charged with the duty of acting 'fairly and impartially' is thus required to show these qualities in circumstances in which they have no meaning; for there can be no such thing as fairness or impartiality except in terms of an accepted code. No one can be impartial in a vacuum. One can only umpire at cricket because there are rules, or at a boxing match so long as certain blows, like those below the belt, are forbidden. Where, therefore, as in wage determinations, there are no rules and no code, the only possible interpretation of impartiality is conservatism." See also Orwell de Ruyter Fönander, *Studies in Australian Law and Relations* (Melbourne: Melbourne University Press, 1952). Also Kenneth Frederick Walker, *Industrial Relations in Australia* (Cambridge, MA: Harvard University Press, 1956), p. 362: "Industrial tribunals, in contrast with ordinary courts, are called upon to decide issues upon which there is not only no defined law, but not even any commonly accepted standards of fairness or justice." Cf. also Lady Gertrude Williams, "The Myth of 'Fair' Wages," *Economic Journal*, 66 (1956): 621–34.

correct the harm done by them but to give the state even greater arbitrary power of coercion. We are indeed already experiencing a pronounced decline of the rule of law in the field of labor.[32] Yet all that is really needed to remedy the situation is a return to the principles of the rule of law and to their consistent application by legislative and executive authorities.

This path is still blocked, however, by the most fatuous of all fashionable arguments, namely, that "we cannot turn the clock back." One cannot help wondering whether those who habitually use this cliché are aware that it expresses the fatalistic belief that we cannot learn from our mistakes, the most abject admission that we are incapable of using our intelligence. I doubt whether anybody who takes a long-range view believes that there is another satisfactory solution which the majority would deliberately choose if they fully understood where the present developments were leading. There are some signs that farsighted union leaders are also beginning to recognize that, unless we are to resign ourselves to the progressive extinction of freedom, we must reverse that trend and resolve to restore the rule of law and that, in order to save what is valuable in their movement, they must abandon the illusions which have guided it for so long.[33]

Nothing less than a rededication of current policy to principles already abandoned will enable us to avert the threatening danger to freedom. What is required is a change in economic policy, for in the present situation the tactical decisions which will seem to be required by the short-term needs of government in successive emergencies will merely lead us further into the thicket of arbitrary controls. The cumulative effects of those palliatives which the pursuit of contradictory aims makes necessary must prove strategically fatal. As is true of all problems of economic policy, the problem of labor unions

---

[32] See Sylvester Petro, *The Labor Policy of a Free Society*, pp. 262ff., esp. 264: "I shall show in this chapter that the rule of law does not exist in labor relations; that there a man is *entitled* in only exceptional cases to a day in court, no matter how unlawfully he has been harmed"; and p. 272: "Congress has given the NLRB [National Labor Relations Board] and its General Counsel arbitrary power to deny an injured person a hearing, Congress has closed the federal courts to persons injured by conduct forbidden under federal law. Congress did not, however, prevent unlawfully harmed persons from seeking whatever remedies they might find in state courts. That blow to the ideal that every man is entitled to his day in court was struck by the Supreme Court."

[33] The Chairman of the English Trades Union Congress, Mr. Charles Geddes, was reported in 1955 to have said: "I do not believe that the trade union movement of Great Britain can live for very much longer on the basis of compulsion. Must people belong to us or starve, whether they like our policies or not? [Is that to be the future of the movement?] No. I believe the trade union card is an honor to be conferred, not a badge which signifies that you have got to do something whether you like it or not. We want the right to exclude people from our union if necessary and we cannot do that on the basis of 'Belong or starve.'" [The story is reported in the *Times* (London), May 21, 1955, p. 5, col. E, in connection with Mr. Geddes's opposition to a closed shop in the Union of Post Office Workers.—Ed.]

cannot be satisfactorily solved by *ad hoc* decisions on particular questions but only by the consistent application of a principle that is uniformly adhered to in all fields. There is only one such principle that can preserve a free society: namely, the strict prevention of all coercion except in the enforcement of general abstract rules equally applicable to all.

NINETEEN

SOCIAL SECURITY

The doctrine of the safety net, to catch those who fall, has been made meaningless by the doctrine of fair shares . . . for those of us who are quite able to stand. —*The Economist*

1. In the Western world some provision for those threatened by the extremes of indigence or starvation due to circumstances beyond their control has long been accepted as a duty of the community.[1] The local arrangements which first supplied this need became inadequate when the growth of large cities and the increased mobility of men dissolved the old neighborhood ties; and (if the responsibility of the local authorities was not to produce obstacles to movement) these services had to be organized nationally and special agencies created to provide them. What we now know as public assistance or relief, which in various forms is provided in all countries, is merely the old poor law adapted to modern conditions. The necessity of some such arrangement in an industrial society is unquestioned—be it only in the interest of those who require protection against acts of desperation on the part of the needy.

It is probably inevitable that this relief should not long be confined to those who themselves have not been able to provide against such needs (the "deserving poor," as they used to be called) and that the amount of relief now given in a comparatively wealthy society should be more than is absolutely necessary to keep alive and in health. We must also expect that the availability of

The quotation at the head of the chapter is taken from "Security through Squalor," *Economist* (London), March 15, 1958, p. 918.

[1] Compare the classic explanation offered by Nassau William Senior in Lionel Robbins, *The Theory of Economic Policy in English Classical Political Economy* (London: Macmillan, 1952), p. 140, who quotes Senior [*Journals Kept in France and England From 1848 to 1852: With a Sketch of the Revolution of 1848* (London: H. M. King and Co., 1871), pp. 57–58]: "to guarantee *subsistence* to all—to proclaim that no man whatever his vices or even his crimes, shall die of hunger or cold—is a promise that in the state of civilization of England, or of France, can be performed not merely with safety but with advantage, because the gift of subsistence may be subjected to conditions which no one will voluntarily accept." With respect to Germany, there is, as far as I know, not a single state in which there do not exist positive and distinct laws that no one shall starve. In all German jurisdictions of which I am aware, the municipality is required to sustain all those who cannot feed themselves.

this assistance will induce some to neglect such provision against emergencies as they would have been able to make on their own. It seems only logical, then, that those who will have a claim to assistance in circumstances for which they could have made provision should be required to make such provision themselves. Once it becomes the recognized duty of the public to provide for the extreme needs of old age, unemployment, sickness, etc., irrespective of whether the individuals could and ought to have made provision themselves, and particularly once help is assured to such an extent that it is apt to reduce individuals' efforts, it seems an obvious corollary to compel them to insure (or otherwise provide) against those common hazards of life. The justification in this case is not that people should be coerced to do what is in their individual interest but that, by neglecting to make provision, they would become a charge to the public. Similarly, we require motorists to insure against third-party risks, not in their interest but in the interest of others who might be harmed by their action.

Finally, once the state requires everybody to make provisions of a kind which only some had made before, it seems reasonable enough that the state should also assist in the development of appropriate institutions. Since it is the action of the state which makes necessary the speeding-up of developments that would otherwise have proceeded more slowly, the cost of experimenting with and developing new types of institutions may be regarded as no less the responsibility of the public than the cost of research or the dissemination of knowledge in other fields that concern the public interest. The aid given out of the public purse for this purpose should be temporary in nature, a subsidy designed to assist in the acceleration of a development made necessary by a public decision and intended only for a transitional period, terminating when the existing institution has grown and developed to meet the new demand.

Up to this point the justification for the whole apparatus of "social security" can probably be accepted by the most consistent defenders of liberty. Though many may think it unwise to go so far, it cannot be said that this would be in conflict with the principles we have stated. Such a program as has been described would involve some coercion, but only coercion intended to forestall greater coercion of the individual in the interest of others; and the argument for it rests as much on the desire of individuals to protect themselves against the consequences of the extreme misery of their fellows as on any wish to force individuals to provide more effectively for their own needs.

2. It is only when the proponents of "social security" go a step further that the crucial issues arise. Even at the beginning stage of "social insurance" in Germany in the 1880s, individuals were not merely required to make provision against those risks which, if they did not, the state would have to provide for, but were compelled to obtain this protection through a unitary organiza-

tion run by the government.[2] Although the inspiration for the new type of organization came from the institutions created by the workers on their own initiative, particularly in England, and although where such institutions had also sprung up in Germany—notably in the field of sickness insurance—they were allowed to continue, it was decided that wherever new developments were necessary, as in the provision for old age, industrial accidents, disability, dependents, and unemployment, these should take the form of a unified organization which would be the sole provider of these services and to which all those to be protected had to belong.

"Social insurance" thus from the beginning meant not merely compulsory insurance but compulsory membership in a unitary organization controlled by the state. The chief justification for this decision, at one time widely contested but now usually accepted as irrevocable, was the presumed greater efficiency and administrative convenience (i.e., economy) of such a unitary organization. It was often claimed that this was the only way to assure sufficient provision at a single stroke for all those in need.

There is an element of truth in this argument, but it is not conclusive. It is probably true that, at any given moment, a unified organization designed by the best experts that authority can select will be the most efficient that can be created. But it is not likely to remain so for long if it is made the only starting point for all future developments and if those initially put in charge also become the sole judges of what changes are necessary. It is an error to believe that the best or cheapest way of doing anything can, in the long run, be secured by advance design rather than by the constant re-evaluation of available resources. The principle that all sheltered monopolies become inefficient in the course of time applies here as much as elsewhere.

True, if we want at any time to make sure that we achieve as quickly as we can all that is definitely known to be possible, the deliberate organization of all the resources to be devoted to that end is the best way. In the field of social security, to rely on the gradual evolution of suitable institutions would undoubtedly mean that some individual needs which a centralized organization would at once care for might for some time get inadequate attention. To the impatient reformer, who will be satisfied with nothing short of the immediate abolition of all avoidable evils, the creation of a single apparatus with full powers to do what can be done now appears therefore as the only appropriate method. In the long run, however, the price we have to pay for this, even in terms of the achievement in a particular field, may be very high. If we

---

[2] About Germany's, and especially Prussia's, role as a model for legislation in the area of social security and public education see Sir Ernest Barker, *The Development of Public Services in Western Europe, 1600–1930* (London: Oxford University Press, 1944), pp. 69, 75, 78, 83–85.

commit ourselves to a single comprehensive organization because its immediate coverage is greater, we may well prevent the evolution of other organizations whose eventual contribution to welfare might have been greater.[3]

If initially it was chiefly efficiency that was stressed in support of the single compulsory organization, there were other considerations clearly also present in the minds of its advocates from the beginning. There are, in fact, two distinct, though connected, aims which a governmental organization with coercive powers can achieve but which are beyond the reach of any agency operating on business lines. A private agency can offer only specific services based on contract, that is, it can provide only for a need which will arise independently of the deliberate action of the beneficiary and which can be ascertained by objective criteria; and it can provide in this manner only for foreseeable needs. However far we extend any system of true insurance, the beneficiary will never get more than satisfaction of a contractual claim—i.e., he will not get whatever he may be judged to need according to his circumstances. A monopolistic government service, on the other hand, can act on the principle of allocation according to need, irrespective of contractual claim. Only such an agency with discretionary powers will be in a position to give individuals whatever they "ought" to have, or make them do whatever they "ought" to do to achieve a uniform "social standard." It will also be in a position—and this is the second chief point—to redistribute income among persons or groups as seems desirable. Though all insurance involves a pooling of risks, private competitive insurance can never effect a deliberate transfer of income from one previously designated group of people to another.[4]

---

[3] Cf. Alfred Marshall's wise statement on a universal scheme for pensions before the Royal Commission on the Aged Poor ("Minutes of Evidence Taken Before the Royal Commission on the Aged Poor, June 5, 1893," *Official Papers of Alfred Marshall*, John Maynard Keynes, ed. [London: Macmillan, for the Royal Economic Society, 1926], p. 244): "My objections to them [universal pension schemes] are that their educational effect, though a true one, would be indirect; that they would be expensive; and that they do not contain, in themselves, the seeds of their own disappearance. I am afraid that, if started, they would tend to become perpetual. I regard all this problem of poverty as a mere passing evil in the progress of man upwards; and I should not like any institution started which did not contain in itself the causes which would make it shrivel up, as the causes of poverty itself shriveled up."

[4] Cf. Eveline Mabel Burns, "Private and Social Insurance and the Problem of Social Security," *Canadian Welfare* (February 1, 1953): 5–10, and (March 15, 1953): 9–13; reprinted in *Analysis of the Social Security System: Hearings Before a Subcommittee on the Committee on Ways and Means, House of Representatives* (83rd Cong., 1st sess.) No. 38458 (Washington, DC: Government Printing Office, 1954), p. 1475: "It is no longer a matter of offering each individual a choice as to how much protection he will buy at the range of premiums yielded by the calculations of the actuary. Unlike the private insurer, the government is not restricted by the fear of competition, and can safely offer differential benefits for uniform contributions, or discriminate against certain insured groups. . . . In private insurance, the purpose is to make a profit out of selling people something they want. The essential criterion governing every decision as to terms and conditions is its effect

Such a redistribution of income has today become the chief purpose of what is still called social "insurance"—a misnomer even in the early days of these schemes. When in 1935 the United States introduced the scheme, the term "insurance" was retained—by "a stroke of promotional genius"[5]— simply to make it more palatable. From the beginning, it had little to do with insurance and has since lost whatever resemblance to insurance it may ever have had. The same is now true of most of those countries which originally started with something more closely akin to insurance.

Though a redistribution of incomes was never the avowed initial purpose of the apparatus of social security, it has now become the actual and admitted aim everywhere.[6] No system of monopolistic compulsory insurance has

upon the continuing existence of the company. Obviously, if the company is to continue operating in a competitive world, it must offer services that people think it worth while to pay for, and run its affairs in such a way that the guarantees offered will be honoured when due. . . . In social insurance the purpose is different." Cf. also the same author's "Social Insurance in Evolution," *American Economic Review*, 34 (1944): 199–211; and her *Social Security and Public Policy* (New York: McGraw-Hill, 1956); and Walter Hagenbuch, *Social Economics* (Cambridge: Cambridge University Press, 1958), p.198.

[5] Lewis Meriam and Karl Schlotterbeck, *The Cost and Financing of Social Security* (Washington, DC: Brookings Institution, 1950), p. 8: "Adoption of the term 'insurance' by the proponents of social security was a stroke of promotional genius. Thus social security has capitalized on the good will of private insurance and, through the establishment of a reserve fund, has clothed itself with an aura of financial soundness. In fact, however, the soundness of old age and survivors insurance rests not on the Social Security Reserve Fund but on the federal power to tax and to borrow."

[6] Cf. the statements of Dr. Arthur Joseph Altmeyer, United States commissioner of social security and at one time chairman of the Social Security Board [in *Analysis of the Social Security System: Hearings Before a Subcommittee on the Committee on Ways and Means, House of Representatives* (83rd Cong., 1st sess.) No. 38458 (Washington, DC: Government Printing Office, 1954), p. 1407]: "I am not suggesting for a moment that social security be used primarily as a method for redistributing income. That problem has to be attacked frontally and frankly through progressive taxes. . . . But I also am very much in favor of having progressive taxation cover a large part of the cost of social security benefits." Similarly M. Pierre Laroque, "From Social Insurance to Social Security: Evolution in France," *International Labour Review*, 57 (1948): 588: "The French social security plan was aimed in essence at no other target than to introduce a little more justice into the distribution of the national income"; and Gerhard Weisser, "Soziale Sicherheit," in *Handwörterbuch der Sozialwissenschaften*, Erwin v. Beckerath, et al., eds. (Stuttgart: Gustav Fischer; Tübingen: J. C. B. Mohr, 1956), vol. 9, p. 401: "Ein weiterer Wesenszug der Sicherungssysteme ist unter *kulturellen* Gesichtspunkten beachtlich. Diese Systeme verwenden Teile des Volkseinkommens *zwangsweise* zur Deckung eines bestimmten Bedarfs, der für *objektiv* gegeben gehalten wird." ["A further tendency of social security schemes arises when one considers it in *cultural* terms. These schemes require, *under compulsion*, that parts of the national income be used to underwrite the costs of a particular demand that is presented as being an *objective* need."—Ed.] Also Alfred Müller-Armack, "Soziale Marktwirtschaft," again in the *Handwörterbuch der Sozialwissenschaften*, p. 391: "Der marktwirtschaftliche Einkommensprozeß bietet der Sozialpolitik ein tragfähiges Fundament für eine staatliche Einkommensumleitung, die in Form von Fürsorgeleistungen, Renten- und Lastenausgleichszahlungen, Wohnungsbauzuschüssen, Subven-

resisted this transformation into something quite different, an instrument for the compulsory redistribution of income. The ethics of such a system, in which it is not a majority of givers who determine what should be given to the unfortunate few, but a majority of takers who decide what they will take from a wealthier minority, will occupy us in the next chapter. At the moment we are concerned only with the process by which an apparatus originally meant to relieve poverty is generally being turned into a tool of egalitarian redistribution. It is as a means of socializing income, of creating a sort of household state which allocates benefits in money or in kind to those who are thought to be most deserving, that the welfare state has for many become the substitute for old-fashioned socialism. Seen as an alternative to the now discredited method of directly steering production, the technique of the welfare state, which attempts to bring about a "just distribution" by handing out income in such proportions and forms as it sees fit, is indeed merely a new method of pursuing the old aims of socialism. The reason why it has come to be so much more widely accepted than the older socialism is that it was at first regularly presented as though it were no more than an efficient method of providing for the specially needy. But the acceptance of this seemingly reasonable proposal for a welfare organization was then interpreted as a commitment to something very different. It was mainly through decisions that seemed to most people to concern minor technical issues, where the essential distinctions were often deliberately obscured by an assiduous and skilful propaganda, that the transformation was effected. It is essential that we become clearly aware of the line that separates a state of affairs in which the community accepts the duty of preventing destitution and of providing a minimum level of welfare from that in which it assumes the power to determine the "just" position of everybody and allocates to each what it thinks he deserves. Freedom is critically threatened when the government is given exclusive powers to provide certain services—powers which, in order to achieve its purpose it must use for the discretionary coercion of individuals.[7]

---

tionen usw. die Einkommensverteilung korrigiert." ["The market economy's method of distributing income provides a solid foundation for a social policy that calls for the diversion of income at the hands of the government, which, in the form of support payments, pensions, equalization payments, allowances for the construction of housing, subsidies, and so on, changes its distribution."—Ed.]

[7] Within the limited space here it is impossible to show in detail how the ambitious aims of the government social security schemes make inevitable the conferment of extensive discretionary and coercive powers on the authorities. Some of these problems are clearly shown in the interesting attempt made by A. D. Watson, *The Principles Which Should Govern the Structure and Provisions of a Scheme of Unemployment Insurance*, to construct a scheme of private insurance achieving the same ends. On this Eveline Mabel Burns, in "Private and Social Insurance and the Problems of Social Security"; reprinted in *Analysis of the Social Security System* [Hearings before a Subcommittee of the Committee on Ways and Means] House of Representatives (83rd Cong., 1st sess.) No. 38458 (Washington, DC: Government Printing Office, 1954), p. 1474, comments: "Thus A. D.

3. The extreme complexity and consequent incomprehensibility of the social security systems create for democracy a serious problem. It is hardly an exaggeration to say that, though the development of the immense social security apparatus has been a chief factor in the transformation of our economy, it is also the least understood. This is seen not only in the persisting beliefs[8] that the individual beneficiary has a moral claim to the services, since he has paid for them, but also in the curious fact that major pieces of social security legislation are sometimes presented to the legislatures in a manner which leaves them no choice but to accept or reject them whole and which precludes any modifications by them.[9] And it produces the paradox that the same majority of the people whose assumed inability to choose wisely for themselves is made the pretext for administering a large part of their income for them is in its collective capacity called upon to determine how the individual incomes are to be spent.[10]

Watson, the author of what is probably the most sustained and consistent effort to relate social to private insurance, states: 'The transgression of sound insurance principles leads into the wilderness, and once in there may be no return.' Yet, in the attempt to devise the specific provisions of an unemployment insurance law, even this author finds himself forced to fall back upon the principles which run in terms of what is 'reasonable,' 'administratively feasible,' or 'practically fair.' But such words can be interpreted only in relation to some underlying purpose, some specific social environment and set of prevailing social values. The decision as to precisely what is 'reasonable' thus involves a balancing of interests and objectives." [Andrew Daniel Watson, at one time Chief Actuary of the Department of Insurance of the Government of Canada, was one of the world's leading authorities on the whole spectrum of social insurance legislation, including unemployment insurance, old-age insurance, and disability insurance. The quotation appears in Watson's *The Principles Which Should Govern the Structure and Provisions of a Scheme of Unemployment Insurance* (Ottawa: The Unemployment Commission, 1948), p. 11.—Ed.] This difficulty arises only if it is assumed that a scheme of private insurance must provide all that a system of government insurance could. Even with more limited objectives, private competing systems may still be preferable.

[8] Ample illustration of the extent to which this erroneous belief has guided policy in the United States is given in Dillard Stokes, *Social Security—Fact and Fancy* (Chicago: H. Regnery, 1956); see especially the Preface (pp. vii–x). Similar illustrations could be given for Great Britain.

[9] See Meriam and Schlotterbeck, *The Cost and Financing of Social Security*, pp. 9–10, where it is reported of the then latest United States social security bill that it "passed the House on October 5, 1949, under a rule that did not permit the offering of amendments from the floor or by the minority members of the Ways and Means Committee. The position taken, not without substantial merit, was that H.R. 6000 was too intricate and technical for piecemeal amendment by persons not conversant with all its complexities." See also Hans Achinger, *Sozialpolitik als Gesellschaftspolitik: Von der Arbeiterfrage zum Wohlfahrtsstaat* (Hamburg: Rowohlt, 1958), p. 135: "Dabei kommt es zu einer Geheimsprache, die es, um ein Beispiel zu nennen, neun Zehnteln der Bundestagsabgeordneten unmöglich macht, sozialpolitischen Debatten mit Verständnis zu folgen." ["There thus emerges a secret language which, for example, makes it impossible for nine out of ten members of parliament to understand the debates on social policy."—Ed.]

[10] Cf. Ludwig von Mises, *Human Action* (New Haven: Yale University Press, 1949), p. 613 [Liberty Fund edition, vol. 2, p. 617]: "One may try to justify [such a system of social security] by declaring that the wage earners lack the insight and the moral strength to provide spontaneously

It is not only the lay members of the general public, however, to whom the intricacies of social security are largely a mystery. The ordinary economist or sociologist or lawyer is today nearly as ignorant of the details of that complex and ever changing system. As a result, the expert has come to dominate in this field as in others.

The new kind of expert, whom we also find in such fields as labor, agriculture, housing, and education, is an expert in a particular institutional setup. The organizations we have created in these fields have grown so complex that it takes more or less the whole of a person's time to master them. The institutional expert is not necessarily a person who knows all that is needed to enable him to judge the value of the institution, but frequently he is the only one who understands its organization fully and who therefore is indispensable. The reasons why he has become interested in and approves of the particular institution have often little to do with any expert qualifications. But, almost invariably, this new kind of expert has one distinguishing characteristic: he is unhesitatingly in favor of the institutions on which he is expert. This is so not merely because only one who approves of the aims of the institution will have the interest and the patience to master the details, but even more because such an effort would hardly be worth the while of anybody else: the views of anybody who is not prepared to accept the principles of the existing institutions are not likely to be taken seriously and will carry no weight in the discussions determining current policy.[11]

It is a fact of considerable importance that, as a result of this development, in more and more fields of policy nearly all the recognized "experts" are, almost by definition, persons who are in favor of the principles underlying the policy. This is indeed one of the factors which tend to make so many contemporary developments self-accelerating. The politician who, in recommending some further development of current policies, claims that "all the

---

for their own future. But then it is not easy to silence the voices of those who ask whether it is not paradoxical to entrust the nation's welfare to the decisions of voters whom the law itself considers incapable of managing their own affairs; whether it is not absurd to make those people supreme in the conduct of government who are manifestly in need of a guardian to prevent them from spending their own income foolishly. Is it reasonable to assign to wards the right to elect their guardians?"

[11] An illuminating illustration of this was provided in a related field by the reception, a few years ago, of a symposium on *The Impact of the Union* [David McCord Wright, ed., Institute on the Structure of the Labor Market held at the American University, May 12–13, 1950 (New York: Harcourt, Brace, 1951)], in which some of the most distinguished economists of our time had taken part [David McCord Wright, John Maurice Clark, Gottfried von Haberler, Frank Hyneman Knight, Kenneth Ewart Boulding, Edward Hastings Chamberlin, Milton Friedman, and Paul Anthony Samuelson]. Although it contained most penetrating discussions of one of our most pressing economic problems, it was treated patronizingly and condescendingly by the "experts in labor relations."

experts favor it," is often perfectly honest, because only those who favor the development have become experts in this institutional sense, and the uncommitted economists or lawyers who oppose are not counted as experts. Once the apparatus is established, its future development will be shaped by what those who have chosen to serve it regard as its needs.[12]

4. It is something of a paradox that the state should today advance its claims for the superiority of the exclusive single-track development by authority in a field that illustrates perhaps more clearly than any other how new institutions emerge not from design but by a gradual evolutionary process. Our modern conception of providing against risks by insurance is not the result of any one's ever having seen the need and devising a rational solution. We are so familiar with the operation of insurance that we are likely to imagine that any intelligent man, after a little reflection, would rapidly discover its principles. In fact, the way in which insurance has evolved is the most telling commentary on the presumption of those who want to confine future evolution to a single channel enforced by authority. It has been well said that "no man ever aimed at creating marine insurance as social insurance was later created" and that we owe our present techniques to a gradual growth in which the successive

---

[12] There is a further effect of the rule of the expert which deserves brief consideration. Any development which is governed by the successive decisions of a series of different experts working within the same organization is liable to be carried further because it meets with fewer real checks than it would in a competitive world. When the medical experts say that this or that is necessary and "must" be done, this is a datum on which the expert in administration bases his decision; and what in consequence he decides to be administratively necessary similarly becomes the datum for the lawyer in drafting the law, and so on. None of these different experts can feel that he is in a position to look at the whole and, in view of the aggregate result, to disregard any of the other experts' "musts." In the past, when things were simpler and the rule was that "the expert should be on tap but not on top," this was the task of the political head of the government department concerned. The complexity of the modern measures makes him almost powerless vis-à-vis the array of experts. In consequence, the resulting measures are more and more not really the result of co-ordination and mutually adjusted decisions but the product of a summation, in which one decision makes the next inevitable, although this was not foreseen by those who made the first, a process in which nobody has the power to say "Stop!" The resulting measures do not rest on the kind of division of labor where at each step a man is free to accept or not to accept as the basis for his decision what some other particular agency offers him. The single scheme that emerges, to which there is no alternative, is determined by the internal necessities of this process, which has little to do with any comprehension of the whole by any one mind.

There can be little doubt, indeed, that, for tasks of the magnitude of, say, the provision of medical services for a whole nation, the single comprehensive organization is not the most efficient method, even for utilizing all the knowledge already available, and still less the method most conducive to a rapid development and spreading of new knowledge. As in many other fields, the very complexity of the task requires a technique of co-ordination which does not rely on the conscious mastery and control of the parts by a directing authority but is guided by an impersonal mechanism.

steps due to "the uncounted contributions of anonymous or historical individuals have in the end created a work of such perfection that in comparison with the whole all the clever conceptions due to single creative intelligences must seem very primitive."[13]

Are we really so confident that we have achieved the end of all wisdom that, in order to reach more quickly certain now visible goals, we can afford to dispense with the assistance which we received in the past from unplanned development and from our gradual adaptation of old arrangements to new purposes? Significantly enough, in the two main fields which the state threatens to monopolize—the provision for old age and for medical care—we are witnessing the most rapid spontaneous growth of new methods wherever the state has not yet taken complete control, a variety of experiments which are almost certain to produce new answers to current needs, answers which no advance planning can contemplate.[14] Is it really likely, then, that in the long run we shall be better off under state monopoly? To make the best available knowledge at any given moment the compulsory standard for all future endeavor may well be the most certain way to prevent new knowledge from emerging.

5. We have seen how the practice of providing out of the public purse for

---

[13]Josef Schreiegg, *Die Versicherung als geistige Schöpfung des Wirtschaftslebens: Eine entwicklungspsychologische Untersuchung* (Leipzig and Berlin: Teubner, 1934), pp. 59 and 58. [The original German reads: "Es hat niemals ein Mensch das Ziel gehabt, eine Seeversicherung zu schaffen wie später eine Sozialversicherung oder Wasserleitungsversicherung" and "Diese Entwicklungsglieder mit ihren unzähligen Einfällen einzelner anonymer oder historischer Persönlichkeiten haben aber schließlich zu einer Vollkommenheit des Schöpfungswerkes geführt, gegenüber der kluge Einfall einer isolierten 'schöpferischen Potenz' begreiflicherweise höchst primitiv erscheinen muß."—Ed.]

[14]On the growth of private pension schemes in Great Britain see particularly the *Report of the Committee on the Economic and Financial Problems of the Provisions for Old Age* (Sir Thomas Phillips, chairman [London: His Majesty's Stationery Office], Cmd. 9333), and the summary of its findings in Arthur Seldon, *Pensions in a Free Society* (London: Institute of Economic Affairs, 1957), pp. 4–5, where it is stated that "in 1936, about 1,800,000 were covered in industry and commerce. By 1951 about 6,300,000 people were covered, 3,900,000 in private employment, 2,400,000 in public employment. By 1953–54 the total had risen to 7,100,000. It is now (June 1957) nearing 8,500,000. This includes about 5,500,000 in private industry." [According to the British Department for Works and Pensions' *Statistical Summary* of June 2005 (p. 4), the number of recipients receiving a state pension in September 2004 was 11,500,000.—Ed.]

The American developments in this field are even more striking, but the most significant fact here is the rapid development of new types of medical or health insurance (see Chester C. Nash, "The Contribution of Life Insurance to Social Security in the United States," *International Labour Review*, 72 (1955): 21–39, reprinted as *The Contribution of Life Insurance to Social Security in the United States* [Geneva: International Labour Office, 1955]; and Wesley Glenn Campbell and Rita Ricardo Campbell, *Voluntary Health Insurance in the United States* [Washington, DC: American Enterprise Association, 1960]; George Bernard de Huszar, ed. *Fundamentals of Voluntary Health Care* [Caldwell, ID: Caxton Printers, 1962], where sections of the Campbell study are reprinted.)

those in great want, in combination with that of compelling people to provide against these wants so that they should not become a burden on the rest, have in the end produced almost everywhere a third and different system, under which people in certain circumstances, such as sickness or old age, are provided for, irrespective of want and irrespective of whether or not they have made provisions for themselves.[15] Under this system all are provided with that standard of welfare which it is thought they should enjoy, irrespective of what they can do for themselves, what personal contributions they have made, or what further contribution they are still capable of making.

The transition to this third system has generally been effected by first supplementing out of public funds what was obtained through compulsory insurance and then giving to the people as a matter of right what they have only to a small extent paid for. Making these compulsory income transfers a legal right cannot, of course, alter the fact that they can be justified only on the score of special need and that they are therefore still charity. But this character is usually disguised by giving this right to all or nearly all and simply taking out of the pockets of those who are better off a multiple of what they receive. The alleged aversion of the majority to receiving anything they know they have not earned and is given only in consideration of personal need, and their dislike of a "means test," have been made the pretext of so wrapping up the whole arrangement that the individual can no longer know what he has and what he has not paid for.[16] This is all part of the endeavor to persuade public opinion, through concealment, to accept a new method of income distribution, which the managers of the new machine seem from the beginning to have regarded as a merely transitional half-measure which must be developed into an apparatus expressly aimed at redistribution.[17] This development can be prevented only if, from the outset, the distinction is clearly made between benefits for

[15] There are, unfortunately, no convenient English equivalents to the German terms describing these stages such as *Fürsorge*, *Versicherung*, and *Versorgung*; see Hans Achinger, *Soziale Sicherheit. Eine historisch-soziologische Untersuchung neuer Hilfsmethoden* (Stuttgart: Frederick Vorwerk, 1953), p. 35, and cf. the same author's contribution to the collective volume, *Neuordnung der sozialen Leistungen: Denkschrift auf Anregung des Herrn Bundeskanzlers* (2 vols. in 1; Cologne: Graven Verlag, 1955) [Essays by Hans Achinger, Joseph Höffner, Hans Muthesius, Ludwig Neundörfer], and Karl-Heinrich Hansmayer, *Der Weg zum Wohlfahrtsstaat: Wandlungen der Staatstätigkeit im Spiegel der Finanzpolitik unseres Jahrhunderts* (Frankfurt am Main: F. Knapp, 1957).

[16] For numerous instances of this see Stokes, *Social Security—Fact and Fancy*.

[17] Cf. the passages quoted in n. 4, above, and, for the extent to which this aim has in fact been achieved in various countries see Alan Turner Peacock, ed., *Income Redistribution and Social Policy* (London: Jonathan Cape, 1954). [For theoretical discussions of income redistribution see Harry Gordon Johnson, "The Macro-Economics of Income Redistribution" (pp. 19–40), and Denstone Berry, "Modern Welfare Analysis and the Forms of Income Redistribution" (pp. 41–51).—Ed.]

which the recipient has fully paid, to which he has therefore a moral as well as a legal right, and those based on need and therefore dependent on proof of need.

In this connection we must note still another peculiarity of the unitary state machine of social security: its power to use funds raised by compulsory means to make propaganda for an extension of this compulsory system. The fundamental absurdity of a majority taxing itself in order to maintain a propaganda organization aimed at persuading the same majority to go further than it is yet willing should be obvious. Although, at least in the United States, the employment by public agencies of "public relations" techniques that are legitimate enough in private business has come to be widely accepted, the propriety of such agencies in a democracy spending public funds on publicity in favor of extending their activities must remain questionable. And in no other field has this become so general a phenomenon, on both a national and an international scale, as in that of social security. It amounts to nothing less than a group of specialists interested in a particular development being allowed to use public funds for the purpose of manipulating public opinion in its favor. The result is that both voters and legislators receive their information almost exclusively from those whose activities they ought to direct. It is difficult to overestimate the extent to which this factor has helped to accelerate development far beyond what the public would otherwise have allowed. Such subsidized propaganda, which is conducted by a single tax-maintained organization, can in no way be compared with competitive advertising. It confers on the organization a power over minds that is in the same class with the powers of a totalitarian state which has the monopoly of the means of supplying information.[18]

Though in a formal sense the existing social security systems have been created by democratic decisions, one may well doubt whether the majority of the beneficiaries would really approve of them if they were fully aware of what they involved. The burden which they accept by allowing the state to divert a part of their incomes to ends of its choosing is particularly heavy in the relatively poor countries, where increase in material productivity is most urgently needed. Does anyone really believe that the average semiskilled worker in Italy is better off because 44 per cent of his employer's total outlay for his work is handed over to the state or, in concrete figures, because of the 49 cents which his employer pays for an hour of his work, he receives only 27

[18] Apart from much of the publications of the International Labor Organization, the lavishly produced volume [George Roger Nelson, ed.] *Freedom and Welfare: Social Patterns in the Northern Countries of Europe* [Sponsored by the Ministries of Social Affairs of Denmark, Finland, Iceland, Norway, and Sweden (Copenhagen: Krohns Bogtrykkeri, 1953)], is a conspicuous example of this propaganda on an international scale, the financing of which it would be interesting to inquire into.

cents, while 22 cents are spent for him by the state?[19] Or that, if the worker understood the situation and were given the choice between this and having his disposable income nearly doubled without social security, he would choose the former? Or that in France, where the figure for all workers amounts to an average of about one-third of total labor cost,[20] the percentage is not more than the workers would willingly surrender for the services that the state offers in return? Or that in Germany, where about 20 per cent of the total national income is placed in the hands of the social security administration,[21] this is not a compulsory diversion of a share of resources much greater than the people would expressly wish? Can it be seriously denied that most of those people would be better off if the money were handed over to them and they were free to buy their insurance from private concerns?[22]

6. We can consider more specifically only the chief branches of social security here: the provision for old age, for permanent disablement from other causes, and for loss of the breadwinner of the family; the provision of medical and hospital care; and the protection against loss of income through unem-

---

[19] Bank for International Settlements, *BIS 24th Annual Report for 1953–1954* [1 April 1953–31 March 1954] (Basel: Bank for International Settlements, 1954), p. 46. [Forty years later conditions in Italy have remained approximately the same as when these figures were generated. According to the Organization for Economic Cooperation and Development, the average effective tax rate on labor in Italy in the period 1991–97 was 47.3% (the comparable figure in France was 47.2% and in Germany 41.4%). See David Carey and Harry Tchilinguirian, *Average Effective Tax Rates on Capital, Labour, and Consumption* (Economics Department Working Papers No. 258; Paris: Organization for Economic Cooperation and Development, 2000), p. 28.—Ed.]

[20] See Laroque, "From Social Insurance to Social Security: Evolution in France," p. 587, and Georges Rottier and Jean François Albert, "The Social Services and Income Redistribution in France," in *Income Redistribution and Social Policy*, Alan T. Peacock, ed., p. 98. [According to the Organization for Economic Cooperation and Development, social security contributions in France in 2004 constituted 38% of labor costs (comparable figures for Italy and Germany were 31.8% and 34.6%), *Organization for Economic Cooperation and Development, Taxing Wages, 2003–2004* (Paris: Organization for Economic Cooperation and Development, 2004), table 1.2.—Ed.]

[21] Weisser, "Soziale Sicherheit," p. 407. The corresponding percentages of the national income devoted in 1950 in the five main English-speaking countries are given by Burns, *Social Security and Public Policy*, p. 5, as Australia 7.3, Canada 7.99, United Kingdom 11.87, New Zealand 13.18, and United States 5.53. Recent figures for European countries, given in "Free Trade and Social Security," *Planning*, 405 (1956): 142–55, are Germany 20.0, France 16.5, Austria 15.8, Italy 11.3, United Kingdom 11.0, and Switzerland 10.0 per cent. [The following figures show expenditures on social security as a percentage of national income for 2003: Japan 25.63%, Germany 38.77%, Sweden 44.14%, France, 39.77%, United Kingdom 26.66%, United States (1997) 20.50%. The source for these data is the Department of Research Planning and Coordination, National Institute of Population and Social Security Research, Tokyo, Japan, "The Cost of Social Security in Japan: Fiscal Year 2004."—Ed.]

[22] In Belgium, I understand, the workers and employed themselves finally put a stop to this development after, in the course of twelve years, the charge had risen from 25 to 41 per cent of wages (see Wilhelm Röpke, *Jenseits von Angebot und Nachfrage* [Erlenbach-Zurich and Stuttgart: Rentsch, 1958], p. 295).

---

ployment. The numerous other services that are supplied in various countries either as part of those or separately, such as maternity and children's allowances, raise distinct problems in that they are conceived as part of what is called "population policy," an aspect of modern policy which we shall not consider.

The field in which most countries have committed themselves furthest and which is likely to create the most serious problems is the provision for old age and dependents (except perhaps in Great Britain, where the establishment of a free National Health Service has created problems of a similar magnitude). The problem of the aged is particularly serious, for in most parts of the Western world today it is the fault of governments that the old have been deprived of the means of support that they may have endeavored to provide for themselves. By failing to keep faith and not discharging their duty of maintaining a stable currency, governments everywhere have created a situation in which the generation going into retirement in the third quarter of our century has been robbed of a great part of what they had attempted to put aside for their retirement and in which many more people than there would otherwise have been are undeservedly facing poverty, despite their earlier efforts to avoid such a predicament. It cannot be said too often that inflation is never an unavoidable natural disaster; it is always the result of the weakness or ignorance of those in charge of monetary policy—though the division of responsibility may be spread so wide that nobody is alone to blame. The authorities may have regarded whatever they tried to avert through inflation as greater evils; it is always their choice of policy, however, that brings about inflation.

Yet, even if we approach the problem of provision for old age, as we ought to, in full awareness of the special responsibility which governments have incurred, we can but question whether the damage done to one generation (which, in the last resort, shares the responsibility) can justify the imposition upon a nation of a permanent system under which the normal source of income above a certain age is a politically determined pension paid out of current taxation. The whole Western world is, however, tending toward this system, which is bound to produce problems that will dominate future policy to an extent yet uncomprehended by most. In our efforts to remedy one ill, we may well saddle future generations with a burden greater than they will be willing to bear, so tying their hands that, after many efforts to extricate themselves, they will probably in the end do so by an even greater breach of faith than we have committed.

The problem arises in serious form as soon as government undertakes to secure not only a minimum but an "adequate" provision for all the aged, regardless of the individual's need or the contributions made by him. There are two critical steps that are almost invariably taken, once the state assumes the monopoly of providing this protection: first, the protection is granted not only to those who have through their contributions gained a claim to it, but to those who have not yet had time to do so; and, second, when the pensions are due, they are not paid out of the yield of an additional capital accumulated for the purpose and therefore out of additional income due to the efforts of the beneficiary, but are a transfer of part of the fruits of the work of those currently producing. This holds equally true whether the government nominally builds up a reserve fund and "invests" it in government securities (i.e., lends it to itself and in fact currently spends the money) or whether it openly covers current obligations by current taxation.[23] (The conceivable, but never practiced, alternative of the government's investing the reserve funds in productive capital would rapidly produce an ever increasing governmental control of the capital of industry.) These two regular consequences of old age pensions' being provided by the state are usually also the chief reasons why this kind of organization is insisted upon.

It is easy to see how such a complete abandonment of the insurance character of the arrangement, with the recognition of the right of all over a certain age (and all the dependents or incapacitated) to an "adequate" income that is currently determined by the majority (of which the beneficiaries form a substantial part), must turn the whole system into a tool of politics, a play ball for vote-catching demagogues. It is vain to believe that any objective standard of justice will set a limit on the extent to which those who have reached the privileged age, even if capable of continued work, can insist on being "adequately" maintained by those still at work—who in turn will find consolation only in the thought that at some future date, when they will be proportionally even more numerous and possess correspondingly greater voting strength, they will be in a still better position to make those at work provide for their needs.

Assiduous propaganda has completely obscured the fact that this scheme of adequate pensions for all must mean that many who have at last reached the long-hoped-for time of retirement and who can retire on their savings will nevertheless be the recipients of a gratuity at the expense of those who have not yet reached it, many of whom would at once retire if they were assured of the same income,[24] and that in a wealthy society not devastated by inflation it is normal that a large proportion of the retired should be more comfortably off than those still at work. How seriously public opinion has been deliberately misguided in this matter is well illustrated by the often quoted assertion (accepted by the United States Supreme Court) that in the United States in 1935, "approximately 3 out of 4 persons 65 and older were probably dependent partly or wholly on others for support"—a statement based on statistics

---

[23] See Alan Turner Peacock, *The Economics of National Insurance* (Edinburgh: W. Hodge, 1952).
[24] Cf. Stokes, *Social Security—Fact and Fancy*, pp. 89ff.

which explicitly assumed that all property held by old couples was owned by the husbands and that consequently all the wives were "dependent"![25]

An inevitable result of this situation, which has become a normal feature in other countries besides the United States, is that at the beginning of every election year there is speculation as to how much social security benefits will again be raised.[26] That there is no limit to the demands that will be pressed for is most clearly shown by a recent pronouncement of the British Labour Party to the effect that a really adequate pension "means the right to go on living in the same neighbourhood, to enjoy the same hobbies and to be able to mix with the same circle of friends."[27] It will probably not be long before it is argued that, because the retired have more time to spend money, they must be given more than those still at work; and, with the age distribution we are approaching, there is no reason why the majority over forty should not soon attempt to make those of a lower age toil for them. It may be only at that point that the physically stronger will rebel and deprive the old of both their political rights and their legal claims to be maintained.

The British Labour document just mentioned is significant also because, besides being motivated by the desire to help the aged, it so clearly betrays the wish to make them unable to help themselves and to make them exclusively dependent on government support. An animosity toward all private pension schemes or other similar arrangements pervades it; and what is even more noteworthy is the cool assumption underlying the figures of the proposed plan that prices will double between 1960 and 1980.[28] If this is the degree of inflation planned for in advance, the real outcome is indeed likely to be such that most of those who will retire at the end of the century will be dependent on the charity of the younger generation. And ultimately not morals but the fact

[25] See Henry D. Allen, "The Proper Federal Function in Security for the Aged," *American Economic Security*, 10 (1953): 50. [Mr. Justice Benjamin N. Cardozo delivered the majority opinion in *Helvering v. Davis* 301 *U.S. Reports* 619 at 643 (1936). Quoting the Social Security Board ("Economic Insecurity in Old Age," 1937, p. 15) Cardozo, on behalf of the Court, noted that "one-fifth of the aged in the United States were receiving old-age assistance, emergency relief, institutional care, employment under the works program, or some other form of aid from public or private funds; two-fifths to one-half were dependent on friends and relatives; one-eighth had some income from earnings; and possibly one-sixth had some savings or property. Approximately three out of four persons 65 or over were probably dependent wholly or partially on others for support." The claim is quoted in Allen's essay as an example of the propaganda circulated by the federal government of the need for broader social programs to aid retired Americans.—Ed.]

[26] See, for example, the *Wall Street Journal*, January 2, 1958: "Social Security: With Elections Near, Chances Grow for New Increase in Benefits. Congress May Hike Monthly Check 5% or 10%," pp. 1, 13. The anticipation has proved correct.

[27] Labour Party (Great Britain), *National Superannuation: Labour's Policy for Security in Old Age* (London: Published by the Labour Party, 1957), p. 30.

[28] Ibid., pp. 104 and 106.

that the young supply the police and the army will decide the issue: concentration camps for the aged unable to maintain themselves are likely to be the fate of an old generation whose income is entirely dependent on coercing the young.

7. The provision against sickness presents not only most of the problems which we have already considered but peculiar ones of its own. They result from the fact that the problem of "need" cannot be treated as though it were the same for all who satisfy certain objective criteria, such as age: each case of need raises problems of urgency and importance which have to be balanced against the cost of meeting it, problems which must be decided either by the individual or for him by somebody else.

There is little doubt that the growth of health insurance is a desirable development. And perhaps there is also a case for making it compulsory since many who could thus provide for themselves might otherwise become a public charge. But there are strong arguments against a single scheme of state insurance; and there seems to be an overwhelming case against a free health service for all. From what we have seen of such schemes, it is probable that their inexpediency will become evident in the countries that have adopted them, although political circumstances make it unlikely that they can ever be abandoned, now that they have been adopted. One of the strongest arguments against them is, indeed, that their introduction is the kind of politically irrevocable measure that will have to be continued, whether it proves a mistake or not.

The case for a free health service is usually based on two fundamental misconceptions. They are, first, the belief that medical needs are usually of an objectively ascertainable character and such that they can and ought to be fully met in every case without regard to economic considerations and second, that this is economically possible because an improved medical service normally results in a restoration of economic effectiveness or earning power and so pays for itself.[29] Both contentions mistake the nature of the problem

---

[29] The most characteristic expression of this view will be found in the "Beveridge Report" (William Henry Beveridge, *Social Insurance and Allied Services* [London: His Majesty's Stationery Office, 1942] [Cmd. 6404], secs. 426–39), where it is proposed that the national health service should "ensure that for every citizen there is available whatever medical treatment he requires, in whatever forms he requires it, domiciliary or institutional, general, specialist, or consultant" (sec. 427, p. 158), and that it should become "a health service providing full preventive and curative treatment of every kind to every citizen without exceptions, without remuneration limit and without an economic barrier at any point to delay recourse to it" (sec. 437, p. 162). It may be mentioned here that the annual cost of the proposed service estimated in the Beveridge Report at £170 million is now running at well over £450 million. See Brian Abel-Smith and Richard Morris Titmuss, *The Cost of the National Health Service in England and Wales* (Cambridge: Cambridge University Press, 1956), pp. 58–61, and Committee of Enquiry into the Cost of the National Health Service, *Report of the Committee of Enquiry into the Cost of the National Health Service*

---

involved in most decisions concerning the preservation of health and life. There is no objective standard for judging how much care and effort are required in a particular case; also, as medicine advances, it becomes more and more clear that there is no limit to the amount that might profitably be spent in order to do all that is objectively possible.[30] Moreover, it is also not true that, in our individual valuation, all that might yet be done to secure health and life has an absolute priority over other needs. As in all other decisions in which we have to deal not with certainties but with probabilities and chances, we constantly take risks and decide on the basis of economic considerations whether a particular precaution is worthwhile, i.e., by balancing the risk against other needs. Even the richest man will normally not do all that medical knowledge makes possible to preserve his health, perhaps because other concerns compete for his time and energy. Somebody must always decide whether an additional effort and additional outlay of resources are called for. The real issue is whether the individual concerned is to have a say and be able, by an additional sacrifice, to get more attention or whether this decision is to be made for him by somebody else. Though we all dislike the fact that we have to balance immaterial values like health and life against material advantages and wish that the choice were unnecessary, we all do have to make the choice because of facts we cannot alter.

The conception that there is an objectively determinable standard of medical services which can and ought to be provided for all, a conception which underlies the Beveridge scheme and the whole British National Health Service, has no relation to reality.[31] In a field that is undergoing as rapid

---

(January 1956) [Guillebaud Report] (London: Her Majesty's Stationery Office, 1956), [Cmd. 9663], pp. 120 and 135; cf. also Charles Anthony Raven Crosland, *The Future of Socialism* (London: Jonthan Cape, 1956), pp. 120 and 135 [In the fiscal year ending 31 March 2006, total outlays on the National Health Service had reached £91.50 billion, or 7.4 percent of GDP (United Kingdom, Office of National Statistics, *Annual Abstract of Statistics*, "Summary of Government Expenditure on Health, 1998–2006," table 10–22, p. 160.).—Ed.]; also John and Sylvia Jewkes, *The Genesis of the British National Heath Service* (Oxford: Blackwell, 1961).

[30] Cf. Ffrangcon Roberts, *The Cost of Health* (London: Macmillan, 1952), and Werner Bosch, *Patient, Arzt, Kasse: eine wirtschaftliche Betrachtung über Krankheit und Gesundheit* (Heidelberg: Quelle und Meyer, 1954); see also Ludwig von Mises, *Socialism* (new ed.; New Haven: Yale University Press, 1951), pt. 5, chap. 34, sec. 3, pp. 476ff. [Liberty Fund edition, p. 431], and earlier German literature quoted there. [Mises refers to two works in German: Erwin Liek, *Der Arzt und seine Sendung: Gedanken eines Ketzers* (4th ed.; Munich: J. F. Lehmanns Verlag, 1927), p. 54, and Erwin Liek, *Die Schäden der sozialen Versicherungen und Wege zur Besserung* (2nd ed.; Munich: J. F. Lehmanns, 1928), pp. 17 et seq.—Ed.]

[31] See Roberts, *The Cost of Health*, p. 129. Cf. also John Jewkes, "The Economist and Economic Change," in *Economics and Public Policy*, Arthur Smithies, ed., Brookings Lectures, 1954 (Washington, DC: Brookings Institution, 1955), p. 96: "The important economic question [about the British National Health Service] was this: if there is a service the demand for which at zero price is almost infinitely great, if no steps are taken to increase the supply, if the cost curve is rising

change as medicine is today, it can, at most, be the bad average standard of service that can be provided equally for all.[32] But since in every progressive field what is objectively possible to provide for all depends on what has already been provided for some, the effect of making it too expensive for most to get better than average service, must, before long, be that this average will be lower than it otherwise would be.

The problems raised by a free health service are made even more difficult by the fact that the progress of medicine tends to increase its efforts not mainly toward restoring working capacity but toward the alleviation of suffering and the prolongation of life; these, of course, cannot be justified on economic but only on humanitarian grounds. Yet, while the task of combating the serious diseases which befall and disable some in manhood is a relatively limited one, the task of slowing down the chronic processes which must bring about the ultimate decay of all of us is unlimited. The latter presents a problem which can, under no conceivable condition, be solved by an unlimited provision of medical facilities and which, therefore, must continue to present a painful choice between competing aims. Under a system of state medicine this choice will have to be imposed by authority upon the individuals. It may seem harsh, but it is probably in the interest of all that under a free system those with full earning capacity should often be rapidly cured of a temporary and not dangerous disablement at the expense of some neglect of the aged and mortally ill. Where systems of state medicine operate, we generally find that those who could be promptly restored to full activity have to wait for long periods because all the hospital facilities are taken up by people who will never again contribute to the needs of the rest.[33]

---

rapidly, if every citizen is guaranteed by law the best possible medical service, and if there is no obvious method of rationing, what will happen? I do not recall any British economist, before the event, asking these simple questions and, after the event, it is the doctors themselves and not primarily the economists, who have raised these questions."

[32] Cf. Roberts, *The Cost of Health*, p. 116: "Our enquiry has shown that medicine, having harnessed itself to science, has acquired the property of perpetual expansion with accelerating velocity; that it feeds upon and is in turn fed by professional ambitions and trade interests; that this process is further accentuated by its own success in that it promotes the prolongation of life in a state of medicated survival rather than cure; and that further factors making for the expansionism of medicine are the raising of the standard of living and the emotion and sentiment inseparable from the contemplation of sickness."

[33] Roberts, *The Cost of Health*, p. 136: "A man of eighty who sustains a fractured hip requires immediate admission to hospital and when he gets there he stays for a long time. On the other hand the person who could be cured, by a brief stay in hospital, of a minor physical defect which nevertheless impairs his working capacity may have to wait a long time." Dr. Roberts adds: "This economic view of the healing art may seem callous. The charge would indeed be justified if our aim were the welfare of the State considered as a superhuman entity; and it need hardly be said that the doctor has no concern with the economic value of his patients. Our aim, however, is the welfare of the members of the State; and since our resources are insufficient

There are so many serious problems raised by the nationalization of medicine that we cannot mention even all the more important ones. But there is one the gravity of which the public has scarcely yet perceived and which is likely to be of the greatest importance. This is the inevitable transformation of doctors, who have been members of a free profession primarily responsible to their patients, into paid servants of the state, officials who are necessarily subject to instruction by authority and who must be released from the duty of secrecy so far as authority is concerned. The most dangerous aspect of the new development may well prove to be that, at a time when the increase in medical knowledge tends to confer more and more power over the minds of men to those who possess it, they should be made dependent on a unified organization under single direction and be guided by the same reasons of state that generally govern policy. A system that gives the indispensable helper of the individual, who is at the same time an agent of the state, an insight into the other's most intimate concerns and creates conditions in which he must reveal this knowledge to a superior and use it for the purposes determined by authority opens frightening prospects. The manner in which state medicine has been used in Russia as an instrument of industrial discipline[34] gives us a foretaste of the uses to which such a system can be put.

8. The branch of social security which seemed the most important in the period before the last war, the provision against unemployment, has become relatively unimportant in recent years. Though there can be no question that the prevention of large-scale unemployment is more important than the method of providing for the unemployed, we cannot be certain that we have permanently solved the former problem and that the latter will not again assume major importance. Nor can we be sure that the character of our provision for the unemployed will not prove to be one of the most important factors determining the extent of unemployment.

We shall again take for granted the availability of a system of public relief which provides a uniform minimum for all instances of proved need, so that no member of the community need be in want of food or shelter. The special problem raised by the unemployed is that of how and by whom any further assistance based on their normal earnings should be provided for them, if at all, and, in particular, whether this need justifies a coercive redistribution of income according to some principle of justice.

The chief argument in support of a provision in excess of the minimum

---

to enable us to treat all disease with the efficiency which under more fortunate conditions the advance of science would make possible, we are compelled to reach a just balance between the short-term direct benefits to the individual and the long-term benefits reflected back to the individual."

[34] See Mark George Field, *Doctor and Patient in Soviet Russia* (Cambridge, MA: Harvard University Press, 1957).

that is assured to all is that sudden and unforeseeable changes in the demand for labor occur as a result of circumstances which the worker can neither foresee nor control. There is force in this argument, so far as widespread unemployment during a major depression is concerned. But there are many other causes of unemployment. Recurrent and foreseeable unemployment occurs in most seasonal trades, and here it is clearly in the general interest either that the labor supply be so limited that the seasonal earnings will suffice to maintain the worker during the year, or that the flow of labor be maintained by periodic movements from and to other occupations. There is also the important instance in which unemployment is the direct effect of wages being too high in a particular trade, either because they have been pushed too high by union action or because of a decline in the industry concerned. In both cases the cure of unemployment demands flexibility of wages and mobility of the workers themselves; however, these are both reduced by a system which assures to all the unemployed a certain percentage of the wages they used to earn.

There is undoubtedly a case for genuine insurance against unemployment wherever practicable, insurance in which the different risks of the various trades are reflected in the premiums paid. Insofar as an industry, because of its peculiar instability, requires a reserve of unemployed most of the time, it is desirable that it induce a sufficient number to hold themselves in readiness by offering wages high enough to compensate for this particular risk. For various reasons, such a system of insurance did not seem immediately practicable in certain occupations (such as agricultural labor and domestic service), and it has been largely for this reason that state schemes for "insurance" were adopted,[35] schemes which in fact subsidized earnings among such groups out of funds levied from contributions by other workers or by general taxation. When, however, the risk of unemployment peculiar to a particular trade is not covered out of the earnings in that trade but from outside, it means that the labor supply of such trades is subsidized to expand beyond the point which is economically desirable.

The chief significance of the comprehensive systems of unemployment compensation that have been adopted in all Western countries, however, is that they operate in a labor market dominated by the coercive action of unions and that they have been designed under strong union influence with the aim of assisting the unions in their wage policies. A system in which a worker is regarded as unable to find employment and therefore is entitled to benefit because the workers in the firm or industry in which he seeks employment are on strike necessarily becomes a major support of union wage pressure. Such a system, which relieves the unions of the responsibility for the

[35] Cf. Eveline Mabel Burns, "Social Insurance in Evolution," pp. 204–5.

unemployment that their policies create and which places on the state the burden not merely of maintaining but of keeping content those who are kept out of jobs by them, can in the long run only make the employment problem more acute.[36]

The reasonable solution of these problems in a free society would seem to be that, while the state provides only a uniform minimum for all who are unable to maintain themselves and endeavors to reduce cyclical unemployment as much as possible by an appropriate monetary policy, any further provision required for the maintenance of the accustomed standard should be left to competitive and voluntary efforts. It is in this field that labor unions, once they have been deprived of all coercive power, can make their most beneficial contribution; indeed, they were well on the way to supplying the need when the state largely relieved them of the task.[37] But a compulsory scheme of so-called unemployment insurance will always be used to "correct" the relative remunerations of different groups, to subsidize the unstable trades at the expense of the stable, and to support wage demands that are irreconcilable with a high level of employment. It is therefore likely in the long run to aggravate the evil it is meant to cure.

9. The difficulties which social insurance systems are facing everywhere and which have become the cause of recurrent discussion of the "crisis of social security" are the consequence of the fact that an apparatus designed for the relief of poverty has been turned into an instrument for the redistribution of income, a redistribution supposedly based on some non-existing principle of social justice but in fact determined by *ad hoc* decisions. It is true, of course, that even the provision of a uniform minimum for all those who cannot provide for themselves involves some redistribution of income. But there is a great deal of difference between the provision of such a minimum for all those who cannot maintain themselves on their earnings in a normally functioning market and a redistribution aiming at a "just" remuneration in all the more important occupations—between a redistribution wherein the great majority earning their living agree to give to those unable to do so, and a redistribution wherein a majority takes from a minority because the latter has more. The former preserves the impersonal method of adjustment under which people

---

[36] As one of the most careful British students of these matters, John Richard Hicks, pointed out some time ago ("The Pursuit of Economic Freedom," in *What We Defend: Essays in Freedom by Members of the University of Manchester*, Ernest Fraser Jacob, ed. [London: Oxford University Press, 1942], p. 105): "One of the reasons why we have high unemployment figures . . . is a direct consequence of our progressive social policy; our unemployment statistics are drawn up in close connection with the administration of unemployment benefit, and the right to that benefit is given very generously."

[37] See Colin Clark, *Welfare and Taxation* (Oxford: Catholic Social Guild, 1954), p. 25.

can choose their occupation; the latter brings us nearer and nearer to a system under which people will have to be told by authority what to do.

It seems to be the fate of all unitary, politically directed schemes for the provision of such services to be turned rapidly into instruments for determining the relative incomes of the great majority and thus for controlling economic activity generally.[38] The Beveridge plan, which was not conceived by its author as an instrument of income redistribution but was promptly turned into such by the politicians, is merely the best-known instance among many. But while in a free society it is possible to provide a minimum level of welfare for all, such a society is not compatible with sharing out income according to some preconceived notion of justice. The assurance of an equal minimum for all in distress presupposes that this minimum is provided only on proof of need and that nothing which is not paid for by personal contribution is given without such proof. The wholly irrational objection to a "means test" for services which are supposed to be based on need has again and again led to the absurd demand that all should be assisted irrespective of need, in order that those who really need help should not feel inferior. It has produced a situation in which generally an attempt is made to assist the needy and at the same time allow them to feel that what they get is the product of their own effort or merit.[39]

[38] Cf. Barbara Wootton, "The Labour Party and Social Services," *Political Quarterly*, 24 (1953): 65–66: "The future design of the social services waits upon some clearer decision as to what these services are supposed to be for. In particular, are they intended to contribute to a policy of social equality? Or are they just part of the national minimum programme enunciated in the earlier work of the Webbs—measures to secure that nobody starves, or is too poor to see a doctor, or lacks a rudimentary education? It is the answers to these questions which must govern the whole future of our social services."

[39] It may be useful to recall here the classical doctrine on these matters as expressed by Edmund Burke, *Thoughts and Details on Scarcity*, in *Works*, vol. 7, pp. 390–91 [Liberty Fund edition, *Selected Works*, vol. 3, p. 72]: "Whenever it happens that a man can claim nothing according to the rules of commerce, and the principles of justice, he passes out of that department, and comes within the jurisdiction of mercy."

Much of the best critical analysis of the present tendencies in this field that I know of is contained in an essay by Walter Hagenbuch, "The Rationale of the Social Services," *Lloyds Bank Review*, n.s., 29 (July 1953): 9–12; partly reproduced in the Epilogue of Walter Hagenbuch, *Social Economics* (Cambridge: Cambridge University Press, 1958), pp. 298–305, where he contends: "Without realizing it, we may be drifting into a system in which everyone becomes permanently dependent on the State for certain basic needs and will inevitably become more and more dependent. Not only are the social services no longer self-liquidating; they are self-propagating. . . . There is surely all the difference in the world between a regime in which a few unfortunate people receive occasional and temporary benefits to tide them over their misfortune and one in which a large slice of everybody's income is continually channelled through the State. The absence of any direct links between what the individual puts in and what he takes out, the political situation that must arise when any kind of inequality of distribution is discussed, and

Though the traditional liberal aversion to any discretionary powers of authority may have played some role in making this development possible, it should be noted that the objection against discretionary coercion can really provide no justification for allowing any responsible person an unconditional claim to assistance and the right to be the ultimate judge of his own needs. There can be no principle of justice in a free society that confers a right to "non-deterrent" or "non-discretionary" support irrespective of proved need. If such claims have been introduced under the disguise of "social insurance" and through an admitted deception of the public—a deception which is a source of pride to its authors[40]—they have certainly nothing to do with the principle of equal justice under the law.

The hope is now sometimes expressed by liberals that "the whole Welfare State apparatus must itself be regarded as a passing phenomenon,"[41] a kind of transitional phase of evolution which the general growth of wealth will soon make unnecessary. It must seem doubtful, however, whether there exists such a distinct phase of evolution in which the net effects of those monopolistic institutions are likely to be beneficial, and still more whether, once they have been created, it will ever be politically possible again to get rid of them. In poor countries the burden of the ever growing machinery is likely to slow down considerably the growth of wealth (not to mention its tendency to aggravate the problem of overpopulation) and thus to postpone indefinitely the time when it will be thought unnecessary, while in the richer countries it

---

the sheer paternalism of it all, suggest a rapid disappearance of that small stream of the national income which does not go through the social service pool, and a move towards the complete State control of all incomes. . . . We may therefore summarize the long term conflict of policy as follows: On the one hand, we may aim at a system of social services which removes poverty by making everybody poor (or everybody rich, according to how you look at it), by giving no benefits unless they are universal, and by socializing the national income. On the other hand, we may aim at a system of social services which removes poverty by raising those below the poverty line above it, by giving selective benefits to groups of people in need, adopting either a means test or the method of insurance categories, and by looking forward to the day when social services will no longer be necessary because the standard of living of even the lowest income groups is above the poverty line." See also the same author's "The Welfare State and Its Finances," *Lloyds Bank Review*, n.s., 49 (July 1958): 1–17; Hans Willgerodt, "Die Krisis der sozialen Sicherheit und das Lohnproblem," *Ordo. Jahrbuch für die Ordnung von Wirtschaft und Gesellschaft*, 7 (1955): 145–87; Hans Achinger, *Soziale Sicherheit*, pp. 45–60; Wilhelm Röpke, *Jenseits von Angebot und Nachfrage*, chap. 4, pp. 210–305; as well as Heddy Neumeister, "Autoritäre Sozialpolitik," in *Ordo*, 12 (1960/1961): 187–252.

[40] Cf. the essay by Eveline Mabel Burns, "Private and Social Insurance and the Problems of Social Security," reprinted in *Analysis of the Social Security System*, esp. p. 1478.

[41] Peter Wiles, "Property and Equality," in *The Unservile State: Essays in Liberty and Welfare*, George Watson, ed. (London: Allen and Unwin, 1957), p. 100. Cf. also Elliott Dodds, "Liberty and Welfare," in *The Unservile State*, George Watson, ed., esp. p. 20: "It has become evident that a State monopoly in Welfare has certain illiberal consequences, and our conviction is that the time has come to provide, not Welfare merely, but a varied and competitive Welfare."

will prevent the evolution of alternative institutions that could take over some of its functions.

There perhaps exists no insuperable obstacle to a gradual transformation of the sickness and unemployment allowance systems into systems of true insurance under which the individuals pay for benefits offered by competing institutions. It is much more difficult to see how it will ever be possible to abandon a system of provision for the aged under which each generation, by paying for the needs of the preceding one, acquires a similar claim to support by the next. It would almost seem as if such a system, once introduced, would have to be continued in perpetuity or allowed to collapse entirely. The introduction of such a system therefore puts a strait jacket on evolution and places on society a steadily growing burden from which it will in all probability again and again attempt to extricate itself by inflation. Neither this outlet, however, nor a deliberate default on obligation already incurred[42] can provide the basis for a decent society. Before we can hope to solve these problems sensibly, democracy will have to learn that it must pay for its own follies and that it cannot draw unlimited checks on the future to solve its present problems.

It has been well said that, while we used to suffer from social evils, we now suffer from the remedies for them.[43] The difference is that, while in former times the social evils were gradually disappearing with the growth of wealth, the remedies we have introduced are beginning to threaten the continuance of that growth of wealth on which all future improvement depends. Instead of the "five giants" which the welfare state of the Beveridge report was designed to combat, we are now raising new giants which may well prove even greater enemies of a decent way of life. Though we may have speeded up a little the conquest of want, disease, ignorance, squalor, and idleness, we may in the future do worse even in that struggle when the chief dangers will come from inflation, paralyzing taxation, coercive labor unions, an ever increasing dominance of government in education, and a social service bureaucracy with far-reaching arbitrary powers—dangers from which the individual cannot escape by his own efforts and which the momentum of the overextended machinery of government is likely to increase rather than mitigate.

[42] As against the proposals for reform in Stokes, *Social Security—Fact and Fancy*, which would amount to a repudiation of obligations already incurred, it must be said that, however great the temptation to "wipe the slate clean" and however great the burden already assumed may appear, this would seem to me a fatal new beginning for any attempt to create more reasonable arrangements.

[43] This phrase was used by Mr. Joseph Wood Krutch in an informal talk.

TWENTY

TAXATION AND REDISTRIBUTION

It lies in the nature of things that the beginnings are slight, but unless great care is taken, the rates will multiply rapidly and finally will reach a point that no one could have foreseen. —Franscesco Guicciardini (ca. 1538)

The quotation at the head of the chapter is taken from Francesco Guicciardini, "La decima scalata," in *Opere inedite*, ed. Piero and Luigi Guicciardini (10 vols.; Florence: Barbàra, Bianchi e comp., 1867), vol. 10, p. 377. The occasion of this observation (now translated into English as "Two Discourses on Progressive Taxation of Land Incomes," *International Economic Papers, No. 9*. Translations prepared for the International Economics Association [London: Macmillan, 1959], pp. 7–19) and the remarkable sixteenth-century discussion of progressive taxation from which it is taken deserve a brief account.

In the fifteenth century the republic of Florence, which for two hundred years had enjoyed a regime of personal freedom under the law as had not been known since ancient Athens and Rome, fell under the rule of the Medici family, who increasingly gained despotic powers by an appeal to the masses. One of the instruments they used for this purpose was progressive taxation, as Guicciardini describes elsewhere ("Del reggimento di Firenze," *Opere inedite*, vol. 2, p. 40): "It is well known how much the nobility and the wealthy were oppressed by Cosimo and in the following time by taxation, and the reason for this, which the Medici never admitted, was that it provided a certain means of destroying in a seemingly legal manner, because they always reserved to themselves the power to knock down arbitrarily anybody they wished." [The Italian reads: "È notissimo quante nobilità, quante ricchezze furono distrutte da Cosimo, e poi ne' tempi seguenti, colle gravezze; e questa è stata la cagione che mai la casa de' Medici non ha consentito, che si truovi uno modo fermo, che le gravezze quasi dalla legge; perchè hanno voluto riservarsi sempre la potestà di battere co'modi arbitrarii chi gli pareva."—Ed.]

When at some time in the following century progressive taxation was again advocated, Guicciardini wrote (the date 1538, suggested by Karl Theodor von Eheberg ["Finanzwissenschaft," *Handwörterbuch der Staatswissenschaften*, Johannes Conrad, Wilhelm Lexis, Edgar Loening, and Ludwig Elster, eds. (3rd ed.; 8 vols.; Jena: Verlag von Gustav Fischer, 1909–11), vol. 4, pp. 292–315, esp. 296], is no more than a conjecture) two brilliant discourses on progressive taxation, one supporting and the second, which evidently represents his opinion, opposing it. They remained in manuscript and were published only in the nineteenth century. His basic objection is (Guicciardini, "La Decima Scalata," vol. 10, p. 368) that "the equality which we must aim at consists in this, that no citizen can oppress another, and that the citizens are all subject to the laws and the authorities, and that the voice of each who is admissible to the Council counts as much as that of any other. This is the meaning of equality in liberty, and not that all are equal in every respect." ["Ma la egualità che si ricerca consiste in questo, che nessuno cittadino possa opprimere l'altro, che ognuno sia egualmente sottoposto alle leggi e a'Magistrati, e che la fava di

1. In many ways I wish I could omit this chapter. Its argument is directed against beliefs so widely held that it is bound to offend many. Even those who have followed me so far and have perhaps regarded my position as on the whole reasonable are likely to think my views on taxation doctrinaire, extremist, and impractical. Many would probably be willing to restore all the freedom for which I have been pleading, provided that the injustice that they believe this would cause were corrected by appropriate measures of taxation. Redistribution by progressive taxation has come to be almost universally accepted as just. Yet it would be disingenuous to avoid discussing this issue. Moreover, to do so would mean to ignore what seems to me not only the chief source of irresponsibility of democratic action but the crucial issue on which the whole character of future society will depend. Though it may require considerable effort to free one's self of what has become a dogmatic creed in this matter, it should become evident, once the issue has been clearly stated, that it is here that, more than elsewhere, policy has moved toward arbitrariness.

After a long period in which there was practically no questioning of the principle of progressive taxation and in which little discussion took place that was new, there has lately appeared a much more critical approach to the problem.[1] There is, however, still a great need for a more searching review of the

---

ognuno che è abile a questo Consiglio, abbia tanta autorità l'una quanto l'altra. Così si intende la egualità nelle libertà, e non generalmente che ognuno sia pari in ogni cosa."—Ed.]

He argues further (vol. 10, p. 372): "It is not liberty when one part of the community is oppressed and maltreated by the rest, nor is it the end for which we have sought liberty, which was that each should with security be able to preserve his proper state." ["Nè si chiama libertà, quando una parte della città è oppressata e male trattata dagli altri, nè è questo il fine a che furono trovate la libertà, che fu che ognuno sicuramente potessi conservare il grado suo."—Ed.] The advocates of progressive taxation are to him (vol. 10, p. 372) "suscitatori del popolo, dissipatori della libertà e de buoni governi delle republiche." [The English reads: "Troublemakers who squander freedom and compromise the good government of the Republic."—Ed.] The main danger he states in the passage quoted at the head of the chapter, which may also be reproduced here in the original Italian: "Ma a la natura delle cose, i principii cominciano piccoli, ma se l'uomo non avvertisce, moltiplicano presto a scorrono in luogo che poi nessuno è a tempo a provvedervi." [The English repeats the epigraph.—Ed.] Cf. on this Giuseppe Ricca-Salerno, *Storia delle dottrine finanziarie in Italia: col raffronto delle dottrine forestiere e delle istituzioni e condizioni di fatto* (2nd ed.; Palermo: A. Reber, 1896), pp. 73–76; and Max Grabein, "Beiträge zur Geschichte der Lehre von der Steuerprogression," *Finanz-archiv*, 12 (1895): 481–96.

See also Günter Schmölders, *Progression und Regression* [Forschungsberichte des Landes Nordrhein-Westfalen No. 624] (Cologne: Westdeutscher Verlag, 1958); Gene Erion, "A Consideration of Some of the Attacks upon the Theory of Progressive Taxation," *The Southwestern Social Science Quarterly*, 38 (March 1958): 344–55; Kurt Schmidt, *Die Steuerprogression* (Basel: Kyklos-Verlag, 1960); Milton Friedman, *Capitalism and Freedom* (Chicago: University of Chicago Press, 1962).

[1] Ten years ago there were only a very few economists left who opposed progressive taxation on principle, among whom Ludwig von Mises, *Human Action* (New Haven: Yale University Press, 1949), pp. 803ff. [Liberty Fund edition, vol. 3, p. 807], and Harley Leist Lutz, *Guideposts to a Free Economy: A Series of Essays on Enterprise and Government Finance* (New York: McGraw-Hill,1945),

whole subject. Unfortunately, we can attempt to present only a brief summary of our objections in this chapter.

It should be said at once that the only progression with which we shall be concerned and which we believe cannot in the long run be reconciled with free institutions is the progression of taxation as a whole, that is, the more than proportionally heavy taxation of the larger incomes when all taxes are considered together. Individual taxes, and especially the income tax, may be graduated for a good reason—that is, so as to compensate for the tendency of many indirect taxes to place a proportionally heavier burden on the smaller incomes. This is the only valid argument in favor of progression. It applies, however, only to particular taxes as part of a given tax structure and cannot be extended to the tax system as a whole. We shall discuss here mainly the effects of a progressive income tax because in recent times it has been used as the main instrument for making taxation as a whole steeply progressive. The question of the appropriate mutual adjustment of the different kinds of taxes within a given system will not concern us.

We shall also not consider separately the problems which arise from the fact that, though progressive taxation is today the chief instrument of income redistribution, it is not the only method by which the latter can be achieved. It is clearly possible to bring about considerable redistribution under a system of proportional taxation. All that is necessary is to use a substantial part of the revenue to provide services which benefit mainly a particular class or to subsidize it directly. One wonders, however, to what extent the people in the lower-income brackets would be prepared to have their freely spendable income reduced by taxation in return for free services. It is also difficult to see how this method could substantially alter the differentials of the higher-income groups. It might well bring about a considerable transfer of income

---

chap. 9 ["Progressive Taxation," pp. 73–82] should be specially mentioned. The first of the younger generation who pointed to its dangers seems to have been David McCord Wright, *Democracy and Progress* (New York: Macmillan, 1948), pp. 94–103. The general reopening of the discussion is due mainly to the careful study of Walter J. Blum and Harry Kalven, Jr., *The Uneasy Case for Progressive Taxation* (Chicago: University of Chicago Press, 1952), first published in the *University of Chicago Law Review*, 19 (1952): 417–520. Two earlier discussions of the problem by myself are, "Die Ungerechtigkeit der Steuerprogression," [The Injustice of the Progressive Income Tax] *Schweizer Monatshefte*, 32 (1952): 508–17 [later translated and published as "The Case Against Progressive Income Taxes," *Freeman*, 4 (December 28, 1953): 229–32] and "Progressive Income Tax Reconsidered," in *On Freedom and Free Enterprise: Essays in Honor of Ludwig von Mises*, Mary Sennholz, ed. [Presented on the Occasion of the Fiftieth Anniversary of his Doctorate, 26 February 1956] (Princeton, NJ: D. Van Nostrand Co., 1956), pp. 265–84. A substantial part of the latter has been incorporated in the present chapter. A recently published non-critical but highly instructive history of progressive taxation in Great Britain is Fakkri Shehab, *Progressive Taxation: A Study in the Development of the Progressive Principle in the British Income Tax* (Oxford: Clarendon Press, 1953).

from the rich as a class to the poor as a class. But it would not produce that flattening of the top of the income pyramid which is the chief effect of progressive taxation. For the comparatively well-to-do it would probably mean that, while they would all be taxed proportionately on their whole incomes, the differences in the services they receive would be negligible. It is in this class, however, that the changes in relative incomes produced by progressive taxation are most significant. Technical progress, the allocation of resources, incentives, social mobility, competition, and investment—the effects of progressive taxation on all these operate mainly through its effects on this class. Whatever may happen in the future, for the present at any rate, progressive taxation is the chief means of redistributing incomes, and, without it, the scope of such a policy would be very limited.

2. As is true of many similar measures, progressive taxation has assumed its present importance as a result of having been smuggled in under false pretenses. When at the time of the French Revolution and again during the socialist agitation preceding the revolutions of 1848 it was frankly advocated as a means of redistributing incomes, it was decisively rejected. "One ought to execute the author and not the project," was the liberal Turgot's indignant response to some early proposals of this sort.[2] When in the 1830s they came to be more widely advocated, J. R. McCulloch expressed the chief objection in the often quoted statement: "The moment you abandon the cardinal principle of exacting from all individuals the *same proportion of their income* or *of their property*, you are at sea without rudder or compass, and there is no amount of injustice and folly you may not commit."[3] In 1848 Karl Marx and Friedrich

[2] Turgot's marginal note, "Il faut exécuter l'auteur, et non le projet, " is reported by Friedrich von Gentz, "Über die Hülfsquellen der französischen Regierung," *Historisches Journal*, 3 (1799): 138. Gentz himself comments there on progressive taxation: "Nun ist schon eine jede Abgabe, bei welcher irgend eine andere, als die reine (geometrische) Progression der Einkünfte oder des Vermögens zum Grunde liegt, jede, die sich auf das Prinzip einer steigenden Progression gründet, nicht viel besser als ein Strassenraub." ["Of course every tax that is not based on a pure (geometric) progression with regard to income or wealth, every tax based on the principle of graduated progression, is not much better than highway robbery."—Ed.] (Gentz, of course, here uses "progression" with regard to the absolute and not to the proportional amount of the tax.) Wilhelm Gerloff, "Steuerwirtschaftslehre," in *Handbuch der Finanzwissenschaft* (4 vols.; Tübingen: J. C. B. Mohr, 1956), vol. 2, p. 288–89, regarded my article as containing "not a single new argument."

[3] [John Ramsay McCulloch], "On the Complaints and Proposals Regarding Taxation" ["art. 7: 1. Scheme for a Graduated Property Tax; 2. Suggestions for the Relief of the Public Burdens"], *Edinburgh Review*, 57 (1833): 164. This early article was largely incorporated into the better-known expanded version in the same author's *A Treatise on the Principles and Practical Influence of Taxation and the Funding System* (London: Printed for Longman, Brown, Green, and Longmans, 1845), p. 143. See also Robert von Mohl in the Frankfurt National Assembly (Franz Wigard, ed., *Stenographischer Bericht über die Verhandlungen der deutschen constituirenden Nationalversammlung zu Frankfurt am Main* [9 vols.; Leipzig: Druck von Breitkopf und Hartel, 1848–49], vol. 7, pp. 5107–09), who contrasts his remarks with the discussions in the French National Assembly of the same year.

Engels frankly proposed "a heavy progressive or graduated income tax" as one of the measures by which, *after* the first stage of the revolution, "the proletariat will use its political supremacy to wrest, by degrees, all capital from the bourgeoisie, to centralize all instruments of production in the hands of the state." And these measures they described as "means of despotic inroads on the right of property, and on the conditions of bourgeois production . . . measures . . . which appear economically insufficient and untenable but which, in the course of the movement, outstrip themselves, necessitate further inroads upon the old social order, and are unavoidable as a means of entirely revolutionizing the mode of production."[4] But the general attitude was still well summed up in A. Thiers's statement that "proportionality is a principle, but progression is simply hateful arbitrariness,"[5] or John Stuart Mill's description of progression as "a mild form of robbery."[6]

But after this first onslaught had been repelled, the agitation for progressive taxation reappeared in a new form. The social reformers, while generally disavowing any desire to alter the distribution of income, began to contend that the total tax burden, assumed to be determined by other considerations, should be distributed according to "ability to pay" in order to secure "equality of sacrifice" and that this would be best achieved by taxing incomes at progressive rates. Of the numerous arguments advanced in support of this, which still survive in the textbooks on public finance,[7] one which looked most scientific carried the day in the end. It requires brief consideration because some still believe that it provides a kind of scientific justification of progressive taxation. Its basic conception is that of the decreasing marginal utility of successive acts of consumption. In spite of, or perhaps because of, its abstract

---

[4] See Karl Marx, *Selected Works*, Vladimir Viktorovich Adoratskii, ed. (2 vols.; London: Lawrence and Wishart, 1942), vol. 1, pp. 227–28. The quotation is from the *Communist Manifesto*. As Ludwig von Mises has pointed out, *Planning for Freedom and Other Essays and Addresses* (South Holland, IL: Libertarian Press, 1952), p. 96 [Liberty Fund edition, p. 86], the words "necessitate further inroads upon the old social order" do not occur in the original version of the Communist Manifesto but were inserted by Friedrich Engels in the English translation of 1888.

[5] Marie Joseph Louis Adolphe Thiers, *De la propriété* (Paris: Paulin, Lheureux et cie., 1848), p. 319: "La proportionnalité est un principe, mais la progression n'est qu'un odieux arbitraire."

[6] John Stuart Mill, *Principles of Political Economy, with some Applications to Social Philosophy* (1st ed.; 2 vols.; London: J. W. Parker, 1848), vol. 2, p. 353. [The first two editions of Mill's *Principles* (1848 and 1849) read: "It is partial [i.e., progressive] taxation that is a mild form of robbery" (bk. 5, chap. 2, sec. 3). It is in the third edition that this passage has been altered to read: "To tax the larger incomes at a higher percentage than the smaller is to lay a tax on industry and economy; to impose a penalty on people for having worked harder and saved more than their neighbours." See the Liberty Fund edition, *Collected Works*, vol. 3, pp. 810–11.—Ed.]

[7] For recent surveys of these arguments in favor of progressive taxation see Elmer D. Fagen, "Recent and Contemporary Theories of Progressive Taxation," *Journal of Political Economy*, 46 (1938): 457–98, and Edgard Allix, "Die Theorie der progressiven Steuer," in vol. 4 of *Die Wirtschaftstheorie der Gegenwart* (4 vols.; Vienna: Springer, 1928), pp. 246–62.

character, it has had great influence in making scientifically respectable[8] what before had been admittedly based on arbitrary postulates.[9]

Modern developments within the field of utility analysis itself have, however, completely destroyed the foundations of this argument. It has lost its validity partly because the belief in the possibility of comparing the utilities to different persons has been generally abandoned[10] and partly because it is more than doubtful whether the conception of decreasing marginal utility can legitimately be applied at all to income as a whole, i.e., whether it has meaning if we count as income all the advantages a person derives from the use of his resources. From the now generally accepted view that utility is a purely relative concept (i.e., that we can only say that a thing has greater, equal, or less utility compared with another and that it is meaningless to speak of the degree of utility of a thing by itself), it follows that we can speak of utility (and of decreasing utility) of income only if we express utility of income in terms of some other desired good, such as leisure (or the avoidance of effort).

[8] I remember that my own teacher, Friedrich von Wieser, one of the founders of modern marginal utility analysis and author of the term "marginal utility" (*Grenznutzen*), regarded it as one of his main achievements to have provided a scientific basis for just taxation. The author who had in this connection the greatest influence in the English-speaking world was Francis Ysidro Edgeworth, *Papers Relating to Political Economy* (3 vols.; London: Published on behalf of the Royal Economic Society by Macmillan, 1925), vol. 2, pp. 234–70. [The relevant essays on taxation in this volume were all originally published elsewhere: "The Subjective Element in the First Principles of Taxation," *Quarterly Journal of Economics*, 14 (1910): 459–70 (published in this collection as "Minimum Sacrifice versus Equal Justice," [pp. 234–42]); "Methods of Graduating Taxes on Income and Capital," *Economic Journal*, 29 (1919):138–53 (published in this collection as "Graduation of Taxes," [pp. 243–59]); and "Mathematical Formulae and the Royal Commission on Income Tax," *Economic Journal*, 30 (1920): 398–408 (published in this collection as "Formulae for Graduating Taxation," [pp. 260–70]).—Ed.]

[9] As late as 1921, Sir Josiah Stamp (later Lord Stamp) could say (*The Fundamental Principles of Taxation in the Light of Modern Developments* [London: Macmillan, 1921], p. 40) that "it was not until the marginal theory was thoroughly worked out on its psychological side, that progressive taxation obtained a really secure basis in principle." Even more recently Tibor Barna, *Redistribution of Incomes through Public Finance in 1937* (Oxford: Clarendon Press, 1945), p. 5, could still argue that "given the total national income, satisfaction is maximized with an equal distribution of income. This argument is based, on the one hand, on the law of diminishing marginal utility of income, and, on the other hand, on the assumption (based on the postulates of political democracy rather than economics) that persons with the same income possess the same capacity of enjoyment. In addition, the currently accepted economic doctrine denies that there is virtue in thrift (made so much easier by the existence of high incomes) *so long as there is unemployment*, and thus the main traditional justification of inequality falls away."

[10] This conclusion can probably be regarded as firmly established in spite of the ever recurring objection that individually most of us have definite views about whether a given need of one person is greater or smaller than that of another. The fact that we have an opinion about this in no way implies that there is any objective basis for deciding who is right if people differ in their views about the relative importance of different people's needs; nor is there any evidence that they are likely to agree.

But if we were to follow up the implications of the contention that the utility of income in terms of effort is decreasing, we would arrive at curious conclusions. It would, in effect, mean that, as a person's income grows, the incentive in terms of additional income which would be required to induce the same marginal effort would increase. This might lead us to argue for regressive taxation, but certainly not for progressive. It is, however, scarcely worthwhile to follow this line of thought further. There can now be little doubt that the use of utility analysis in the theory of taxation was all a regrettable mistake (in which some of the most distinguished economists of the time shared) and that the sooner we can rid ourselves of the confusion it has caused, the better.

3. Those who advocated progressive taxation during the latter part of the nineteenth century generally stressed that their aim was only to achieve equality of sacrifice and not a redistribution of income; also they generally held that this aim could justify only a "moderate" degree of progression and that its "excessive" use (as in fifteenth-century Florence, where rates had been pushed up to 50 per cent) was, of course, to be condemned. Though all attempts to supply an objective standard for an appropriate rate of progression failed and though no answer was offered when it was objected that, once the principle was accepted, there would be no assignable limit beyond which progression might not be carried with equal justification, the discussion moved entirely in a context of contemplated rates which made any effect on the distribution of income appear negligible. The suggestion that rates would not stay within these limits was treated as a malicious distortion of the argument, betraying a reprehensible lack of confidence in the wisdom of democratic government.

It was in Germany, then the leader in "social reform," that the advocates of progressive taxation first overcame the resistance and its modern evolution began. In 1891, Prussia introduced a progressive income tax rising from 0.67 to 4 per cent. In vain did Rudolf von Geist, the venerable leader of the then recently consummated movement for the *Rechtsstaat*, protest in the Diet that this meant the abandonment of the fundamental principle of equality before the law, "of the most sacred principle of equality," which provided the only barrier against encroachment on property.[11] The very smallness of the burden involved in the new schemes made ineffective any attempt to oppose it as a matter of principle.

---

[11] Prussian Parliament, *Stenographische Berichte über die Verhandlungen der durch die Allerhöchste Verordnung vom 16. Dezember 1890 einberufenen beiden Häuser des Landtages: Haus der Abgeordneten* (2 vols.; Berlin, 1891), vol. 2, p. 907: "Die allerheiligsten politischen Grundsätze der Gleichheit werden sich aber untreu, wenn wir an die Frage der Progressivsteuer herangehen. Da verleugnet selbst die absolute Demokratie in Hunderttausenden von Stimmen ihre Grundsätze, wenn es sich darum handelt, den Reichen schärfer zu treffen." ["The most sacred political principles of equality are betrayed, however, when dealing with the question of progressive taxation. Here extreme democracy contravenes these principles with hundreds of thousands of votes should the issue concern encroaching upon the wealth of the rich."—Ed.]

Though some other Continental countries soon followed Prussia, it took nearly twenty years for the movement to reach the great Anglo-Saxon powers. It was only in 1910 and 1913 that Great Britain and the United States adopted graduated income taxes rising to the then spectacular figures of 8¼ and 7 per cent, respectively. Yet within thirty years these figures had risen to 97½ and 91 per cent.

Thus in the space of a single generation what nearly all the supporters of progressive taxation had for half a century asserted could not happen came to pass. This change in the absolute rates, of course, completely changed the character of the problem, making it different not merely in degree but in kind. All attempt to justify these rates on the basis of capacity to pay was, in consequence, soon abandoned, and the supporters reverted to the original, but long avoided, justification of progression as a means of bringing about a more just distribution of income.[12] It has come to be generally accepted once more that the only ground on which a progressive scale of over-all taxation can be defended is the desirability of changing the distribution of income and that this defense cannot be based on any scientific argument but must be recognized as a frankly political postulate, that is, as an attempt to impose upon society a pattern of distribution determined by majority decision.

4. An explanation of this development that is usually offered is that the great

---

[12] See particularly Henry Calvert Simons, *Personal Income Taxation: The Definition of Income as a Problem of Fiscal Policy* (Chicago: University of Chicago Press, 1938), pp. 17ff. Cf. also Alan Turner Peacock, "Welfare in the Liberal State," in *The Unservile State: Essays in Liberty and Welfare*, George Watson, ed. (London: Allen and Unwin, 1957), pp. 113–30: "Liberal support for such measures as progressive taxation does not rest on the utilitarian belief that an extra pound is more 'valuable' or will 'afford a greater utility' to a poor man than to a rich man. It rests on a positive dislike of gross inequality." [Since Hayek wrote this, substantial changes have been made in the income tax structure of most developed nations, where the top tax rates were, on average, nearly 20% lower in 2004 than they were in the 1970s. This was especially true in the United States and the United Kingdom, where the top rates were 38% and 40%, respectively. Initiated by Margaret Thatcher in Britain and Ronald Reagan in the United States, tax rates were reduced and its progressive features were sharply curtailed. In the United States, the following income tax rates on taxable income for those who filed single returns prevailed in 2007:

From $1.00 to 7,825.00	10%
From 7,826.00 to 31,850.00	15%
From 31,851.00 to 77,100.00	25%
From 77,101.00 to 160,850.00	28%
From 160,850.00 to 349,700.00	33%
Over 349,701.00	35%

The rates in the United Kingdom on earned income for 2005–2006 were:

From £1.00 to 2,230.00	10%
From 2,231.00 to 33,300.00	22%
Over 33,301.00	40%

It should be kept in mind that these rates did not include social security "contributions," which, in the United States and the United Kingdom, were quite substantial, nor, in the United States, did they include state or local income taxes.—Ed.]

increase in public expenditure in the last forty years could not have been met without resort to steep progression, or at least that, without it, an intolerable burden would have had to be placed on the poor and that, once the necessity of relieving the poor was admitted, some degree of progression was inevitable. On examination, however, the explanation dissolves into pure myth. Not only is the revenue derived from the high rates levied on large incomes, particularly in the highest brackets, so small compared with the total revenue as to make hardly any difference to the burden borne by the rest; but for a long time after the introduction of progression it was not the poorest who benefited from it but entirely the better-off working class and the lower strata of the middle class who provided the largest number of voters. It would probably be true, on the other hand, to say that the illusion that by means of progressive taxation the burden can be shifted substantially onto the shoulders of the wealthy has been the chief reason why taxation has increased as fast as it has done and that, under the influence of this illusion, the masses have come to accept a much heavier load than they would have done otherwise. The only major result of the policy has been the severe limitation of the incomes that could be earned by the most successful and thereby gratification of the envy of the less-well-off.

How small is the contribution of progressive tax rates (particularly of the high punitive rates levied on the largest incomes) to total revenue may be illustrated by a few figures for the United States and for Great Britain. Concerning the former it has been stated (in 1956) that "the entire progressive super structure produces only about 17 per cent of the total revenue derived from the individual [income] tax"—or about 8½ per cent of all federal revenue—and that of this, "half . . . is taken from the taxable income brackets up through $16,000–$18,000, where the tax rate reaches 50 per cent" while "the other half comes from the higher brackets and rates."[13] As for Great Britain, which has an even steeper scale of progression and a greater proportional tax burden, it has been pointed out that "*all* surtax (on both earned and unearned incomes) only brings in about 2½ per cent of all public revenue, and that if we collared every £1 of income over £2.000 p. a. [$5.600], we would only net an extra 1½ per cent of revenue. . . . Indeed the massive contribution to income tax and surtax comes from incomes between £750 p.a. and £3.000 p.a. [$2.100–$8.400]—i.e., just those which begin with foremen and end with managers, or begin with public servants just taking responsibility and end with those at the head of our Civil and other services."[14]

<hr>

[13] National Association of Manufacturers, Taxation Committee, *Facing the Issue of Income Tax Discrimination: In Support of the Five-Year Plan for Income Tax Reduction* (rev. and expanded ed.; New York: National Association of Manufacturers, 1956), p. 14.

[14] David Graham Hutton, "The Dynamics of Progress," in *The Unservile State*, pp. 161–86. This seems to be recognized now even in Labour party circles (see, for example, Charles Anthony Raven Crosland, *The Future of Socialism* [London: Jonthan Cape, 1956], p.190).

Generally speaking and in terms of the progressive character of the two tax systems as a whole, it would seem that the contribution made by progression in the two countries is between 2½ and 8½ per cent of total revenue, or between ½ and 2 per cent of gross national income. These figures clearly do not suggest that progression is the only method by which the revenue required can be obtained. It seems at least probable (though nobody can speak on this with certainty) that under progressive taxation the gain to revenue is less than the reduction of real income which it causes.

If the belief that the high rates levied on the rich make an indispensable contribution to total revenue is thus illusory, the claim that progression has served mainly to relieve the poorest classes is belied by what happened in the democracies during the greater part of the period since progression was introduced. Independent studies in the United States, Great Britain, France, and Prussia agree that, as a rule, it was those of modest income who provided the largest number of voters that were let off most lightly, while not only those who had more income but also those who had less carried a much heavier proportional burden of total taxation. The best illustration of this situation, which appears to have been fairly general until the last war, is provided by the results of a detailed study of conditions in Britain, where in 1936–37 the total burden of taxation on fully earned income of families with two children was 18 per cent for those with an annual income of £100 per annum, which then gradually fell to a minimum of 11 per cent at £350 and then rose again, to reach 19 per cent only at £1,000.[15] What these figures (and the similar data for other

[15] Cf. George Finlay Shirras and László Rostas, *The Burden of British Taxation* (Cambridge: Cambridge University Press, 1943), p. 56. The main results of this investigation are shown in the accompanying table. See also the earlier discussions in Committee on the National Debt and

Income (£)	Per Cent Taken by Taxation	Income (£)	Per Cent Taken by Taxation
100	18	1,000	19
150	16	2,000	24
200	15	2,500	25
250	14	5,000	33
300	12	10,000	41
350	11	20,000	50
500	14	50,000	58

Taxation, *Report* [chaired by Frederick Henry Smith, Baron Colwyn] (London: His Majesty's Stationery Office, 1927) [Cmd. 2800]; for the United States, Gerhard Colm and Helen Tarasov, *Who Pays the Taxes? (Allocation of Federal, State, and local taxes to consumer income brackets)*, Temporary National Economic Committee, Monograph No. 3 (Washington, DC: Government Printing Office, 1940); and John Hans Adler, "The Fiscal System: The Distribution of Income and Public Welfare," in *Fiscal Policies and the American Economy*, Kenyon Edward Poole, ed. (New York: Prentice-Hall, 1951), pp. 359–409; for France, see Hubert Brochier, *Finances publiques et redistribution des revenus* (Paris: Presse de la Fondation nationale des sciences politiques, 1950); and, for an earlier similar result for Prussia, Friedrich Julius Neumann, *Die persönlichen Steuern vom Einkommen:*

countries) clearly show is not only that, once the principle of proportional taxation is abandoned, it is not necessarily those in greatest need but more likely the classes with the greatest voting strength that will profit, but also that all that was obtained by progression could undoubtedly have been obtained by taxing the masses with modest incomes as heavily as the poorest groups.

It is true, of course, that developments since the last war in Britain, and probably elsewhere, have so increased the progressive character of the income tax as to make the burden of taxation progressive throughout and that, through redistributive expenditure on subsidies and services, the income of the very lowest classes has been increased (so far as these things can be meaningfully measured: what can be shown is always only the cost and not the value of the services rendered) by as much as 22 per cent.[16] But the latter development is little dependent on the present high rates of progression but is financed mainly by the contributions of the middle and upper ranges of the middle class.

5. The real reason why all the assurances that progression would remain moderate have proved false and why its development has gone far beyond the most pessimistic prognostications of its opponents[17] is that all arguments in support of progression can be used to justify any degree of progression. Its advocates may realize that beyond a certain point the adverse effects on the efficiency of the economic system may become so serious as to make it inexpedient to push it any further. But the argument based on the presumed justice of progression provides for no limitation, as has often been admitted by its supporters, before all incomes above a certain figure are confiscated and those below left untaxed. Unlike proportionality, progression provides no principle which tells us what the relative burden of different persons ought to be. It is no more than a rejection of proportionality in favor of a discrimination against the wealthy without any criterion for limiting the extent of this discrimination.

Verbunden mit Ertrags- oder mit Vermögenssteuern mit besonderer Beziehung auf württembergische Verhältnisse (Tübingen: Laupp'sche Buchhandlung, 1896).

[16] Allan Murray Cartter, *The Redistribution of Income in Postwar Britain: A Study of the Effects of the Central Government Fiscal Program in 1948–1949* (New Haven: Yale University Press, 1955), pp. 54–79 [chap. 11, "The Redistribution of Income in 1948–1949"], esp. p. 57); see also Alan Turner Peacock and P. R. Browning, "The Social Services in Great Britain and the Redistribution of Income," in *Income Redistribution and Social Policy*, Alan Turner Peacock, ed. (London: Jonathan Cape, 1954), pp. 139–77; and Richard Abel Musgrave, John Joseph Carroll, L. D. Cooke, and Lenore Frane, "Distribution of Tax Payments by Income Groups: A Case Study for 1948," *National Tax Journal*, 4 (1951): 1–53.

[17] The best-known of these pessimistic prognostications is that by William Edward Hartpole Lecky, *Democracy and Liberty* (2 vols.; new ed.; New York: Longmans, Green, and, Co. 1899), vol. 1, p. 347 [Liberty Fund edition, vol. 1, p. 293]: "Highly graduated taxation realises most completely the supreme danger of democracy, creating a state of things in which one class imposes on another burdens which it is not asked to share, and impels the State into vast schemes of extravagance, under the belief that the whole costs will be thrown upon others."

Because "there is no ideal rate of progression that can be demonstrated by formula,"[18] it is only the newness of the principle that has prevented its being carried at once to punitive rates. But there is no reason why "a little more than before" should not always be represented as just and reasonable.

It is no slur on democracy, no ignoble distrust of its wisdom, to maintain that, once it embarks upon such a policy, it is bound to go much further than originally intended. This is not to say that "free and representative government is a failure"[19] or that it must lead to "a complete distrust in democratic government,"[20] but that democracy has yet to learn that, in order to be just, it must be guided in its action by general principles. What is true of individual action is equally true of collective action, except that a majority is perhaps even less likely to consider explicitly the long-term significance of its decision and therefore is even more in need of guidance by principles. Where, as in the case of progression, the so-called principle adopted is no more than an open invitation to discrimination and, what is worse, an invitation to the majority to discriminate against a minority, the pretended principle of justice must become the pretext for pure arbitrariness.

What is required here is a rule which, while still leaving open the possibility of a majority's taxing itself to assist a minority, does not sanction a majority's imposing upon a minority whatever burden it regards as right. That a majority, merely because it is a majority, should be entitled to apply to a minority a rule which does not apply to itself is an infringement of a principle much more fundamental than democracy itself, a principle on which the justification of democracy rests. We have seen before (in chaps. 10 and 14) that if the classifications of persons which the law must employ are to result neither in privilege nor in discrimination, they must rest on distinctions which those inside the group singled out, as well as those outside it, will recognize as relevant.

It is the great merit of proportional taxation that it provides a rule which is likely to be agreed upon by those who will pay absolutely more and those who will pay absolutely less and which, once accepted, raises no problem of a separate rule applying only to a minority. Even if progressive taxation does not name the individuals to be taxed at a higher rate, it discriminates by introducing a distinction which aims at shifting the burden from those who determine the rates onto others. In no sense can a progressive scale of taxation be regarded as a general rule applicable equally to all—in no sense can it be said

[18] Royal Commission on Taxation of Profits and Income, *Second Report* (London: Her Majesty's Stationery Office, 1954) [Cmd. 9105], p. 43 [sec. 142].

[19] Justice [Edward Douglass] White in *Knowlton v. Moore* 178 *U.S.* 41 at 109 (1899), quoted in Blum and Kalven, "The Uneasy Case for Progressive Taxation," *University of Chicago Law Review*, 19 (1952): 425.

[20] Edwin Robert Anderson Seligman, *Progressive Taxation in Theory and Practice* (2nd ed., completely rev. and enl.; Princeton, NJ: American Economic Association Quarterly, 1908), p. 298.

that a tax of 20 per cent on one person's income and a tax of 75 per cent on the larger income of another person are equal. Progression provides no criterion whatever of what is and what is not to be regarded as just. It indicates no halting point for its application, and the "good judgment" of the people on which its defenders are usually driven to rely as the only safeguard[21] is nothing more than the current state of opinion shaped by past policy.

That the rates of progression have, in fact, risen as fast as they have done is, however, also due to a special cause which has been operating during the last forty years, namely, inflation. It is now well understood that a rise in aggregate money incomes tends to lift everybody into a higher tax bracket, even though their real income has remained the same. As a result, members of the majorities have found themselves again and again unexpectedly the victims of the discriminatory rates for which they had voted in the belief that they would not be affected.

This effect of progressive taxation is often represented as a merit, because it tends to make inflation (and deflation) in some measure self-correcting. If a budget deficit is the source of inflation, revenue will rise proportionately more than incomes and may thus close the gap; and if a budget surplus has produced deflation, the resulting fall of incomes will soon bring an even greater reduction in revenue and wipe out the surplus. It is very doubtful, however, whether, with the prevailing bias in favor of inflation, this is really an advantage. Even without this effect, budgetary needs have in the past been the main source of recurrent inflations; and it has been only the knowledge that an inflation, once started, is difficult to stop that in some measure has acted as a deterrent. With a tax system under which inflation produces a more than proportional increase in revenue through a disguised increase in taxes which requires no vote of the legislature, this device may become almost irresistibly tempting.

6. It is sometimes contended that proportional taxation is as arbitrary a principle as progressive taxation and that, apart from an apparently greater mathematical neatness, it has little to recommend it. There are, however, other strong arguments in its favor besides the one we have already mentioned—i.e., that it provides a uniform principle on which people paying different amounts are likely to agree. There also is still much to be said for the old argument that, since almost all economic activity benefits from the basic services of government, these services form a more or less constant ingredient of all we consume and enjoy and that, therefore, a person who commands more of the resources of society will also gain proportionately more from what the government has contributed.

More important is the observation that proportional taxation leaves the relations between the net remunerations of different kinds of work unchanged.

---

[21] Royal Commission on Taxation of Profits and Income, *Second Report*, p. 45 [sec. 150].

This is not quite the same as the old maxim, "No tax is a good tax unless it leaves individuals in the same relative position as it finds them."[22] It concerns the effect, not on the relations between individual incomes, but on the relations between the net remunerations for particular services performed, and it is this which is the economically relevant factor. It also does not, as might be said of the old maxim, beg the issue by simply postulating that the proportional size of the different incomes should be left unchanged.

There may be a difference of opinion as to whether the relation between two incomes remains the same when they are reduced by the same amount or in the same proportion. There can be no doubt, however, whether or not the net remunerations for two services which before taxation were equal still stand in the same relation after taxes have been deducted. And this is where the effects of progressive taxation are significantly different from those of proportional taxation. The use that will be made of particular resources depends on the net reward for services, and, if the resources are to be used efficiently, it is important that taxation leave the relative recompenses that will be received for particular services as the market determines them. Progressive taxation alters this relation substantially by making net remuneration for a particular service dependent upon the other earnings of the individual over a certain period, usually a year. If, before taxation, a surgeon gets as much for an operation as an architect for planning a house, or a salesman gets as much for selling ten cars as a photographer for taking forty portraits, the same relation will still hold if proportional taxes are deducted from their receipts. But with progressive taxation of incomes this relation may be greatly changed. Not only may services which before taxation receive the same remuneration bring very different rewards; but a man who receives a relatively large payment for a service may in the end be left with less than another who receives a smaller payment.

This means that progressive taxation necessarily offends against what is probably the only universally recognized principle of economic justice, that of "equal pay for equal work." If what each of two lawyers will be allowed to retain from his fees for conducting exactly the same kind of case as the other depends on his other earnings during the year—they will, in fact, often derive very different gains from similar efforts. A man who has worked very hard, or for some reason is in greater demand, may receive a much smaller reward for further effort than one who has been idle or less lucky. Indeed, the more

[22] McCulloch in ["On the Complaints and Proposals Regarding Taxation,"] *Edinburgh Review*, p. 162; reprinted in *Treatise on the Principles and Practical Influence of Taxation*, p. 141. The phrase was later used often and occurs, for example, in Francis Amasa Walker, *Political Economy* (2nd ed., rev. and enl.; New York: H. Holt and Co., 1887), p. 491. [Walker's formulation differs slightly. He writes: "No tax is a just tax unless it leaves individuals in the same relative condition in which it finds them."—Ed.]

the consumers value a man's services, the less worthwhile will it be for him to exert himself further.

This effect on incentive, in the usual sense of the term, though important and frequently stressed, is by no means the most harmful effect of progressive taxation. Even here the objection is not so much that people may, as a result, not work as hard as they otherwise would, as it is that the change in the net remunerations for different activities will often divert their energies to activities where they are less useful than they might be. The fact that with progressive taxation the net remuneration for any service will vary with the time rate at which the earning accrues thus becomes a source not only of injustice but also of a misdirection of resources.

There is no need to dwell here on the familiar and insoluble difficulties which progressive taxation creates in all instances where effort (or outlay) and reward are not approximately coincident in time, i.e., where effort is expended in expectation of a distant and uncertain result—in short, in all instances where human effort takes the form of a long and risky investment. No practicable scheme of averaging incomes can do justice to the author or inventor, the artist or actor, who reaps the rewards of perhaps decades of effort in a few years.[23] Nor should it be necessary to elaborate further on the effects of steeply progressive taxation on the willingness to undertake risky capital investments. It is obvious that such taxation discriminates against those risky ventures which are worthwhile only because, in case of success, they will bring a return big enough to compensate for the great risk of total loss. It is more than likely that what truth there is in the alleged "exhaustion of investment opportunities" is due largely to a fiscal policy which effectively eliminates a wide range of ventures that private capital might profitably undertake.[24]

We must pass rapidly over these harmful effects on incentive and on investment, not because they are unimportant but because they are on the whole well enough known. We shall devote our limited space, then, to other effects which are less understood but at least equally important. Of these, one which perhaps still deserves emphasis is the frequent restriction or reduction of the

---

[23] See the detailed discussion in the Royal Commission on the Taxation of Profits and Income, *Final Report* (London: Her Majesty's Stationery Office, 1955) [Cmd. 9474], p. 60 [secs. 186–207, esp. 186]: "It is inherent in a graduated tax that it should fall with different incidence on the uneven and the even income."

[24] It deserves notice that the same authors who were loudest in their emphasis on the alleged "exhaustion of investment opportunities" are now demanding that "the effective progressivity of the income tax must be strengthened" and emphasizing that "the most important single other grounds confronting American politics today is the issue of progressivity of our income tax" and seriously contend that "we are in a situation in which the marginal *tax dollar* can clearly yield a much higher social utility than the marginal *pay envelope* dollar" (Alvin Harvey Hansen, "The Task of Promoting Economic Growth and Stability." Address to the National Planning Association, February 26, 1956 [mimeographed].).

division of labor. This effect is particularly noticeable where professional work is not organized on business lines and much of the outlay that in fact would tend to increase a man's productivity is not counted as part of the cost. The tendency to "do it yourself" comes to produce the most absurd results when, for instance, a man who wishes to devote himself to more productive activities may have to earn in an hour twenty or even forty times as much in order to be able to pay another whose time is less valuable for an hour's services.[25]

We can also only briefly mention the very serious effect of progressive taxation on the supply of savings. If twenty-five years ago the argument that savings were too high and should be reduced may have had some degree of plausibility, few responsible persons today will doubt that, if we are to achieve even part of the tasks we have set ourselves, we want as high a rate of saving as people are prepared to supply. The socialist answer to those who are concerned about this effect on savings is, in fact, no longer that these savings are not needed but that they should be supplied by the community, i.e., out of funds raised from taxation. This, however, can be justified only if the long-term aim is socialism of the old kind, namely, government ownership of the means of production.

7. One of the chief reasons why progressive taxation has come to be so widely accepted is that the great majority of people have come to think of an appropriate *income* as the only legitimate and socially desirable form of reward. They think of income not as related to the value of the services rendered but as conferring what is regarded as an appropriate status in society. This is shown very clearly in the argument, frequently used in support of progressive taxation, that "no man is worth £10,000 a year, and, in our present state of poverty, with the great majority of people earning less than £6 a week, only a few very exceptional men deserve to exceed £2,000 a year."[26] That this contention lacks all foundation and appeals only to emotion and

---

[25] This seems to have shaken even an author so firmly convinced of the justice of progressive taxation that he wanted to apply it on an international scale (see James Edward Meade, *Planning and the Price Mechanism: The Liberal-Socialist Solution* (London: Allen and Unwin, 1948), p. 40: "Thus a skilled author who is taxed 19s 6d in the £ [i.e., 97 ½ per cent] must earn £200 in order to have the money to pay £5 to get some housework done. He may well decide to do the housework himself instead of writing. Only if he is forty times more productive in writing than housework will it be profitable for him to extend the division of labour and to exchange his writing for housework."

[26] Sir William Arthur Lewis, *The Principles of Economic Planning: A Study Prepared for the Fabian Society* (London: D. Dobson, 1949), p. 30; the argument appears to have been used first by Leonard Trelawney Hobhouse, *Liberalism* (Home University Library; London: Williams and Norgate, 1911), pp. 199–201, who suggests that the argument for a supertax is "a respectful doubt whether any single individual is worth to society by any means as much as some individuals obtain" and suggests that "when we come to an income of some £5,000 a year, we approach the limit of the industrial value of the individual."

prejudice will be at once obvious when we see that what it means is that no act that any individual can perform in a year or, for that matter in an hour, can be worth more to society than £10,000 ($28,000). Of course, it can and sometimes will have many times that value. There is no necessary relation between the time an action takes and the benefit that society will derive from it.

The whole attitude which regards large gains as unnecessary and socially undesirable springs from the state of mind of people who are used to selling their time for a fixed salary or fixed wages and who consequently regard a remuneration of so much per unit of time as the normal thing.[27] But though this method of remuneration has become predominant in an increasing number of fields, it is appropriate only where people sell their time to be used at another's direction or at least act on behalf of and in fulfilment of the will of others. It is meaningless for men whose task is to administer resources at their own risk and responsibility and whose main aim is to increase the resources under their control out of their own earnings. For them the control of resources is a condition for practicing their vocation, just as the acquisition of certain skills or of particular knowledge is such a condition in the professions. Profits and losses are mainly a mechanism for redistributing capital among these men rather than a means of providing their current sustenance. The conception that current net receipts are normally intended for current consumption, though natural to the salaried man, is alien to the thinking of those whose aim is to build up a business. Even the conception of income itself is in their case largely an abstraction forced upon them by the income tax. It is no more than an estimate of what, in view of their expectations and plans, they can afford to spend without bringing their prospective power of expenditure below the present level. I doubt whether a society consisting mainly of "self-employed" individuals would ever have come to take the concept of income so much for granted as we do or would ever have thought of taxing the earnings from a certain service according to the rate at which they accrued in time.

It is questionable whether a society which will recognize no reward other than what appears to its majority as an appropriate income, and which does not regard the acquisition of a fortune in a relatively short time as a legitimate form of remuneration for certain kinds of activities, can in the long run preserve a system of private enterprise. Though there may be no difficulty in widely dispersing ownership of well-established enterprises among a large number of small owners and in having them run by managers in a position intermediate between that of an entrepreneur and that of a salaried employee, the building-up of new enterprises is still and probably always will

[27] Cf. Wright, *Democracy and Progress*, p. 96: "It must be remembered that our income-tax laws have been for the most part drawn up and enacted by people on steady salaries for the benefit of people on steady salaries."

be done mainly by individuals controlling considerable resources. New developments, as a rule, will still have to be backed by a few persons intimately acquainted with particular opportunities; and it is certainly not to be wished that all future evolution should be dependent on the established financial and industrial corporations.

Closely connected with this problem is the effect of progressive taxation on an aspect of capital formation which is different from that already discussed, namely, the place of formation. It is one of the advantages of a competitive system that successful new ventures are likely for a short time to bring very large profits and that thus the capital needed for development will be formed by the persons who have the best opportunity of using it. The large gains of the successful innovator meant in the past that, having shown the capacity for profitably employing capital in new ventures, he would soon be able to back his judgment with larger means. Much of the individual formation of new capital, since it is offset by capital losses of others, should be realistically seen as part of a continuous process of redistribution of capital among the entrepreneurs. The taxation of such profits, at more or less confiscatory rates, amounts to a heavy tax on that turnover of capital which is part of the driving force of a progressive society.

The most serious consequence, however, of the discouragement of individual capital formation where there are temporary opportunities for large profits is the restriction of competition. The system tends generally to favor corporate as against individual saving and particularly to strengthen the position of the established corporations against newcomers. It thus assists to create quasi-monopolistic situations. Because taxes today absorb the greater part of the newcomer's "excessive" profits, he cannot, as has been well said, "accumulate capital; he cannot expand his own business; he will never become big business and a match for the vested interests. The old firms do not need to fear his competition: they are sheltered by the tax collector. They may with impunity indulge in routine, they may defy the wishes of the public and become conservative. It is true, the income tax prevents them, too, from accumulating new capital. But what is more important for them is that it prevents the dangerous newcomer from accumulating any capital. They are virtually privileged by the tax system. In this sense progressive taxation checks economic progress and makes for rigidity."[28]

[28] Ludwig von Mises, *Human Action*, pp. 804–5 [Liberty Fund edition, vol. 3, pp. 808–9]. Cf. also Colin Clark, *Welfare and Taxation* (Oxford: Catholic Social Guild, 1954), pp. 51–52: "Many upholders of high taxation are sincere opponents of monopoly; but if taxation were lower and, especially, if undistributed profits were exempted from taxation, many businesses would spring up which would compete actively with the old established monopolies. As a matter of fact, the present excessive rates of taxation are one of the principal reasons for monopolies now being so strong." Similarly, Lionel Robbins, "Notes on Public Finance," *Lloyds Bank Review*, n.s., 38 (October 1955): 10: "The fact that it has become so difficult to accumulate even a com-

An even more paradoxical and socially grave effect of progressive taxation is that, though intended to reduce inequality, it in fact helps to perpetuate existing inequalities and eliminates the most important compensation for that inequality which is inevitable in a free-enterprise society. It used to be the redeeming feature of such a system that the rich were not a closed group and that the successful man might in a comparatively short time acquire large resources.[29] Today, however, the chances of rising into the class are probably already smaller in some countries, such as Great Britain, than they have been at any time since the beginning of the modern era. One significant effect of this is that the administration of more and more of the world's capital is coming under the control of men who, though they enjoy very large incomes and all the amenities that this secures, have never on their own account and at their personal risk controlled substantial property. Whether this is altogether a gain remains to be seen.

It is also true that the less possible it becomes for a man to acquire a new fortune, the more must the existing fortunes appear as privileges for which there is no justification. Policy is then certain to aim at taking these fortunes out of private hands, either by the slow process of heavy taxation of inheritance or by the quicker one of outright confiscation. A system based on private property and control of the means of production presupposes that such property and control can be acquired by any successful man. If this is made impossible, even the men who otherwise would have been the most eminent capitalists of the new generation are bound to become the enemies of the established rich.

8. In those countries where taxation of incomes reaches very high rates, greater equality is, in effect, brought about by setting a limit to the net income that anybody can earn. (In Great Britain, during the last war, the largest net income after taxation was approximately £5,000, or $14,000—though this was partly tempered by the fact that capital gains were not treated as income.) We have seen that, considering the insignificant contribution which progressive taxation of the higher brackets makes to revenue, it can be justified only by the view that nobody should command a large income. But what a large income is depends on the views of the particular community and, in the last

---

paratively small fortune must have the most profound effects on the organization of business; and it is by no means clear to me that these results are in the social interest. Must not the inevitable consequence of all this be that it will become more and more difficult for innovation to develop save within the ambit of established corporate enterprise, and that more and more of what accumulation takes place will take place within the large concerns which—largely as a result of individual enterprise in the past—managed to get started before the ice age descended?"

[29] See Wright, *Democracy and Progress*, pp. 94–103; cf. also John Keith Butters and John Lintner, *Effects of Federal Taxes on Growing Enterprises* (Boston: Division of Research, Harvard University Graduate School of Business Administration, 1945).

resort, on its average wealth. The poorer a country, therefore, the lower will its permissible maximum incomes be, and the more difficult for any of its inhabitants to reach income levels that in wealthier countries are considered only moderate. Where this may lead is illustrated by a recent proposal, only narrowly defeated, of the National Planning Commission of India, according to which a ceiling of $6,300 per annum was to be fixed for all incomes (and a ceiling of $4,300 for salary incomes).[30] One need only to think of the same principle being applied to the different regions of any one country, or internationally, to see its implications. These consequences certainly are a commentary on the moral basis of the belief that the majority of a particular group should be entitled to decide on the appropriate limit of incomes and on the wisdom of those who believe that in this manner they will assist the well-being of the masses. Can there be much doubt that poor countries, by preventing individuals from getting rich, will also slow down the general growth of wealth? And does not what applies to the poor countries apply equally to the rich?

In the last resort, the problem of progressive taxation is, of course, an ethical problem, and in a democracy the real problem is whether the support that the principle now receives would continue if the people fully understood how it operates. It is probable that the practice is based on ideas which most people would not approve if they were stated abstractly. That a majority should be free to impose a discriminatory tax burden on a minority; that, in consequence, equal services should be remunerated differently; and that for a whole class, merely because its incomes are not in line with those of the rest, the normal incentives should be practically made ineffective—all these are principles which cannot be defended on grounds of justice. If, in addition, we consider the waste of energy and effort which progressive taxation in so many ways leads to,[31] it should not be impossible to convince reasonable people of

---

[30] See the report in the *New York Times*, "Ceiling on Income Proposed in India," January 8, 1956, p. 24.

[New Delhi, India, January 7—India's National Planning Commission has suggested putting a ceiling of the equivalent of $6,300 a year on all incomes.

That would be the most an Indian could earn from business or dividends. Salaried Indians would be limited to $4,300 a year after taxes.

The suggestions were contained in the latest memorandum on the second five-year plan. The new plan is supposed to go into operation in April and will be directed toward building up India's industrial strength.—Ed.]

[31] Much of the expense-account waste is indirectly a consequence of progressive taxation, since, without it, it would often be in the better interest of a firm so to pay its executives as to induce them to pay their representation expenditure out of their own pockets. Much greater than is commonly understood are also the legal costs caused by progressive taxation; cf. Blum and Kalven, "The Uneasy Case for Progressive Taxation," p. 431: "It is remarkable how much of the day to day work of the lawyer in the income tax field derives from the simple fact that the tax is progressive. Perhaps the majority of his problems are either caused or aggravated by that fact."

its undesirability. Yet experience in this field shows how rapidly habit blunts the sense of justice and even elevates into a principle what in fact has no better basis than envy.

If a reasonable system of taxation is to be achieved, people must recognize as a principle that the majority which determines what the total amount of taxation should be must also bear it at the maximum rate. There can be no justified objection to the same majority deciding to grant to an economically weak minority some relief in the form of a proportionately lower taxation. The task of erecting a barrier against abuse of progression is complicated by the fact that, as we have seen, some progression in personal income taxation is probably justified as a way of compensating for the effects of indirect taxation. Is there a principle which has any prospect of being accepted and which would effectively prevent those temptations inherent in progressive taxation from getting out of hand? Personally, I do not believe that setting an upper limit which progression is not to exceed would achieve its purpose. Such a percentage figure would be as arbitrary as the principle of progression and would be as readily altered when the need for additional revenue seemed to require it.

What is needed is a principle that will limit the maximum rate of direct taxation in some relation to the total burden of taxation. The most reasonable rule of the kind would seem to be one that fixed the maximum admissible (marginal) rate of direct taxation at that percentage of the total national income which the government takes in taxation. This would mean that if the government took 25 per cent of the national income, 25 per cent would also be the maximum rate of direct taxation of any part of individual incomes. If a national emergency made it necessary to raise this proportion, the maximum admissible rate would be raised to the same figure; and it would be correspondingly reduced when the over-all tax burden was reduced. This would still leave taxation somewhat progressive, since those paying the maximum rate on their incomes would also pay some indirect taxes which could bring their total proportional burden above the national average. Adherence to this principle would have the salutary consequence that every budget would have to be prefaced by an estimate of the share of national income which the government proposed to take as taxes. This percentage would provide the standard rate of direct taxation of incomes which, for the lower incomes, would be reduced in proportion as they were taxed indirectly. The net result would be a slight over-all progression in which, however, the marginal rate of taxation of the largest incomes could never exceed the rate at which incomes were taxed on the average by more than the amount of indirect taxation.

TWENTY-ONE

THE MONETARY FRAMEWORK

There is no subtler, no surer means of overturning the existing basis of society than to debauch the currency. The process engages all the hidden forces of economic law on the side of destruction, and does it in a manner which not one man in a million is able to diagnose. —J. M. Keynes

1. The experience of the last fifty years has taught most people the importance of a stable monetary system. Compared with the preceding century, this period has been one of great monetary disturbances. Governments have assumed a much more active part in controlling money, and this has been as much a cause as a consequence of instability. It is only natural, therefore, that some people should feel it would be better if governments were deprived of their control over monetary policy. Why, it is sometimes asked, should we not rely on the spontaneous forces of the market to supply whatever is needed for a satisfactory medium of exchange as we do in most other respects?

It is important to be clear at the outset that this is not only politically impracticable today but would probably be undesirable if it were possible. Perhaps, if governments had never interfered, a kind of monetary arrangement might have evolved which would not have required deliberate control; in particular, if men had not come extensively to use credit instruments as money or close substitutes for money, we might have been able to rely on some self-regulating mechanism.[1] This choice, however, is now closed to us. We know of no sub-

---

The quotation at the head of the chapter is taken from John Maynard Keynes, *The Economic Consequences of the Peace* (London: Macmillan, 1919), pp. 220–21. Keynes's observation was prompted by a similar remark attributed to Lenin to the effect that "the best way to destroy the capitalist system was to debauch the currency." Cf. also Keynes's later statement in *A Tract on Monetary Reform* (London: Macmillan, 1923), p. 40. "The Individualistic Capitalism of to-day, precisely because it entrusts saving to the individual investor and production to the individual employer, *presumes* a stable measuring-rod of value, and cannot be efficient—perhaps can not survive—without one." [The statement attributed to Lenin is possibly spurious. The Library of Congress has failed to uncover this or any similar statement in Lenin's writings. However, it has recently been suggested that he made the claim in an interview in 1919.—Ed.]

[1] Cf. Ludwig von Mises, *Human Action*, pp. 429–45 [Liberty Fund edition, vol. 2, pp. 432–448].

stantially different alternatives to the credit institutions on which the organization of modern business has come largely to rely; and historical developments have created conditions in which the existence of these institutions makes necessary some deliberate control of the interacting money and credit systems. Moreover, other circumstances which we certainly could not hope to change by merely altering our monetary arrangements make it, for the time being, inevitable that this control should be largely exercised by governments.[2]

The three fundamental reasons for this state of affairs are of different degrees of generality and validity. The first refers to all money at all times and explains why changes in the relative supply of money are so much more disturbing than changes in any of the other circumstances that affect prices and production. The second refers to all monetary systems in which the supply of money is closely related to credit—the kind on which all modern economic life rests. The third refers to the present volume of government expenditure and thus to a circumstance which we may hope to change eventually but which we must accept, for the time being, in all decisions about monetary policy.

The first of these facts makes money a kind of loose joint in the otherwise self-steering mechanism of the market, a loose joint that can sufficiently interfere with the adjusting mechanism to cause recurrent misdirections of production unless these effects are anticipated and deliberately counteracted. The reason for this is that money, unlike ordinary commodities, serves not by being used up but by being handed on. The consequence of this is that the effects of a change in the supply of money (or in the demand for it) do not directly lead to a new equilibrium. Monetary changes are, in a peculiar sense, "self-reversing." If, for example, an addition to the stock of money is first spent on a particular commodity or service, it not merely creates a new demand which in its nature is temporary and passing, but also sets up a train of further effects which will reverse the effects of the initial increase in demand. Those who first received the money will in turn spend it on other things. Like the ripples on a pool when a pebble has been thrown into it, the increase in demand will spread itself throughout the whole economic system, at each point temporarily altering relative prices in a way which will persist as long as the quantity

[2] Though I am convinced that modern credit banking as it has developed, requires some public institutions such as the central banks, I am doubtful whether it is necessary or desirable that they (or the government) should have the monopoly of the issue of all kinds of money. The state has, of course, the right to protect the name of the unit of money which it (or anybody else) issues and, if it issues "dollars," to prevent anybody else from issuing tokens with the same name. And as it is its function to enforce contracts, it must be able to determine what is "legal tender" for the discharge of any obligation contracted. But there seems to be no reason whatever why the state should ever prohibit the use of other kinds of media of exchange, be it some commodity or money issued by another agency, domestic or foreign. One of the most effective measures for protecting the freedom of the individual might indeed be to have constitutions prohibiting all peacetime restrictions on transactions in any kind of money or the precious metals.

of money continues to increase but which will be reversed when the increase comes to an end. Exactly the same applies if any part of the stock of money is destroyed, or even if people start holding larger or smaller amounts of cash, in relation to their receipts and outlay, than they normally do; each change of this sort will give rise to a succession of changes in demand which do not correspond to a change in the underlying real factors and which will therefore cause changes in prices and production which upset the equilibrium between demand and supply.[3]

If, for this reason, changes in the supply of money are particularly disturbing, the supply of money as we know it is also particularly apt to change in a harmful manner. What is important is that the rate at which money is spent should not fluctuate unduly. This means that when at any time people change their minds about how much cash they want to hold in proportion to the payments they make (or, as the economist calls it, they decide to be more or less liquid), the quantity of money should be changed correspondingly. However we define "cash," people's propensity to hold part of their resources in this form is subject to considerable fluctuation both over short and over long periods, and various spontaneous developments (such as, for instance, the credit card and the travelers' check) are likely to affect it profoundly. No automatic regulation of the supply of money is likely to bring about the desirable adjustments before such changes in the demand for money or in the supply of substitutes for it have had a strong and harmful effect on prices and employment.

Still worse, under all modern monetary systems, not only will the supply of money not adjust itself to such changes in demand, but it will tend to change in the opposite direction. Whenever claims for money come to serve in the place of money—and it is difficult to see how this can be prevented—the supply of such substitutes for money tends to be "perversely elastic."[4] This is a result of the simple fact that the same considerations which will make people want to hold more money will also make those who supply claims for money by lending produce fewer such claims, and vice versa. The familiar fact that, when everybody else wants to be more liquid, the banks for the same reasons will also wish to be more liquid and therefore supply less credit, is merely one instance of a general tendency inherent in most forms of credit.

These spontaneous fluctuations in the supply of money can be prevented only if somebody has the power to change deliberately the supply of some generally accepted medium of exchange in the opposite direction. This is a

[3] The most important of these temporary and self-reversing shifts of demand which monetary changes are likely to cause are changes in the relative demand for consumers' goods and investment goods; this problem we cannot consider here without entering into all the disputed problems of business-cycle theory.

[4] See the more detailed discussion of these problems in my *Monetary Nationalism and International Stability* (London: Longmans, Green, and Co., 1937).

function which it has generally been found necessary to entrust to a single national institution, in the past the central banks. Even countries like the United States, which long resisted the establishment of such an institution, found in the end that, if recurrent panics were to be avoided, a system which made extensive use of bank credit must rest on such a central agency which is always able to provide cash and which, through this control of the supply of cash, is able to influence the total supply of credit.

There are strong and probably still valid reasons which make it desirable that these institutions should be independent of government and its financial policy as much as possible. Here, however, we come to the third point to which we have referred—a historical development which, though not strictly irrevocable, we must accept for the immediate future. A monetary policy independent of financial policy is possible so long as government expenditure constitutes a comparatively small part of all payments and so long as the government debt (and particularly its short-term debt) constitutes only a small part of all credit instruments.[5] Today this condition no longer exists. In consequence, an effective monetary policy can be conducted only in co-ordination with the financial policy of government. Co-ordination in this respect, however, inevitably means that whatever nominally independent monetary authorities still exist have in fact to adjust their policy to that of the government. The latter, whether we like it or not, thus necessarily becomes the determining factor.

This more effective control over monetary conditions by government which, it would seem, can thus be achieved is welcomed by some people. Whether we have really been placed in a better position to pursue a desirable monetary policy we shall have to consider later. For the moment the important fact is that, as long as government expenditure constitutes as large a part of the national income as it now does everywhere, we must accept the fact that government will necessarily dominate monetary policy and that the only way in which we could alter this would be to reduce government expenditure greatly.

[5] See Richard Sidney Sayers, *Central Banking after Bagehot* (Oxford: Clarendon Press, 1957), pp. 85–107 [chap. 7, "The Variation of Cash Reserve Requirements," pp. 85–91, and chap. 8, "The Determination of the Volume of Bank Deposits: England 1955–56," pp. 92–107]. In light of the common assumption that "fiscal policy" as a means of controlling the economy was unknown when liberal policy was at its peak, two quotations from John Morley, Viscount Morley (*Life of William Ewart Gladstone* [3 vols.; London: Macmillan, 1903]) are of interest. Morley, writing of Gladstone's first budget in 1853 (vol. 1, bk. 4, p. 461) observes: "its initial boldness lay in the adoption of the unusual course of estimating the national income roughly for a period of seven years, and assuming that expenditure would remain tolerably steady for the whole period," and, earlier, he cites a remark made by Gladstone (vol. 2, bk. 5, p. 57): "If you want to benefit the labouring classes and to do the maximum of good, it is not enough to operate upon the articles consumed by them; you should rather operate upon the articles that give the maximum of employment."

2. With government in control of monetary policy, the chief threat in this field has become inflation. Governments everywhere and at all times have been the chief cause of the depreciation of the currency. Though there have been occasional prolonged falls in the value of a metallic money, the major inflations of the past have been the result of governments' either diminishing the coin or issuing excessive quantities of paper money. It is possible that the present generation is more on its guard against those cruder ways in which currencies were destroyed when governments paid their way by issuing paper money. The same can be done nowadays, however, by subtler procedures that the public is less likely to notice.

We have seen how every one of the chief features of the welfare state which we have considered tends to encourage inflation. We have seen how wage pressures from the labor unions, combined with the current full-employment policies, work in this manner and how the heavy financial burden which governments are assuming through old age pensions are likely to lead them to repeated attempts to lighten them by reducing the value of money. We should also note here, although this may not necessarily be connected, that governments seem invariably to have resorted to inflation to lighten the burden of their fixed obligations whenever the share of national income which they took exceeded about 25 per cent.[6] And we have also seen that, because under a system of progressive taxation inflation tends to increase tax revenue proportionately more than incomes, the temptation to resort to inflation becomes very great.

If it is true, however, that the institutions of the welfare state tend to favor inflation, it is even more true that it was the effects of inflation which strengthened the demand for welfare measures. This is true not only of some of those measures we have already considered but also of many others which we have yet to examine or can merely mention here, such as rent restrictions on dwellings, food subsidies, and all kinds of controls of prices and expenditures. The extent to which the effects of inflation have in recent times provided the chief arguments for an extension of government controls is too well known to need more illustration. But the extent to which, for over forty years now, developments throughout the whole world have been determined by an unprecedented inflationary trend is not sufficiently understood. It is perhaps best seen in the influence that it has had on the efforts of the generation whose working life covers that period to provide for their old age.

It will help us to see what inflation has done to the savings of the genera-

---

[6] See Colin Clark, "Public Finance and Changes in the Value of Money," *Economic Journal*, 55 (1945): 371–89, and compare the discussion of his thesis by Joseph A. Pechman and Thomas Mayer, "Mr. Colin Clark on the Limits of Taxation," *Review of Economics and Statistics*, 34 (1952): 232–42.

tion now on the point of retiring if we look at the results of a little statistical inquiry.[7] The aim of the inquiry was to determine what would be the present value in various countries of the accumulated savings of a person who for a period of forty-five years, from 1913 to 1958, had put aside every year the equivalent in money of the same real value and invested it at a fixed rate of interest of 4 per cent. This corresponds approximately to the return which the small saver in Western countries could have obtained from the kind of investment accessible to him, whether its actual form was a savings account, government bonds, or life insurance. We shall represent as 100 the amount that the saver would have possessed at the end of the period if the value of money had remained constant. What part of this real value would such a saver actually have had in 1958?

It seems that there is only one country in the world, namely, Switzerland, where the amount would have been as much as 70 per cent. The saver in the United States and Canada would still have been relatively well off, having been able to retain about 58 per cent. For most of the countries of the British Commonwealth and the other members of the "sterling bloc" the figure would have been around 50 per cent, and for Germany, in spite of the loss of all pre-1924 savings, still as much as 37 per cent. The investors in all those countries were still fortunate, however, compared with those in France or Italy, who would have retained only between 11 and 12 per cent of what the value of their savings over the period ought to have been at the beginning of 1958.[8]

---

[7] The figures quoted in the text are the result of calculations made for me by Mr. Salvator V. Ferrera, whose assistance I gratefully acknowledge. They were necessarily confined to those countries for which cost-of-living index numbers were readily available for the whole of the forty-year period. I am deliberately giving in the text only round figures, because I do not believe that the results of this kind of calculation can give us more than rough indications of the orders of magnitude involved. For those who are interested I give here the results (up to one decimal place) for all the countries for which the calculation was made:

	Per Cent		Per Cent		Per Cent
Switzerland	70.0	New Zealand	49.9	Germany	37.1
Canada	59.7	Norway	49.4	Belgium	28.8
United States	58.3	Egypt	48.2	Peru	20.6
Union of South Africa	52.3	Denmark	48.1	Italy	11.4
United Kingdom	50.2	Netherlands	44.0	France	11.4
Sweden	50.1	Ireland	42.1	Greece	8.4

The comparatively good results these statistics show for Germany are probably due to the fact that the currency reform of 1948 was not taken into account.

[8] So far as France is concerned, this, of course, does not take into account the effects of the considerable further depreciation (and consequent devaluation) of the French franc in the course of 1958.

It is usual today to dismiss the importance of this long and world-wide inflationary trend with the comment that things have always been like that and that history is largely a history of inflation. However true this may be in general, it is certainly not true of the period during which our modern economic system developed and during which wealth and incomes grew at an unprecedented rate. During the two hundred years preceding 1914, when Great Britain adhered to the gold standard, the price level, so far as it can be meaningfully measured over such a period, fluctuated around a constant level, ending up pretty well where it started and rarely changing by more than a third above or below that average level (except during the period of the Napoleonic wars, when the gold standard was abandoned).[9] Similarly, in the United States, during the period 1749–1939 there also does not seem to have occurred a significant upward trend of prices.[10] Compared with this, the rate at which prices have risen during the last quarter of a century in these and other countries represents a major change.

3. Although there are a few people who deliberately advocate a continuous upward movement of prices, the chief source of the existing inflationary bias is the general belief that deflation, the opposite of inflation, is so much more to be feared that, in order to keep on the safe side, a persistent error in the direction of inflation is preferable. But, as we do not know how to keep prices completely stable and can achieve stability only by correcting any small movement in either direction, the determination to avoid deflation at any cost must result in cumulative inflation. Also, the fact that inflation and deflation will often be local or sectional phenomena which must occur necessarily as part of the mechanism redistributing the resources of the economy means that attempts to prevent any deflation affecting a major area of the economy must result in over-all inflation.

It is, however, rather doubtful whether, from a long-term point of view, deflation is really more harmful than inflation. Indeed, there is a sense in which inflation is infinitely more dangerous and needs to be more carefully

---

[9] There is no continuous index number available for the whole of this two-hundred-year period, but the approximate trend of prices can be gauged by piecing together the data given by Elizabeth Waterman Gilboy, "The Cost of Living and Real Wages in Eighteenth Century England," *Review of Economics and Statistics*, 18 (1936): 134–43, and Rufus Stickney Tucker, "Real Wages of Artisans in London, 1729–1935," *Journal of the American Statistical Association*, 31 (1936): 73–84. For another later study, see Phyllis Deane and William Alan Cole, *British Economic Growth, 1688–1959: Trends and Structure* (Cambridge: Cambridge University Press, 1962).

[10] This statement is based on the index number of wholesale prices for the United States (see United States Department of Labor, Bureau of Labor Statistics, *Bureau of Labor Statistics Chart Series* [1948] (Washington, DC: Government Printing Office, 1948), chart E-11. [The Bureau of Labor Statistics calculates that wholesale prices for all commodities (1926 = 100) was 53.5 in 1749 and 77.1 in 1939, or an annual increase in prices of approximately .1925% over the course of 190 years.—Ed.]

guarded against. Of the two errors, it is the one much more likely to be committed. The reason for this is that moderate inflation is generally pleasant while it proceeds, whereas deflation is immediately and acutely painful.[11] There is little need to take precautions against any practice the bad effects of which will be immediately and strongly felt; but there is need for precautions wherever action which is immediately pleasant or relieves temporary difficulties involves much greater harm that will be felt only later. There is, indeed, more than a mere superficial similarity between inflation and drug-taking, a comparison which has often been made.

Inflation and deflation both produce their peculiar effects by causing unexpected price changes, and both are bound to disappoint expectations twice. The first time is when prices prove to be higher or lower than they were expected to be and the second when, as must sooner or later happen, these price changes come to be expected and cease to have the effect which their unforeseen occurrence had. The difference between inflation and deflation is that, with the former, the pleasant surprise comes first and the reaction later, while, with the latter, the first effect on business is depressing. The effects of both, however, are self-reversing. For a time the forces which bring about either tend to feed on themselves, and the period during which prices move faster than expected may thus be prolonged. But unless price movements continue in the same direction at an ever accelerating rate, expectations must catch up with them. As soon as this happens, the character of the effects changes.

Inflation at first merely produces conditions in which more people make profits and in which profits are generally larger than usual. Almost everything succeeds, there are hardly any failures. The fact that profits again and again prove to be greater than had been expected and that an unusual number of ventures turn out to be successful produces a general atmosphere favorable to risk-taking. Even those who would have been driven out of business without the windfalls caused by the unexpected general rise in prices are able to hold on and to keep their employees in the expectation that they will soon share in the general prosperity. This situation will last, however, only until people begin to expect prices to continue to rise at the same rate. Once they begin to count on prices being so many per cent higher in so many months' time, they will bid up the prices of the factors of production which determine the costs to a level corresponding to the future prices they expect. If prices then rise no more than had been expected, profits will return to normal, and the proportion of those making a profit also will fall; and since, during the period of exceptionally large profits, many have held on who would otherwise have been forced to change the direction of their efforts, a higher proportion than usual will suffer losses.

[11] Cf. Wilhelm Röpke, *Welfare, Freedom and Inflation* (London: Pall Mall Press, 1957).

The stimulating effect of inflation will thus operate only so long as it has not been foreseen; as soon as it comes to be foreseen, only its continuation at an increased rate will maintain the same degree of prosperity. If in such a situation prices rose less than expected, the effect would be the same as that of unforeseen deflation. Even if they rose only as much as was generally expected, this would no longer provide the exceptional stimulus but would lay bare the whole backlog of adjustments that had been postponed while the temporary stimulus lasted. In order for inflation to retain its initial stimulating effect, it would have to continue at a rate always faster than expected.

We cannot consider here all the complications which make it impossible for adaptations to an expected change in prices ever to become perfect, and especially for long-term and short-term expectations to become equally adjusted; nor can we go into the different effects on current production and on investment which are so important in any full examination of industrial fluctuations. It is enough for our purpose to know that the stimulating effects of inflation must cease to operate unless its rate is progressively accelerated and that, as it proceeds, certain unfavorable consequences of the fact that complete adaptation is impossible become more and more serious. The most important of these is that the methods of accounting on which all business decisions rest make sense only so long as the value of money is tolerably stable. With prices rising at an accelerating rate, the techniques of capital and cost accounting that provide the basis for all business planning would soon lose all meaning. Real costs, profits, or income would soon cease to be ascertainable by any conventional or generally acceptable method. And, with the principles of taxation being what they are, more and more would be taken in taxes as profits that in fact should be reinvested merely to maintain capital.

Inflation thus can never be more than a temporary fillip, and even this beneficial effect can last only as long as somebody continues to be cheated and the expectations of some people unnecessarily disappointed. Its stimulus is due to the errors which it produces. It is particularly dangerous because the harmful aftereffects of even small doses of inflation can be staved off only by larger doses of inflation. Once it has continued for some time, even the prevention of further acceleration will create a situation in which it will be very difficult to avoid a spontaneous deflation. Once certain activities that have become extended can be maintained only by continued inflation, their simultaneous discontinuation may well produce that vicious and rightly feared process in which the decline of some incomes leads to the decline of other incomes, and so forth. From what we know, it still seems probable that we should be able to prevent serious depressions by preventing the inflations which regularly precede them, but that there is little we can do to cure them, once they have set in. The time to worry about depressions is, unfortunately, when they are furthest from the minds of most people.

The manner in which inflation operates explains why it is so difficult to resist when policy mainly concerns itself with particular situations rather than with general conditions and with short-term rather than with long-term problems. It is usually the easy way out of any temporary difficulties for both government and private business—the path of least resistance and sometimes also the easiest way to help the economy get over all the obstacles that government policy has placed in its way.[12] It is the inevitable result of a policy which regards all the other decisions as data to which the supply of money must be adapted so that the damage done by other measures will be as little noticed as possible. In the long run, however, such a policy makes governments the captives of their own earlier decisions, which often force them to adopt measures that they know to be harmful. It is no accident that the author whose views, perhaps mistakenly interpreted, have given more encouragement to these inflationary propensities than any other man's is also responsible for the fundamentally antiliberal aphorism, "in the long run we are all dead."[13] The inflationary bias of our day is largely the result of the prevalence of the short-term view, which in turn stems from the great difficulty of recognizing the more remote consequences of current measures, and from the inevitable preoccupation of practical men, and particularly politicians, with the immediate problems and the achievement of near goals.

Because inflation is psychologically and politically so much more difficult to prevent than deflation and because it is, at the same time, technically so much more easily prevented, the economist should always stress the dangers of inflation. As soon as deflation makes itself felt, there will be immediate attempts to combat it—often when it is only a local and necessary process that should not be prevented. There is more danger in untimely fears of deflation than in the possibility of our not taking necessary countermeasures. While nobody is likely to mistake local or sectional prosperity for inflation, people often demand wholly inappropriate monetary countermeasures when there is a local or sectional depression.

These considerations would seem to suggest that, on balance, probably some mechanical rule which aims at what is desirable in the long run and ties

[12] Cf. my essay, "Full Employment, Planning, and Inflation," *Review of the Institute of Public Affairs* (Melbourne, Australia), 4 (1950): 174–84; reprinted in *Studies in Philosophy, Politics and Economics* (Chicago: University of Chicago Press, 1967), pp. 270–79; the German version of this essay, ["Vollbeschäftigung, Planwirtschaft und Inflation"] appears in *Vollbeschäftigung, Inflation und Planwirtschaft* [Schweizerisches Institut für Auslandforschung], Albert Hunold, ed. (Erlenbach-Zurich: Eugen Rentsch Verlag, 1951), pp. 184–97; and Friedrich August Lutz, "Inflationsgefahr und Konjunkturpolitik," *Schweizerische Zeitschrift für Volkswirtschaft und Statistik / Revue suisse d'économie politique*, 93 (1957): 195–205, and "Cost- and Demand-Induced Inflation," *Banca Nazionale del Lavoro Quarterly Review*, 11 (1958): 3–18.

[13] John Maynard Keynes, *A Tract on Monetary Reform* (London: Macmillan, 1923), p. 80.

the hands of authority in its short-term decisions is likely to produce a better monetary policy than principles which give to the authorities more power and discretion and thereby make them more subject to both political pressure and their own inclination to overestimate the urgency of the circumstances of the moment. This, however, raises issues which we must approach more systematically.

4. The case for "rules versus authorities in monetary policy" has been persuasively argued by the late Henry Simons in a well-known essay.[14] The arguments advanced there in favor of strict rules are so strong that the issue is now largely on of how far it is practically possible to tie down monetary authority by appropriate rules. It may still be true that if there were full agreement as to what monetary policy ought to aim for, an independent monetary authority, fully protected against political pressure and free to decide on the means to be employed in order to achieve the ends it has been assigned, might be the best arrangement. The old arguments in favor of independent central banks still have great merit. But the fact that the responsibility for monetary policy today inevitably rests in part with agencies whose main concern is with government finance probably strengthens the case against allowing much discretion and for making decisions on monetary policy as predictable as possible.

It should perhaps be explicitly stated that the case against discretion in monetary policy is not quite the same as that against discretion in the use of the coercive powers of government. Even if the control of money is in the hands of a monopoly, its exercise does not necessarily involve coercion of private individuals.[15] The argument against discretion in monetary policy rests on the view that monetary policy and its effects should be as predictable as possible. The validity of the argument depends, therefore, on whether we can devise an automatic mechanism which will make the effective supply of money change in a more predictable and less disturbing manner than will any discretionary measures likely to be adopted. The answer is not certain. No automatic mechanism is known which will make the total supply of money adapt itself exactly as we would wish, and the most we can say in favor of any mechanism (or action determined by rigid rules) is that it is doubtful whether in practice any deliberate control would do better. The reason for this doubt is partly that the conditions in which monetary authorities have to make their decisions are usually not favorable to the prevailing of long views, partly that we are not too certain what they should do in particular circumstances and

[14] Henry Calvert Simons's essay of that title, originally published in "Rules versus Authorities in Monetary Policy," *Journal of Political Economy*, 44 (1936): 1–30; reprinted in Henry Calvert Simons, *Economic Policy for a Free Society* (Chicago: University of Chicago Press, 1948), pp. 160–83.

[15] This applies at least to the traditional instruments of monetary policy though not to such newer measures as the changes in the required reserves of the banks.

that, therefore, uncertainty about what they will do is necessarily greater when they do not act according to fixed rules.

The problem has remained acute ever since the destruction of the gold standard by the policies of the 1920s and1930s.[16] It is only natural that some people should regard a return to that tried system as the only real solution. And an even larger number would probably agree today that the defects of the gold standard have been greatly exaggerated and that it is doubtful whether its abandonment was a gain. This does not mean, however, that its restoration is at present a practical proposition.

It must be remembered, in the first place, that no single country could effectively restore it by independent action. Its operation rested on its being an international standard, and if, for example, the United States today returned to gold, it would chiefly mean that United States policy would determine the value of gold and not necessarily that gold would determine the value of the dollar.

Second, and no less important, the functioning of the international gold standard rested on certain attitudes and beliefs which have probably ceased to exist. It operated largely on the basis of the general opinion that to be driven off the gold standard was a major calamity and a national disgrace. It is not likely to have much influence even as a fair-weather standard when it is known that no country is prepared to take painful measures in order to preserve it. I may be mistaken in my belief that this *mystique* of gold has disappeared for good, but, until I see more evidence to the contrary, I do not believe that an attempt to restore the gold standard can be more than temporarily successful.[17]

---

[16] The fatal errors begin with the British attempt after the first World War to restore the pound to its former value rather than to relink it with gold at a new parity corresponding to its reduced value. Besides the fact that this was not required by the principles of the gold standard, it was contrary to the best classical teaching. David Ricardo had explicitly said of a similar situation one hundred years earlier that he "never should advise a government to restore a currency, which was depreciated 30 pct., to par; I should recommend, as you propose, but not in the same manner, that the currency should be fixed at the depreciated value by lowering the standard, and that no further deviations should take place" (David Ricardo, letter to John Wheatley, September 18, 1821, *The Works and Correspondence of David Ricardo*, Piero Sraffa, ed. (11 vols.; Cambridge: Cambridge University Press, 1951), vol. 9, p. 73 [Liberty Fund edition, vol. 9 (*Letters 1821–1823*), p. 73].

[17] There is, of course, a strong case for completely freeing the trade in gold. Indeed, it would seem desirable to go considerably further in this direction; probably nothing would contribute more to international monetary stability than the different countries mutually binding themselves by treaty to place no obstacles whatever in the way of free dealing in one another's currencies. (There would probably also be a strong case for going still further and permitting their respective banks to operate freely in their territories.) But, though this would go far in the direction of restoring a stable international standard, the control of the value of this standard would still be in the hands of the authorities of the biggest countries participating in it.

The case for the gold standard is closely connected with the general argument in favor of an international, as against a national standard. Within the limitations we have accepted here, we cannot pursue this problem further. We will merely add that if a standard is desired which is highly automatic and can at the same time be made international, a commodity reserve standard which has been worked out in some detail appears to me still the best plan for achieving all the advantages attributed to the gold standard without its defects.[18] But, though the proposals for such a standard deserve more attention than they have received, they hardly offer a practical alternative for the near future. Even if there were a chance of such a scheme being immediately adopted, there would be very little prospect of its being run as it should be, i.e., for the purpose of stabilizing only the aggregate price of the large group of commodities selected and not the prices of any of the individual commodities included.

5. I certainly have no wish to weaken the case for any arrangement that will force the authorities to do the right thing. The case for such a mechanism becomes stronger as the likelihood of the monetary policy's being affected by considerations of public finance becomes greater; but it would weaken, rather than strengthen, the argument if we exaggerated what can be achieved by it. It is probably undeniable that, though we can limit discretion in this field, we never can eliminate it; in consequence, what can be done within the unavoidable range of discretion not only is very important but is likely in practice to determine even whether or not the mechanism will ever be allowed to operate.

There is one basic dilemma, which all central banks face, which makes it inevitable that their policy must involve much discretion. A central bank can exercise only an indirect and therefore limited control over all the circulating media. Its power is based chiefly on the threat of not supplying cash when it is needed. Yet at the same time it is considered to be its duty never to refuse to supply this cash at a price when needed. It is this problem, rather than the general effects of policy on prices or the value of money, that necessarily preoccupies the central banker in his day-to-day actions. It is a task which makes it necessary for the central bank constantly to forestall or counteract developments in the realm of credit, for which no simple rules can provide sufficient guidance.[19]

The same is nearly as true of the measures intended to affect prices and employment. They must be directed more at forestalling changes before they

---

[18] Cf. my essay on "A Commodity Reserve Currency," *Economic Journal*, 53 (1943): 176–84; reprinted in Friedrich August Hayek, *Individualism and Economic Order*, pp. 209–19.[*Collected Works* edition, vol. 6, pp. 106–14.]

[19] See my essay *Monetary Nationalism and International Stability*, (London: Longmans, Green, and Co., 1937). [*Collected Works* edition, vol. 6, pp. 37–105.]

occur than at correcting them after they have occurred. If a central bank always waited until rule or mechanism forced it to take action, the resulting fluctuations would be much greater than they need be. And if, within the range of its discretion, it takes measures in a direction opposite to those which mechanism or rule will later impose upon it, it will probably create a situation in which the mechanism will not long be allowed to operate. In the last resort, therefore, even where the discretion of the authority is greatly restricted, the outcome is likely to depend on what the authority does within the limits of its discretion.

This means in practice that under present conditions we have little choice but to limit monetary policy by prescribing its goals rather than its specific actions. The concrete issue today is whether it ought to keep stable some level of employment or some level of prices. Reasonably interpreted and with due allowance made for the inevitability of minor fluctuations around a given level, these two aims are not necessarily in conflict, provided that the requirements for monetary stability are given first place and the rest of economic policy is adapted to them. A conflict arises, however, if "full employment" is made the chief objective and this is interpreted, as it sometimes is, as that maximum of employment which can be produced by monetary means in the short run. That way lies progressive inflation.

The reasonable goal of a high and stable level of employment can probably be secured as well as we know how while aiming at the stability of some comprehensive price level. For practical purposes, it probably does not greatly matter precisely how this price level is defined, except that it should not refer exclusively to final products (for if it did, it might in times of rapid technological advance still produce a significant inflationary tendency) and that it should be based as much as possible on international rather than local prices. Such a policy, if pursued simultaneously by two or three of the major countries, should also be reconcilable with stability of exchange rates. The important point is that there will be definite known limits which the monetary authorities will not allow price movements to exceed—or even to approach to the point of making drastic reversals of policy necessary.

6. Though there may be some people who explicitly advocate continuous inflation, it is certainly not because the majority wants it that we are likely to get it. Few people would be willing to accept it when it is pointed out that even such a seemingly moderate increase in prices as 3 per cent per annum means that the price level will double every twenty-three and a half years and that it will nearly quadruple over the normal span of a man's working life. The danger that inflation will continue is not so much due to the strength of those who deliberately advocate it as to the weakness of the opposition. In order to prevent it, it is necessary for the public to become clearly aware of the things we can do and of the consequences of not doing them. Most competent students agree that the difficulty of preventing inflation is only political and not eco-

nomic. Yet almost no one seems to believe that the monetary authorities have the power to prevent it and will exercise it. The greatest optimism about the short-term miracles that monetary policy will achieve is accompanied by a complete fatalism about what it will produce in the long run.

There are two points which cannot be stressed enough: first, it seems certain that we shall not stop the drift toward more and more state control unless we stop the inflationary trend; and, second, any continued rise in prices is dangerous because, once we begin to rely on its stimulating effect, we shall be committed to a course that will leave us no choice but that between more inflation, on the one hand, and paying for our mistake by a recession or depression, on the other. Even a very moderate degree of inflation is dangerous because it ties the hands of those responsible for policy by creating a situation in which, every time a problem arises, a little more inflation seems the only easy way out.

We have not had space to touch on the various ways in which the efforts of individuals to protect themselves against inflation, such as sliding-scale contracts, not only tend to make the process self-accelerating but also increase the rate of inflation necessary to maintain its stimulating effect. Let us simply note, then, that inflation makes it more and more impossible for people of moderate means to provide for their old age themselves; that it discourages saving and encourages running into debt; and that, by destroying the middle class, it creates that dangerous gap between the completely propertyless and the wealthy that is so characteristic of societies which have gone through prolonged inflations and which is the source of so much tension in those societies. Perhaps even more ominous is the wider psychological effect, the spreading among the population at large of that disregard of long-range views and exclusive concern with immediate advantages which already dominate public policy.

It is no accident that inflationary policies are generally advocated by those who want more government control—though, unfortunately, not by them alone. The increased dependence of the individual upon government which inflation produces and the demand for more government action to which this leads may for the socialist be an argument in its favor. Those who wish to preserve freedom should recognize, however, that inflation is probably the most important single factor in that vicious circle wherein one kind of government action makes more and more government control necessary. For this reason, all those who wish to stop the drift toward increasing government control should concentrate their efforts on monetary policy. There is perhaps nothing more disheartening than the fact that there are still so many intelligent and informed people who in most other respects will defend freedom and yet are induced by the immediate benefits of an expansionist policy to support what, in the long run, must destroy the foundations of a free society.

TWENTY-TWO

HOUSING AND TOWN PLANNING

If the government simultaneously abolished housing subsidies and cut working class taxation by an amount exactly equal to the subsidies the working classes would be no worse off financially; but they would then without any doubt prefer to spend the money in other ways than on housing, and would live in overcrowded and inadequately provided houses, some because they do not know the advantages of better housing, and others because they value these too lightly in comparison with other ways of spending their money. That is the case, and the only case for housing subsidies, and it is put here in its crudest form because the matter is so often discussed in left wing literature without facing reality. —William Arthur Lewis

1. Civilization as we know it is inseparable from urban life. Almost all that distinguishes civilized from primitive society is intimately connected with the large agglomerations of population that we call "cities," and when we speak of "urbanity," "civility," or "politeness," we refer to the manner of life in cities. Even most of the differences between the life of the present rural population and that of primitive people are due to what the cities provide. It is also the possibility of enjoying the products of the city in the country that in advanced civilizations often makes a leisured life in the country appear the ideal of a cultured life.

Yet the advantages of city life, particularly the enormous increases in productivity made possible by its industry, which equips a small part of the population remaining in the country to feed all the rest, are bought at great cost. City life is not only more productive than rural life; it is also much more costly. Only those whose productivity is much increased by life in the city will reap a net advantage over and above the extra cost of this kind of life. Both the costs and the kinds of amenities which come with city life are such that the minimum income at which a decent life is possible is much higher than in the country. Life at a level of poverty which is still bearable in the country not

The quotation at the head of the chapter is taken from Sir William Arthur Lewis, *The Principles of Economic Planning: A Study Prepared for the Fabian Society* (London: D. Dobson, 1949), p. 32.

only is scarcely tolerable in the city but produces outward signs of squalor which are shocking to fellow men. Thus the city, which is the source of nearly all that gives civilization its value and which has provided the means for the pursuit of science and art as well as of material comfort, is at the same time responsible for the darkest blotches on this civilization.

Moreover, the costs involved in large numbers living in great density not only are very high but are also to a large extent communal, i.e., they do not necessarily or automatically fall on those who cause them but may have to be borne by all. In many respects, the close contiguity of city life invalidates the assumptions underlying any simple division of property rights. In such conditions it is true only to a limited extent that whatever an owner does with his property will affect only him and nobody else. What economists call the "neighborhood effects," i.e., the effects of what one does to one's property on that of others, assume major importance. The usefulness of almost any piece of property in a city will in fact depend in part on what one's immediate neighbors do and in part on the communal services without which effective use of the land by separate owners would be nearly impossible.

The general formulas of private property or freedom of contract do not therefore provide an immediate answer to the complex problems which city life raises. It is probable that, even if there had been no authority with coercive powers, the superior advantages of larger units would have led to the development of new legal institutions—some division of the right of control between the holders of a superior right to determine the character of a large district to be developed and the owners of inferior rights to the use of smaller units, who, within the framework determined by the former, would be free to decide on particular issues. In many respects the functions which the organized municipal corporations are learning to exercise correspond to those of such a superior owner.

It must be admitted that, until recently, economists gave regrettably little attention to the problems of the co-ordination of all the different aspects of city development.[1] Though some of them have been among the foremost critics of the evils of urban housing (some fifty years ago a satirical Ger-

---

[1] A valuable attempt to remedy this position has recently been made in Ralph Turvey, *Economics of Real Property: An Analysis of Property Values and Patterns of Use* (London: Allen and Unwin Ltd., 1957). Of earlier works the discussions of local taxation by Edwin Cannan, *History of Local Rates in England, in Relation to the Proper Distribution of the Burden of Taxation* (2nd ed., much enl.; London: P. S. King and Son, 1912), and his "Memorandum," in Royal Commission on Local Taxation, *Memoranda Chiefly Relating to the Classification and Incidence of Imperial and Local Taxes* [Alexander Hugh Bruce Balfour, Baron Balfour, Chairman] (London: Her Majesty's Stationery Office, 1899) [Cmd. 9528], pp. 160–75, are still among the most helpful on the crucial issues. [See also Cannan's *Answers to the Questions Submitted to Him by the Royal Commission on Local Taxation* (London, 1898).—Ed.] See also Jane Jacobs, *The Death and Life of the Great American Cities* (New York: Random House, 1961).

man weekly could suggest that an economist be defined as a man who went around measuring workmen's dwellings, saying they were too small!) so far as the important issues of urban life are concerned, they have long followed the example of Adam Smith, who explained in his lectures that the problem of cleanliness and security, "to wit, the proper method of carrying dirt from the streets, and the execution of justice, so far as it regards regulations for preventing crimes or the method of keeping a city guard, though useful, are too mean to be considered in a general discourse of this kind."[2]

In view of this neglect by his profession of the study of a highly important subject, an economist perhaps ought not to complain that it is in a very unsatisfactory state. Development of opinion in this field has, in fact, been led almost exclusively by men concerned with the abolition of particular evils, and the central question of how the separate efforts are to be mutually adjusted has been much neglected. Yet the problem of how the effective utilization of the knowledge and skill of the individual owners is to be reconciled with keeping their actions within limits where they will not gain at somebody else's expense is here of peculiar importance. We must not overlook the fact that the market has, on the whole, guided the evolution of cities more successfully, though imperfectly, than is commonly realized and that most of the proposals to improve upon this, not by making it work better, but by superimposing a system of central direction, show little awareness of what such a system would have to accomplish, even to equal the market in effectiveness.

Indeed, when we look at the haphazard manner in which governments, with seemingly no clear conception of the forces that determined the development of cities, have generally dealt with these difficult problems, we wonder that the evils are not greater than they are. Many of the policies intended to combat particular evils have actually made them worse. And some of the more recent developments have created greater potentialities for a direct control by authority of the private life of the individual than may be seen in any other field of policy.

2. We must first consider a measure which, though always introduced as a device to meet a passing emergency and never defended as a permanent arrangement, has in fact regularly become a lasting feature and in much of western Europe has probably done more to restrict freedom and prosperity than any other measure, excepting only inflation. This is rent restriction or the placing of ceilings on the rents of dwellings. Originally introduced to prevent rents from rising during the first World War, it was retained in many countries for more than forty years through major inflations, with the result

---

[2] Adam Smith, *Lectures on Justice, Police, Revenue, and Arms: Delivered in the University of Glasgow* (delivered in 1763–64) Edwin Cannan, ed. (Oxford: Clarendon Press, 1896), p. 154 [Liberty Fund edition, *Lectures on Jurisprudence*, p. 486].

that rents were reduced to a fraction of what they would be in a free market. Thus house property was in effect expropriated. Probably more than any other measure of this kind, it worsened in the long run the evil it was meant to cure and produced a situation in which administrative authorities acquired highly arbitrary powers over the movement of men. It also contributed much toward weakening the respect for property and the sense of individual responsibility. To those who have not experienced its effects over a long period, these remarks may seem unduly strong. But whoever has seen the progressive decay of housing conditions and the effects on the general manner of life of the people of Paris, of Vienna, or even of London, will appreciate the deadly effect that this one measure can have on the whole character of an economy—and even of a people.

In the first place, any fixing of rents below the market price inevitably perpetuates the housing shortage. Demand continues to exceed supply, and, if ceilings are effectively enforced (i.e., the appearance of "premiums" prevented), a mechanism for allocating dwelling space by authority must be established. Mobility is greatly reduced and in the course of time the distribution of people between districts and types of dwellings ceases to correspond to needs or desires. The normal rotation, in which a family during the period of full earning power of the head occupies more space than a very young or retired couple, is suspended. Since people cannot be ordered to move around, they just hold on to what they have, and the rented premises become a sort of inalienable property of the family which is handed down from generation to generation, irrespective of need. Those who have inherited a rented dwelling are often better off than they would be otherwise, but an ever increasing proportion of the population either cannot get a separate dwelling at all or can do so only by grace of official favor or by a sacrifice of capital they can ill afford or by some illegal or devious means.[3]

At the same time, the owner loses all interest in investing in the maintenance of buildings beyond what the law allows him to recover from the ten-

[3] Cf. Milton Friedman and George Joseph Stigler, *Roofs or Ceilings? The Current Housing Problem* (New York: Foundation for Economic Education, 1946); Bertrand de Jouvenel, *No Vacancies* (New York: Foundation for Economic Education, 1948); Sir Roy Forbes Harrod, *Are These Hardships Necessary?* (London: Rupert Hart-Davis, 1947); Frank Walter Paish, "The Economics of Rent Restriction," *Lloyds Bank Review*, n.s., 14 (April 1950): 1–17, reprinted in Frank Walter Paish, *The Post-War Financial Problem, and Other Essays* (London: Macmillan, 1950), pp. 74–93; Wilhelm Röpke, *Wohnungszwangswirtschaft—ein europäisches Problem* (Düsseldorf: Deutsche Wohnungswirtschaft, 1951); Alfred Amonn, "Normalisierung der Wohnungswirtschaft in grundsätzlicher Sicht," *Schweizer Monatshefte*, 33 (June 1953): 129–138; and my own earlier essays, *Das Mieterschutzproblem: nationalökonomische Betrachtungen* [The Rent-Control Problem: Political-Economic Considerations] (Vienna: Steyrermühl Verlag, 1929) and "Wirkungen der Mietzinsbeschränkungen" [The Repercussions of Rent Restrictions], *Schriften des Vereins für Sozialpolitik*, 182 (Leipzig: Duncker und Humblot, 1930), pp. 253–70.

ants for that specific purpose. In cities like Paris, where inflation has reduced the real value of rents to a twentieth or less of what they once were, the rate at which houses are falling into an unprecedented state of decay is such that their replacement will be impracticable for decades to come.

It is not the material damage, however, that is the most important. Because of rent restriction, large sections of the population in Western countries have become subject to arbitrary decisions of authority in their daily affairs and accustomed to looking for permission and direction in the main decisions of their lives. They have come to regard it as a matter of course that the capital which pays for the roof over their heads should be provided free by somebody else and that individual economic well-being should depend on the favor of the political party in power, which often uses its control over housing to assist its supporters.

What has done so much to undermine the respect for property and for the law and the courts is the fact that authority is constantly called upon to decide on the relative merits of needs, to allocate essential services, and to dispose of what is still nominally private property according to its judgment of the urgency of different individual needs. For example, whether "an owner, with an invalid wife and three young children, who wishes to obtain occupation of his house [would] suffer more hardship if his request were refused than the tenant, with only one child but a bed-ridden mother-in-law, would suffer if it were granted"[4] is a problem that cannot be settled by appeal to any recognized principles of justice but only by the arbitrary intervention of authority. How great a power this sort of control over the most important decisions of one's private life confers on authority is clearly shown by a recent decision of the German Administrative Court of Appeal, which found it necessary to declare as illegal the refusal of a local government labor exchange to find work for a man living in a different area unless he first obtained from the housing authority permission to move and promise of accommodation—not because neither authority was entitled to refuse his request but because their refusal involved an "inadmissible coupling of separate interests of administration."[5] Indeed, the co-ordination of the activities of different authorities, which the planners

---

[4] The illustration is given by Frank Walter Paish in his essay, "The Economics of Rent Restriction," p. 4; reprinted in *The Post-War Financial Problem, and Other Essays*, pp. 77–78.

[5] Ernst Forsthoff, *Lehrbuch des Verwaltungsrechts*. Vol. 1: *Allgemeiner Teil* (Munich: C. H. Beck, 1950), p. 222. [The citation to which Hayek refers reads: "Mit anderen Worten: die Verwaltungsbehörde darf die Erledigung ihrer Obliegenheiten nicht mit den Interessen oder Ansprüchen anderer Behörden oder mit der Erledigung anderer Verwaltungszwecke verkuppeln, sofern nicht eine Verbindung in der Sache selbst gegeben ist." ("In other words, the administrative authority may not couple the execution of its responsibilities with the interests or demands of other authorities or with the pursuit of other administrative goals, unless such a coupling follows from the matter itself.")—Ed.]

so dearly want, is liable to turn what otherwise is merely arbitrariness in particular decisions into despotic power over the whole life of the individual.

3. While rent restriction, even where it has been in force as far back as most people can remember, is still regarded as an emergency measure which has become politically impossible to abandon,[6] efforts to reduce the cost of housing for the poorer sections of the population by public housing or building subsidies have come to be accepted as a permanent part of the welfare state. It is little understood that, unless very carefully limited in scope and method, such efforts are likely to produce results very similar to those of rent restriction.

The first point to note is that any group of people whom the government attempts to assist through a public supply of housing will benefit only if the government undertakes to supply all the new housing they will get. Provision of only part of the supply of dwellings by authority will in effect be not an addition to, but merely a replacement of, what has been provided by private building activity. Second, cheaper housing provided by government will have to be strictly limited to the class it is intended to help, and, merely to satisfy the demand at the lower rents, government will have to supply considerably more housing than that class would otherwise occupy. Third, such limitation of public housing to the poorest families will generally be practicable only if the government does not attempt to supply dwellings which are both cheaper and substantially better than they had before; otherwise the people thus assisted would be better housed than those immediately above them on the economic ladder; and pressure from the latter to be included in the scheme would become irresistible, a process which would repeat itself and progressively bring in more and more people.

A consequence of this is that, as has again and again been emphasized by the housing reformers, any far-reaching change in housing conditions by public action will be achieved only if practically the whole of the housing of a city is regarded as a public service and paid for out of public funds. This means, however, not only that people in general will be forced to spend more on housing than they are willing to do, but that their personal liberty will be gravely threatened. Unless the authority succeeds in supplying as much of this better and cheaper housing as will be demanded at the rents charged,

---

[6] Only recently have determined, systematic efforts been made in both Great Britain and Germany to abolish the whole system of rent controls. Even in the United States they still exist in New York City. [In 1969 New York City enacted a rent stabilization law to replace the older rent control law. As rent controlled apartments in New York City become vacant, they normally become subject to rent stabilization, which limits the rate of rent increases and stipulates the grounds on which a landlord may evict a tenant, including the manner of eviction. Allowable rent increases are determined by a Rent Guidelines Board. In 1993, high-rent units were decontrolled.—Ed.]

a permanent system of allocating the available facilities by authority will be necessary—that is, a system whereby authority determines how much people should spend on housing and what sort of accommodation each family or individual ought to get. It is easy to see what powers over individual life authority would possess if the obtaining of an apartment or house were generally dependent on its decision.

It should also be realized that the endeavor to make housing a public service has already in many instances become the chief obstacle to the general improvement of housing conditions, by counteracting those forces which produce a gradual lowering of the cost of building. All monopolists are notoriously uneconomical, and the bureaucratic machinery of government even more so; and the suspension of the mechanism of competition and the tendency of any centrally directed development to ossify are bound to obstruct the attainment of the desirable and technically not impossible goal—a substantial and progressive reduction of the costs at which all the housing needs can be met.

Public housing (and subsidized housing) can thus, at best, be an instrument of assisting the poor, with the inevitable consequence that it will make those who take advantage of it dependent on authority to a degree that would be politically very serious if they constituted a large part of the population. Like any assistance to an unfortunate minority, such a measure is not irreconcilable with a general system of freedom. But it raises very grave problems that should be squarely faced if it is not to produce dangerous consequences.

4. The greater earning power and other advantages that city life offers are to a considerable degree offset by its higher costs, which generally increase with the size of the city. Those whose productivity is greatly increased by working in the city will derive a net advantage, even though they have to pay much more for their limited dwelling space and may also have to pay for daily transportation over long distances. Others will gain a net advantage only if they do not have to spend money on travel or expensive quarters or if they do not mind living in crowded conditions so long as they have more to spend on other things. The old buildings which at most stages of the growth of a city will exist in its center, on land which is already in such great demand for other purposes that it is no longer profitable to build new dwellings on it, and which are no longer wanted by the better-off, will often provide for those of low productivity an opportunity to benefit from what the city offers at the price of very congested living. So long as they are prepared to live in them, to leave these old houses standing will often be the most profitable way of using the land. Thus, paradoxically, the poorest inhabitants of a city frequently live in districts where the value of the land is very high and the landlords draw very large incomes from what is likely to be the most dilapidated part of the city. In such a situation property of this sort continues to be available for housing

only because the old buildings, with little spent on them for repair or maintenance, are occupied at great density. If they were not available or could not be
used in this manner, the opportunities for increasing their earnings by more
than the additional costs of living in the city would not exist for most of the
people who live there.

The existence of such slums, which in a more or less aggravated form
appear during the growth of most cities, raises two sets of problems which
ought to be distinguished but are commonly confused. It is unquestionably
true that the presence of such unsanitary quarters, with their generally squalid
and often lawless conditions, may have a deleterious effect on the rest of the
city and will force the city administration or the other inhabitants to bear costs
which those who come to live in the slums do not take into account. Insofar as
it is true that the slum dwellers find it to their advantage to live in the center
of the city only because they do not pay for all the costs caused by their decision, there is a case for altering the situation by charging the slum properties with all these costs—with the probable result that they will disappear and
be replaced by buildings for commercial or industrial purposes. This would
clearly not assist the slum dwellers. The case for action here is not based on
their interest; the problems are raised by "neighborhood effects" and belong
to the questions of city planning, which we shall have to consider later.

Quite different from this are the arguments for slum clearance based on the
presumed interests or needs of slum dwellers. These pose a genuine dilemma.
It is often only because people live in crowded old buildings that they are able
to derive some gain from the extra earning opportunities of the city. If we
want to abolish the slums, we must choose one of two alternatives: we must
either prevent these people from taking advantage of what to them is part of
their opportunity, by removing the cheap but squalid dwellings from where
their earning opportunities lie, and effectively squeeze them out of the cities
by insisting on certain minimum standards for all town dwellings;[7] or we must
provide them with better facilities at a price which does not cover costs and
thus subsidize both their staying in the city and the movement into the city of
more people of the same kind. This amounts to a stimulation of the growth
of cities beyond the point where it is economically justifiable and to a deliberate creation of a class dependent on the community for the provision of what
they are presumed to need. We can hardly expect this service to be provided
for long without the authorities also claiming the right to decide who is and
who is not to be allowed to move into a given city.

As happens in many fields, the policies pursued here aim at providing for a
given number of people without taking into account the additional numbers

---

[7] This possibility has not infrequently been used in various parts of the world to drive out
unpopular racial minorities.

that will have to be provided for as a result. It is true that a part of the slum population of most cities consists of old inhabitants who know only city life and who would be even less able to earn an adequate living in rural conditions. But the more acute problem is that raised by the influx of large numbers from poorer and still predominantly rural regions, to whom the cheap accommodation in the old and decaying buildings of the city offers a foothold on the ladder that may lead to greater prosperity. They find it to their advantage to move into the city in spite of the crowded and unsanitary conditions in which they have to live. Providing them with much better quarters at an equally low cost will attract a great many more. The solution of the problem would be either to let the economic deterrents act or to control directly the influx of population; those who believe in liberty will regard the former as the lesser evil.

The housing problem is not an independent problem which can be solved in isolation: it is part of the general problem of poverty and can be solved only by a general rise in incomes. This solution, however, will be delayed if we subsidize people to move from where their productivity is still greater than the cost of living to places where it will be less, or if we prevent from moving those who believe that, by doing so, they can improve their prospects at the price of living in conditions which to us seem deplorable.

There is no space here to consider all the other municipal measures which, though designed to relieve the needs of a given population, really tend to subsidize the growth of giant cities beyond the economically justifiable point. Most of the policies concerning public utility rates which are immediately aimed at relieving congestion and furthering the growth of the outlying districts by providing services below costs only make matters worse in the long run. What has been said of current housing policies in England is equally true about most other countries: "We have drifted into a practice of encouraging financially, out of taxes collected from the whole nation, the maintenance of over-grown and over-concentrated urban fabrics and, in the case of large cities still growing, the continuance of fundamentally uneconomic growth."[8]

5. A different set of problems is raised by the fact that in the close contiguity of city living the price mechanism reflects only imperfectly the benefit or harm to others that a property owner may cause by his actions. Unlike the situation which generally prevails with mobile property, where the advantages or disadvantages arising from its use are usually confined to those who control it, the use made of a piece of land often necessarily affects the usefulness of neighboring pieces. Under the conditions of city life this applies to the actions of private owners and even more to the use made of communally owned land, such as that used for streets and the public amenities which are

---

[8] Sir Frederick Osborn, "How Subsidies Distort Housing Development," *Lloyds Bank Review*, n.s., 36 (April 1955): 36.

so essential to city life. In order that the market may bring about an efficient co-ordination of individual endeavors, both the individual owners and the authorities controlling communal property should be so placed as to enable them to take into account at least the more important effects of their actions on other property. Only when the value of the property of individuals as well as of the city authorities reflects all the effects of the use they make of it, will the price mechanism function as it should. Without special arrangements, this condition will exist only to a limited degree. The value of any piece of property will be affected by the manner in which the neighbors use theirs and even more by the services provided and the regulations enforced by the authorities; and unless the various decisions take these effects into account, there is little likelihood that total benefits will exceed total costs.[9]

But though the price mechanism is an imperfect guide for the use of urban land, it is still an indispensable guide if development is to be left to private initiative and if all the knowledge and foresight dispersed among many men is to be used. There is a strong case for taking whatever practical measures can be found to cause the mechanism to operate more efficiently by making owners take into consideration all the possible effects of their decisions. The framework of rules within which the decisions of the private owner are likely to agree with the public interest will therefore in this case have to be more detailed and more adjusted to particular local circumstances than is necessary with other kinds of property. Such "town planning," which operates largely through its effects on the market and through the establishing of general conditions to which all developments of a district or neighborhood must conform but which, within these conditions, leaves the decisions to the individual owner, is part of the effort to make the market mechanism more effective.

There is a very different type of control, however, which is also practiced under the name of "town planning." Unlike the other, this is motivated by the desire to dispense with the price mechanism and to replace it by central direction. Much of the town planning that is in fact carried out, particularly by architects and engineers who have never understood the role that prices play in co-ordinating individual activities,[10] is of this kind. Even where it is not aimed at tying future developments to a preconceived plan which prescribes

[9] On these problems see Ralph Turvey, *Economics of Real Property*, and Allison Dunham, "City Planning: An Analysis of the Content of the Master Plan," *Journal of Law and Economics*, 1 (1958): 170–86.

[10] The extent to which the movement for town planning, under the leadership of such men as Frederick Law Olmsted, Patrick Geddes, and Lewis Mumford, has developed into a sort of anti-economics would make an interesting study. [Frederick Law Olmsted, Jr. (1870–1957), the son of America's greatest landscape architect and a founder of the American town planning movement; Patrick Geddes (1854–1932), Scottish biologist and an outspoken adherent of urban planning; Lewis Mumford (1895–1990), social critic who developed a theory that urban sprawl, the undirected and uncontrolled growth of cities, was responsible for most modern social ills.—Ed.]

the use of every piece of land, it tends to lead to this by making the market mechanism increasingly inoperative.

The issue is therefore not whether one ought or ought not to be for town planning but whether the measures to be used are to supplement and assist the market or to suspend it and put central direction in its place. The practical problems which policy raises here are of great complexity, and no perfect solution is to be expected. The beneficial character of any measures will show itself in contributing to a desirable development, the details of which, however, will be largely unpredictable.

The main practical difficulties arise from the fact that most measures of town planning will enhance the value of some individual properties and reduce that of others. If they are to be beneficial, the sum of the gains must exceed the sum of the losses. If an effective offsetting is to be achieved, it is necessary that both gains and losses due to a measure accrue to the planning authority, who must be able to accept the responsibility of charging the individual owners for the increase in the value of their property (even if the measures causing it have been taken against the will of some of the owners) and of compensating those whose property has suffered. This can be achieved without conferring on authority arbitrary and uncontrollable powers by giving it only the right of expropriation at fair market value. This is generally sufficient to enable the authority both to capture any increments in value that its actions will cause and to buy out those who oppose the measure because it reduces the value of their property. In practice, the authority will normally not have to buy, but, backed by its power of compulsory purchase, it will be able to negotiate an agreed charge or compensation with the owner. So long as expropriation at market value is its only coercive power, all legitimate interests will be protected. It will be a somewhat imperfect instrument, of course, since in such circumstances "market value" is not an unambiguous magnitude and opinions about what is a fair market value may vary widely. The important point, however, is that such disputes can be decided in the last resort by independent courts and need not be left to the discretion of the planning authority.

The dangers come largely from the desire of many planners to be released from the necessity of counting all the costs of their schemes. They often plead that if they are made to compensate at market value, the cost of carrying out some improvements becomes prohibitive. Wherever this is the case, it means, however, that the proposed plan should not be carried out. Nothing ought to be treated with more suspicion than arguments used by town planners to justify expropriation below fair market value, arguments regularly based on the false contention that they can thereby reduce the social costs of the scheme. All that such a scheme amounts to is that certain costs will not be taken into account: the planners make it appear advantageous simply by placing some of the costs on the shoulders of private persons and then disregarding them.

Most of what is valid in the argument for town planning is, in effect, an argument for making the planning unit for some purposes larger than the usual size of individually owned property. Some of the aims of planning could be achieved by a division of the contents of the property rights in such a way that certain decisions would rest with the holder of the superior right, i.e., with some corporation representing the whole district or region and possessing powers to assess benefits and charges to individual subowners. Estate development in which the developer retains some permanent control over the use of the individual plots offers at least one alternative to the exercise of such control by political authority. There is also the advantage that the larger planning unit will still be one of many and that it will be restrained in the exercise of its powers by the necessity of competing with other similar units.

To some extent, of course, even competition between municipalities or other political subdivisions will have a similar restraining effect. Town planners, however, frequently demand town planning on a regional or even national scale. It is true that there will always be some factors in planning which only the larger units can consider. But it is still more true that, as the area of unified planning is extended, particular knowledge of local circumstances will, of necessity, be less effectively used. Nation-wide planning means that, instead of the unit of competition becoming larger, competition will be eliminated altogether. This is certainly not a desirable solution. There is probably no perfect answer to the real difficulties which the complexity of the problem creates. But only a method which operates mainly through the inducements and data offered to the private owner and which leaves him free in the use of a particular piece of land is likely to produce satisfactory results, since no other method will make as full use of the dispersed knowledge of the prospects and possibilities of development as the market does.

There still exist some organized groups who contend that all these difficulties could be solved by the adoption of the "single-tax" plan, that is, by transferring the ownership of all land to the community and merely leasing it at rents determined by the market to private developers. This scheme for the socialization of land is, in its logic, probably the most seductive and plausible of all socialist schemes. If the factual assumptions on which it is based were correct, i.e., if it were possible to distinguish clearly between the value of "the permanent and indestructible powers of the soil," on the one hand, and, on the other, the value due to the two different kinds of improvement—that due to communal efforts and that due to the efforts of the individual owner—the argument for its adoption would be very strong. Almost all the difficulties we have mentioned, however, stem from the fact that no such distinction can be drawn with any degree of certainty. In order to give the necessary scope for private development of any one piece of land, the leases that would have to be granted at fixed rents would have to be for such long periods (they would also have to be made freely transferable) as to become little different from private property, and all the problems of individual property would reappear. Though we might often wish that things were as simple as the single-tax program assumes, we will find in it no solution to any of the problems with which we are concerned.

6. The administrative despotism to which town planners are inclined to subject the whole economy is well illustrated by the drastic provisions of the British Town and Country Planning Act of 1947.[11] Though they had to be repealed after a few years, they have not lacked admirers elsewhere and have been held up as an example to be imitated in the United States.[12] They provided for nothing less than the complete expropriation of all gains by the owner of urban property from any major change in the use made of his land—and a gain was defined as any increase in the value of the land over what it would be if a change in its use were altogether prohibited, which might, of course, be zero.[13] The compensation for this confiscation of all development rights was to be a share in a lump sum set aside for that purpose.

The conception underlying the scheme was that people should be free to sell and buy land only at a price based on the assumption that the particular piece of land would be permanently devoted to its present use: any gain made from changing its use was to go to the planning authority as the price for the

[11] It should perhaps be said, in exculpation of the British economists, that it would hardly have been possible for these absurdities ever to have become law if the decisive stage of the preparation of the legislation had not taken place at a time when the economists were almost entirely occupied with the war effort, and when the town planners had the time and a free field to put through their conception of a better postwar world. It is hardly an exaggeration to say that, at the time the act was passed, scarcely anybody in Parliament understood its implications and that probably nobody at all foresaw that the responsible minister would use the powers given to him to decree a complete confiscation of the development gain. See on the act Sir Arnold Plant, "Land Planning and the Economic Functions of Ownership," *The Journal—Chartered Auctioneers and Estate Agents Institute*, 29 (1949): 284–305 [While the title of the volume in which this article appears is as shown, this varies slightly from those of subsequent numbers, which carry the title *The Journal of the Chartered Auctioneers' and Estate Agents' Institute*.—Ed.]; and, in addition to Ralph Turvey, *Economics of Real Property*, see his article, "Development Charges and the Compensation-Betterment Problem," *Economic Journal*, 63 (1953): 299–317, and my article "A Levy on Increasing Efficiency," *Financial Times* (London), pt. 1 (April 26, 1949), "The Economics of Development Charges," p. 4; pt. 2 (April 27, 1949), "Detrimental Effects of Development Charges," p. 4; and pt. 3 (April 28, 1949), "Too Little Evidence of Planning," p. 4.

[12] Charles Monroe Haar, *Land Planning Law in a Free Society: A Study of the British Town and Country Planning Act* (Cambridge, MA: Harvard University Press, 1951); cf. my "Review of C. M. Haar's *Land Planning Law in a Free Society*," *University of Chicago Law Review*, 19 (1952): 620–26; reprinted as an Appendix under the title "The Economics of Development Charges," in *Studies in Philosophy, Politics and Economics* (Chicago: University of Chicago Press, 1967), pp. 331–38.

[13] Strictly speaking, this act was implemented by the responsible minister who had been authorized to fix the development charges at some percentage of the development gain and chose to fix them at 100 per cent.

permission to make the change, while any loss caused by a fall in the value of the land in its present use would affect only the owner. In instances where a piece of land had ceased to bring any return in its present use, the "development charges," as the levy was called, would therefore have amounted to the full value of the land in any new use to which it could be put.

As the authority created to administer these provisions of the law was thus given complete control of all changes in the use of land outside agriculture, it was in effect given a monopoly in deciding the use of any land in Britain for new industrial or commercial uses and complete authority to employ this power to exercise effective control of all such developments. This is a power which, by its nature, cannot be limited by rules, and the Central Land Board entrusted with it made it clear from the beginning that it did not mean to limit itself by any self-imposed rules to which it would consistently adhere. The *Practice Notes* it issued at the beginning of its activities stated this with a frankness that has rarely been equaled. They explicitly reserved the right to deviate from its announced working rules whenever "for special reasons the normal rules do not apply" and "from time to time to vary [its] policy" and to treat the "general working rule [as] variable if it does not fit a particular case."[14]

It is not surprising that these features of the act were found unworkable and had to be repealed after seven years and before any of the compensations for the "nationalization of the development value" of all land had been paid. What remains is a situation in which all development of land is by permission of the planning authority, which permission, however, is presumed to be obtainable if the development is not contrary to an announced over-all plan. The individual owner thus again has an interest in putting his land to better use. The whole experiment might be regarded as a curious episode and an illustration of the follies of ill-considered legislation, if it were not in fact the logical outcome of conceptions which are widely held. All endeavors to suspend the market mechanism in land and to replace it by central direction must lead to some such system of control that gives authority complete power over all development. The abortive British experiment has not attracted wider attention because, while the law was in force, the mechanism which its administration required never came into full operation. The law and the apparatus required to administer it were so complex that nobody except the unfortunate few who got caught in its meshes ever came to understand what it was all about.

7. Similar to the problems of general town planning in many respects are those of building regulations. Though they do not raise important questions

---

[14] Central Land Board, *Practice Notes (First Series): Being Notes on Development Charges Under the Town and Country Planning Act, 1947* (London: His Majesty's Stationery Office, 1949), Preface, pp. ii–iii.

of principle, they must be briefly considered. There are two reasons why some regulation of buildings permitted in cities is unquestionably desirable. The first is the now familiar consideration of the harm that may be done to others by the erection of buildings which constitute fire or health hazards; in modern conditions the people to be considered include the neighbors and all the users of a building who are not occupants but customers or clients of occupants and who need some assurance (or at least some means of ascertaining) that the building they enter is safe. The second is that, in the case of building, the enforcement of certain standards is perhaps the only effective way of preventing fraud and deception on the part of the builder: the standards laid down in building codes serve as a means of interpreting building contracts and insure that what are commonly understood to be appropriate materials and techniques will in fact be used unless the contract explicitly specifies otherwise.

Though the desirability of such regulations can hardly be disputed, there are few fields in which government regulations offer the same opportunity for abuse or have in fact been used so much to impose harmful or wholly irrational restrictions on development and so often help to strengthen the quasi-monopolistic positions of local producers. Wherever such regulations go beyond the requirement of minimum standards, and particularly where they tend to make what at a given time and place is the standard method the only permitted method, they can become serious obstructions to desirable economic developments. By preventing experimentation with new methods and by supporting local monopolies of enterprise and labor, they are often partly to blame for the high building costs and are largely responsible for housing shortages and overcrowding. This is particularly true where regulations not merely require that the buildings satisfy certain conditions or tests but prescribe particular techniques to be employed. It should be especially emphasized that "performance codes" of the former kind impose less restrictions on spontaneous developments than "specification codes" and are therefore to be preferred. The latter may at first seem to agree more with our principles because they confer less discretion on authority; the discretion which "performance codes" confer is, however, not of the objectionable kind. Whether or not a given technique satisfies criteria of performance laid down in a rule can be ascertained by independent experts, and any dispute, if it arises, can be decided by a court.

Another issue of some importance and difficulty is whether building regulations should be laid down by local or by central authorities. It is perhaps true that local regulations will be more liable to be abused under the influence of local monopolies and are also in other respects more likely to be obstructive. There are probably strong arguments in favor of a carefully thought-out national standard or pattern which local authorities can adopt with whatever modifications seem appropriate to them. In general, however, it seems probable that if the codes are determined locally, the competition between local authorities will bring about a more rapid elimination of obstructive and unreasonable restrictions than would be possible if the codes were uniformly laid down by law for a whole country or large region.

8. Problems of the kind raised by town planning are likely to assume great importance in the future in connection with the location of industries on a national scale. The subject is beginning to occupy the attention of the planners more and more, and it is in this area that we now encounter most often the contention that the results of free competition are irrational and harmful.

How much is there in this alleged irrationality of the actual location of industry and the supposed possibility of improving upon it by central planning? It is, of course, true that, had developments been correctly foreseen, many decisions about the location of plants would have been different and that in this sense what has happened in the past appears in retrospect as unwise. This does not mean, however, that, with the knowledge which was then available, a different decision could have been expected or that the results would have been more satisfactory if developments had been under the control of a national authority. Though we again have to deal here with a problem wherein the price mechanism operates only imperfectly and does not take into account many things we would wish to see taken into account, it is more than doubtful whether a central planner could guide developments as successfully as the market does. It is remarkable how much the market does accomplish in this respect by making individuals take into account those facts which they do not know directly but which are merely reflected in the prices. The best-known critical examination of these problems has indeed led August Lösch to conclude that "the most important result of this book is probably the demonstration of the surprising extent to which the free forces operate favorably." He then goes on to say that the market "respects all human wishes, sight unseen, whether these are wholesome or unwholesome" and that "the free market mechanism works much more to the common good than is generally supposed, though with certain exceptions."[15]

---

[15] August Lösch, *The Economics of Location*, William Henry Woglom, trans. (New Haven: Yale University Press, 1954), pp. 343–44.

TWENTY-THREE

AGRICULTURE AND NATURAL RESOURCES

My opinion is against an overdoing of any sort of administration, and more especially against this most momentous of all meddling on the part of authority; the meddling with the subsistence of the people. —Edmund Burke

1. The increase in the urban and industrial population which always accompanies the growth of wealth and civilization has in the modern Western world brought about a decrease not only in the proportion but in the absolute numbers of the agricultural population. Technological advance has so increased the productivity of human effort in the production of food that fewer men than ever before can supply the needs of a larger population. But, though an increase in population causes a proportional increase in the demand for food, as the population increase slows down and further advance mainly takes the form of a growth of income per head, less and less of this additional income is spent on an increased consumption of food. People may still be induced to spend more on food if preferred kinds are offered, but, after a certain point, per capita consumption of the cereal staples ceases to increase and may actually decrease. This increase in productivity combined with an inelastic demand means that if those engaged in agriculture are to maintain their average income (let alone keep up with the general increase in incomes), their number will have to decrease.

If such a redistribution of manpower between agriculture and other occupations takes place, there is no reason why in the long run those remaining in agriculture should not derive as much benefit from economic advance as the rest. But as long as the agricultural population is relatively too large, the change, while it proceeds, is bound to operate to their disadvantage. Spontaneous movements out of agriculture will be induced only if incomes in agriculture are reduced relative to those in urban occupations. The greater the reluctance of the farmers or peasants to shift to other occupations, the greater

The quotation at the head of the chapter is the concluding sentence of Edmund Burke, *Thoughts and Details upon Scarcity* (1795), in *Works*, vol. 7, p. 419 [Liberty Fund edition, *Selected Works*, vol. 3, p. 92].

the differences in incomes will be during the transitional period. Particularly when the change continues over several generations, the differences will be kept small only if the movements are relatively fast.

Policy, however, has everywhere delayed this adjustment, with the result that the problem has steadily grown in magnitude. The part of the population which has been kept in agriculture by deliberate acts of policy has grown so large that equalizing productivity between the agricultural and the industrial population would in many cases require a shift of numbers which seems altogether impracticable within any limited period of time.[1]

This policy has been pursued for a variety of reasons. In the European countries in which industrialization proceeded rapidly, the policy initially resulted from some vague notion about a "proper balance" between industry and agriculture, where "balance" meant little more than the maintenance of the traditional proportion between the two. In the countries which, as a consequence of their industrialization, tended to become dependent on imported food, those arguments were supported by the strategic consideration of self-sufficiency in wartime. Also it was often believed that the necessity of a transfer of population was a non-recurring one and that the problem could therefore be eased by spreading the process over a longer period. But the dominant consideration which almost everywhere led governments to interfere with it was the assurance of an "adequate income" to the people engaged in agriculture at the moment.

The support which the policy received from the general public was often due to the impression that the whole of the agricultural population, rather than only the less productive sections of it, was unable to earn a reasonable income. This belief was founded on the fact that the prices of agricultural products tended to fall much lower before the necessary readjustments were effected than they would have to do permanently. But it is also only this pressure of prices, which not only produces the necessary reduction in the agricultural population but leads to the adoption of the new in agricultural techniques, that will lower cost and make the survival of the suitable units possible.

---

[1] See Eric Mervyn Ojala, *Agriculture and Economic Progress* (London: Oxford University Press, 1952); Kenneth Ewart Boulding, "Economic Analysis and Agricultural Policy," *Canadian Journal of Economic and Political Science*, 13 (1947): 436–46, reprinted in *Contemporary Readings in Agricultural Economics*, Harold Graham Halcrow, ed. (New York: Prentice-Hall, 1955), pp. 195–220; Theodore William Schultz, *Agriculture in an Unstable Economy* (New York: McGraw-Hill, 1945); Jean Fourastie, *Le grand espoir du XXe siècle: progrès technique, progrès économique, progrès sociale* (Paris: Presses universitaires de France, 1949); Heinrich Niehaus, *Leitbilder der Wirtschafts- und Agrarpolitik in der modernen Gesellschaft* (Stuttgart: H. Seewald, 1957); and Heinrich Niehaus and Hermann Priebe, *Agrarpolitik in der sozialen Marktwirtschaft. Wortlaut der Vorträge und Diskussion auf der Fünften Arbeitstagung der Aktionsgemeinschaft Soziale Marktwirtschaft am 13. März 1956 in Bad Godesberg* (Ludwigsburg: M. Hoch, 1956). Also William H. Peterson, *The Great Farm Problem* (Chicago: Henry Regnery, 1959).

The elimination of the marginal land and farms, which will reduce average costs and, by reducing supply, stop and perhaps even partly reverse the fall in product prices, is only part of the necessary readjustment. Equally important for restoring the prosperity of agriculture are the changes in its internal structure which will be induced by the changes in the relative prices of its different products. The policies pursued to assist agriculture in its difficulties, however, usually prevent those very adjustments that would make it profitable.

We can give here only one significant instance of this. As has already been said, once the general rise in incomes has exceeded a certain level, people are not likely to increase their expenditure on food unless they are offered preferred kinds. In the Western world this means mainly a substitution of high-protein foods, such as meat and dairy products, for cereals and other starchy foods. This process would be assisted if agriculture were led to produce more of these desired products at reduced relative costs. This would be brought about if the cereals were allowed to fall in price until it became profitable to use them as feed for cattle and thus indirectly produce the food that the consumers want. Such a development would prevent the total consumption of grain from shrinking as much as it would otherwise and, at the same time, decrease the costs of meat, etc. It is usually made impossible, however, by a policy of maintaining the prices of cereals at such a level that human consumption will not absorb the supply and they cannot be profitably put to other uses.

This example must suffice here as an illustration of the various ways in which the policies pursued have prevented agriculture from adapting itself to the changed conditions. With proper adaptation, a smaller number of producers (but still larger than would otherwise succeed) could increase their productivity so as to share in the general growth of prosperity. It is true, of course, that part of the trouble of agriculture is that both the character of its processes and that of the producers tend to make it peculiarly sluggish in its adaptation to change. But the remedy clearly cannot lie in making it still more resistant to adaptation. This, however, is what most of the important measures of control adopted by governments, and particularly all measures of price control, do.

2. It should hardly be necessary to repeat that in the long run price controls serve no desirable purpose and that, even for a limited period, they can be made effective only if combined with direct controls of production. If they are to benefit the producers, they must be supplemented in one way or another by decisions of authority as to who is to produce, how much, and what. Since the intention is to enable the people now tilling the land to stay there and to earn an income which satisfies them, and since consumers are not willing to spend enough on food to maintain them at that level, authority must resort to forcible transfer of income. How far this is likely to be carried is best shown

by the example of Great Britain, where it is expected that the total financial assistance to agriculture will soon reach "something like two-thirds of the aggregate net income of agriculture."[2]

Two things should be especially noted about this development. One is that in most countries the process of taking agriculture out of the market mechanism and subjecting it to increasing government direction began before the same was done in industry and that it was usually carried out with the support, or even on the initiative, of the conservatives, who have shown themselves little averse to socialistic measures if they serve ends of which they approve. The second is that the tendency was perhaps even stronger in countries where the agricultural population constituted a comparatively small part of the total but, because of a peculiar political position, was given privileges which no similar group had yet attained and which could be granted to all in no sort of system. There are few developments which give one so much cause for doubt concerning the ability of democratic government to act rationally or to pursue any intelligent designs, once it throws principles to the wind and undertakes to assure the status of particular groups. We have reached a state of affairs in agriculture where almost everywhere the more thoughtful specialists no longer ask what would be a rational policy to pursue but only which of the courses that seem politically feasible would do the least harm.

In a book such as this we can pay no attention, however, to the political necessities which the existing state of opinion imposes upon current decisions. We must confine ourselves to showing that agricultural policy has been dominated in most Western countries by conceptions which not only are self-defeating but, if generally applied, would lead to a totalitarian control of all economic activity. We cannot apply the principles of socialism for the benefit of one group only; if we do, we cannot expect to resist the demand of other groups to have their incomes similarly determined by authority according to supposed principles of justice.

The best illustration of the consequences of such policies is probably the situation which has arisen in the United States after twenty years of effort to apply the conception of "parity."[3] The attempt to assure to the agricultural

---

[2] Sir Ralph Enfield, "How Much Agriculture?" *Lloyds Bank Review*, n.s., 32 (April 1954): 30. [In 2001, total support to agriculture in the United States amounted to 64% of the sector's contribution to GDP, while the figure for the European Union was 66% and for Japan 127%! (See the World Trade Organization, *Annual Report, 2003* [Geneva: World Trade Organization, 2003]).—Ed.].

[3] It perhaps deserves mention, since this is little known, that in this field, too, the inspiration for the control measures seems to have come from Germany. Cf. the account in Arthur Meier Schlesinger, Jr., *The Age of Roosevelt: The Crisis of the Old Order, 1919–1933* (Boston: Houghton Mifflin, 1957), p. 110: "In the late twenties Beardsley Ruml of the Laura Spelman Rockefeller Foundation, impressed by a program of agricultural control he observed in operation in Germany, asked John Black, now at Harvard, to investigate its adaptability to the American farm prob-

producers prices that stand in a fixed relation to the prices of industrial products must lead to a suspension of the forces which would bring about the necessary restriction of agricultural production to those producers operating at the lowest costs and to those products which can still be profitably produced. It is undeniable that, if these forces are to operate, the growth of incomes in agriculture during the period of transition will lag behind that of the rest of the population. But nothing we can do, short of stopping the progress of technology and wealth, will avoid the necessity of these adaptations; and the attempt to mitigate its effects by compulsory transfers of income from the urban to the agricultural population must, by delaying it, produce an ever greater backlog of postponed adaptations and so increase the difficulty of the problem.

The results of this policy in the United States—the ever mounting accumulation of surplus stocks, the existence of which has become a new threat to the stability not only of American but of world agriculture, the fundamentally arbitrary and yet ineffective and irrational allocation of acreages, and so on— are too well known to need description. Few people will deny that the main problem has become that of how policy can extricate itself from the situation it has produced and that American agriculture would be in a healthier state if the government had never meddled with prices and quantities and methods of production.

3. Though the irrationality and absurdity of modern agricultural policy is perhaps most easily seen in the United States, we must turn to other countries if we are to become aware of the full extent to which such policies, systematically pursued, are liable to impose restrictions on the farmer (whose "sturdy independence" is at the same time often referred to as an argument for maintaining him at public expense) and turn him into the most regimented and supervised of all producers.

This development has probably gone furthest in Great Britain, where a degree of supervision and control of most farming activities has been established that is not equaled this side of the iron curtain. Perhaps it is inevitable that, once farming is conducted largely at public expense, certain standards should also be enforced, and even that the penalty for what the authorities regard as bad farming should be that the offender is driven from his own

---

lem. In 1929 Black worked out the details of what he christened the voluntary domestic allotment plan." [Beardsley Ruml was at one point Treasurer of R. H. Macy, the department store, and went on to become Chairman of the Federal Reserve Bank of New York and a close advisor to President Franklin D. Roosevelt. Among his many contributions to the modern state was the idea of withholding income taxes from workers' paychecks. John Black, an advisor in farm policy in the Roosevelt administration, later joined the Harvard faculty, where he became one of the most persistent voices supporting more extensive government. Black's protegé, John Kenneth Galbraith, was brought into the department largely at Black's urging.—Ed.]

property. It is, however, a curious illusion to expect that farming will more effectively adapt itself to changing conditions if methods of cultivation are made subject to the control of a committee of neighbors and if what the majority or some superior authority regards as good farming is made the standard method universally enforced. Such restrictions may be the best way of preserving the kind of farming which we know and which many people (most of whom, one suspects, live in the city) wish to see preserved for sentimental reasons; but they can result only in the agricultural population's becoming more and more dependent.

In fact, the remarkable solicitude which the public shows in England for the fate of farming is probably due more to aesthetic than to economic considerations. The same is true to an even greater degree of the concern shown by the public in countries like Austria or Switzerland for the preservation of the mountain peasants. In all these instances a heavy burden is accepted because of the fear that the familiar face of the countryside would be changed by the disappearance of the present farming techniques and that the farmer or peasant, if he were not specially protected, would disappear altogether. It is this apprehension which causes people to be alarmed over any reduction in the agricultural population and to conjure up in their minds a picture of completely deserted villages or valleys as soon as some homesteads are abandoned.

It is, however, this very "conservation" which is the archenemy of a viable agriculture. It is hardly ever true that all farmers or peasants are equally threatened by any development. There are as great gaps between prosperity and poverty among farmers working under similar conditions as exist in any other occupation.[4] As in all other fields, if there is to be a continuous adaptation to changing circumstances in agriculture, it is essential that the example of those individuals who are successful because they have discovered the appropriate response to a change be followed by the rest. This always means that certain types will disappear. In agriculture in particular, it means that the farmer or peasant, if he is to succeed, must progressively become a businessman— a necessary process that many people deplore and want to prevent. But the alternative for the agricultural population would be to become more and more a sort of appendage to a national park, quaint folk preserved to people the scenery, and deliberately prevented from making the mental and technological adjustments that would enable them to be self-supporting.

Such attempts to preserve particular members of the agricultural population by sheltering them against the necessity of changing strong traditions and habits must turn them into permanent wards of government, pensioners

---

[4] Cf. Hilde Weber, *Die Landwirtschaft in der volkswirtschaftlichen Entwicklung: eine Betrachtung über Beschäftigung und Einkommen* [inaugural dissertation, Universität Bonn; Sonderheft No. 161] (Hamburg: P. Parey, 1955).

living off the rest of the population, and lastingly dependent for their liveli-hood on political decisions. It would certainly be the lesser evil if some remote homesteads disappeared and in some places pastures or even forests replaced what in different conditions had been arable land. Indeed, we should be show-ing more respect for the dignity of man if we allowed certain ways of life to disappear altogether instead of preserving them as specimens of a past age.

4. The contention that there is in agriculture no case for control of prices or production or for any kind of over-all planning, and that most of the mea-sures of this sort have been both economically unwise and a threat to individ-ual liberty, does not mean that there are not genuine and important problems of agricultural policy, or that government has no important functions to per-form in this field. But here, as elsewhere, these tasks involve, on the one hand, the gradual improvement of the legal institutions which will make the mar-ket function more effectively and induce the individual to take fuller account of the effects of his actions and, on the other, those true service activities in which government as the agent of the people provides certain facilities, mainly in the form of information, which, at least in certain stages of develop-ment, is not likely to be provided in any other way, though here, too, govern-ment should never arrogate to itself exclusive rights but rather facilitate the growth of voluntary efforts which may in time take over these functions.

To the first category belong all those problems which in agriculture no less than in urban affairs arise from the neighborhood effects and from the more far-reaching consequences which the use of a particular piece of land may have for the rest of the community.[5] Some of these problems we shall have to consider a little later in connection with the general problem of the con-servation of natural resources. There are also, however, specifically agricul-tural problems with regard to which our legal framework and particularly the law concerning ownership and tenure could be improved. Many of the more serious defects in the working of the price mechanism can be remedied only by the evolution of appropriate units of enterprise under single control, and sometimes perhaps only by appropriate groups collaborating for certain pur-poses. How far such an evolution of appropriate forms of organization will go will depend largely on the character of the land law, including the possibili-ties that it provides, under the necessary safeguards, for compulsory expropri-ation. There can be little question that the consolidation of dispersed holdings inherited in Europe from the Middle Ages or the enclosures of the commons in England were necessary legislative measures to make improvements by indi-

---

[5] On the extent to which "soil conservation" has often served merely as a pretext for economic controls see Charles Meyer Hardin, *The Politics of Agriculture: Soil Conservation and the Struggle for Power in Rural America* (Glencoe, IL: Free Press, 1952), and Frederic Benham, *Economic Aid to Under-developed Countries* (Oxford: Oxford University Press, 1959).

vidual efforts possible. And it is at least conceivable, though the actual experience with "land reforms" gives little ground for confidence, that in certain circumstances changes in the land law may assist the breakup of latifundia which have become uneconomical but are kept in existence by certain features of the existing law. While there is room for such gradual improvement in the legal framework, the greater the freedom of experimentation allowed in the existing arrangements, the greater will be the likelihood that the changes will be made in the right direction.

There is also much scope for government action of a service character, especially in the form of spreading information. One of the real difficulties of agriculture in a dynamic society is that the very character of an agricultural population makes it likely that it will be less in touch with the advances and changes in knowledge than others. Where this means, as it often does with a peasantry adhering to traditional methods of cultivation, that most individuals do not even know that there is useful knowledge available and worth paying for, it will often be an advantageous investment for the community to bear some of the costs of spreading such knowledge. We all have an interest in our fellow citizens' being put in a position to choose wisely, and if some have not yet awakened to the possibilities which technological developments offer, a comparatively small outlay may often be sufficient to induce the individuals to take advantage of new opportunities and thence to advance further on their own initiative. Again the government should not become the sole dispenser of knowledge, with the power of deciding what the individual should and should not know. It is also possible that too much activity on the part of government will do harm by preventing the growth of more effective forms of voluntary effort. At any rate, there can be no objection of principle against such services being rendered by government; and the question as to which of these services will be worth while and to what extent they should be carried is one of expediency and raises no further fundamental issues.

5. Though we cannot attempt here to consider seriously the peculiar problems of "underdeveloped countries,"[6] we cannot leave the subject of agriculture without commenting briefly on the paradoxical fact that, while the old countries involve themselves in the most absurd complexities to prevent a shrinkage of their agricultural population, the new countries seem even more anxious to speed up the growth of the industrial population by arti-

---

[6] On the problems of undeveloped countries and assistance to their economic development see particularly Peter Tamás Bauer, *Economic Analysis and Policy in Underdeveloped Countries* (Cambridge: Cambridge University Press, 1957); Sally Herbert Frankel, *The Economic Impact on Under-developed Societies: Essays on International Investment and Social Change* (Oxford: Blackwell, 1953); Frederic Benham, " Reflexiones sobre los países insuficientemente desarrollados," *El Trimestre económico*, 19 (1952): 45–57; and Milton Friedman, "Foreign Economic Aid, Means and Objectives," *Yale Review*, n.s., 47 (1958): 500–516.

ficial means.[7] Much of this endeavor on the latter's part seems to be based on a rather naïve fallacy of the *post hoc ergo propter hoc* variety: because historically the growth of wealth has regularly been accompanied by rapid industrialization, it is assumed that industrialization will bring about a more rapid growth of wealth. This involves a clear confusion of an intermediate effect with a cause. It is true that, as productivity per head increases as a result of the investment of more capital in tools, and even more as a result of investment in knowledge and skill, more and more of the additional output will be wanted in the form of industrial products. It is also true that a substantial increase in the production of food in those countries will require an increased supply of tools. But neither of these considerations alters the fact that if large-scale industrialization is to be the most rapid way of increasing average income, there must be an agricultural surplus available so that an industrial population can be fed.[8] If unlimited amounts of capital were available and if the mere availability of sufficient capital could speedily change the knowledge and attitudes of an agricultural population, it might be sensible for such countries to impose a planned reconstruction of their economies on the model of the most advanced capitalist countries. This, however, is clearly not within the range of actual possibilities. It would seem, indeed, that if such countries as India and China are to effect a rapid rise in the standard of living, only a small portion of such capital as becomes available should be devoted to the creation of elaborate industrial equipment and perhaps none of it to the kind of highly automatized, "capital-intensive" plants that are characteristic of countries where the value of labor is very high, and that these countries should aim at spreading such capital as widely and thinly as possible among those uses that will directly increase the production of food.

The essentially unpredictable developments that may be produced by the application of advanced technological knowledge to economies extremely poor in capital are more likely to be speeded up if opportunity for free development is provided than if a pattern is imposed which is borrowed from societies in which the proportion between capital and labor is altogether different

[7] This has its complement in the fact, first pointed out, I believe, by Frank Walter Paish, that today the wealthy countries regularly overpay their farmers while the poor countries generally underpay them.

[8] The important and well-established fact of the necessity of the development of an agricultural surplus before rapid industrialization can bring a growth of wealth is particularly well brought out by Kenneth Ewart Boulding, "Economic Analysis and Agricultural Policy," esp. p. 440, reprinted in *Contemporary Readings in Agricultural Economics*, esp. p. 197: "The so called 'industrial revolution' was not created by a few rather unimportant technical changes in the textile industry; it was the direct child of the agricultural revolution based on turnips, clover, four-course rotation, and livestock improvement which developed in the first half of the eighteenth century. It is the turnip, not the spinning jenny, which is the father of industrial society." See Samuel Pfrimmer Hays, *Conservation and the Gospel of Efficiency: The Progressive Conservation Movement, 1890–1920* [Harvard Historical Monographs, No. 40] (Cambridge, MA: Harvard University Press, 1960).

from what it will be in the newer economies in the foreseeable future. However strong a case there may exist in such countries for the government's taking the initiative in providing examples and spending freely on spreading knowledge and education, it seems to me that the case against over-all planning and direction of all economic activity is even stronger there than in more advanced countries. I say this on both economic and cultural grounds. Only free growth is likely to enable such countries to develop a viable civilization of their own, capable of making a distinct contribution to the needs of mankind.

6. Most sensible people in the West are aware that the problem of agricultural policy now is to extricate governments from a system of controls in which they have become entangled and to restore the working of the market. But in the related field of the exploitation of natural resources, prevalent opinion still is that the peculiar situation existing here requires governments to undertake far-reaching controls. This view is particularly strong in the United States, where the "conservation movement" has to a great extent been the source of the agitation for economic planning and has contributed much to the indigenous ideology of the radical economic reformers.[9] Few arguments have been used so widely and effectively to persuade the public of the "wastefulness of competition" and the desirability of a central direction of important economic activities as the alleged squandering of natural resources by private enterprise.

There are several reasons why, in a new country that was rapidly settled by immigrants bringing with them an advanced technology, the problem of resource conservation should become more acute than it ever did in Europe. While there the evolution had been gradual and some sort of equilibrium had established itself long before (partly, no doubt, because exploitation had done its worst at an early stage, as in the deforestation and consequent erosion of much of the southern slopes of the Alps), the rapid occupation in America of enormous tracts of virgin lands raised problems of a different order of magnitude. That the changes involved in bringing the whole of a continent for the first time under cultivation in the course of a single century should have caused upsets in the balance of nature which in retrospect seem regrettable need not surprise us.[10] Most of those who complain about what has happened, however, are being wise after the event, and there is little reason to believe that, with

[9] It is significant that, as has been pointed out by Anthony Scott, *National Resources: The Economics of Conservation* (Toronto: University of Toronto Press, 1955), p. 37, "the whole school of land economics (and its cousin, institutional economics)" largely traces back to this concern of Americans.

[10] Cf. Paul Bigelow Sears, "Science and National Resources," *American Scientist*, 44 (1956): 331–46, and "The Processes of Environmental Change by Man," in *Man's Role in Changing the Face of the Earth*, William Leroy Thomas, Jr., ed. [International Symposium on Man's Role in Changing the Face of the Earth, Princeton, NJ, 1955] (Chicago: University of Chicago Press, 1956), pp. 471–84.

the knowledge available at the time, even the most intelligent governmental policy could have prevented those effects which are now most deplored.

It is not to be denied that there has been real waste; it must be emphasized, however, that the most important instance of this—the depletion of the forests—was largely due to the fact that they did *not* become private property but were retained as public land and given over to private exploitation on terms which gave the exploiters no incentive for conservation. It is true that, with some kinds of natural resources, property arrangements that are generally adequate will not secure an efficient use and that special provisions of the law may be desirable with regard to them. Different kinds of natural resources raise separate problems in this respect which we must consider in turn.

With some natural resources, such as deposits of minerals, their exploitation necessarily means that they are gradually used up, while others can be made to bring a continuous return for an indefinite period.[11] The usual complaint of the conservationists is that the former—the "stock resources"—are used up too rapidly, while the latter the "flow resources"—are not used so as to give as high a permanent return as they would be capable of. These contentions are based partly on the belief that the private exploiter does not take a long enough view or does not have as much foreknowledge of future developments as the government and partly, as we shall see, on a simple fallacy which invalidates a great part of the usual conservationist argument.

There arises also in this connection the problem of the neighborhood effects, which may in certain instances lead to wasteful methods of exploitation unless the units of property are of such size that at least all the more important effects of any one owner's actions are reflected in the value of his own property. This problem arises in particular in connection with the various types of "fugitive resources," such as game, fish, water, oil, or natural gas (and perhaps rain, too, in the near future) which we can appropriate only by using them up and which no individual exploiter will have an interest in conserving, since what he does not take will be taken by others. They give rise to situations in which either private property cannot exist (as with deep-sea fisheries and most other forms of wild-life resources), and we have, in consequence, to find some substitute arrangement, or where private property will lead to rational use only if the scope of unified control is made coextensive with the range within which the same resource can be tapped, as with a pool of oil. It is undeniable that where for such technological reasons we cannot have exclusive control of particular resources by individual owners, we must resort to alternative forms of regulation.

---

[11] See mainly Scott, *National Resources*; Scott Gordon, "Economics and the Conservation Question," *Journal of Law and Economics*, 1 (1958): 110–21; and Siegfried von Ciriacy-Wantrup, *Resource Conservation: Economics and Policies* (Berkeley: University of California Press, 1952).

In a sense, of course, most consumption of irreplaceable resources rests on an act of faith. We are generally confident that, by the time the resource is exhausted, something new will have been discovered which will either satisfy the same need or at least compensate us for what we no longer have, so that we are, on the whole, as well off as before. We are constantly using up resources on the basis of the mere probability that our knowledge of available resources will increase indefinitely—and this knowledge does increase in part because we are using up what is available at such a fast rate. Indeed, if we are to make full use of the available resources, we must act on the assumption that it will continue to increase, even if some of our particular expectations are bound to be disappointed. Industrial development would have been greatly retarded if sixty or eighty years ago the warning of the conservationists about the threatening exhaustion of the supply of coal had been heeded; and the internal combustion engine would never have revolutionized transport if its use had been limited to the then known supplies of oil (during the first few decades of the era of the automobile and the airplane the known resources of oil at the current rate of use would have been exhausted in ten years). Though it is important that on all these matters the opinion of the experts about the physical facts should be heard, the result in most instances would have been very detrimental if they had had the power to enforce their views on policy.

7. The chief arguments that have persuaded people of the necessity of central direction of the conservation of natural resources are that the community has a greater interest in and a greater foreknowledge of the future than the individuals and that the preservation of particular resources raises problems different from those of the provision for the future in general.

The implications of the contention that the community has a greater interest in providing for the future than do individuals go far beyond the problems of the conservation of natural resources. The contention is not merely that certain future needs, such as security or defense, can be provided for only by the community as a whole. It is also that the community should generally devote a larger proportion of its resources to provision for the future than will result from the separate decisions of the individuals. Or, as it is often put, future needs should be valued more highly (or discounted at a lower rate of interest) by the community than is done by individuals. If valid, this contention would indeed justify central planning of most economic activity. There is, however, nothing to support this but the arbitrary judgment of those who maintain it.

There is no more justification in a free society for relieving the individuals of the responsibility for the future than there is for claiming that past generations ought to have made more provision for us than they did. The contention is made no more conclusive by the often used fallacious argument that, because government can borrow at cheaper rates, it is in a better position to take care of future needs. It is fallacious because the advantage which governments have in this respect rests solely on the fact that the risk of failure in its investments is not borne by them but by the taxpayer; in fact, the risk is no less, so far as judgment of the worthwhileness of the particular investment is concerned. But, since governments that can recoup themselves by taxation if the investment does not bring the expected return usually count only the interest they actually pay as costs of the capital they are using, the argument operates in fact against, rather than in favor of, government investment.

The claim that the government possesses superior knowledge raises a more complex problem. It cannot be denied that there are some facts concerning probable future developments which the government is more likely to know than most of the individual owners of natural resources. Many of the more recent achievements of science illustrate this. There will always exist, however, an even greater store of knowledge of special circumstances that ought to be taken into account in decisions about specific resources which only the individual owners will possess and which can never be concentrated within a single authority. Thus, if it is true that the government is likely to know some facts known to few others, it is equally true that the government will be necessarily ignorant of an even greater number of relevant facts known to some others. We can bring together all the knowledge that is relevant to particular problems only by dispersing downward the generic knowledge available to the government, not by centralizing all the special knowledge possessed by individuals. There is probably no instance where authority can possess superior knowledge of all the facts that ought to influence a specific decision; and, while it is possible to communicate to the owners of particular resources the more general considerations that they ought to take into account, it is not possible for authority to learn all the different facts known to the individuals.

This appears perhaps most clearly where the problem concerns the rate at which stock resources, such as mineral deposits, ought to be used up. An intelligent decision presupposes a rational estimate of the future course of prices of the materials in question, and this in turn depends on forecasts of future technological and economic developments which the small individual owner is usually not in a position to make intelligently. This does not mean, however, that the market will not induce individual owners to act as if they took these considerations explicitly into account, or that such decisions should not be left to them who alone know many of the circumstances which determine the present usefulness of a particular deposit. Though they may know little about probable future developments, they will be influenced in their decisions by the knowledge of others who make it their concern to estimate such probabilities and who will be prepared to offer for the resources prices determined by these estimates. If the owner can get a higher return by selling to those who want to conserve than by exploiting the particular resource himself, he will do so.

There will normally exist a potential sale price of the resource which will reflect opinion about all the factors likely to affect its future value, and a decision based on the comparison of its value as a salable asset with what it would bring if exploited now will probably take into account more of all the relevant knowledge than could any decision of a central authority.

It has often been demonstrated that, in the case of rare natural resources, exploitation by a monopoly is likely to extend their use over a longer period and that this is perhaps the only instance where such monopolies are likely to be formed and to persist in a free economy.[12] I cannot go all the way with those who use this as an argument in favor of such monopolies, because I am not persuaded that the greater degree of conservation which a monopoly would practice is desirable from a social point of view. But for those who want more conservation because they believe that the market habitually underestimates future needs, the monopolies that are likely to develop spontaneously in such instances provide the answer.

8. Much of the argument for conservation, however, rests simply on an unreasoned prejudice. Its proponents take for granted that there is something particularly desirable about the flow of services that a given resource can provide at any one time and that this rate of output should be permanently maintained. Though they recognize that this is impossible with regard to stock resources, they consider it a calamity if the rate of return of flow resources is diminished below the level at which it is physically possible to maintain it. This position is often taken with regard to both the fertility of the soil in general and the stock of game, fish, etc.

To bring out the crucial point most strongly, we shall consider here the most conspicuous instance of this prejudice, where most people are inclined to accept uncritically the fallacy of much of the conservationist argument. It is the belief that the natural fertility of the soil should in all circumstances be preserved and that what is branded as "soil mining" should in all circumstances be avoided. It can be easily shown that as a general proposition, this is unsound and that the level at which fertility ought to be maintained has little to do with the initial condition of a given piece of land. In fact, "soil mining" may in certain circumstances be as much in the long-range interest of a community as the using up of any stock resource.

A tract of land is often built up by cumulative deposits of organic substance to a level of fertility which, once the land is brought under cultivation, can be maintained only at costs in excess of the returns. As in certain circumstances it will be desirable to build up the fertility of a piece of land by artificially enriching it to a level at which what is annually put in will be repaid by the

---

[12] Cf. Ludwig von Mises, *Socialism*, p. 392 [Liberty Fund edition, p. 350], and Scott, *National Resources*, pp. 82–85.

increase of the product, so in certain other circumstances it will be desirable to allow the fertility to decline to the level at which investments will still pay. In some instances this may even mean that it is uneconomical to aim at permanent cultivation and that, after the accumulated natural fertility has been exhausted, the land ought to be abandoned, because in the given geographic or climatic conditions it cannot with advantage be permanently cultivated.

To use up a free gift of nature once and for all is in such instances no more wasteful or reprehensible than a similar exploitation of a stock resource. There may, of course, be other effects, known or probable, which a lasting change in the character of a tract of land may have and which ought to be taken into account: for example, as a result of temporary cultivation it may lose properties or potentialities that it possessed before and which could have been utilized for some other purpose. But this is a separate problem, one which does not concern us. We are concerned solely with examining the belief that, wherever possible, the flow of services from any natural resource should be kept at the highest level attainable. This may be accidentally valid in a particular instance, but never because of considerations which concern the attributes of a given piece of land or some other resource.

Such resources share with most of the capital of society the property of being exhaustible, and if we want to maintain or increase our income, we must be able to replace each resource that is being used up with a new one that will make at least an equal contribution to future income. This does not mean, however, that it should be preserved in kind or replaced by another of the same kind, or even that the total stock of natural resources should be kept intact. From a social as well as from an individual point of view, any natural resource represents just one item of our total endowment of exhaustible resources, and our problem is not to preserve this stock in any particular form, but always to maintain it in a form that will make the most desirable contribution to total income. The existence of a particular natural resource merely means that, while it lasts, its temporary contribution to our income will help us to create new ones which will similarly assist us in the future. This normally will not mean that we should replace any one resource with one of the same kind. One of the considerations which we shall have to keep in mind is that if one kind of resource becomes scarcer, the products depending on it will also be more scarce in the future. The foreseeable rise in the prices of products consequent upon the growing scarcity of a natural resource will indeed be one of the factors determining the amount of investment that will go to preserving this kind of resource.[13]

---

[13] Cf. my *The Pure Theory of Capital* (London: Macmillan, 1941), chap. 7, pp. 85–94, esp. p. 88n [reprinted as vol. 12 of *The Collected Works of F. A. Hayek*, Lawrence H. White, ed. (Chicago: University of Chicago Press, 2007), pp. 100–107, esp. p. 104, n. 2].

Perhaps the best way of concisely stating the chief point is to say that all resource conservation constitutes investment and should be judged by precisely the same criteria as all other investment.[14] There is nothing in the preservation of natural resources as such which makes it a more desirable object of investment than man-made equipment or human capacities; and, so long as society anticipates the exhaustion of particular resources and channels its investment in such a manner that its aggregate income is made as great as the funds available for investment can make it, there is no further economic case for preserving any one kind of resource. To extend investment in the conservation of a particular natural resource to a point where the return is lower than the capital it uses would bring elsewhere would reduce future income below what it would otherwise be. As has been well said, "the conservationist who urges us 'to make greater provision for the future' is in fact urging a *lesser* provision for posterity."[15]

9. While most of the arguments advanced in favor of governmental control of private activity in the interest of conservation of natural resources are thus invalid and while there is little in them beyond an argument for providing more information and knowledge, the situation is different where the aim is the provision of amenities of or opportunities for recreation, or the preservation of natural beauty or of historical sites or places of scientific interest, etc. The kinds of services that such amenities render to the public at large, which often enable the individual beneficiary to derive advantages for which he cannot be charged a price, and the size of the tracts of land usually required make this an appropriate field for collective effort.

The case for natural parks, nature reservations, etc., is exactly of the same sort as that for similar amenities which municipalities provide on a smaller scale. There is much to be said for their being provided as far as possible by voluntary organizations, such as the National Trust in Great Britain, rather than through the compulsory powers of government. But there can be no objection to the government's providing such amenities where it happens to be the owner of the land in question or, indeed, where it has to acquire it out of funds raised by taxation or perhaps even by compulsory purchase, so long as the community approves this, in full awareness of the cost, and realizes that this is one aim competing with others and not a unique objective overriding all other needs. If the taxpayer knows the full extent of the bill he will have to foot and has the last word in the decision, there is nothing further to be said about these problems in general terms.

[14] See Scott, *National Resources*, p. 8.
[15] Ibid., p. 97.

TWENTY-FOUR

EDUCATION AND RESEARCH

education as coercion

A general State education is a mere contrivance for moulding people to be exactly like one another: and as the mould in which it casts them is that which pleases the predominant power in the government, whether this be a monarch, a priesthood, an aristocracy, or the majority of the existing generation; in proportion as it is efficient and successful, it establishes a despotism over the mind, leading by natural tendency to one over the body.

—John Stuart Mill

1. Knowledge is perhaps the chief good that can be had at a price, but those who do not already possess it often cannot recognize its usefulness. More important still, access to the sources of knowledge necessary for the working of modern society presupposes the command of certain techniques—above all, that of reading—which people must acquire before they can judge well for themselves what will be useful to them. Though our case for freedom rests to a great extent on the contention that competition is one of the most powerful instruments for the dissemination of knowledge and that it will usually demonstrate the value of knowledge to those who do not possess it, there is no doubt that the utilization of knowledge can be greatly increased by deliberate

---

The quotation at the head of the chapter is taken from John Stuart Mill, "On Liberty," in *On Liberty and Considerations on Representative Government*, Ronald Buchanan McCallum, ed. (Oxford: B. Blackwell, 1946), p. 95. Cf. also Bertrand Russell, commenting on the same problem ninety-five years later in his lecture, "John Stuart Mill," *Proceedings of the British Academy*, 41 (1955): 57: "State education, in the countries which adopt [Johann Gottfried Fichte's] principles, produces, so far as it is successful, a herd of ignorant fanatics, ready at the word of command to engage in war or persecution as may be required of them. So great is this evil that the world would be a better place (at any rate, in my opinion) if State education had never been inaugurated." [At the heart of Fichte's philosophical system is a passion for a system of universal education that will liberate all men from their instincts to a life based on reason.—Ed.] Also consider the directives issued by one of Napoleon's ministers (quoted in Pieter Geyl, *The Revolt of the Netherlands, 1555–1609* [London: Williams and Norgate Ltd., 1932], p. 140): "Education must impart the same knowledge and the same principles to all individuals living in the same society, so that they will make, as a whole, one body, informed with one and the same understanding, and working for the common good, on the basis of uniformity of views and desires."

efforts. Ignorance is one of the chief reasons why men's endeavors are often not channeled so that they are most useful to their fellows; and there are various reasons why it may be in the interest of the whole community that knowledge be brought to people who have little incentive to seek it or to make some sacrifice to acquire it. These reasons are particularly compelling in the case of children, but some of the arguments apply no less to adults.

With regard to children the important fact is, of course, that they are not responsible individuals to whom the argument for freedom fully applies. Though it is generally in the best interest of children that their bodily and mental welfare be left in the care of their parents or guardians, this does not mean that parents should have unrestricted liberty to treat their children as they like. The other members of the community have a genuine stake in the welfare of the children. The case for requiring parents or guardians to provide for those under their care a certain minimum of education is clearly very strong.[1]

In contemporary society, the case for compulsory education up to a certain minimum standard is twofold. There is the general argument that all of us will be exposed to fewer risks and will receive more benefits from our fellows if they share with us certain basic knowledge and beliefs. And in a country with democratic institutions there is the further important consideration that democracy is not likely to work, except on the smallest local scale, with a partly illiterate people.[2]

---

[1] Cf. Mill, "On Liberty," pp. 94–95: "It is in the case of children that misapplied notions of liberty are a real obstacle to the fulfilment by the State of its duties. One would almost think that a man's children were supposed to be literally, and not metaphorically, a part of himself, so jealous is opinion of the smallest interference of law with his absolute and exclusive control over them; more jealous than of almost any interference with his own freedom of action; so much less do the generality of mankind value liberty than power. Consider, for example the case of education. Is it not almost a self-evident axiom, that the State should require and compel the education, up to a certain standard, of every human being who is born its citizen? . . . If the government would make up its mind to require for every child a good education, it might save itself the trouble of providing one. It might leave to parents to obtain the education where and how they pleased, and content itself with helping to pay the school fees of the poorer classes of children, and defraying the entire school expenses of those who have no one else to pay for them. The objections which are argued with reason against State education do not apply to the enforcement of education by the State, but to the State's taking upon itself to direct that education; which is a totally different thing."

[2] Historically, the needs of universal military service were probably much more decisive in leading most governments to make education compulsory than the needs of universal suffrage. It is also significant that (according to Max Pohlenz, *Griechische Freiheit: Wesen und Werden eines Lebensideals* [Heidelberg: Quelle und Meyer, 1955], p. 42): "es unter den Bürgern des alten Athen keine Analphabeten gegeben haben soll, obwohl dessen 'freie Demokratie jede Einmischung in das Privatleben [vermied]. Es gab keinen Schulzwang und keine staatlichen Schulen.'" ["There were allegedly no illiterate persons among the citizens of ancient Athens, though their 'free democracy

[It is important to recognize that general education is not solely, and perhaps not even mainly, a matter of communicating knowledge. There is a need for certain common standards of values, and, though too great emphasis on this need may lead to very illiberal consequences, peaceful common existence would be clearly impossible without any such standards] If in long-settled communities with a predominantly indigenous population, this is not likely to be a serious problem, there are instances, such as the United States during the period of large immigration, where it may well be one. That the United States would not have become such an effective "melting pot" and would probably have faced extremely difficult problems if it had not been for a deliberate policy of "Americanization" through the public school system seems fairly certain.

The fact that all education must be and ought to be guided by definite values is, however, also the source of real dangers in any system of public education. One has to admit that in this respect most nineteenth-century liberals were guided by a naïve overconfidence in what mere communication of knowledge could achieve. In their rationalistic liberalism they often presented the case for general education as though the dispersion of knowledge would solve all major problems and as though it were necessary only to convey to the masses that little extra knowledge which the educated already possessed in order that this "conquest of ignorance" should initiate a new era. There is not much reason to believe that, if at any one time the best knowledge which some possess were made available to all, the result would be a much better society. [Knowledge and ignorance are very relative concepts, and there is little evidence that the difference in knowledge which at any one time exists between the more and the less educated of a society can have such a decisive influence on its character]

2. If we accept the general argument for compulsory education, there remain these chief problems: How is this education to be provided? How much of it is to be provided for all? How are those who are to be given more to be selected and at whose expense? It is probably a necessary consequence of the adoption of compulsory education that for those families to whom the cost would be a severe burden it should be defrayed out of public funds. There is still the question, however, how much education should be provided at public expense and in what manner it should be provided. It is true that, historically, compulsory education was usually preceded by the governments' increasing opportunities by providing state schools. The earliest experiments with making education compulsory, those in Prussia at the beginning of the eighteenth century, were in fact confined to those districts where the govern-

---

also avoided all interference with private life. There was no compulsory education nor state schools.'"—Ed.]

ment had provided schools. There can be little doubt that in this manner the process of making education general was greatly facilitated. Imposing general education on a people largely unfamiliar with its institutions and advantages would indeed be difficult. This does not mean, however, that compulsory education or even government-financed general education today requires the educational institutions to be run by the government.

It is a curious fact that one of the first effective systems under which compulsory education was combined with the provision of most educational institutions by the government was created by one of the great advocates of individual liberty, Wilhelm von Humboldt, only fifteen years after he had argued that public education was harmful because it prevented variety in accomplishments and unnecessary because in a free nation there would be no lack of educational institutions. "Education," he had said, "seems to me to lie wholly beyond the limits within which political agency should be properly confined."[3] It was the plight of Prussia during the Napoleonic wars and the needs of national defense that made him abandon his earlier position. The desire for "the development of the individual personalities in their greatest variety" which had inspired his earlier work became secondary when desire for a strong organized state led him to devote much of his later life to the building of a system of state education that became a model for the rest of the world. It can scarcely be denied that the general level of education which Prussia thus

[3] Wilhelm von Humboldt, *Über die Grenzen der Wirksamkeit des Staates* (Nuremberg: Verlag Hans Carl, 1946) (written in 1792, but first completely published in Breslau in 1851 under the title *Ideen zu einem Versuch, die Gränzen der Wirksamkeit des Staats zu bestimmen*), chap. 6, summary at the beginning and the concluding sentence. [The English quotation can be found in the standard English edition, *The Sphere and Duties of Government*, Joseph Coulthard, Jr., trans. (London: John Chapman, 1854), p. 71 (Liberty Fund edition, p. 52). The sentence Hayek here quotes is indeed the concluding sentence of chapter 6, which in German reads: "Öffentliche Erziehung scheint mir daher ganz außerhalb der Schranken zu liegen, in welchen der Staat seine Wirksamkeit halten muß" (*Über die Grenzen*, p. 85). The summary reads: "Having seen in a preceding chapter that it is not only a justifiable but necessary end of Government to provide for the mutual security of the citizens, it here becomes our duty to enter on a more profound and explicit investigation into the nature of such a solicitude, and the means through which it acts. For it does not seem enough merely to commit the care for security to the political power as a general and unconditional duty, but it further becomes us to define the especial limits of its activity in this respect or, at least, should this general definition be difficult, or wholly impossible, to exhibit the reasons for that impossibility, and discover the characteristics by which these limits may, in given cases, be recognized" (p. 62; Liberty Fund edition, p.46). ("Eine tiefere und ausführlichere Prüfung erfordert die Sorgfalt des Staats für die innere Sicherheit der Bürger unter einander, zu der ich mich jetzt wende. Denn es scheint mir nicht hinlänglich, demselben bloß allgemein die Erhaltung derselben zur Pflicht zu machen, sondern ich halte es vielmehr für notwendig, die besondern Grenzen dabei zu bestimmen oder wenn dies allgemein nicht möglich sein sollte, wenigstens die Gründe dieser Unmöglichkeit auseinanderzusetzen und die Merkmale anzugeben, an welchen sie in gegebenen Fällen zu erkennen sein möchten." The quotation falls on p. 77 of the 1946 German edition.)—Ed.]

attained was one of the chief causes of her rapid economic rise and later that of all Germany. One may well ask, however, whether this success was not bought at too high a price. The role played by Prussia during the succeeding generations may make one doubt whether the much lauded Prussian school-master was an unmixed blessing for the world, or even for Prussia.

The very magnitude of the power over men's minds that a highly central-ized and government-dominated system of education places in the hands of the authorities ought to make one hesitate before accepting it too readily. Up to a point, the arguments that justify compulsory education also require that government should prescribe some of the content of this education. As we have already mentioned, there may be circumstances in which the case for authority's providing a common cultural background for all citizens becomes very strong. Yet we must remember that it is the provision of education by government which creates such problems as that of the segregation of Negroes in the United States—difficult problems of ethnic or religious minor-ities which are bound to arise where government takes control of the chief instruments of transmitting culture. In multinational states the problem of who is to control the school system tends to become the chief source of fric-tion between nationalities. To one who has seen this happen in countries like the old Austria-Hungary, there is much force in the argument that it may be better even that some children should go without formal education than that they should be killed in fighting over who is to control that education.[4]

Even in ethnically homogeneous states, however, there are strong argu-ments against entrusting to government that degree of control of the contents of education which it will possess if it directly manages most of the schools that are accessible to the great masses. Even if education were a science which provided us with the best of methods of achieving certain goals, we could hardly wish the latest methods to be applied universally and to the complete exclusion of others—still less that the aims should be uniform. Very few of the problems of education, however, are scientific questions in the sense that they can be decided by any objective tests. They are mostly either outright questions of value, or at least the kind of questions concerning which the only ground for trusting the judgment of some people rather than that of others is that the former have shown more good sense in other respects. Indeed, the very possibility that, with a system of government education, all elemen-tary education may come to be dominated by the theories of a particular group who genuinely believe that they have scientific answers to those prob-

---

[4] Cf. Ludwig von Mises, *Nation, Staat und Wirtschaft. Beiträge zur Politik und Geschichte der Zeit* (Vienna and Leipzig: Manzscher Verlag, 1919). [This work was translated into English as *Nation, State, and Economy: Contributions to the Politics and History of Our Time,* Leland B. Yeager, trans. (New York: New York University Press, 1983). A Liberty Fund edition was released in 2006.—Ed.]

lems (as has happened to a large extent in the United States during the last thirty years) should be sufficient to warn us of the risks involved in subjecting the whole educational system to central direction.

3. In fact, the more highly one rates the power that education can have over men's minds, the more convinced one should be of the danger of placing this power in the hands of any single authority. But even if one does not rate its power to do good as highly as did some of the rationalistic liberals of the nineteenth century, however, the mere recognition of this power should lead us to conclusions almost the opposite of theirs. And if, at present, one of the reasons why there should be the greatest variety of educational opportunities is that we really know so little about what different educational techniques may achieve, the argument for variety would be even stronger if we knew more about the methods of producing certain types of results—as we soon may.

In the field of education perhaps more than in any other, the greatest dangers to freedom are likely to come from the development of psychological techniques which may soon give us far greater power than we ever had to shape men's minds deliberately. But knowledge of what we can make of human beings if we can control the essential conditions of their development, though it will offer a frightful temptation, does not necessarily mean that we shall by its use improve upon the human being who has been allowed to develop freely. It is by no means clear that it would be a gain if we could produce the human types that it was generally thought we needed. It is not at all unlikely that the great problem in this field will soon be that of preventing the use of powers which we do possess and which may present a strong temptation to all those who regard a controlled result as invariably superior to an uncontrolled one. Indeed, we may soon find that the solution has to lie in government ceasing to be the chief dispenser of education and becoming the impartial protector of the individual against all uses of such newly found powers.

Not only is the case against the management of schools by government now stronger than ever, but most of the reasons which in the past could have been advanced in its favor have disappeared. Whatever may have been true then, there can be little doubt that today, with the traditions and institutions of universal education firmly established and with modern transportation solving most of the difficulties of distance, it is no longer necessary that education be not only financed but also provided by government.

As has been shown by Professor Milton Friedman,[5] it would now be entirely practicable to defray the costs of general education out of the public purse

---

[5] Milton Friedman, "The Role of Government Education," in *Economics and the Public Interest*, Robert Alexander Solo, ed. (New Brunswick, NJ: Rutgers University Press, 1955), pp. 123–44, and Friedman, *Capitalism and Freedom* (Chicago: University of Chicago Press, 1962).

without maintaining government schools, by giving the parents vouchers covering the cost of education of each child which they could hand over to schools of their choice.]It may still be desirable that government directly provide schools in a few isolated communities where the number of children is too small (and the average cost of education therefore too high) for privately run schools. But with respect to the great majority of the population, it would undoubtedly be possible to leave the organization and management of education entirely to private efforts, with the government providing merely the basic finance and ensuring a minimum standard for all schools where the vouchers could be spent. Another great advantage of this plan is that parents would no longer be faced with the alternative of having to accept whatever education the government provides or of paying the entire cost of a different and slightly more expensive education themselves; and if they should choose a school out of the common run, they would be required to pay only the additional cost.]

4. A more difficult problem is how much education is to be provided at public expense and for whom such education is to be provided beyond the minimum assured to all. It can hardly be doubted that the number of those whose contribution to the common needs will be increased by education extended beyond a certain stage sufficiently to justify the cost will always be only a small proportion of the total population. Also, it is probably undeniable that we have no certain methods of ascertaining beforehand who among the young people will derive the greatest benefit from an advanced education. Moreover, whatever we do, it seems inevitable that many of those who get an advanced education will later enjoy material advantages over their fellows only because someone else felt it worthwhile to invest more in their education, and not because of any greater natural capacity or greater effort on their part.

We shall not stop to consider how much education is to be provided for all or how long all children should be required to attend school. The answer must depend in part on particular circumstances, such as the general wealth of the community, the character of its economy, and perhaps even climatic conditions affecting the age of adolescence. In wealthier communities the problem usually is no longer one of what schooling will increase economic efficiency but rather one of how to occupy children, until they are allowed to earn a living, in a manner that will later assist them in better using their leisure.

The really important issue is that of the manner in which those whose education is to be prolonged beyond the general minimum are to be selected. The costs of a prolonged education, in terms of material resources and still more of human ones, are so considerable even for a rich country that the desire to give a large fraction of the population an advanced education will always in some degree conflict with the desire to prolong the education for all. It also seems probable that a society that wishes to get a maximum economic return from a limited expenditure on education should concentrate on the higher education of a comparatively small elite,[6] which today would mean increasing that part of the population getting the most advanced type of education rather than prolonging education for large numbers. Yet, with government education, this would not seem practicable in a democracy, nor would it be desirable that authority should determine who is to get such an education.

As in all other fields, the case for subsidization of higher education (and of research) must rest not on the benefit it confers on the recipient but on the resulting advantages for the community at large. There is, therefore, little case for subsidizing any kind of vocational training, where the greater proficiency acquired will be reflected in greater earning power, which will constitute a fairly adequate measure of the desirability of investing in training of this kind. Much of the increased earnings in occupations requiring such training will be merely a return on the capital invested in it. The best solution would seem to be that those in whom such investment would appear to promise the largest return should be enabled to borrow the capital and later repay it out of their increased earnings, though such an arrangement would meet with considerable practical difficulties.[7]

The situation is somewhat different, however, where the costs of a higher education are not likely to result in a corresponding increase in the price at which the services of the better-trained man can be sold to other individuals (as is the case in the professions of medicine, the law, engineering, and so on) but where the aim is the further dispersion and increase in knowledge throughout the community at large. The benefits that a community receives from its scientists and scholars cannot be measured by the price at which these men can sell particular services, since much of their contribution becomes freely available to all. There is therefore a strong case for assisting at least some of those who show promise and inclination for the pursuit of such studies.

It is a different matter, however, to assume that all who are intellectually capable of acquiring a higher education have a claim to it. That it is in the general interest to enable all the specially intelligent to become learned is by no means evident or that all of them would materially profit by such an advanced education, or even that such an education should be restricted to those who have an unquestionable capacity for it and be made the normal or perhaps the exclusive path to higher positions. As has been pointed out recently, a much sharper division between classes might come to exist, and the less fortunate might become seriously neglected, if all the more intelli-

[6] Cf. George Joseph Stigler, "The Economic Theory of Education" [in an unpublished essay]. [This brief essay, twelve pages in typescript, was written in 1957. It has never appeared in print.—Ed.]

[7] See the interesting proposals suggested by Milton Friedman in "The Role of Government Education," which deserve careful study, though one may feel doubt about their practicability.

gent were deliberately and successfully brought into the wealthy group and it became not only a general presumption but a universal fact that the relatively poor were less intelligent. There is also another problem which has assumed serious proportions in some European countries and which we ought to keep in mind, and this is the problem of having more intellectuals than we can profitably employ. There are few greater dangers to political stability than the existence of an intellectual proletariat who find no outlet for their learning.

The general problem we are faced with in all higher education, then, is this: by some method, certain young people must be selected, at an age when one cannot know with any certainty who will profit most, to be given an education that will enable them to earn a higher income than the rest; and to justify the investment, they must be selected so that, on the whole, they will be qualified to earn a higher income. Finally, we have to accept the fact that, since as a rule somebody else will have to pay for the education, those who benefit from it will thus be enjoying an "unearned" advantage.

5. In recent times the difficulties of this problem have been greatly increased and a reasonable solution made almost impossible by the increasing use of government education as an instrument for egalitarian aims. Though a case can be made for assuring opportunities for an advanced education as far as possible to those most likely to profit from them, the control of government over education has in large measure been used to equalize the prospects of all, which is something very different. Though egalitarians usually protest against the imputation that their goal is any sort of mechanical equality which would deprive some people of advantages which cannot be provided for all, there is in education a clear indication that such is the tendency. This egalitarian stand is usually not so explicitly argued as in R. H. Tawney's *Equality*, in which influential tract the author contends that it would be unjust "to spend less liberally on the education of the slow than on that of the intelligent."[8] But to some extent the two conflicting desires of equalizing opportunity and of adjusting opportunity to capacity (which, as we know, has little to do with merit in any moral sense) have become everywhere confused.

It should be admitted that, so far as education at public expense is concerned, the argument for equal treatment of all is strong. When it is combined, however, with an argument against permitting any special advantages to the more fortunate ones, it means in effect that all must be given what any child gets and that none should have what cannot be provided for all. Consistently pursued, it would mean that no more must be spent on the education of any child than can be spent on the education of every child. If this were the necessary consequence of public education, it would constitute a strong argu-

[8] Richard Henry Tawney, *Equality*, Halley Stewart Lectures, 1929 (London: Allen and Unwin, 1931), p. 52.

ment against government's concerning itself with education beyond the elementary level, which can indeed be given to all, and for leaving all advanced education in private hands.

At any rate, the fact that certain advantages must be limited to some does not mean that a single authority should have exclusive power to decide to whom they should go. It is not likely that such power in the hands of authority would in the long run really advance education or that it would create social conditions that would be felt to be more satisfactory or just than they would otherwise have been. On the first point it should be clear that no single authority should have the monopoly of judging how valuable a particular kind of education is and how much should be invested in more education or in which of the different kinds of education. There is not—and cannot be in a free society—a single standard by which we can decide on the relative importance of different aims or the relative desirability of different methods. Perhaps in no other field is the continued availability of alternative ways as important as in that of education, where the task is to prepare young people for an ever changing world.

So far as justice is concerned, we should be clear that those who in the general interest most "deserve" an advanced education are not necessarily those who by effort and sacrifice have earned the greatest subjective merit. Natural capacity and inborn aptitude are as much "unfair advantages" as accidents of environment, and to confine the advantages of higher education to those that we can confidently foresee profiting most from them will necessarily increase rather than decrease the discrepancy between economic status and subjective merit.

The desire to eliminate the effects of accident, which lies at the root of the demand for "social justice," can be satisfied in the field of education, as elsewhere, only by eliminating all those opportunities which are not subject to deliberate control. But the growth of civilization rests largely on the individuals' making the best use of whatever accidents they encounter, of the essentially unpredictable advantages that one kind of knowledge will in new circumstances confer on one individual over others.

However commendable may be the motives of those who fervently desire that, in the interest of justice, all should be made to start with the same chances, theirs is an ideal that is literally impossible to realize. Furthermore, any pretense that it has been achieved or even closely approached can only make matters worse for the less successful. Though there is every case for removing whatever special obstacles existing institutions may put in the way of some, it is neither possible nor desirable to make all start with the same chances, since this can be achieved only by depriving some of possibilities that cannot be provided for all. While we wish everybody's opportunities to be as great as possible, we should certainly decrease those of most if we were to prevent them from being any greater than those of the least fortunate. To say that all who live at the same time in any given country should start at the same place is no more reconcilable with a developing civilization than to say that this kind of equality should be assured to people living at different times or at different places.

It may be in the interest of the community that some who show exceptional capacities for scholarly or scientific pursuits should be given an opportunity to follow them irrespective of family means. But this does not confer a right on anyone to such opportunity; nor does it mean that only those whose exceptional capacities can be ascertained ought to have the opportunity or that nobody should have it unless it can be assured to all who can pass the same objective tests.

Not all the qualities which enable one to make special contributions are ascertainable by examinations or tests, and it is more important that at least some of those who possess such qualities have an opportunity than that it be given to all who satisfy the same requirements. A passionate desire for knowledge or an unusual combination of interests may be more important than the more visible gifts or any testable capacities; and a background of general knowledge and interests or a high esteem for knowledge produced by family environment often contributes more to achievement than natural capacity. That there are some people who enjoy the advantages of a favorable home atmosphere is an asset to society which egalitarian policies can destroy but which cannot be utilized without the appearance of unmerited inequalities. And since a desire for knowledge is a bent that is likely to be transmitted through the family, there is a strong case for enabling parents who greatly care for education to secure it for their children by a material sacrifice, even if on other grounds these children may appear less deserving than others who will not get it.[9]

6. The insistence that education should be given only to those of proved capacity produces a situation in which the whole population is graded according to some objective test and in which one set of opinions as to what kind of person qualifies for the benefits of an advanced education prevails throughout. This means an official ranking of people into a hierarchy, with the cer-

[9] A problem which is not taken care of in present conditions is that presented by the occasional young person in whom a passionate desire for knowledge appears without any recognizable special gifts in the standard subjects of instruction. Such a desire ought to count for much more than it does, and the opportunity of working through college does not really solve the problem on a higher level. It has always seemed to me that there is a strong case for institutions which fulfill the functions that the monasteries fulfilled in the past, where those who cared enough could, at the price of renouncing many of the comforts and pleasures of life, earn the opportunity of devoting all the formative period of their development to the pursuit of knowledge.

tified genius on top and the certified moron at the bottom, a hierarchy made much worse by the fact that it is presumed to express "merit" and will determine access to the opportunities in which value can show itself. Where exclusive reliance on a system of government education is intended to serve "social justice," a single view of what constitutes an advanced education—and then of the capacities which qualify for it—will apply throughout, and the fact that somebody has received an advanced education will be presumed to indicate that he had "deserved" it.

In education, as in other fields, the admitted fact that the public has an interest in assisting some must not be taken to mean that only those who are judged by some agreed view to deserve assistance out of public funds should be allowed access to an advanced education, or that nobody should be allowed to assist specific individuals on other grounds. There is probably much to be said for some members of each of the different groups of the population being given a chance, even if the best from some groups seem less qualified than members of other groups who do not get it. For this reason, different local, religious, occupational, or ethnic groups should be able to assist some of the young members, so that those who receive a higher education will represent their respective group somewhat in proportion to the esteem in which the latter hold education.

It must at least seem doubtful that a society in which educational opportunities were universally awarded according to presumed capacity would be more tolerable for the unsuccessful ones than one in which accidents of birth admittedly played a great role. In Britain, where the postwar reform of education has gone a long way toward establishing a system based on presumed capacity, the consequences already cause concern. A recent study of social mobility suggests that it now "will be the grammar schools which will furnish the new *elite*, an elite apparently much less assailable because it is selected for 'measured intelligence.' The selection process will tend to reinforce the prestige of occupations already high in social status and to divide the population into streams which many may come to regard, indeed already regard, as distinct as sheep and goats. Not to have been to a grammar school will be a more serious disqualification than in the past, when social inequality in the educational system was known to exist. And the feeling of resentment may become more rather than less acute just because the individual concerned realizes that there is some validity in the selection process which has kept him out of grammar school. In this respect apparent justice may be more difficult to bear than injustice."[10] Or, as another British writer has observed more generally, "it is

[10] David Victor Glass, "Introduction," in the volume edited by him and entitled *Social Mobility in Britain* (London: Routledge and Kegan Paul, 1954), pp. 25–26; see also the review of this

one unexpected result of the Welfare State that it should make the social pattern not less rigid but more so."[11]

Let us by all means endeavor to increase opportunities for all. But we ought to do so in the full knowledge that to increase opportunities for all is likely to favor those better able to take advantage of them and may often at first increase inequalities. Where the demand for "equality of opportunity" leads to attempts to eliminate such "unfair advantages," it is only likely to do harm. All human differences, whether they are differences in natural gifts or in opportunities, create unfair advantages. But, since the chief contribution of any individual is to make the best use of the accidents he encounters, success must to a great extent be a matter of chance.

7. On the highest level the dissemination of knowledge by instruction becomes inseparable from the advance of knowledge by research. The introduction to those problems which are on the boundaries of knowledge can be given only by men whose main occupation is research. During the nineteenth century the universities, particularly those on the European Continent, in fact developed into institutions which, at their best, provided education as a by-product of research and where the student acquired knowledge by working as an apprentice to the creative scientist or scholar. Since then, because of the increased amount of knowledge that must be mastered before the boundaries of knowledge are reached, and because of the increasing numbers receiving a university education without any intention of ever reaching that stage, the character of the universities has greatly changed. The greater part of what is still called "university work" is today in character and substance merely a continuation of school instruction. Only the "graduate" or "postgraduate" schools—in fact, only the best of these—are still mainly devoted to the kind of work that characterized the Continental universities of the last century.

There is no reason to think, however, that we are not as much in need of the more advanced type of work. It is still this kind of work on which the general level of the intellectual life of a country chiefly depends. And while in the experimental sciences research institutes in which the young scientists serve

work by Adam Curle, "The Scale of Prestige: Review of D. V. Glass, *Social Mobility in Britain*," in *The New Statesman and Nation*, n.s., 48 (August 14, 1954): 190, col. 2, where it is suggested that "the educational dilemma is that the desire to produce a more 'open' society may simply end in one which, while flexible so far as individuals are concerned, is just as rigidly stratified on an I.Q. basis as it was once by birth." Cf. also Michael Young, *The Rise of the Meritocracy, 1870–2033: An Essay on Education and Equality* (London: Thames and Hudson, 1958).

[11] Sir Charles Percy Snow, quoted in *Time*, May 27, 1957, p. 106. [The quotation originates in a letter by Snow to the (London) *Sunday Times* of January 8, 1956. The original reads: "it is an unexpected result of the Welfare State that in this sense it should make the social pattern not less rigid but much more so." The quotation as Hayek has it is an exact transcription of the *Time* article.—Ed.]

their apprenticeship are in some measure fulfilling this need, there is danger that in some fields of scholarship the democratic broadening of education may be detrimental to the pursuit of that original work that keeps knowledge alive.

There is probably less cause for concern about the supposedly inadequate number of university-trained specialists that are currently being produced in the Western world[12] than about the inadequate output of men of really top quality. And though, at least in the United States, and to an increasing extent also elsewhere, the responsibility for this rests mainly with the inadequate preparation by the schools and with the utilitarian bias of institutions concerned primarily with conferring professional qualifications, we must not overlook the democratic preference for providing better material opportunities for large numbers over the advancement of knowledge, which will always be the work of the relatively few and which indeed has the strongest claim for public support.

The reason why it still seems probable that institutions like the old universities, devoted to research and teaching at the boundaries of knowledge, will continue to remain the chief sources of new knowledge is that only such institutions can offer that freedom in the choice of problems and those contacts between representatives of the different disciplines that provide the best conditions for the conception and pursuit of new ideas. However greatly progress in a known direction may be accelerated by the deliberate organization of work aiming at some known goal, the decisive and unforeseeable steps in the general advance usually occur not in the pursuit of specific ends but in the exploitation of those opportunities which the accidental combination of particular knowledge and gifts and special circumstances and contacts have placed in the way of some individual. Though the specialized research institution may be the most efficient for all tasks that are of an "applied" character, such institutional research is always in some measure directed research, the aim of which is determined by the specialized equipment, the particular team assembled, and the concrete purpose to which the institution is dedicated. But in "fundamental" research on the outskirts of knowledge there are often no fixed subjects or fields, and the decisive advances will frequently be due to the disregard of the conventional division of disciplines.

8. The problem of supporting the advance of knowledge in the most effective manner is therefore closely connected with the issue of "academic freedom." The conceptions for which this term stands were developed in the countries of the European Continent, where the universities were generally state

---

[12] David Mordecai Blank and George Joseph Stigler, *The Demand and Supply of Scientific Personnel* (New York: National Bureau of Economic Research, 1957).

institutions; thus they were directed almost entirely against political interference with the work of these institutions.[13] The real issue, however, is a much wider one. There would be nearly as strong a case against any unitary planning and direction of all research by a senate composed of the most highly reputed scientists and scholars as there is against such direction by more extraneous authorities. Though it is natural that the individual scientist should most resent interference with his choice or pursuit of problems when it is motivated by what to him seem irrelevant considerations, it might be still less harmful if there were a multiplicity of such institutions, each subject to different outside pressures, than if they were all under the unified control of one single conception of what at a given moment was in the best scientific interest.

Academic freedom cannot mean, of course, that every scientist should do what seems most desirable to him. Nor does it mean self-government of science as a whole. It means rather that there should be as many independent centers of work as possible, in which at least those men who have proved their capacity to advance knowledge and their devotion to their task can themselves determine the problems on which they are to spend their energies and where they can expound the conclusions they have reached, whether or not these conclusions are palatable to their employer or the public at large.[14]

In practice, this means that those men who have already proved themselves in the eyes of their peers, and who, for this reason, have been given senior positions in which they can determine both their own work and that of their juniors, should be given security of tenure. This is a privilege conferred for reason similar to those which have made it desirable to make the position of judges secure, and it is conferred not in the interest of the individual but because it is rightly believed that persons in such positions will, on the whole, serve the public interest best if they are protected against pressure from outside opinion. It is of course not an unlimited privilege, and it means merely that, once it is granted, it cannot be withdrawn except for reasons specifically provided for in the original appointment.

There is no reason why these terms should not be altered for new appointments as we gain new experience, though such new conditions cannot apply to those who already possess what in the United States is called "tenure." For example, recent experience seems to suggest that the terms of appointment should specify that the occupant of such a position forfeits the privilege if he

---

[13] It is significant that in England, where the universities were endowed corporations, each consisting of a large number of self-governing bodies, academic freedom has never become a serious issue in the manner in which it did where universities were government institutions.

[14] Cf. Michael Polanyi, *The Logic of Liberty: Reflections and Rejoinders* (London: Routledge and Kegan Paul, 1951), p. 33: "Academic freedom consists in the right to choose one's own problems for investigation, to conduct research free from any outside control, and to teach one's subject in the light of one's own opinion."

knowingly joins or supports any movement that is opposed to the very principles on which this privilege rests. Tolerance should not include the advocacy of intolerance. On this ground I feel that a Communist should not be given "tenure," though, once he has been given it without such explicit limitations, it would have to be respected like any other similar appointment.

All this applies, however, only to the special privilege of "tenure." Apart from these considerations pertinent to tenure, there exists little justification for anyone claiming as a matter of right the freedom to do or teach what he likes or, on the other hand, for any hard-and-fast rule stating that anyone holding a particular opinion should be universally excluded. Though an institution aiming at high standards will soon discover that it can attract first-class talent only if it grants even its youngest members a wide choice of pursuits and opinions, no one has the right to be employed by an institution irrespective of the interests and views he holds.

9. The need for protecting institutions of learning against the cruder kind of interference by political or economic interests is so well recognized today that there is not much danger of its being successfully exercised in reputable institutions. There is still need for watchfulness, especially in the social sciences, where the pressure is often exercised in the name of highly idealistic and widely approved aims. Pressure against an unpopular view is more harmful than opposition to a popular one. It should certainly be a warning to us that even Thomas Jefferson argued that in the field of government the principles taught and the texts to be followed in the University of Virginia should be prescribed by authority, because the next professor might be "one of the school of quondam federalism"![15]

Today the danger lies, however, not so much in obvious outside interference as in the increased control which the growing financial needs of research give to those who hold the purse strings. It constitutes a real threat to the interests of scientific advance because the ideal of a unified and centralized direction of all scientific efforts which it might be made to serve is shared by some of the scientists themselves. Although the first great attack which, in the name of

[15] Thomas Jefferson [to Joseph Carrington Cabell], February 3, 1825, in *The Writings of Thomas Jefferson: Being his Autobiography, Correspondence, Reports, Messages, Addresses, and Other Writings, Official and Private*, Henry Augustine Washington, ed. [Published by the Order of the Joint Committee of Congress on the Library, from the original manuscripts, deposited in the Department of State] (9 vols.; New York: J. C. Riker, 1853–54), vol. 7, p. 397. It should be said that Jefferson's opposition to academic freedom was quite consistent with his general position on such matters, which, in the manner of most doctrinaire democrats, made him equally oppose the independence of judges. See also his report to the President and Directors of the Literary Fund, October 5, 1824, in *Early History of the University of Virginia, as Contained in the Letters of Thomas Jefferson and Joseph C. Cabell*, Nathaniel Francis Cabell, ed. (Richmond, VA: J. W. Randolph, 1856), p. 482. See also *Letters and Other Writings of James Madison, Fourth president of the United States, Published by Order of Congress* (4 vols.; Philadelphia: J. B. Lippincott and Co., 1865), vol. 3, pp. 481–83.

planning of science and under strong Marxist influence, was launched in the 1930s has been successfully repelled,[16] and the discussions to which it gave rise have created a greater awareness of the importance of freedom in this field, it seems probable that the attempts to "organize" scientific effort and to direct it to particular goals will reappear in new forms.

The conspicuous successes which the Russians have achieved in certain fields and which are the cause of the renewed interest in the deliberate organization of scientific effort should not have surprised us and should give us no reason for altering our opinion about the importance of freedom. That any one goal, or any limited number of objectives, which are already known to be achievable, are likely to be reached sooner if they are given priority in a central allocation of all resources cannot be disputed. This is the reason why a totalitarian organization is indeed likely to be more effective in a short war—and why such a government is so dangerous to the others when it is in a position to choose the most favorable moment for war. But this does not mean that the advance of knowledge in general is likely to be faster if all efforts are directed to what now seem the most important goals or that, in the long run, the nation that has more deliberately organized its efforts will be the stronger.[17]

Another factor that has contributed to the belief in the superiority of directed research is the somewhat exaggerated conception of the extent to which modern industry owes its progress to the organized teamwork of the great industrial laboratories. In fact, as has been shown recently in some detail,[18] a much greater proportion than is generally believed even of the chief technological advances of recent times has come from individual efforts, often from men pursuing an amateur interest or who were led to their problems by accident. And what appears to be true of the more applied fields is certainly even more true of basic research, where the important advances are, by their nature, more difficult to foresee. In this field there may indeed be danger in the current emphasis on teamwork and co-operation, and it may well be the greater individualism of the European (which is partly owing to his being less used to and therefore less dependent on ample material support) which still seems to give him some advantage over the American scientist in the most original sphere of fundamental research.

[16] Cf. John Randal Baker, *Science and the Planned State* (London: Allen and Unwin, 1945).

[17] This is not the place to enter into a discussion of the Russian educational system. But it may be briefly mentioned that its chief differences from the American system have little to do with the different social order and that, in fact, the Russians are merely following a Continental European tradition. In the critical aspects the achievements of the German or French or Scandinavian schools would repay study as much as the Russian ones.

[18] See John Jewkes, David Sawers, and Richard Stillerman, *The Sources of Invention* (London: Macmillan, 1958), esp. pp. 197–222.

There is perhaps no more important application of our main theses than that the advance of knowledge is likely to be fastest where scientific pursuits are not determined by some unified conception of their social utility, and where each proved man can devote himself to the tasks in which he sees the best chance of making a contribution. Where, as is increasingly the case in all the experimental fields, this opportunity can no longer be given by assuring to every qualified student the possibility of deciding how to use his own time, but where large material means are required for most kinds of work, the prospects of advance would be most favorable if, instead of the control of funds being in the hands of a single authority proceeding according to a unitary plan, there were a multiplicity of independent sources so that even the unorthodox thinker would have a chance of finding a sympathetic ear.

Though we still have much to learn about the best manner of managing independent funds devoted to the support of research and though it may not be certain whether the influence of the very large foundations (with their inevitable dependence on majority opinion and consequent tendency to accentuate the swings of scientific fashion) has always been as beneficial as it might have been, there can be little doubt that the multiplicity of private endowments interested in limited fields is one of the most promising features of the American situation. But though present tax laws may have temporarily increased the flow of such funds, we should also remember that the same laws make the accumulation of new fortunes more difficult, and that to that extent these sources are likely to dry up in the future. As elsewhere, the preservation of freedom in the spheres of the mind and of the spirit will depend, in the long run, on the dispersal of the control of the material means and on the continued existence of individuals who are in a position to devote large funds to purposes which seem important to them.

10. Nowhere is freedom more important than where our ignorance is greatest—at the boundaries of knowledge, in other words, where nobody can predict what lies a step ahead. Though freedom has been threatened even there, it is still the field where we can count on most men rallying to its defense when they recognize the threat. If in this book we have been concerned mainly with freedom in other fields, it is because we so often forget today that intellectual freedom rests on a much wider foundation of freedom and cannot exist without it. But the ultimate aim of freedom is the enlargement of those capacities in which man surpasses his ancestors and to which each generation must endeavor to add its share—its share in the growth of knowledge and the gradual advance of moral and aesthetic beliefs, where no superior must be allowed to enforce one set of views of what is right or good and where only further experience can decide what should prevail.

It is wherever man reaches beyond his present self, where the new emerges and assessment lies in the future, that liberty ultimately shows its value. The problems of education and research have thus brought us back to the leading theme of this book, from where the consequences of freedom and restriction are more remote and less visible to where they most directly affect the ultimate values. And we cannot think of better words to conclude than those of Wilhelm von Humboldt which a hundred years ago John Stuart Mill put in front of his essay *On Liberty:* "The grand, leading principle, towards which every argument hitherto unfolded in these pages directly converges, is the absolute and essential importance of human development in its richest diversity."[19]

[19] Wilhelm von Humboldt, *The Sphere and Duties of Government,* Joseph Coulthard, Jr., trans. (London: John Chapman, 1854), p. 65 [Liberty Fund edition, p. 48]. [The German reads: "Nach dem ganzen vorigen Räsonnement kommt schlechterdings alles auf Ausbildung des Menschen in der höchsten Mannigfaltigkeit an." (*Über die Grenzen der Wirksamkeit des Staates* [Nuremberg: Verlag Hans Carl, 1946], p. 80)—Ed.] John Stuart Mill took the quotation from this translation.

WHY I AM NOT A CONSERVATIVE

At all times sincere friends of freedom have been rare, and its triumphs have been due to minorities, that have prevailed by associating themselves with auxiliaries whose objects often differed from their own; and this association, which is always dangerous, has sometimes been disastrous, by giving to opponents just grounds of opposition. —Lord Acton

The quotation at the head of the Postscript is taken from Acton, *History of Freedom*, p. 1 [Liberty Fund edition, *Essays in the History of Liberty*, p. 1].

WHY I AM NOT A CONSERVATIVE

1. At a time when most movements that are thought to be progressive advocate further encroachments on individual liberty,[1] those who cherish freedom are likely to expend their energies in opposition. In this they find themselves much of the time on the same side as those who habitually resist change. In matters of current politics today they generally have little choice but to support the conservative parties. But, though the position I have tried to define is also often described as "conservative," it is very different from that to which this name has been traditionally attached. There is danger in the confused condition which brings the defenders of liberty and the true conservatives together in common opposition to developments which threaten their different ideals equally. It is therefore important to distinguish clearly the position taken here from that which has long been known—perhaps more appropriately—as conservatism.

Conservatism proper is a legitimate, probably necessary, and certainly widespread attitude of opposition to drastic change. It has, since the French Revolution, for a century and a half played an important role in European politics. Until the rise of socialism its opposite was liberalism. There is nothing corresponding to this conflict in the history of the United States, because what in Europe was called "liberalism" was here the common tradition on which the American polity had been built: thus the defender of the American tradition was a liberal in the European sense.[2] This already existing confusion was made worse by the recent attempt to transplant to America the European type of conservatism, which, being alien to the American tradition, has acquired a somewhat odd character. And some time before this, American radicals

---

[1] This has now been true for over a century, and as early as 1855 John Stuart Mill in a letter to Harriet Taylor, Rome, 15 January 1855 (Friedrich August Hayek, *John Stuart Mill and Harriet Taylor: Their Correspondence and Subsequent Marriage* [London: Routledge and Kegan Paul, 1951], p. 216) could say that "almost all the projects of social reformers of these days are really *liberticide*."

[2] Bernard Crick, "The Strange Quest for an American Conservatism," *Review of Politics*, 17 (1955): 365, says rightly that "the normal American who calls himself 'a conservative' is, in fact, a liberal." It would appear that the reluctance of these conservatives to call themselves by the more appropriate name dates only from its abuse during the New Deal era.

and socialists began calling themselves "liberals." I will nevertheless continue for the moment to describe as liberal the position which I hold and which I believe differs as much from true conservatism as from socialism. Let me say at once, however, that I do so with increasing misgivings, and I shall later have to consider what would be the appropriate name for the party of liberty. The reason for this is not only that the term "liberal" in the United States is the cause of constant misunderstandings today, but also that in Europe the predominant type of rationalistic liberalism has long been one of the pacemakers of socialism.

Let me now state what seems to me the decisive objection to any conservatism which deserves to be called such. It is that by its very nature it cannot offer an alternative to the direction in which we are moving. It may succeed by its resistance to current tendencies in slowing down undesirable developments, but, since it does not indicate another direction, it cannot prevent their continuance. It has, for this reason, invariably been the fate of conservatism to be dragged along a path not of its own choosing. The tug of war between conservatives and progressives can only affect the speed, not the direction, of contemporary developments. But, though there is need for a "brake on the vehicle of progress,"[3] I personally cannot be content with simply helping to apply the brake. What the liberal must ask, first of all, is not how fast or how far we should move, but where we should move. In fact, he differs much more from the collectivist radical of today than does the conservative. While the last generally holds merely a mild and moderate version of the prejudices of his time, the liberal today must more positively oppose some of the basic conceptions which most conservatives share with the socialists.

2. The picture generally given of the relative position of the three parties does more to obscure than to elucidate their true relations. They are usually represented as different positions on a line, with the socialists on the left, the conservatives on the right, and the liberals somewhere in the middle. Nothing could be more misleading. If we want a diagram, it would be more appropriate to arrange them in a triangle with the conservatives occupying one corner, with the socialists pulling toward the second and the liberals toward the third. But, as the socialists have for a long time been able to pull harder, the conservatives have tended to follow the socialist rather than the liberal direction and have adopted at appropriate intervals of time those ideas made respectable by radical propaganda. It has been regularly the conservatives who have compromised with socialism and stolen its thunder. Advocates of the Middle Way[4]

---

[3] The expression is that of Robin George Collingwood, *The New Leviathan; or, Man, Society, Civilization and Barbarism* (Oxford: Clarendon Press, 1942), p. 209.

[4] Cf. the characteristic choice of this title for the programmatic book by British Prime Minister Harold Macmillan, *The Middle Way: A Study of the Problem of Economic and Social Progress in a Free and Democratic Society* (London: Macmillan, 1938). [Harold Macmillan became prime minis-

with no goal of their own, conservatives have been guided by the belief that the truth must lie somewhere between the extremes—with the result that they have shifted their position every time a more extreme movement appeared on either wing.

The position which can be rightly described as conservative at any time depends, therefore, on the direction of existing tendencies. Since the development during the last decades has been generally in a socialist direction, it may seem that both conservatives and liberals have been mainly intent on retarding that movement. But the main point about liberalism is that it wants to go elsewhere, not to stand still. Though today the contrary impression may sometimes be caused by the fact that there was a time when liberalism was more widely accepted and some of its objectives closer to being achieved, it has never been a backward-looking doctrine. There has never been a time when liberal ideals were fully realized and when liberalism did not look forward to further improvement of institutions. Liberalism is not averse to evolution and change; and where spontaneous change has been smothered by government control, it wants a great deal of change of policy. So far as much of current governmental action is concerned, there is in the present world very little reason for the liberal to wish to preserve things as they are. It would seem to the liberal, indeed, that what is most urgently needed in most parts of the world is a thorough sweeping-away of the obstacles to free growth.

This difference between liberalism and conservatism must not be obscured by the fact that in the United States it is still possible to defend individual liberty by defending long-established institutions. To the liberal they are valuable not mainly because they are long established or because they are American but because they correspond to the ideals which he cherishes.

3. Before I consider the main points on which the liberal attitude is sharply opposed to the conservative one, I ought to stress that there is much that the liberal might with advantage have learned from the work of some conservative thinkers. To their loving and reverential study of the value of grown institutions we owe (at least outside the field of economics) some profound insights

---

ter and leader of the Conservative Party on the resignation of Anthony Eden in January 1957. He remained in that office until he himself resigned in October 1963, when he was replaced as prime minister by his foreign secretary, Alec Douglas-Home.—Ed.] Unfortunately, for the most part this is the social doctrine adopted by the Roman Catholic Church and certain conscientious German social democrats, who were able to cite one of the nation's leading Catholic social philosophers, Oswald von Nell-Breuning, in their recent publication, Sozialdemokratische Partei Deutschlands, *Godesberger Programm: Zur Situation nach Mater Magistra* (Bonn: Sozialdemokratische Partei, 1962), p. 25: "Soweit auf sozialem und ökonomischem Gebiet Differenzen in der Christlichen Soziallehre bestehen, sind sie auf jeden Fall geringer als die Differenzen zwischen Neoliberalismus und christlicher Soziallehre." ["As far as there are differences within Christian social teaching in social and economic matters, these are in any case smaller than the differences between neoliberalism and Christian social teaching."—Ed.]

which are real contributions to our understanding of a free society. However reactionary in politics such figures as Coleridge, Bonald, De Maistre, Justus Möser, or Donoso Cortès may have been, they did show an understanding of the meaning of spontaneously grown institutions such as language, law, morals, and conventions that anticipated modern scientific approaches and from which the liberals might have profited. But the admiration of the conservatives for free growth generally applies only to the past. They typically lack the courage to welcome the same undesigned change from which new tools of human endeavors will emerge.

This brings me to the first point on which the conservative and the liberal dispositions differ radically. As has often been acknowledged by conservative writers, one of the fundamental traits of the conservative attitude is a fear of change, a timid distrust of the new as such,[5] while the liberal position is based on courage and confidence, on a preparedness to let change run its course even if we cannot predict where it will lead. There would not be much to object to if the conservatives merely disliked too rapid change in institutions and public policy; here the case for caution and slow process is indeed strong. But the conservatives are inclined to use the powers of government to prevent change or to limit its rate to whatever appeals to the more timid mind. In looking forward, they lack the faith in the spontaneous forces of adjustment which makes the liberal accept changes without apprehension, even though he does not know how the necessary adaptations will be brought about. It is, indeed, part of the liberal attitude to assume that, especially in the economic field, the self-regulating forces of the market will somehow bring about the required adjustments to new conditions, although no one can foretell how they will do this in a particular instance. There is perhaps no single factor contributing so much to people's frequent reluctance to let the market work as their inability to conceive how some necessary balance, between demand and supply, between exports and imports, or the like, will be brought about without deliberate control. The conservative feels safe and content only if he is assured that some higher wisdom watches and supervises change, only if he knows that some authority is charged with keeping the change "orderly."

This fear of trusting uncontrolled social forces is closely related to two other characteristics of conservatism: its fondness for authority and its lack of understanding of economic forces. Since it distrusts both abstract theories and general principles,[6] it neither understands those spontaneous forces on which

---

[5] Cf. Hugh Richard Heathcote, Lord Cecil, *Conservatism* (Home University Library; London: Williams and Norgate, 1912), p. 9: "Natural Conservatism . . . is a disposition averse from change; and it springs partly from a distrust of the unknown."

[6] Cf. the revealing self-description of a conservative in Sir Keith Grahame Feiling, *Sketches in Nineteenth Century Biography* (London: Longmans Green, and Co.,1930), p. 174: "Taken in bulk, the Right have a horror of ideas, for is not the practical man, in Disraeli's words, 'one who prac-

a policy of freedom relies nor possesses a basis for formulating principles of policy. Order appears to the conservatives as the result of the continuous attention of authority, which, for this purpose, must be allowed to do what is required by the particular circumstances and not be tied to rigid rule. A commitment to principles presupposes an understanding of the general forces by which the efforts of society are co-ordinated, but it is such a theory of society and especially of the economic mechanism that conservatism conspicuously lacks. So unproductive has conservatism been in producing a general conception of how a social order is maintained that its modern votaries, in trying to construct a theoretical foundation, invariably find themselves appealing almost exclusively to authors who regarded themselves as liberal. Macaulay, Tocqueville, Lord Acton, and Lecky certainly considered themselves liberals, and with justice; and even Edmund Burke remained an Old Whig to the end and would have shuddered at the thought of being regarded as a Tory.

Let me return, however, to the main point, which is the characteristic complacency of the conservative toward the action of established authority and his prime concern that this authority be not weakened rather than that its power be kept within bounds. This is difficult to reconcile with the preservation of liberty. In general, it can probably be said that the conservative does not object to coercion or arbitrary power so long as it is used for what he regards as the right purposes. He believes that if government is in the hands of decent men, it ought not to be too much restricted by rigid rules. Since he is essentially opportunist and lacks principles, his main hope must be that the wise and the good will rule—not merely by example, as we all must wish, but by authority given to them and enforced by them.[7] Like the socialist, he is less concerned with the problem of how the powers of government should be limited than with that of who wields them; and, like the socialist, he regards himself as entitled to force the value he holds on other people.

When I say that the conservative lacks principles, I do not mean to suggest that he lacks moral conviction. The typical conservative is indeed usually a

---

tises the blunders of his predecessors'? For long tracts of their history they have indiscriminately resisted improvement, and in claiming to reverence their ancestors often reduce opinion to aged individual prejudice. Their position becomes safer, but more complex, when we add that this Right wing is incessantly overtaking the Left; that it lives by repeated inoculation of Liberal ideas, and thus suffers from a never-perfected state of compromise."

[7] I trust I shall be forgiven for repeating here the words in which on an earlier occasion I stated an important point: "The main merit of the individualism which [Adam Smith] and his contemporaries advocated is that it is a system under which bad men can do least harm. It is a social system which does not depend for its functioning on our finding good men for running it, or on all men becoming better than they now are, but which makes use of men in all their given variety and complexity, sometimes good and sometimes bad, sometimes intelligent and more often stupid" (*Individualism and Economic Order* [Chicago: University of Chicago Press, 1948], pp. 11–12). [*Collected Works* edition, vol. 13, p. 57.]

man of very strong moral convictions. What I mean is that he has no political principles which enable him to work with people whose moral values differ from his own for a political order in which both can obey their convictions. It is the recognition of such principles that permits the coexistence of different sets of values that makes it possible to build a peaceful society with a minimum of force. The acceptance of such principles means that we agree to tolerate much that we dislike. There are many values of the conservative which appeal to me more than those of the socialists; yet for a liberal the importance he personally attaches to specific goals is no sufficient justification for forcing others to serve them. I have little doubt that some of my conservative friends will be shocked by what they will regard as "concessions" to modern views that I have made in Part III of this book. But, though I may dislike some of the measures concerned as much as they do and might vote against them, I know of no general principles to which I could appeal to persuade those of a different view that those measures are not permissible in the general kind of society which we both desire. To live and work successfully with others requires more than faithfulness to one's concrete aims. It requires an intellectual commitment to a type of order in which, even on issues which to one are fundamental, others are allowed to pursue different ends.

It is for this reason that to the liberal neither moral nor religious ideals are proper objects of coercion, while both conservatives and socialists recognize no such limits. I sometimes feel that the most conspicuous attribute of liberalism that distinguishes it as much from conservatism as from socialism is the view that moral beliefs concerning matters of conduct which do not directly interfere with the protected sphere of other persons do not justify coercion. This may also explain why it seems to be so much easier for the repentant socialist to find a new spiritual home in the conservative fold than in the liberal.

In the last resort, the conservative position rests on the belief that in any society there are recognizably superior persons whose inherited standards and values and position ought to he protected and who should have a greater influence on public affairs than others. The liberal, of course, does not deny that there are some superior people—he is not an egalitarian—but he denies that anyone has authority to decide who these superior people are. While the conservative inclines to defend a particular established hierarchy and wishes authority to protect the status of those whom he values, the liberal feels that no respect for established values can justify the resort to privilege or monopoly or any other coercive power of the state in order to shelter such people against the forces of economic change. Though he is fully aware of the important role that cultural and intellectual elites have played in the evolution of civilization, he also believes that these elites have to prove themselves by their capacity to maintain their position under the same rules that apply to all others.

Closely connected with this is the usual attitude of the conservative to democracy. I have made it clear earlier that I do not regard majority rule as an end but merely as a means, or perhaps even as the least evil of those forms of government from which we have to choose. But I believe that the conservatives deceive themselves when they blame the evils of our time on democracy. The chief evil is unlimited government, and nobody is qualified to wield unlimited power.[8] The powers which modern democracy possesses would be even more intolerable in the hands of some small elite.

Admittedly, it was only when power came into the hands of the majority that further limitation of the power of government was thought unnecessary. In this sense democracy and unlimited government are connected. But it is not democracy but unlimited government that is objectionable, and I do not see why the people should not learn to limit the scope of majority rule as well as that of any other form of government. At any rate, the advantages of democracy as a method of peaceful change and of political education seem to be so great compared with those of any other system that I can have no sympathy with the anti-democratic strain of conservatism. It is not who governs but what government is entitled to do that seems to me the essential problem.

That the conservative opposition to too much government control is not a matter of principle but is concerned with the particular aims of government is clearly shown in the economic sphere. Conservatives usually oppose collectivist and directivist measures in the industrial field, and here the liberal will often find allies in them. But at the same time conservatives are usually protectionists and have frequently supported socialist measures in agriculture. Indeed, though the restrictions which exist today in industry and commerce are mainly the result of socialist views, the equally important restrictions in agriculture were usually introduced by conservatives at an even earlier date. And in their efforts to discredit free enterprise many conservative leaders have vied with the socialists.[9]

4. I have already referred to the differences between conservatism and liberalism in the purely intellectual field, but I must return to them because the characteristic conservative attitude here not only is a serious weakness of conservatism but tends to harm any cause which allies itself with it. Con-

---

[8] Cf. Lord Acton, *Letters of Lord Acton to Mary, Daughter of the Right Hon. W. E. Gladstone*, Herbert Woodfield Paul, ed. (2nd ed.; London: Macmillan, 1913), p. 73: "The danger is not that a particular class is unfit to govern. Every class is unfit to govern. The law of liberty tends to abolish the reign of race over race, of faith over faith, of class over class."

[9] John Richard Hicks has rightly spoken in this connection of the "caricature drawn alike by the young Disraeli, by Marx and by Goebbels" (Hicks, "The Pursuit of Economic Freedom," in *What We Defend: Essays in Freedom by Members of the University of Manchester*, Ernest Fraser Jacob, ed. [London: Oxford University Press, 1942], p. 96). On the role of the conservatives in this connection see also my "Introduction: History and Politics," *Capitalism and the Historians* (Chicago: University of Chicago Press, 1954), pp. 19ff. [*Collected Works* edition, vol. 3, pp. 56–72.]

servatives feel instinctively that it is new ideas more than anything else that cause change. But, from its point of view rightly, conservatism fears new ideas because it has no distinctive principles of its own to oppose to them; and, by its distrust of theory and its lack of imagination concerning anything except that which experience has already proved, it deprives itself of the weapons needed in the struggle of ideas. Unlike liberalism with its fundamental belief in the long-range power of ideas, conservatism is bound by the stock of ideas inherited at a given time. And since it does not really believe in the power of argument, its last resort is generally a claim to superior wisdom, based on some self-arrogated superior quality.

This difference shows itself most clearly in the different attitudes of the two traditions to the advance of knowledge. Though the liberal certainly does not regard all change as progress, he does regard the advance of knowledge as one of the chief aims of human effort and expects from it the gradual solution of such problems and difficulties as we can hope to solve. Without preferring the new merely because it is new, the liberal is aware that it is of the essence of human achievement that it produces something new; and he is prepared to come to terms with new knowledge, whether he likes its immediate effects or not.

Personally, I find that the most objectionable feature of the conservative attitude is its propensity to reject well-substantiated new knowledge because it dislikes some of the consequences which seem to follow from it—or, to put it bluntly, its obscurantism. I will not deny that scientists as much as others are given to fads and fashions and that we have much reason to be cautious in accepting the conclusions that they draw from their latest theories. But the reasons for our reluctance must themselves be rational and must be kept separate from our regret that the new theories upset our cherished beliefs. I can have little patience with those who oppose, for instance, the theory of evolution or what are called "mechanistic" explanations of the phenomena of life simply because of certain moral consequences which at first seem to follow from these theories, and still less with those who regard it as irreverent or impious to ask certain questions at all. By refusing to face the facts, the conservative only weakens his own position. Frequently the conclusions which rationalist presumption draws from new scientific insights do not at all follow from them. But only by actively taking part in the elaboration of the consequences of new discoveries do we learn whether or not they fit into our world picture and, if so, how. Should our moral beliefs really prove to be dependent on factual assumptions shown to be incorrect, it would be hardly moral to defend them by refusing to acknowledge facts.

Connected with the conservative distrust of the new and the strange is its hostility to internationalism and its proneness to a strident nationalism. Here is another source of its weakness in the struggle of ideas. It cannot alter the fact that the ideas which are changing our civilization respect no boundaries. But refusal to acquaint one's self with new ideas merely deprives one of the power of effectively countering them when necessary. The growth of ideas is an international process, and only those who fully take part in the discussion will be able to exercise a significant influence. It is no real argument to say that an idea is un-American, un-British, or un-German, nor is a mistaken or vicious ideal better for having been conceived by one of our compatriots.

A great deal more might be said about the close connection between conservatism and nationalism, but I shall not dwell on this point because it may be felt that my personal position makes me unable to sympathize with any form of nationalism. I will merely add that it is this nationalistic bias which frequently provides the bridge from conservatism to collectivism: to think in terms of "our" industry or resource is only a short step away from demanding that these national assets be directed in the national interest. But in this respect the Continental liberalism which derives from the French Revolution is little better than conservatism. I need hardly say that nationalism of this sort is something very different from patriotism and that an aversion to nationalism is fully compatible with a deep attachment to national traditions. But the fact that I prefer and feel reverence for some of the traditions of my society need not be the cause of hostility to what is strange and different.

Only at first does it seem paradoxical that the anti-internationalism of the conservative is so frequently associated with imperialism. But the more a person dislikes the strange and thinks his own ways superior, the more he tends to regard it as his mission to "civilize" others[10]—not by the voluntary and unhampered intercourse which the liberal favors, but by bringing them the blessings of efficient government. It is significant that here again we frequently find the conservatives joining hands with the socialists against the liberals— not only in England, where the Webbs and their Fabians were outspoken imperialists, or in Germany, where state socialism and colonial expansionism went together and found the support of the same group of "socialists of the chair," but also in the United States, where even at the time of the first Roosevelt it could be observed: "the Jingo and the Social Reformer have gotten together and have formed a political party, which threatened to capture the Government and use it for their program of Caesaristic paternalism, a danger which appears now to have been averted only by the other parties having themselves adopted this programme in a somewhat milder degree and form."[11]

---

[10] Cf. John Stuart Mill, "On Liberty," in *On Liberty and Considerations on Representative Government*, Ronald Buchanan McCallum, ed. (Oxford: B. Blackwell, 1946), p. 83: "I am not aware that any community has a right to force another to be civilized."

[11] John William Burgess, *The Reconciliation of Government with Liberty* (New York: Charles Scribner's Sons, 1915), p. 380.

5. There is one respect, however, in which there is justification for saying that the liberal occupies a position midway between the socialist and the conservative: he is as far from the crude rationalism of the socialist, who wants to reconstruct all social institutions according to a pattern prescribed by his individual reason, as from the mysticism to which the conservative so frequently has to resort. What I have described as the liberal position shares with conservatism a distrust of reason to the extent that the liberal is very much aware that we do not know all the answers and that he is not sure that the answers he has are certainly the right ones or even that we can find all the answers. He also does not disdain to seek assistance from whatever non-rational institutions or habits have proved their worth. The liberal differs from the conservative in his willingness to face this ignorance and to admit how little we know, without claiming the authority of supernatural sources of knowledge where his reason fails him. It has to be admitted that in some respects the liberal is fundamentally a skeptic[12]—but it seems to require a certain degree of diffidence to let others seek their happiness in their own fashion and to adhere consistently to that tolerance which is an essential characteristic of liberalism.

There is no reason why this need mean an absence of religious belief on the part of the liberal. Unlike the rationalism of the French Revolution, true liberalism has no quarrel with religion, and I can only deplore the militant and essentially illiberal antireligionism which animated so much of nineteenth-century Continental liberalism. That this is not essential to liberalism is clearly shown by its English ancestors, the Old Whigs, who, if anything, were much too closely allied with a particular religious belief. What distinguishes the liberal from the conservative here is that, however profound his own spiritual beliefs, he will never regard himself as entitled to impose them on others and that for him the spiritual and the temporal are different spheres which ought not to be confused.

6. What I have said should suffice to explain why I do not regard myself as a conservative. Many people will feel, however, that the position which emerges is hardly what they used to call "liberal." I must, therefore, now face the question of whether this name is today the appropriate name for the party of liberty. I have already indicated that, though I have all my life described

---

[12] Cf. Learned Hand, "The Spirit of Liberty" [Address delivered at the "I Am an American Day," in Central Park, New York City, on May 21, 1944], in *The Spirit of Liberty: Papers and Addresses of Learned Hand*, Irving Dillard, ed. (New York: Alfred A. Knopf, 1952), p. 190: "The spirit of liberty is the spirit which is not too sure that it is right." See also Oliver Cromwell's often quoted statement in his *Letter to the General Assembly of the Church of Scotland* [*A letter sent to the General Assembly of the kirke of Scotland (August 3, 1650) by Oliver Cromwell Lord General of the army of the Common-wealth of England now in Scotland*] (London: Printed for Hanna Allen, 1650), p. 4: "I beseech you, in the bowels of Christ, think it possible you may be mistaken." It is significant that this should probably be the best-remembered saying of the only "dictator" in British history!

myself as a liberal, I have done so more recently with increasing misgivings—not only because in the United States this term constantly gives rise to misunderstanding, but also because I have become more and more aware of the great gulf that exists between my position and the rationalistic Continental liberalism or even the English liberalism of the utilitarians.

If liberalism still meant what it meant to an English historian who in 1827 could speak of the revolution of 1688 as "the triumph of those principles which, in the language of the present day, are denominated liberal or constitutional"[13] or if one could still, with Lord Acton, speak of Burke, Macaulay, and Gladstone as the three greatest liberals, or if one could still, with Harold Laski, regard Tocqueville and Lord Acton as "the essential liberals of the nineteenth century,"[14] I should indeed be only too proud to describe myself by that name. But, much as I am tempted to call their liberalism true liberalism, I must recognize that the majority of Continental liberals stood for ideas to which these men were strongly opposed, and that they were led more by a desire to impose upon the world a preconceived rational pattern than to provide opportunity for free growth. The same is largely true of what has called itself Liberalism in England at least since the time of Lloyd George.

It is thus necessary to recognize that what I have called "liberalism" has little to do with any political movement that goes under that name today. It is also questionable whether the historical associations which that name carries today are conducive to the success of any movement. Whether in these circumstances one ought to make an effort to rescue the term from what one

[13] Henry Hallam, *The Constitutional History of England, Henry VII to George II* (1827) (Everyman edition; 3 vols.; London: J. M. Dent and Sons, 1930), vol. 3, p. 90. It is often suggested that the term "liberal" derives from the early nineteenth-century Spanish party of the *liberales*. I am more inclined to believe that it derives from the use of the term by Adam Smith in such passages as *Wealth of Nations*, vol. 2, p. 41 [Liberty Fund edition, vol. 1, p. 538]: "the liberal system of free exportation and free importation"; and vol. 2, p. 216 [Liberty Fund edition, vol. 2, p. 664]: "allowing every man to pursue his own interest his own way, upon the liberal plan of equality, liberty, and justice."

[14] Lord Acton, in *Letters to Mary Gladstone*, p. 44. [In a letter dated December 27, 1880, Acton writes: "I do think that, of the three greatest Liberals, Burke is equally good in speaking and writing; Macaulay better in writing, and Mr. Gladstone better in speaking."—Ed.] Cf. also his judgment of Tocqueville in *Lectures on the French Revolution* (London: Macmillan, 1910), p. 357 [Liberty Fund edition, p. 308]: "Tocqueville was a Liberal of the purest breed—a Liberal and nothing else, deeply suspicious of democracy and its kindred, equality, centralisation, and utilitarianism." Similarly in "Noticeable Books: Tocqueville's Souvenirs," in *The Nineteenth Century*, 33 (1893): 885. The statement by Harold Joseph Laski occurs in "Alexis de Tocqueville," in *The Social and Political Ideas of Some Representative Thinkers of the Victorian Age: A Series of Lectures delivered at King's College, University of London, During the Session 1931–1932*, Fossey John Cobb Hearnshaw, ed. (London: G. G. Harrap and Co., 1933), p. 100, where he says that "a case of unanswerable power could, I think, be made out for the view that he [Tocqueville] and Lord Acton were the essential liberals of the nineteenth century."

feels is its misuse is a question on which opinions may well differ. I myself feel more and more that to use it without long explanations causes too much confusion and that as a label it has become more of a ballast than a source of strength.

In the United States, where it has become almost impossible to use "liberal" in the sense in which I have used it, the term "libertarian" has been used instead. It may be the answer; but for my part I find it singularly unattractive. For my taste it carries too much the flavor of a manufactured term and of a substitute. What I should want is a word which describes the party of life, the party that favors free growth and spontaneous evolution. But I have racked my brain unsuccessfully to find a descriptive term which commends itself.

7. We should remember, however, that when the ideals which I have been trying to restate first began to spread through the Western world, the party which represented them had a generally recognized name. It was the ideals of the English Whigs that inspired what later came to be known as the liberal movement in the whole of Europe[15] and that provided the conceptions that the American colonists carried with them and which guided them in their struggle for independence and in the establishment of their constitution.[16] Indeed, until the character of this tradition was altered by the accretions due to the French Revolution, with its totalitarian democracy and social-

---

[15] As early as the beginning of the eighteenth century, an English observer could remark that he "scarce ever knew a foreigner settled in England, whether of Dutch, German, French, Italian, or Turkish growth, but became a Whig in a little time after his mixing with us" (quoted by George Herbert Guttridge, *English Whiggism and the American Revolution* [Berkeley: University of California Press, 1942], p. 3). [The "English observer" is Francis Atterbury, *English Advice to the Freeholders of England* (London, 1714), p. 24.—Ed.]

[16] In the United States the nineteenth-century use of the term "Whig" has unfortunately obliterated the memory of the fact that in the eighteenth it stood for the principles which guided the revolution, gained independence, and shaped the Constitution. It was in Whig societies that the young James Madison and John Adams developed their political ideals (cf. Edward McNall Burns, *James Madison: Philosopher of the Constitution* [New Brunswick, NJ: Rutgers University Press, 1938], p. 4); it was Whig principles which, as Jefferson tells us, guided all the lawyers who constituted such a strong majority among the signers of the Declaration of Independence and among the members of the Constitutional Convention (see Thomas Jefferson, *Writings of Thomas Jefferson*, Andrew Adgate Lipscomb and Albert Ellery Bergh, eds. [20 vols.; Washington, DC: Issued under the auspices of the Thomas Jefferson Memorial Association of the United States, 1903–4], vol. 16, p. 156). The profession of Whig principles was carried to such a point that even Washington's soldiers were clad in the traditional "blue and buff" colors of the Whigs, which they shared with the Foxites in the British Parliament and which was preserved down to our own days on the covers of the *Edinburgh Review*. If a socialist generation has made Whiggism its favorite target, this is all the more reason for the opponents of socialism to vindicate the name. It is today the only name which correctly describes the beliefs of the Gladstonian liberals, of the men of the generation of Maitland, Acton, Bryce, Pollock, Sidgwick, and Leslie Stephen, the last generation for whom liberty rather than equality or democracy was the main goal.

ist leanings, "Whig" was the name by which the party of liberty was generally known.

The name died in the country of its birth partly because for a time the principles for which it stood were no longer distinctive of a particular party, and partly because the men who bore the name did not remain true to those principles. The Whig parties of the nineteenth century, in both Britain and the United States, finally brought discredit to the name among the radicals. But it is still true that, since liberalism took the place of Whiggism only after the movement for liberty had absorbed the crude and militant rationalism of the French Revolution, and since our task must largely be to free that tradition from the overrationalistic, nationalistic, and socialistic influences which have intruded into it, Whiggism is historically the correct name for the ideas in which I believe. The more I learn about the evolution of ideas, the more I have become aware that I am simply an unrepentant Old Whig—with the stress on the "old."

To confess one's self an Old Whig does not mean, of course, that one wants to go back to where we were at the end of the seventeenth century. It has been one of the purposes of this book to show that the doctrines then first stated continued to grow and develop until about seventy or eighty years ago, even though they were no longer the chief aim of a distinct party. We have since learned much that should enable us to restate them in a more satisfactory and effective form. But, though they require restatement in the light of our present knowledge, the basic principles are still those of the Old Whigs. True, the later history of the party that bore that name has made some historians doubt where there was a distinct body of Whig principles; but I can but agree with Lord Acton that, though some of "the patriarchs of the doctrine were the most infamous of men, the notion of a higher law above municipal codes, with which Whiggism began, is the supreme achievement of Englishmen and their bequest to the nation"[17]—and, we may add, to the world. It is the doctrine which is at the basis of the common tradition of the Anglo-Saxon countries. It is the doctrine from which Continental liberalism took what is valuable in it. It is the doctrine on which the American system of government is based. In its pure form it is represented in the United States, not by the radicalism of

---

[17] Lord Acton, "The Rise of the Whig," *Lectures on Modern History,* John Neville Figgis and Reginald Vere Laurence, eds. (London: Macmillan, 1906), pp. 217–18 [Liberty Fund edition, *Essays in the History of Liberty,* p. 107]. (I have slightly rearranged Acton's clauses to reproduce briefly the sense of his statement). [The original phrasing reads: "Burke's address to the colonists is the logical outcome of the principles of liberty and the notion of a higher law above municipal codes and constitutions, with which Whiggism began. It is the supreme achievement of Englishmen and their bequest to the nation; but the patriarchs of the doctrine were the most infamous of men."—Ed.]

Jefferson, nor by the conservatism of Hamilton or even of John Adams, but by the ideas of James Madison, the "father of the Constitution."[18]

I do not know whether to revive that old name is practical politics. That to the mass of people, both in the Anglo-Saxon world and elsewhere, it is today probably a term without definite associations is perhaps more an advantage than a drawback. To those familiar with the history of ideas it is probably the only name that quite expresses what the tradition means. That, both for the genuine conservative and still more for the many socialists turned conservative, Whiggism is the name for their pet aversion shows a sound instinct on their part. It has been the name for the only set of ideals that has consistently opposed all arbitrary power.

8. It may well be asked whether the name really matters so much. In a country like the United States, which on the whole still has free institutions and where, therefore, the defense of the existing is often a defense of freedom, it might not make so much difference if the defenders of freedom call themselves conservatives, although even here the association with the conservatives by disposition will often be embarrassing. Even when men approve of the same arrangements, it must be asked whether they approve of them because they exist or because they are desirable in themselves. The common resistance to the collectivist tide should not be allowed to obscure the fact that the belief in integral freedom is based on an essentially forward-looking attitude and not on any nostalgic longing for the past or a romantic admiration for what has been.

The need for a clear distinction is absolutely imperative, however, where, as is true in many parts of Europe, the conservatives have already accepted a large part of the collectivist creed—a creed that has governed policy for so long that many of its institutions have come to be accepted as a matter of course and have become a source of pride to "conservative" parties who created them.[19] Here the believer in freedom cannot but conflict with the conservative and take an essentially radical position, directed against popular

[18] Cf. Saul Kussiel Padover, ed., "Introduction: Madison as a Political Thinker," *The Complete Madison: His Basic Writings* (New York: Harper, 1953), p. 10: "In modern terminology, Madison would be labeled a middle-of-the-road liberal and Jefferson a radical." This is true and important, though we must remember what Edwin Samuel Corwin ("James Madison: Layman, Publicist, and Exegete," *New York University Law Review*, 27 [1952]: 285) has called Madison's later "surrender to the overweening influence of Jefferson."

[19] Cf. the British Conservative party's statement of policy, Conservative and Unionist Central Office, *The Right Road for Britain: The Conservative Party's Statement of Policy* (London: Conservative and Unionist Central Office, 1949), pp. 41–42, which claims, with considerable justification, that "this new conception [of the social services] was developed [by] the Coalition Government with a majority of Conservative Ministers and the full approval of the Conservative majority in the House of Commons. . . . [We] set out the principle for the schemes of pensions, sickness and unemployment benefit, industrial injuries benefit and a national health scheme."

prejudices, entrenched positions, and firmly established privileges. Follies and abuses are no better for having long been established principles of policy.

Though *quieta non movere* may at times be a wise maxim for the statesman, it cannot satisfy the political philosopher. He may wish policy to proceed gingerly and not before public opinion is prepared to support it, but he cannot accept arrangements merely because current opinion sanctions them. In a world where the chief need is once more, as it was at the beginning of the nineteenth century, to free the process of spontaneous growth from the obstacles and encumbrances that human folly has erected, his hopes must rest on persuading and gaining the support of those who by disposition are "progressives," those who, though they may now be seeking change in the wrong direction, are at least willing to examine critically the existing and to change it wherever necessary.

I hope I have not misled the reader by occasionally speaking of "party" when I was thinking of groups of men defending a set of intellectual and moral principles. Party politics of any one country has not been the concern of this book. The question of how the principles I have tried to reconstruct by piecing together the broken fragments of a tradition can be translated into a program with mass appeal, the political philosopher must leave to "that insidious and crafty animal, vulgarly called a statesman or politician, whose councils are directed by the momentary fluctuations of affairs."[20] The task of the political philosopher can only be to influence public opinion, not to organize people for action. He will do so effectively only if he is not concerned with what is now politically possible but consistently defends the "general principles which are always the same."[21] In this sense I doubt whether there can be such a thing as a conservative political philosophy. Conservatism may often be a useful practical maxim, but it does not give us any guiding principles which can influence long-range developments.

[20] Adam Smith, *Wealth of Nations*, vol. 1, p. 432 [Liberty Fund edition, vol. 1, p. 468].
[21] Ibid.

ANALYTICAL TABLE
OF CONTENTS

CITATION INDEX

SUBJECT INDEX

absolutism: administrative, 362; in Continental Europe, 288–289; law and, 234
abstraction: manifestations of, 217n5;
rules governing society and, 217–218
Abuse of Reason project, 6
accidents: innovation and, 81–82, 85,
514; social justice and, 507
Act of Athens, 365, 365n91
Act of Settlement of 1701 (England), 254
Acton, John Emerich Edward Dalberg
(Lord Acton), 529, 529n14
Adams, John, 270n26, 530n16
Adams, Samuel, 261, 263–264n10
adaptation: growth of knowledge and,
84–85; origins of institutions and, 115;
progress and, 94; rules and, 226
administration: arbitrariness and, 361–
362n81, 364; versus business, 321,
321n26; in Continental Europe, 288,
294–295n15, 298–299; delegation of
power and, 320, 353n38; despotism
and, 372n11, 478; discretion and, 319–
323, 319n23, 320–321nn25–26, 334–
335, 360, 372n11; employed majority
and, 189–190; English, 301, 314–
315n12; excessively powerful, 357–362,
357–358nn66–9, 361–362nn81–82;
housing and, 471–472; judiciary and,
302–304, 306–307, 322–323, 364–
365; labor unions and, 398; versus law,
323n29, 352–353, 352n33; legal limitation of, 301, 305; legislation and, 319–
320; versus market, 401; overdoing by,
482; public administration movement

and, 359; public and private spheres
and, 315, 324; of social insurance,
407–408; tribunals and, 355–356,
357, 364; welfare state and, 378–379;
zealousness of, 378. *See also* executive
branch of government
Agenda for a Free Society (Seldon), 21
agriculture: aesthetics and, 487–488; costs
and prices and, 483–484, 486, 488; in
developing world, 489–491; farmers'
earnings and, 490n7; government control and, 486–487; government subsidy
of, 484–485, 485n2; industry and, 483,
489–490, 490n8; information provision
and, 489; land reform and, 489; parity
and, 485–486; politics and, 485; population shifts and, 482–483; protectionism
and, 525; soil conservation and, 488n5,
495–496; surplus produce of, 486
All Things Considered, 18–19
altruism, responsibility and, 141–143
America. *See* United States
American Revolution: British constitution and, 263–264; English ideals and,
261–262n2; French Revolution and,
292; higher law and, 266; liberalism
and, 530; Whigs and, 530n16
anarchy, 69n28
antirationalism: British tradition and,
91–92n; Christian tradition and, 120;
David Hume and, 112, 131n52; evolutionary tradition and, 124; faith and,
131n51; versus irrationalism or mysticism, 131

formations: general laws and, 85; versus
institutions, 85n15
Fortune (magazine), 17
Foxites, 530n16
France: administration in, 293, 293n12,
306; antirationalism and, 131n51; conception of free society in, 14; constitutional law and, 294n14; Declaration of
the Rights of Man and, 212n18; depreciation of currency of, 456n8; French
Code and, 226n18; inflation in, 456;
July Monarchy in, 293; liberal tradition in, 8, 65n17; Napoleonic regime
in, 292–293; rationalist tradition in,
119, 259; separation of powers in, 298;
social insurance in, 409–410n6, 417,
417nn20–21; theories of liberty and,
108–113, 108n1, 109–110nn6–8. *See
also* French Revolution
franchise. *See* suffrage
Frankfurter, Felix, 327n34
Franks, Oliver, 378–379n20
Frederick II (Prussia), 295, 295n16, 297,
297n2
Frederick the Great. *See* Frederick II
(Prussia)
freedom: as absence of coercion, 65, 199;
as absence of restraint, 68n27; versus absolute power, 342; of action, 87;
altruism versus selfishness and, 141–
143; in antiquity, 115–116n23, 238–
239; of association, 385; attributes of
legal systems and, 8; benefits to majority of, 83–84; bound service and religious vows and, 63; certainty of, 297;
in Christianity, 115–116n23; coercion and, 58n3, 59, 60n8; collective,
63–64; conservatism and, 532–533;
of contract, 339–340, 397; creation of
law and, 236; criteria for, 51; definition of, 53, 57–61, 57–58nn1–2, 59n5,
60–61nn7–9, 237–238n10; delayed
recognition of, 107–108, 107n; dignity
of the individual and, 141–142; dispersal of knowledge and, 82; economic,
65–66n18, 246, 329; employment and,

143–145, 185–187; expansionism and,
465; fear of, 133–134; free sphere and,
324–326; guarantees of, 326; ignorance and, 80, 82, 515; individual initiative and, 49; inequality and, 148n1,
372n11; injury to others and, 212,
212n18; inner, 64–65, 69–70n29, 71;
intellectual foundations for, 110n8;
judgment and, 133; labor unions and,
403; law and, 245–246, 245n37; versus liberty, 61n10; manumission and,
70–71; metaphysical, 64–65; morality and, 129–130, 142n10; national,
63–64; new, 65–66n18, 71; as omnipotence, 65; personal, 11; philosophy of,
50; political, 61–62, 62n11, 62–63n13;
positive versus negative, 67n25; power
and, 65, 65n17, 67n25, 69n28; predictability and, 231; as primary human
need, 53n8; property and, 62n11;
range of choice and, 61; rarity of
friends of, 517; rationalists as enemies
of, 122; reduction of coercion and,
13; restatement of ideal of, 48, 48n2;
restrictions on legislative activity and,
12; rule of law and, 11n28, 12, 21,
62–63n13, 254n74, 350; rules of conduct and, 123–125; science and, 135,
135n3; security and, 67n24, 87n19;
slavery and, 59n6, 63, 70–71; socialism
and, 343n1; social security and, 410;
social versus physical circumstances
and, 60, 60n8; societal versus individual, 52–53; subjective, 64–65; tradition
and, 122; uncertainty and, 83; as undesigned, 107; values and, 52n7; from
want, 57n1; welfare state and, 375,
377–378n17; of will, 65, 134–137,
135–136n4, 137–138nn7–8, 142n10,
221–222, 222n10; youth and, 62. *See
also* unfreedom
Freedom and the Law (Leoni), 12n31
"Freedom and the Rule of Law in F. A.
Hayek" (Hamowy), 11n28
"free law" school, 344, 344n4
free-trade doctrines, 82n13

on, 3–4n4; apology over errors by, 39; autobiographical writings of, 5, 6; background of, 39–40; hostility to work of, 3–4; influence of, 2–3; Nobel Prize and, 21–22; as Old Whig, 17, 531; political philosophy of, 21; reputation of, 21–22; rigidity of writings of, 3n3
Hazlitt, Henry, 17
health care: Beveridge Report and, 421–422n29; government provision and, 333, 414, 414n13, 421–424, 421–422n29; in Great Britain, 418; insurance and, 414n14, 421; medical decisions and, 422; productivity of recipients of, 423, 423–424n33; prolongation of life and, 423, 423n32; self-accelerating policy and, 413n12; as social security, 417; standard of service and, 422–423
Hegel, Georg Wilhelm Friedrich, 345n8
Heveningham, John, 308n
historians, 256
historicism, 344–345
history, economics and, 373–374n12
History of England (Hume), 256
Hitler, Adolf, 3–4n4, 328n35, 349–350
Hobbes, Thomas: critique of Edward Coke by, 114–115n22; law as command and, 218n7; legal positivism and, 345n8; Mathew Hale's critique of, 114, 252n63; rationalism and, 111; sovereignty and, 269
Hobhouse, Leonard Trelawny, 373–374n12
homosexuality, 212n19
Hook, Sidney, 18
housing: bureaucratic allocation of, 471–472; overcrowding in, 473, 474; price mechanisms and, 474–475; productivity and, 474; public, 471, 472; rent control and, 468–471, 471n6; shortage of, 469; subsidies for, 466, 471; urbanization and, 467–468
human nature: good and bad people and, 120, 120n32; morality and, 126; ratio-

nalism versus evolutionism and, 120; self-love and, 118; variety of, 149
Humboldt, Wilhelm von, 116–118n26
Hume, David: antirationalism and, 112, 131n52; British tradition of liberty and, 110; Enlightenment and, 131, 131n52; history of England and, 256; influence of, 259; liberal society and, 14; political affiliation of, 256n83; reason and morality and, 124, 124n39; Roman influences on, 244n34
Hungary, 1
Hurtado v. California, 313n10
Hutton, James, 116n24

Iceland, 297n2
ideas, influence of, 178–180, 178–179nn15–16
ignorance: culture and, 75; freedom and, 80, 82, 515; institutionalization of, 80–81n10; versus knowledge, 73–74; political theory and, 82; range of, 77–78; slavery to passions and, 64; tolerance and, 82; versus uncertainty, 80–81n10
immigration, 500
imperialism, 527, 527n10
income. *See* distribution of income
independence: civil society and, 190, 190–191n9; versus employment, 184–185; intellectual class and, 193–194n10; liberty and, 251–252n61; as privilege, 184
India, 449, 449n30
individual initiative: in developing world, 49; judgment and, 225n16
individualism, 14, 523n7
"Individualism: True and False" (Hayek), 14
individual responsibility. *See* responsibility, individual
individual rights: versus rights of majority, 65–66n18; state coercion and, 72
industry: agriculture and, 483, 489–490, 490n8; natural resources and, 493; town planning and, 481

realism, legal, 344

reason: constitutions and, 273n35; liberal and conservative distrust of, 528; limits to power of, 268; limits to uses of, 130–132. *See also* rationalism

Rechtsstaat: abandonment of, 304; battles over, 301; development of, 299–301, 299–300n26; disappearance of, 349; English rule of law and, 305n35, 354–355; formalization of, 348–349; German liberal tradition and, 8; from ideal to practice and, 303–304; justicialism and, 301, 303; legal positivism and, 346–347; origins of, 300–301; praise for, 363; Prussian government and, 299; significance of, 304–305; versus socialism, 349; state incapacity and, 350n25; taxation and, 436; theory of, 299–300n26; as word, 299–300n26, 305n35. *See also* rule of law

redistribution of income. *See* distribution of income

redistribution of wealth: on basis of group membership, 164–165; command economy and, 341; distributive justice and, 156n12; versus economic growth, 102–103n16, 105; extreme poverty and, 96n10; long-term versus short-term view and, 101–102; poor countries and, 105; versus progress, 99–100; rule of law and, 341; substantive versus formal justice and, 342–343; taxation and, 431. *See also* distribution of income

regulatory agencies, versus law, 9

Rehberg, August Wilhelm, 299–300n26

relief. *See* public relief

religion: for conservatives, socialists, and liberals, 524, 528; enforced conformity and, 212; law and, 223. *See also* Christianity

Renaissance, origins of liberty and, 232–233n1

responsibility, individual: altruism and, 141–143; assignment of, 137–141, 145–146; versus collective responsibility, 146n12, 147; consequences and, 138, 145; decline of, 133–137; dread of, 133–134n1; education and, 499; employment and giftedness and, 143–145; freedom of the will and, 137; liberty and, 139–140; natural resources and, 493–494; necessity of, 133; scientific determinism and, 65, 136n6; success and, 145

Restoration (England), 249, 250–251

restraint: absence of, 66, 66n19, 68n27, 69n28; versus coercion, 66, 66n20; rules of government and, 72

rights: bills of, 270–271, 270n23, 275–277, 276n41, 324, 325; to education, 508; employment and, 145; enumeration of, 277; federalism and, 274–275, 274n36; *garantisme* system and, 293n12; German approach to, 235–236n6; law and, 267, 267n16, 287–288n, 310n2; in nineteenth-century Prussia, 294–295n15; private sphere and, 206–209, 211–212; as procedural, 13–14; property, 226; rule of law and, 287n; social justice and, 15–16; U.S. Constitution and, 275–277; to work, 398, 398n24

Rights of Man, 261

right to vote. *See* suffrage

risk: employment and, 186, 187; natural disasters and, 165; value and, 159–160

Road to Reaction, The (Finer), 3–4n4

Road to Serfdom, The (Hayek), 3–4, 3–4n4, 6–8, 17

Robespierre, 114, 114n21

Robson, William Alexander, 355–356

romanticism, English liberalism and, 110n7

Rome, ancient: constitution of, 113; economy in, 246; hostility toward, 237n9; individual liberty in, 237; legal tradition of, 243–246, 244–245nn33–8; legislation in, 235–236n6; limited constitution and, 264n11

Roosevelt, Franklin D.: administrative agencies under, 361–362n81; agricultural policy and, 485–486n3; Court